A SURVEY
OF ISRAEL'S
HISTORY

A SURVEY OF ISRAEL'S HISTORY

LEON J. WOOD

Revised by
DAVID O'BRIEN

Academie Books Grand Rapids, Michigan
Zondervan Publishing House

A SURVEY OF ISRAEL'S HISTORY
Copyright © 1970 by Leon J. Wood
Copyright © 1986 by The Zondervan Corporation
Grand Rapids, Michigan

ACADEMIE BOOKS
is an imprint of
Zondervan Publishing House
1415 Lake Drive S.E.
Grand Rapids, Michigan 49506

Library of Congress Cataloging in Publication Data

Wood, Leon James.
    A survey of Israel's history.

    Bibliography: p.
    Includes indexes.
    1. Bible.   O.T.—History of Biblical events.
2. Jews—History—To A.D. 70.   I. O'Brien, David, 1940–   II. Title.

BS1197.W66   1986   221.9'5   85–26500

ISBN   0–310–34770–X

Designed by Louise Bauer

Printed in the United States of America
90 91 92 93 94 95 96 / DH / 14 13 12 11 10 9 8
This edition is printed on acid-free paper and meets the American National Standards Institute Z39.48 standard.

CONTENTS

LIST OF MAPS

FOREWORD

The view has been prevalent for some years that the traditional conservative position regarding the Bible is unacceptable to the modern mind. It is held that anyone is uninformed who believes that the autographs of the biblical books were free from error. In keeping with this view is the fact that liberal works have long dominated the scene in scholarship, making it sometimes difficult to find acceptable texts for a conservative class in Bible. The number of scholars who disagree with this viewpoint, however, has been growing in recent years, and some volumes have appeared to make a change. It is with the intention of aiding in that change that this book has been written.

A knowledge of Israel's history is important if one is to understand the message of the Old Testament. Both message and history are inseparably intertwined. This is especially true for the student who accepts the supernatural origin of the Bible, for then Israel's history is seen to be divinely ordained as preparatory for the coming of Christ. One cannot understand Him without knowing of those events which called for and led to His coming.

This book has been written especially with the undergraduate theological student in mind, but its language and level of content should make it useful to a much wider range of readers. One does not need to have a wide background in ancient history to follow the thought. No attempt has been made to provide full documentation, but it is hoped that sufficient references have been included to lend credence to positions taken and to give direction to students interested in further study.

The reader may be surprised that all of one chapter (chapter 5) is devoted to a discussion of chronology and so includes details of a kind and quantity not found elsewhere in the book. The reason is that this chronology has long been a matter of discussion, being basic in importance. It is my conviction that the viewpoint held traditionally by conservatives remains as defensible as ever, and a presentation of the matter in sufficient detail to support this conviction was thought appropriate.

Biblical references have been included with the history, and the student is urged to make use of them. The chapter and verse references are taken from the English translation and not the Hebrew text, where differences exist. The name "Yahweh" has been used for God instead of the more common "Jehovah," because it represents more closely what is generally thought to be the original pronunciation of the sacred name.

A word of gratitude is due to Professor David Egner, a former student and now a faculty member of the English department of the Grand Rapids Baptist Bible College, who read the entire work and made helpful suggestions; to Mrs. Joyce VanderMeer, who gave so much of her time to typing the manuscript; and to my wife and family for patience as well as assistance in various ways.

LEON J. WOOD
1970

PUBLISHER'S FOREWORD

Since 1970, when Leon Wood wrote this work, it has become a respected and widely used textbook and source for the diligent student of the Old Testament. In the same interval, however, a number of archaeological discoveries and historical insights have been made. So David O'Brien has revised Wood's book, incorporating this recent scholarship and adding a final chapter (covering the intertestamental period). It is hoped that, thus updated, the present volume will be even more useful in Old Testament studies than its popular predecessor.

THE PUBLISHERS
1986

ABBREVIATIONS

AASOR   *Annual of the American Schools of Oriental Research*
AB   George A. Barton, *Archaeology and the Bible*, 7th ed. (Philadelphia: American Sunday School Union, 1937)
ABH   Joseph P. Free, *Archaeology and Bible History*, 8th ed. (Wheaton: Scripture Press, 1964)
AJ   Josephus, *Antiquities of the Jews*
AJSL   *American Journal of Semitic Languages and Literatures*
ANE   Cyrus H. Gordon, *The Ancient Near East*, 3d ed. (New York: W. W. Norton, 1965); formerly published as *The World of the Old Testament* (Garden City, N.Y.: Doubleday, 1958)
ANEP   James B. Pritchard, *The Ancient Near East in Pictures* (Princeton: Princeton University Press, 1954)
ANET   James B. Pritchard, ed., *Ancient Near Eastern Texts Relating to the Old Testament*, 3d ed. with suppl. (Princeton: Princeton University Press, 1969)
ANF   Alexander Roberts and James Donaldson, eds., *The Ante-Nicene Fathers*, 10 vols. (Buffalo: Christian Literature, 1885–96; reprint, Grand Rapids: Eerdmans, 1950)
AOOT   Kenneth A. Kitchen, *Ancient Orient and Old Testament* (Chicago: InterVarsity, 1966)
AOT   Merrill F. Unger, *Archaeology and the Old Testament*, 4th ed. (Grand Rapids: Zondervan, 1960)
AOTS   D. Winton Thomas, ed., *Archaeology and Old Testament Study* (Oxford: Clarendon, 1967)
AP   William F. Albright, *The Archaeology of Palestine* (Baltimore: Penguin, 1949)
ARI   William F. Albright, *Archaeology and the Religion of Israel*, 3d ed. (Baltimore: Johns Hopkins University Press, 1953)
ASV   The American Standard Version
BA   *The Biblical Archaeologist*
BAR   George Ernest Wright, *Biblical Archaeology*, rev. ed. (Philadelphia: Westminster, 1962)
BAREV   *Biblical Archaeology Review*
BASOR   *Bulletin of the American Schools of Oriental Research*
BETS   *Bulletin of the Evangelical Theological Society*
BHI   John Bright, *A History of Israel*, 3d ed. (Philadelphia: Westminster, 1981)
BJRL   *Bulletin of the John Rylands Library*
BP   William F. Albright, "The Biblical Period," in Louis Finkelstein, ed., *The Jews: Their History, Culture and Religion* (New York: Harper & Row, 1949; reprint, Pittsburg: The Biblical Colloquium, 1950), pp. 3–65
BS   *Bibliotheca Sacra*
BW   Kenneth A. Kitchen, *The Bible in Its World: The Bible and Archaeology Today* (Downers Grove, Ill.: InterVarsity, 1978)
DOTT   D. Winton Thomas, ed., *Documents from Old Testament Times* (New York: Harper Torchbooks, 1958)
EAEHL   Michael Avi-Yonah and Ephraim Stern, eds., *Encyclopedia of Archeological Excavations in the Holy Land*, 4 vols. (Englewood Cliffs, N.J.: Prentice-Hall, 1978)
EHI   Roland De Vaux, *The Early History of Israel* (Philadelphia: Westminster, 1978)
EPN   Donald J. Wiseman and A. R. Millard, eds., *Essays on the Patriarchal Narratives* (Winona Lake, Ind.: Eisenbrauns, 1983)

FSAC	William F. Albright, *From Stone Age to Christianity*, 2d ed. (Garden City, N.Y.: Doubleday/Anchor, 1957)
GTT	J. Simons, *The Geographical and Topographical Texts of the Old Testament* (Leiden: Brill, 1959)
HDB	Hastings' *Dictionary of the Bible*
HIOT	Roland Kenneth Harrison, *Introduction to the Old Testament* (Grand Rapids: Eerdmans, 1969)
IJH	John H. Hayes and J. Maxwell Miller, eds., *Israelite and Judean History* (Philadelphia: Westminster, 1977)
ISBE	*The International Standard Bible Encyclopedia*, rev. ed., 5 vols. (Grand Rapids: Eerdmans, 1946)
JAOS	*Journal of the American Oriental Society*
JBL	*Journal of Biblical Literature*
JCS	*Journal of Cuneiform Studies*
JETS	*Journal of the Evangelical Theological Society*
JNES	*Journal of Near Eastern Studies*
JTVI	*Journal of Transactions of the Victoria Institute*
KD	C. F. Keil and F. Delitzsch, *Old Testament Commentaries*, 25 vols. (reprint, Grand Rapids: Eerdmans, 1971)
KJV	The King James Version (Authorized Version)
LAP	Jack Finegan, *Light from the Ancient Past*, 2d ed. (Princeton: Princeton University Press, 1959)
LB	Yohanan Aharoni, *The Land of the Bible*, trans. A. F. Rainey (Philadelphia: Westminster, 1962, 1967)
MNHK	Edwin R. Thiele, *The Mysterious Numbers of the Hebrew Kings*, rev. ed. (Grand Rapids: Eerdmans, 1965)
NASB	*The New American Standard Bible*
NBD	Francis Davidson, A. M. Stibbs, and E. F. Kevan, *The New Bible Dictionary* (Grand Rapids: Eerdmans, 1953)
NEB	*The New English Bible*
NHI	Martin Noth, *The History of Israel*, 2d ed. (London: A. & C. Black, 1958)
OHH	J. Barton Payne, *An Outline of Hebrew History* (Grand Rapids: Baker, 1954)
OTS	Samuel J. Schultz, *The Old Testament Speaks* (New York: Harper & Row, 1960)
PBW	Claire Epstein, *Palestinian Bichrome Ware* (Leiden: Brill, 1966)
PEQ	*Palestine Exploration Quarterly*
RB	*Revue Biblique*
SE	W. C. Hayes, *The Scepter of Egypt* (Cambridge: Harvard University Press; Part 1, 1953; Part 2, 1959)
SOTI	Gleason L. Archer, Jr., *A Survey of Old Testament Introduction* (Chicago: Moody, 1964)
TH	John Van Seters, *The Hyksos* (New Haven, Conn.: Yale University Press, 1966)
WTJ	*The Westminster Theological Journal*
WJ	Josephus, *The Jewish War*

A SURVEY
OF ISRAEL'S
HISTORY

CHAPTER ONE

INTRODUCTION

Though the beginning of Israel's national history must be placed at the time of her departure from Egypt, an account of her history must start with Abraham.[1] Only after Israel had moved across Egypt's border did she have size and identity with which other nations would have to reckon; but she already had a history that stretched back through the years in Egypt to her patriarchal fathers, Jacob and Abraham. To Jacob the twelve heads of the respective tribes had been born, and to Abraham God had given His promises concerning this unique posterity.

A. SOURCE MATERIAL

Source material for Israel's history is found mainly in the Old Testament. Because of this rich treasure of information, her history can be written in greater detail than that of any of her neighbors. In fact, though archaeological research has filled out their histories in remarkable detail, none of the great countries of her day has a document that is comparable to the Old Testament.

This invaluable book tells of Israel's ancestral background, her period of development in Egypt, her beginnings as separate tribes in the Promised Land, the uniting of these tribes in a monarchy (with the names, reign durations, and main activities of all her kings), the deportation to eastern countries as God's punishment for her sin, the return from that captivity by many of her people, and their subsequent experiences back in Palestine. The Old Testament contains not only history but also law, philosophy, dissertation, and sermon. The reader learns not only what the people did but also how they thought, spoke, and behaved. One becomes acquainted both with historical events and with the people who made them happen.

---

[1] Liberal scholars commonly begin their treatments of Israel's history with the Exodus, giving only cursory remarks concerning the patriarchal periods. For instance, Noth, *NHI;* or Bernhard Anderson, *Understanding the Old Testament* (Englewood Cliffs, N.J.: Prentice-Hall, 1957).

This wealth of information is given, though the primary purpose of the Old Testament is not history but rather to portray God's interest in, and preparation for, His redemptive provision for sinful humanity. The sin of Adam (the first and representative man) in the Garden of Eden made redemption necessary. The Old Testament is God's record of how He prepared for the coming of Jesus Christ, who provided redemption through His death. Because Scripture's purpose is to point humanity to redemption, the historical material pertinent to this preparation was included; what was not pertinent was normally omitted. For this reason, though the history is remarkably complete in many respects, events and facts a history book would normally include are often omitted.

Happily another source of information—archaeological research—helps fill in these omissions and supply general background. Diligent work by excavators has gone on in the Bible lands for many years, a work that continues and grows more productive with each new season. The information contributed is of the greatest value.

B. IMPORTANCE OF ISRAEL

Israel was one of the smaller countries of the pre-Christian era, but her history has had a major impact on the world. In fact, the history of no other ancient nation has had more influence on the western world. Israel's law contains God's standards for a just law, suitable for a country of Israel's size and situation. Its basic principles, when observed, have provided guidelines for lawmakers since.

Among Israel's prophets are the greatest thinkers and writers of their day. Parallels to their writings have been seen in the Egyptian "Admonitions of Ipuwer"[2] and "Prophecies of Neferti,"[3] both, and the Assyrian "Oracles of Arbella."[4] The Ebla documents name two classes of prophets.[5] The most extensive extrabiblical references to prophets are found in the Mari texts; over twenty tablets describe prophets of three different types and prophetic messages on various topics.[6] None of these, however, rivals the work of Israel's prophets in length, literary quality, ethical orientation, or power.

In Israel's wisdom literature her view

---

[2]The "prophetic" nature of Ipuwer is seen in his unprecedented criticism of the Pharaoh. Traditionally viewed as a work reflecting the chaotic conditions of the First Intermediate Period, Ipuwer charges the king with responsibility for these conditions and demands a change in style of leadership. See J. Breasted, *The Dawn of Conscience* (New York: Scribner, 1935). Dated by many around 2000 B.C., prior to the rise of the powerful Twelfth Dynasty, some Egyptologists would see it as a general tract on the theme of "national distress" with no particular historical setting. For a recent translation, see Miriam Lichtheim, *Ancient Egyptian Literature* (Berkeley: University of California Press, 1975), 1:149–62; or the older *ANET*, pp. 441–44.

[3]Also dated around 2000 B.C., this work is set in the distant past (the reign of Snefru [Fourth Dynasty]). Neferti "predicts" the fall of the current dynasty, the troubles of the First Intermediate Period, and the rise of "Ameny," or Amenemhet I, of the Twelfth Dynasty. See Breasted, *Dawn of Conscience;* Lichtheim, *Ancient Egyptian Literature,* 1:139–44; and *ANET,* pp. 444–46. Van Seters has argued (*TH,* 1966, p. 103) that both Ipuwer and Neferti belong to the Thirteenth Dynasty.

[4]A. Guillaume, *Prophecy and Divination Among the Hebrews and Other Semites* (London: Hodder & Stoughton, 1938), pp. 42–43, finds parallels to Hebrew prophecy in these oracles as follows: "Like the Hebrew prophets, the priestesses employed the first person in speaking on behalf of Ishtar. The frequent injunction to 'fear not,' the promise of help, and the overthrow of the king's enemies, the assertion of the goddess's greatness, are all suggestive of Hebrew prophecy."

[5]Kitchen, *BW*.

[6]Herbert B. Huffmon, "Prophecy in the Mari Letters" in *BA* 31 (1968): 101–24.

of God, the world, and life are presented in a more philosophical vein. Here dialogue, drama, psalm, and proverb make their appeal to the emotions, the will, and the mind. The call to social justice and, supremely, to commitment to God, in both this wisdom literature and the prophets, has continued to be as significant for subsequent generations as it was for its first readers.

The abiding value of the Old Testament is mainly religious and moral, but its artistic merit must not be overlooked. It contains the finest literature to survive from its day. In fact, the Book of Job, the Psalms, or Isaiah's brilliant chapters are among the finest of any day. Everywhere since, not only writers but also musicians, painters, sculptors, and artists in almost every field have thrilled to these books. Much of the western world's fine music, painting, and statuary finds its theme in the pages of the Old Testament. Many volumes have been penned with its history in view. Its moral and cultural influence have been enormous in shaping the Christian West, which has been a major economic, political, and cultural force in the world for centuries.

C. ISRAEL'S STRATEGIC LOCATION

Contributing also to Israel's political importance was her strategic location. Wedged between the Arabian Desert and the Mediterranean, her narrow sixty miles afforded the only caravan routes for north-south traffic between the major nations of the ancient world. To the south lay Egypt, a continuing world power throughout the Old Testament period. The annual flooding of the Nile changed arid desert to fertile soil for productive farming and provided convenient transportation for both people and merchandise. Because of the Nile, Egypt prospered and pursued extensive trade with countries to the north.

The countries with which she traded occupied what is often called the Fertile Crescent. This area also was dependent on the benefits of rivers, especially the Euphrates and the Tigris. Both rise in the Armenian mountains, and both flow southeastward by different routes, separated at one point by a distance of 450 miles, gradually converging until they join near the Persian Gulf.[7] The shorter Tigris descends more rapidly. Both of Assyria's capitals, Assur and later Nineveh, lay on its banks and were dependent on it. The Euphrates provided a main avenue of travel to the west for Babylonians, Assyrians, Armenians, and Mittanians in their respective periods. All of these countries wished to trade with prosperous Egypt to the south. Their caravans joined with those of Northern Canaan, and even of Anatolia farther to the north, employing the much-used routes through the length of Israel.

D. GEOGRAPHY OF PALESTINE[8]

The name *Palestine*[9] is derived from "Philistia," meaning "land of the Philis-

---

[7] It is believed that they entered the Persian Gulf separately in Abraham's day. However, the great burden of silt they carry has filled the Gulf to its present shoreline over one hundred miles from where it was then, within which distance they now join.

[8] Color map 15 in the map section at the end of the book should be consulted while reading this section of the chapter.

[9] For good geographical discussion, see Aharoni, *LB*, pp. 3–57.

Map 1. The Fertile Crescent

Map 2. Ancient World — Physical Features

tines." Philistia originally referred only to the southwest portion of the land (where the Philistines dwelt), but, in its slightly different form, it came to denote all the land of Israel.

Palestine was not a large country. It lay along the southern portion of the east Mediterranean coastline and extended little more than 150 miles north to south and 60 east to west. Natural limitations confined it on three sides: the vastness of the Syrian-Arabian desert (east), the desertlike Negeb (south), and the great Mediterranean (west). Only on the north did arable land continue. There, for much of Old Testament times, lay two countries—Phoenicia along the Mediterranean and Aram-Damascus farther inland. Phoenicia became a leading maritime power, and because relations between Israel and Phoenicia were usually good, the benefits of her merchandising were partly shared by Israel. Aram-Damascus, on the other hand, was poorer, largely because of extensive areas of desert waste within her border, and often she fought with Israel, apparently trying to better her position.

1. The Jordan rift

The most distinctive feature in Palestinian topography is the Jordan Valley, a remarkable rift in the earth's surface. It is lined by slopes that are generally abrupt and steep, sometimes forming sharply rising cliffs. Through this great fissure, averaging ten miles in width, runs the Jordan River. It drops from an altitude of about three hundred feet near the base of Mount Hermon to a depth of more than twelve hundred feet below sea level at the Dead Sea, the lowest place on earth.

The Jordan River is formed by four small tributaries,[10] that join just north of Lake Huleh,[11] 210 feet above sea level. Ten miles farther south the Jordan empties into the Sea of Galilee, thirteen miles long, seven miles wide, and 630 feet below sea level. This sweet water lake is unusually blue in color, abounds in fish today as it did in Bible times, and is famous for its sudden storms which transform its normally placid surface into a boiling cauldron. The Jordan Valley runs about seventy miles from the Sea of Galilee to the Dead Sea. The Jordan River, because of its winding and twisting course, is almost double that length; it averages between ninety and a hundred feet in width and from three to ten feet in depth. Flood season has seen it flow over its banks, however, for a width of up to a mile. Extensive irrigation projects of recent years have reduced the flow of water measurably.[12]

The Dead Sea is one of the most remarkable bodies of water in the world. Its concentrated chemical content[13] gives it great buoyancy but makes it fatal for most forms of marine life. Potash extracted from it provides Israel with a source of revenue today. The Sea is about forty-seven miles long and six to nine miles wide; its northern two-thirds is very deep and is divided

---

[10] The Bareighit, the Hasbany, the Leddan, and the Banias. These vary from five and one-half to twenty-four miles in length.

[11] Work was completed in 1957 in straightening and deepening the Jordan, which served to drain most of Lake Huleh as well as extensive marshy areas, thus reclaiming many acres of fertile farmland.

[12] Both Jordan and Israel take water, Jordan especially from the Yarmuk River before it flows into the Jordan, and Israel directly out of the Sea of Galilee.

[13] This concentration is twenty-five percent, made up of salt, potash, magnesium, and calcium chlorides and bromide.

from the shallower southern part by the *Lisan,* a boot-shaped peninsula extending from the eastern shore and leaving only a two and one-half mile expanse remaining at one point. A passable ford existed across this expanse for centuries.

South of the Dead Sea the great rift continues in what is called the Arabah.[14] It runs to the Gulf of Aqaba (over a hundred miles in distance). Sealed off by the mountains of the Negeb to the west and the high peaks of old Edom to the east, this narrow stretch is hot and arid, receiving only sporadic rainfall. It carried economic importance, especially after the time of Solomon, for its fine copper mines. Solomon developed these and built efficient smelters to refine the ore. Then he employed Elath as a port nearby on the Gulf of Aqaba from which to ship ore for trade with countries south.

2. Transjordan

On the east of the Jordan rift lies Transjordan. This is rolling plateau land, long known for its grazing value. Little farming is done there because hot winds (siroccos) burn it in the spring and fall, and cold desert winds sweep across it quite unhindered in the winter. The high ridges running up from the Jordan, arresting and cooling the air, do cause substantial rainfall, however. Much of this water drains back into the Jordan through four principal river systems: the Yarmuk (just below the Sea of Galilee), the Jabbok (about midway between the Sea of Galilee and the Dead Sea), the Arnon (emptying directly into the Dead Sea), and the Zered (at the southern extreme of the Dead Sea).

The area north of the Yarmuk was known as Bashan, a fertile tableland highly prized by, and a source of contention between, Israel and Aram-Damascus for many years. Gilead extended from Bashan as far south as Moab. This region attains altitudes of over three thousand feet both north and south of the Jabbok River, which bisects it. Fine forests covered many of its slopes in ancient times. Moab at times was confined between the Zered and Arnon rivers but more often controlled as far north as a latitudinal line approximately even with the northern tip of the Dead Sea. North of the Arnon the land is lower (averaging 2000–2400 feet high) than south of it (over 4000 feet high). South of the Zered River stretched Edom, long and narrow, confined mainly to Mount Seir ("the hairy mountain"), the mountain ridge east of the Arabah. These mountains, formed of red Nubian sandstone, exceed five thousand feet. Nestled among them is one of the world's most unusual cities, old Petra, a city carved from the cliffs and entered only by a long defile called the Sik.

3. The central mountains

On the west of the Jordan runs what is often called the backbone of Palestine proper, a series of three blocks of mountain country. The northern block was called Galilee, separated from the central block by the expansive Esdraelon Valley, fertile for farming in Bible days and even more so today. Elevations in Upper Galilee reach to over three thousand feet; in Lower Galilee they attain about two thousand, and

---

[14]This name is limited today to this southern portion of the rift. However, the Bible uses it in reference to the rift as far north as the Sea of Galilee (see Deut. 3:17; Josh. 3:15; 2 Sam. 2:29).

the peaks are more widely separated by valleys suitable for farming.

The middle block was early called Mount Ephraim (from the tribe of Ephraim, which occupied its southern half) and later Samaria. The mountains of its northern half are not as high as those of the southern half and again are separated more by valleys. Here the two mountains, Ebal and Gerizim, with the important city Shechem between, were especially significant.

The southern block was Judea. Its steep slopes were well farmed in Bible times by means of terracing. As one moves toward the Dead Sea, however, these slopes become arid and bare and form the Judean Desert. Apart from the oasis of En-gedi and a few less significant settlements, this wilderness region never knew permanent habitation. It was in this area that the invaluable Dead Sea Scrolls were found.

4. The coastal region

Between the mountains of Palestine proper and the Mediterranean run the coastal plains. The shoreline itself is marked by shifting sand dunes, but inland only a short distance is good farmland. The coastal plains are interrupted at one point by the ridge of Carmel, which forms a jutting irregularity into the Mediterranean on a latitudinal line about even with the Sea of Galilee. North of this ridge, running angularly east and west, is the Esdraelon Valley. South, to modern Tel Aviv, extends the beautiful Sharon Plain, dotted today by fine orchards.

Below the Sharon was the excellent land controlled so long by the Philistines. Here the Mediterranean begins to sweep westward and makes the plain wider. Here, too, heavy alluvial soil predominates, making excellent crops

possible. Rainfall decreases toward the south but is still sufficient at Gaza for agriculture. Old Gaza appears to have been the metropolis of the region, with Ashkelon, slightly north, the main port. The name "Shephelah" is given to the gradually rising ground between the coastal plain and the central mountains. It, too, is well suited for farming.

Though the Mediterranean extends along the entire length of Palestine, it never influenced Palestinians the way one might think. The reason is the lack of natural harbors. The shore is remarkably straight, so that only Ashkelon, Joppa, Dor, and Acco did any appreciable shipping, and this was limited. The Israelites did little fishing and trading by water; instead, they depended on the Phoenicians, who had fine harbors at Tyre, Sidon, and Byblos.

5. Climate

Palestine is located in a subtropical zone. Its temperatures are suited, for instance, to growing oranges, lemons, and grapefruit. The year is divided almost equally into a dry season and a rainy season, the wet season extending from about November to April: the early rains (November), the heaviest rains (December–February), and the latter rains (March–April). About the time the rains cease, the hot desert winds (siroccos) begin to blow and rapidly dry the soil; then no rain falls for up to six months. Vegetation soon becomes brown. Rainfall amounts vary throughout the land; the coastal region and the northern highlands receive the most. Many streams carry water only when rain falls. Only the larger streams are perennial—e.g., the Yarkon (flowing into the Mediterranean at Tel Aviv) and the Yarmuk, Jabbok, Arnon, Zered, and Jalud (all flowing into the

Jordan rift). Even these fall to low levels in the dry season.

E. HISTORY DIVISIONS

Old Testament history may be divided into seven periods: first, the patriarchal, running from Abraham to Jacob's twelve sons, the heads of the respective tribes; second, the Egyptian (from Jacob's descent into Egypt to the Exodus); third, the time of wilderness travel and Palestinian conquest; fourth, the period of the Judges, when the tribes lived as quite separate entities unified by their common faith in God, their ancestral heritage, and the central sanctuary at Shiloh; fifth, the time of the united monarchy (Saul to Solomon); sixth, the years of the divided monarchy, ending for Israel at the fall of Samaria (722 B.C.) and for Judah at the fall of Jerusalem (586 B.C.); and seventh, the exilic and postexilic period, running until the close of the fourth century.

CHAPTER TWO

PATRIARCHAL BACKGROUND

A. HISTORICAL ACCURACY

Since the last decades of the nineteenth century, when archaeology was first beginning to assert itself as a fledgling science, discoveries in the Near East have tended to support and illuminate Scripture. The discipline of "Biblical Archaeology" became a favorite subject among church men and women as find after find opened new vistas on the world and language of the Old Testament, holding out the promise that archaeology would one day put the charges of the radical critics to rest for good.

No area of biblical scholarship felt the impact of biblical archaeology as forcefully as the patriarchal narratives. The viewpoint of Julius Wellhausen (that no reliable historical information about the patriarchs was available in the Old Testament)[1] had reigned unchallenged until discoveries in the Near East began to fill out the picture of an ancient civilization in which the activities of the patriarchs seemed to fit perfectly. As recently as 1972, conservatives could say with confidence that most liberals had been forced to accept the historicity of these accounts on the basis of finds at such places as Mari and, especially, Nuzi.[2]

In the years since, liberal scholarship has mounted a concerted assault on the archaeological approach. The publication of two major works[3]—with their massive reinterpretation of data to support a position not far removed from that of Wellhausen—placed the conservative community on notice that the war was not over. Predictably, these have been cheerfully accepted in those circles where the unreliability of Scripture is an article of faith.[4] Thompson

[1] For instance, Julius Wellhausen, *Prolegomena to the History of Israel,* trans. Black and Menzies (Edinburgh: A. & C. Black, 1885), pp. 318–19.

[2] Edwin Yamauchi, *The Stones and the Scriptures* (Philadelphia: J. B. Lippincott, 1972), p. 36.

[3] T. L. Thompson, *The Historicity of the Patriarchal Narratives* (Berlin: de Gruyter, 1974); and John Van Seters, *Abraham in History and Tradition* (New Haven: Yale University Press, 1975). DeVaux, *EHI,* anticipated some of the criticisms of the Nuzi material.

[4] For example, George W. Ramsey, *The Quest for the Historical Israel* (Atlanta: John Knox, 1981), pp. 28–44.

and Van Seters have initiated a period of reexamination that, from the conservative perspective, may produce more benefit than harm. They have accurately identified areas where argumentation has been less than rigorous and motivated conservatives to stop resting on their archaeological laurels and seek new and stronger evidence for the patriarchal milieu.

None of this should suggest, however, that these reactionary critics have proven anything. While they have refuted some of the parallels used to explain patriarchal customs, others have stood up to closer scrutiny. In addition, serious scholars from both ends of the theological spectrum have leveled telling criticisms against their reconstructions.[5]

Fortunately for conservative Old Testament scholarship, little of real value has been lost in the recent debate, although many of the parallels from Nuzi have had to be abandoned as pertinent for understanding the patriarchs. There is still a significant body of data on which to base an understanding of the patriarchal milieu in the early second millennium.

1. Names

One set of data often cited comes from the numerous examples of names like those in Genesis being used in ancient extrabiblical texts. The name *Jacob,* for instance, has been found in the form *Ya῾qob-el*; in an eighteenth-century text from Chagar-bazar in Upper Mesopotamia it is used to designate a person, and in a list of Thutmose III it designates a place in Palestine. It also occurs in the form *Ya῾qob-har* as the name of a Hyksos chief.[6] The name *Abraham* has been found in Babylonian texts of the sixteenth century in the form *Abamram,* and in other forms at Mari.[7] A Mari text uses the name of Abraham's brother, Nahor, in the form *Nakhur,* as the name of a city in the vicinity of Haran. Mari texts speak further of a people called *Banu-yamina* (Benjamin),[8] and use names built on the same roots as Gad, Dan, Levi, and Ishmael.

Later Assyrian texts speak of two cities, *Til-turakhi* and *Sarugi,* the equivalents of *Terah* and *Serug,* Abraham's father and great-grandfather respectively. While it is still impossible to be certain about the contents of the Ebla tablets, the names *Ishmael* (*Ishmail*) and *Israel* (*Ishrail*) do seem to be attested.[9] These names and others appear in texts from the first half of the second millennium or earlier. Though the texts do not refer to a specific biblical person or

---

[5] The work of British conservatives has been especially helpful. Kitchen, *BW,* pp. 59–68, proposes an argument for the historicity of the patriarchal narratives on the basis of literary comparison with works from the ancient world as well as the more familiar legal and customary practices. Millard and Wiseman, eds., *EPN* contains several essays by different scholars written in response to recent criticism. See also, J. T. Luke, "Abraham and the Iron Age: Reflections on the New Patriarchal Studies," *JOTS* 4 (1977): 35–47. For a devastating critique of Thompson from a non-Evangelical perspective, see William G. Dever, "New Vistas on the EB IV ("MB I") Horizon in Syria-Palestine," *BASOR* 237 (Winter 1980): 54, 56.

[6] See Albright, *JAOS* 74 (1954): 231; DeVaux, *EHI,* p. 199. On p. 200 DeVaux affirms the historicity of the narratives on the strength of the patriarchal names.

[7] For three such texts, see Barton, *AB,* pp. 344–45. On names generally at Mari see H. B. Huffmon, *Amorite Personal Names in the Mari Texts* (1965).

[8] See Gelb, *JCS* 15 (1961): 37–38; and Tadmore, *JNES* 17 (1958): 130n.12.

[9] Kitchen, *BW,* p. 53.

place, they do indicate that the names in Genesis were in common use then.[10]

2. Customs

Further evidence concerns customs of the time. Some actions of the patriarchs seem strange in view of Mosaic Law and later practices but are understandable in the light of customs then. The Nuzi texts[11] have often been cited for their significant parallels with patriarchal customs. Despite a concerted effort to discredit them, some are still pertinent, though in some cases stronger evidence exists. For instance, Abraham was concerned lest his servant Eliezer, not a son, be his heir (Gen. 15:1-4). Nuzi texts show it was normal for childless parents to adopt a servant as a son; he served them until they died and then became heir.

A difficulty with this interpretation is that no inheritance for Eliezer is mentioned after the birth of Isaac, yet cuneiform texts indicate that the adopted person did not forfeit his inheritance even after the birth of a natural son.[12] However, Scripture's silence concerning an inheritance for Eliezer is no proof that he received none. Arguments from silence are never strong. At any rate, if Eliezer's inheritance was set aside, it was God who did it (Gen. 15:4); Abraham seems to have had every intention of honoring that right (Gen. 15:2-3).

That Rachel should take her father's teraphim (Gen. 31:19, 34, 35) also finds explanation at Nuzi. Such family idols signified right of heirship. Laban had natural sons, apparently born after Jacob's arrival (Gen. 31:1). Rachel, by her action, was trying to maintain Jacob's right to be principal heir. Nuzi texts further show that oral blessings were considered binding. A court record says that the court held binding a father's blessing for his sons. This explains Isaac's refusal of Esau's entreaty to change the blessing given to Jacob, even though deceit had been involved. This is in keeping, too, with the prominent place Genesis gives to blessings. Again it seems strange that Sarah gave her slave, Hagar, to Abraham as second wife (Gen. 21:9-11); similarly, Rachel and Leah gave their maids to Jacob (Gen. 30:1-13). Such actions may shock the modern reader, but they fit well in the "fundamental legal traditions and cultural milieu of ancient Mesopotamia."[13]

The weakness inherent in earlier use of the Nuzi texts, a weakness exploited skillfully by Thompson and Van Seters, is that the parallels are so numerous and superficially convincing that they have been accepted uncritically. When the focus of attention is broadened to include the mainstream of Mesopotamian culture, viewing Nuzi as one of many sources of information, the over-

---

[10] For further discussion and references, see Unger, *AOT,* pp. 127-28; Bright, *BHI,* pp. 70-71; Gordon, *ANE,* pp. 113-33; and Kitchen, *AOOT,* pp. 48-49, 153-54.

[11] Nuzi texts date from the fifteenth century and represent Hurrian customs, many of which were adopted from prior Amorites; see C. H. Gordon, *BA* 3 (1940): 1-12; Wright, *BAR,* pp. 43-44. Gordon's assumption that these parallels imply a date for the patriarchs in the fifteenth century does not hold, for similar parallels exist in tablets from Ur of the nineteenth and eighteenth centuries; see D. J. Wiseman, *JTVI* 88 (1956): 124.

[12] Kitchen, *BW,* p. 70. DeVaux, *EHI,* pp. 247-49, rejects the idea of adoption in connection with the Eliezer episode. He suggests rather that Abraham merely intends to will his property to a trusted servant who would also be set free.

[13] Tikva Frymer-Kensky, "Patriarchal Family Relationships and Near Eastern Law," *BA* 44:4 (Fall 1981): 209-14. See Nuzi tablet H. 67; Speiser, *AASOR* 10 (1930): 30.

all picture of patriarchal customs fits effortlessly into the early second millennium B.C.[14] As in hermeneutics, the more the sources, the stronger the interpretation.

3. Conditions in Palestine

General conditions in Palestine during the patriarchal period lend credence to the picture of the patriarchs' lives as painted by Genesis, but the nature of the biblical narrative itself precludes any detailed application of historical or archaeological discoveries as proof of historicity. The patriarchs are described as ordinary people—landless, mobile sojourners, tent-dwelling and living by means of herding and agriculture. For them, the assurance of children, the search for water and grazing land for their flocks, and the maintenance of peaceful relations with their usually more powerful neighbors are the dramatic stuff of everyday life. Their comings and goings would not be recorded in the state archives that constitute our principal source of documents from the ancient world. Neither are they the kind of lives that can be accounted for by the theories of Wellhausen and his latter-day disciples. The world of centralized powers and urbanism that the documentary hypothesis insists gave rise to the Pentateuch is totally absent from any but the most unrestrainedly imaginative reading of the biblical text.

A detail that is particularly telling for establishing an early date for Abraham is the account of the invasion of the four kings in Genesis 14. This chapter, which most liberals have trouble fitting into their systems,[15] depicts a war between two coalitions of kings, one from Mesopotamia and the other from Canaan. Such coalitions fit best into the general time frame offered by Genesis, as they tend to disappear in Mesopotamia with the rise of the Old Babylonian Dynasty, especially under Hammurabi (c. 1800 B.C.).

Similarly, this early period in Canaan was one of weak, minor kingdoms with limited territorial jurisdiction that tended to form alliances for mutual protection and advantage.[16] The consolidation of power during the latter half of the second millennium brought city-state coalitions of this sort to an end as well. The political realities of the ancient world changed radically enough after this time that the invention of such coalitions by people of a much later period is highly unlikely, if not impossible.

Until recently, conservatives have been able to argue that the sparse population of Palestine during the late third/early second millennium provided an ideal setting for the patriarchs. As Genesis attests, they moved about the land with no apparent outside interference; and if there was a limited popula-

---

[14] In response to the negativism that has arisen concerning the Nuzi materials, Evangelicals have begun to acknowledge the weakness of some comparisons and stress others. Kitchen (*BW,* pp. 61–68), by comparing the patriarchal narratives with ancient Near Eastern literature, concludes that, on the basis of literary type and content, one must grant Genesis 12–50 the status of historical narrative. Selman ("Comparative Customs and the Patriarchal Age" in Millard and Wiseman, *EPN,* pp. 91–139) proposes numerous parallels that must be considered valid even under the closest examination.

[15] See E. A. Speiser's moderate treatment in his Anchor Bible commentary on Genesis (Garden City, N.Y.: Doubleday/Anchor, 1964), pp. 105–9; or Gerhard von Rad, *Genesis* (Philadelphia: Westminster, 1972), pp. 174–80 for a more radical treatment.

[16] Kitchen, *BW,* p. 72.

tion during the time, that would explain their freedom of movement.

Unfortunately, this argument is a two-edged sword that cuts both ways. More recent archaeological work not only confirms the sparseness of population; it argues that the major patriarchal cities did not exist at the time of Abraham.[17] Thus, what had once figured as an argument for the historicity of the Genesis narratives has been turned around and now is being used as an argument against it.

Conservatives will agree that the occupation history of such cities as Jerusalem (Salem?), Shechem, Hebron, Bethel, Beersheba, and Dothan creates difficulties—but not insurmountable ones. Bimson, for example, points to the great length of time spanned by the three patriarchs and insists that the centuries described in the biblical narrative allow more than adequate time for the repopulation of appropriate sites before the end of the period involved.[18] His rather lengthy and technical explanation must be considered a plausible one by conservatives.

This dramatic reversal in the interpretation of the archaeological data is another illustration of the danger of an overly enthusiastic appeal to archaeology. It would be wise to bear in mind that the body of information available to modern scholarship is pathetically small, and what is available is always subject to interpretation or reinterpretation. Since Genesis is our only ancient source for the lives of the patriarchs, it deserves the pride of place. Let the critics offer archaeological proof that Abraham did not exist! In the absence of such unattainable proof, it is only intellectual honesty to admit the evidence of the biblical text, without the kind of special pleading and arguments from silence that characterize liberal attacks on Scripture. Archaeology can still provide illumination for the patriarchal milieu without being forced to bear the impossible burden of proving their existence.

Another idea that is being revised is that of regarding the patriarchs as nomads. Earlier works, which characterized them as "seminomads," were depending on a faulty understanding of nomadism.[19] Nomads—once considered to be enemies of civilization, hovering on the fringes of the desert, awaiting the opportunity to invade and possess the land—are now seen as an important link in a series of symbiotic relationships between urban dwellers and agriculturalists.[20] A far more com-

---

[17] Dever, *IJH*, pp. 99–101.

[18] See John J. Bimson, "Archaeological Data and the Dating of the Patriarchs," in A. R. Millard and D. J. Wiseman, *Essays on the Patriarchal Narratives* (Winona Lake, Ind.: Eisenbrauns, 1983), pp. 88–89, for his conclusions. Bimson acknowledges archaeological problems but deals with them in a way that supports both Scripture and archaeology.

[19] J. W. Rogerson, *Anthropology and the Old Testament* (Atlanta: John Knox, 1979), pp. 12–16, discusses the anthropological assumptions that shaped the idea of "seminomads." Rogerson writes from the "functionalist" perspective and reflects an almost nihilistic pessimism about our ability to know anything at all about biblical nomadism (pp. 41–43) because it is impossible to observe the patriarchs firsthand. He follows one of the leading functionalist experts in nomadic studies, Neville Dyson-Hudson, "The Study of Nomads," in *Perspectives on Nomadism,* ed. William Irons and Neville Dyson-Hudson (Leiden: Brill, 1972), pp. 2–29.

[20] The bibliography here is extensive. Norman K. Gottwald, *The Tribes of Yahweh* (Maryknoll, N.Y.: Orbis, 1979); J. T. Luke, "Pastoralism and Politics in the Mari Period," (Ph.D. diss., University of Michigan, 1965; University Microfilm 66–5094); Victor H. Matthews, *Pastoral Nomadism in the Mari Kingdom* (ASOR Dissertation Series #3, 1978); George Mendenhall, *The Tenth Generation*

plex social structure than was once appreciated, nomadism is an economic adaptation by which a family or tribe provides insurance against crop failure, especially in such agriculturally marginal areas as characterize much of Canaan.[21]

Our improved understanding of nomadism has helped to clarify some elements of the patriarchal lifestyle. Jacob's taking up residence near Shechem (Gen. 34) and later near Hebron (Gen. 37:12–18) is similar to the practices of the leaders of nomadic tribes near Mari.

In what has been described as "enclosed nomadism,"[22] the nomad is never far from the economic, political, and military control of the city, negotiating grazing rights within the very shadow of the city. Even if the sites of the patriarchal period were sparsely populated, without walls, it would have been in the best interest of townspeople and herdsmen to carry on their respective lifestyles without conflict.

The concern of Jacob after the massacre at Shechem (Gen. 34:30–31) reflects the nomad's fear that his migratory routes and grazing lands might be denied him if the towns turn against him. His apparently permanent residence near Shechem, and then later in the valley of Hebron (Gen. 37:12–18), is also congruent with the tendency of

more affluent nomads to establish residences in town while leaving the herding of sheep to their sons and hired men. Even Abraham's uncharacteristically warlike behavior in Genesis 14 fits with the picture of nomadic military prowess that can be clearly seen in the Mari documents. While the field of nomadic studies has only recently been applied to the Old Testament, it promises to illuminate the patriarchal narratives.[23]

4. Extensive travel

The last area of evidence concerns the existence of extensive travel in the Near East of patriarchal times. This is shown to be the same as that reflected in the patriarchal narratives. Abraham traveled more than one thousand miles moving from Ur of the Chaldees to southern Canaan (Gen. 11:31–12:9). Later he sent his chief servant Eliezer more than four hundred miles north to Haran in Upper Mesopotamia to acquire a bride for his son, Isaac (Gen. 24:1–10). Then Jacob traveled to the same area in flight from Esau, acquired a family and possessions, and returned to southern Canaan (Gen. 28–33). Numerous texts from archaeological research show that travel of this kind was not uncommon for the time. Letters from Mari indicate that her envoys visited all the way from Hazor in

---

(Baltimore: Johns Hopkins University Press, 1973). A significant series of articles by M. B. Rowton is indexed in M. B. Rowton, "Dimorphic Structure and Topology," *Oriens Antiquus* 15 (1976): 2–3. A thirteenth article not included in this bibliography is Rowton, "Dimorphic Structure and the Parasocial Element," *JNES* 36 (1977): 181–98.

[21] M. B. Rowton, "Dimorphic Structure and Topology," *Oriens Antiquus* 15 (1976): 19–22, defines the agriculturally marginal zone as it appears in Mesopotamia.

[22] For a brief definition, see David O'Brien, "David the Hebrew," *JETS,* 23:3 (September 1980): 194n.4; or for a full development, M. B. Rowton, "Enclosed Nomadism," *Journal of the Economic and Social History of the Orient,* 17:1 (1974): 1–30.

[23] In spite of Thompson's rejection of much of the related data as being too far removed in time from the patriarchal period (*Historicity of the Patriarchal Narratives,* pp. 85–88), the inherent conservatism of traditional cultures must be recognized, along with the tenacity of culture traits in the Near East. See Carol Kramer, ed., *Ethnoarchaeology* (New York: Columbia University Press, 1979).

Palestine to southern Mesopotamia and even Elam.[24] Somewhat earlier, the Cappadocian Texts from Kanish in Asia Minor tell of extensive trade relations between the Hittites and Assur. Assyrian trade colonies existed among the Hittites, where Assyrian wares were exchanged for native merchandise.[25] Earlier still, both Sargon and his grandson, Naram-sin, of the Akkadian period in southern Mesopotamia, conducted military campaigns as far distant as the Mediterranean coast and held, at least intermittently, an empire that extended from there all the way to central Persia.[26]

B. SIGNIFICANCE OF ABRAHAM'S CALL

God's call of Abraham introduced a new phase in His dealings with mankind. Until Abraham, God had dealt with the human race in a general way. There had been no select nation, chosen in distinction from others. Accordingly, when mankind did not obey, mankind was punished in the Flood. But with the call of Abraham, this worldwide approach was changed. No longer did God address Himself generally, but particularly. He chose one man alone. He separated him from others and gave him individual instruction.

The intention was to rear a new, select nation, with Abraham as the father.

People at large had refused God's way and so, for a time, had forfeited their opportunity. God would now make a special people through whom to work in effecting His plan of redemption. Through them now the written Word, the Scriptures, would come into existence, and also through them the Living Word, Jesus Christ, would be born in due time. In this manner the redemptive provision would be brought to reality in spite of the wickedness of the world at large. When complete and ready, however, it would be made available to all the world, and God would once more work with the whole race generally.

C. DATE OF ABRAHAM

Both biblical and extrabiblical materials bear on the date of Abraham. Considerable difference in evaluation of these materials exists among scholars, especially between conservatives and liberals, but even among Evangelicals there is a broad range of opinions. The conclusions of liberal scholars vary from a date in the latter half of the fifteenth century[27] to sometime in the twentieth.[28] Conservative scholars gen-

---

[24] See Kitchen, *AOOT,* p. 50, for references.

[25] The texts date from the nineteenth century, but the colonies existed from the last of the third millennium; see William F. Albright, *BASOR* 139 (October 1955): 15. See Kitchen, *AOOT,* for references describing colony activities.

[26] See pp. 27, 38–40.

[27] So Cyrus Gordon, who argues from reflected Nuzi customs, from Egypt being called "land of Rameses" in Jacob's time (Gen. 47:11), and from his belief that there were only four generations from Moses back to Joseph (Gen. 15:16; Exod. 6:16–20), with Moses dating in the thirteenth century; Gordon, *ANE,* pp. 115–16. H. H. Rowley argues for the seventeenth century in his *From Joseph to Joshua* (London: Oxford University Press, 1948).

[28] So Albright, who believes Abraham's move to Canaan could have been part of the Amorite migration, and Jacob's to Egypt part of the Hyksos occupation there; Albright, *AP,* p. 83. So also N. Glueck, *BA* 18 (1955): 4, 6–9; and Wright, *BAR,* p. 50. The discovery of the Ebla tablets has given rise to yet another proposed theory on the date of Abraham, although one that has received as little general support as Gordon's. David Noel Freedman, ("The Real Story of the Ebla Tablets: Ebla and the Cities of the Plain," *BA* 4 [December 1978]: 143–64) argues for a date for the patriarchs in Early

erally favor an earlier date, many placing Abraham's birth at the middle of the twenty-second century.[29] The matter depends on the establishment of three sets of dates: the date of Israel's Exodus from Egypt, the duration of Israel's stay in Egypt, and the length of time between Abraham's birthdate and Jacob's descent into Egypt with his family.

1. Biblical evidence

The Bible has much to say on all three matters, but not all Evangelical scholars agree on the interpretation of the biblical data. According to a literal reading of the relevant passages, Abraham was 100 years old when Isaac was born (Gen. 21:5), Isaac was 60 when Jacob was born (Gen. 25:26), and Jacob was 130 when he went down into Egypt (Gen. 47:9), giving a total of 290 years.

a. Date of the Exodus. The date of the Exodus, while debated even among conservative scholars, probably occurred shortly after the middle of the fifteenth century.[30] This date, commonly placed c. 1446 B.C., is called the "early" date in contrast to one in the thirteenth century called the "late" date.[31] Extensive evidence, both biblical and extrabiblical,[32] bears on this determination. Suffice it now simply to list four biblical items that favor the early date. First, according to 1 Kings 6:1, the Exodus preceded the time when Solomon began to build the temple (c. 966 B.C.) by 480 years. Second, Jephthah says that by his day Israel had been in possession of the land for three hundred years (Judg. 11:26). Third, an analysis of the duration of the Judges' period seems to require more years than possible with the late date. Fourth, in looking at the sequence of events in Egyptian history, it may be safely argued that the biblical account fits well the fifteenth century but not in the thirteenth.

b. Duration of Egyptian sojourn. Regarding the duration of the Egyptian sojourn, even greater difference of opinion exists among conservative scholars, but here, too, a conclusion based on biblical data can be reached. These data can be interpreted to say either that the sojourn lasted 430 years

Bronze III (2650–2350 B.C.) on the basis of excavations at Bab edh-Dhra, the since retracted reading of one of the Ebla texts and the appearance of the name *Ebr(i)um* at Ebla. Biblical chronology can no more support this construction, however, than it can the theory of Gordon.

[29] So J. B. Payne, who holds to the early date of the Exodus with Israel's sojourn in Egypt lasting 430 years and so finds Abraham born 2166 B.C. (Payne, *OHH,* pp. 34–36); see Unger, *AOT,* pp. 106–7, and Archer, *SOTI,* pp. 203–5. However, Schultz, *OTS,* pp. 30–31, 48–49, holds to a date more in keeping with Albright, apparently believing that Israel's sojourn in Egypt lasted less than 430 years; and Kitchen, *AOOT,* pp. 41–56, generally agrees, only he finds his evidence in a late date for the Exodus.

[30] A number of conservative writers take a contrary position. For instance, F. F. Bruce, *Israel and the Nations* (Grand Rapids: Eerdmans, 1963), pp. 13–14; Charles Pfeiffer, *Egypt and the Exodus* (Grand Rapids: Baker, 1964), pp. 84–88; Kitchen, *AOOT,* pp. 57–75; or Harrison, *HIOT,* pp. 174–77.

[31] Often placed early (c. 1290 B.C.) in the reign of Rameses II (1304–1238; see p. 89n.30, for discussion of these dates). A former popular view that Merneptah (1238–1228) was the Pharaoh of the Exodus has been generally abandoned with the finding of Merneptah's inscription claiming to have defeated Israel in the land of Palestine. However, Cyrus Gordon still favors the "third quarter of the thirteenth century," *ANE,* p. 115; and see H. H. Rowley, "Israel's Sojourn in Egypt," *BJRL* 22 (1938): 263, for a date of c. 1225 B.C.

[32] See pp. 69–86.

or, alternatively, 215 years. Once again several matters bear on the question.[33] At this point we will list only the main arguments for the longer period: first, the statement of the Hebrew text in Exodus 12:40 that the period in question lasted 430 years; second, God's prediction to Abraham (Gen. 15:13) that his posterity would be afflicted in a foreign land "four hundred years" (a round number); third, Stephen's similar statement in Acts 7:6, using again the figure 400; and fourth, the high improbability that Jacob's family multiplying in size to a nation of over two million people could have occurred in a period substantially less than 430 years.

Abraham's birthdate can be easily calculated by understanding these texts literally. To 966 B.C., the date when Solomon began to build the temple, one must add three periods of time: (1) 480 years, the time between the Exodus and this start of temple construction (1 Kings 6:1), (2) 430 years, the time between Jacob's descent to Egypt and the Exodus (assuming the longer Egyptian sojourn), and (3) 290 years, the time between Jacob's descent to Egypt and Abraham's birth. The resultant date is 2166 B.C.[34]

2. Extrabiblical evidence

Extrabiblical evidence also lends substantial testimony. Three areas call for attention.

a. Conditions in Canaan. If Abraham was born c. 2166 B.C., his arrival in Canaan at the age of seventy-five (Gen. 12:4) can be dated c. 2091 B.C. Do conditions in Canaan, as reflected in the Genesis narratives, agree with indications of archaeological research for this date? The answer is that they do.[35]

For one thing, there is agreement as to sparseness of population in Canaan at the time. This condition did not last long, since many cities west of the Jordan were reoccupied during the nineteenth century.[36] This too is significant because both Isaac and Jacob[37] also enjoyed comparative ease of movement in the land, which may indicate that Abraham lived before this time. The twenty-first century, indicated in the above chronology, fits well.

Further, there is agreement as to the existence yet in Abraham's day of vigorous population in the region of Sodom and Gomorrah.[38] Though Abraham moved freely through a sparse area in the highlands of Palestine, Lot found

---

[33] See pp. 65–69.

[34] This date cannot be pressed within a possible variation of a few years due to possible roundness of number in the biblical figures. This still leaves the date near the middle of the twenty-second century, however.

[35] Besides the two items listed here, Kitchen mentions the matter of "seasonal occupation of the Negeb region on the southwest border of Palestine" as attested by archaeology for the "twenty-first to nineteenth centuries B.C." but "*not* for a thousand years earlier or for eight hundred years afterwards," citing many references from especially Albright and Glueck in evidence (*AOOT*, pp. 49–50). Both Abraham and Isaac spent time in this area (Gen. 20:1; 24:62).

[36] Evidenced especially by the Egyptian Execration Texts, which mention many more Palestinian cities for the nineteenth century than for the twentieth; see Wright, *BAR*, p. 47; Aharoni, *LB*, pp. 131–35. Van Seters (*TH*, pp. 9–19), finding confirmation from Kenyon (*Archaeology in the Holy Land* [New York: Praeger, 1960], pp. 158–59), recently argued that this condition existed 2200–1950, which still fits our dating and allows it to be as early as indicated.

[37] Isaac remained mostly in the south (Hebron, Beersheba, Gerar), but Jacob, after his return from Padan-aram, moved freely to Shechem, on to Bethel, and then further south to Hebron, from where his sons later took the family flocks back north for pasture, first to Shechem and then on to Dothan (Gen. 35:1–8; 37:12–17).

[38] For discussion of the destruction, see p. 42.

numerous cities in the Jordan plain (Gen. 13:12; 14:2–7; 19:29). But the research of Nelson Glueck[39] has demonstrated that it was sometime in the twentieth or nineteenth century that these cities were destroyed. He points out that they, along with other population centers of Transjordan and the Negeb generally, were still occupied when the cities of Palestine proper were destroyed, but that they were all abandoned for some reason at this slightly later time.

This means that Abraham and Lot must have lived in the land sometime following the general destruction in the highland region and prior to the destruction of the cities in the Jordan plain; in other words, sometime between c. 2100 B.C. and c. 1900 B.C. According to our chronology, Abraham lived in Canaan from c. 2091 B.C. to c. 1991 B.C.

b. Conditions in Egypt. The second area of evidence concerns whether or not Egyptian history of the early nineteenth century (c. 1876 B.C.)[40] fits conditions reflected in the biblical account regarding Jacob's descent there. The answer again is in the affirmative. Two matters are worthy of note.

One concerns freedom of travel between Canaan and Egypt. Jacob's sons experienced no difficulty in crossing the Egyptian border two different times to buy corn, and later Jacob himself went to Egypt with his whole family (Gen. 42–46). Prior to this, Abraham too had traveled to Egypt in time of famine (Gen. 12:10–20). These occasions suggest that movement between the two countries was common for the time. Evidence from archaeology lends credence to the picture painted by Genesis. Particularly significant is an Egyptian tomb painting, dated c. 1900 B.C., which pictures a group of Semites entering Egypt as Jacob and Abraham must have. There are thirty-seven of them, dressed in colored garments that appear in marked contrast to the plain white of the Egyptians.[41] Pictured thus in a tomb, this type of movement is indicated to have been well known in Egypt.[42]

The other matter concerns the existence of a Pharaoh who, as the biblical account says, "did not know about Joseph" (Exod. 1:8); one who arose sometime after Joseph and enslaved the Israelites. The Genesis account implies that, whoever he was, he began a line of kings different from those who had befriended Israelites previously. Does Egyptian history of this general time reveal such a king? The answer is that it does; in fact, it reveals two. One was the first king of the foreign, Semitic rulers, the Hyksos.[43] These outsiders

---

[39] See Glueck, "The Age of Abraham in the Negeb," *BA* 18 (February 1955): pp. 2–9; see also Glueck, *The Other Side of the Jordan* (New Haven: American Schools of Oriental Research, 1940), p. 21. Van Seters (*TH*, pp. 9–19) places this destruction at 1950 B.C.

[40] Jacob entered Egypt 430 years before the Exodus (Exod. 12:40). Adding 430 to c. 1446 B.C. (Exodus date) gives c. 1876 for Jacob's entry.

[41] Tomb of Khnum-hotep III from the Twelfth Dynasty Period (see p. 87) at Beni Hasan. For picture, see *ANEP*, fig. 3.

[42] George E. Wright (*BAR*, p. 56), cites two inscriptions from the thirteenth and fourteenth centuries that show that similar ease of entrance to Egypt by Asiatics continued for several centuries.

[43] A Semitic people who gradually infiltrated Egypt and finally took over the rule. Their names suggest a northwest Semitic background, but their exact origin is still unknown. Manetho, as quoted by Josephus, says that the name, Hyksos, means "king-shepherds," evidently relating the element *hyk* to an Egyptian word for "ruler," and the element *sos* to a word meaning, in the later stages of the

drove the native dynasty from the throne sometime prior to 1700 B.C. (c. 1730), and so did establish a new line that could easily have taken a new attitude toward multiplying Israelites. The other was the first king of the Eighteenth Dynasty, Ahmose, who was able, in turn, to drive these foreign Hyksos back out of the land and reestablish the native line. He could also have inaugurated new attitudes toward Israelites who were ethnically related to the hated Hyksos just expelled.[44]

c. Pharaoh identity. The third area of evidence concerns the specific identity of this Pharaoh who "did not know about Joseph." We have observed that two rulers fit the general pattern, but can a choice be made between them? The literal reading of the chronology of the sojourn, which requires a nineteenth-century B.C. date for Jacob's entrance into Egypt, would have to favor the Hyksos ruler. A considerable period of time would have been required from the descent into Egypt until the rise of this unnamed Pharaoh to allow for Joseph's long life in Egypt[45] and for

the alarming multiplication of Israel (Exod. 1:8–11). The century and a half between Jacob's entrance and the accession of the Hyksos ruler would be adequate but none too much for this.

If, on the other hand, the second of the two rulers, Ahmose, who expelled the Hyksos from Egypt, were the one, then Jacob's entrance could have been correspondingly later, even during the Hyksos period itself.[46] It should be noted that differing opinions exist among Evangelicals concerning the chronology of this period, but four factors may be cited as evidence in favor of the Hyksos ruler.[47]

First, the Egyptian cities Pithom and Raamses, which were built by enslaved Israelites for the unfriendly Pharaoh (Exod. 1:11), must have been constructed either before or after the period of the Eighteenth Dynasty, when Ahmose lived, for archaeological evidence indicates that they were not constructed during that time. Excavation at old Raamses (identified with Avaris, capital of the Hyksos) has revealed "not a single object of the Eighteenth Dynasty."[48]

language, "shepherd." However, this explanation may be only a later popular idea. The name more likely comes from the Egyptian *heku shoswet* (later pronounced *hyku shose*) meaning "rulers of foreign lands." See Steindorf and Seele, *When Egypt Ruled the East*, 2d ed. (Chicago: University of Chicago Press, 1957), p. 24; R. M. Engberg, *The Hyksos Reconsidered* (Chicago: University of Chicago Press, 1939); and Van Seters, *TH*, pp. 181–90.

[44] A possible objection to a nineteenth-century entry to Egypt—that Egyptians (strong Twelfth Dynasty then ruling) considered shepherds "detestable" (Gen. 46:34) and so would not have been likely to give choice farmland to Jacob's family, who were shepherds—may be answered as follows. The Pharaoh's willingness to bestow this favor was prompted by his gratitude toward Joseph for his excellent work in time of famine. Further, the amount of land given would not have been extensive, for the days of great multiplication for Jacob's family were yet future.

[45] Joseph was 39 years old when Jacob entered Egypt (Gen. 41:46, 53, 54; 45:6) and lived to be 110 (Gen. 50:22); hence he died 71 years after c. 1876 B.C. or c. 1805 B.C.

[46] See above, n. 28. With the first Hyksos ruler dating at c. 1730 B.C. and Ahmose at 1584 B.C., the entrance could have been up to a century and a half later.

[47] See John Rea, "The Time of the Oppression and the Exodus," *BETS* 3 (Summer 1960): 58–59; also Archer, *SOTI*, pp. 205–8.

[48] Wright, *BAR*, p. 60; see Finegan, *LAP*, pp. 118–19. The identification of Raamses with Tanis, as held by Wright, is widely accepted. The site, Qantir, is favored by some, for instance, Hayes, *SE,*

G. E. Wright says this is evidence for the late date of the Exodus, believing that the city was built by Rameses II (1304–1238) of the Nineteenth Dynasty, but it can be used just as well in favor of the Hyksos time preceding the Eighteenth Dynasty. At that time the city, Raamses, was even the capital of the country, and so the Hyksos kings, especially the first, would certainly have been interested in building and enlarging it. The fact that nothing from the Eighteenth Dynasty has been found in that city argues strongly against Ahmose or any of his successors in that dynasty having built it. In fact, Wright observes that the city was destroyed by Ahmose[49] and not occupied again until the close of the fourteenth century.

Second, a statement in the Book of Exodus attributed to this Pharaoh who "did not know about Joseph" is more easily understood if he were a Hyksos ruler rather than one of the Eighteenth Dynasty:

> "Look," [the Pharaoh] said to his people, "the Israelites have become much too numerous for us. Come, we must deal shrewdly with them or they will become even more numerous and, if war breaks out, will join our enemies, fight against us and leave the country" (Exod. 1:9–10).

One matter to notice is that this king spoke of Israel as being "more and mightier than we" (KJV). The statement was made long before Israel grew in size to her eventual number of two million at the Exodus; it would have been a gross exaggeration if said in comparison to all Egyptians, who would have been the ones compared if this was said by Ahmose. However, if said by the first Hyksos ruler, it would not have been an exaggeration; for he would have been comparing only with Hyksos people, who never were numerous in Egypt. The Hyksos ruled by holding key positions, not by force of numbers.

Another matter is that this ruler feared that the Israelites might join with an enemy against his people. Once more this is understandable, if the speaker was a Hyksos; for the enemy was always so close at hand, namely the Egyptians, whose native rulers still held sway in the southern part of the land. But if the speaker was Ahmose, who would then have just driven the enemy, the Hyksos, out of Egypt and well up into Palestine,[50] this is not so understandable. The enemy had just been thoroughly defeated and driven far away.

Third, a statement made by God to Abraham is more in keeping with Israel's enslavement having been earlier, with the Hyksos, rather than later, with the Eighteenth Dynasty. The statement is, "Know for certain that your descendants will be strangers in a country not their own, and *they will be enslaved and mistreated four hundred years*" (Gen. 15:13, italics mine; see Acts 7:6). During the first years of Jacob's descendants dwelling in Egypt, they were

---

2:339, and Van Seters, *TH,* pp. 128–49. However, no Eighteenth Dynasty remains have been found there either.

[49] Wright, *BAR,* p. 60.

[50] Ahmose pursued the Hyksos as far as Sharuhen in southern Palestine (see Josh. 19:6), then besieged this city for six years, and finally destroyed it. This decisively ended any relation of the Hyksos with Egypt. A direct account of these events is available from the pen of a naval officer under Ahmose; see *Ancient Records of Egypt,* vol. 2, secs. 1–16.

not afflicted. This hardship started only when the Pharaoh who "did not know about Joseph" came to the throne. But if this Pharaoh was Ahmose, then the enslavement condition would have lasted only about a century and a third,[51] a period far short of four centuries and out of keeping with the above statement. However, if he was the first of the Hyksos kings, this enslavement would have lasted nearly three centuries.

Fourth, it is difficult to understand why the Eighteenth Dynasty, in driving the Asiatic Hyksos from Egypt, would not have driven the Asiatic Israelites out also at the same time. Those who believe that the Eighteenth Dynasty was the first to enslave Israel commonly argue that, because the two groups had been ethnically related, Israel was enslaved after the Hyksos were expelled. One group was driven out and the other made bondmen. But would it not have been more likely for both groups to have been expelled? Why would Ahmose have wanted to chance a new rebellion by leaving a group the size of Israel (who were very likely more numerous than those put out) yet in the land? Further, if the two groups had been friendly, intermarriage would have occurred and it might have been difficult to distinguish one Asiatic group from the other to be able to treat them separately. However, if the two groups had been enemies, as would be true on the basis of the enslaving king having been Hyksos, then a clear distinction between them (and a different treatment for each) is certainly understandable.

As an argument in favor of Ahmose of the Eighteenth Dynasty having been Israel's enslaver, it is asserted that such an action by a foreign people like the Egyptians, is more easily understood than if by a related people like the Hyksos. However, it is also understandable that also Hyksos, whether related or not, would have wanted to enslave Israel under the circumstances then existent. As has been observed, the Hyksos were not themselves very numerous. Consequently, they could well have considered this close-knit, separated, rapidly growing group of Israelites, located in the choice farmland of Goshen,[52] a threat to their reign and, at the same time, a potential source of valuable labor if they were to become enslaved.[53]

D. ABRAHAM'S COUNTRY

The words of God's initial call to Abraham were, "Leave your country

---

[51] This is on the basis of the Exodus having occurred at the early date of c. 1446 B.C., evidence for which will be developed in chapter 5. With Ahmose coming to the throne in 1584 B.C., this leaves only 138 years intervening.

[52] Goshen is best identified with the region of Wadi Tumilat, a valley over thirty miles long, extending from the Nile River to Lake Timsah. It has long been considered one of Egypt's richest farming areas; see Wright, *BAR,* p. 56.

[53] See p. 39n.44, for answer to a further objection that free acceptance into Egypt accorded Jacob's family is more easily understood if granted by ethnically related Hyksos than by foreign Egyptians (an objection voiced often by those who hold that the Egyptian sojourn lasted only 215 years, thus placing Jacob's entry well into the Hyksos period). Then, even favoring the idea that Joseph's Pharaoh was Egyptian rather than Hyksos are two other factors: first, that this Pharaoh gave a wife to Joseph (Gen. 41:45) from the priests of On (Heliopolis), and these priests served particularly the sun-god Ra who was disfavored by many of the Hyksos (see George Wishart Anderson, *The History and Religion of Israel* [London: Oxford University Press, 1966], p. 25); and second, the requirements of this Pharaoh appear Egyptian in that Joseph shaved (Gen. 41:14) before going to see him.

and your people and go to a land I will show you."[54] The question rises as to what sort of land this was from which God called this man. The call was given at Ur of the Chaldees,[55] still generally recognized as the well-known Ur of the lower Mesopotamian Valley.[56] The possibility that it was an Ur in upper Mesopotamia has been suggested in recent years, but supporting evidence is meager.[57] So we look for information concerning conditions in the traditionally accepted site of Ur—and lower Mesopotamia generally—at the close of the twenty-second century, when Abraham would have been growing to adulthood and still been living in this country.

1. Third Dynasty of Ur

In making the inquiry, we are fortunate that the period involved (the Third Dynasty of Ur)[58] is well-known from extrabiblical sources. It lasted 108 years, and the city of Ur was the capital of all lower Mesopotamia.

The time covered by this period either included or just followed the close of the twenty-second century, the time of our interest. The exact determination depends on the much-discussed date of Hammurabi, from which this period can be fixed. Scholars suggest three main dates for the beginning of Hammurabi's reign: a "low" date of 1728 B.C., a "middle" date of 1792 B.C., and a "high" date of 1848 B.C.[59] To any of these dates must be added approximately 340 years to arrive at the beginning of the Third Dynasty of Ur. This places that period on the basis of the low date at c. 2070–1962, the middle date at c. 2130–2022, and the high date at c. 2190–2082.[60] With Abraham born c. 2166 B.C., and migrating c. 2100 B.C.,[61] this means that, on the

---

[54] Acts 7:3. The similar words of Genesis 12:1 are given in reference to God's call later at Haran.

[55] Because it was after 1000 B.C. that Chaldeans became dominant in lower Mesopotamia and finally even established the Neo-Babylonian Empire, many scholars hold that the name used in Genesis, *Ur of the Chaldees,* must be anachronistic. M. Unger explains it as "a later scribal gloss to explain to a subsequent age, when Ur and its location had utterly perished, that the city was located in southern Babylonia" (*AOT,* p. 108).

[56] Excavation was first carried out at Ur by J. E. Taylor in 1854, more extensively by H. R. Hall in 1918, and with care by C. L. Woolley between 1922 and 1934. For description, see Woolley, *Ur of the Chaldees* (New York: Penguin, 1940).

[57] Cyrus Gordon, "Abraham and the Merchants of Ura," *JNES* 17 (1958): 28–31, advocates an Ura somewhere in western Mesopotamia as Ur. A text from Ugarit speaks of merchants to Ugarit from this Ura. Gordon's reason is that Haran was somewhat out of the way for Abraham if he traveled from Ur in lower Mesopotamia on his way to Canaan; also that Abraham later speaks of his home territory as being the Haran region (Gen. 24:4, 7, 10). However, it is likely that this Ura was also out of position for Haran to have been a logical stopping place, for it seems to have been further west than Haran, more in the Ugarit area. From there a traveler would have gone straight south to Canaan. Further, Abraham's "homeland" references may have been only in view of the family of his one living brother, Nahor, who had apparently moved from Ur to Haran (Gen. 24:10, 15; 28:2). Abraham's interest was not in a particular land, but in blood relatives where a wife might be found.

[58] For a brief summary of this period, see J. S. Schwantes, *A Short History of the Ancient Near East* (Grand Rapids: Baker, 1965); or Finegan, *LAP,* pp. 49–53; or for a summary of cultural conditions, G. Childe, *What Happened in History,* rev. ed. (New York: Penguin, 1954), pp. 89–112.

[59] For a discussion of the complex evidence, see M. B. Rowton, "The Date of Hammurabi," *JNES* 17 (1958): 97–111; for a brief summary, see Archer, *SOTI,* p. 204. Rowton himself favors the middle date.

[60] P. Van Der Meer, *The Chronology of Ancient Western Asia and Egypt* (Leiden: Brill, 1963), p. 46, argues to a beginning date for the period of 2044 B.C., still later than the low date given. Albright follows the low date, which he gives as 2060–1950 (*BASOR* 88 [December 1942]: 28–33; and 144 [April 1956]: 26–30).

[61] With Abraham seventy-five years old when leaving Haran (Gen. 12:4) and not likely having

basis of the low date, he left Ur about thirty years before this period began, and, on the basis of either the middle or the high date, he lived and left during that period. It is difficult to choose which position is best, but fortunately it is unnecessary for our purpose, for even if the period began a few years after Abraham left, conditions would not have changed greatly in this length of time.

What were conditions during the Third Dynasty of Ur? This was the classical time of Sumerian civilization, the era when Sumerian culture reached its highest development. Sumerian culture had progressed toward this peak during all the Early Dynastic Period preceding,[62] but then it suffered eclipse approximately two centuries before with the rise to power of the city of Agade (Akkad) and its Semitic culture. This eclipse had come when Sargon, capable ruler of Agade, had defeated powerful Lugal-zaggisi, king of Erech (Uruk), who had only recently succeeded in unifying lower Mesopotamia. Sargon was a Semite, speaking the Akkadian language rather than Sumerian. While a few Semitic names had appeared in the king list of lower Mesopotamia during the prior Early Dynastic Period, indicating some Semitic influence, for the most part Sumerian civilization had dominated until Sargon's rise. The period he inaugurated continued for more than a century. Akkadian control extended for a time from central Persia to the Mediterranean, making this the first true empire in history.[63]

This Akkadian period was brought to an end by a barbaric people called Guti who invaded the region apparently from the Zagros Mountains. A dark age resulted, but it paved the way for the resurgence of Sumerian culture in the Third Dynasty of Ur. It was actually the king of Erech, Utu-hegal, who broke the hold of the Guti, but then Ur-nammu, king of Ur, in turn defeated him and began the period of our concern.

2. Rulers

Ur never controlled as much land as Agade. Her kings claimed to perpetuate Sargon's empire, however, styling themselves as "Kings of Sumer and Akkad," and "Kings of the Four Parts of the World." They likely did control as far north as Ashur and certainly over all lower Mesopotamia. The names of the five successive rulers are known: Ur-nammu, who ruled eighteen years; Shulgi, forty-eight years; Amar-sin, nine years; Shu-sin, nine years; and Ibbi-sin, twenty-five years. Power waned during the reign of Ibbi-sin, and finally the city was sacked by Elamites who came down from the mountains to the east.

Ur-nammu, the first ruler, is probably best known for his code of laws. This code is the oldest found, antedating the better known and more complete code of Hammurabi. A brief text accompanies the code and states that

---

remained there more than a very few years, it is likely he was at least seventy when he left Ur, making the date for his departure just after the turn of the century.

[62] See Bright, *BHI,* pp. 27–28, for a brief survey of conditions during this lengthy period.

[63] Military expeditions ranged even farther, at least into Asia Minor and southeastern Arabia and possibly Egypt. Trade contacts extended as far as the Indus Valley eastward. A victory stele of Naram-sin, grandson of Sargon, who rivaled his grandfather in power, was found at Susa and is a beautiful work of art showing high cultural progress; see J. Finegan, *LAP,* pp. 47–48, for picture and description.

Ur-nammu had been appointed by the god Nanna to rule over the land. It says that he had removed dishonest practices in respect to weights and measures and had shown concern that orphans and widows not be exploited by the wealthy. Many of the laws themselves are not legible, but those that are manifest a marked similarity with those of Hammurabi.[64] They show an understanding of basic problems in society and a concern for justice. The desire to have them recorded in the form found would also have provided for their enforcement. Abraham lived in a society controlled by a developing legal system.

3. Religion

The society of Abraham's day was religious. The remains of fine religious structures so testify. The best preserved example of an ancient ziggurat dates from this period. Ur-nammu's name and title are stamped on its bricks, showing that he directed much of its construction. It seems to have been built on the top of a smaller, earlier ziggurat, and its upper part was the work of Nabonidus (of the much later Neo-Babylonian era). The completed structure measured 200 feet by 150 feet by 70 feet high and had the customary shape for ziggurats then (square and pyramidal). The religious shrine at the top no longer existed at the time of excavation, but there remained a number of the blue-glazed bricks that apparently covered it. C. L. Woolley, mainly responsible for laying bare the massive

structure, believes that trees and shrubs were planted on its various levels.[65] It was a masterpiece of workmanship and testifies of the engineering skills of the day.

Around the ziggurat lay numerous other sacred structures, one a splendid temple to Ningal, a moon-goddess and wife of Nanna. Other buildings provided living quarters for priests and storehouses for ceremonial materials. These surrounded a brick-paved open court stretching 225 feet in front of the ziggurat. One can imagine the busy coming and going of both official personnel and visiting worshipers in such a complex.

4. Living conditions

Regarding the general living conditions, as much or more is known from artifacts left by Gudea, *ensi* at Lagash, as from any of the main rulers at Ur. Gudea apparently held greater power than the average subruler, claiming 216,000 subjects. He left numerous hymn and prayer texts that show the Sumerian language at its highest point of development.[66] One of these texts tells of instructions given to Gudea by the god Ningirsu for restoring the Lagash temple, Eninnu. We are told that Gudea proceeded quickly to the task, bringing wood from as far away as the Amanus Mountains in northern Syria, a part of the same general range from which Solomon later brought cedar for the Jerusalem temple (1 Kings 5:6).[67] Gudea also left many statues, often of himself, sculptured in

---

[64] See S. N. Kramer, *Archaeology* 7 (1954): 143–44.

[65] Woolley, *Ur of the Chaldees,* pp. 143–44.

[66] Not long after this period, the Akkadian took its place as the common language, but Sumerian continued as the classical language of the whole Mesopotamian area until the Akkadian itself disappeared in the first century A.D.; see Gordon, *ANE,* p. 17.

[67] See *ANET,* pp. 268–69, for texts.

the round, revealing the artistic ability of the skilled craftsmen of his day.

The times generally were prosperous. Some one hundred thousand business documents discovered in the general area, most of which concern this period, give helpful insight.[68] Concerning transactions in grain, vegetables, fruit, cattle, slaves, and other commodities, they show prices and general methods of doing business. Economic conditions in general appear to have been stable, though inflation was not unknown. They also reveal that, in spite of the large place religion held in people's lives, the main evidence of prosperity and cultural advance is an impressive number of cylinder seals, all excellently carved, and a host of finely worked metal trinkets, indicating that the science of metallurgy was unsurpassed here in antiquity.

All of this comprised the world of Abraham when he was called by God. It was a progressive world, where cultural advantage was notable. Artists were skilled, builders competent, business active, and times good. Religion, centering in the worship of the moon-god Nanna, was extremely important. Writing was comparatively common, and apparently there were schools where this art and various subjects might be learned.[69] We may believe that Abraham, clearly a capable person, would have availed himself of educational opportunities. Perhaps he learned to write and then recorded some historical events later put in Holy Writ by Moses. Certainly he had gained an appreciation for cultural niceties when he found it necessary to leave and go where standards could only be lower. But he had been able to profit from these advantages before leaving.

5. Abraham's call to leave

Such advantages undoubtedly would have made Abraham's leaving more difficult. Genesis does not portray him as one of an adventuresome spirit, easily given to moving. He was a staid person, thoughtful, a man of judgment and foresight, who calculated before he acted. We may be sure that he would have much preferred to remain in surroundings he knew, where he could continue to enjoy old friends and comfortable living conditions. But he heeded God's call, and this response indicates his remarkable faith.

The question rises as to why God asked him to leave. Could not the nation of Israel have come to existence in lower Mesopotamia instead of Canaan? The answer seems to involve three considerations. First, Abraham needed to be removed from old friends and situations that might hinder his full obedience to God. Second, this departure provided a definite step of faith that contributed of itself to his further spiritual development. If he could obey God in leaving Ur, he would be able to do so in still more difficult matters later on. Third, there was a need at this historical juncture to shift the center of God's working from lower Mesopotamia to strategically located Canaan. Abraham's posterity should inhabit this narrow neck of land that would soon become the crossroad of the Near East.

---

[68] See *ANET,* p. 217, for texts.

[69] See Free, *ABH,* pp. 49–50. Foundations of what appears to have been a school were uncovered, and clay tablets for learning the cuneiform signs were found. Some tablets show reading lessons of hymns and others of multiplication and division tablets.

E. DEPARTURE

In Genesis 11:31, we read that "Terah took his son Abram,"[70] and departed "from Ur of the Chaldeans," suggesting that Terah, the father, was the one who led in the departure rather than Abraham. However, Stephen (Acts 7:2) speaks of Abraham as the one to whom God appeared, not mentioning Terah. Likely the son persuaded the father to accompany him, and the father, then according to patriarchal propriety, became the official leader of the party.

Question rises as to whether or not Abraham knew his destination when he left Ur. In Genesis 11:31 again, we read that the party left "to go to Canaan." But Hebrews 11:8 states that Abraham left Ur "even though he did not know where he was going." It is likely that the latter passage refers to the specific place, while the former refers to the general area. Abraham knew that he should go to Canaan, which to him at the time would have meant a country in the West near the Mediterranean,[71] without knowing the exact location of that large area.

Accompanying Terah and Abraham were Sarai, Abraham's wife, and Lot, the son of Abraham's brother, Haran. Haran seems to have died prior to this departure (Gen. 11:28), and Abraham's other brother (Nahor) did not join the party, though apparently he moved north to the city of Haran at some later time (Gen. 24:10, 15).

1. Stop at Haran

The four travelers did not get to Canaan, however, before they stopped. They set up residence at the city of Haran, nearly seven hundred miles along the way (about two-thirds of the total distance). Haran lay on the Balikh River about sixty miles north of where the Balikh empties into the Euphrates. *Haran* means "road," and the city was located on a main caravan road connecting cities of the East with Damascus and Egypt. Considered a strategic location by successive nations that controlled it, it is mentioned often in letters and documents of that time. Excavations since 1951 indicate that it was occupied at least from the third millennium. It (as Ur) was a center of moon-god worship. Abraham stayed there till Terah died (Acts 7:4).

2. Reason for stopping

Since Abraham's destination was Canaan, and Haran (being sixty miles north of the normal line of travel along the Euphrates) was out of Abraham's way,[72] the question arises as to why Abraham stopped and then remained for a substantial period of time. A common answer is that his father found affinity in Haran and its moon-god[73] worship being practiced as in Ur and simply persuaded his son, whose faith

---

[70] Abraham's name was changed from Abram ("exalted father") to Abraham ("father of a multitude") at the time of God's announcement to him regarding Isaac's birth (Gen. 17:4–5).

[71] The region was known in general terms. Lugal-zaggisi (c. 2360 B.C.) claims to have marched troops to the area, and both Sargon and Naram-sin ruled as far as the Mediterranean; see pp. 27, 38–40. Naram-sin calls the area, "The land of the Amorites." See Finegan, *LAP,* pp. 44, 47, 48, and Bright, *BHI,* p. 30.

[72] It may be that Abraham traveled up the Tigris, however, rather than the Euphrates, and if so, would have taken the normal road west which did lead directly to Haran.

[73] The name used for the moon-god in this northern, Semitic area was Sin, the equivalent of the Sumerian Nanna.

Map 3. Route of Abraham

too may have waned because of the long trip, to interrupt their journey at this point. This explanation assumes that Terah worshiped this god, Nanna. For support for the assumption, adherents point to Joshua 24:2, which states that Israel's "forefathers" (naming Terah specifically) "worshiped other gods." Among these gods, it is asserted, would have been Nanna.

However, there are problems with this explanation. Abraham himself was devoted to Yahweh,[74] so he had been instructed regarding the true God. This is not easy to understand if his father worshiped the false deity Nanna. Neither does it fit that Terah would have heeded God's orders to leave culturally advanced Ur if he did not himself give allegiance to the God whom Abraham was obeying.

Another explanation is needed. One that fits the biblical record better is that Terah suffered ill health on the journey and could go no further than Haran. Abraham, knowing that Haran held at least a religious kinship with Ur, and so might present an atmosphere more familiar to the aged man, detoured sixty miles from his intended route so that Terah might either regain his strength or else live out what might be only a few remaining days.

In favor of this explanation is the fact that Terah was very old when he left Ur,[75] and that he did die while Abraham was still with him at Haran, and so not very long after his arrival there.[76] Also, this explanation gives reason for Abraham being willing to remain with his father. It is doubtful that Abraham would have even made the detour, much less remained any length of time, if his father had only wished to worship at the shrine of Nanna. As an explanation of Joshua 24:2, it may be that Terah, while earlier in life giving allegiance to Nanna and other deities as well as Yahweh, later changed. He may never have arisen to Abraham's truly monotheistic belief, but at least he may have introduced his son to the worship of Yahweh and been willing to respond to Abraham's urging to leave Ur when Yahweh called.

In keeping with this explanation, we may think of Abraham, aware that he was not yet where God had called him, accepting the filial responsibility. He persuaded his father to go with him, thinking no doubt that it would be good for him to leave former religious associations and be with him where they might worship Yahweh together. But now he had to tarry while his father passed his closing days. Though perhaps anxious, Abraham properly stayed the few months, and possibly years. Then, when Terah died, Abraham was ready to hear God's further call to move on to the land of His choice.

---

[74] Because the personal name of God was not pronounced by the Jews after their return from Exile, no one knows for sure how the name was pronounced originally. *Yahweh* is generally accepted as the nearest we know, certainly much closer than *Jehovah;* and so this form is used in this book.

[75] Terah died at 205 (Gen. 11:32), when Abraham was 75 (Gen. 12:4); so was 130 at Abraham's birth (the Gen. 11:26 mention of 70 is in reference only to the eldest son, likely Haran). Abraham was a married adult when the party left Ur, which means that Terah must have been near 200 at the time. Marriages do not seem to have been made early: Isaac was 40 (Gen. 25:20) and Jacob 77 (Gen. 47:9; 41:46, 47, 54; 45:11; 31:41; 30:25) when they married.

[76] It is not likely that Abraham would have remained long and extensively interrupted his trip to Canaan. However, for Abraham later to refer to the Haran region as his homeland calls for him to have stayed at least several months and maybe even a few years. This follows, too, in that it was appropriate for God again to call him from there (Gen. 12:1–3).

CHAPTER THREE

ABRAHAM

Genesis 12:1–25:18

A. THE NEW LAND

The destination God intended for Abraham proved to be the land of Canaan, named after the son of Ham who settled in the region.[1] In its broader sense,[2] Canaan included Syria-Palestine, defined in Genesis 10:19 as extending from Sidon south to Gaza, east to Sodom and Gomorrah, and north to Lasha (location unknown). In the Amarna Letters (fourteenth century B.C.),[3] "Canaan" is referred to as equivalent to Egypt's Syro-Palestinian territories at the time, which would include land also well north of Sidon. The land to which Abraham came, however, was southern Canaan, later called Palestine.

1. Canaan

The third millennium, which approximates the Early Bronze Age in Canaan, was drawing to a close when Abraham arrived. Canaan had been a progressive

land during the prior centuries. Excavation reveals that Early Bronze people had effected remarkable urban development under a city-state form of government. Cities like Megiddo, Bethshan, Shechem, Ai, Jericho, and Lachish, later to be important in biblical events, already existed and were well built, boasting strong fortifications. Many of the fine Early Bronze cities (Megiddo, Jericho, Ai, etc.) were destroyed and abandoned, beginning about 2200 B.C.[4]

Archaeologically, this period is difficult to assess, as, in recent years, the dating and terminology used to deal with the Early Bronze/Middle Bronze has been experiencing a radical reevaluation that has not yet stabilized. Consensus is possible on some elements, but not others. It is generally agreed that the period from about 2200 to 2000 B.C. is one of transition from the urban culture of the Early Bronze to

---

[1] According to Genesis 10:15–18 and a native tradition preserved by Philo of Byblos.
[2] A narrower sense confines Canaan to the coastland, especially Phoenicia proper (see Num. 13:29; Josh. 5:1; 11:3; Judg. 1:27–33).
[3] See pp. 82–84.
[4] See Wright, *BAR,* pp.41–42; Albright, *FSAC,* pp. 118–20; Aharoni, *LB,* pp. 125–26.

the characteristic "Canaanite" culture of the Middle and Late Bronze, i.e., c. 2000–1200 B.C.[5] The decline of urban life during this period was apparently accompanied by a shift of the population to marginal areas and a consequent swing from an agrarian economy to one based on pastoral nomadism.[6] This picture disagrees with the older "Amorite incursion" theory championed by such giants of biblical archaeology as Kenyon[7] and DeVaux[8] but presents a more comprehensive explanation of all the data than does the older theory.[9]

Recently, Old Testament scholars have increasingly questioned the "Amorite incursion," and it seems to be generally losing support among them. While the reasons for the abandonment of this theory are complex[10] and beyond the scope of the present work, the emerging consensus offers some benefits to the Evangelical interpreter of the patriarchal narrative.

The picture of land-hungry nomads hovering on the fringes of civilization that is at the center of the idea of the Amorite invasion arises out of an inadequate understanding of the institution of nomadism. The migration of Abraham has been placed in the context of this large-scale Amorite movement, making his obedience to the call of God a response to a larger societal movement rather than the supreme call to faith that the Bible makes it. The significance of Abraham's migration is that it involves a complete break with his homeland and his people (Gen. 12:1). This equation of Abraham with "seminomadic" migrations has been one of the weak points of the conservative position, and, understandably, it has been criticized vigorously by liberal scholars.

It is much more defensible to understand Abraham as part of what has been termed a "dimorphic society" (with sedentary elements coexisting alongside nomadic elements in a symbiotic relationship). This understanding, substantiated by a sizable and growing body of literature,[11] supports the biblical picture of Abraham moving freely through Palestine and does not depend on archaeological evidence for (or against) the occupation of specific sites. As the chronology of this work would argue, Abraham arrived in Canaan c. 2091 B.C., in the middle of the deurbanized period between Early Bronze and Middle Bronze. Archaeology has, to date, found an embarrassing absence of settlement at some of the major patriarchal sites at this time. If, however, Abraham is a pastoral nomad grazing his flock within the sphere of influence of the few remaining cities or the

---

[5] Patty Gerstenblith, "A Reassessment of the Beginning of the Middle Bronze Age in Syria-Palestine," *BASOR* 237 (Winter 1980): 65; and DeVaux, *EHI,* p. 55.

[6] William G. Dever, "New Vistas on the EB IV ("MB I") Horizon in Syria-Palestine," *BASOR* 237 (Winter 1980): 38.

[7] Kathleen Kenyon, "Syria and Palestine c. 2160–1780 B.C.," *Cambridge Ancient History,* 1:2 (1971): 532–94.

[8] DeVaux, *EHI,* pp. 55–71.

[9] A summary of the burgeoning literature is conveniently available in M. Liverani's summary, "The Amorites," in *Peoples of Old Testament Times,* ed. Donald J. Wiseman (London: Oxford University Press, 1973), pp. 100–133.

[10] The complexity of archaeological theories for this period is discussed in a review article by Kay Prag in *PEQ* (January–June 1984): 67.

[11] See p. 17n.20.

scattered, unwalled villages that characterized this period in the south,[12] then many elements of the Genesis narrative are easily explained.

While Hebron, Jerusalem, Beersheba, Bethel, and others are currently thought to have been vacant at the time of Abraham,[13] this is primarily on the assumption that these sites had to have been cities, i.e., walled urban centers. On the basis of the model now being proposed, a settlement near the site of these cities would satisfy the biblical text. With the historical emphasis on the excavation of *tells* rather than the one-period sites that have caught the attention of excavators more recently,[14] occupation in the vicinity of the patriarchal sites would easily be missed. In fact, most of the locations associated with Abraham could be nonurban and not do violence to the literal reading of the text of Genesis.

The idea that Abraham entered Canaan as part of a larger movement of Amorites is also under attack. While ably defended in some circles,[15] it is refuted with equal vigor in others.[16] On balance, it seems wise to divorce the question of patriarchal historicity from the Amorite question. As in so many other areas of Old Testament research, it is a serious mistake to link the factuality of Scripture with prevailing scholarly opinion.

What can be asserted is that the Canaan into which Abraham entered was a Canaan in transition. The urban society of the first three quarters of the third millennium had disintegrated, leaving a largely agrarian, decentralized land in which political power, where it existed, was never great and resided in the hands of local "kings" whose domains were geographically limited city-states. Abraham, the herdsman, would have enjoyed relative freedom of movement with no major political entities in the areas where he established himself. This emerging picture of Canaan in the time of Abraham fits well with the narratives in Genesis.

2. Egypt

Some notice must be taken of Egypt at this juncture also, for her influence was felt in Canaan during the patriarchal day, and Abraham was himself soon to make direct contact there. During the third millennium, Egypt had experienced marked progress.[17] From 2600 to 2200 B.C., the Third to the Sixth Dynasties ruled in the Old Kingdom Period, the first flowering of Egyptian culture, shown especially by the giant pyramids. Sozer, founder of the Third Dynasty, built the first, the Step Pyramid, and Khafre, Khefren, and Menkure of the Fourth Dynasty built the three largest. Other pyramids built during the Fifth and Sixth Dynasties were smaller, but were important. In these, the so-called Pyramid Texts, incantations for assuring the Pharaoh safe passage into the life to come, were found.

---

[12] Dever, "New Vistas," p. 38.

[13] Dever, "The Second Millennium BCE: The Archaeological Picture," *IJH,* pp. 99–101.

[14] Dever, "New Vistas," pp. 42–45.

[15] See p. 34nn.7,8.

[16] An Evangelical assessment is available in William Sanford LaSor, David Allan Hubbard, and Frederic William Bush, *Old Testament Survey* (Grand Rapids: Eerdmans, 1982), p. 98. Also, J. J. Bimson, "Archaeological Data and the Dating of the Patriarchs," *EPN,* pp. 59–62.

[17] For discussion of both Egypt's Old Kingdom and First Intermediate periods, see Hayes, *SE,* 1:58–131; or A. Gardiner, *Egypt of the Pharaohs* (Oxford: Clarendon, 1961), pp. 72–106.

But Egypt too fell upon difficult days between 2200 and 2000 B.C., in what is called the First Intermediate Period. Rival Pharaohs claimed the throne, provincial administrators became feudal lords, and numerous cities came to act quite independently of any outside authority. Economic hardship and famine became widespread, and this resulted in a gloom of hopelessness and depression among the people. From this condition arose an appealing literature, however, among which are found *The Eloquent Peasant, The Admonitions of Ipuwer,* and *The Instruction for King Merikare.*[18] Religion played a dominant role in people's lives, but it was never a unitary whole in Egypt overall. Every community had particular local gods, with identities of national deities varying with political changes. Priests held great power, and people generally were kept in a state of fear.

B. SHECHEM, BETHEL, EGYPT, BETHEL (Genesis 12:4–13:18)

1. Arrival at Shechem (Genesis 12:4–9)

Abraham's journey into Canaan took him to Shechem,[19] (about thirty-five miles north of Jerusalem). Here God told him he had arrived at the intended destination ("To your offspring I will give this land," Gen. 12:7). Abraham thus learned that he was where God had planned for him to come. Reassured at the good news, he built an altar. After stopping for a time between Bethel and Ai, where he built another altar, he moved on to the southern part of Canaan.

2. Down to Egypt (Genesis 12:10–20)

When a famine developed in Canaan, Abraham journeyed southwest to Egypt. On reaching Egypt, Abraham told a half-truth concerning his wife Sarai, a form of subterfuge probably devised when he had first left Ur (Gen. 20:13). He presented her to the Egyptians as his sister (she was, in fact, his half-sister, Gen. 20:12), for he feared that the Pharaoh, seeing the attractiveness of Sarai, might so desire her for himself that, in order to get her, she might have taken the life of any husband.

Pharaoh, one of the rival rulers of the First Intermediate Period, did want her and did take her to the palace, but God intervened; he sent plagues on Pharaoh's house. This served to bring Abraham's deception to the ruler's attention, and he then dismissed Abraham from the land, though he gave him parting gifts.

3. Separation from Lot (Genesis 13:1–18)

When Abraham returned to Canaan, a new problem faced him (Gen. 13:1–18). He and Lot owned too

---

[18] For these and other Egyptian texts, see Erman and Blackmann, *Literature of the Ancient Egyptians,* 1927; and for numerous selections, *ANET.* A more recent and extensive set of documents can be found in Miriam Lichtheim, *Ancient Egyptian Literature,* 3 vols. (Berkeley and Los Angeles: University of California Press, 1975, 1976, 1980).

[19] Shechem lay between the twin peaks of Mount Ebal and Mount Gerizim. Toward the east stretches a small plain in which Joshua later heard Abraham's posterity respond to blessings and curses of the law (Josh. 8:30–35), and here also Jesus met a woman of Samaria at Jacob's well and led her to faith in Himself (John 4). For an account of the significant discoveries made at Shechem by the Drew-McCormick Expedition, see G. Wright, *Shechem: The Biography of a Biblical City* (New York: McGraw-Hill, 1965).

much livestock between them to find adequate pasture, and they dealt with the situation in a way that is traditional among pastoralists. They divided their herds and agreed on separate grazing areas.[20] Abraham magnanimously gave his nephew first choice as to which part of the land he would choose. Lot took the valley region of the Jordan.

Scholars have long debated the location of the notorious "Cities of the Plain." Until only recently, however, the case has seemed to be closed. Based on work done early in the 1924 season, Albright proposed that the sites of Sodom, Gomorrah, Admah, and Zeboiim were located along four of the fresh-water streams that flow into the Dead Sea at its southeast edge and had, at some time in the past, been submerged in the rising waters of the sea. Zoar, the fifth city (also called Bela in the biblical text) has been identified with modern Zoar, also located on the bank of one of the many *wadis* that flows down from the Plains of Moab, almost a mile above the Dead Sea.[21]

This became the basis for the dominant theory on the location of the cities and has been ably defended in the ensuing decades.[22] While some have argued for a northern location,[23] this "submersion" theory has not been seriously challenged until recently. Ironically, it has been work at Bab edh-Dhra, one of the sites that led Albright

to advance his idea in the first place, that has given rise to this new approach. He identified Bab edh-Dhra as a cultic center for the proposed submerged cities, since he found no evidence of permanent occupation at the site. However, the survey and excavations of Walter Rast and Thomas Schaub, beginning in the 1973 season, have brought several important Early Bronze settlements to light on the southwest edge of the Dead Sea.

Contrary to Albright's conclusion, Bab edh-Dhra was a heavily populated area, as were its four neighboring cities, Numeira (suggested by some as the site of Gomorrah), Safi, Feifah, and Khanazir. Bab edh-Dhra was apparently the largest and most important of these cities, but all share similar occupation histories, town plans, location, and (in three of the five cities) destruction by burning. The excavators, while not claiming a positive identification, have acknowledged possible connections with the biblical Cities of the Plain.[24]

In addition to the archaeological evidence that has been advanced for a southwestern location, the documents from Ebla have been used to validate this location. On the basis of a now discredited reading of one of the tablets, a case has been made for a patriarchal age in the Early Bronze Age, prior to 2350 B.C.[25]

---

[20] Victor Matthews, "Pastoralists and Patriarchs," *BA,* 44:4 (Fall 1981): 215.

[21] W. F. Albright, "The Archaeological Results of an Expedition to Moab and the Dead Sea," *BASOR* 14 (April 1924): 2–12. J. Penrose Harlan, "The Location of the Cities of the Plain," *BAR,* ed. George Ernest Wright and David Noel Freedman (Garden City, N.Y.: Anchor, 1961), 1:41–58, presents a comprehensive treatment of this theory. Appreciation is in order for David M. Howard, Jr., Bethel Theological Seminary, St. Paul, Minn., for access to an early draft of his article, "Sodom and Gomorrah Revisited," *JETS* 27:4 (December 1984): 385–400.

[22] It would be safe to say that this is currently the dominant approach.

[23] Most recently, *GTT,* p. 406.

[24] Walter E. Rast and R. Thomas Schaub, "Expedition to the Southeastern Dead Sea Plain," *ASOR Newsletter* (June 1980): 16–17.

[25] David Noel Freedman, "The Real Story of the Ebla Tablets," *BA* 4 (December 1978): 152. Also,

Of possibly greater significance is an article by William H. Shea that claims to have identified the city of Sodom on the eastern edge of the Dead Sea near the Lisan, in an Eblaite geographical text.[26] It is still too early, unfortunately, to place credence in readings of the Ebla texts. It may eventually be proven that Shea is right, but for the time being his suggestion is more tantalizing than conclusive.

Although there seems to be a general move in the direction of the Bab edh-Dhra hypothesis, it should be noted that significant problems still exist for it. Most damaging for those who hold to a literal reading of Scripture is the chronological problem. The five cities that were discovered by Rast and Schaub, while all apparently experienced destruction—and possibly at the same period—would seem to date from a time almost three hundred years before Abraham.[27] Attempts to identify Sodom and Gomorrah on the basis of Bab edh-Dhra founder on this inconsistency.

While it is not possible to change the reading of the biblical text to accommodate archaeological findings, it may well be that the archaeological data, when better understood, will support this identification. Until then, it seems best to not follow the current trend but to admit that there is no certainty regarding the location of Sodom and Gomorrah.

C. RESCUE OF LOT
(Genesis 14)

1. Abraham's courageous rescue (Genesis 14:1–16)

Sometime after settling into his new surroundings, Lot needed Abraham's assistance. A confederacy of four kings from Mesopotamia, far to the east, led by Chedorlaomer, king of Elam, attacked Sodom, Gomorrah, and other cities of the area, taking many people, including Lot and his family, captive. News soon came to Abraham, who, with 318 of his own servants, plus help from his neighbors (Mamre, Aner, and Eschol), gave pursuit. This coalition overtook and defeated the four-king confederacy at Dan, set free those taken captive, and recovered a large amount of booty. In this action, Abraham displayed outstanding courage, resourcefulness, and especially faith in God.

2. Extrabiblical evidence

This account, perhaps more than any other from patriarchal times, was challenged by liberal scholars for its historical value until recent years. The thinking was that kings as far away as Mesopotamia did not make military expeditions this far from home. However, archaeological research has prompted marked change in the viewpoint today. The biblical facts are now found to fit conditions of Abraham's time. For instance, as observed earlier, both Sargon and his grandson, Naramsin, conquered all the way to the

William C. van Hattem, "Once Again: Sodom and Gomorrah," *BA* 1 (Spring 1981): 87–92, who depends primarily on the Bab edh-Dhra excavations, makes passing reference to "new discoveries in the north of Syria (Ebla)."

[26] William H. Shea, "Two Palestinian segments from the Eblaite Geographical Atlas," in *The Word of the Lord Shall Go Forth,* ed. Carol Meyers and M. O'Connor (Winona Lake, Ind.: Eisenbrauns, 1983), pp. 601–5.

[27] If Abraham entered Canaan in 2091 B.C. (pp. 21, 22, 34) and Sodom was destroyed in 2068 B.C. (p. 41n.34), Bab edh-Dhra cannot be Sodom, since it was destroyed c. 2350 B.C.

Map 4. The Campaign of Genesis 14 and main areas of population

Mediterranean and held substantial territory along its coast[28] three centuries before Abraham. One Akkadian text from the time, concerning a condition for renting a wagon, is particularly significant for indicating frequency of travel to the west. The condition was that the renter not drive the wagon "unto the land of Kittim," meaning the Mediterranean coastland.[29]

Further, the names of the kings involved are all compatible with known names from that period. Some older scholars went so far as to propose specific identifications with kings from Near Eastern history (for example, Amraphel being equated with the great lawgiver Hammurabi[30] and Arioch with one of his contemporaries mentioned in the Mari texts, Arriwuk). However, as the chronology of the period has been refined, these identifications have been recognized as impossible. They are simply incompatible with any conservative chronology for Abraham, but the general suitability of the names to the nomenclature of the day is beyond dispute.[31]

Some have pointed out that the mention of Dan as the place where Abraham caught the retreating kings must be anachronistic, and so, in this sense, an exception. It is true that the name *Dan* was not given to the city formerly called "Laish" until the migration of the Danites in the days of the Judges (Judg. 18:29), but the reference may be to another Dan. In 2 Samuel 24:6, a Dan-jaan in the Gilead area is mentioned, and Gilead is more likely to have provided the path these eastern kings would have taken as they headed home than Coele-Syria (where the better-known Dan was located).[32] It might also be argued that a later scribe, in the interest of clarity, substituted Dan for the city's older, less familiar, name.

3. Kings of Sodom and Salem (Genesis 14:17–24)

When Abraham returned from his remarkable victory over these armies, two kings of his own country met him. One was the king of Sodom, who urged Abraham to retain the booty recovered and return only the people to their king and city. Abraham, however, refused the generous offer on the basis that people might say this earthly king had made him rich, and Abraham desired that all credit be rendered to God.

The other was Melchizedek, king of

---

[28] Naram-sin claims to have conquered even Magan (used in later texts for Egypt). Most scholars doubt this, but agree that he did control substantial areas along the Mediterranean. See Wright, *BAR,* p. 34; Bright, *BHI,* p. 30.

[29] For the text, see Barton, *AB,* pp. 346–47.

[30] Until comparatively recent time, when Hammurabi's date was found to be in the eighteenth century rather than the twentieth, this identification was held as valid by numerous scholars, such as Pinches, Hommel, Sayce, Clay, et al. It may be added, too, that Chedorlaomer, king of Elam, held a name of excellent Elamite type, having the likely spelling, *Kudur-lagamar.* A parallel name, *Kudur-mabug,* has been found for a king of West Elam, *Yamutbal;* the element *Kudur* is also a deity name. Further, the name *Tidal* is recognized as equivalent to Tudkhula, the name of several Hittite kings. See T. G. Pinches, *The Old Testament in the Light of the Historical Records of Assyria and Babylonia,* 3d ed. (London: Society for Promoting Christian Knowledge, 1908), pp. 209–33; Barton, *AB,* pp. 347–53.

[31] As to names of places also fitting, both Ashteroth Karnaim and Ham (Gen. 14:5) have been identified as having existed at the time; see Unger, *AOT,* p. 117.

[32] The Anti-Lebanon range was also a factor, for it would have had to be crossed if the better-known Dan was the city involved. It is not likely either that Abraham would have had to give chase as far north as the better-known Dan, making a Dan somewhere in Gilead more likely in terms of distance.

Salem (Jerusalem). His name is well-known because he is made typical of Christ in the Book of Hebrews. His name means "king of righteousness." Melchizedek brought bread and wine to Abraham's weary troops, and Abraham in turn gave him, as "priest of God Most High," a tenth of the booty. This gracious gesture was made apparently before Abraham returned the remainder of the spoil to the Sodom ruler. By this gesture Abraham recognized Melchizedek to be a priest of the true God, which is significant in illustrating that there did exist in the world a few beside God's chosen line who continued to worship Him. Abraham's act also demonstrated that the principle of tithing was recognized this early as a proper basis for giving to God.[33]

D. DESTRUCTION OF SODOM (Genesis 18:1–19:38)

1. Abraham intercedes for Lot (Genesis 18)

Several years had passed[34] when Lot needed assistance again. The occasion concerned God's destruction of Sodom and surrounding cities. Three "men" came to Abraham as he sat at the entrance to his tent in Mamre. As the account later indicates, two were angels (Gen. 18:22; 19:1), and one was the "Angel of Yahweh"[35] The Angel of Yahweh, indicated here directly as "Yahweh" (Gen. 18:1, 13, 17, 20, et al.), warned Abraham about the plan for destruction, which prompted the patriarch to intercede for the city (Gen. 18:23–33). He urged that if there were even only a few righteous in the city—"bargaining" with the Angel as to how few—the city might be spared. He was assured that if there were only ten his request would be granted. We may believe that this assurance gave Abraham relief, for the fact that he used the expedient of intercession at all shows that he believed there must be some others beside Lot who could be classified as righteous.

2. Lot delivered from Sodom (Genesis 19)

While Abraham made this intercession, the two angels, who earlier had departed, were making their way toward Sodom and were eventually received by Lot into his house. After a night in which men of the city gave shocking witness to the grave wickedness of Sodom,[36] Lot, his wife, and his two daughters were persuaded to leave the city.[37] There were not ten

---

[33] The Mosaic Law later established this principle clearly (e.g., Lev. 27:30–31; Num. 18:21–22; Deut. 12:5–18; 14:22–26).

[34] If we knew how long a time had intervened between Abraham's entry into Canaan and the military attack by the four kings, we could know exactly how many years elapsed here. We know the time when Sodom was destroyed, namely when Abraham was ninety-nine (Gen. 18:10; 21:5), and that Abraham was seventy-five when he entered the land. But where during the intervening twenty-four years this episode of the four kings fell is not indicated, though probably in the first half.

[35] The "Angel of Yahweh" is not called by that name here as elsewhere but corresponds in description to other places where the name is used, being called both a "man" (18:2) and "Yahweh." This is considered by some to be a pre-Incarnation appearance of Christ (see Josh. 5:13–6:5; Judg. 6:11–22; 13:2–21; et al.).

[36] The extent of desire on the part of these men to "know" (KJV) Lot's guests is accentuated by the number involved, their insistence, and Lot's expedient of offering his two daughters to them in an attempt to spare the guests (Gen. 19:4–9).

[37] Lot could not persuade his sons-in-law. The Hebrew is not clear whether these were only betrothed to the two daughters, who did escape, or whether they had married other daughters otherwise unknown, who then also refused to accompany their parents (Gen. 19:14).

righteous people there, as Abraham had hoped, and so the city had to be destroyed. But God showed favor toward Abraham's entreaty in at least having these four led to safety. The city was consumed as the four moved away, and Lot's wife, in a gesture of longing and regret, turned to look back, for which God brought death by changing her into what is called a "pillar of salt" (Gen. 19:26).

Later, Lot's two daughters, apparently under the false impression that they were the last people alive on earth, tricked their father into having incestuous relations, which issued in the births of Moab and Ben-ammi.[38] Lot's earlier choice of the cities of the plain, which had seemed so attractive at the time, indeed worked to his regret in these closing days of life.

3. Destruction of Sodom (Genesis 19:24–25, 27–28)

The destruction of Sodom was effected by a rain of "burning sulfur." In examining the meaning of this expression, scholars have ruled out volcanic action because the geology of the region does not lend itself to this type of activity. Many believe that it refers to an earthquake resulting in an enormous explosion.[39] Several factors favor this view. The idea of brimstone and fire (KJV) suggests incendiary materials raining upon the city as the result of an

explosion. Another descriptive word used is "overthrew" (Gen. 19:29), and this fits the thought of an earthquake. That Abraham saw smoke rising in the direction of the city indicates that there was fire. Inflammable asphalt has long been known in the area. Moreover, records from ancient writers speak of strong sulphuric odors, which suggests that quantities of sulphur were there in past time.[40] Further, the whole Jordan Valley constitutes an enormous fault in the earth's surface, given to earthquake conditions.

It is possible, then, that God did see fit miraculously to time an earthquake at this precise moment, which could have released great quantities of gas, mixed sulphur with various salts found in abundance, and measurably increased the flow of asphalt seepage. Lightning could have ignited all, the entire country being consumed as indicated. The Bible is clear that God does sometimes use natural means to accomplish His purpose when and to the extent that they are available. He may have done so in this instance. Whatever the method employed, God did bring the destruction.

E. COVENANT

On five different occasions, Abraham received promises from God, which, taken together, constitute what is called the Abrahamic covenant. The first in-

---

[38] These became fathers of the Moabites and Ammonites respectively, enemies of Israel in later years.

[39] For discussion, see J. Penrose Harlan, "The Destruction of the Cities of the Plain," *BA* 6 (September 1943): 41–52.

[40] Harlan quotes Strabo of the first century B.C., Josephus his successor, and Tacitus of about A.D. 100. All testify to severe odors, asphalt seepages, and a general burned complexion of the area now called the southern end of the Dead Sea. The area, identified by Harlan as the "Valley of Siddim" (Gen. 14:8), was not under water at that time. Writes Tacitus, "Not far from the lake (Dead Sea) is a plain which, according to report, was once fertile and the site of great cities, but which was later devastated by lightning; and it is said that traces of this disaster still exist there; and that the very ground looks burnt and has lost its fertility"; bk. 5, chap. 7 of his *Histories*.

stance was before Abraham arrived in the Promised Land (Gen. 12:1–3), the second was after Lot's separation from him (Gen. 13:14–17), the third was after Abraham's deliverance of Lot from the four kings (Gen. 15:1–21), the fourth was when Abraham was ninety-nine, just prior to the Sodom destruction (Gen. 17:1–22), and the fifth was several years later, following God's command to sacrifice Isaac (Gen. 22:15–18).

Analyzing what God said these five times, three principal areas of promise can be distinguished. First, Abraham's posterity would grow to the size of a nation and be His special people (Gen. 12:2; 13:16; 15:2–5; 17:4–6; 22:17). Second, the country to which God had brought Abraham would be this nation's homeland (Gen. 13:14–17; 15:19; 17:8). Third, his posterity would be a blessing to the world, to the extent that all nations would be blessed (Gen. 12:2–3; 18:18; 22:18).[41]

Genesis 15:6 states that Abraham "believed the LORD, and he credited it to him as righteousness" (see Rom. 4:1–4). That is, Abraham believed that God would perform what He promised. The promises were great, but so was Abraham's faith. He believed that God could and would do what He said. The additional element—that God then reckoned this faith to Abraham for righteousness—indicates that God's declared principle of salvation by faith alone, and not by works, was in effect at the time. Abraham's righteous stand-

ing before God was established by his belief in the promises of God.

F. WAITING THE PROMISED CHILD (Genesis 16:1–18:15)

God's promise to Abraham that he would have a large posterity came the first time just before he entered Palestine at the age of seventy-five. No doubt he thought in terms of a child being born very soon. He and Sarah had no children at the time and both were already advanced in years, Sarah being only ten years younger than he. But no child was born.

After waiting ten years (Gen. 16:3)—a period that must have seemed long—Sarah suggested the expedient that Abraham take Hagar as a secondary wife to beget a child (Gen. 16:1–4). Abraham did so, likely reasoning that this must be God's way of accomplishing what He had promised, since no child had been born through Sarah. But Abraham was out of God's will in this, for the seed was to come through Sarah in God's own time. Abraham's actions, however, wrong as they were, must be understood and judged in terms of customs of the day.[42] A son, Ishmael, was now born to Hagar, but God indicated that he was not the one through whom the promised posterity should come (Gen. 16:7–16; 17:20–21).[43] After the birth, Sarah became bitter and wanted Abraham to drive Hagar with her son from the household, causing severe distress for the patriarch, who did not

---

[41] Such detailed aspects as "I will make your name great and you will be a blessing" (Gen. 12:2) and "I will bless those who bless you, and whoever curses you I will curse" (Gen. 12:3), are part of these three main promises.

[42] See p. 15.

[43] God did promise a plenteous seed to Hagar, however (though not the seed of the covenant promise).

wish to compound the error already committed.[44]

Abraham thought he had a long wait before Ishmael was born, but he had fourteen more years to wait before the son of promise arrived. Finally, when Abraham was ninety-nine (Gen. 17:1), God specifically told him concerning Isaac (Gen. 17:15–19; 18:10–15). By this time, however, so many years had passed that both Abraham (Gen. 17:17) and Sarah (Gen. 18:12–15) laughed in their hearts. Apparently their faith had waned.

But Isaac was indeed born when Abraham was one hundred and Sarah was ninety. Twenty-five years had passed since God's first promise. God commemorated the occasion in both their lives by changing each one's name. Abraham's name was changed from Abram (Gen. 17:5) and Sarah's from Sarai (Gen. 17:15). The significance was that now Abraham became in truth a "father of many nations" and Sarah, as mother of this posterity, a "princess" before God.[45]

In addition, it was at this time that God directed that every male of Abraham's household should be circumcised as a "sign of the covenant" made with Abraham.[46] The propriety of inaugurating the sign at this time is found in the fact that Isaac's birth was the first tangible fulfillment of the several promises of the covenant. As it were, the covenant now began in tangible form.

The question presses as to why it was necessary for Abraham to wait twenty-five years for Isaac's birth. What was accomplished by this lapse of time? At least two matters seem to bear on the answer. One is that this delay constituted a major test of Abraham's faith. Could Abraham yet believe God would fulfill His promise after so long a time? The Bible shows that God often brings similar tests of faith into the lives of His children that He might stimulate further growth in that faith.[47] Abraham's faith would be stronger for meeting new challenges, if he could keep believing God here. His faith did wane to a degree, as we have observed, but in view of overall developments, it did not suffer serious decline.

The other matter is that this delay forced Abraham to realize that the nation to be raised from him was to be of God alone. God waited until Sarah was past her natural time of bearing children so as to demonstrate that Abraham's promised posterity would truly be of supernatural origin. Isaac was to be uniquely God's child, though born to Abraham and Sarah.

G. ABIMELECH AND THE PHILISTINES (Genesis 20–21)

1. Second half-truth regarding Sarah (Genesis 20)

Between the time of the announcement of Isaac's birth and the happy

---

[44] Hagar was actually driven away twice, and the second time Abraham's displeasure at the act was more pronounced (Gen. 21:9–12). Custom, as noted in the prior chapter, was against driving her away; as was also, of course, moral obligation.

[45] Abram means "high father"; Abraham means "father of a multitude" (see p. 30n.70). Sarai is obscure in meaning, with the idea "contentious" perhaps being the most likely, from the root *sarah*. Sarah means "princess."

[46] Circumcision was not unique to Israel. Arabians, Moabites, Edomites, Ammonites, and Egyptians practiced it; see G. L. Robinson, *The Bearing of Archaeology on the Old Testament* (New York: American Tract Society, 1941), p. 26, for a tomb picture of a circumcision operation. Circumcision was unique, however, in being used as a sign of God's covenant with His people.

[47] A prime example is Job, tried so severely by Satan to make him curse God.

event itself, Abraham was again guilty of telling a half-truth regarding his wife; this time to Abimelech, king of Gerar, a city west of Beersheba. About twenty-five years had elapsed since the similar occasion in Egypt, and perhaps Abraham's memory had dimmed regarding the reprimand and humiliation then experienced. Abimelech took Sarah to his palace, as had Pharaoh at the earlier time, but God once more intervened to protect her. God revealed to Abimelech her true relationship to Abraham through a dream.

2. Early Philistines

The land where Abimelech lived is called "the land of the Philistines" (Gen. 21:32, 34). Also, later when Isaac had further dealings in the area, the people themselves are called Philistines (Gen. 26:1, 8, 14, 15, 18). Were these people indeed the ancestors of those of the same name following Israel's conquest?

Liberal scholars commonly answer negatively, taking these mentions as anachronistic.[48] But reason exists for at least a partially positive answer. It is true that the major number of Philistines came to Palestine as a member group of the Sea Peoples that were repulsed by Rameses III of Egypt c. 1190 B.C.[49]

But this does not preclude the possibility that some ancestors came many years before. Archaeological evidence testifies that they did. Caphtorian type pottery, like that which Philistines left later in Palestine, since their earlier home had been the region of Caphtor, has been found both in Philistia proper and as far inland as Bethshan and Jericho, dating at least to 1500 B.C. Furthermore, that there was communication in patriarchal times between Canaan and Caphtor has been evidenced—first, by discovery of Middle Minoan II pottery at both Hazor and Ugarit and, second, by an eighteenth-century Mari document that mentions the king of Hazor sending gifts to Kaptara (Caphtor).[50]

Flinders Petrie years ago suggested that rationale for this early coming of Philistines—namely, that there was a desire to export grain back to the rocky, non-self-supporting homeland.[51] Petrie's discovery of sickles in the Philistine region from the early period indicates that grain was grown.

---

[48] For instance, Wright, *BAR*, p. 40; Burrows, *What Mean These Stones?* (New Haven: American Schools of Oriental Research, 1951), p. 277. Another item said to be anachronistic is the mention of camels (e.g., Gen. 24:10, 11, 14, 19), asserting that "the camel had not been generally domesticated as yet" (Wright, *BAR,* p. 40). However, Free, *ABH,* p. 55 (see his article, "Abraham's Camels," *JNES* [July 1944]: 187–93; also Kitchen, *AOOT,* pp. 79–80; and R. DeVaux, *Theology Digest* 12 [1964]: 233), says that camels were known in Egypt even before Abraham, listing as evidence "statuettes and figurines of camels, plaques bearing representations of camels, rock carvings and drawings, camel bones, a camel skull, and a camel hair rope" all dating "from the seventh century B.C. to the period before 3000 B.C."

[49] The Sea Peoples were constituted of at least five ethnic groups who moved from the Aegean area, particularly Crete, perhaps pushed in turn by European migrators. The *prst* group is identified with the Philistines, the hieroglyphic script using *r* for *l,* a change not uncommon; see Albright, *AASOR* 12 (1934): 53–58; Wright, *BAR,* pp. 87–88; Freedman, *BA* 26 (December 1963): 145–49.

[50] C. Gordon calls the Philistine migration of 1200 B.C. only a late migration "in a long series of migrations that had established various Caphtor folk in Canaan long before 1500 B.C."; *ANE,* pp. 121–22. Gordon believes that Caphtor is a name for the whole "Aegean and Minoan sphere"; *ANE,* p. 85.

[51] Flinders Petrie, *Palestine and Israel* (London: Society for Promoting Christian Knowledge, 1934), p. 62, as cited by Free, *ABH,* p. 6.

H. NEAR SACRIFICE
OF ISAAC
(Genesis 22)

1. Birth of Isaac
(Genesis 21:1–21)

Shortly after Abraham's encounter with Abimelech, the wonderful promise regarding Isaac's birth was fulfilled (Gen. 21:1–8). The long-awaited child was born. This was certainly a memorable day for Abraham and Sarah. It led Sarah, however, to request a second time that Hagar and Ishmael be sent away, Ishmael now being fourteen years old. The "Angel of God" found the mother and son in the desert, suffering from lack of food, and then provided for their need (Gen. 21:9–21).

2. Abraham's most severe test
(Genesis 22:1–14)

After a few years,[52] God brought Abraham his most severe test. He called him to sacrifice this promised son. No other request could have been quite so difficult to fulfill. The boy meant much to Abraham in terms of personal affection, in view of his miraculous birth, but even more in terms of the fulfillment of God's promise. How could a nation be formed through him if he were now sacrificed? But still Abraham was able to obey. He had grown in faith as God had led and blessed him, and he was now able to meet even this challenge.

God had designated the place for the sacrifice as Mount Moriah,[53] and Abraham took three days to get there. This means that he traveled slowly, perhaps with the thought that God might give him counterorders. But none came—that is, not until the boy had been bound and Abraham had raised the knife to perform the actual sacrifice. Then God did intervene. He told Abraham that he should substitute for Isaac a ram caught in a nearby thicket. God let Abraham go this far, to prove his sincerity of faith. One can hardly think of a greater test. At no time did Abraham's faith shine more brightly. The Book of Hebrews says in explanation that Abraham believed that God would even raise Isaac from the dead in order to fulfill the promise regarding the nation (11:9).

I. DEATH AND BURIAL
OF SARAH
(Genesis 23)

Sarah died at the age of 127. Isaac was 37 at the time; Abraham still had 38 years to live. Sarah had been married to Abraham while they were yet in Ur of the Chaldees (Gen. 11:29–31). She was Abraham's half-sister, the daughter of his father, but not of his mother (Gen. 20:12). She had been an obedient wife to Abraham, even acceding to his sinful request that she pass herself off as his sister, first to the Egyptian Pharaoh and later to Abime-

---

[52] The passage does not say how many, but likely Isaac was not more than ten years old. He goes with his father quite as a matter of course, even permitting himself to be bound without apparent protest. His question, "Where is the lamb for the burnt offering?" indicates that he was old enough to reason but also shows that he was young enough not to have asked the question prior to the arrival at the mountain or for the father to have shared such information with him.

[53] The designation "Moriah" occurs only twice in the Old Testament: here in the form "region of Moriah" and in 2 Chronicles 3:1 as "on Mount Moriah," where the reference is to the mountain where Solomon built the temple. Some scholars have objected that the distance is not great enough from Beersheba to this Moriah of Solomon for Abraham's three days of travel. However, he was in no hurry. The identification is likely.

lech. She had displayed a vindictive spirit, however, in turning against Hagar when the latter bore her son Ishmael to Abraham.

A Hittite named Ephron sold Abraham the cave of Machpelah at Kirjatharba (Hebron) as a burial place for Sarah. The business transaction is briefly described (Gen. 23:3–16) and—though recent scholars have challenged the parallel—may reveal the possible influence in Ephron's thinking of a law of the Hittites to which he apparently felt bound.[54] The law was that the owner of any property obligated himself to the state for military duties as long as he owned it. When Abraham asked to buy only the cave of Machpelah, Ephron urged him to take the whole field in which it was located. If he was to be rid of a part of his property, he apparently wanted to be rid of it all and so avoid this military obligation.

Abraham finally did buy the whole field, paying four hundred shekels for it, weighing the money to Ephron.[55] The transaction was effected before the "children of Heth" (KJV) and so made public and binding. This was the only real estate that Abraham purchased of the total land God had promised to give him for his posterity.

J. A BRIDE FOR ISAAC
(Genesis 24:1–25:11)

1. Rebekah is found
(Genesis 24)

Three years after Sarah's death, when Isaac was forty years old (Gen. 25:20), Abraham sought a bride for his son. He did not want Isaac to marry a daughter of Canaanite neighbors. He apparently recognized that marriage with the Canaanites—now by his son and later by future generations—would result in amalgamation. A distinction must be maintained if Abraham's posterity was to develop into a separate nation.[56]

Abraham, thus, thought of his relatives[57] who lived in northern Mesopotamia[58] (where he had stopped years before with his father, Terah). Isaac's wife should come from these. So decided, Abraham sent his senior servant, probably Eliezer (Gen. 15:2), on the long journey to find the one whom Abraham believed God Himself would select (Gen. 24:7).

[54] For discussion, see Cyrus Gordon, "Abraham and the Merchants of Ura," *JNES* 17 (1958): 29; also Charles F. Pfeiffer, *The Patriarchal Age* (Grand Rapids: Baker, 1961), pp. 115–16. Kitchen, *BW*, p. 71, considers the question to be open at this point.

[55] Coinage was not yet practiced, and money was valued in terms of weight. Earliest evidence of coinage (striking of a piece of metal with a seal authenticating its title and weight) comes from the Lydians of Asia Minor perhaps as early as the late eighth century B.C. By the late seventh century, coined money was plentiful in the Aegean region. Probably Cyrus the Great introduced the practice to the Persian world about 540 B.C.

[56] Abraham's example was followed by Isaac in his direction to Jacob that he take his wife from elsewhere (Gen. 28:1–5). Esau, knowing that Canaanite wives displeased his father, married a daughter of Ishmael, though he had previously married two Hittite girls (Gen. 26:34), which was "a source of grief to Isaac and Rebekah."

[57] Persons indicated as living there are those of Nahor's family, particularly his son, Bethuel, and two children of Bethuel, Rebekah and Laban. Nahor had either accompanied Terah and Abraham in going there or else made the journey from Ur himself later.

[58] The term used here for the area is Aram-naharaim (Gen. 24:10), also employed in Deuteronomy 23:4 and Judges 3:8. It means "Aram of the two rivers," referring to the Euphrates and Tigris, and so speaks of all northern Mesopotamia. Another term used in the account is Padan-aram (Gen. 25:20; 28:2; 31:18), meaning "Field of Aram." This term seems to have more specifically designated the region near Haran.

The servant went and arrived at the "town of Nahor" (likely Haran), so called in the account because Nahor, Abraham's brother, now lived there.[59] Under God's blessing and guidance, the servant met Rebekah, Nahor's granddaughter, at a well on the edge of town as she came to draw water. Displaying kindness and hospitality, Rebekah drew water not only for the servant but also for his camels, an action that served as a confirming sign to the servant that this was the person whom God had selected. Highly encouraged, the servant went with the young lady into the city, met her family (Gen. 24:29–50)—including Bethuel (her father) and Laban (her brother)—told of his mission, and received consent for Rebekah to accompany him to become Isaac's wife. Rebekah was agreeable to this arrangement and went with him to meet and begin her life with Isaac.

2. Abraham's marriage to Keturah (Genesis 25:1–11)

Abraham still lived thirty-five years after Isaac's marriage. He married Keturah, of whom nothing is known before this time. Six sons were born to them: Zimran, Jokshan, Medan, Midian, Ishbak, and Shuah,[60] all of whom became ancestors of various Arabian peoples. Nothing is known of Abraham's life during this period. He died at the advanced age of 175 (Gen. 25:7), and Isaac and Ishmael buried him next to Sarah in the cave of Machpelah. Isaac alone was designated as heir, though Abraham set aside certain gifts for Ishmael and Keturah's six sons.

K. ABRAHAM, MAN OF FAITH

Abraham was truly one of the great men of the Old Testament. He was a man of outstanding faith, demonstrated especially in his willingness to leave Ur of the Chaldees for an unidentified land and to sacrifice his own son, even believing God would raise him from the dead to fulfill the promise of a great nation. He was magnanimous, giving Lot first choice of the land he desired. He was forgiving, willing to aid Lot after Lot's selfish choice—first by delivering him from invaders and then by interceding for him (after learning that the wicked city of Sodom, Lot's chosen home, was to be destroyed). He was courageous, daring to pursue an army to effect Lot's deliverance.

His one weakness was his prevarication regarding his wife when they came in contact with foreign kings. How to assess or understand this weakness is not easy to know. It does not fit the pattern of his life otherwise. But one should not let this deficiency cloud the other splendid characteristics of the man. He was one who loved God, for which reason the high accolade is accorded him that he was the "friend" of God (2 Chron. 20:7; Isa. 41:8; James 2:23).

---

[59] It could mean a city named Nahor, too, for a Mari text speaks of a city of this name (see p. 14). Its mound has not been identified with certainty but is commonly believed to be near Haran (see Wright, *BAR,* p. 41).

[60] To account for Abraham here having children when previously said to be "as good as dead" (Rom. 4:19) in this respect, Keil suggests that he had married Keturah well before Sarah's death (*KD,* 1:261). This is difficult to understand, however, in view of (1) his reluctance even to take Hagar while Sarah lived and (2) the clear implication of the Genesis account. It is better to think either that his rejuvenation in begetting Isaac as continued on or else that his "deadness" had been only in connection with Sarah, not he, being incapable of having children.

CHAPTER FOUR

ISAAC, JACOB, JOSEPH

Genesis 25:9–50:26

In this chapter our interest remains with the patriarchal period, but now as centered in the three descendants of Abraham: Isaac, Jacob, and Joseph. They represent three successive generations which intervened between Abraham and the period of sojourn for Abraham's posterity in Egypt. Isaac and Jacob differ from Joseph in that, for their generations, they alone lived as members of the line of promise. Joseph, however, had eleven brothers in that line, each one to be head of a respective tribe. But Joseph stands out among them for special consideration, for he was easily the most significant, the one upon whom God had chosen to place special favor, and the one, accordingly, of whom more is said in the sacred record.

A. ISAAC
(Genesis 25:9–26:35)

Isaac[1] is the least known of the three. Considerably more is related in Genesis regarding Jacob and Joseph. Because of this, one tends to think of Isaac more as either the son of Abraham or the father of Jacob, rather than an individual in his own right. Isaac was the least conspicuous of the patriarchs. He was not given to daring action or unusual exploits. But he still constituted an important link in the ancestral chain of Israel and is honored throughout Scripture in parallel with Abraham and Jacob. He was granted longer life than either.

Earlier, in our consideration of Abraham, we have noted some aspects of Isaac's life. We will now take up matters that followed the death of his father.

1. Jacob and Esau born
(Genesis 25:21–34)

The first matter recorded is the birth of Isaac's twin sons, Jacob and Esau. These were born only when Isaac had reached the age of sixty (Gen. 25:26),

---

[1] The name *Isaac* means "one laughs." The reference is to the fact that both Abraham and Sarah laughed (Gen. 17:17–19; 18:9–15) in incredulity that they, at their age, would be promised a child.

twenty years after his marriage to Rebekah. Abraham had waited twenty-five years for Isaac, and now Isaac had waited twenty years for Jacob and Esau. Isaac's faith was tried even as Abraham's, but he, like his father, continued to believe God. It is stated that he "prayed to the LORD on behalf of his wife, because she was barren" (Gen. 25:21). It must have been difficult, however, to understand why God should delay so long in fulfilling the promise of a large posterity. But finally God heard Isaac's prayer, and Rebekah conceived.

Even before birth, the twins struggled within the womb of Rebekah. She inquired as to the significance and God told her that this was a sign that the two, followed in turn by their respective posterities, would struggle with each other in years to come, with the elder being made to serve the younger. Esau was born first, with Jacob grasping his heel.[2]

Growing up, the twins little resembled each other. Jacob was fair, a man of the house, beloved of his mother. Esau was rugged, a man of the outdoors, favored by his father. In keeping with God's prediction, they did clash (Gen. 25:27–34). They had grown to be young men when Jacob one day took advantage of his home position to persuade Esau to sell him his birthright. Having been born first, Esau enjoyed the inheritance rights of the eldest son. Jacob wanted these rights and persuaded Esau to exchange them for a portion of food Jacob was preparing.[3] Esau, having been in the field, was hungry and foolishly made the trade urged by Jacob. Jacob is to be criticized for coveting something that was not his own, but, at the same time, Esau gave up a legal right of lifelong value for the satisfaction of a moment. The birthright secured for its owner the headship of the family and the possession of a major share of family property. How poorly Esau measured relative values!

2. Relations With Philistines (Genesis 26:1–33)

A famine in the land prompted Isaac to move, as an earlier famine had prompted a similar action on the part of his father. God warned him not to go to Egypt, however, but only to a place He would designate. The location proved to be near the city of Gerar,[4] where Philistines[5] lived, an area where Abraham had similarly sojourned (Gen. 20:1–18).

Here Isaac followed in the sin which his father had twice committed—telling an untruth regarding his wife. Rebekah was fair, as Sarah had been, and Isaac feared for his life. He spread the word that Rebekah was his sister, a deception still more serious than Abraham's, for Sarah at least had been Abraham's half-sister. It was sometime

---

[2] The name *Jacob* derives from a root that means both "to grasp the heel" and "to deceive." The Hebrew love of puns is evident in the naming of one who was born grasping his brother's heel and who would be characterized, in his early life, by deception. "Cheater" or "deceiver" may catch the implications of Jacob's name. The name *Esau* means "hairy," in description of him at birth.

[3] Nuzi tablets give instances of similar negotiation in inheritance rights between brothers. In one a brother sells a grove, which was his inheritance, to another brother for three sheep; see Gordon, *ANE,* p. 126; also Wright, *BAR,* p. 43.

[4] Formerly identified with Tell Jemmeh, eight miles south of Gaza, but now thought to be Tell Abu Hureira, eleven miles southeast of Gaza (Albright, *BASOR* 163 [October 1961]: 47–48).

[5] See p. 45.

later that Abimelech,[6] the Gerar ruler, learned of the deception, warned his people against familiarity with Rebekah, and graciously permitted Isaac to remain in his land.

Isaac accepted this hospitality, planted crops, and reaped a fine harvest. His wealth, inherited and now increased, made Abimelech's people jealous, and Abimelech finally asked him to leave. Isaac did so, but went only as far as a valley in the general vicinity. Here he reopened wells which Abraham had dug and which the Philistines had later refilled. Isaac experienced continued ill will from the people who claimed each well Isaac reopened. At last he moved back to Beersheba and there received a visit from Abimelech, who now wished to make a covenant with him regarding land rights; and this was done.

A bright aspect of this otherwise unhappy period is that God confirmed His covenant with Isaac, as He had with Abraham; in fact, this happened two different times. The first was just before Isaac went to Gerar, when God not only told him not to go to Egypt, but promised him great seed and possession of the land in which he lived (Gen. 26:2–5); and the second was just after his return from Gerar, when God promised to be with him, to bless him, and to multiply his seed for Abraham's sake (Gen. 26:24).

3. The stolen blessing (Genesis 27:1–46)

At the age of 137,[7] Isaac took steps to bestow the parental blessing on his eldest son. In spite of God's clear indication at the birth of the two boys that the elder should serve the younger (Gen. 25:23), Isaac determined to perform the rite in favor of Esau, who was his favorite. However, Rebekah wanted it for Jacob. She persuaded Jacob, who at first was reticent, to disguise himself as his brother in order to procure it. She placed goat skin on his hands and neck so that he would appear to be his hairy brother Esau and dressed him in his brother's clothing. Isaac, who was nearly blind, had to depend on touch and smell for identification, and so was deceived. Isaac's intensive questioning of his visitor seems to indicate a high level of suspicion on his part, but, unable to confirm his suspicion, he bestowed the blessing, calling for the recipient to receive abundant material provisions and rule over both his mother's posterity and surrounding nations.

Jacob had scarcely left his father's presence when Esau came expecting to receive the blessing. When both father and son realized the deception that had been perpetrated, each experienced remorse and anger. But what had been done, even though in this manner, was binding,[8] and all Isaac could do for Esau was grant a secondary blessing, promising all that was left, the arid lands out of reach of the winter rains and subservience to his younger brother. Bitter hatred stirred in Esau's heart, and he resolved to kill Jacob as soon as their father died. Accordingly, at Rebekah's urging, Jacob made ready to flee north to the home country of Rebekah in Haran.

---

[6] Probably a descendant of the Abimelech visited by Abraham.

[7] Isaac would live to be 180 years old (Gen. 35:28), so he still had 43 years to live, but he could not know this. His age here is figured on the basis that Jacob was now 77 (see below, n.11) and he was born when Isaac was 60.

[8] See p. 15.

4. Isaac the man

Isaac as a person is not easy to understand. He is accorded a high place in Scripture as an important member in Israel's lineage, and yet there is comparatively little in the record for which to admire him. It is true that he showed faith when he continued to trust God for children after twenty years of waiting. But many of his actions and omissions otherwise call for criticism. He followed his father in the sin of telling an untruth regarding his wife. Moreover, his two sons seem not to have been properly instructed and disciplined in religious matters; Jacob came to be known as a deceiver and demonstrated little understanding of the greatness of God (Gen. 28:16–22), and Esau married pagan girls (Gen. 26:34; 36:1–2). Even Isaac's wife exhibited little fear of God and less respect for her husband as she schemed with her son to steal a blessing intended for another.

Clearly, Isaac (in contrast with Abraham and Jacob) was not a man of action. This must be borne in mind in evaluating him. Almost never is he seen in situations which called for initiative or a display of faith. He left the matter of choice of wife entirely to his father and readily accepted the one provided. When Philistines successively claimed wells he had reopened, he did not greatly protest but moved on to dig others. He seems never to have traveled outside the confines of southern Canaan in all his 180 years.[9] And never is he said to have been asked by God, as was Abraham, to perform actions calling for great faith.

One reason may be that in early life he had been dominated by an outstanding father and later was simply content to bask in the greatness Abraham had displayed. No doubt, too, he was naturally one of more retiring personality, not given to aggressive, outward demonstration, a characteristic that in itself can be commendable. In fact, one can admire Isaac for being willing to receive his chosen wife Rebekah so readily and also, without serious protest, to give up wells to enemies; certainly meekness is high on the list of godly virtues. But still, if Isaac were truly a great man of God, one would expect more evidence of this than exists, particularly of his good influence on those who were near him. He knew God and was a worthy member of the patriarchal line, but certainly he fell short of the measure of either Abraham or Jacob.

B. JACOB
(Genesis 28:1–36:43)

Jacob, the third patriarch, contrasts markedly with his father. Like Abraham, he was a man of action, but unlike him, Jacob was a man whose recorded actions demonstrate a consistent deceitfulness. He is known then for his deceptions. We have already noted his schemes against his brother and father; and he would later take advantage of his uncle Laban, who, it must be admitted, probably deserved his treatment. In later life, however, God changed him, and he became truly devoted. Much more is said regarding him than Isaac.

---

[9]Most references show him near either Beersheba or Gerar (Gen. 24:62; 25:11; 26:1, 23; 28:10), though he was at Hebron when Jacob returned from Haran (Gen. 35:27–29).

1. The flight to Haran
(Genesis 28:1–29:13)

Before Jacob departed for Rebekah's homeland, Isaac summoned him. Though Jacob had wronged his father, Isaac loved him and had his best interest in mind. Isaac bestowed further blessing on him and then charged him not to take a wife from the Canaanites, but rather from his mother's relation in Haran.[10] It should be realized that Jacob at this time was no longer young. A comparison of Scriptures reveals that he was seventy-seven years of age.[11]

Jacob departed and had proceeded as far as Bethel when, resting for the night, he had a dream of a ladder reaching to heaven, with angels ascending and descending upon it (Gen. 28:10–22).[12] In the morning, properly impressed that God was with him, he poured oil on the stone that he used for a pillow, called the place Bethel (house of God), and made solemn promises to God. His pouring oil on the stone was a symbolic way of giving religious importance to the place, for God had here reassured him of His abiding presence. Jacob needed this reassurance because he was carrying a deserved guilty conscience for his action toward Esau. Also, all that we know of him points to spiritual immaturity on his part at the time, and we may believe that little thought of God had crossed his mind as he had left home.

His response to the dream, accordingly, was one of amazement, appreciation, and then determination to reciprocate with proper conduct of life. This new thinking was to be of great importance for him as he would soon enter a land where false deities were worshiped (Gen. 31:19, 30) and where he would encounter an uncle who would work treachery against him.

Jacob met Rachel, his bride-to-be, as she came to water her flock of sheep at a well near Haran. Jacob had arrived somewhat sooner and found shepherds awaiting removal of the well's covering stone. He now proceeded to move the stone himself so that he could water Rachel's flock. Jacob apparently was physically strong and not one to wait long for others or to be hindered by local customs. No one objected to the brusque action, and Rachel's flock was watered early that day. Jacob told her who he was; she in turn called her father, Laban, who came and greeted Jacob; and then all went to the uncle's house. Here Jacob was to spend twenty unusual years.

2. Twenty years in Haran
(Genesis 29:14–31:20)

a. Jacob's two wives (Gen. 29:14–31). Jacob loved Rachel from the beginning and agreed with Laban to serve him seven years for her hand in marriage. When the seven years were completed, Laban showed his deceitfulness by giving Leah, his eldest

---

[10] Isaac's urging of Jacob to seek a wife in the north does not contradict Rebekah's interest that he flee north to escape from Esau. The prime reason for his going was to escape from his brother, but in addition Isaac wanted him to find a wife. Rebekah and Isaac were agreed on this as shown by their mutual anxiety that Esau had married local girls (Gen. 26:34–35).

[11] When Jacob was 130 at his descent to Egypt (Gen. 47:9), Joseph was 39 (41:46, 47, 54; 45:11), which means that Jacob was 90 when Joseph was born. Joseph was born 14 years after Jacob's arrival in Haran (31:41; 30:25), which, subtracted from 91, leaves 77.

[12] The significance of this God-sent dream was to show Jacob that God was maintaining a constant means of communication between Jacob and Himself. In other words, Jacob was important to Him and could know that God was with him to help as he would look to Him.

daughter, to Jacob in place of Rachel. Laban explained that the custom of the country was that the elder sister should marry first.[13] He could have told Jacob this seven years before but had not, and now Jacob found it necessary to work another seven years for the one he loved. To be deceived in terms of seven years employment is not a small matter. Jacob could not have helped but remember the similar deceptions he had perpetrated against his brother and father.

Jacob did not have to wait seven years before Rachel was given to him, however.[14] He waited only one week, while wedding festivities for Leah were completed (Gen. 29:27–28). He was then permitted to marry Rachel also, but he was expected to work seven additional years in payment for her, which he did.[15]

b. Jacob's children (Gen. 29:32–30:24). It was at this point that the promise to Abraham of more than a century and a half earlier[16] began to be fulfilled in greater degree. Jacob was now given a large family (Gen. 29:31–30:24). Though Jacob favored Rachel, it was through Leah that God gave Jacob his first and most children. Leah bore in succession Reuben (see, a son), Simeon (hearing), Levi (joining), and Judah (praise). Rachel, who continued to be barren, now urged Jacob to raise up children unto her through her handmaid, Bilhah.[17] Jacob did so, and

Bilhah gave birth to Dan (judge) and Naphtali (wrestling). Leah then countered by giving her handmaid, Zilpah, to Jacob; and to her were born Gad (troop) and Asher (gladness). At this point, God again blessed Leah with children, and she bore Issachar (he brings wages) and Zebulon (dwelling). She also gave birth to a daughter, Dinah (judgment). Finally, God permitted Rachel to conceive, and she bore Joseph (adding). This gave Jacob eleven sons and one daughter. The twelfth son, Benjamin (son of my right hand), was born to Rachel, too, but not until the family had moved back to Canaan (Gen. 35:16–20).

c. The last six years (Gen. 30:25–31:21). Following Joseph's birth, and with the completion of the fourteen years of service owed, Jacob asked permission of Laban to leave the land; but Laban persuaded him to remain longer (Gen. 30:25–34). Apparently Jacob had been a good worker and his employment thus far had cost Laban little. Laban wanted more of this advantageous relationship.

Jacob set as his new wage all Laban's sheep and goats that were other than solid white or solid black (or dark brown), including those living and those to be born while he worked. Laban agreed, since he knew that normally few animals were born spotted. Jacob now sought to better his own interests through selective breeding

---

[13] This custom seems to have been only local, for no other evidence of it exists. Jacob, however, acceded in apparent recognition of it.

[14] Evidenced both by the episode as told (Gen. 29:27–30) and that strife existed between Leah and Rachel from the first in respect to bearing Jacob children (Gen. 29:31–30:24).

[15] What would have happened had Jacob left for Palestine before completing these additional years (which normal reaction to Laban's treachery could have indicated) is not made clear. It is to Jacob's credit that he paid what he owed. Sometimes Jacob's deficiencies in character are overemphasized.

[16] Adding 25 years until Isaac's birth, 60 until Jacob's, and then Jacob's age here of 77 gives 162 total years.

[17] See p. 15.

measures (Gen. 30:40) and devices for prenatal influence.[18] Jacob apparently felt justified in this course of action in light of Laban's earlier trickery. God prospered Jacob, and the spotted animals became unusually numerous. Laban, probably pressured by his sons,[19] countered by changing the agreement, as Jacob later says, ten times (Gen. 31:7, 41), but still Jacob prospered. His flocks and herds became very large; indeed, so large that, when he later left for home, after working for this wage only six years, he could afford a gift of 580 animals[20] at one time to his brother Esau (Gen. 32:13–16).

Recognizing that his prosperity at his father-in-law's expense did not endear him to the Haran relation, Jacob left after six years (for a total of twenty years) of this arrangement (Gen. 31:1–20). His own desire to leave was reinforced by a dream in which God gave direct instruction. Even his wives, daughters of Laban that they were, supported his action.

Jacob waited until a day when Laban was away for sheepshearing, apparently lest his uncle try to hinder or make matters unpleasant by claiming a substantial portion of Jacob's property. Then Jacob took his two wives, twelve children, servants, and abundant livestock, and departed for home. Unknown to Jacob, Rachel took the family idols also, which some have suggested were significant for symbolizing inheritance rights,[21] possibly in a desire thus to have evidence of Jacob's right to all he possessed. As he left, Jacob recognized that God had been good to him. Jacob had come to Haran as one person alone and now, after twenty years, was departing as a wealthy man with a large family (Gen. 32:10).

3. Return to Canaan (Genesis 31:21–33:20)

a. Laban's pursuit (Gen. 31:22–55). Laban was angry when he discovered Jacob's secret departure. Immediately he pursued Jacob's slower moving company, but was unable to catch the group until it had reached Mount Gilead, at least 275 miles from Haran.[22] While it is no longer possible to equate possession of the idols with inheritance rights with certainty, recovery of the household gods does seem to have been an important motivation for Laban. For all the effort, however, Laban accomplished little. God warned him in a dream not to speak harshly to Jacob, and his own daughter tricked him so that he was unable to locate the idols (Gen. 31:32–35). The matter ended with an agreement that neither he nor Jacob would impose on the other again.

b. Jacob's wrestling match (Gen. 32:24–32). As Jacob now continued

---

[18] Genesis 30:37–39 says that he peeled white stripes on tree branches and set these before the animals as they bred. He believed that these would effect spotted offspring. Many spotted animals did result, but only because God blessed to that end.

[19] Genesis 31:1 suggests this thought. It may be that these sons had been born since Jacob's arrival, for none are mentioned earlier and apparently they were still too young to be a factor when the bargain was first made with Laban.

[20] Mostly sheep and goats. However, also camels, asses, and cattle were included, indicating that Jacob had been able to accumulate these from Laban as well.

[21] See p. 15.

[22] It is this distance to the northernmost fringes of Mount Gilead which was likely the region. To travel this far in seven days (Gen. 31:23) is fast travel. Jacob had started three days earlier and had moved quickly also, particularly since he had to drive sheep and goats.

his journey, he feared an inevitable meeting with Esau; but before that meeting could occur, he experienced another confrontation of much greater significance. This came in the form of a wrestling match with the Angel of Yahweh. Jacob was alone on the north bank of the Jabbok River. He had sent his family and possessions across the stream the prior evening and had remained by himself apparently for a time of private devotion.

During the night, the Angel drew near and began to wrestle with him. Jacob was now ninety-seven years old but evidently still in good physical condition. He realized as the match progressed that his opponent was more than human, and accordingly he asked for a blessing. He remembered well the dream of twenty years before (when he had left the land) and the resulting benefit in his life. He wished now for a renewed blessing. He wanted to be assured that God would continue to be with him.

The Angel gave this assurance. As tangible evidence, he changed Jacob's name to Israel[23] and touched his thigh, apparently dislocating the hip. From now on, Jacob would limp, but it would be a constant reminder of both God's gracious favor and his own responsibility for proper life conduct. From this time on, Jacob is not seen scheming or deceiving.

c. Jacob's meeting with Esau (Gen. 32:1–23; 33:1–17). On the next day, Jacob received clear evidence that God indeed was blessing him. He met Esau, and no bitterness was shown (Gen. 33:1–17). Jacob had dreaded this meeting, especially after having learned that Esau, accompanied by four hundred men, was coming to meet him (Gen. 32:3–6). Jacob had sent three droves of animals as presents in an attempt to appease his brother's anticipated anger, but these presents proved to be unnecessary.

Somehow Esau's heart had mellowed through the intervening twenty years. He, too, possessed material wealth, and at first he refused Jacob's gifts; but Jacob urged him to accept, and he did. The brothers embraced each other warmly, exchanged pleasantries, and parted—with all previous barriers removed. Jacob's heart was now much lighter for moving on. Esau returned to his chosen territory of Mount Seir, south of the Dead Sea, and Jacob continued across the Jordan to Shechem.[24]

4. Back in Canaan (Genesis 34–36)

Arriving at Shechem, Jacob was unable to remain long as a result of the slaughter of Shechemites by two of his sons, Simeon and Levi (Gen. 34:1–31). A young man, Shechem, son of Hamor, leader in the city of Shechem, took Dinah, violated her, and requested permission of Jacob to marry her. Jacob's sons devised a plan for revenge. All Shechemites would have to

---

[23] The name *Israel* comes from the verb, *sarah,* meaning "to strive," from which also the noun, *sar,* meaning "prince" or "striver" comes. The last element of the name, *'el,* means "God." The full name means "prince (striver) with God."

[24] Jacob here purchased a tract of land from Hamor (Gen. 33:18–20). Today one can view a site known to tradition as Jacob's well just outside old Shechem, supposedly located on the tract that Jacob bought. Here Jesus met the woman of Samaria years later (John 4). For discussion of the well, see George E. Wright, *Shechem* (New York: McGraw-Hill, 1965), pp. 215–17. It is not known when the well was dug, but very likely it was in Old Testament time.

be circumcised if Shechem's request were granted. Hamor and Shechem agreed, and all Shechemites were circumcised. Then, while they were incapacitated and unable to defend themselves, they were killed by Simeon and Levi. Dinah was brought home. Jacob, fearing reprisal from other inhabitants of the area, quickly moved further south.

Jacob now came again to Bethel, where he had experienced his memorable dream (Gen. 35:1–10). Once more God appeared to him, this time renewing the promises given to both Abraham and Isaac concerning a large posterity and the land of Canaan as an inheritance (Gen. 35:11–13). He traveled farther south. When he drew near Bethlehem, Rachel died while giving birth to Benjamin (Gen. 35:16–20), and Jacob set a monument on the grave[25] of this one whom he dearly loved. He then moved on to Hebron where he found his father yet living. Jacob now seems to have lived with, or at least near, his father for the remainder of Isaac's life.[26] When Isaac died, Esau came to join Jacob for his burial (Gen. 35:27–29).

At this point in the record, Esau's generations are enumerated, closing with the words, "This was Esau the father of the Edomites" (Gen. 36:1–43). In later years Edom proved to be a perennial enemy of Israel.

5. Jacob, a transformed man

The biblical portions that deal with Jacob present the picture of a man who has been transformed by the power of God. In his early life, he was a schemer and deceiver, but in later days he became a devout follower of God. Before the change, he bargained for his brother's birthright, deceived for his father's blessing, and schemed for his uncle's flocks; after the change, he lived a life of quiet meditation, was grieved at his sons' sinful activities, and was a proper recipient for God's further revelation of covenantal blessing.

One should not judge Jacob too harshly for his early wrong actions, however, for it was his mother who persuaded him to deceive his father, and surely his uncle gave him severe provocation for retaliation while he was in Haran. Nevertheless, Jacob did find it easy to fit into these roles, and it should be remembered that the bargain for his brother's birthright was of his own doing.

The great change in Jacob's life came at two points. The first was at Bethel, on his way to Haran, where he encountered God in a way he had never experienced before; yet afterwards he could still engage his uncle in their standoff of wrongdoing. The second was at the brook Jabbok, where, on his return from the north, he wrestled with the Angel of Yahweh. That Jacob did experience change at this time was important for the rearing of his sons, who by this time were growing old enough to experience his influence.

C. JOSEPH
(Genesis 37–50)

The account continues with the life of Joseph. As noted earlier, he was the

---

[25] A grave for her is still marked today by a small Moslem mosque on the northern outskirts of Bethlehem, but the actual site is probably farther north (see 1 Sam. 10:2).

[26] Isaac far outlived expectations (see above, n.7). Esau had said twenty years earlier that he would kill Jacob when his father was dead (Gen. 27:41), but Isaac had lived all during Jacob's absence and still was to live twenty-three years more until he reached the age of 180 (Gen. 35:28).

outstanding son of Jacob's twelve. He was a person of remarkable gifts and sense of dedication. He had the faith of Abraham, the gentleness of Isaac, and the courage of Jacob. Above all, he was a man of obedience to God and one of the most admirable persons in all the Old Testament. The closing chapters of Genesis center mainly on his experiences.

1. Sold Into Egypt
(Genesis 37)

At the age of seventeen,[27] Joseph was sold into Egypt by his brothers. Their ill will toward him had been prompted by his father's favoritism and his own unwise action of relating dreams that predicted his superiority over both them and his parents (Gen. 37:5–11).

The treachery occurred at Dothan. Father Jacob had sent Joseph from Hebron to the area where the brothers were pasturing the family flocks. They had gone north some fifty miles to Shechem for this purpose; but, when Joseph came there, he found that they had now moved on another fifteen miles to Dothan. Pasture apparently was scarce in southern Canaan. The brothers recognized Joseph while he was still some distance off and immediately plotted against him. Most wished to take his life, but Reuben, the oldest, and Judah, who often assumed leadership, urged in different ways that his life be spared. The matter was settled when a caravan of Midianites[28] traveling to Egypt passed by, and Joseph was sold as a slave for the price of twenty pieces of silver.[29]

The emotional shock to Joseph must have been severe, not only for being sold as a slave into a foreign country, but for being rejected and treacherously treated by his own brothers. The brothers then deceived their father into thinking that Joseph had been killed by a wild beast. They presented him with Joseph's fine, specially made robe, which they had dipped in the blood of a goat, letting it serve as mute evidence of his death.

2. Judah and Tamar
(Genesis 38)

The record of Joseph's life is interrupted at this point by a sad episode in the life of Judah, involving Tamar, his daughter-in-law. When Judah's son Er died without progeny, Tamar, wife of Er, was given to Onan, the younger brother, in keeping with the levirate principle.[30] When Onan also died childless, Tamar waited for still a younger brother, Shelah, to reach maturity that she might marry him and still have hope of children. Judah did not give Shelah to her, however, and when some time had passed, Tamar took a bold step in posing as a prosti-

---

[27] Genesis 37:2. Joseph was born when his father had served Laban fourteen years (Gen. 30:23–26) and so was six when Jacob returned to Canaan. This means eleven years had elapsed since his return.

[28] Called both Midianites and Ishmaelites (Gen. 37:28). As Midianites, they were descendants of Abraham by Keturah; as Ishmaelites, they were descendants of Hagar. On the basis of Judges 8:1, 24, it is obvious that the two names are synonymous or overlapping.

[29] Twenty shekels was the average price of a slave at this time. In prior centuries the price had been less, averaging ten to fifteen shekels, and by the fifteenth century, thirty to forty shekels. This is further confirmation of this episode occurring in the early centuries of the second millennium. For references, see Kitchen, *AOOT*, pp. 52–53.

[30] Indicating that the principle of levirate marriage was recognized at this period in history.

tute in order to have a child by Judah himself. Her scheme worked, and twins were born to her.[31]

The influence of Hittite law may be reflected in Tamar's action, for it held that, when no brother-in-law existed to fulfill the levirate duty, the father-in-law was responsible.[32] Accordingly, Judah said to Tamar, even though she had tricked him, that she was more righteous than he (Gen. 38:26). Also, Ugarit sources attest the custom of showing three different items to prove identification in such a situation, as Tamar did in presenting Judah's signet, cord, and staff as evidence that Judah indeed was the father of her twins.[33]

3. Joseph in Egypt (Genesis 39–41).

Joseph's trials did not end when he reached Egypt. The betrayal of his brothers had been enough to bear, but more injustices awaited him.

a. Injustice in Egypt (Gen. 39–40). He was sold by the Midianites to one Potiphar,[34] officer of Pharaoh. Joseph suffered a major wrong while working for him (Gen. 39:1–20). The young man worked diligently for the new master and was rewarded at first by being elevated to a place of trust. But in this position, Potiphar's wife became

attracted to him, sought to entice him, and, when he resisted her, had him consigned to prison.[35]

Young and away from home restraints, Joseph must be highly admired for this fine behavior in a tempting, difficult situation. Even more must he be commended for not becoming bitter and morose when thrown into prison. Instead, he distinguished himself and was once more rewarded with a position of trust (Gen. 39:21–23).

But again disappointment came (Gen. 40:1–23). Joseph favored two of Pharaoh's servants, a butler and a baker, by interpreting their respective dreams.[36] They expressed appreciation to Joseph at the time, but when the butler was reinstated to his position (according to the interpretation Joseph had given), he promptly forgot Joseph's favor, though Joseph had specifically requested that he try to effect his release.

b. Honored in Egypt (Gen. 41). However, God intervened. Pharaoh himself was made to dream; and the butler, made aware of the ruler's desire that the dream be interpreted, remembered the prisoner who had interpreted his dream (Gen. 41:1–37). He told Pharaoh of Joseph, who was immediately summoned. Joseph's interpreta-

---

[31] One of them, Pharez, apparently became ancestor to David (Ruth 4:18), thus giving this episode, sad in itself, unusual historical significance.

[32] For discussion, see Gordon, *ANE,* p. 136.

[33] Ibid.

[34] Some scholars consider the name *Potiphar* to be of late origin (see DeVaux, *EHI,* pp. 307–9), but for refutation of this view, see Free, *ABH,* pp. 77–78.

[35] A parallel story is found in the Egyptian Tale of Two Brothers. A younger brother, Bitis, resisted the advances of the wife of his older brother Anubis. Like Potiphar's wife, she then charged mistreatment by the younger brother, who had to flee for his life. For text, see Barton, *AB,* pp. 365–67.

[36] The interpretations were that the butler would be reinstated to his former position within three days, while the baker would be killed within that time (Gen. 40:12–23). Both predictions came true. The titles "butler" and "cupbearer" probably derive originally from a time when Pharaoh's court was much simpler. By the time of Joseph, the simple titles of household retainers had come to refer to high government officials.

tion of Pharaoh's dream was that Egypt would soon experience seven years of unusual abundance followed by seven years of terrible famine. He then advised the ruler to procure an able superintendent to store great quantities of food during the plentiful years in preparation for the lean.

Pharaoh followed this advice and promptly placed Joseph himself in that position, reasoning quite correctly that a man through whom God would give this kind of information would be one also able to perform the important task involved (Gen. 41:38–44). Joseph was given authority next to that of Pharaoh himself.[37] What a remarkable elevation this was! One day a prisoner and the next a virtual prime minister!

Of course, this was the high position God had predicted for Joseph years before in his dreams. Other people were now to bow before him, even his brothers and father. We may believe that Joseph had wondered how those dreams could ever come true, particularly after being sold into slavery. But now God had shown him. God had rewarded faithfulness in a manner far surpassing what he could have ever imagined!

Joseph immediately addressed himself to the new work (Gen. 41:45–57), being first given an Egyptian name, Zaphenath-paneah,[38] and an Egyptian wife, Asenath, daughter of a priest of the god Ra.[39] Joseph was thirty years old at the time. During the seven plentiful years he gathered an immense store of food, and during the seven lean years he dispensed it to the people for a price. News of this possible source of supply reached outside of Egypt and people from other countries came.

During the plentiful years Joseph's two sons, Ephraim (*fruitful*) and Manasseh (*causing to forget*), who later took Joseph's place as heads of Israelite tribes, were born to Asenath (Gen. 41:50–52).

4. Extrabiblical matters

Contemporary Egyptian practices and customs illustrate the accuracy of the details of the biblical record.[40] The titles "chief cupbearer" and "chief baker" occur both in Genesis (40:2) and extant Egyptian texts.[41] Famines were known in Egypt, and the idea of persons being assigned to dispense food during these famines is borne out in tomb inscriptions. One inscription speaks even of a seven-year famine at the time of the Third Dynasty (c. 2700 B.C.).[42]

Indication is made on the Rosetta Stone that the Pharaoh had a custom of releasing prisoners on his birthday, as he did the butler (Gen. 40:20). Joseph shaved before seeing Pharaoh (Gen. 41:14), and shaving was a distinctive custom in Egypt. Pharaoh gave Joseph

---

[37] The degree of his authority is revealed by the freedom he exercised in making decisions, apparently without consulting the Pharaoh. For instance, he set the price the people were to pay for the food, even telling them they could pay in animals when their money was gone and later in land when the animals were gone (Gen. 47:14–26).

[38] "The one who furnishes the sustenance of the land." Von Rad, *Genesis: A Commentary* (Philadelphia: Westminster, 1972), renders it, "The God speaks and he lives."

[39] See p. 25n.53.

[40] See Gordon, *ANE*, pp. 139–40 for discussion.

[41] See George Ernest Wright and Floyd Vivian Filson, eds., *The Westminster Atlas to the Bible* (Philadelphia: Westminster, 1945), p. 28b.

[42] Ibid.

a signet ring, linen clothing, and a gold chain (Gen. 41:42), all three of which were mentioned in Egyptian texts for similar use.

Some scholars have objected to the idea of Joseph, a Semite, being elevated to such a high position in Egypt; but a letter dating from the Amarna period has been found written to a person in a similar position having the Semitic name Dudu (David).[43] Given the preferred early date for the Exodus, the Twelfth Dynasty ruled at the time of Joseph.[44] Under this dynasty, the southern capital at Thebes had been abandoned in favor of a northern location at Memphis.[45] Joseph was thus more accessible to his brothers coming down from Canaan, as the continuing account indicates, and also to them living later in Goshen after Jacob's arrival.

5. Jacob moves to Egypt (Genesis 42:1–47:11)

The Scriptures frequently depict God accomplishing His goals in ways man little understands or recognizes at the time. The sale of Joseph into Egyptian slavery, and the years of famine which brought his brothers there in search of food, ultimately led to the descent of all Jacob's family to Egypt. There it increased to the size of a nation during the 430-year sojourn. It was no doubt difficult at the time to see the good in many of these developments, but God saw them working together to bring about His plan for Israel (Gen. 45:7–8).

a. Joseph and his brothers (Gen. 42–45). The record of the visits to

Egypt is given in some detail. The brothers made the four hundred-plus mile round trip twice, both times to get food in the only country where it was available. Both times they spoke with Joseph personally; but because of the many years since they had seen him last, his Egyptian dress and speech, and the "impossible" position he now held, they did not recognize him. Joseph treated them harshly both times, not in retaliation but apparently in an effort to discover their present attitudes toward their father and toward their younger brother Benjamin.

At the first visit (Gen. 42), Joseph accused them of being spies, demanded that they prove their integrity by returning to him with Benjamin, kept Simeon as hostage until they should, and caused considerable consternation among them by giving back the money they had paid for the food, placing it in the mouths of their sacks of grain.

At the second visit (Gen. 43–45), when Benjamin was brought along in spite of Jacob's reluctance to risk Rachel's only surviving son, Joseph startled the brothers by dining with them in his own home where he seated each according to his respective age. Since they had brought Benjamin, he released Simeon; and he asked regarding the father at home and then sent them away, once again placing their money in the sacks. In Benjamin's sack he also placed his own silver cup.

Soon after they left he ordered the arrest of the one with the cup. This brought further remorse and a show of extreme humiliation on the part of all as they returned and again appeared

---

[43] See Barton, *AB,* pp. 368–69.
[44] See pp. 20–25.
[45] See Bright, *BHI,* p. 46.

before Joseph. Finally, Joseph could restrain himself no longer and revealed himself to them. He told them that he was indeed their brother and asked once more regarding the father at home. Then he urged that the entire family be brought to Egypt because of the famine. Pharaoh, informed of the situation, himself gave his approval by supplying wagons to facilitate the move.

b. Jacob's move (Gen. 46–47:11). Back in Palestine, Jacob rejoiced at the news regarding Joseph. He immediately decided to heed Joseph's invitation and to set out for Egypt. On the way, he stopped at Beersheba to sacrifice, and there God indicated His divine approval and restated the promises first given to Abraham over two centuries before. With this reassurance, the aged father, now 130 years old, moved on to Egypt with all his family.[46] There Joseph presented him to Pharaoh, whom Jacob blessed. Pharaoh, in turn, assigned the family a home in Goshen.[47]

Divine guidance is apparent in the relocation of Jacob's family to Egypt. Egypt was a country in which his descendants would have to remain a separate, distinct people, for Jacob and his sons were shepherds, and shepherds were an abomination to Egyptians (Gen. 43:32; 46:34). The fact would remain a natural barrier to intermarriage. In Canaan there had already been some intermarriage,[48] and continued residence there would certainly have brought more. This could only have led to assimilation with the Canaanites, destroying distinctness as a nation. Further, Egypt afforded excellent living conditions for Israel's rapid growth in numbers. The land of Goshen was fertile and regularly watered by the flooding Nile which provided an adequate food supply. Still further, Egypt was now the world leader in cultural advances.[49]

6. Death of Jacob and Joseph (Genesis 47:27–50:26)

Jacob lived yet seventeen years after coming to Egypt, dying at the age of 147 (Gen. 47:28). These were probably the happiest years of his life. His family was together again, and living conditions were fine. Certainly he took great pride in Joseph, whom he had favored in early life anyway and who was now next in power to the Pharaoh. We may be sure that Joseph, in turn,

---

[46] Genesis 46:27 says their number totaled seventy, and Genesis 46:8–27 tells who they were: thirty-two descendants of Leah (v. 15 says thirty-three, but in this figure Jacob is included, and it should be realized that both figures count Dinah, the daughter, and do not include Er and Onan who had died, v. 12), eleven of Rachel (v. 22 gives fourteen, but this includes Joseph and his two sons already in Egypt), sixteen of Zilpah (vv. 16–18), and seven of Bilhah (vv. 23–25), for a total of sixty-six (v. 26)—the addition of Jacob, Joseph, and Joseph's two sons bringing the total to seventy. Stephen, in Acts 7:14, gives the total figure as seventy-five, apparently following the Septuagint rendition of both Genesis 46:27 and Exodus 1:5, where the additional persons in mind are the five (total) sons and grandsons of Ephraim and Manasseh (see Num. 26:28–37; 1 Chron. 7:14–21).

[47] See p. 25n.52.

[48] In Genesis 46:10, Simeon's son Shaul is called "the son of a Canaanite woman." Genesis 38:2 tells of Judah having children with Shuah, a Canaanite. And if Shechem wanted Dinah for his wife (Gen. 34), though he did not get her, other Canaanites could have desired the same. On the other hand, since Genesis 46:10 does single out Shaul as the son of a Canaanite, we may infer that this was not common. If it were not, this means that most of Jacob's sons had taken wives of Haran (returning for them, then, for the oldest could only have been about twelve when Jacob left) or other areas outside Canaan

[49] See Bright, *BHI,* pp. 46–47 for description of life under the Twelfth Dynasty.

saw to it that his family, and especially his father, lacked for nothing that wealth and position could provide.

One day, when he heard that his father was sick, Joseph brought his two sons to Jacob for his blessing (Gen. 48:1–22). Joseph brought the boys so that Jacob's right hand, the one of highest blessing, would rest on the head of Manasseh, the oldest, and his left hand on Ephraim. But Jacob, guided by God, crossed his hands so that the right rested on Ephraim. Joseph objected, but Jacob told him that the younger would indeed be the more favored of the two. Jacob blessed each and then pronounced similar blessings on each of his twelve own sons (Gen. 49:1–28).

When Jacob died, his body was embalmed and he was mourned in the Egyptian manner.[50] His sons took him back to Canaan for burial in the cave of Machpelah, according to his directions (Gen. 49:29–50:14). Joseph accompanied them with a large group ordered by Pharaoh to show his respect for Jacob. Upon returning to Egypt, Joseph's brothers feared reprisal by Joseph with Jacob now dead, but Joseph reassured them that no revenge was intended (Gen. 50:15–21).

Joseph died at the age of 110 (Gen. 50:26), fifty-four years after Jacob. His body also was embalmed but remained in Egypt until the Exodus, when Israel took it along for final burial in Canaan (Exod. 13:9).

7. Joseph, man of integrity

Joseph stands with Abraham as a person to be admired. He was a man of the highest integrity. Few in Scripture compare with him for righteous conduct in tempting, trying circumstances. Sold treacherously by his own brothers, he did not react with bitterness or a defeated life of sin. Tempted by a woman of Egypt, he did not deviate from what he knew was right. Betrayed by her so wrongly, he did not become morose and moody when cast into prison. Joseph also was capable. Not only was he given a high position in Egypt, but he was able to hold it and distinguish himself in it. Joseph remained in high position apparently for the rest of his life. God placed him in this exalted position so that he might prepare the way for Jacob's coming to Egypt. Had not Joseph been prime minister, Jacob would not have thought of bringing the family to the foreign land, nor would Pharaoh have received him or given him the fine land of Goshen if he had. Joseph was God's instrument to bring the family into this fine country where it would grow to the appropriate size for nationhood.

8. The patriarchal period

The patriarchal period closed with the death of Joseph. Religiously, it was a time of simple faith in God. All four of its principals—Abraham, Isaac, Jacob, and Joseph—displayed this faith, though in different ways and degrees. All four were unusual men, each making his respective contribution. The patriarchs built altars and offered sacrifices, which suggests that God had given general directions concerning sacrifice,[51] even though the Mosaic Law had not yet been revealed.

---

[50] For description of embalming, see Free, *ABH,* pp. 80–81.

[51] Some indication must have been given even prior to Abel's sacrifice (Gen. 4:4) to make his experience understandable.

The patriarch acted as priest for the family.[52] Prayer was simple and direct. Abraham spoke face to face with the Angel of Yahweh (Gen. 18). Abraham's servant felt free to request God's aid in finding Isaac's bride (Gen. 24:12–24).

Revelation was given to the patriarchs in a variety of ways. God used dreams, visions, and appearances of the Angel of Yahweh for the purpose. By various means, the covenant promises were repeated to Abraham, Isaac, and Jacob. Abraham's presentation of tithes to Melchizedek witnesses to the antiquity of this practice. The principal requirement in all this was true obedience to God's revealed will. In contrast to the merely ritualistic requirements among the neighboring peoples, the patriarchs knew their responsibility consisted in proper ethical conduct. God told Isaac that because "Abraham obeyed me and kept my requirements, my commands, my decrees and my laws," the blessings of the covenant would come on his posterity (Gen. 26:5).

---

[52] Job's intercession for his children provides a clear illustration (Job 1:5). Job is best dated during the patriarchal period.

CHAPTER FIVE

SOJOURN AND EXODUS CHRONOLOGY*

While in Egypt, Jacob's posterity grew to a size that could class them as a nation. Until this time, fulfillment of God's promise of descendants like the sands of the sea had been very slow; but during this period it became very rapid. When Moses led Israel across Egypt's border at the time of the Exodus, Jacob's seventy had become more than two million.

The historical period during which this growth took place is debated vigorously among Evangelicals. While the effort to correlate biblical history with Egyptian history is difficult, it is possible, given the establishment of two key pieces of data—the length of Jacob's descendants' stay in Egypt and the date of the Exodus. Both matters were briefly discussed earlier when Abraham's date was considered, but now the fuller study will be undertaken.

A. DURATION OF EGYPTIAN SOJOURN

Indication was made at the earlier time that there are two main views as to the duration of Israel's sojourn in Egypt—that the sojourn lasted 430 years, or that it lasted 215 years. Some of the principal reasons favoring the longer period have been pointed out but without discussion or consideration of evidence set forth by adherents of the shorter time.[1]

1. Evidence for 430 years

a. Exodus 12:40. The first reason listed in favor of the longer period was that Exodus 12:40 in the Masoretic Hebrew text gives 430 years for the Egyptian sojourn. It reads, "Now the time that the children of Israel dwelt in Egypt was four hundred and thirty

---

*Reviser's note: The chronologies presented in this book are in keeping with the traditional, literal reading of the biblical text. Dates for specific events within the traditional framework may vary considerably from source to source. Biblical chronology is notoriously difficult, and the establishment of specific dates depends upon such a multiplicity of variable assumptions that it is unlikely that, even among conservatives, consensus can be reached at every point. Other conservative scholars champion chronologies that differ significantly from that presented here.

[1] See pp. 20–21.

years." However, a textual problem exists. The Septuagint and the Samaritan Pentateuch include both the patriarchs' sojourning in Canaan and their posterity's sojourn in Egypt in the 430 years.[2] This reading favors the 215-year view, for it requires that the time of the patriarchal activity in Canaan, which lasted 215 years,[3] be subtracted from the total 430 years.

Which reading represents the original? A well-known rule in textual criticism is that the Masoretic Hebrew text should be favored unless the evidence from other testimony is strong. In this instance the strength of that evidence is lessened in that the Septuagint and Samaritan Pentateuch do not reflect the exact same original and also that neither reading is supported by the Syriac or Vulgate versions, both of which are primary in value. It may be added that the affirmation of Exodus 12:41, that at the end of 430 years, "on that very day" (KJV), the people went out of Egypt, is more impressive if it was the anniversary of the beginning of life in Egypt only.[4] For these reasons, the Hebrew rendition seems best.

b. Genesis 15:13.

The second reason listed was that God predicted to Abraham that his posterity would be "strangers in a country not their own" and that they would be "mistreated four hundred years." One matter to notice is that the land for this sojourn of Abraham's posterity would be "not their own." But if Canaan was included in the "country not their own," this does not seem to fit the situation; for Abraham was happily dwelling in Canaan at the time and had already received God's promise that this land would be the home of his descendants.

Another matter is that affliction would be involved in this land, but the patriarchs were not afflicted in Canaan. Affliction came later in Egypt. As to the figure used here being 400, rather than the more exact 430 of Exodus 12:40, this is an employment of a round number, something not uncommon in Scripture. The mention in Genesis 15:16 that the return would be "in the fourth generation"[5] may be explained in terms of the length of a generation in Abraham's experience. God knew that Abraham would be one hundred at Isaac's birth and here employed this length of time in a multiple of four to stress how long Abraham's posterity would remain in Egypt.

c. Acts 7:6–7.

The third reason listed was that Stephen used language similar to Genesis when he spoke before the Sanhedrin and referred to God's warning that Israel would be treated ill in a strange land four hundred years. Since Stephen said essentially the same thing as Genesis, similar arguments may be drawn from his words. The foreign land is called a "strange" (KJV; Greek, *allotria*) land, hardly proper for Canaan; and Israel would be "enslaved" and "mistreated."

---

[2] The Septuagint (Codex Vaticanus) read, "And the sojourning of the children of Israel, while they sojourned in the land of Egypt and the land of Canaan, was 430 years." The Samaritan Pentateuch is the same in thought though not entirely in words.

[3] Abraham had been in Canaan twenty-five years when Isaac was born (Gen. 12:4; 21:5), Isaac was 60 when Jacob was born (Gen. 25:26), and Jacob was 130 when he went down to Egypt (Gen. 47:9).

[4] Finegan, *LAP*, p. 72, makes a similar observation.

[5] This mention has been related by some scholars to the four listed generations of Exodus 6:16–20 and taken as evidence for an even shorter period than 215 years. See discussion, pp. 67–68.

d. Population increase. The fourth reason concerned the high improbability of Jacob's family multiplying to over two million[6] in a period substantially less than 430 years. Jacob's grandsons had been born before he moved to Egypt. They numbered forty-one,[7] excluding those of Levi, whose descendants are not numbered in the final count. Doubling this number to include wives, yields eighty-two individuals, from whom came the two million.

It may be that to these eighty-two should be added numerous servants whose descendants would also have come to be counted as Israelites in time.[8] How many servants Jacob's family had is not known, but even if as many as two thousand total persons are conjectured, the increase to reach two million is still one thousand times. Nowhere else in history has anything like this rate of growth transpired, even if we think in terms of 430 years for the time involved.[9]

The reason for the rapid growth was God's unusual blessing. There was need that the population develop to a size that, when the people returned to Canaan in due time, they would be a full-fledged nation; so God simply provided accordingly. Mathematically this increase in 430 years is possible under such blessing, the birth rate being kept high and the death rate low. However, an increase of this size in only 215 years is quite unthinkable.

e. "Children of Israel" sojourned. Still a fifth reason may be taken from Exodus 12:40, which uses the phrase "children of Israel" (KJV; *bene yisra'el*), for those who sojourned the 430 years. Adherents of the 215-year view must accept this as a suitable designation for Abraham, Isaac, and Jacob as individuals, prior to the birth of Jacob's children. Evidently the transcribers of the Samaritan Pentateuch saw difficulty in this, however, for they wrote, "and the sojourning of the children of Israel *and of their fathers*" (italics mine),[10] a reading that must be rejected otherwise for lack of supporting textual evidence. If one takes "children of Israel" in its normal meaning, he is limited to subtracting at most 33 years[11] from the total 430 as the sojourning time in Egypt, for Jacob's children lived in Canaan no longer than this before moving to Egypt.

2. Evidence for 215 years

a. Four generations. In favor of the shorter period of time is the genealogy in Exodus 6:16–20, which makes Moses the great-grandson of Levi (i.e., Levi, Kohath, Amram, and Moses). The four generations involved could be

---

[6] See the discussion on pp. 124–26.

[7] For discussion of this number, see *KD*, 2:28–29.

[8] Certainly Jacob's family, being wealthy, did have servants, and it is likely (especially in view of shepherds being an abomination to Egyptians) that intermarriage occurred between their descendants and Jacob's. Some scholars have thought in terms of "several thousand" servants, but this seems unlikely. Even the near two thousand here suggested is probably too high.

[9] Speaking comparably, if Israelites had continued to multiply one thousand times in each succeeding period of 430 years, they would have numbered two billion by the time of David, two trillion by the captivity, and over two quadrillion by the time of Christ.

[10] Codex Alexandrinus carries a similar thought: "which they and their fathers sojourned in Egypt and in Canaan."

[11] Evidence for thirty-three years: Joseph was thirty-nine when the family joined him in Egypt (Gen. 41:46, 47, 54; 45:11), and he had been six (born when his father had served Laban fourteen years, Gen. 30:23–26, and all came to Canaan after twenty years) when Jacob left Haran.

the four generations anticipated in Genesis 15:16. Since generations really did not last 100 years, it can be argued that this listing makes the 430-year position impossible.[12] On the other hand, it must be remembered that not all Israelite genealogies are complete.[13] In this case, a parallel genealogy, running from Ephraim to Joshua (1 Chron. 7:22–27) lists ten generations. It would be possible, but not probable, to reconcile ten generations with 215 years.[14]

b. Church fathers.

Sometimes early church fathers, like Tertullian,[15] are quoted in support of the 215-year position. However, another, Hippolytus,[16] favored 430 years. In one place Josephus seems to hold to 215 years;[17] in another, to 430.[18] Such quotations simply show that both views were held in the early church, even as now. The reason for both views existing then is probably to be found in the variant reading of Exodus 12:40 in the Septuagint, the Greek Bible of the day.

c. Galatians 3:17.

The strongest evidence for the 215-year position is taken from Galatians 3:17, where Paul says, "The law, introduced 430 years later, does not set aside the covenant previously established by God and thus do away with the promise." Paul has been speaking in prior verses of the covenant given to Abraham; he seems to say here that the Law came 430 years later. Since the promises of that covenant were given to Abraham first at his entry into Canaan (Gen. 12:1–3), which was 215 years before Jacob took his family to Egypt, it would appear that the actual time in Egypt could only have been the remaining 215 years. It is often pointed out as well that Paul was likely referring here to the Septuagint reading of Exodus 12:40, thus in this indirect way showing his approval of it.

However, Paul, while familiar with the Septuagint, would also have known

---

[12] Indeed, it could be taken as evidence for less than 215 years. The exact average length of generations at this time is difficult to determine, but it was certainly much less than 50 years.

[13] For instance, Ezra (7:1–5) gives sixteen generations for his genealogy back to Aaron, a period of one thousand years, which calls for at least twice that many, and Matthew 1:8 lists "Uzziah" as son of "Jehoram," but from both 2 Kings and 2 Chronicles we know that Ahaziah, Joash, and Amaziah intervened.

[14] Some believe that another problem with identifying the Amram of Exodus 6:20 (the father of Moses) with the Amram of Exodus 6:18 (the son of Kohath) is found in Numbers 3:27–28, which states that Kohath's male descendants from a month old and upward numbered 8,600 by the time Moses and the Israelites reached Mount Sinai after leaving Egypt. These were divided into four groups (Amramites, Izeharites, Hebronites, and Uzzielites), so approximately one-fourth (2,150) would have descended from Amram; thus, Moses would have had this many male descendants, brothers, and male descendants of his brothers. This is certainly not impossible, especially considering the large number of children in some families then (e.g., Jacob's family).

[15] Tertullian writes, "For thus, after the above mentioned patriarchs, was the law given to Moses, at that well-known time after their exode [sic] from Egypt, after the interval and space of four hundred years. In fact it was after Abraham's 'four hundred and thirty years' that the law was given" ("An answer to the Jews," ANF, 3.153).

[16] Hippolytus says, "That means that they may be slaves to the nations, not four hundred and thirty years as in Egypt, nor seventy as in Babylon, . . ."; "Expository Treatise Against the Jews," ANF, 4.220.

[17] "They left Egypt . . . four hundred and thirty years after our forefather Abraham came into Canaan, but two hundred and fifteen years only after Jacob removed into Egypt" (AJ, 2.15.2).

[18] "And four hundred years did they spend under these afflictions; for they strove one against the other which should get the mastery, the Egyptians desiring to destroy the Israelites by these labours, and the Israelites desiring to hold out to the end under them" (ibid., 2.9.1).

the Hebrew text. He had been educated in the rabbinical schools of Jerusalem. So he would have known the chronological difference involved with the reading of the two texts. Therefore, any figure employed by him, whether 430 or 645 (430 plus 215), would have been well pondered and the result of careful choice.

At least three factors should be kept in mind. First, Paul's main point was not one in chronology. It was that the Law could not disannul the covenant given many years prior to it. Really, the number of those years, so long as it was large, was quite unimportant; but a specific number made Paul's argument more concrete. Second, there was reason to use a number that would bring the least chance of distracting readers from the main point; 645 could do this for those who knew only the Septuagint. And third, the covenant had been not only given to Abraham but repeated to Isaac and even Jacob,[19] the last time, indeed, just before Jacob moved down to Egypt (Gen. 46:1–4). This made any chronological conclusion by Paul's readers necessarily indefinite and allowed him to use a figure that would at the same time not be distracting and yet historically accurate.

B. DATE OF THE EXODUS[20]

The former discussion of Abraham's date set forth the year c. 1446 B.C. as the date of the Exodus. The main reasons favoring this early date were cited without discussion or consideration of arguments set forth by adherents of the late date (of approximately two centuries following).[21]

1. Direct biblical evidence

a. 1 Kings 6:1. The first reason listed for the early date is the statement of 1 Kings 6:1 that the Exodus preceded the time when Solomon began to build the temple (c. 966 B.C.) by 480 years. Adding 480 years to 966 B.C. gives the date 1446 B.C. To offset this evidence, adherents of the late date assert that the number 480, being the twelfth multiple of 40 (40 years is said to represent a generation),[22] is indicative of twelve generations,[23] and that, since a generation was really much less than 40 years, one is justified in reducing 480 by as much as 200 years,[24] bringing it into agreement with the late date.

However, the text in no way states or implies the thought of twelve generations. It refers merely to the definite number 480; any idea of generations must be read into the text. If this plain number can be reduced so drastically by

---

[19] Significantly, in the prior verse, Galatians 3:16, Paul speaks of the promises having been made not only to Abraham but to "his seed"; see Psalm 105:9, 10. Meredith Kline, "Law Covenant," *WTJ* 27 (1964): 7n.11, holds a similar view.

[20] Material here contained is largely dependent on a paper read at the annual meeting of the Evangelical Theological Society, December 26–28, 1968.

[21] See p. 20.

[22] This is argued from the many times that the number forty is used in the Old Testament. For instance, Israel was forty years in the wilderness, Moses was forty years old when he fled to Midian and then remained there for forty years, Saul ruled forty years, and so did both David and Solomon. However, many other numbers appear along with these and in parallel with them which argues that these, too, must be taken as exact numbers.

[23] See Finegan, *LAP*, p. 121; Wright, *BAR*, pp. 84–85.

[24] The exact amount of reduction varies with the date for the Exodus respectively favored. Most late-date scholars favor a time in the early part of the reign of Rameses II (1304–1238), but H. H. Rowley, for instance, favors c. 1225 B.C.; see p. 20n.31 for references.

this manner of analysis, then many other biblical numbers can be similarly adjusted by parallel methods, making scriptural numbers very uncertain indeed.

b. Jephthah's statement. The second reason listed is that Jephthah speaks of Israel as having possessed the land of Palestine by his day for a period of three hundred years (Judg. 11:26).[25] Jephthah was the eighth judge of Israel. Following him came four other judges,[26] Samuel's time of leadership, the kingships of Saul and David, and four years of Solomon's reign, all prior to the beginning of the building of the temple. The total years represented by these successive leaders[27] must be added to the date c. 966 B.C., when the construction of the temple began, to arrive at Jephthah's date. This works out to approximately 1100 B.C., which is just three hundred years after 1400 B.C., the time of the conquest on the basis of the early date. There is simply no way to harmonize Jephthah's statement

with the late date, apart from a denial of its historical accuracy.

c. Length of the Judges Period. The third reason listed is that an analysis of the length of the Judges Period requires a total time longer than possible with the late date. The Judges Period occupied a major part of the time between the Exodus and the establishment of Israel's monarchy in c. 1050 B.C., but not all. Not included were the years of the wilderness journey, of Joshua's leadership, and of the period between Samson's demise and Saul's inauguration: totally about sixty. Therefore, between the date of the Exodus and 1050 B.C., enough time must be allowed for both these sixty years and the Judges Period. On the basis of the early date, this leaves about three and one-third centuries for the Judges Period;[28] with the late date, it is less than a century and a half. Admittedly, some overlapping of judgeships and times of rest existed in the period, but only enough to suit the three-century allotted time of the early date.[29] Again there

---

[25] His words are, "For three hundred years Israel occupied Heshbon, Aroer, the surrounding settlements and all the towns along the Arnon."

[26] See Judges 12:8–15, listing Ibzan for seven years, Elon ten years, and Abdon eight years. After this came Samson for twenty years (Judg. 16:31), but he was contemporary with Samuel.

[27] The reigns of Saul, David, and four years of Solomon add to eighty-four years. Samuel's time (contemporary of Samson) may be figured as about twenty-five years (see p. 192n.93). The three judges overlap, but their years plus Jephthah's six, after he made the statement, add to more than twenty (see pp. 184n.63 and 187n.72 for suggested exact date of 1096 B.C.).

[28] From 1446 B.C. to 1050 B.C. is 396 years, less 61 leaves 335. For greater detail, see pp. 175–92.

[29] When added together, all the judgeships and periods of rest of the Judges Period total 410 years,

seems to be no way to harmonize the late date and the biblical indication of the length of this period.

d. Historical correlations. The fourth reason listed concerns a better correlation between the events of Scripture and Egyptian history on the basis of the early date. The biblical account of the Exodus fits Egyptian history well if the Exodus transpired in the fifteenth century, not if it was in the thirteenth.

Two aspects of the record call for particular notice. One concerns the order by an Egyptian Pharaoh for the building of Pithom and Raamses (Exod. 1:11) by enslaved Israelites. Late date adherents commonly identify Rameses II (1304–1238)[30] as both the one who gave the order[31] and the Pharaoh of the Exodus. But if he were, then the order could not have preceded the Exodus by many years, thirty at the most.[32]

The biblical account, however, implies a much longer time. The mention of the order falls in a context showing that it was part of Egypt's initial afflictions of the Israelites.[33] It was following this order that other methods for curtailing their population growth were taken—first ordering Hebrew midwives to kill Hebrew male babies (Exod. 1:15–21) and later directing that all Hebrew male children be cast into the Nile (Exod. 1:22). Then to the years implied for these measures must be added eighty more, for Moses was not born till the time of the last directive, and he was that old by the time of the Exodus. The total number of years implied is in keeping with the conclusion that was reached earlier[34]— that the Pharaoh who gave the order to build these two cities was the first of the Hyksos (about 1730 B.C.)—but not with any suggestion of late-date adherents.

The other aspect concerns the identity of the king who died while Moses was in Midian (Exod. 2:23–25). The rationale for the mention of his death in the biblical record is that the death made possible Moses' return to Egypt, which strongly suggests that the one

---

which is 75 more than the 335 available even on the early-date basis. See pp. 170–71 for discussion of hints in the Book of Judges itself that overlapping existed.

[30] The date of Rameses II is determinative for the Eighteenth and Nineteenth Dynasties. From the mention of a new moon in his fifty-second year, astronomical calculations make his accession year either 1304 or 1290 B.C. In the article "Comparative Chronology at the Time of Dynasty XIX," *JNES* 19 (January 1960): 15–22, M. B. Rowton reverses his former opinion in favor of the earlier year. E. Hornung, *Untersuchungen zur Chronologie und Geschichte des Neuen Reiches,* 1964, however, still argues for the later. Herein, dates in keeping with the earlier year are followed.

[31] Sometimes Seti I (1316–1304), predecessor of Rameses II, is suggested as the one who gave the order, but still this does not allow enough time as indicated.

[32] Most late-date adherents place the Exodus no later than c. 1275 B.C. Merneptah (1238–1228), successor of Rameses II, defeated Israelites in Canaan (see Kitchen, *AOOT,* 1966, pp. 59–60, for good discussion of evidence), which means the Exodus had to precede this time by at least the forty years of the wilderness wanderings.

[33] Kitchen, *AOOT,* p. 57n.3, defending the late date, argues that Exodus 1:7–14 provides merely a general summary of Egypt's total oppression of Israel, so that events listed later need not be taken as necessarily having followed chronologically. He believes the very fact that the Pithom and Raamses matter is mentioned at all argues that it came last when it would have been best remembered. However, two questions come quickly to mind on this basis. Why, if Exodus 1:7–14 is such a general summary, was the specific matter of Pithom and Raamses mentioned within it when other events are listed later? And why, if the Pithom and Raamses matter came last in the overall account, was its mention made rather early in the summary rather than last where one would expect it?

[34] See pp. 23–25.

Early Date Reckoning

Late Date Reckoning

who died was the same as the one from whom Moses fled forty years before (Exod. 2:15). Whenever the Exodus occurred, then, a Pharaoh who had ruled at least forty years must have just died. On the basis of the early date, such a death had just occurred; namely of Thutmose III, who died in 1450 B.C., just four years before our accepted date for the Exodus (1446 B.C.). Also, he had ruled alone since 1482 B.C., and before this he had ruled jointly with his famous aunt-stepmother Hatshepsut (1504–1482),[35]—long enough to be the one from whom Moses had fled.

For the late date, however, there is no death of a long-ruling Pharaoh that fits. Seti I (1316–1304) was the ruler who immediately preceded Rameses II, but he reigned only twelve years. Furthermore, late-date adherents normally place the Exodus well into the reign of Rameses II,[36] which locates the death of Seti I too many years prior to the Exodus to suit the rationale for the reference of Exodus 2:23.

At one time, late-date adherents identified the successor of Rameses II, Merneptah (1238–1228), as the Exodus Pharaoh, thus making Rameses II the one who died, permitting Moses to return to Egypt; and Rameses II did rule long enough to qualify as the one from whom Moses fled. Very few make this identification today, however, due to the discovery of the so-called "Israel Stele," which commemorates a victory by Merneptah in his fifth year (c. 1234 B.C.) over the Libyans and lists places and peoples in the Canaan region, significantly including Israel, that Merneptah claims are conquered.[37] If Israel was defeated by Merneptah in Canaan, she must have left Egypt at least forty years before.[38]

2. Extrabiblical considerations

Numerous scholars believe that matters thus far discussed, all involving direct biblical evidence, are sufficient to settle the question in favor of the early

[35] This most unusual person has been suggested by some as the Pharaoh's daughter who found Moses in the Nile and adopted him; see pp. 93–95 for discussion regarding her and the nature of the joint rule between herself and the younger Thutmose III.

[36] If Rameses II was the one who gave the order for Pithom and Raamses to be built, as commonly held, there is need to put several years between this order and the actual Exodus.

[37] Found in Merneptah's mortuary temple at Thebes. The stele has twenty-eight lines of closely spaced writing. See p. 71n.32.

[38] Israel was forty years in the wilderness. By greatly reducing this forty-year time, however, Rowley still finds place for the Exodus under Merneptah; *From Joseph to Joshua* (London: Oxford University Press, 1950), pp. 133–34. This suggestion is correctly rejected by most scholars.

date, in view of the Bible's authority and the clarity of the evidence given. However, there are other matters, more extrabiblical in nature, that have bearing and must be considered. Among these are items that are presented as evidence for the late date.

a. Pithom and Raamses. The first concerns the building of Pithom and Raamses by enslaved Israelites. In spite of the chronological difficulty in harmonizing the biblical statements with Egyptian history in the thirteenth century, many late-date adherents say that this reference in Exodus 1:11 supports their position. It is pointed out that at Pithom, generally identified today with Tell er-Retabeh,[39] the oldest royal building uncovered was a temple attributed to Rameses II. Hence, if the Israelites built for royalty in this city, it could not have been earlier than his time.[40] Then it is pointed out that it was this same ruler who gave the name *Pi-Ramesse* (House of Rameses) to the old Hyksos capital Avaris; and so, since Exodus 1:11 uses the name *Raamses* for the city ordered built by the Pharaoh, this one must have been Rameses II.

This is impressive evidence, not so much respecting Pithom, the identification of which with Tell er-Retabeh is not certain, but with Raamses. For wherever the site of the ancient Hyksos capital Avaris,[41] Evidently it was Rameses II who first named it Pi-Ramesse, and at this time there does not appear to be any other old Egyptian city called Raamses to correspond to the mention of Exodus 1:11.

The most likely explanation[42] in support of the fifteenth-century date is that the name *Raamses* had already been used by the Hyksos kings many years before the Nineteenth Dynasty.[43] As has already been argued,[44] the Hyksos were probably the ones who forced the Israelites to build Pithom and Raamses.

Several lines of argument make the Hyksos use of Raamses highly plausible—arguments that show ties between the Nineteenth Dynasty and those earlier rulers. For instance, it is known that the Nineteenth Dynasty traced its ancestry back to the Hyksos line.[45] Then, as indicated earlier, the old Hyksos city, Avaris, was once again made capital in the North by the Nineteenth Dynasty. Further, Rameses

---

[39] In 1883 the Swiss archaeologist Naville suggested that Tell el-Mashkuta (also in Wadi Tumelat, six miles east of Tell er-Retabeh) was Pithom. He found the word *Pi-Tum* ("House of the god Tum") on certain inscriptions there. Now, however, Tell er-Retabeh is generally accepted.

[40] Wright, *BAR*, p. 58.

[41] See p. 23, 23n.48.

[42] Unger's explanation is that the name is "a modernization of an archaic place name" by a later writer (*AOT*, p. 149). This writer wanted to make the original name more easily identified by later readers. However, this explanation, though possible, fits the rationale for change in Exodus 1:11 better than for a similar use of the name in Genesis 47:11, where the phrase "land of Rameses" is used for the area still better known as Goshen. For a work defending Unger's position, see Charles Aling, "The Biblical City of Ramses," *JETS* 25:2 (June 1982): 129–38.

[43] Held by J. Rea, "The Time of the Oppression and the Exodus," *BETS* 3 (Summer 1960): 63; and Archer, *SOTI*, pp. 207–8.

[44] See pp. 23–25. Note that Genesis 47:11 gives evidence that the term *Rameses* was used in the Goshen area even before the Hyksos time.

[45] Albright, *FSAC*, p. 223, writes, "The Ramesside house actually traced its ancestry back to a Hyksos king whose era was fixed 400 years before the date commemorated in the '400-year Stele' of Tanis. The great-grandfather of Rameses II evidently came from an old Tanite family, very possibly of Hyksos origin, since his name was Sethos (Suta) . . . . Rameses II established his capital and residence at Tanis . . . where he built a great temple to the old Tanite, later Hyksos, god Seth."

II built a temple to the god Seth, adopted from the Egyptians by the Hyksos. Still further, the father of Rameses II took his official name from this deity, calling himself Seti (or Sethos) I. The name *Raamses* (Egyptian *Ra'amessu*), meaning "begotten of Ra," was a suitable Hyksos name since the Hyksos also recognized the god Ra. If Raamses is indeed a Hyksos name, it might have been used for the capital city at the earlier time as well as later.

b. Jericho. Another matter concerns the date of Jericho's fall. At one time a majority of scholars believed that evidence from Jericho favored the early date of the Exodus. While Garstang's interpretation is widely rejected today, it will be considered with some care for the contribution it can make in support of the early date of the Exodus.

(i) Conclusions of John Garstang. John Garstang, while professor at the University of Liverpool, led an expedition to excavate old Jericho (Tell es Sultan) for that school's Institute of Archaeology, working from 1930 to 1936. He came to three principal conclusions.[46] First, Jericho fell to Joshua during the reign of Amenhotep III (1414–1378), since both pottery and scarabs were found still existing for that pharaoh's time but none for that of his successor, Akhenaton. Second, a small amount of pottery found in one lone building, dating toward the close of the fourteenth century, was from the brief occupation of Eglon, king of Moab (Judg. 3:12–14), a view supported by the fact that none of this same pottery was found in the tombs nearby, showing that whoever lived there at the time did not bury in Jericho's cemetery. Third, a few pieces of still later pottery (including imitation Mycenaean), dating to Late Bronze II and Early Iron I, were from a few sporadic residents, since the pieces were so few in number, intrusive in nature, and appeared in only two of forty-two tombs examined, with none from the tell itself.

For several years, scholars generally accepted Garstang's conclusions.[47] Gradually, however, doubt arose,[48] not because of declining value in the Jericho evidence, but because Garstang's date for Jericho's fall did not agree with evidence arising that other cities taken by Joshua showed a layer of destruction dating nearly two centuries later.[49] It was believed that the two areas of evidence should agree, and desire existed to have more work done at Jericho.

(ii) Excavations and conclusions of Kathleen Kenyon. From 1952 to 1958, Kathleen Kenyon of the British School of Archaeology headed an expedition to Jericho.[50] But though her effort was rewarding relative to early Jericho, she found little to add to Garstang's evidence regarding Joshua's Jericho.[51]

---

[46] John Garstang and J. B. E. Garstang, *The Story of Jericho*, 2d ed. (Marshall, Morgan & Scott, 1948), esp. pp. 120–29, 177–80.

[47] For instance, Albright did; see his *The Archaeology of Palestine and the Bible* (New York: Revell, 1933), p. 234; or Frederic Kenyon, father of Kathleen Kenyon, *The Bible and Archaeology* (New York: Harper, 1949), p. 189.

[48] Aware of this doubt, Garstang writes in the preface of the second edition of *The Story of Jericho*, "We are aware that varying opinions have appeared in print which conflict with our interpretation," but he continues to say that he has found no evidence to change his former views.

[49] For discussion regarding these other cities, see pp. 78–80.

[50] Admittedly undertaken, in large part, to clear up this seeming conflict; see A. Tushingham, *BA* 16 (September 1953): 49–60.

[51] Kathleen Kenyon, *Digging Up Jericho* (New York: Frederick A. Praeger, 1957), pp. 51–102.

Her interpretation of the evidence (walls, mound, and pottery) was quite different, however. First, Garstang's well-known "double-wall,"[52] which he believed was the wall that fell at the time of Joshua, was not a double wall at all, but two separate walls, dating at different times and both more than five hundred years before Joshua.[53] Second, the city mound was severely denuded of all remains of Late Bronze occupancy (i.e., after 1550 B.C.), except on the mound "above the spring," which, she believed, minimizes the strength of evidence regarding this period.[54]

Third, regarding the pottery, what Garstang found either on this portion of the mound or else in tombs, which he said was continuous into the reign of Amenhotep III at 1400 B.C., actually ceased with Middle Bronze II (probably about 1550 B.C.), meaning that a layer of ash found by Garstang in connection with this pottery does not represent Joshua's destruction but probably one effected by Egyptians shortly after the Hyksos expulsion.[55] Fourth, the few pottery pieces Garstang found in the lone building above the spring,[56] which he ascribed to the occupation of Eglon, king of Moab, are actually the only evidence of the city Joshua devastated—a city, then, apparently small and destroyed c. 1325 B.C.[57] Fifth, the few pottery pieces Garstang found in two tombs are of the same date as the pottery of the city Joshua overthrew and not of Late Bronze II and Early Iron I, as Garstang thought.

Notice should be taken that, though these conclusions do not agree with Garstang's view, neither do they support the position of late-date adherents. Their thinking has been that, since at least some habitation existed at Jericho for the fourteenth century, of which a little evidence remains, there could have been a city there which Joshua destroyed also in the thirteenth century, even though almost no evidence remains.[58] But Kenyon's view is that "the latest Bronze Age occupation" must be dated "to the third quarter of the fourteenth century";[59] and, speaking directly regarding the thirteenth-century position, she says, "It is impossible to associate the destruction of Jericho with such a date."[60]

(iii) Evaluation. With the evidence and conclusions of both archaeologists before us, an evaluation is called for. As concerns Kenyon's first two conclusions, she is certainly correct. The evidence she gathered regarding the "double wall" is convincing that Gar-

---

Her reports appeared in *PEQ*—1952 (pp. 62–82), 1953 (pp. 81–95), 1954 (pp. 45–63), 1955 (pp. 108–17), and 1956 (pp. 67–82).

[52] Garstang believed that he had located a double wall which fell when Joshua destroyed the city. Though this wall really did not enter into his evidence for Jericho's date of fall, he made quite a little of it, and Kenyon reacts in stressing his error.

[53] Garstang, *Story of Jericho,* pp. 112–14; Kenyon, *Digging Up Jericho,* pp. 45–46.

[54] Kenyon, *Digging Up Jericho,* pp. 44–47; 261–62. This denudation was due to the mound lying unoccupied from Joshua's destruction to the time of Ahab (1 Kings 16:34; see Josh. 6:26).

[55] Ibid., p. 229.

[56] Kenyon found one more in a room of a house nearby; see *Digging Up Jericho,* p. 261.

[57] Ibid., p. 262.

[58] For instance, Finegan, *LAP,* p. 159. Kitchen indeed argues, following Albright, *BP,* p. 100n.59, "Positive evidence that a settlement existed in the thirteenth century B.C. comes from the tombs, these yielding Mycenaean pottery and imitations of such"; *AOOT,* p. 63n.22.

[59] Kenyon, *Digging Up Jericho,* p. 262.

[60] "Jericho," *AOTS,* p. 273.

stang was wrong. It is true also that the city mound was severely denuded. However, neither item makes any difference as to Garstang's real evidence. The section of the wrongly dated wall found is well removed from the area where he located his significant material. Also, Garstang realized, as did Kenyon, that the city mound was denuded, though he did not make as much of it. Both based their conclusions on materials found on the mound above the spring.

As to her fifth conclusion, Kenyon conflicts with late-date adherents more than with Garstang; for, in assigning the few pottery pieces, found by Garstang in only two of forty-three tombs, to the fourteenth century, she removed the only evidence they had for a thirteenth-century city.

Regarding her fourth conclusion, it may be fairly stated that the explanation of Garstang fits the evidence measurably better than that of Kenyon. This item concerns the several pottery pieces found mainly by Garstang in or near the lone building above the spring. Both Garstang and Kenyon date these pieces to the latter half of the fourteenth century,[61] but she believes they represent the city of Joshua's destruction, while Garstang attributes them to the temporary occupancy of Eglon, king of Moab. Her reason is only that this is the one occupancy that can date to Joshua's time, the former one having closed at c. 1550 B.C., with a long gap intervening. She admits that the idea of

a small (apparently wall-less) city for the time is out of keeping with the biblical record but argues that evidence for the city having been larger and walled may have simply washed away in the general denudation. Garstang's explanation, however, fits well. That the city was small fits, for Eglon, occupying Jericho only temporarily, would not have rebuilt extensively; and that none of the pottery found in the city was located in the tombs also fits, for Eglon, being king of Moab, would not have buried at Jericho.

The most significant conclusion is her third one. This concerns the extensive pottery[62] found on both the mound above the spring and in the tombs, which Garstang contends represents occupancy until c. 1400 B.C. but which Kenyon says terminated before 1500 B.C. A thick burned layer of ash lies below this pottery, representing a major destruction, which Garstang takes as the destruction by Joshua, while Kenyon ascribes it to Egyptians. She defends her view on the basis that Late Bronze I pottery is better known now than when Garstang made his evaluation, particularly since the publication of the Megiddo excavations.[63]

Garstang did not change his position, however, in view of Megiddo,[64] and with seemingly adequate reason. For one thing, along with the pottery he had dated to c. 1400 B.C., he had found scarabs, and these dated to, and ended with, the reign of Amenhotep III at c. 1400 B.C. Of these Kenyon only

---

[61] It is noteworthy that both Albright and Wright agree with this dating; see Wright, *BAR,* p. 79.

[62] In contrast to only eight pieces dating, according to Garstang, to LB II or EI I, Garstang identifies 320 pieces for this time (also 419 to MB III and 1,012 to MB II); Garstang, *Story of Jericho,* pp. 128, 129, n. 3.

[63] Kenyon, *Digging Up Jericho,* p. 260; see her *Archaeology in the Holy Land* (New York: Frederick A. Praeger, 1960), p. 198.

[64] Garstang, *Story of Jericho,* preface, p. xiv, written in 1947, eight years after completion of work at Megiddo.

remarks that scarabs are not safe as evidence for dating, for they "are the sort of thing liable to be heirlooms."[65] Though, generally speaking, this is true, one cannot help but wonder at the remarkable coincidence of these scarabs ceasing exactly at the time of Jericho's fall on the early-date basis. Furthermore, if they were heirlooms, they would have had to be sometime after c. 1400 B.C., and those found seem to appear in context only with pre-1400 B.C. pottery.[66]

Another aspect of evidence presented by Garstang, which appears as valid as ever, concerns imported Cypriot pottery, especially well-known wishbone milk bowls and pipe-necked bilbils found as part of the pottery he dates to c. 1400 B.C. At Megiddo, the site Kenyon believes is determinative, the same were found in Levels X to VII, with the major number in Levels VIII and VII which date 1479 to 1150 B.C.[67] Since Jericho was well inland, in contrast to Megiddo, it is to be expected that this imported ware would have reached Jericho later than Megiddo and quite possibly only after it had become plentiful there, which means after 1479 B.C.[68] If so, it supplies evidence that this pottery context did indeed extend to c. 1400 B.C.[69] And if this is true, the layer of ash below this pottery may be attributed to the thorough burning of the city by Joshua (Josh. 6:24).

Given the ambiguity of the evidence and the subjective nature of its interpretation, a plausible, although not conclusive, case may be presented for an early-date conquest of Jericho. Future excavations may yet provide the desired evidence, but for the present it is probably prudent to recognize that for all the confidence of some liberal pronouncements, archaeological evidence

---

[65] Kenyon, *Digging Up Jericho*, p. 260.

[66] Garstang reports none with the small amount of pottery from the fourteenth and thirteenth centuries, and Kenyon states that she found nothing in tombs she excavated from after "the end of the Middle Bronze Age" (*Digging Up Jericho*, p. 260), and only one pottery piece on the mound (p. 261).

[67] See G. Loud, *Megiddo II: Seasons of 1935–39*, Vol. Plates (Chicago: University of Chicago Press, 1948), plates 45, 54, 58, 61, 65, 69, 72, 130, 133–34, 137–41. Garstang includes a picture of the four principal types he found (*Story of Jericho*, p. 121).

[68] Kenyon herself states, "Cypriot imports during the Middle Bronze Age are rare. . . . But in the transitional period covered by Megiddo IX they become much more numerous, until during the Late Bronze Age almost as much pottery of Cypriot connections is found as that in the native tradition"; *Archaeology in the Holy Land*, p. 200.

[69] The particular type of pottery lacking at Jericho, on which Kenyon seems to base her conclusion mainly, is a bichrome ware using red and black geometric lines enclosing stylized figures of fish, birds, and animals (see Epstein, *Palestinian Bichrome Ware* [Leiden: Brill, 1966]). The pottery is attractive, distinctive, and attributed by some to the genius of an itinerant artist (see Kenyon, *Digging Up Jericho*, p. 200; Thomas, *AOTS*, p. 317; Epstein, however, argues for its introduction to Palestine by the Hurrian migration). Found in both north and south Palestine, it is commonly taken as marking the transition point between MB and LB periods. However, the use of this pottery was really quite limited, which gives reason to doubt that simply because it is lacking at Jericho, one may conclude that Jericho was then uninhabited. Its duration is generally agreed not to have exceeded a century (c. 1575–1475 B.C.), and its extent of coverage was not over all the land. It seems to have spread out from Megiddo, east in the Esdraelon Valley, to Ta'anach, and north to Hazor, in respect to the North; and from Tell el-'Ajjul to numerous sites but only as far east as the foothills of Judah, in the South. It has not been found in the mountain region of central Palestine, nor in the Jordan Valley (see Epstein's map, ibid., facing p. 188). It should be noted also that numerous sites in the areas where it has not been found have been worked sufficiently to show it, if there. Even Bethshan, located on the quite accessible crossroad of the Esdraelon and Jordan Valleys, though still fifty miles north of Jericho, has revealed no bichrome ware proper, and the uninterrupted occupancy of Bethshan during this time is generally asserted (Epstein, ibid., p. 118).

is still fragmentary and open to interpretation. Jericho should stand as a reminder that the believer's faith is not dependent on the discoveries of archaeology, and the reliability of Scripture on the presence of Late Bronze artifacts. In the absence of archaeological data, the literary record of Joshua's conquest is the only clear-cut evidence available for this event.

c. Lachish, Debir, and Hazor. Since many scholars have been reluctant to accept the date of c. 1400 B.C. for Jericho's fall, due in substantial part to alleged conflicting evidence regarding the dates for the destruction of other cities captured by Joshua, it is well now to turn our attention to this matter. Three principal cities are involved: Lachish, Debir, and Hazor.[70] Joshua captured Lachish and Debir in his southern campaign (Josh. 10:32, 38,

39), Hazor in his northern campaign (Josh. 11:10).

(i) A thirteenth-century destruction.
Lachish has been well identified with modern Tell ed-Duweir.[71] Besides scarabs that date from Amenhotep III and Rameses II, also found here was a broken bowl generally accepted as coming from the "year four" of Merneptah (1238–1228), successor of Rameses II. The fragments of the bowl, discovered in a burned layer of destruction, particularly date this layer to the latter half of the thirteenth century.[72]

Debir (Kiriath-sepher, Josh. 15:15) was identified by Albright as Tell Beit Mirsim,[73] but Khirbet Rabud has been advanced more recently as the correct site. A burned layer of destruction was found also here; and it is dated to the same general time, since it was found at the cessation point of Late Bronze material.[74] Neither Tell ed-Duweir nor

---

[70] Bethel and Eglon are commonly included in this list (see Wright, *BAR,* pp. 80–85). Evidence respecting Bethel, however, is largely dependent on identifying it as the city captured by Joshua in Joshua 8, rather than Ai. But this is doubtful (as an answer to the problem of Ai) if only because Joshua 7:2 says specifically that Ai, as attacked by Israel, lay "on the east side of Bethel." Thus, the burned layer at Bethel, dating to the thirteenth century, could well represent only its capture by the "house of Joseph" (Judg. 1:22–25). Also, Bethel's pottery, being superior to that of Lachish and Debir at the time of destruction, suggests a different date for Bethel's fall. It should also be added that Bethel's identification with Tell Beitin is now being challenged. Eglon suffers in evidential value both because its identification with Tell el-Hesy is not certain and because the evidence for the date of destruction of this tell, excavated already in the last century by Petrie and Bliss, is not clearly determinative. It should be noted here that J. J. Bimson's important work, *Redating the Exodus and Conquest* (Sheffield, England: University of Sheffield, 1978), raises significant questions about the correlation of archaeology and the Bible as it applies to a thirteenth-century date.

[71] Excavated 1932–38 by the Wellcome-Marston Archaeological Expedition led by J. L. Starkey. Lachish was formerly thought to be Tell el-Hesy (see H. Torczyner, Lachish I: *The Lachish Letters,* 1935; O. Tufnell et al., Lachish II: *The Fosse Temple,* 1940; Lachish III: *The Iron Age,* 1953; Lachish IV: *The Bronze Age,* 1957).

[72] See Finegan, *LAP,* pp. 161–63. A scarab of Rameses III (1195–1164) found there, however, has suggested a date even in the twelfth century, which does not fit the late-date view so well; see O. Tufnell, Lachish IV, p. 97, and her article, "Lachish," *AOTS,* p. 302.

[73] Excavated in 1926 and following years by a joint effort of the Pittsburgh-Xenia Theological Seminary and the American School of Oriental Research (Melvin G. Kyle and William F. Albright, directors). It is located twelve miles southwest of Hebron. See Melvin G. Kyle, *Excavating Kiriath-Sepher's Ten Cities,* 1934; Albright, *AASOR,* 12 (1930–31); 17 (1936–37); 21–22 (1941–43); and Albright, "Debir," in Thomas, *AOTS,* pp. 207–19, for recent treatment. For Khirbet Rabud, see *EAEHL,* 4:995, but note Albright's article in 1:171–78.

[74] The Late Bronze Age closes c. 1200 B.C. However, this city may have lain waste for several years so that it cannot be dated precisely.

Tell Beit Mirsim shows a similar burned layer for c. 1400 B.C.[75]

Hazor has been well identified with Tell el-Qeday, nine miles north of the Sea of Galilee.[76] The site boasts an oval-shaped tell of about 25 acres and a much larger plateau next to it of about 175 acres, indicating that Hazor was by far the largest city of ancient Palestine.[77] There is evidence of violent destruction sometime in the thirteenth century; this indicates that nearly all habitation ceased on the plateau and that life on the main tell was able to continue only in a poor and modest way. Such a change in living pattern speaks of a major defeat, and late-date adherents take the enemy to have been Israel, thus linking the date of Hazor's destruction with that of Lachish and Debir. Once more an exact time in the thirteenth century for the destruction cannot be determined, but a date is assumed which fits the Lachish information. Some observations regarding this evidence are pertinent.

(ii) Earlier burning at Hazor. First concerning Hazor, Yadin found no indication of burning regarding the destruction of the thirteenth century (Stratum I on the plateau), whereas Joshua 11:11 states definitely that the city destroyed by Joshua was burned.

However, at Stratum III, Yadin did find evidence of burning, stating that this level "was effectively destroyed by fire, most probably by one of the Egyptian Pharaohs of the New Kingdom, Amenophis II or more probably Thutmose III."[78] Since it is at this level that burning is indicated, and since a destruction by Amenhotep II or Thutmose III[79] is less than half a century prior to the early-date time for Joshua's destruction, the suggestion is in order that this city of Stratum III—and not that of the thirteenth-century Stratum I—was really the one that Joshua destroyed. In keeping, too, is the fact that Hazor still appears strong at the time of Deborah and Barak. Though they fought their battle with Sisera, this man was only a military underling of "Jabin, king of Canaan, that reigned in Hazor" (Judg. 4:2, 17), which means that Hazor was still the leading city of the north. If so, a time for Joshua's destruction well before the thirteenth century, and the condition of semi-demise for Hazor then existent, is far more suitable.[80]

(iii) Lachish and Debir not burned by Joshua. Concerning Lachish and Debir, contrary to the case with Hazor, the Bible does not say that these cities were burned by Joshua. This omission

[75] Thomas, *AOTS,* p. 215, believes there was a nonoccupancy period which began c. 1564 B.C. (see Epstein, *Palestinian Ware,* p. 185). Even if not, it is very possible that Tell Beit Mirsim is not ancient Debir (see Simons, *GTT,* p. 282).

[76] Excavation began in 1955 under direction of Yigael Yadin, who gives summaries in *BA* 19–22 (1956–59). As many as two hundred laborers and forty-five technicians worked on this major project. For Yadin's profusely illustrated account of the dig, written for the lay reader, see Yigael Yadin, *Hazor: The Rediscovery of a Great Citadel of the Bible* (New York: Random House, 1975).

[77] This size of two hundred acres compares with Lachish at eighteen acres, Megiddo at fourteen, and Jericho at eight.

[78] Yadin, *BA* 20 (1957), p. 44.

[79] The spelling of names of various Egyptian Pharaohs varies among scholars, as indicated in Yadin's quotation.

[80] Kitchen, *AOOT,* pp. 67–68, argues against this conclusion, stating that the stress in the biblical account of Deborah and Barak's battle is elsewhere than on Hazor. However, this is because the battle took place elsewhere, namely farther south near Megiddo.

cannot be considered insignificant either, for when Joshua did burn cities, as Jericho (Josh. 6:21) and Ai (Josh. 8:28), the fact is mentioned. Further, Joshua 11:13 states specifically that "Israel did not burn any of the cities built on their mounds—except Hazor, which Joshua burned." Admittedly the primary reference in this passage is to cities of northern Palestine, but there is no reason to think that the general practice differed greatly in the South, and both Lachish and Debir did stand on "mounds."[81] Regarding these cities, it is stated only that Joshua "took" (*lakadh*) them, smiting them with "the edge of the sword" (KJV), which could well mean merely that the people were thoroughly subdued, without doing great material harm. After all, Israel could use these cities and so reason existed not to destroy more than necessary. The point to notice is that, if Joshua did not burn Lachish and Debir, the burned layers found must represent some other destruction,[82] and the fact that no such layer is found for c. 1400 B.C. is only as should be expected on the early-date basis.

d. Transjordan evidence. Another reason cited frequently in favor of the late date concerns an alleged absence of sedentary occupation in the Transjordan and Negeb regions between c. 1900 and c. 1300 B.C.[83] Nelson Glueck's presentation of evidence to this effect is well known.[84] The biblical account tells of Israel being refused a travel route through the land of Edom by the king of that country (Num. 20:14–21); of defeating great nations east of the Jordan ruled by kings Sihon and Og (Num. 21:21–35); and of being the object of a plot by Balak, king of Moab, who had called for the prophet Balaam to "curse" Israel (Num. 22–25). All these occasions transpired in the Transjordan–Negeb region, which suggests that there was a sedentary habitation there at the time of Israel's wilderness experiences. Glueck and others have concluded from this that Israel, therefore, must have traveled through this region on her way to Palestine sometime after 1300 B.C., when a sedentary occupation did exist.

Concerning this evidence, however, it must be said that Glueck's assertion, regarding absence of settled living con-

---

[81] The Hebrew word used is the very word *tell*, which has come to be employed as the technical designation for such mounds. Tuffnell agrees that Israel did not cause the burned layer at Lachish; see her "Lachish," *AOTS*, p. 302.

[82] There is no difficulty in finding other possible destroyers. Simply intercity warfare, known to have been common, could have been responsible. Or Merneptah of Egypt, who campaigned in the area c. 1234 B.C., could have burned both. Or, perhaps even more likely, the Sea Peoples, in their destructive migration, could have done this. These people swept down the eastern Mediterranean coast and destroyed cities from Ugarit to Ashkelon (see p. 61n.49 for references). They moved on to Egypt and there were repulsed, one group by Merneptah in this fifth year (1234 B.C.) and another by Rameses III from his fifth to eleventh years (c. 1190–1184). If these migrating peoples destroyed other coastal cities, why not Lachish and Debir; indeed, why not thirteenth-century Hazor? Martin Noth, *NHI*, p. 82, agrees: "These destructions were more probably due, . . . circa 1200 B.C. to the warlike emergence of the 'Sea Peoples' in the regions of the city-states of Palestine."

[83] Nelson Glueck states that occupation of Transjordan did not start again until "the beginning of Iron Age I" (*BA* 18 [February 1955]: 9). Iron Age I is normally dated as beginning c. 1200 B.C. However, Glueck and others regularly use the date c. 1300 B.C. in reference to Transjordan, perhaps because Israelite travel cannot be placed, even on the late-date basis, after c. 1250 B.C. Is the archaeological evidence being forced here, however?

[84] Glueck, ibid., pp. 8–9; *BA* 10 (1947): 77–84; also *The Other Side of the Jordan* (New Haven: American School of Oriental Research, 1940), pp. 125–47.

ditions in this area, is being challenged today. Scholars have admired the long and painstaking efforts of Glueck, but some have reserved full acceptance of his conclusions since they have been based almost solely on surface exploration. Recently, other discoveries have borne out the wisdom in this reservation. The 1978 survey of Central Moab[85] covered some of the same area as that surveyed by Glueck and led the team to conclude that "Glueck was premature in concluding that the plateau was abandoned in the Middle and Late Bronze Ages." While this recent survey did not find evidence of extensive occupation, it did find enough evidence of occupation during MB and LB to conclude that there is no period in the history of the occupation of Moab during which Moses and the Israelites would not have encountered people there. With this major link in the late-date argument broken, the chain of evidence is becoming increasingly difficult to maintain.

e. Egyptian capital location. A further reason cited in favor of the late date concerns the location of the Egyptian capital. During the period of the Eighteenth Dynasty, ruling at the time of the Exodus on the early-date basis, the capital was at Thebes, nearly four hundred miles south of the Delta. But during the reign of the Nineteenth Dynasty, involved with the late date, a northern capital was established once more at the old Hyksos site, Avaris. Since the biblical account implies that the Pharaoh concerned was near the northern area of Goshen, when Moses

was able to make his frequent contacts during the period of the plagues, it is asserted that the capital can only have been in the North at the time and that the general date, then, must have been that of the Nineteenth Dynasty.

However, good evidence exists that, though the Eighteenth Dynasty did maintain its capital in the South, some of the rulers—particularly Thutmose III and his son, Amenhotep II, the two most concerned in the early-date position—still conducted extensive operations in the North and even resided there for substantial periods of time. Speaking first of the father, it is known that he appointed a vizier for the northern area at Heliopolis, besides the vizier who continued at Thebes. This can only mean that he had unusually important interest there, which called for this kind of supervision.

Further, Thutmose III had himself called "Lord of Heliopolis," on two red granite obelisks that he erected in the city of Heliopolis,[86] indicating particular attachment for this northern center of Ra worship. Again, a scarab was found stating that his son Amenhotep II was born at Memphis, the ancient northern capital. This is especially significant, for the mother, at least, must have resided there for several months— and likely the father, too, who would have been interested in the birth of the crown prince. Indeed, that he permitted his son to be born in the ancient capital carries important implications.

Lastly, the general fact that Thutmose III campaigned extensively against the Hittites and the kingdom of Mitanni far to the north, a matter well

---

[85] James R. Kautz, "Tracking the Ancient Moabites," in *BAR,* 44:1 (Winter 1981): 27–35.

[86] See W. C. Hayes, *SE,* 2:118; and John Rea, "The Time of the Oppression and the Exodus," *BETS* 3 (Summer 1960): 65. One of these obelisks now stands in Central Park, New York City, and the other on the Thames embankment in London.

known,[87] argues that he must have maintained substantial supply bases in northern Egypt. These military forays could hardly have started from Thebes, far to the south. In fact, they probably constituted a prime cause for the other matters noted. Thutmose III had to maintain a strong interest in the North in order to conduct these ambitious Asiatic endeavors.

As for Amenhotep II, the son, pertinent discoveries were made at Tell Basta, the ancient city of Bubastis (Pibeseth of Ezek. 30:17) by the Swiss archaeologist Naville, as early as 1887–1889. On a red granite slab of two carved panels, this king is shown in worship before Amon-Ra, "he who dwells in Perunefer."[88] Amenhotep II had been appointed as a youth to serve as commandant at Perunefer, a dockyard near Memphis, and there exists evidence that he spent much time there. W. Hayes states that he "seems to have maintained large estates" in the vicinity of Perunefer, where not only he but "his successors appear to have resided for extended periods of time."[89] This is substantiated further by the discovery of a temple that his grandson Amenhotep III had erected at the same site. All of this indicates that Amenhotep II, the

Pharaoh of the Exodus on the early-date basis, could have been residing in the north at the time Moses needed to contact him relative to the plagues.

f. The Amarna Tablets. Now to be considered is the matter of the Amarna Tablets[90] and their mention of Habiru invading Canaan. This is admittedly a complex question. Once commonly believed that these tablets constituted good evidence for the early date of the Exodus, many scholars' opinions have changed in recent years.

(i) The evidence. The Tablets are letters written between c. 1400 and 1367 B.C. to the Egyptian courts of Amenhotep III and of Akhenaton, mostly by Canaanite city-kings. The letters reveal a chaotic condition of plot, counterplot, and contradictory accusations among Canaanite rulers. Particularly pertinent is the frequent mention of trouble from a people called Habiru.[91] Since there is possible equivalency in name between "Habiru" and "Hebrew" (ʿibri),[92] and since the disturbances wrought by these people are approximately at the time of the Israelite conquest on the basis of the early date, there is attraction toward identi-

---

[87] Thutmose III is considered the greatest of the Egyptian Pharaohs. In seventeen campaigns he pushed the Egyptian boundary across the Euphrates, thus fashioning the Egyptian Empire.

[88] John Rea, "Time of Oppression," p. 65, who refers to Naville, *Bubastis* (London: Kegan Paul, Trench, Trubner, 1891), p. 30.

[89] Ibid., p. 141.

[90] The first of them were found by an Egyptian peasant woman in 1887 at Tell el-Amarna, Akhenaton's capital. Total collection now numbers 378 of which about 300 were written by Canaanite scribes in Palestine, Phoenicia, and southern Syria. They are written in a conventional vulgar Akkadian filled with Canaanitisms. See S. A. B. Mercer's two-volume work, *The Tell el-Amarna Tablets* (Toronto, 1939) for full treatment; *ANET,* pp. 483–90 for translations by Albright and Mendenhall of 28 representative letters; or F. F. Bruce, "Tell el-Amarna," *AOTS,* for recent brief discussion.

[91] Also called ʿApiru, especially in Canaan, the frequently occurring idiogram *SA.GAZ* being used interchangeably.

[92] For discussion on name equivalency and other matters, as well as listing of significant works, see M. Greenberg, *The Hab/piru* (New Haven: American Oriental Society, 1955). See also H. H. Rowley, *From Joseph to Joshua* (London: Oxford University Press, 1950), pp. 46–56, for good discussion and many references.

fying these Habiru with Joshua's invading forces.

In recent years, however, this attraction has been measurably reduced by the discovery that Habiru are mentioned also in many other texts, found as far distant as Boghazkoi, Mari, Nuzi, and Babylon, and dating back as early as the Third Dynasty of Ur. Also, scholars have come to recognize more fully that the letters speak of Habiru causing trouble in northern Canaanite cities (where Joshua did not campaign) as well as southern. Still further, it has been learned that the term *Habiru* was a social and descriptive term, not an ethnic one, of a person without citizenship, an undesirable, a migrant, even a bandit or raider. As a result, many late-date adherents today believe that there is no connection between the Habiru of the Tablets and the Hebrews of Joshua and see no bearing of the letters on the date of the Exodus.

(ii) One explanation: Hebrews were Habiru. Numerous early-date adherents, however, believe they are still relevant. Among these scholars, many directly identify the Habiru with the Hebrews, as formerly commonly held.[93] That is, they identify those Habiru involved in southern Canaan with the Hebrews. Other Habiru in other places and at other times obviously were not; but it is believed that those who invaded southern Canaan could have been, for the disturbed city-kings of that area could have classed Joshua's forces as Habiru in type, since they were without country and seeking to seize Canaanite land. This view considers the Canaanites to have used the name quite as an epithet, a derogatory term, at least at first.[94] Supporting this viewpoint is the fact that the southern Canaanite Amarna letters were written only from cities late in being captured by Israel, among them Megiddo, Gezer, Ashkelon, and Acco, and not from cities captured early, like Jericho, Bethel, Gibeon, and Hebron. Since the letters date after Joshua's initial conquests, this is the way it would have had to be if the view is correct.[95]

---

[93] See Unger. *AOT,* pp. 124–25, 145–46; also Archer, *SOTI* , pp. 164, 214, 253–59. It is believed that this view makes an observation of J. W. Jack, *The Date of the Exodus* (Edinburgh, 1925), p. 128, still pertinent: "Who were these invaders of southern Palestine? . . . Who could they be but the Hebrews of the Exodus, and have we not here the native version of their entry into the land?"

[94] The term is not always used derogatorily, however. At Alalakh, for instance, Habiru held official positions in the city government and were among the chariot-owning *maryannu* (highest warrior class). Abraham was already called a Hebrew (Gen. 14:13) and certainly not derogatorily. The name continued on after the conquest, too (1 Sam. 4:6, 9; 13:3, 7; 29:3, et al., though not often), and not with the derogatory connotation; but the Canaanites could have so used it while being divested of their land. For an attempt to explain *Habiru* as applying to a larger class to which Israel belonged, see David O'Brien, "David the Hebrew," *JETS* 23:3 (September 1980): 194–99.

[95] Arguments are raised against this view, but they can be satisfactorily answered. It is asserted (Wright, *BAR,* pp. 75–76) that the Habiru are represented in the letters as resident within Canaan, often even serving Canaanite princes, whereas the Hebrews were invaders; but, in answer, it should be realized that the Hebrews were already in the land by the time the Amarna letters were written, with Joshua's initial campaigns completed and the various tribes active in occupying their allotted areas. Again, it is pointed out (Finegan, *LAP,* p. 118) that correspondence from the ruler of Jerusalem, Abdi-Hiba, indicates that Jerusalem was in imminent danger of falling to the Habiru, whereas the city does not appear to have been a real objective of Joshua; but, since Joshua's campaigns were past, the concern of Abdi-Hiba could have been due simply to all the country around Jerusalem having been occupied and his city now having to survive alone. Third, it is commonly argued that the names of persons in the letters do not correspond to those in the text of Joshua, with the king of Jerusalem, for instance, being called Abdi-Hiba and in Joshua 10:3 Adoni-zedec; but it should be realized that

(iii) Second explanation: Hebrews preceded the Habiru. There is also a second viewpoint as to a relation between Habiru and the Hebrews, espoused by Meredith Kline.[96] It does not identify the two but places Joshua's conquest just prior to the time of the Habiru notices,[97] rather than many decades later as with the late-date view.

Kline argues against identification by showing first that the term "Hebrew" is not used in the Old Testament with a social connotation (true for the term "Habiru"), but ethnical, harking back to Eber, ancestor of Abraham; second, that there is difficulty in etymologically equating the two terms "Habiru" and "Hebrew" (asserted also by numerous late-date adherents, though not all); and third, that there are a few difficulties in completely harmonizing the activities of the Habiru in the Amarna letters and those of the Hebrews in Joshua's conquest.

Further, to show that the conquest preceded the Habiru references, Kline develops an attractive historical reconstruction. He states that Joshua's main campaigns had been completed by the time Habiru raiders entered southern Canaan. Then he suggests that these southern raiders were sent by a larger group of Habiru already established in northern Canaan, and that coming into the South where Joshua's people had recently arrived, they did not at first

take notice of them since they were new and not yet settled. He continues to suggest that later, upon becoming stronger themselves, they did recognize them and then proceeded to force them into subjection, which occasion Kline identifies with Israel's oppression at the hands of Cushan-rishathaim of Mesopotamia (Judg. 3:8–10). This last point lends measurable credence to Kline's view, for otherwise there is a real problem in harmonizing this first oppression of Israel with the Habiru mentioned, for they date at the same time.[98]

It is unnecessary to choose which of these two views is best. Perhaps there is more to commend the second at the present time. What is significant is that either view gives a satisfactory explanation in keeping with the early-date position. It should be observed further that either position sees the letters as contemporary with Israel's early years in Canaan and finds in them helpful commentary on conditions Israel encountered.

g. Military campaigns of Seti I and Rameses II. The last matter to notice concerns the Palestinian military campaigns of two Egyptian Pharaohs, Seti I and Rameses II. Late-date adherents argue that, if Israel were in Palestine at the time of these campaigns, which would have been true on the early-date basis, the campaigns should be men-

---

Joshua's nomenclature is earlier than that of the letters, and in a troubled time, such as represented in this correspondence, local rulers rise and fall with marked rapidity. It may be added, however, that one correlation in name does exist, namely for Japhia of Joshua 10:3, said to be king of Lachish; and also a letter from Megiddo refers to a Benenima and Yashuya which could be Benjamin and Joshua.

[96] Meredith G. Kline, "The Ha-Bi-Ru—Kin or Foe of Israel?—II," *WTJ* 20 (November 1957): 54–61.

[97] If the conquest began in 1406 B.C. (forty years after 1446), it likely was completed in its initial stages by c. 1400 B.C., the date of the first of the Amarna letters. The letters indicate that the main Habiru threat came about two decades later.

[98] The first oppression lasted eight years and is best dated c. 1375–1367 (see p. 176), exactly during the years of Akhenaton (1384–1367) when the Habiru seem to have been the most active.

tioned in the Book of Judges, a book given largely to military activities; and, since they are not, Israel must not yet have been there.

(i) The evidence. Seti I campaigned northward already in his first year (1316 B.C.), encountering enemy forces in northern Palestine and slightly beyond. In a later campaign he pressed as far as Kadesh on the Orontes River, where he made a treaty with the Hittite king, Muwatallis.[99] Rameses II followed with other campaigns, notably in his fifth and twenty-first years, in the last of which he made his famous treaty with the Hittite Hattusilis III (1283 B.C.).[100] In each of these campaigns, the Egyptian army had to march through the length of Palestine and must have come in contact with Israelites, if indeed they were there. Then, besides, both Seti I and Rameses II appear to have engaged in actual warfare in Palestine itself. At least both left a stele at Bethshan;[101] and Seti I tells of his clashing with Apiru near that city, a reference certainly to the Hebrews in which the term "Habiru-Apiru" is used again. These Palestinian activities do make the question pertinent as to why, if Israel was in the land at the time, the

Book of Judges gives no record of them.

(ii) The explanation. In reply, two observations may be made. First, later military inroads into Palestine by Merneptah (1238–1228) and Rameses III (c. 1195–1164)[102] are not mentioned in the Book of Judges either, and the campaigns of each did follow the time of Israel's entrance into Canaan, even on the late-date basis.

Merneptah, as already noted,[103] claims to have wrought extensive havoc in Palestine, stating that "Israel is laid waste, his seed is not; Hurru is become a widow for Egypt."[104] Rameses III of the Twentieth Dynasty boasts of having reduced both the "Tjeker and the Philistines" to ashes.[105] He even had scenes of the campaign he conducted into Palestine depicted on the walls of his famous temple of Medinet Habu. He seems to have had a major interest in the Bethshan area, even as Seti I and Rameses II, for he rebuilt the city, including a fine temple, and made the city a sort of Egyptian frontier post.[106]

It is clear that both Ramses III and Merneptah centered attacks on the Palestine sector itself and did not merely pass through, as was true mainly for both Seti I and Rameses II (whose

---

[99] See Hayes, *SE*, 2:327. This agreement continued to place all Palestine under Egyptian control. The main intention of both Seti I and Rameses II was to restore the northern borders of empire days, but in this they did not succeed.

[100] Copies of this treaty have been found both in cuneiform and hieroglyphic writing, respectively at Boghazkoi and Karnak. Cordial relations followed this treaty, with Rameses II even marrying the eldest daughter of Hattusilis in Rameses' forty-fifth year of reign. See Hayes, *SE*, 2:344–45; and *ANET*, pp. 201–3 for copy of the treaty.

[101] See *ANET*, p. 155, for text of each. See G. M. Fitzgerald, "Beth-Shean," *AOTS*, pp. 185–96, for recent brief treatment of discoveries at Bethshan.

[102] Date uncertain. Albright, *FSAC*, p. 289, prefers 1175 as first year of Rameses III.

[103] See p. 71n.32 and p. 72.

[104] See *ANET*, pp. 376–78, for text. "Hurru" is Syria, here no doubt including Palestine.

[105] See *ANET*, p. 262, for text. "Tjeker" (*tkr*) is the name of one of the Sea Peoples who in part, along with the Philistines (*prst*), took up residence in Palestine. The Egyptian Wenamon (1100 B.C.) speaks of the *tkr* occupying the coastal town, Dor, just south of Mount Carmel; see *ANET*, p. 26n.5.

[106] See Wright, *BAR*, p. 95; and *ANET*, p. 262, n. 21.

activities are likewise omitted in the Book of Judges). One may conclude from this that, if their campaigns are not mentioned when Israel surely was in the land, then that the earlier campaigns are not mentioned need not be evidence that Israel was not in the land at this time.

The other observation concerns the reason for this omission in the Book of Judges, whether of the earlier or the later campaigns. The book does not constitute a history as such of the period of time covered. It is rather an accounting of Israel's deviant behavior and corresponding punishments. In keeping with this idea, those military encounters with other nations, which served as a means of punishment or correction, are mentioned, and those which did not, are omitted. An outside power would strike, Israel would be defeated and then suffer a period of oppression, and finally a delivering judge would often arise to bring relief. Several outside powers were so involved,[107] but Egypt was not among them. Her military encounters did not lead to servitude and punishment for Israel.*

---

[107] Mesopotamians (Judg. 3:8), Moabites (Judg. 3:12), Canaanites (Judg. 4:2), Midianites (Judg. 6:1), Ammonites (Judg. 10:7), and Philistines (Judg. 10:7).

*Reviser's note: Little new archaeological data relevant to the date of the Exodus has come to light since the first edition of this work, but the available data have been rearranged extensively. (Albright's identification of Tell-Beit-Mirsim with Debir is under serious attack. Moshe Kochavi ["Rabud, Khirbet" in *EAEHL,* 4:995], identifies Khirbet Rabud as Debir without reference to Tell Beit Mirsim. Glueck's Moab survey, a major element in the late-date formulation, has been revised significantly in recent years [above, p. 99].) While some of the older material has been called into question, Professor Wood's treatment is still a fair presentation of arguments for the early date. For a detailed reassessment of the archaeological data relating to the dates of the conquest and Exodus, see J. J. Bimson, *Redating the Exodus and Conquest* (Sheffield, England: University of Sheffield, 1978). Bimson argues convincingly for a fifteenth-century Exodus by calling the major archaeological arguments for the late date into question. It should be noted that Bimson's arguments against the late date have won a hearing among some non-Evangelicals (George W. Ramsey, *The Quest for the Historical Israel* [Atlanta: John Knox, 1981]), who also reject the arguments for the early date (pp. 73–77).

The lack of new evidence may be reflected in the increasingly bizarre formulations of some scholars. Hans Goedicke, a highly respected Egyptologist, has proposed that a contingent of Israelite mercenaries fleeing from Egypt were saved from the pursuing army when, after taking up a defensive position on Tell-Hazzob, a tidal wave swept the surrounding area, leaving only the Israelites safe on the high ground. The tidal wave, according to Goedicke, was caused by the eruption of a volcano on Thera/Santorini Island around 1475 (Hershel Shanks, "The Exodus and the Crossing of the Red Sea, According to Hans Goedicke," *BARev* 7:5 [September–October 1981]: 42–50). The nature of this theory, and others presented in response to it, underscores the sober nature of Professor Wood's treatment.

CHAPTER SIX

LIFE IN EGYPT

Exodus 1–14; *Psalm* 105:17–39; *Acts* 7:15–36; *Hebrews* 11:22–29

A. FOUR PERIODS OF EGYPTIAN RULE

The second millennium B.C. in Egyptian history was marked by four distinctive periods of rule. First came the powerful Twelfth Dynasty, lasting from c. 1991 to c. 1786 B.C.[1] During this time the country was stabilized, following a period of divided feudal lordship, and the Pharaoh ruled once more with full authority. Lower and Upper Egypt were united. The capital was located at Ith-taui, south of the great capital of the Old Kingdom, Memphis. The country prospered, and conditions for the most part pleased the people. Egyptian pottery found in neighboring countries indicates that extensive trade relations existed. The period was one of Egypt's strongest, and her influence in the world extended far beyond her borders.[2]

The second period was that of the Hyksos,[3] a foreign people who now came into Egypt and took over the throne. Though their exact origin still remains a mystery, it is quite clear that they were Asiatics who gradually infiltrated Egypt during the latter half of the eighteenth century. The strong Twelfth Dynasty had been succeeded by much weaker kings of the short-lived Thirteenth and Fourteenth Dynasties,[4] in whose days the infiltration took place.

About 1730 the newcomers took over rule in the northeastern Delta,

---

[1] These dates are from R. A. Parker, *The Calendars of Egypt* (Chicago: University of Chicago Press, 1950), pp. 63–69, with which Albright, *BASOR* 127 (October 1952): 27–30, agrees. See W. F. Edgerton, "The Chronology of the Twelfth Dynasty," *JNES* 1 (1942): 307–14, who differs slightly. For general discussion, see H. E. Winlock, *The Rise and Fall of the Middle Kingdom* (New York: Macmillan, 1947).

[2] This period is known as Egypt's Middle Kingdom. The fascinating story of Sinuhe occurred at this time. He fled from Egypt, traveled through the East, and returned, the story giving valuable information regarding life of the day; see *ANET*, p. 418.

[3] This period is called the Second Intermediate. See R. M. Engberg, *The Hyksos Reconsidered* (Chicago: University of Chicago Press, 1939); Hayes, *SE*, 2:3–8; Van Seters, *TH*.

[4] These dynasties, so designated by Manetho, apparently ruled contemporaneously.

establishing their capital at Avaris,[5] and about 1680 they succeeded in displacing the Egyptian ruler at the main capital, Memphis, and so assumed control over all Egypt, even including, for a time, Nubia to the south.[6] The Hyksos were not really numerous during these years but remained dominant by holding key positions. They adopted Egyptian ways[7] and appear to have made every effort to rule in an acceptable Egyptian fashion.

In spite of what seems to have been a period of stability and prosperity, later history painted the Hyksos as brutal, hated rulers. Josephus preserves a tradition of the Egyptian priest Manetho that speaks of burned cities, ruined temples, and enslaved Egyptians. Whether this tradition is true or not, it reflects an attitude that led to the attempt to eradicate all traces of the Hyksos from the records. Because of this, information on the Hyksos is scant.

The third period was that of one of the strongest dynasties of all, the Eighteenth.[8] Under the leadership of the vigorous and able Pharaohs of this dynasty, Egypt for the first time turned its attention to the building of an empire.

The first step required driving out the Hyksos and reestablishing Egyptian autonomy. This had been begun already by the Seventeenth Dynasty;[9] but it was Ahmose (1584–1560), first ruler of the Eighteenth, who captured the Hyksos capital, Avaris, and drove the foreigners far north into Palestine. With him, native rule was solidified, and with his grandson, Thutmose I (1539–1514), came the dawn of empire for Egypt. This Pharaoh's army campaigned as far south as the Third Cataract of the Nile and as far north along the Mediterranean coast as the Euphrates River. Later his grandson, the great Thutmose III (1504–1450), generally considered Egypt's most capable ruler, surpassed him in marching yet farther and establishing recognized boundaries. The son of Thutmose III, Amenhotep II, was also gifted as a military commander.

At this time, Egypt's army was the strongest in the world, spearheaded by the chariot corps. With good crops at home, advantageous trade relations with neighbors near and far, and now rich booty from successful conquests, Egypt reached a zenith of prosperity. The country also enjoyed the finest in educational and cultural advantages.

The fourth period was that of the Nineteenth Dynasty,[10] nearly as strong

---

[5] This occasion is commemorated on the New Kingdom stele, stating that it took place four hundred years prior to the reign of Horemhab, the last king of the Eighteenth Dynasty. For discussion, see Van Seters, *TH*, pp. 97–103.

[6] Manetho names the ruler who took Memphis in 1680 as Salutis and says the Fifteenth Dynasty began with him. Manetho assigns both the Fifteenth and Sixteenth Dynasties to Hyksos, though these were likely contemporary like the Thirteenth and Fourteenth.

[7] The rulers used Egyptian titles and throne names, writing them in the Egyptian hieroglyphics. They admired Egyptian art, for they made copies of Middle Kingdom originals of statues, reliefs, and other works. That they took over the Egyptian gods, Seth and Ra, shows that they even accepted much of the Egyptian religion.

[8] See Steindorff and Seele, *When Egypt Ruled the East,* rev. ed. (Chicago: University of Chicago Press, 1957); also Hayes, *SE,* 2:42–325.

[9] The Seventeenth Dynasty dates from about 1660 B.C. It took over in Thebes from the Thirteenth, which had continued in the Thebes area after the Hyksos conquest. The last ruler of the Seventeenth, Kamose, already took back much Egyptian territory from the Hyksos, pushing at least as far as the Delta. Ahmose, first of the Eighteenth Dynasty, was his younger brother; see Hayes, *SE,* 2:8–9.

[10] See Hayes, *SE,* 2:326–434, besides general works. It should be realized that the Eighteenth, Nineteenth, and Twentieth Dynasties constituted Egypt's New Kingdom period.

in world influence as the Eighteenth. The period lasted 109 years, of which 66 were under the rule of Rameses II (1304–1238).[11] He and his predecessor, Seti I, sought to reestablish the northern boundary of Thutmose III, and, though they fell short of this goal, did secure full control once more over all Palestine and southern Syria.[12] Rameses II was a builder as well as military strategist, as witnessed by structures he erected or enlarged in nearly every major city of both Lower and Upper Egypt.[13] Throughout the Nineteenth Dynasty prosperity continued and Egypt remained the dominant world power.

B. EGYPTIAN LIFE

Egyptians lived near and depended greatly on the Nile River.[14] Annual flooding by this long waterway brought new fertile soil and initial deep wetting so that continued irrigation through the growing season produced excellent crops. Without the Nile, Egypt would have been mere desert. The country was long and narrow, with most of the people living within a few miles of the Nile's banks. A delta, formed by the Nile fanning out into numerous branches as it neared the Mediterranean, provided broader areas for farming. The land of Goshen, given to Jacob's family, lay on the east of the Delta. Present day Cairo lies at its southern end just over one hundred miles from the Mediterranean. The Delta region was called Lower Egypt and the area south, Upper Egypt, these terms given in view of the Nile flowing from south to north.

Religion played a major role in Egyptian life.[15] The people believed in many gods, often identifying them with birds and animals. Every community had gods which were particularly venerated. The will of these gods, thought to be discernible in a variety of ways, governed decisions of life.

In addition to the local gods there were national deities, thought to be higher in rank, though actually not influencing personal life patterns as much as the local gods. Horus, the falcon god, rose from local to national status when Lower and Upper Egypt were first united under King Menes.[16] During the Old Kingdom, the god Ra was honored as chief deity. For most of the second millennium, however, Amon (sometimes identified with Ra as Amon-Ra) carried this distinction. Thebes was his main center of worship, and immense temples, particularly Karnak and Luxor, were erected to him there. His priesthood wielded enormous power, controlling vast tracts of land and insisting on contributions from people already poor. The priests exerted extensive influence politically. Amenhotep IV (1384–1367), of the Eighteenth Dynasty, sought to break from their hold and establish a revolutionary new cult to the god Aton (changing his own name to Akhenaton,

---

[11] For discussion of this date, see p. 71n.30.

[12] See p. 85n.99.

[13] Hayes, *SE*, 2:342.

[14] For a recent popular study, see Bruce Brander, *The Nile River* (Washington, D.C.: National Geographic Society, 1966).

[15] Hayes, *SE*, vol. 1, chap. 6, "The Religion and Funerary Beliefs in Ancient Egypt," pp. 75–83.

[16] Manetho identifies Menes as the first king of permanently united Egypt, the first of the First Dynasty. See Alan Gardner, *Egypt of the Pharaohs* (London: Oxford University Press, 1961), pp. 66–67; Finegan, *LAP*, pp. 82–83.

accordingly) in a new capital at Tell el-Amarna; but when he died, all reverted to the established pattern.

A major feature in Egyptian religion was the belief in life after death. People believed that a record of their deeds was weighed after death to determine what would be their continuing status in the afterlife. Also, because people desired adequate material provisions for the future existence, they stressed the importance of burial preparation. Bodies were embalmed and fine tombs constructed. Pharaohs of the Old Kingdom built the immense pyramids as their places to be buried. Food, drink, furniture, and other necessities of life were included in the tombs. In earlier days the Pharaoh and those close to him were assured entry to the afterlife, but over the course of centuries this expectation extended to anyone who could afford the necessary funerary equipment.

C. JACOB'S DESCENDANTS IN EGYPT

On the basis of the chronology established in the prior chapter, Jacob and his family arrived in this Egyptian milieu during the first period of rule in the second millennium, that of the Twelfth Dynasty. Since the date of the arrival was c. 1876 B.C.,[17] the Pharaoh would likely have been Senusert (Sesostris) III (1878–1871), one of the most aggressive of the Dynasty. He conquered as far south as the Second Cataract and north through all of Palestine. He dug a canal from the Delta to the Red Sea and reopened another at the first Cataract. His predecessor, Senusert II (1894–1878), would have been the man whose dream Joseph interpreted and who made Joseph his vizier.

Given the fertile land of Goshen, and being unusually blessed by God, Jacob's descendants prospered. God gave Jacob seventeen years to see this prosperity, and the satisfaction he experienced must have been gratifying after suffering so much disappointment earlier in life. Crops grew, and the population increased until "the land was filled" (Exod. 1:7) with the children of Israel. This does not mean that they spread throughout all the land, in both Lower and Upper Egypt. This would not have occurred, because every shepherd was "detestable to the Egyptians" (Gen. 46:34). The Egyptians would not have permitted this kind of intermingling. For the most part, the descendants of Jacob remained together and expanded their holdings to fill the Goshen area completely.

Joseph lived seventy-one years after his family came to Egypt.[18] This means that he died c. 1805 B.C., during the reign of Amenemhet III (1841–1797), approximately twenty-five years prior to the end of the Twelfth Dynasty. Apparently Joseph continued in high office even after the famine and, if so, would have been able to do much for the benefit of his loved ones. It is easy to believe that the finest irrigation equipment, farming tools, and home conveniences were provided. Life

---

[17] See p. 22n.40. Considerable evidence exists in Egyptian papyri that a large Asiatic slave population lived in Egypt during the latter part of the Twelfth and especially the Thirteenth Dynasty. This cannot reflect Israel's enslavement as a nation, however, for this did not ensue until the Hyksos period. Some Israelites may have been taken earlier as slave-servants, but probably most of these were Asiatics of other origins. See Van Seters, *TH,* pp. 90–92, for discussion and references.

[18] See p. 23n.45.

would have been good for Israelites as long as Joseph lived.

D. ISRAEL IN SERVITUDE
(Exodus 1:8—22)

Prior discussion has contended that the king who arose and "did not know about Joseph" was the first of the Hyksos,[19] who, in the initial stages of their control, ruled only northeastern Egypt and established Avaris as the capital. Goshen was in the area and no doubt was included in this first stage of conquest. If so, the year was about 1730 B.C.,[20] some seventy-five years after Joseph's death. These intervening years likely had continued as years of prosperity for the Israelites. The Egyptian Pharaohs would have permitted them to live quite as before, both because of respect for the memory of Joseph and because there was no urgent reason to change. It is probable that the special benefits that had been provided by Joseph ceased, but these would not have been so needed by this time, since the people had already attained a position of strength.

1. Slavery imposed
(Exodus 1:8—14)

But now matters changed. A rigorous servitude was imposed on the dwellers of Goshen. Exodus 1:8—10 records the reasons. First, the new ruler "did not know about Joseph"; that is, he did not have historical knowledge of Joseph, nor did he have reason to respect it if he had. He headed a new dynasty of a foreign rule, so that former allegiances or obligations were of little

consequence. Second, Israelites were seen to be more and mightier than the Hyksos. As has been pointed out, the Hyksos were never of great number, and Jacob's family could have outnumbered them easily by this time. The new ruling family would not have wanted a strong, unified, foreign group to continue unchecked as a potential source of trouble. Third, a military alliance with the former regime was seen as a possible way in which this trouble might come. The deposed rulers, whose dynasty had befriended this group of people, might now call upon them for support in reestablishing the status quo.

Accordingly, a decision was made to enslave Israel. Their potential for trouble would be removed both by restricting freedom of movement and employment and by placing "slave masters" over them to make sure that all energy was expended in hard labor. Further, this would not only keep them in control but also provide valuable labor for building projects, such as the cities of Pithom and Raamses (Avaris), the new capital.[21]

The Hyksos did gain in labor contributed, and they also prevented any alliance between deposed Egyptians and Israel—if indeed such a possibility really existed—but they did not succeed in curtailing Israelite population growth. Exodus 1:12 states that "the more they were oppressed, the more they multiplied and spread." Population growth was necessary if Israel was to become nation-size by the time of

---

[19] See p. 24.

[20] The alternative is that this one was Salutis, the Hyksos who took over all Egypt about 1680 B.C. He was likely a still more aggressive person.

[21] See p. 23n.48.

the Exodus, and God blessed them to that end. The rapid rate of increase[22] continued as before.

2. Male babies ordered killed (Exodus 1:15–22)

In time another measure was instituted to curtail this growth: all male children were ordered to be killed. This order was not given by the Hyksos, however, but by one of the Eighteenth Dynasty.[23] This follows from the fact that Moses was born while the order was in effect. Since Moses was eighty years old[24] at the time of Exodus (1446 B.C.), his birthdate may be figured as c. 1526 B.C., during the reign of Thutmose I (1539–1514), the third ruler of that dynasty.

The order came in two stages, which may have been separated by many years. The first stage was a directive to Hebrew midwives[25] to kill every male Hebrew child at the moment of birth (Exod. 1:15–21). It was probably issued by either Ahmose (1584–1560) or Amenhotep I (1560–1539), the first two rulers of the Eighteenth Dynasty. It was a vicious order and would have been very effective had it been obeyed. However, thanks to courageous midwives, it was not, the excuse being given that the Hebrew women were quick in giving birth so that midwives could not arrive in time to do the evil deed.

The second stage of the order was issued, as observed, by Thutmose I, the first great empire builder of Egypt. It was a public order, directed to every Egyptian, that all male children of the Hebrews be thrown in the Nile to drown (Exod. 1:22). This was surely an inhuman directive; but it is, in a measure, understandable in view of the circumstances. The Israelites were becoming very numerous now that three and one-half centuries of rapid growth had elapsed. Thutmose I was involved in enlarging Egypt's borders, which meant that most of his army was out of the country for extensive periods of time. He did not want this foreign people to increase and become still a greater threat while his home force was so small.

E. MOSES[26] (Exodus 2:1–10)

While the new order was more effective than the first,[27] it did not keep one very important person from entering Israelite history. That was Moses, the one whom the king, had he known his destiny, would have been the most interested in disposing. God's special protection was over him, however, for

---

[22] See p. 67.

[23] Any Egyptian dynasty now would have desired such a controlling measure for several reasons: first, the historical tie with Israelites would now have been forgotten; second, an awareness of Asiatic kinship between these who remained and the hated, departed Hyksos would have existed; and third, the numbers of the Israelites would now have grown much larger than at any time prior to the Hyksos period.

[24] Exodus 7:7. Moses spent forty years in the wilderness and was 120 at his death (Deut. 34:7).

[25] Only two midwives are named, Shiphrah and Puah (Exod. 1:15), but these may have been the superintendents. Likely there were more than two to serve the number of Hebrew families then living.

[26] The name *Moses* finds meaning both in Hebrew and Egyptian. In Hebrew *mosheh* means "drawn out" (Exod. 2:10), and in Egyptian *mos* means "child," it being the same element as found, for instance, in Thutmose, which means "child of Thoth."

[27] At least Moses' parents found it advisable to hide the baby and then make an ark in which to place him in the river.

he was planned as Israel's great deliverer.

1. Early home
(Exodus 2:1–10)

Moses' father, Amram,[28] and his mother, Jochebed, were both descendants of Levi (Exod. 6:16–20). They already had two children: Aaron, three years old, and Miriam, perhaps about seven.[29] It is certain that the home was a center of godly instruction, for Moses, there only during his beginning years, was still highly influenced by it years later in the Egyptian palace. At that time he chose to identify himself with his own people and so "be mistreated along with the people of God," rather than enjoy "the pleasures of sin for a short time" (Heb. 11:25). Other homes among the Israelites, after so many years since Joseph, may have become cold toward the God of their fathers, but not that of Amram and Jochebed. Their piety, no doubt, was a factor in God's selection of them to be the parents of Moses.

Moses is described as a "fine" child, which would only have intensified the parents' desire to have his life spared (Exod. 2:2–10). They hid him at home three months, in defiance of the king's commandment, and then, when this was no longer possible, laid him in a basket of bulrushes (papyri), which they placed in the river, leaving his sister to watch.

Under God's providential care, the daughter of Pharaoh came to bathe,[30] found the baby crying, and, at the sister's suggestion, hired Jochebed to care for the child until he should be weaned, apparently not knowing that Jochebed was the baby's own mother. Jochebed thus had her son back, now legally safe, and was even to be paid for caring for him. In perhaps four or five years,[31] however, she had to give him up to the palace where he became the legal son of Pharaoh's daughter.

2. Hatshepsut, Pharaoh's daughter?*

This daughter may have been the renowned Hatshepsut, who in time came to declare herself supreme ruler in Egypt. For a woman to assume such a position in that day was most unusual, but Hatshepsut was a most unusual person.[32] She had a strong personality and remarkable gift for leadership, which she used in advantageous cir-

---

[28] See p. 68n.14, for discussion of whether or not Moses' father was the same Amram as the grandson of Levi (Exod. 6:16–18).

[29] Exodus 7:7 gives Aaron's age. Miriam is probably correctly identified with the older sister who watched Moses when he was placed in the river. If so, she was old enough to assume this responsibility.

[30] With the capital then at Thebes, this princess must have been visiting in the north near the Goshen area. Such trips were not unusual, however; see pp. 81–82.

[31] Moses would hardly have been younger than this, for he certainly was influenced by early home instruction years later in his choice to go to his own people, and also the princess would not likely have wanted to care for him much younger.

*Reviser's note: Pharaohs of the New Kingdom were known to maintain large harems with large numbers of children. Rameses II, for example, had eighty or ninety children. While it has been popular in some circles to see Hatshepsut as the "Pharaoh's daughter," there is no evidence to support the idea. The likelihood of this is small. Hatshepsut was, however, a woman of such strength and accomplishment that she deserves notice regardless, of her connection, or lack thereof, with Moses.

[32] Two prior queens in Egypt's history had assumed supreme headship, but neither had posed and dressed as a man as did Hatshepsut; see Gardner, *Egypt of the Pharaohs* (London: Oxford University Press, 1961), p. 183.

cumstances to claim the throne.[33] She proclaimed herself ruler of both Lower and Upper Egypt and took a special king's name, Kamare, as well as most of the normal royal titles.

Hatshepsut was the only living child of Thutmose I and his chief wife, Ahmose.[34] Four children had been born: two sons (Wadmose and Amenmose) and two daughters (Hatshepsut and Nefruibity). It is all but certain, however, that three of these died early in life, leaving Hatshepsut as the only one of the four who could be identified as the daughter of Pharaoh who found Moses.[35]

Because she was not male, Hatshepsut could not accede to the throne directly. A son of Thutmose I by a lesser wife was now married[36] to Hatshepsut, so that her legal title might work in his behalf. He took the name Thutmose II (1514–1504). This man was weak both in body and personality, quite in contrast to the robust Hatshepsut; and he was dominated in his rule by her and the queen-mother, Ahmose, also a woman of strength.

One daughter only, Nefrure, was born to Thutmose II and Hatshepsut, and so once again a son of the Pharaoh by a lesser wife was brought forward as successor. He, too, may have been married to the daughter, royal in blood from both parents, though no certain evidence has been found in this instance.[37]

This successor assumed the name Thutmose III (1504–1450). It was when Thutmose II had died and this young Thutmose III was about ten years of age that Hatshepsut took the daring step of assuming full control of the kingdom. Thutmose III clearly had been crowned before she did so and reigned perhaps a year.[38] But then she seized his crown; and it was not until her death twenty-two years later (1503–1482), following a most impressive reign,[39] that he was finally able to take the headship back again. That he harbored great bitterness toward her as a result is witnessed by his multiple defacements of her name and representation from monuments and temples.[40]

---

[33] Since the Egyptian word for *king* is written the same as *queen*, it cannot be said for sure that she applied the masculine term to herself. However, her reliefs and statues depict her often in masculine clothing, wearing the ceremonial beard.

[34] See Steindorff and Seele, *When Egypt Ruled the East*, rev. ed. (Chicago: University of Chicago Press, 1957), pp. 36–46; Hayes, *SE*, 2:78–83.

[35] It is possible that this daughter may have been of a lesser wife, of course. However, it seems more than coincidental that one of Hatshepsut's stature, who could provide every advantage for Moses, lived at this very time. Also, it would have taken someone of her strength and daring to rescue a Hebrew baby and even rear him right at the palace in defiance of the king's command.

[36] Brother-sister marriages were accepted in ancient Egypt, where it was believed that even the god Osiris had married his sister Isis.

[37] See discussion by Hayes, *SE*, 2:81–82; 105–6.

[38] During this year, Hatshepsut permitted herself to be represented on public monuments standing behind her stepson, bearing only titles which were hers as wife of the deceased Thutmose II.

[39] During her reign, Egypt enjoyed the highest economic prosperity since the Twelfth Dynasty. She built extensively in Thebes, particularly her magnificent temple, Deir el Bahri, as well as in other cities. Sanctuaries, destroyed or neglected by the Hyksos, were restored. She was devoted to Amon, adding courts and halls to his immense temple of Karnak and erecting there two giant obelisks each about ninety-seven feet high. She gave attention to trade and also mining ventures in the copper and turquoise mines of Sinai.

[40] For instance at Hatshepsut's great funerary complex at Deir el Bahri, though the buildings were spared, the names and figures of Hatshepsut were methodically obliterated wherever found. This

He clearly wished to obliterate her memory from the minds of the people. This same man went on to become the greatest ruler Egypt ever knew.[41]

3. Moses at the palace

We may picture Moses, if he was reared by this remarkable woman, in the palace at Thebes as her adopted son. Thebes was a city of splendor at the time and offered the finest in cultural benefits. Being the center of Amun worship, great religious buildings abounded and educational advantages were the best the world afforded.

Hatshepsut, intellectually endowed herself, would not have been satisfied with anything less than the finest education for her son. Her own daughter, Nefrure, died while still little more than a child,[42] which left Moses to receive all Hatshepsut's attention.[43] He would have been provided the finest in tutors, and his own mental capacity would have been able to absorb all that was taught. That he did profit greatly was verified years later by Stephen saying, "Moses was educated in all the wisdom of the Egyptians" (Acts 7:22).

F. MOSES' CHOICE
(Exodus 2:11–25; Acts 7:23–29; Hebrews 11:24–27)

1. A commendable decision
(Heb. 11:24–27)

In view of these matters, the words of Hebrews 11:24 carry deep meaning:

"Moses, when he had grown up, refused to be known as the son of Pharaoh's daughter." That is, he turned down opportunities this position afforded. This occurred when he was forty years old. He chose to aid his own people in their plight of bondage.

Had he not done do, he might have commanded a fine office in Egypt. Some have suggested that Hatshepsut might even have tried to make him Pharaoh to succeed her, especially in view of the bitterness between herself and the young deposed Thutmose III. This is hardly likely, however, for Thutmose III had already been given this position before Hatshepsut's assumption of it, and he was extremely capable and strong-willed in his own right. He would certainly have done everything possible to prohibit such a move. Moses' Hebrew origin, a fact Hatshepsut probably sought to hide, would have given Thutmose III a strong weapon to use in a struggle. Moses, however, with his ability and advantageous position, may well have had other offices open to him.[44] But when he chose to identify himself with his people, the enslaved Hebrews, all this was forfeited. Hatshepsut certainly had warned him of the result, but Moses would not be deterred.

2. Unwise procedure
(Exodus 2:11–22; Acts 7:23–29)

Having made the commendable choice, however, Moses did not carry it

---

involved destruction of much relief sculpture and more than two hundred statues and sphinxes which adorned the courts and colonades.

[41] Hayes describes him as "incontestably the greatest Pharaoh ever to occupy the throne of Egypt," *SE*, 2:116. Steindorff and Seele state, "If any Egyptian ruler deserves to be honored by being designated 'the great,' he is a far more fitting candidate than any other" (*When Egypt Ruled*, p. 66).

[42] If she married Thutmose III, it was when both were still ten years of age or less.

[43] Moses was older than the daughter, too. Born c. 1526 B.C., he would have been twenty-two years old when Thutmose III was made king in 1504 B.C. Hatshepsut was married to Thutmose II probably just before his accession in 1514 B.C., which makes their daughter something less than ten at this time.

[44] Indeed, he may already have held office, here at the age of forty. Thutmose III, on returning to the throne, would likely have left him alone, too, as long as he was himself Pharaoh.

out wisely. He went out among his kindred Hebrews, saw one abused by a slave master, and killed the cruel fellow.[45] He hid the body, thinking no one had seen him. The next day he attempted to settle a difference between two struggling Hebrews, and in doing so he learned that his action of the previous day was known.

Hearing this, he immediately fled the country, thus giving up in a moment what he had achieved through nearly forty years. But the reason is not difficult to see. He knew the danger from Thutmose III if he stayed. This rival[46] of many years would now have all the excuse necessary to take his life. Moses would not be able to defend himself, having shown his identity with the enslaved foreigners. He saw safety only in flight—and that as quickly as possible.[47]

Moses' escape led him eastward into the Sinaitic peninsula to the home of one Jethro,[48] a priest of Midian (Exod. 2:15–22). He married this man's daughter, Zipporah, and, for employment, tended his sheep. Forty years passed in quietness and solitude, much in contrast to the bustling court activity of Egypt. Moses' area of work seems to have been near the Gulf of Aqaba and Mount Sinai, the very region through which he would lead Israel not many years hence. No doubt geographical information gained aided significantly in the later day.

3. Thutmose III

Most of Moses' forty-year period in the desert had elapsed when finally the great Thutmose III died (Exod. 2:23–25). By this time the mighty king had ruled thirty-two years since his return to full control. These had been years of great accomplishment.[49] He excelled as a statesman and administrator, and he was one of the accomplished horsemen, archers, and all-around athletes of his day. He was a patron of the arts.

But it was as a military strategist that he distinguished himself. Immediately upon Hatshepsut's death, he was faced with a major revolt by northern Palestine and Syria. This he put down decisively with a brilliant victory at Megiddo. In later campaigns he pushed Egypt's northern border once more beyond the Euphrates, even farther than his grandfather had. Then two quick campaigns south along the Nile fixed this boundary as far as Napata below the Fourth Cataract.

Egypt's borders were now brought to their maximum limits, a true empire. Gold, silver, and valuable merchandise of all kinds poured into the land, both in the form of seized booty and products of trade. Egypt flourished as seldom in her history. But finally the great ruler died, and Moses was able to return to Egypt.

---

[45] This event, too, would have had to occur in Goshen, far north of Moses' usual home in Thebes. However, Moses may have spent much of his time in the north on government business.

[46] The animosity existing between Thutmose III and Hatshepsut would have been shared by the two young men. Thutmose would now have been about twenty-eight years old, right at his prime and ever becoming stronger as Hatshepsut grew older. Her death about four years later may even have been unnatural.

[47] Unless Thutmose III was also in the North, Moses would have had ample time to get away, however, before news reached the young ruler in Thebes.

[48] Also called Reuel (Exod. 2:18; see 3:1). *Reuel,* meaning "friend of God," may have been his personal name, and *Jethro,* meaning "excellence," his title.

[49] See Hayes, *SE,* 2:114–15; Steindorff and Seele, *When Egypt Ruled,* pp. 53–54.

G. MOSES' RETURN
TO EGYPT
(Exodus 3:1–4:31)

The idea of returning to Egypt, however, did not originate with Moses. He even resisted the thought. God called Moses as he tended sheep on Mount Horeb, the very mountain where God later would impart Israel's law (Exod. 3:1–4:17). Using the miracle of a nonconsumed, burning bush as a sign, the Angel of Yahweh[50] informed Moses that he was indeed to go back to Egypt and there lead Israel out from her bondage. He also gave Moses the name of God that he was to tell the Israelites (Exod. 3:13–14).[51] Translated "I AM," it is the first-person form of the verb *hayah* ("to be"), the verb from which (in the third person) the name *Yahweh* comes. The simplest understanding of the meaning of this name is "I am"—or, in the form *Yahweh,* "He is."

Various attempts have been made at explaining its significance, but the best seems to be a promise of God's faithful presence with His people.[52] He would not fail Israel in any of His promises, for He knew no contingencies. Nothing could hinder Him in His faithfulness, for He controlled all existence, and nothing could exist to effect a hindrance unless He permitted it.

When Moses protested that the people would not believe him, God gave him two miracles to perform as credentials. The first was having his staff turn into a live serpent when cast upon the ground; and the second involved his hand becoming leprous when placed within his clothing, followed by removal of the leprosy when inserted a second time (Exod. 4:2–7). Again Moses protested, this time claiming inability to speak well enough, and to this God replied that Aaron would act as his spokesman.[53]

Moses bade farewell to his father-in-law and departed for Egypt with his wife Zipporah and two sons (Exod. 4:18–31). On the way, a dispute arose concerning the circumcision of one of the boys; and after Zipporah performed the operation, Moses sent her back home with both sons.[54] It was not until Moses came back to Horeb much later with the Israelites that the family rejoined him.

Now Moses went on alone and was met by his brother, Aaron, whom God had previously instructed to go to Sinai for this meeting. Moses shared God's instructions with him, and the two then made their way to the land of Israel's

---

[50] See p. 41n.35.

[51] The name *Yahweh* had been known to the patriarchs, but, according to Exodus 6:3, had not been understood in its full meaning. Critics assert that the name only now came to be used, but this must be rejected.

[52] J. Barton Payne, יהוה, *Theological Wordbook of the Old Testament*, 2 vols. (Chicago: Moody, 1978) 1:210. Walter C. Kaiser, Jr. *Toward an Old Testament Theology* (Grand Rapids: Zondervan, 1978), p. 107, renders the name, "I am the God who will be there," stressing the name as a promise of God's "dynamic, active *presence.*"

[53] In view of Moses' early experience in the palace and later abilities to communicate with Israel, it is not likely that his speech was seriously impaired, although Jewish tradition interprets Moses' excuse as a genuine speech impediment. His forty years of solitude may have given him a sense of insecurity in meeting Pharaoh. Aaron apparently was known for his greater ease in oral communication.

[54] It is stated that God was "about to kill" Moses in this instance. Apparently Moses had been lax in circumcising one of the boys, probably the younger, Eliezer (Gershom was likely circumcised earlier properly). Zipporah had clearly opposed the idea but here circumcised him herself to save Moses' life. The account is one of the most difficult in the Pentateuch to interpret.

bondage. Their first act on arrival was to assemble Israel's elders as representatives of the people and relay God's words to them, along with displaying the confirming signs. Happily, Moses and Aaron were well received at this time, and their words and signs were believed.

H. THE CONTEST WITH PHARAOH
(Exodus 5:1–12:36)

This done, Moses and Aaron went to see the Pharaoh, now Amenhotep II, son of Thutmose III. A ruler of valor and strength in his own right, Amenhotep II had been carefully trained by his outstanding father. Ascending the throne at the age of eighteen, he prided himself in his horsemanship and claimed to be a better handler of ships and more expert with the bow than any other.[55] He conducted at least three successful military campaigns north in Syria, maintaining his father's holdings there, and was able to continue Egypt's southern boundary at Napata near the Fourth Cataract. Moses and Aaron would have encountered this man when he was yet young in life and in the early years of his reign.[56]

Moses first requested of Pharaoh only that Israel be permitted to take a "three-day journey into the desert to offer sacrifices to the LORD our God" (Exod. 5:1–3). Apparently Moses desired to test the king and observe his reaction before presenting the request for complete release of the people. The reaction was immediate and decisive (Exod. 5:4–11).

The king flatly refused the request and, in fact, imposed increased hardship on the Israelites. The Israelites had already been laboring in making a large quota of bricks, but now they would have to do so without straw being provided for them. They would have to gather their own straw in the form of stubble.[57] The Israelites, angered at this, blamed Moses and Aaron for adding to their burden (Exod. 5:12–21). The effect on Moses and Aaron, now resented by both Pharaoh and the people, was one of crushing discouragement and a sense of need for a fresh revelation from God.

God knew the need and did reveal further instructions (Exod. 5:22–6:13; 6:28–7:9). Moses and Aaron were renewed in spirit and returned to Pharaoh to effect the first step indicated. They performed one of the miracle-signs that God had given as a credential: that of turning the rod into a serpent (Exod. 7:10–13). Pharaoh's magicians, however, appeared able to duplicate the miracle which left the king unconvinced regarding the credential,[58] and he refused to comply with the request to let Israel go.

1. The ten plagues
(Exodus 7:14–12:33)

With the king having been given this much opportunity to grant the request

---

[55] Hayes, *SE,* 2:140–41; see Steindorff and Seele, *When Egypt Ruled,* pp. 67–71, and J. Breasted, *A History of Egypt* (New York: Scribner, 1912), p. 326.

[56] Coming to the throne at the age of eighteen in 1450 B.C., he would have been about twenty-two in 1446 B.C. and in his fourth year of rule.

[57] See Free, *ABH,* pp. 91–92, for discussion of Egyptian manufacture of bricks with and without straw.

[58] Magic and religion were closely linked in Egypt. There were two patron deities of magic: the god Thoth and the goddess Isis. In all areas of mystery, whether involving man and man, or god and man, magic was employed to obtain answers and ends. Magicians attained great skill in their art.

without the use of force by Yahweh, Moses now proceeded with the second step, in which force indeed was employed. Ten severe plagues were brought upon the country. God gave particular instruction regarding each as the time came to bring it: (1) the water turning to blood (Exod. 7:14−25); (2) the frogs (Exod. 8:1−15); (3) the lice[59] (Exod. 8:16−19); (4) the flies (Exod. 8:20−32); (5) the cattle disease (Exod. 9:1−7); (6) the boils (Exod. 9:8−12); (7) the hail (Exod. 9:13−35); (8) the locusts (Exod. 10:1−20); (9) the darkness (Exod. 10:21−29); and (10) the death of the firstborn (Exod. 12:29−33).

An examination of the nature of these plagues reveals an increasing degree in capacity to inflict suffering and loss on the Egyptians. The first four would have been extremely unpleasant, but none of these would have brought great suffering or material loss. The fifth (cattle disease), however, would have caused real material loss in the death of livestock. The sixth (boils) would have inflicted severe human suffering. The seventh (hail) and eighth (locusts) would again have brought great material loss, this time in the form of severe destruction of crops. The ninth (darkness) would have dealt a serious psychological blow. The tenth (death of the firstborn) would have been the worst of all, taking the lives of family heirs. God thus gradually increased pressure on Pharaoh to accede to Moses' request.

2. Pharaoh's magicians

Pharaoh's magicians were able to convince Pharaoh that they could duplicate the first two of the plague miracles,[60] in addition to the miracle-sign of the rod turning into a serpent. It is definitely stated that they did turn the river to blood and brought frogs onto the land (Exod. 7:22; 8:7). The explanation for this apparent duplication must be sought in one of two directions. One is trickery. Ancient magicians were highly skilled in trickery. It may be that they performed the first trick by making the serpents immobile and then bringing them back to normal functioning. It is known, for instance, that the Egyptian cobra can be rendered immobile by first charming the reptile and then applying pressure at the nape of the neck.[61]

The other possible explanation is demon power. These Egyptian magicians were religious personnel, devoted to the temple and to the false gods. This means that they were apt subjects for demon empowerment. In fact, history records many remarkable acts by similar "holy men" in the propagation of false religions, all apparently in the pattern of the "counterfeit miracles, signs and wonders" of Satan that are mentioned in 2 Thessalonians 2:9.

It should be observed, however, that the inadequacy of these magicians, in comparison with God, was displayed in three clear respects: first, the serpent of Moses and Aaron swallowed their serpents (Exod. 7:12); second, they could

---

[59] The Hebrew word here used, *kinnam*, means some type of insect which may have been lice, gnats, mosquitoes, or some other.

[60] Though most of the plagues involved phenomena natural to Egypt, they were still miraculous in several ways: (1) intensification of the natural phenomena; (2) prediction as to exactly when each would occur; (3) distinction between Goshen and the rest of Egypt as to where each would occur; and (4) the overall plan and purpose involved with them. See Free, *ABH*, p. 95.

[61] See Kenneth A. Kitchen, "Magic and Sorcery," *NBD*, pp. 769−70, for discussion and references.

not duplicate any miracle after the second, being stopped by their inability to bring lice to life, even admitting that this was "the finger of God" (Exod. 8:18–19); and third, they were themselves afflicted by the boils of the sixth plague (Exod. 9:11). It is of interest that the names of these magicians are given in 2 Timothy 3:8—Jannes and Jambres.

3. Goshen exempted

With the fourth plague (flies), God made a distinction between Goshen and the rest of Egypt: the last seven plagues, by far the more serious, affecting only the latter. This relieved God's people from major suffering, but, more significantly, it provided additional evidence that Israel's Yahweh was indeed sending the plagues. With the third plague, as noted, the magicians admitted the existence of a supernatural power, but there was need yet to prove that this God was Yahweh. The distinction made regarding the fourth plague demonstrated that this was so. It is noteworthy, too, that with the fifth plague (cattle disease) Pharaoh specifically sent to Goshen to ascertain if this distinction really existed (Exod. 9:7).

4. Pharaoh's gradual change of mind

The continued increase in severity of the plagues caused Pharaoh gradually to become more inclined toward acceding to Moses' request. He made a series of promises to let the people go— promises he broke each time when the plague was removed—which became more and more in keeping with Moses' petition.

As early as the second plague (frogs), he made a general promise to let the people go if the frogs would be withdrawn (Exod. 8:8), though, in view of the later promises being more specific, this one likely was not seriously intended. No promise was given with the third plague (lice); but with the fourth (flies), he promised again (Exod. 8:25–28)—this time more specifically and no doubt more seriously—that if the flies were removed, the people could go a little distance to do the sacrificing.

Again, no promise came with the fifth (cattle disease) or sixth (boils), but with the seventh (hail), eighth (locusts), and ninth (darkness) he went much further than before. Twice he admitted sin on his part (Exod. 9:27–28; 10:16), even naming Yahweh as the one sinned against; and with the eighth he promised that all Israelites with their animals could go (Exod. 10:8–11), though with the ninth again he retracted to speaking only of the people departing (Exod. 10:24). The significance is that, though he remained adamant in never keeping a promise, he was being psychologically conditioned for granting the full request with the tenth.

5. Duration of plagues

A few clues exist for determining the length of time between the first and last plagues. While no certain conclusion can be reached, the probable time is just under six months. The first clue is one of limitation. Amenhotep II, the Pharaoh concerned, would certainly have had to be in the Delta region during the period, and, since the capital was at Thebes, far south, he would hardly have been there an extensive time.

The other clues all suggest, however, that the period covered at least a few months. One concerns the time of year when it ended: in the Spring, on the fourteenth of Nisan (March/April), the date of the Passover. This was the time of the tenth plague. Another is equally sure in identifying the time of the seventh plague (hail), for it destroyed the barley and flax crops when they were mature.[62] These crops ripen in the first half of February, six to eight weeks before Passover. A third clue is less certain but suggests that the first plague was timed near the height of the Nile's flood stage. The Nile flooded each year, reaching its maximum depth in September and slowly receding through October.[63] To have timed the turning of its water to blood at a moment when the water was covering much of the country would have brought the greatest impression on the people.[64] A fourth clue is that since the second plague (frogs) is said to have come only seven days after the first (Exod. 7:25), and a situation of muddy conditions such as would result from a flood drying up would suit this type of plague, it is likely that the specific time of the first plague was just after the height of the high-water period, which means sometime in October.[65] All this argues for a total period from sometime in October to the latter part of March.

6. Purpose of the plagues

God's purpose in the plagues was not only to persuade Pharaoh to let Israel depart from Egypt, important as that was,[66] but also to demonstrate His reality and power in this foreign country. Pharaoh had significantly asked Moses, when first approached, "Who is the LORD, that I should obey him and let Israel go?" (Exod. 5:2). This question is understandable in terms of standards of deity evaluation accepted in that day. Since Yahweh's people had no land of their own, no army, and no independent status,[67] Pharaoh thought that Egypt's gods were much greater. But God would not let this thinking stand; Pharaoh and the Egyptians should be forced to recognize who Yahweh really was before Israel left the land. God stated this clearly to Moses before bringing the first plague, foretelling that Pharaoh would refuse the request so that God's hand might be on Egypt to reveal to them that He was Yahweh (Exod. 7:4–5; see 9:14). Later God declared further that Pharaoh's very rule was to the end that God's power might be demonstrated and that God's name might be known throughout all the earth (Exod. 9:16).

This means that every time Pharaoh changed his mind and broke his promise, rather than demonstrating his own

---

[62] The need for the eighth plague (locusts), in destroying more crops, is to be found in the wheat and spelt not being mature as early as the barley and flax and not being destroyed by the hail.

[63] The Nile was at its lowest in May, gradually began to rise in June, and flooded in July and August, reaching maximum height in September.

[64] It is not likely, however, that this plague involved merely flood stage reddening due to red silt, as some have suggested. Such reddening does not normally kill fish (Exod. 7:20–21) nor does it occur suddenly as at the precise command of Moses on a particular day.

[65] The mention in Exodus 7:19 of so many different types of bodies of water being affected (rivers, streams, pools, and ponds) suggests that the flood had started to decrease, leaving these.

[66] Had this been the only purpose, God could have used fewer plagues, or some other means entirely, to accomplish it in much shorter time.

[67] People believed that the domain of the gods of a country extended as far as the borders of that country, and measured their strength by the size of it, the victories of its armies, and the degree of its prosperity.

personal authority, as he thought, he was actually helping to fulfill God's purpose.[68] It was God's plan that all ten plagues occur to allow the display of His power to make its fullest impact on Egypt and on the nations. That this purpose was truly accomplished, even to the extent of God's name being made known in foreign countries, finds witness in the Philistines' repeated mention of these plagues some four hundred years later, far north from Egypt in Palestine, at the time that they captured Israel's ark (1 Sam. 4:7–9; 6:5–6).

7. The tenth plague (Exodus 12:29–30)

The tenth and final plague was the slaying of Egyptian firstborn. The eldest male child[69] of every Egyptian household was killed (Exod. 11:5) during the night of the fourteenth of Nisan. Only the firstborn of Israel escaped.

Even Pharaoh's son was included in the slaughter, a fact possibly confirmed by an extrabiblical text. A curious "dream" inscription was left by the successor of Amenhotep II, Thutmose IV. Since the eldest son of Amenhotep II would have died on that night, Thutmose IV must not have been the eldest. This "dream" inscription supports that conclusion. Written on a granite stele placed between the paws of the great Sphinx of Gizeh, it states that the god Harmakhis, with whom the Sphinx was identified, had promised the young man in a dream that the kingship would be his if he uncovered the Sphinx from the desert sand. The point is that, in order for the young man to have been emotionally conditioned to have such a dream, and to record it in this way, he must have been fearful that he would not receive the throne. But he would not have been fearful if he had been the eldest son, for heirship to the crown then was all but automatic.[70]

The severity of the tenth plague brought quick results from Pharaoh (Exod. 12:29–36). He called for Moses and Aaron that same night and told them that Israel could leave the land as requested. No exceptions nor variations were now stated.

Moses must have given careful directions ahead of time to the Israelites regarding preparations for departure, for, according to Numbers 33:3, the people were able to leave on the fifteenth of Nisan, the very next day. Much packing and loading of wagons would have had to be done beforehand.[71] Moses did relay the message to his waiting couriers, and they in turn took it to the people. The next day all Israel began the long-awaited move out of the land of bondage.

---

[68] Pharaoh's refusal is said twice (plagues 2 and 4) to have been the result of Pharaoh hardening his own heart; three times the result simply of hardening of heart without specifying the agent (plagues 1, 3, 5, 7, and the initial sign). This is a remarkable illustration of human responsibility and divine sovereignty working together to accomplish God's will.

[69] Even the firstborn of animals were killed (Exod. 11:5).

[70] The comment of Hayes (SE, 2:147) is noteworthy: "This fanciful tale, . . . suggests that Thutmose IV was not his father's heir apparent, but had obtained the throne through an unforeseen turn of fate, such as the premature death of an older brother."

[71] The people must also have done their "borrowing" (Exod. 12:35–36 KJV) from the Egyptians before the fifteenth, for there would have been little time then. The Hebrew word translated "borrowed" in the KJV is simply the word "to ask" (sha'al). They asked the Egyptians for gifts, and the Egyptians, now highly respectful of them after the plagues, gave what they asked.

8. The Passover
(Exodus 12:1—28)

The last plague was eventful, not only for the Egyptians, but also for the Israelites. They escaped death in their homes because they observed the Passover prescribed by God. Moses had delivered the instructions a few days before (Exod. 12:1—23), when he no doubt also had given the directions for departure. Every Israelite household was to select an unblemished year-old male lamb or goat on the tenth day of Nisan and kill it on the fourteenth in the evening.[72] The blood from this lamb was to be sprinkled on the two sideposts and lintel of each doorway, using a sprig of hyssop as an applicator. Then the roasted flesh of the lamb was to be eaten by the family along with unleavened bread and bitter herbs. While eating, the family members were to be ready to leave quickly, for the order to march might come at any time.

When the designated days arrived, the Israelites followed these instructions, and their firstborn were spared. They killed the lambs, applied the blood to the doorways, and ate the roasted flesh. When the death-cry arose from all the homes of Egypt, their homes, identified by the applied blood, were silent, having been spared the terrible loss. Lambs had died in place of sons. God instructed that an annual Passover Feast should be observed in memory of this significant occasion (Exod. 12:14—28).[73]

I. DEPARTURE FROM EGYPT

1. Route through Egypt
(Exodus 12:37; 13:20; 14:2).

Israel's assembly point on the fifteenth of Nisan was the city of Raamses (Exod. 12:37). If the common identification of Raamses with ancient Tanis is correct,[74] the people assembled well north of their main area of dwelling, for old Tanis was at the northern extreme of Goshen.[75] The route taken from Raamses led through Succoth (Exod. 12:37; 13:20) which commonly is identified with Tell el-Maskuta. This Tell lies thirty-two miles southeast of ancient Tanis, in the likely direction of Israel's march. Israel then came to Etham, which is unknown, but may be the name of a district lying along both sides of the northern end of the Red Sea.[76] Here some change in direction of travel occurred as instruction came to "turn back"[77] and "en-

---

[72] The Hebrew says, "between the evenings" (*ben ha'arbayim*), which likely means between sunset and complete darkness.

[73] The significance was more than commemorative. It was also predictive in that the slain lamb was typical of Christ, as the Lamb of God who would in due time die in the place of sinners.

[74] Some favor Qantir (p. 23n.48), however, which is sixteen miles southwest of Tanis and so within the Goshen area, though still in the northwest portion.

[75] This fact in itself argues against the identification and more in favor of Qantir, for the rationale of assembling to the north, when the route lay southeast, is not apparent. Simons, *GTT,* pp. 245—46n.209, makes the observation that a significant part of the people may have started from Raamses, as stated, but that a major portion joined the march as it proceeded through Goshen proper, which idea could apply for either Tanis or Qantir.

[76] The area through which Israel traveled south for three days after crossing the Red Sea is also called Etham (Num. 33:6—8).

[77] Wright, *BAR,* pp. 60—62, follows Albright, *BASOR,* 109 (February 1948), pp. 15—16, in arguing that the "turn" at Etham was back north several miles, so that the eventual crossing of water was not far from Raamses where they had started. The evidence given deserves notice, but is hardly sufficient to offset the unreasonableness of such retracting steps. J. Simons (*GTT,* p. 247) argues

camp near Pi Hahiroth, between Midgol and the sea, before Baal Zephon" (Exod. 14:2), these places being unknown.[78]

At this point they were on the shore of an extensive body of water that barred further progress. This body of water is called *yam suph,* meaning literally "Sea of Reeds" (Exod. 13:18). Though it is said that the Red Sea did not have reeds (from which fact it is often argued that *yam suph* could not mean Red Sea),[79] still this term is clearly used elsewhere to designate the Red Sea, being employed in reference both to the Gulf of Suez (Exod. 10:19; Num. 33:10–11; western arm) and the Gulf of Aqaba (Num. 14:25; Deut. 1:40; eastern arm).

However, three matters argue that the body of water here concerned was not the Red Sea proper (Gulf of Suez): first, the Gulf of Suez is too far south to have provided a logical place of exit from the country; second, the biblical account (Exod. 13:20–14:3; Num. 33:6–8) implies that the *yam suph* divided between productive Egyptian soil and the desert, while, if the people went as far south as the Gulf of Suez, they would have encountered much desert before reaching it; and third, when they had crossed this body of water, they found themselves in the "Desert of Shur" (Exod. 15:22), which was in the northern part of the Sinaitic peninsula, hardly as far south as the Gulf of Suez.[80]

A more likely identification for *yam suph,* then, is the water of the Bitter Lakes, which may even have been an extension of the Gulf of Suez in that day. This identification in no way militates against the miraculous character of the crossing, for the water is deep here, too.[81]

2. The people

The number of people who moved out from Egypt was very large. Several biblical references give the approximate figure 600,000 as the number of men twenty years and above (Exod. 12:37; 38:26; Num. 1:46; 2:32; 11:21; 26:51).[82] This means a probable total figure of more than two million.[83]

---

against such a turn back north, which would have been toward the center of enemy power, in favor of a more southwesterly route around the Bitter Lakes.

[78] Both Pi-hahiroth and Migdol are found mentioned in Egyptian inscriptions, but have not been identified. On the basis of a Phoenician letter, which indicates that a temple to the god Baal-zephon was located at ancient Tahpanhes (modern Tell Defneh, where Jeremiah was brought, Jer. 43:7–9), Wright, *BAR,* pp. 60–62, argues that the mention of Baal-zephon here is a reference to this temple. This constitutes one of his arguments for the retraced northern route (see n.77). The rational for the biblical account mentioning a temple in a city, however, rather than the city itself, Tahpanhes, is hard to see, particularly when this temple was to a pagan deity. Baal-zephon is better thought of as a place farther south. See further, Albright, "Baal-Zephon," *Festschrift Alfred Bertholet* (Tubingen: Mohr, 1950), pp. 1–14. For concise treatment and references in respect to various proposed routes, see C. de Wit, "Encampment by the Sea," *NBD,* pp. 368–69; for more detail, Simons, *GTT,* pp. 234–41; also Aharoni, *LB,* pp. 179–81.

[79] Jonah 2:5 uses *suph* to mean "seaweed," and certainly the Red Sea had plenty of this.

[80] Shur is mentioned five other times in the Old Testament and always as located just south of Canaan or on the way to Egypt (Gen. 16:7; 20:1; 25:18; 1 Sam. 15:7; 27:8).

[81] Liberal scholars argue for an area merely marshy in order to avoid the miraculous. It may be added that Lake Timsah, also deep, still farther north is another possible identification.

[82] This repetition of the 600,000 figure, in different contexts, makes it unlikely that it is a copyist error as some assert. A wilderness journey for such a large number of people certainly posed immense problems. But God, working through Moses, was able to work out the problems.

[83] The 600,000 must be doubled to include women, and to this number the children under twenty years must be added. See pp. 124–26 for further discussion.

Most all of those were descendants of the household of Jacob. They had remained a people distinct from the Egyptians through the 430 years.

At least three factors would have contributed to the maintenance of this distinctness. One factor, which would have tended to keep Israelites from marrying Egyptians, was a sense of heritage from, and corresponding loyalty to, the patriarchal fathers. Many Israelites would have simply wanted to keep the line of descent pure. The other two, which would have tended to keep Egyptians from marrying Israelites, were first, that shepherds were an abomination to Egyptians, and second, that Israelites had been despised slaves of the Egyptians now for two and one-half centuries. The last two certainly would have been unpleasant in the minds of God's people but would at least have served this good purpose.

There was also a minority group which accompanied the Israelites proper. They are called by the term, "mixed multitude" (Exod. 12:38 KJV, 'erebh rabh; Num. 11:4, 'asaphsuph).[84] These people were non-Israelites and made up of two basic types: a helpful, welcome group who had been influenced by the plague miracles to go with a people whose God could wield such power; and a critical, undesirable number who were dissidents looking for an easier life elsewhere. No doubt it was the second group who led in much of the complaining by the people during the wilderness experiences (Num. 11:4).

A multitude this size could not have traveled very fast, particularly when they had flocks and herds (Exod. 12:38). It would have taken nearly a week to travel the approximately sixty miles to the *yam suph*. Their path was directed by a miraculous, moving cloud which at night became a "pillar of fire," providing light (Exod. 13:21–22). They moved when it moved, followed the direction of its leading, and stopped when it stopped.

3. The plight at the *yam suph* (Exodus 14:1–12)

On reaching the *yam suph*, the people found themselves in a serious plight. They were barred from further progress by this extensive body of water. In addition, they learned that they were being pursued. Pharaoh, hearing of the direction in which they were headed and calculating that they would encounter the water, had changed his mind[85] and sent his elite chariot corps after them (Exod. 14:6–10). The chariot corps were a major factor in the world-feared Egyptian army, and here, coming against the defenseless Israelites, would have struck terror into their hearts (Exod. 14:11–12). Certain return to bondage, if not death, seemed inevitable. All their preparation and flight appeared to have been fruitless.

4. Three great miracles (Exodus 14:14–31)

a. Moving the cloud (Exod. 14:19–20). At this point, God intervened to deliver His people with three distinct miracles. The first was a shift in position of the cloud which had been

---

[84] The word ʿerebh ("mixture") is used again (Neh. 13:3) of a similar group who returned with Jews from Babylon. KJV translates it "mingled people" four times (Jer. 25:20, "foreign people" NIV; 50:37, "foreign people" NIV; 50:37, "foreigners" NIV; Ezek. 30:5, "people of the covenant" NIV).

[85] That Pharaoh had been so reluctant to let Israel go before and now here changed his mind again, even after so many terrible plagues, shows how valuable Israelite labor had been to Egypt.

leading. From standing out over the water before the camp, it now moved directly overhead to stand behind it. This accomplished two things: it stopped the Egyptians, settling down on them like a fog so that they could not see,[86] and it provided light on the Israelite side so that the people there could see better. The cloud's normal lighting property was at this time confined to one side only. This illumination enabled the people to make preparations for crossing the water and allowed them to witness the second miracle God performed.

b. Opening the water (Exod. 14:21–22). The second miracle was the dividing of the water so that the people could cross to the other side. We are told that as part of the miracle, God "all that night drove the sea back with a strong east wind" (Exod. 14:21). The wind is said to be particularly effective on the Bitter Lakes in changing water levels.

But certainly wind alone did not do all that was necessary in this instance. God had to intervene with additional, supernatural power.[87] We know that the water involved was deep, and not merely that of a marshy area, for later the Egyptians were drowned in it (Exod. 14:27–28). Moreover, the lake bottom was made sufficiently dry (Exod. 14:22, the Hebrew using *yabbashah*) so that Israelites could drive their wagons over it. Still further, the path had to be very wide, perhaps as much as a mile, to permit more than two million Israelites to cross during part of one night.[88] To push back water for a half mile on one side and a half mile on the other would indeed take the miraculous power of almighty God. The startled Israelites, after watching under the blaze of the illuminating cloud, moved into the broad path that was now open to them. The great amount of water pushed back was now a wall on both sides of them (Exod. 14:22).

Since there is no way to know exactly where the crossing was made, the length of this miraculous path is uncertain. Three factors, however, have a bearing on the matter. The first is that the length could not have been greater than the distance the people could travel in perhaps five or six hours. Darkness apparently had fallen by the time the first of the people started, since the light from the cloud was already needed; and it was "during the last watch" (Exod. 14:24; between three and six o'clock) that all were across, because by then the Egyptians were already in the path pursuing. A second factor concerns the length of the Israelite line going through the path. Numbering so many, even on a front of up to a mile wide, the column would have extended close to two miles, which means that an hour or more would have been consumed in merely

---

[86] Fog is quite unknown otherwise in Egypt. Being unaccustomed to this type of interference probably contributed to the frustration of these men and to their decision to stop entirely.

[87] A study of biblical miracles reveals that God normally employs natural law when, and to the extent that, it is available to do His work; and that He only uses supernatural force when the natural is insufficient. It should be realized that as much divine power is required to effect natural processes as supernatural interventions.

[88] A marching line of two million people, walking ten abreast with an average of five feet separating each rank, would be 190 miles long. Had this path been only as wide as a modern highway, the first Israelites through would have been in Canaan before the last started, and several days would have elapsed.

passing over its own length, or in entering the path. Still a third factor is that progress would have been slow, with wagons having to be driven and flocks and herds shepherded. These matters together suggest that the distance was not more than three or four miles.

c. Closing the water (Exod. 14:23–31). The third miracle was the closing of the water so that the pursuing Egyptians were drowned. As the last of the Israelites moved into the dried path, the cloud began to move ahead of the Egyptians so that they could once more see to take up the chase. They found the footprints and wheelmarks of the Israelites leading down to where the water had been, and they directly followed. They thought, no doubt, that if the Israelites had been able to go through, so could they.

When all were well between the great walls of water, however, God intervened to bring trouble: chariot wheels began to come off. The Egyptians, remembering the plagues, realized that again Yahweh was fighting for His people (Exod. 14:24–25). But as they started to flee back to the shoreline, God released the pent-up waters, enormous in amount as they were, and they rolled down upon the helpless Egyptians with speed and crushing power. In the resulting maelstrom, neither man nor animal had a chance to survive. Israelites, watching in the planned, opportune light of morning, saw the mighty, awesome elite of Egypt destroyed.

It is not likely that Pharaoh himself was in this group. The record does not say so,[89] and Amenhotep II did not die at this time. He lived twenty-two years after this, and his mummy has been found in the Valley of the Tombs of the Kings along with those of the many other Pharaohs buried there.[90]

d. The reason for the experience. The question rises as to why God led His people to a place where they would be trapped between water and pursuing Egyptians. A slightly different route, really no longer in distance, would have missed the Bitter Lakes entirely.[91] The answer is clear that there was need for just this sort of experience by the Israelites at the beginning of their long weary march through the wilderness. They needed a strong impression of the greatness of Yahweh's power, for they had long been in the land of Egypt, where false gods were worshiped. They

---

[89] Exodus 14:6 suggests that Pharaoh did personally assemble the army and possibly even accompanied them at the start, but no indication is made that he was involved in the closing waters. He is not mentioned after Exodus 14:10, and the drowning is not described until verses 26–27. Psalm 136:15 is poetical, with a figure of speech to be expected.

[90] His mummy was found in 1898 by Loret. The discovery was unusual, for the mummy was found in its own coffin and tomb, whereas most royal tombs had been robbed and the mummies taken elsewhere. In one of the side rooms of his tomb were found nine other royal mummies, including those of Thutmose IV, Amenhotep III, and Merneptah, which had been brought here from their tombs. See G. F. Owen, *Archaeology and the Bible* (Westwood, N.J.: Revell, 1961), pp. 214–17.

[91] It has been suggested that the need for Israel coming to this water was to avoid Egyptian fortifications elsewhere. Seti I, in inscriptions at Karnak, does speak of fortifications along the eastern approaches to Egypt. One is known to have been at Zilu (Thel) north, and one toward the southern end of the Bitter Lakes, which seems to have been there also during the Eighteenth Dynasty; see Simons, *GTT,* p. 248. However, not enough is known regarding either location or purpose of these "forts" (*mktl*) to make certain conclusions. Furthermore, it is doubtful if a small garrison would have done much to stop two million people or would have been a necessary reason to detour.

had forgotten how great in power the true God really was.

The demonstrations of His power in the plagues had helped, but most of these had occurred, intentionally, only in the Egyptian area. Israelites certainly had heard of them, but hearsay is never as impressive as direct experience. The people needed to see God's power for themselves, and here they did. They saw most vividly what their God could do in controlling and redirecting forces of nature, employing them to overthrow the world-renowned Egyptian army. The memory fortified the Israelites for meeting days of trial that lay ahead during the forty years of wilderness travel.

CHAPTER SEVEN

ISRAEL IN THE WILDERNESS

Exodus 15:22–40:38; *Leviticus* 8–10; *Numbers* 1–4; 10:11–14:45; 16–17; 20–27; 31–36; *Deuteronomy* 1–4; 34

Israel's task, now that she was out of Egypt and across the *yam suph*, was to go to Canaan. The sojourn in Egypt had served to fulfill God's promise to Abraham of a nation-size posterity. Another promise was now to be fulfilled: that of a homeland. The shortest way to Canaan lay northeast. From Israel's present location on the east side of the *yam suph* to southern Canaan was approximately 150 miles, which, had the people gone directly, would have taken less than a month to traverse. However, God did not so lead them, one reason being that they would have encountered Philistines and been wearied by fighting them (Exod. 13:17).[1] The route God did select has been the subject of much discussion.

A. ISRAEL'S ROUTE OF TRAVEL

The route of Israel (held traditionally and by most scholars today)[2] runs south along the Red Sea for over one hundred miles and then diagonally inland toward modern Jebel Musa (Mount Sinai) nearly fifty miles. From this point, where Israel remained for nearly a year, it leads north to Kadesh-barnea at the southern extremity of Canaan.

The key to determining the route is the location of Mount Sinai. The traditional view identifies it with Jebel Musa in the southern Sinai peninsula. Some scholars believe, however, that it must be found somewhere east of the Gulf of Aqaba. Their reasoning is that apparently Mount Sinai was a volcano, as evidenced by the fire, smoke, clouds, and sound that issued from it as the people one day stood at its base (Exod. 19:16–18); and no volcanos are found in the Sinaitic peninsula. The nearest is beyond the Gulf of Aqaba. In reply, it must be observed that these phenomena were supernatural in origin; and

---

[1] For existence of Philistines here at this time, see p. 45.

[2] Held for instance by Bright, *BHI*, 3d ed., if somewhat tentatively, pp. 124–25; Wright, *BAR*, pp. 62–64; *Westminster Historical Atlas to the Bible* (1956), pp. 38–39; Anderson, *Understanding the Old Testament* (Englewood Cliffs, N.J.: Prentice-Hall, 1957), p. 46.

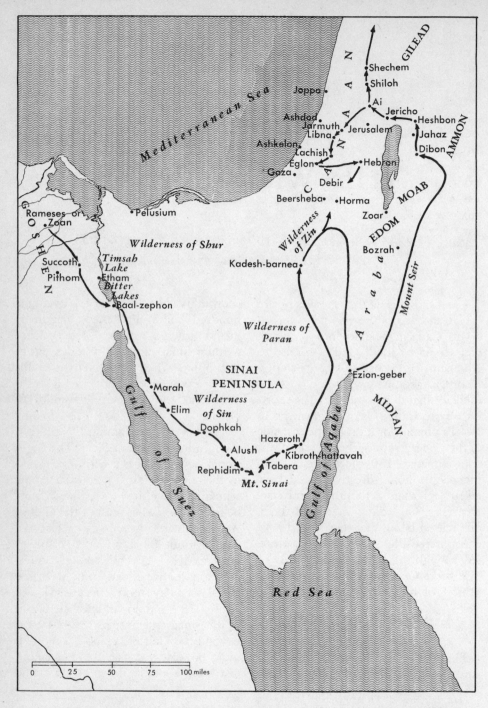

Map 5. The Route of the Exodus and the Conquest of Canaan

the mountain itself need not have produced them.

Another view is that Mount Sinai must have been in the north of the Sinaitic peninsula, because Amalekites waged battle with Israel there (Exod. 17:8–16), and Amalekites were never otherwise found as far south as Jebel Musa (Num. 14:43–45; 1 Sam. 15:7; 27:8). In reply to this, it may be pointed out that, though Amalekites did normally remain farther north, in this instance they had apparently followed Israel south for the purpose of preying on them (Deut. 25:18). A roving tribe, they lived by looting wherever there was opportunity; and it is not surprising that they should here have left their ordinary territory in pursuit of Israel as a likely victim.

Several matters favor the traditional location. For one thing, it has been held as correct for many centuries—in fact, from early Christian times and probably before. For another, Mount Sinai must have been some distance from the point of Israel's exodus from Egypt, for a number of stopping places are listed between the two locations (Num. 33:2–18), some of which can be identified with a degree of probability. For a third, Mount Sinai must have been well south of Canaan, for it was an eleven-day journey from there to Kadesh-barnea (Deut. 1:2), and years later Elijah even took forty days to make the trip from Beersheba, though he likely moved slowly and indirectly

(1 Kings 19:8).[3] For a fourth, it may be pertinent that Moses' father-in-law is called a Kenite, meaning "smith," for near Jebel Musa lay the copper mines of Serabit el-Khadim, which could have prompted smiths to live in the vicinity.

B. TO MOUNT SINAI
(Exodus 15:22–18:27)

1. Marah, Elim, Wilderness of Sin (Exodus 15:22–16:36)

a. Water (Exod. 15:22–27). Israel watched the overthrow of the Egyptian army from the eastern shore of the *yam suph,* paused to give praise to God (Exod. 15:1–21), and proceeded to follow the directing cloud southward. Three days they traveled without finding water.[4] They finally came to a small oasis called Marah, but its water was bitter. Marah has commonly been identified with modern Hawarah, where the water is still bitter.[5] Moses, at God's direction, cast a piece of wood into the water, and it immediately became sweet and drinkable.

The people moved on to Elim—which is believed to be present-day Wadi Ghurundel,[6] about six miles south of Hawarah, where plenty of sweet water is still to be found. Israel discovered here twelve wells and seventy palm trees, which made it a place of welcome refreshment for both water and shade. This location is yet a favorite stop for travelers, and Israel may have remained for several days.

Then the people moved on to a

---

[3] He is said to have traveled to Mount Horeb, but Mount Sinai and Mount Horeb were identical, except that the former may have been the entire mountain of which the latter formed only one peak.

[4] Simons, *GTT,* p. 251, states that Israel must have moved inland for some distance here or else they would have found water in several places near the Red Sea before coming to Hawarah.

[5] Described as a basin some five feet wide and eighteen inches deep, containing water disagreeably bitter and salty; see W. G. Blaikie, *A Manual of Bible History,* rev. C. D. Matthews (New York: Ronald, 1957), p. 65; also Simons, *GTT,* p. 252n.218.

[6] George E. Wright and Floyd V. Filson, *Westminster Historical Atlas to the Bible,* rev. ed. (Philadelphia: Westminster, 1956), pp. 38–39.

region called "Desert of Sin" (Exod. 16:1). This is best identified with a sandy, easily traveled plain along the shore of the Red Sea, since the terrain just inland is rugged. They arrived in this plain "on the fifteenth day of the second month" (Exod. 16:1), exactly one month after departure from Raamses.

b. Manna (Exod. 16:1–36). It was here that Israel's food supply ran out. The people had brought considerable provisions but one month had depleted them. The Israelites became anxious and cried to Moses. With so many people, besides flocks and herds, and with the wilderness barren, their anxiety is understandable. Where would adequate food be found in such a desolate region?[7] However, the people should have realized that God, who had already miraculously delivered them at the *yam suph,* would also be able to meet this need. They should have trusted rather than doubted.

God's provision turned out to be a nourishing food in the form of "thin flakes like frost,"[8] described as "white like coriander seed and tasted like wafers made with honey," which the people called "manna"[9] (Exod. 16:14, 15, 31). It lay on the ground fresh each morning except the Sabbath. The peo-ple were instructed to gather as much as they needed for one day, and on the sixth day to gather a double portion to last over the Sabbath. They were told that unused food gathered on normal days would spoil, but not when gathered on the sixth.[10]

c. Quail (Exod. 16:12–13). In the evening prior to the first morning on which the manna appeared, another provision of food was made, though only for one day. It was meat and was supplied through a great flight of quail. It is stated that "quail came and covered the camp." Perhaps the birds were caused to fly near enough to the ground for the people to strike them in flight, as seems to have been the case approximately one year later in a similar instance.[11] Whatever the method of capture, the people were provided abundant meat from these quail that night. The next morning the manna first appeared.

Certainly no one hungered in camp that day! God had marvelously supplied. It should be added that the provision of manna continued daily, from this time until the Jordan had been crossed forty years later (Exod. 16:35; Josh. 5:11–12).

---

[7] A modern city of two million by comparison calls for hundreds of food markets. The Israelites needed an enormous amount of food.

[8] This was not the honeydew excretion of scale-insects sucking sap from the tamarisk thickets of Sinai, as suggested by some scholars (Wright, *BAR,* pp. 64–65). Such excretion would not have sufficed for so many and, furthermore, is seasonal.

[9] Hebrew *man,* meaning "what?" The people asked "What is it?" and from this question took the name *manna.*

[10] God could have kept the manna over other days, too, of course, but did not, no doubt, to make each day a fresh experience of trusting God to supply. Jesus taught the disciples to pray, "Give us this day our daily bread" (Matt. 6:11). God's people are to trust Him for each day's provision.

[11] On the second occasion, the quail flew about three feet above the ground (see Free, *ABH,* p. 116). Wright's suggestion, *BAR,* p. 65, that both instances may have involved an annual crossing of the Mediterranean by quail must be rejected for two reasons: the Israelites were not near the Mediterranean either time; and this annual migration today comes in September and October, while both these instances for Israel were in the spring.

2. Rephidim and Mount Sinai (Exodus 17:1–19:3)

From the wilderness of Sin, Israel turned inland, perhaps moving up Wadi Feiran, which leads toward Jebel Musa, and came to a place called Rephidim, sometimes identified with Wadi Refayid. Rephidim was near Mount Sinai, for it was here that God told Moses to smite the "rock in Horeb" to bring water for the people; Horeb being identical with, or at least inclusive of, Sinai.

a. Water from the rock (Exod. 17:1–7).

At Rephidim the people found their water depleted. The region contains a few springs, but these apparently were not flowing strongly this year. The people complained bitterly to Moses, who brought the need to God. Following instructions, Moses struck[12] the rock of Horeb, and water in great quantity gushed forth.[13] The people's thirst was satisfied. It is very possible that this stream continued to flow all the time that the people were at Sinai.[14] There are sources of water near Jebel Musa today,[15] but, in view of the shortage of water at Rephidim, this particular year had evidently seen little rainfall, and so there was need for such a special stream. Rephidim and the plain before Sinai were not so far apart but what the stream could have flowed by natural course near enough to the plain to make its water available to the encampment there.

b. Amalekite battle (Exod. 17:8–16).

Also at Rephidim, the Israelites encountered a roving band called Amalekites in battle. This band may have descended from Esau[16] (Gen. 36:12), even as the Edomites (Gen. 36:1). The Amalekites moved about, preying on

---

[12] The suggestion of Wright, *BAR,* p. 65, and others, that Moses merely opened a vein of water in the rock must be rejected. Such a small amount could not have satisfied two million people. Actually, Moses' action in striking the rock was unnecessary for making this water flow, for it was produced supernaturally. The only reason for the act was to provide a typical picture of Christ who in due time would be smitten on Calvary to provide spiritual water for lost sinners (1 Cor. 10:4). See Numbers 20:8.

[13] In Psalm 105:41, the amount is called a "river" (*nahar*). It would have taken a river to satisfy the needs of so many people and animals.

[14] Some matters suggest this. Deuteronomy 9:21 speaks of the brook, on which Moses later spread ashes from the burned golden calf, as "stream that flowed down the mountain." The descriptive phrase used here is unnecessary if this was a natural brook. Also 1 Corinthians 10:4 speaks of the rock from which the water flowed at Rephidim as the "spiritual rock that accompanied them," which could mean that the water from this rock followed them by natural course the short distance to the plain before Mount Sinai. Further, since the people ate food supplied supernaturally while at Sinai, it would be in keeping if God desired them to drink water supplied supernaturally and so be daily reminded of their continual dependence on Him in these two basic ways.

[15] C. Conder, *ISBE,* 4:2804, quotes F. Holland, *Recovery of Jerus,* p. 524, as follows: "With regard to water supply there is no spot in the whole Peninsula which is nearly so well supplied as the neighborhood of *Jebel Musa.* Four streams of running water are found there: one in *Wady Leja;* a second in *Wady et Ti'ah,* which waters a succession of gardens extending more than three miles in length, and forms pools in which I have often had a swim; a third stream rises to the N. of the watershed of the plain of *er Rahah* and runs W. into *Wady et Ti'ah;* and a fourth is formed by the drainage from the mountains of *Umm 'Alawy,* to the E. of *Wady Sebaiyeh* and finds its way into that valley by a narrow ravine opposite *Jebel ed Deir.* In addition to these streams there are numerous wells and springs, affording excellent water throughout the whole of the granitic district."

[16] One problem exists in this identification, however, in that eastern kings are said to have devastated "the whole territory of the Amalekites" already in Abraham's day (Gen. 14:7). If this is not proleptic speech, Amalekites must have existed before Esau. If so, his descendants probably joined with them.

others,[17] in distinction from many tribes of the day which were more sedentary. Though not directly stated, the Amalekites apparently had been attacking the weak and stragglers of Israel since the crossing of the *yam suph* (Deut. 25:17–18), but now had become bolder in their hit-and-run tactics.[18] Consequently, Moses instructed Joshua, one in whom he had learned to place confidence,[19] to choose men for engaging the raiders in battle.

This was not an easy task for Joshua, for the people, fresh from Egyptian slavery, were not trained for warfare and would not have had many weapons. Certainly Joshua could not have expected many to volunteer for fighting in these circumstances, especially when the enemy lived by his very expertness in combat. However, some did respond, probably in large part out of respect for Joshua. The battle was fought the following day, and God gave a most unusual victory. Moses, observing from a nearby hill, raised his arms toward God in a gesture of supplication, and, as long as his arms were held upright, Joshua's troops advanced; but, when his arms tired and were lowered, his soldiers were forced to retreat. Finally, Aaron and Hur,[20] standing on either side of Moses, assisted their leader in maintaining his arms upright until full victory was achieved. In this way, the Israelites were given an impressive lesson that victory was not won through their own abilities but through trust in God's might.

c. Organization (Exod. 18:1–27). Also at Rephidim, Moses was visited by his father-in-law, Jethro. This was Jethro's home country, and he did not have far to come to make the visit. He brought with him Moses' wife Zipporah, and Moses' two sons, Gershom and Eliezer, whom Moses had earlier sent home when on his way back to Egypt (Exod. 4:24–26; 18:2).

Upon arriving in the camp and making some observations, Jethro offered counsel to Moses.[21] He suggested that Moses appoint assistants to aid in superintending the host of Israel. Moses followed the counsel and did appoint "officials over thousands, hundreds, fifties and tens" (Exod. 18:25). This means that at least several hundred, if not a few thousand,[22] persons

---

[17] Clearly illustrated in their attack years later on the Philistine city of Ziklag in the time of David (1 Sam. 30).

[18] Moses probably had hoped that Israel's journey southward, directly away from the Amalekites' natural habitat, would dissuade this enemy from continuing to pursue. From the fact that Joshua seemingly knew when and where to expect their attack at the time of the battle, it is clear that the raids had been increasing in frequency, however.

[19] This is the first mention of Joshua in the biblical record. To cause Moses to entrust him now means that Joshua had already been found capable and dependable.

[20] Aaron we know was Moses' brother, and Hur may have been his brother-in-law, the husband of Miriam, as Josephus states (*JA*, 3.2.4). Later Hur was given responsibility, along with Aaron, in superintending Israel while Moses was absent receiving the Law (Exod. 24:14). He may have died soon after this, however, for he is not mentioned later in the historical record.

[21] Jethro here voiced praise to Yahweh and even performed sacrifice to Him (Exod. 18:10–12), which means that Moses had strongly influenced him during the prior forty years. He also said, "Now I know that the LORD is greater than all other gods." The view of liberal scholars that Moses had learned of Yahweh from Jethro (see H. H. Rowley, *The Rediscovery of the Old Testament* [Philadelphia: Westminster, 1946], chap. 5) must be rejected.

[22] It is impossible to figure the exact number, for insufficient information is given regarding the

then became official personnel in the camp of Israel. Without question, this action proved of great value to Moses. The work of these assistants appears to have been mainly judicial, for it is stated that "difficult cases they brought to Moses," but "the simple ones they decided themselves." In addition, the divisions of the people thus formed would have provided natural lines of organization for dispensing information and effecting regulations.

d. Arrival at Mount Sinai (Exod. 19:1-2).

The next stop was at Mount Sinai itself, best identified with one end of a mountain ridge about two miles long and one mile wide.[23] Only the southern peak of this mountain is Jebel Musa (7,363 feet high), while the northern peak is called Ras es-safsafeh (6,540 feet). Before each peak stretches a plain adequate for the Israelite encampment, but scholars generally favor the one before Jebel Musa as the one used. Here Israel arrived in the third month of the journey (Exod. 19:1) on what is called "the very day"; likely meaning the same day of this third month as that of the first month on which the journey had started from Raamses, which was the fifteenth. The people were to be here eleven months and five days, for they departed finally on the twentieth day of the second month, a year later (Num. 10:11). During this time the Law was to be given and the central tabernacle built.

C. GIVING THE LAW
(Exodus 19:3-24:18; 32:1-34:35)

As Israel made her way from Egypt to Sinai, she was a vast host of people with little order or organization. Except for size, she could scarcely be called a nation. Slavery in Egypt had prohibited anything like self-government. She had no law of her own nor any real identity as an organized people. Neither did she have a true consciousness of God or the manner of life He required.

This situation would be corrected during the long encampment at Sinai. In fact, it is reasonable to suggest that a prime reason for the long detour through the peninsula is to be found in this intention.[24] Sinai offered an advantageous setting. Here the people would be quite undisturbed by others, for population was scarce. Here, too, the people would be entirely dependent on God's physical provisions. Here, then, God did choose to weld them into a true nation; to give them a law and organization; to unify them as a people with a sense of identity and mission; and above all to make them a people of faith and confidence in their God.

1. Giving the Decalogue
(Exodus 19:3-20:17)

The first aspect of God's communication to Israel at Sinai was His proclamation of the Decalogue or Ten Commandments (Exod. 20:1-17). To ready the people to receive these ten laws in a proper spirit, God gave instructions for two days of preparation (Exod. 19:3-15). The people were to realize the importance of what God was about to impart to them. Moses called for the people to declare their willingness to obey the laws God was about to give; and the people respond-

---

particular units over which these officials ruled. They likely were family units, but these could be figured either larger or smaller.
[23] See above, n.3.
[24] There was little reason to go this far south merely to avoid Philistines (Exod. 13:17).

ed that they would (Exod. 19:3–8). Then he drew a boundary line at the foot of the mountain beyond which both people and animals were not to pass, or else they would die. Further, the people were to wash themselves physically and sanctify themselves spiritually and so be "ready by the third day." The washing was necessary both as physical cleansing, in view of many days of dusty walking, and as a symbol of inner spiritual cleansing which brought their minds and heart-attitudes to a state befitting the occasion.

The anticipated third day began with an awe-inspiring display on Mount Sinai (Exod. 19:16–25). A thick cloud rested on the mountain, from which came thunder, lightning, and an increasing sound of a blowing trumpet. Smoke ascended as from a great furnace. An earthquake shook the mountain. This demonstration was to prepare the people further. They were to be impressed with the great might and authority of Him who was about to speak. During the display, Moses once more, at God's command, instructed the people not to cross the boundary line.

At the proper moment, God began to speak audibly from the mountain so that all could hear.[25] Probably these spoken words now took the place of the trumpet sound, but the other phenomena apparently continued to make the setting awesome. Certainly the emotional effect on the people was marked, as out from this fearful, majestic background words were heard without the appearance of a human speaker.

That which was communicated was the Decalogue. One by one ten basic laws of life were delineated. The people listened and were afraid. When the Voice ceased, the people urged Moses to act as their mediator, so that they would not have to hear more in this direct, fearful manner (Exod. 20:19). After this, Moses "approached the thick darkness where God was" (Exod. 20:21), so that he alone could hear, and God continued His communication.

2. The Book of the Covenant (Exodus 20:22–24:4)

What Moses now received from God is called the "Book of the Covenant" (Exod. 24:7). Its record covers more than three chapters. All of it was apparently revealed to Moses that same third day, after which Moses returned to the people[26] and relayed it orally to them.[27] In response, the people once more declared that they would obey what God commanded. This response was more meaningful than the first, for now there was content to what God demanded. Still that same day Moses recorded the material in writing (Exod. 24:3–4). The hour must have been late when Moses retired.

3. The ratification ceremony (Exodus 24:4–8)

The following day, when Israel ratified God's covenant, was one of her

---

[25] See Exodus 20:1, 19; Deuteronomy 5:4, 22. This miraculous, oral declaration, and then permanent recording on tables of stone, of the Ten Commandments should have impressed the people with their great importance.

[26] There was hardly time for Moses to climb all the way to the top of Sinai either this time or the ones previous. He may have gone that far only later when he was to be there for forty days.

[27] A great feat of memory. God may have especially gifted him, or perhaps Moses had been instructed to take notes.

most important days. If one were to pick out a particular day when Israel became a true nation, this would be the day. For here God's covenant with Israel went into effect. It is true that all the Law had not yet been revealed—in fact, only a small part of the total[28]—but enough so that this could represent the remainder. Since nearly three months would be occupied in giving the remainder, and it was now that the people had been duly prepared in mind and heart for the ratification, this was the most opportune day for it.

Moses first built an altar and placed twelve stone pillars around it, the altar clearly representing God and the pillars representing the twelve tribes of Israel. Then young men were appointed to kill oxen for sacrifice. Half of the blood was caught in containers and half was applied to the altar.[29] This done, Moses read aloud the entire "Book of the Covenant,"[30] recorded just the night before as noted, and the people responded for the third time that they would obey.[31] With this affirmative response given, Moses took the blood in the containers and sprinkled it out toward the people in a gesture representing the covering of their sin. The people's sin thus covered, and their promise to keep God's law formally declared, the covenant was made binding and Israel became God's chartered nation.

In representation of this new intimate relationship, Moses, Aaron, and Aaron's two eldest sons, Nadab and Abihu, besides seventy elders, ascended Mount Sinai the same day and ate in God's presence, a presence symbolized to them by a majestic vision (Exod. 24:9–11).

4. The Law given and broken (Exodus 24:12–18; 32:1–34:35)

a. First forty days (Exod. 24:12–18). God now called Moses up into the mountain to begin a period of revelation lasting forty days. Moses took Joshua with him, leaving Aaron and Hur in charge of the camp. For six days Moses stayed at a point only part way up the mountain, apparently still with Joshua, but on the seventh day God called him on alone.[32] He remained in God's presence continuously for forty days as God revealed the Law to him.[33] At some point during this time, God also inscribed the Ten Commandments on two hewn tables of stone.

---

[28] In that it included the moral law, however, it was the most important part and that on which the remainder was based.

[29] With more than one animal killed, there would have been sufficient blood to cover this altar completely. This blood so applied symbolized purification of the altar, as did the blood which came to be sprinkled on the "mercy seat" and brazen altar on the Day of Atonement (Lev. 16:14–20). Representing God, this altar had to be symbolized as perfectly pure.

[30] Likely Moses had recorded also what God had said orally, the Ten Commandments, which means that he here read what is now in Exodus 20–23.

[31] This third time counted much more than the first two. The first time the people had only assented to what they thought God would command. The second time was more meaningful, in that they now knew what God commanded. But this third time was in full ceremony, which constituted their formal pledge to obey. The first two had been more preliminary, giving them occasion to reflect before making the formal promise.

[32] Joshua remained on the mountain while Moses was gone, for Moses found him there on returning (Exod. 32:17), and Joshua knew no more about the people's sin than did Moses at that time.

[33] This first period of forty days was probably occupied mainly with plans for the tabernacle, in view of these plans being included in the immediately following chapters (Exod. 25–31).

b. Golden calf (Exod. 32). On the fortieth day, God told Moses that the people had sinned in making a golden calf as an object of worship. Moses immediately returned to camp, meeting Joshua again on the way. On his arrival, Moses, in a display of righteous indignation, broke the two inscribed stone tablets in the sight of the people,[34] utterly destroyed the gold calf, reprimanded a flustered Aaron who had consented to the sin, and instructed Levites to slay guilty Israelites, which they did to the number of three thousand. The next morning Moses pleaded with God that no more Israelites be destroyed in punishment for the sin, but instead, if more retribution were necessary, that Moses himself be blotted out of the "book" which God had "written"[35] (Exod. 32:30–32).

Why Israelites, within forty days of ratifying the covenant, should have sinned so seriously in breaking that covenant is not easy to explain. Apparently they believed that Moses, who had now been gone from them for several days,[36] had died on the mountain in the fearful presence of God (Exod. 32:1). So believing, they thought themselves leaderless, and this prompted the idea of returning to Egypt.

This in turn somehow led to the thought of a bull image, no doubt influenced by memories of Egyptian bull worship.[37] It may be that Aaron thought to stop the movement by demanding that the people contribute their gold earrings as material to make the image and was caught by his own demand when the people complied. It may also be that Israel, only newly separated from the idolatrous environment of Egypt, had not yet come to a full appreciation of the God they now served and thought they could please Him by the construction of an extravagant idol. Whatever the details, the image was made and the great sin committed.

c. Moses' commendable spirit (Exod. 32:11–14, 30–33). But if the people are to be condemned, Moses, in contrast, is to be applauded. When God first made Moses aware of His people's sin, He offered him a choice. Moses could either allow God to destroy all the Israelites and begin again with him or he could intercede on their behalf and forfeit this great honor. In other words, all Moses needed to do in order to become head of a new nation was refrain from interceding in Israel's behalf.

But Moses chose to intercede, and he did so to safeguard God's reputation, thus putting his own interest below that of God's and of the people's. Then, after returning to camp and effecting considerable retribution, Moses went still further and asked to be destroyed himself, even eternally, rather than have Israel be further punished. Aside from

---

[34] Deuteronomy 9:17 implies that this action was deliberate on Moses' part, as he symbolized before the people their sin in breaking God's covenant.

[35] This "book" is the Book of Life (Ps. 69:28; Dan. 12:1). The figure is taken from the practice of the time in maintaining registers of accepted people in a community or tribe.

[36] Very likely Moses had not absented himself from them for any extended length of time before this. Even when he had received the "Book of the Covenant" he had been gone only a part of one day.

[37] Egypt had Apis bull worship at Memphis and Mnevis bull worship at Heliopolis, but both of these were at some distance from Goshen. Nearer, and no doubt more influential, were bull cults connected with Horus worship. The bull was a symbol of fertility and strength. See Steindorff and Seele, *When Egypt Ruled the East* (Chicago: University of Chicago Press, 1957), pp. 140–41.

Christ, only one other person demonstrated this degree of selflessness: the apostle Paul, who wrote, "I could wish that I myself were cursed and cut off from Christ for the sake of my brothers" (Rom. 9:3). God's response to Moses was that only those who had sinned would experience punishment.

d. Two further actions (Exod. 33:7–23). Before returning to the mountain to continue receiving the Law, Moses did two more things. First, he pitched a tent[38] outside the camp for himself, and, when he entered it, the pillar of cloud moved to stand at its door. The intention was to show the people how displeased God was with them, for the cloud left them to move where Moses dwelt, and to encourage full repentance toward God for their sin. Moreover, it demonstrated that God's approval was on Moses, and the people should again rally to his leadership, if they were to be blessed.

Second, Moses requested that he be permitted to see God's own glory. Moses, discouraged by Israel's disobedience, needed reassurance. God promised that His own "Presence" would surely go with Moses, but Moses still wanted tangible evidence. God graciously acceded by hiding His servant in the "cleft of the rock," somewhere on Sinai, and allowing him to see what is called the "back" of God.[39]

e. Second forty days (Exod. 34:1–35). Moses was now instructed to cut two more tables of stone and return to the top of Sinai. He did so the following morning, and for forty more days God revealed the Law to him. When Moses descended this time, his face shone with the brightness of God's presence, and he had to cover himself with a veil that he might converse with others. It was likely soon after this return to camp that Moses recorded all that God had told him on the mountain, while it was still fresh in his mind.[40]

D. THE LAW

The Mosaic Law includes the Ten Commandments given orally to all the people, the "Book of the Covenant" given to Moses alone later the same day, and the lengthy, detailed regulations revealed to Moses, again alone, during the two forty-day periods on Mount Sinai. The total content may be divided into moral, civil, and ceremonial law.

1. Moral law

The moral law is the Decalogue, or Ten Commandments. It supplies the broad moral foundation for conducting life generally, and it presents the basis for the more specific civil and ceremonial regulations. Its importance was stressed in that it was orally proclaimed by God and then inscribed supernaturally on stone tables. It is of two parts:[41]

---

[38] This tent is called the "tent of meeting" (*'ohel mo'edh*), the same name given to the later tabernacle. However, that structure had not yet been built and so should not be confused with this simple tent.

[39] This language is highly anthropomorphic. God is pure spirit (John 4:24) and cannot be seen by physical eyesight; and if He could, the man that should see Him would die, as God Himself says (Exod. 33:20). What Moses saw, however, was real and represented God in His glory, although, as the language implies, only a small proportion of that glory.

[40] For discussion as to when Moses wrote the Pentateuch as such, see p. 135–36.

[41] This twofold division was recognized by Christ in speaking of the two great commandments of the Law (Matt. 22:34–40).

the first concerning man's duties to God, regarding God's being, His worship, His name, and His day; the second concerning man's duties to man, regarding honoring parents, not murdering, not committing adultery, not stealing, not bearing false witness, and not coveting.[42] It is likely that every person was expected to memorize these precepts and esteem them of the highest importance.

2. Civil law

The civil law gives specific instruction about daily social relationships. It concerns administration of justice, rights of property, care of the poor, training of children, punishment of criminals, and many other matters. Numerous laws deal with personal interrelationships: fathers and children, husbands and wives, masters and servants, and kindness to strangers. Nearly all of the "Book of the Covenant" concerns civil laws, many of which can be rightly understood only in the light of contemporary cultures. Regulations were especially needed that many Egyptian customs and practices might be avoided.

3. Ceremonial law

The ceremonial law has to do with religious matters, with much of it concerning priestly functions at the tabernacle. Specifications are given for the tabernacle itself, the dress and duties of the priests and Levites, and the various sacrifices and offerings.[43] The great annual feasts are prescribed, and every male was required to celebrate the three main ones[44] annually at the central sanctuary. The ceremonial law is the longest of the three divisions. It should be added that many of the ceremonial and civil laws were only temporary in nature, being valid for as long as conditions made them appropriate, whereas the moral laws were designated to be permanent.

4. Comparison with other laws

The Mosaic Law has often been compared with other legal codes of early time. Six are known: (1) the Ur-nammu code, c. 2050 B.C., from the Third Dynasty of Ur; (2) the code of Bilalama, c. 1925 B.C., from Eshnunna; (3) the code of Lipit-Ishtar, c. 1860 B.C., from Isin; (4) the code of Hammurabi, c. 1700 B.C., from Babylon; (5) the Hittite code, c. 1450 B.C., from Boghazkoi; and (6) the Assyrian code, c. 1350 B.C., from Assur.[45]

The analysis of these codes has revealed numerous parallels with the laws of the Old Testament. This should present no problem for the Evangelical, however. The Bible is clear in portraying the Mesopotamian origin of Israel and, as is true elsewhere in the Old Testament, God used compatible cultural forms to frame the transcendent elements of His Word. The recognition

---

[42] Another division combines the first two (God's being and worship) and divides the last (not coveting) into two (not coveting a neighbor's house and not coveting a neighbor's other property or wife).

[43] For discussion, see pp. 158–63.

[44] The Feast of Passover in the spring (Exod. 12:1–28; Num. 28:16–25; Deut. 16:1–8), the Feast of Pentecost fifty days later (Exod. 34:22; Lev. 23:15–22; Deut. 16:10), and the Feast of Tabernacles in the fall (Lev. 23:34–42; Num. 29:12–40). See pp. 163–65.

[45] George Mendenhall, "Ancient Oriental and Biblical Law," *BA* 17 (May 1954): 23n.18. For discussion, see his *Law and Covenant in Israel and the Ancient Near East* (Pittsburgh: Biblical Colloquium, 1955); also for texts and discussion, see *ANET*, pp. 159–98.

of similarities does not negate the uniqueness of Old Testament law. This uniqueness is to be found in the context of God's covenant relationship with Israel.

It has been a commonplace in Old Testament scholarship to equate the covenant form of the Hittite suzerainty treaty with the covenant form found in the Bible. While not without challengers,[46] this idea provides a congenial context for understanding Israel's covenant with God. In the Hittite covenant, the king bound a subject nation to himself and, in return for promised benefits or punishments, established a set of stipulations that would govern their relationship.

An understanding of Israel's relationship with Yahweh that sees the covenant as a mutually binding agreement is essential to an understanding of much of the prophetic literature, which is dependent on covenant for its force. God's benefits to Israel, under the covenant, were fulfilled in the conquest of Canaan when the land God promised was given to His people. Israel's obligation, in return for God's benefits, was to live in accordance with the stipulations God established in the Law. This is seen most clearly in Deuteronomy 27 and 28. It is on the basis of this kind of covenant language that the judgment of the Exile was proclaimed.

The laws of the Old Testament are to be understood as the stipulations assigned to the subject people by the Great King, who in this case is God. Even those laws that have direct parallels in the codes of other ancient people have religious import. What they teach us is that God is concerned with humanity's relationship with Him, but is also concerned that that relationship demonstrate itself in justice and equitable treatment of one person by another.

The laws have been described in two categories, casuistic and apodictic. Casuistic, or case laws, are usually framed as conditional statements, describing an action and then the consequences. For example, "*If* a bull gores a man or a woman to death, the bull must be stoned to death, and its meat must not be eaten. But the owner of the bull will not be held responsible" (Exod. 21:28). Apodictic laws, on the other hand, are unconditional statements such as, "You shall have no other gods before me" (Exod. 20:3). In many respects, the casuistic laws of the Old Testament are expansions and specific explanations of the apodictic statements of the Ten Commandments.

E. THE TABERNACLE
(Exodus 25–31; 35–40)

One of the main subjects in God's communication to Moses was the tabernacle. In contrast to Egypt and other countries where many temples existed, Israel was to have only one place of worship. For the period of wilderness travel, and also for many years after occupying Palestine, this place was to be a portable sanctuary called the taber-

---

[46] George Mendenhall, "Covenant Forms in Israelite Tradition" in E. F. Campbell, Jr., and David Noel Freedman, eds., *The Biblical Archaeologist* (New York: Anchor, 1970), 3:25–53. The classic conservative formulation of this position is Meredith Kline's *Treaty of the Great King* (Grand Rapids: Eerdmans, 1963). More recent treatments from the more liberal point of view are: K. Baltzer, *The Covenant Formulary* (Philadelphia: Fortress, 1971); and D. J. McCarthy, *Treaty and Covenant*, 2d ed. (Rome: Pontifical Biblical Institute, 1978). McCarthy takes issue with the idea of Deuteronomy having analogies in the suzerainty treaty.

nacle, for which God gave Moses the plan. Bezaleel of the tribe of Judah and Aholiab of the tribe of Dan, both skilled by special enablement of the Spirit of God, were to lead in the construction (Exod. 35:30–35). Free-will offerings of the people quickly provided ample building material, though the amount needed was large and of great value (Exod. 35:4–29). The importance of this structure was stressed by the large place given to it in the Law and its assigned central location among the tribes. There was need for it to be central, for, being God's own sanctuary, it represented His presence among the people.

1. Description

The tabernacle consisted of a portable building located within a rectangular court. The court measured 150 feet[47] by 75 feet, and was enclosed by linen curtains hung from silver hooks on silver-covered rods attached to posts of acacia wood. Entrance was from the east through a gate of curtains. Two articles of furniture were located in the eastern half of the court. Nearest the entrance was the brazen altar where the priest offered sacrifices for the people (Exod. 27:1–8; 38:1–7). It measured 7½ feet square and 4½ feet high, was made of acacia wood covered with bronze, and had horns at each corner. Beyond the altar was the laver (Exod. 30:17–21; 38:8; 40:30). This was made of bronze and was the place where priests washed prior to engagement in ceremony.

In the western half of the court stood the tabernacle proper, a rectangular building 45 feet long, 15 feet wide, and 15 feet high, constructed of forty-eight frames[48] of acacia wood covered with gold (Exod. 26:1–37; 36:8–38). It consisted of two compartments: the first, called the Holy Place, comprising two-thirds of the area and containing the seven-light lampstand, the table of showbread, and the altar of incense; and the second, called the Holy of Holies, containing the ark of the covenant,[49] which supported two golden cherubim with outstretched wings. The building had four layers of covering: the first of linen, the second of goat's hair, the third of dyed rams' skins, and the fourth of dugong[50] skins.

2. Location

God directed that the tabernacle be located in the exact center of the tribes,

---

[47] Figuring the standard cubit as approximately 18 inches (more precisely, 17.51 inches); see R. B. Y. Scott, *JBL* 78 (1958): 210–12.

[48] "Frames" (*qerashim;* Exod. 26:15–16; 36:20–21) is better than "boards" of KJV because (1) a plank fifteen feet by twenty-seven inches would be extremely heavy and very difficult to obtain, whereas a framework of this dimension would be lighter and easily constructed; (2) frames would have let one see through to the beautiful covering curtain; and (3) the best analysis of the Hebrew word favors "frameworks." See A. R. S. Kennedy, "Tabernacle," *HDB,* pp. 559–661.

[49] The Ark was the most sacred object. The high priest alone was to enter the Holy of Holies where it was, and this only once a year on the Day of Atonement. Made of acacia wood, overlaid on the inside and out with gold, and with a solid gold plate for a lid, called the mercy seat, the ark represented the presence of God among His people. The Decalogue forbade any image of God, and this ark in a way took the place of one without the element of attempted physical resemblance. The ark contained the two inscribed tables of stone representing the Covenant, a gold pot of manna, and later Aaron's rod that budded (Num. 17:1–13; Heb. 9:4).

[50] The dugong is a marine animal, averaging five to nine feet long, which lives in the seas around Egypt and Sinai. It was likely the skin of this animal which was used, rather than that of the badger, the Hebrew word employed being properly so rendered and badgers are not known to have lived in this part of the world; see Free, *ABH,* pp. 106–7.

	Asher		Dan		Naphtali	
Manasseh						Issachar
Ephraim		Tabernacle				Judah
Benjamin						Zebulon
	Simeon		Reuben		Gad	

Tribes Encamped

when encamped during the wilderness journey. On the east were to be the tribes of Judah, Issachar, and Zebulon; on the south, Reuben, Simeon, and Gad; on the west, Ephraim, Manasseh, and Benjamin; and on the north, Dan, Asher, and Naphtali (Num. 2).[51] When marching, the three eastern tribes were to go first, followed by the Levitic families of Gershon and Merari bearing the dismantled tabernacle material;[52] then the three southern tribes, followed by the Levitic family of Kohath bearing the tabernacle furniture;[53] then the three western tribes, and finally the three northern tribes (Num. 3–4; 10:11–28). Even when marching, the tabernacle furniture was to be kept in the center, though the tabernacle itself was to go earlier so that it might be erected in time for the furniture to be set in place on arrival (Num. 10:21). One item of furniture went before all, the ark of the covenant, which led the way, with the priests carrying it as they followed the pillar of cloud moving overhead.

3. Service instituted

A main task for the approximate year that Israel remained at Sinai was the construction of this tabernacle. Presumably work began shortly after Moses returned from the mountain, which would have been about three months after the people's first arrival at Sinai.[54] The date of completion is given as the first day of the first month in the second year (Exod. 40:17), which means about five and one-half months later. On the day of completion, the cloud, which otherwise led the people, settled over the tabernacle, and the glory of God filled it (Exod. 40:34).

The next matter was the consecration of Aaron and his sons, Nadab, Abihu, Eleazar, and Ithamar, to act as priests for ministering at the tabernacle (Exod. 29:1–37; 40:12–15; Lev. 8:1–36). All five were washed with water, clothed in the prescribed priestly garments, and anointed with oil. A series of offerings was presented to God, with blood from a slain ram applied to the

---

[51] This grouping is according to mother ancestry: Leah's posterity, Reuben, Simeon (Levi removed as priestly tribe), Judah, Issachar, and Zebulon, are on the east and south; Rachel's posterity, Ephraim, Manasseh (sons of Joseph), and Benjamin, are on the west; Bilhah's (Rachel's maid) posterity, Dan and Naphtali, are on the north; and Zilpah's (Leah's maid) posterity, Gad and Asher, are divided, one on the north and one on the south.

[52] The Gershonites transported the fabrics of the tabernacle (Num. 4:21–28) in two wagons drawn by four oxen (Num. 7:7), and the Merarites transported the wood and metal items (Num. 4:29–33) in four wagons drawn by eight oxen (Num. 7:8).

[53] The Kohathites did not need wagons, for the furniture was carried on poles inserted through supporting rings (Num. 4:1–15).

[54] Besides Moses' eighty days on the mount, there had been four days spent prior to his going there and a few days at the midpoint when the golden calf had been made, for a total of nearly ninety days.

Judah			Reuben		Ephraim	Dan
Ark	Issachar	Tabernacle Material (Gershon Merari)	Simeon	Tabernacle Furniture (Kohath)	Manasseh	Asher
	Zebulon		Gad		Benjamin	Naphtali

Tribes Marching

right thumb, right ear, and large toe of the right foot of all five persons. Wave offerings followed, and lastly a sacrificial meal was eaten by Moses and the priests. The ceremony was repeated on seven successive days.

After this week of consecration, the priests began their ministry (Lev. 9:1–24). The inaugural day was most impressive. Several offerings were presented to God, both for the priests and the people, before Aaron was escorted by Moses into the tabernacle for general orientation. When the two came out, miraculous fire appeared on the brazen altar, apparently consuming the offerings that were on the altar in an instant. This was not the initial kindling of altar fire, however, as is sometimes believed, for offerings had been made all during the prior week of priestly consecration. This fire served more to climax the eight days of festivities, showing God's approval, both of all that had been done and what would be done in days and years to come.

4. Sin of Nadab and Abihu (Leviticus 10:1–7)

This happy atmosphere was now saddened, however, by unexpected, serious sin on the part of Aaron's two older sons, Nadab and Abihu. They had just been highly honored by inclusion in Israel's priesthood, but now they offered what is called "unauthor-

ized fire" on the altar of incense. The implication is that they used coals of fire not taken from the prescribed place, the brazen altar. The fire on the brazen altar was never to go out (Lev. 6:13), one reason being that there would always be coals available for burning the incense. Nadab and Abihu certainly knew this and should have been particularly conscious of the altar as the place to get coals, after the miraculous fire had so recently burned upon it. But somehow they were negligent, or else deliberately rebellious, and took coals from elsewhere. It seems evident as well that they offered the incense at an unprescribed time, that is, other than at the morning or evening sacrifice.

Perhaps their new position had made them proud and spoiled them for obeying orders carefully, or perhaps they had partaken of too much wine—a possibility that finds support in God's immediate warning to Aaron (Lev. 10:9) that wine and strong drink should be avoided at the time of tabernacle service. Whatever the full reason, the sin of the two was serious. God in judgment sent forth fire again, this time to take the lives of each, both as punishment on them and as warning for those observing.

F. THE NUMBER OF PEOPLE

The need for organization of the people gave reason for a census. One

124

was taken early in the second month of the second year, beginning on the first day, exactly one month after completion of the tabernacle (Num. 1:1).[55] Twenty days later, Israel broke camp (Num. 10:11), which means that the census was one of the last matters undertaken at Sinai. In this activity, Moses' knowledge from Egypt would have benefited, for Egypt is known to have had good methods in census taking.

Those numbered were the men available for military service from twenty years of age and above. Their total proved to be 603,550 (Num. 1:46). Others were not counted, but the grand total can be approximated. To the number of military men should be added an equal number of women, making them over 1,200,000; and to this the number of young people under twenty.

This last group is difficult to esti-mate. In the United States, those under twenty years of age number approximately 60 percent of those over twenty.[56] If this had been the ratio for Israel, there would have been 720,000 young people, making the total figure 1,920,000. In view of the rapid growth rate while in Egypt, however, the family size in Israel was probably larger than that in the United States,[57] which would have increased the number of young people to a million or more, making a grand total of between 2 million and 2.5 million people.

Liberal critics* commonly object to the idea of this large number of people living in the wilderness. Wright[58] and Albright[59] do, believing that these large figures really come from the later time of David and were misplaced in the records. This explanation finds two difficulties, however: the misplacement would have had to occur in no less than six different biblical texts,[60] and the

---

[55] This may have been the completion of a census actually begun nine months before when the offering was taken for the tabernacle. Every male then had to give one-half shekel, and the number who did is given the same as here (603,550; Exod. 30:11–12; 38:25–28). The count may have been taken then and the formal registration made here for the purpose of military availability.

[56] The 1960 census gave 113,974,000 age twenty and over, and 66,009,000 under twenty, for 58 percent. In Grand Rapids, Michigan (the author's own city), it was 125,804 to 75,863, for 60 percent. Some countries with higher birth rates show a figure of 80 percent. While there is fluctuation above and below these percentages, they provide a benchmark by which to estimate population.

[57] It should be borne in mind, however, that the birth rate may well have slowed by this time, this especially in view of actual loss in population during the wilderness journey (see Num. 26).

*Reviser's note: Some conservatives also have difficulty with these numbers, primarily because the number seems to clash with what is known of population and army sizes in the ancient world. (But see n.58 below.) Most conservative attempts to reduce the number to coincide with population estimates involve the Hebrew word 'eleph, "thousand." There are varieties of theories, but most substitute another word for thousand, (family unit, squad, armed men), giving readings like "57 armed men, 23 'hundreds' (military unit)." (John G. Wenham, "The Large Numbers of the Old Testament," Eerdmans' Handbook to the Bible, ed. David Alexander [Grand Rapids: Eerdmans, 1973], pp. 191–92.) All of these reconstructions have problems.

[58] BAR, p. 66. Wright argues also that an army of 600,000 could have crushed any opposing army by "sheer weight of numbers." However, the possibility exists that populations in the ancient world may have been underestimated. The 260,000-person (!) population claimed for Ebla (Giovanni Pettinato, "The Royal Archives of Tell-Mardikh-Ebla," BA, 2 [May 1976]: 47) is far larger than the populations estimated for other cities of that era.

[59] Albright, ARI, p. 123.

[60] Exodus 12:37; 38:26; Numbers 1:46; 2:32; 11:21; and 26:51. It is significant, too, that the figures of Numbers 1:46 (the first census) and 26:51 (the second) are not the same—not only in the totals, but for all the separate tribes, some varying considerably.

census for David's day is given in its appropriate place and is much larger.[61] The census figures must be accepted as correct.

In doing so, however, one must not minimize the enormity of Moses' task in superintending a host so large. This was a vast number of people to keep together and control, especially in the unpleasant conditions of desert travel, for no less than forty years. Probably no other person ever carried greater responsibility. It is pertinent to remember that Moses had been well trained, that he had the tribes well organized following the year at Sinai, that there was a general signal for travel in the pillar of cloud which all could see, and, most important, that the supernatural provision and blessing of God was attendant at all times.

G. SINAI TO KADESH-BARNEA
(Numbers 10:11–17:13; 33:16–19)

Eleven months and five days had elapsed at Sinai (Num. 10:11) when the pillar of cloud lifted, leading Israel north in the direction of Canaan. A covenant had been made between God and the people, an organization established, and the tabernacle built. The people were ready to move on to the Promised Land.

1. The route
(Numbers 10:12, 34, 35; 33:16–19)

The route north led to Kadesh-barnea,[62] a city located at the southern extremity of Canaan. Its location is reasonably sure. Two sites in close proximity, lying about fifty miles southwest of Beersheba, qualify for general position and water supply, Ain Qudeis and Ain Qudirat. The first retains the basic name *Kadesh,* and the second boasts the best springs. Lying only five miles apart, both sites may have contributed water to the large encampment.

Israel's itinerary to Kadesh, however, is less certain. The names of only two places en route are given: Kibroth-hattaavah and Hazeroth (Num. 11:34–35; 12:16; 33:16–18).[63] Hazeroth has been suggested as modern ʿain hudrah, a site about thirty miles northeast of Mount Sinai, which would make Kibroth-hattaavah to be modern el-ebeirig, an oasis between the two.[64] Little evidence exists in support of these suggestions, however, and Numbers 12:16 is opposed, for it implies that Hazeroth was really much nearer Kadesh than modern ʿain hudrah, in that it lists the "Desert of Paran," which included Kadesh, as having been reached next after Hazeroth.[65]

---

[61] This census gives 1,300,000 men of army age, which means more than 4,000,000 total population (2 Sam. 24:9).

[62] Earlier at Kadesh the four eastern kings of Genesis 14 defeated Amalekites (Gen. 14:7). Hagar was found by the angel between Kadesh and Bered on the way to Shur (Gen. 16:7–14). Kadesh is associated with Shur also in Genesis 20:1.

[63] Numbers 33:16–36 gives twenty-one names of places between Sinai and Kadesh. However, these include names not only from this early trip from Sinai to Kadesh, but also from the later wanderings as the people left Kadesh and finally returned there again. This is clear from the places and events cited after Numbers 33:36 which are all from the last year of the wilderness journey. They most likely place in the listing of twenty-one cities, for the break between the two portions of the total journey is with Rithmah (v. 19), making Rithmah the same as Kadesh and leaving only the two names given, Kibroth-hattaavah and Hazeroth, as stopping places on this earlier leg of the trip.

[64] Simons, *GTT,* p. 255.

[65] Also Kibroth-hattaavah is where the people ate the quail, and this incident transpired after the people had traveled at least three days and probably longer (Num. 10:33; 11:31–34).

Two matters suggest that the route was not direct between Sinai and Kadesh but veered to the east. In Numbers 11:31 it is stated that quail were brought "from the sea" as food for Israel, which is likely a reference to the Gulf of Aqaba to the east; and Deuteronomy 1:2, 19 implies that at some time the people were in the vicinity of Mount Seir, also to the east.

2. Four incidents en route (Numbers 11:1–33; 12:1–15)

Though the time of travel for this leg of the journey was not long,[66] four events are recorded from it. The first was a time of severe complaint by the people and occurred after only three days of travel from Sinai (Num. 10:33; 11:1–3). It apparently was hard for them to adjust again to the rigors of desert travel, and three days were enough to bring strong discontent. God sent fire to consume the fringes of the camp as punishment for their complaining. Moses' prayer stopped the burning, and then he called the place "Taberah" (*tab'erah*, "burning") because of the punishment.

The second recorded event was the appointment of seventy elders of Israel to act as Moses' assistants in bearing "the burden of the people" (Num. 11:4–30). This action was taken when Moses despaired after hearing further complaint from the people. The objec-

tion this time, initiated by the "mixed multitude,"[67] concerned food, for the people had become weary of manna. They wanted fish, cucumbers, melons, leeks, onions, and garlic, which they remembered from Egypt.

When Moses cried to God that he was unable to bear the burden of such a difficult people alone, God gave the directive that seventy elders be appointed to help him. God "took of the Spirit that was on" Moses "and put the Spirit on the seventy elders," to enable them for the task.[68] As a concomitant to this enablement, the seventy joined in a chorus of praise[69] to God. When two of the seventy, Eldad and Medad, continued to sing longer than the others, Joshua was disturbed and questioned their behavior before Moses, but Moses approved of what they were doing.

The relationship in office between these seventy and those appointed previously as rulers of thousands, hundreds, fifties, and tens (Exod. 18:25) is not indicated. It may be that these were higher in authority, helping Moses solve problems that the earlier appointees, as lesser officials, brought to him.[70]

The third event was another provision of quail (Num. 11:31–34), in response to a complaint regarding the manna. God told Moses that the people, because of their sinful attitude,

---

[66] Deuteronomy 1:2 calls it a journey of eleven days. However, since the distance is nearly 150 miles, it is doubtful if Israel made it in this time. Eleven days may have been a normal time of travel, but Israel went much slower. It would seem that three weeks would have sufficed, however.

[67] See p. 105.

[68] The Holy Spirit came upon persons in the Old Testament particularly for the purpose of enablement for some task, as with Bezaleel (Exod. 35:30) and such later judges as Othniel (Judg. 3:10), Gideon (Judg. 6:34), Jephthah (Judg. 11:29), and Samson (Judg. 13:25; 14:6, 19; 15:14).

[69] The text says that they "prophesied," but since the idea of a spoken message does not fit the occasion, and according to 1 Chronicles 25:1–3 a proper meaning for "prophesy" (*yithnabbe'*) is "praise," it is best to take this meaning here since it fits very well.

[70] Based on the fact that this group was much fewer in number, and also that they were especially endowed with the Holy Spirit in distinction from the others.

would now eat meat for "a whole month—until it [came] out of [their] nostrils" (Num. 11:20). Moses found this difficult to believe, but God indeed brought quail in immense number. The best interpretation of the description given, as to how so many were killed, is that the quail were caused to fly about three feet above the ground at a level where Israelites could hit them easily in flight. The striking continued for two days and a night and extended for a "day's walk" on either side of the camp, resulting in an average take of more than ten homers.[71] When the people began to eat in a greedy manner, thus displaying their belief that God had not been supplying adequately before, God struck them "with a severe plague," bringing death to many.

The fourth event was an act of insubordination by Aaron and Miriam, Moses' brother and sister (Num. 12:1–15). The immediate occasion was Moses' marriage to a Cushite woman,[72] but clearly the true reason was jealousy. These two, already enjoying places of honor,[73] wanted greater authority, claiming that God had spoken by them as well as by Moses. God called all three before the tabernacle, and, speaking out of the pillar of cloud, made known His appointment of Moses, saying that Moses had been honored above even the prophets in being privileged to speak with God

"face to face." He then brought punishment on Miriam, who apparently had led in the brief rebellion, by smiting her with leprosy for one week.

3. Refusal to enter the land (Numbers 13–14)

When Israel arrived at Kadesh, the first matter of business was to reconnoiter Canaan. To that end God directed the appointment of twelve men, one from each tribe, to act as spies. These were instructed to investigate the food production of the land and the people's strength for self-defense.

For forty days the twelve traversed the land as far north as Rehob.[74] All agreed in their report. The land was good for food supply but would be very difficult to conquer because the people were strong, giants lived in the land, and the cities were walled (Num. 13:27–28). They differed, however, in their evaluation. Ten said the difficulties were too great, which meant returning to Egypt (Num. 13:31–33); two, Caleb and Joshua, asserted that God could give victory in spite of the difficulties, pleading that Israel not rebel against God by refusing to enter the land (Num. 13:30; 14:6–9). The people heeded the ten, even threatening to kill the two, and began planning to return to Egypt—under new leadership, if need be.[75]

As a result, God threatened to anni-

---

[71] R. B. Y. Scott, *BA* 22 (1959): 22–40, states that the homer was equal to six and one-quarter bushels, which means that the average take here was more than sixty bushels. For other discussion and references, see p. 133n.11.

[72] Probably not Zipporah, who could have been Cushite, but Moses' marriage to her had taken place over forty years earlier. Probably she had died and Moses had married again. The marriage was not contrary to the Law which forbade marriage to Canaanites (Exod. 34:16).

[73] Miriam is called "the prophetess" and seemingly held a leading position among Israelite women (Exod. 15:20). Aaron of course had been made high priest.

[74] Located near the city of Laish, later called Dan (Judg. 18:28–29).

[75] This action was inexcusable. It is difficult to see why the people would have thought that God, who had led and provided so miraculously thus far, had brought them all the way to Canaan's southern border only now to fail in the original objective.

hilate Israel in punishment, but again Moses interceded[76] for the people, this time on the basis of God's own reputation (Num. 14:11–20). God then stipulated the nature of the punishment that would be inflicted, now milder in view of Moses' prayer but still severe. He said that the entire nation, rather than entering the land, would remain in the desert wilderness for a total of forty years, one year for each day of the spies' search, and that every Israelite twenty years and older (hence, responsible for his rebellious decision), with the exception of Caleb and Joshua, would die during this time and never enter the Promised Land (Num. 14:20–35). Following this, all ten of the faithless spies died immediately in a plague (Num. 14:36–38). The people, witnessing these events, now reversed their thinking and wanted to storm the land immediately. But this no longer was pleasing to God; and when they made an attempt, they were sorely defeated by the Amalekites and Canaanites (Num. 14:39–45).

H. THIRTY-SEVEN YEARS AND SIX MONTHS OF FRUITLESS WANDERING (Numbers 15–19; 33:19–36)

At this point, Israel began approximately thirty-seven and one-half years[77] of fruitless wandering in the Sinai desert. Very little is recorded from these years, for clearly this was a time intentionally devoid of profit or progress for a disobedient people. The nation had been given opportunity to move into the land of blessing but had refused. Now the people should wander in unpleasant conditions, with nothing positive accomplished, until all over twenty years of age had died.[78]

During these years the people did move about some within a confined area, going from Kadesh as far southeast as Ezion-geber at the tip of the Gulf of Aqaba (Num. 33:36), about eighty-five miles distant. Sixteen other stopping places are listed, all probably between these two extremes, though none can be identified. Likely much of the time was spent at Kadesh, although they must have moved periodically to provide fresh pasturage for their livestock. Back at Kadesh in the first month of the fortieth year, Miriam died (Num. 20:1, 28; 33:38).

Only one incident is recorded from all these years. That was a revolt of 250 people led by two Reubenites (Dathan and Abiram) and the Levite Korah (Num. 16–17). Jealousy again seems to have been the reason. These leaders desired places of authority along with, or in place of, Moses and Aaron. God vindicated Moses and Aaron by (1) opening the earth to swallow Korah and Dathan and Abiram, along with their households,[79] (2) bringing

---

[76] Similar to the occasion in connection with Israel's sin with the golden calf (Exod. 32:11–13).

[77] The length of this period is figured as follows. The time spent in the journey until the rebellion at Kadesh had been something less than eighteen months. Then beginning with Numbers 20:1, all events concern the fortieth year of travel (Num. 20:1, 28: 33:38), thus leaving thirty-seven and one-half years intervening between Numbers 14 and 20, the chapters concerned with this period.

[78] Figuring 1,200,000 (600,000 of both men and women) as having to die in 14,508 days (thirty-eight and one-half years), gives eighty-five per day. Figuring twelve hours per day maximum for funerals, gives an average of seven funerals per hour for all thirty-eight and one-half years, a continuous foreboding reminder of God's punishment upon them.

[79] The "men that appertained unto Korah" (Num. 16:32 KJV), indicated here as among those swallowed by the earth, must mean Korah's servants, for Numbers 26:11 says that "the line of Korah

129

fire to consume the 250 supporters of the rebels, and (3) when many Israelites complained at this harsh treatment, sending a plague through the camp, which took the lives of 14,700 of these complainers (Num. 16:23–35, 41–50). Further, to show Aaron's approved position, God caused Aaron's rod,[80] placed in the tabernacle at God's direction, to bud, in contrast to the rods placed there by other tribal heads (Num. 17:1–11). Then God instructed Moses to continue to keep Aaron's budded rod in the tabernacle as a constant reminder and evidence that Aaron had been divinely chosen as the religious leader of Israel (see Heb. 9:4).

I. KADESH-BARNEA TO THE JORDAN
(Numbers 20–21; 33:37–48; Deuteronomy 2:1–3:14)

1. Death of Miriam (Numbers 20:1)

About the time of Israel's final arrival in Kadesh, following the years of fruitless wandering, Miriam died. The date is given as the "first month," and the year clearly was the fortieth year of the sojourn, for it was the same year at that of Aaron's death five months later (Num. 20:23–29), which is definitely designated as the fortieth (Num. 33:38).

It should be realized that even the head family of Miriam, Aaron, and Moses had to die before Canaan could be taken, for God had exempted only Caleb and Joshua in His earlier pronouncement of judgment (Num. 14:30). The three were allowed to live, however, until this closing year of wandering.

2. Water again from a rock (Numbers 20:2–13)

On arriving back in Kadesh at this time, the people lacked water once more. Since the area normally boasted good springs, the people may have looked forward to getting back. But apparently the springs were running low this year. The people complained, and Moses brought the matter to God. The reply was that Moses and Aaron were to gather the people at a certain rock; water would flow from it,[81] as had occurred earlier at Rephidim (Exod. 17:1–7).

This time, however, God instructed Moses only to "speak" to the rock,[82] saying nothing about striking it. But Moses struck it, even twice, and cried to the people, "Must we bring you water out of this rock?" Water came forth, but Moses' action and words made it appear as though his human effort had helped to produce it. God was displeased and pronounced punishment on Moses, stating that now he would not be permitted to enter the

---

. . . did not die out." This was in contrast to the children of Dathan and Abiram and was no doubt for the purpose of continuing this priestly line, which may have later contributed celebrated singers (1 Chron. 6:18–22; 9:19; Pss. 42, 44; et al.).

[80] Rods (*matteh*), undescribed in kind, were here labeled with the names of heads of each of the tribes, apparently symbolizing the authority of each. When Aaron's budded, representing life, his divinely appointed supremacy over the others was demonstrated.

[81] The article is used with "rock," showing that the rock must have been one well known at Kadesh. The idea that it was the same as the one struck in Rephidim, having been carried along since, however, is not correct; see *KD*, 3:131n 1.

[82] Typology is involved here. In 1 Corinthians 10:4 Paul's reference to this Old Testament event brings to mind Jesus' statement to the woman at the well, to whom He said, "Whoever drinks of the water I give him will never thirst" (John 4:14).

Promised Land (Num. 20:12; 27:12–14; Deut. 32:48–52), a fact that can be inferred from Numbers 14:30, as just observed, but here definitely stated in the context of God's particular reason.[83]

3. Request to pass through Edom (Numbers 20:14–21)

While at Kadesh, Moses sent messengers to the king of Edom requesting passage through his land. The plan now was to skirt the southern end of the Dead Sea, march north on its east side, and enter Canaan heading west. But Edom lay in the way, stretching in its narrow width from the Dead Sea south to the Gulf of Aqaba. Moses promised to stay strictly to the "king's highway." Many scholars believe that, using this term, he referred to an ancient, well-known, north-south road, identified in recent times and traced as far north as Syria.[84] It had been used by the four eastern kings of Genesis 14, was later paved by the Romans, and is today followed closely by a modern Jordanian highway. But even though Moses promised not to stray from this "highway," the Edomite king refused passage. This meant a tedious journey south to Ezion-geber again (Deut. 2:8),[85] where the people had been only shortly before (Num. 33:35), and then a return on the eastern side of Edom.

4. Death of Aaron (Numbers 20:23–29; 33:38)

En route Aaron died on Mount Hor at the age of 123. Since Mount Hor is best located roughly on an east-west parallel with Kadesh (though nearer to Edom),[86] it is possible that until this time Moses still hoped to be able to pass through the territory of Edom. Perhaps a return message from the Edomite ruler did not reach him until his arrival at Mount Hor.

Aaron died the first day of the fifth month of the fortieth year (Num. 33:38), just five months after Miriam's passing. Instructed of God, Moses accompanied Aaron, with Eleazar, Aaron's son and successor, to the top of the mountain, and there he placed Aaron's clothes on Eleazar before Aaron's life was taken. The people remained in mourning at Mount Hor for thirty days.

While they were there, a brief battle occurred (Num. 21:1–3). Arad, king in the southern part of Canaan, led an assault against Israel. Initially defeated, Israel looked to God for help and then thoroughly routed the foe, even pressing on to destroy several of the cities in Arad's kingdom.

5. Edom detour (Numbers 21:4–20; 33:41–49)

Israel now began the long southern detour around Edom. Several uniden-

---

[83] Apparently Moses, in view of his work and position, would have merited entrance to Canaan along with Caleb and Joshua had he not sinned here.

[84] This road, however, does not cross from east to west through the mountains of Edom. Israel would only have reached it after traversing Edom.

[85] From Jebel Madeira (see n.86) south to Ezion-geber is approximately 90 miles. This means that Israel had about 180 miles extra to walk because of this refusal.

[86] Exact location uncertain, but either Jebel Madeira or Jebel el-Hamrah, both roughly parallel with Kadesh (though slightly north), is the most likely. A traditional site, Jebel Nebi Harun ("mountain of the prophet Aaron"), near Petra, must be rejected, for it is east of the Arabah and too far out of position to fit the account. See Simons, *GTT,* p. 258.

tified stopping places are listed,[87] but only one event is described.

God again punished Israel for complaining about food and drink (Num. 21:5–9).[88] Apparently the people had found little water as they had marched south through the barren Arabah Valley, and they also had grown weary of eating manna. God brought punishment by sending "fiery serpents" (KJV) among them so that many died.[89] This brought a repentant spirit to the people, and God instructed Moses to provide a remedy for those bitten, in the form of a brazen serpent placed high on a pole where it might be easily seen.[90] This he did, and when any who were afflicted looked upon it, they were instantly healed.[91]

6. Return north and victory over Sihon and Og (Numbers 21:10–35)

Following God's instructions not to interfere with the Edomites (Deut. 2:4–5), Israel skirted their territory on the east and again made her way northward. Coming to the brook Zered,[92] Moab's southern boundary, God forbade interference with Moab also (Deut. 2:9). Israel obeyed and followed a path well to the east.

However, interference from King Sihon's kingdom was unavoidable. His land stood between Israel and the Jordan River. Moses asked for permission to cross the land but was refused, even as by the king of Edom (Num. 21:21–32). Sihon mustered his army at Jahaz, and Moses met and defeated him. Then Israel occupied all Sihon's territory to the Jabbok River.

With this victory Israel's forces were not far from the country of Og, the powerful king of Bashan,[93] who ruled from the Yarmuk River as far north as Mount Hermon. Now Moses took the offensive and defeated Og at his important city, Edrei (Num. 21:33–35),[94] before moving on to occupy his land. Israel now controlled most of the land from the Arnon River in the South (Moab's northern boundary) to Mount Hermon in the north, a distance of 130 miles. The defeat of these kings was really the beginning of the conquest,

---

[87] Some scholars believe that Israel reversed direction shortly after leaving Mount Hor and actually marched around the north end of Edom rather than the south. The view is based largely on identifying Punon and Oboth (Num. 33:42–44; 21:10–11) with modern Feinan and el-Weibeh, both of which are on Edom's west side rather than the east. However, these identifications should be rejected since little evidence exists for them. Deuteronomy 2:8 says that the "turn" was made at Elath and Eziongeber, which are at the head of the Gulf of Aqaba. See Aharoni, *LB,* p. 51, for opposing view.

[88] This is the first recorded incident of complaint regarding food since the time of quail provision thirty-eight years before, though numerous incidents could have occurred during the silent years.

[89] Perhaps "fiery" due to color or due to a resulting sore on the one bitten. Reddish, poisonous snakes are known in the Arabah today.

[90] This brazen serpent was later worshiped by the people, and finally Hezekiah had to destroy it (2 Kings 18:4).

[91] Used by Christ as an illustration of how a sinner is saved: by looking in faith to Him as the Israelites looked to the serpent (John 3:14–15).

[92] The Zered is a small stream that flows into the southern extremity of the Dead Sea from the southeast. In Deuteronomy 2:14 it is stated that Israel crossed this stream just thirty-eight years after the Kadesh rebellion.

[93] This was a man of large stature, perhaps a descendant of the Rephaites mentioned in Abraham's time (Gen. 14:5; 15:20), having an iron bed over thirteen feet long and six feet wide (Deut. 3:11). His country boasted many cities, of which sixty were walled (Deut. 3:4–5).

[94] It should be realized that Moses, in bringing the army here, was about sixty miles north of where the Jordan was later crossed.

for the territory east of the Jordan would eventually be allotted to Gad, Ephraim, and half of the tribe of Manasseh. These victories were important, too, in impressing the Canaanites across the Jordan with the power of God exercised on Israel's behalf (Josh. 2:9–11; 9:8–10).

J. AT THE JORDAN
(Numbers 22–27; 31–32; Deuteronomy 31, 34)

1. Balaam and the Moabites (Numbers 22–25; 31)

With these significant victories won, Moses assembled the army near the Jordan River opposite Jericho. Here Balak, king of Moab, viewed Israel as a menace to his country[95] and, in cooperation with elders of Midian, sent messengers far north to Pethor on the Euphrates River[96] to bring Balaam, a prophet whose reputation had reached this far south,[97] to place a curse on Israel (Num. 22–24).[98] At first Balaam refused to accompany the messengers, but a second visit persuaded him.

However, once with Balak, Balaam only blessed Israel instead of cursing her, much to the frustration of the Moabite king. Balak took him to three different vantage points from which to view the Israelite encampment, hoping that the prophet would change his pronouncement, but to no avail. In each place, Balaam spoke words of blessing desired by God. Then after Balak had dismissed him in disgust, Balaam uttered yet a fourth message (Num. 24:14–25), in which he gave a remarkable prediction regarding the coming Messiah and future blessing of Israel. Finally, however, the strange prophet did work in Moab's favor. He advised[99] Balak to entice Israelite men to take part in the cult activities of Baal-peor (Num. 25:1–18).[100]

Balak followed Balaam's advice and many Israelites were ensnared. As a result of this excursion into idolatry, God sent a punishing plague, which took twenty-four thousand Israelite lives. The plague was stopped only when Phinehas, son of the high priest Eleazar, killed an Israelite man and a Midianite woman who had openly

---

[95] Balak was here north of his Arnon border. Perhaps with Sihon recently defeated by Israel, he had thought to reoccupy land formerly taken from him by Sihon (Num. 21:26).

[96] Pethor was in Mesopotamia (Deut. 23:4) and is commonly identified with Pitru of Assyrian texts (see *ANET,* p. 278) located twelve miles south of Carchemish. These messengers had a trip of over four hundred miles each way.

[97] Balaam was a Mesopotamian diviner-prophet. In spite of this, God could communicate with him and even use him to present a remarkable messianic prophecy (Num. 24:17–19). Still, Balaam was in the employ of Balak and ultimately gave his employer advice that would lead Israel into idolatry at Baal-Peor. In 1976 a seventh-century B.C. text from Deir Alla in the Transjordan beginning, "The sayings of Balaam . . . ," was published. These sayings, only partially preserved, were written on the wall of a temple and purport to record the words of a message he received from the gods in a dream. Of interest in this text is a notation that his mournful reaction to the message caught the attention of "his people" suggesting that, as in Numbers 24:14, he is considered a foreigner in Moab (P. Kyle McCarter, Jr., "The Balaam Texts from Deir Alla: The First Combination," *BASOR* 239 [Summer 1980]: 49–60).

[98] It was thought that such a curse would weaken the one cursed; see Egyptian execration texts, *ANET,* pp. 328–29.

[99] That this idea was indeed Balaam's is not indicated until later when Moses had sent the army to punish the offenders (Num. 31:8, 16).

[100] Two matters suggest that the tribe of Simeon was involved in this defection more than other tribes: first, the one man named was a leading Simeonite; second, the census taken just after this shows Simeon's number greatly reduced, as if by such a plague as here sent (Num. 26:14; see 1:23).

entered the Israelite encampment together. While the biblical account is discreet, the Israelite man was probably guilty of introducing the sexual rites of Baal worship into the vicinity of the tabernacle.

Moses then dispatched an army of twelve thousand to punish Midian, which had been partner with Moab from the start and here apparently had assumed leadership. The Midianites were soundly defeated, and all the males, the kings of Midian, and Balaam himself were killed (Num. 31:1–54). All the married women were slain later, and a great amount of booty was divided among the Israelites.

2. A request granted (Numbers 32)

With the land east of the Jordan conquered and found to be well adapted for pasture, the tribes of Reuben, Gad, and later half of Manasseh, all having extensive flocks, asked permission to make this region their home. Moses' first reaction was unfavorable. However, these tribes assured Moses that their men of military age would accompany the other tribes in conquest of the west side of the Jordan, too, and would not return to their families until that task had been completed. Moses finally acceded but made it clear that they would have to fulfill their responsibility to the rest of Israel. When agreement was reached, the Transjordanian tribes set about building sheep pens for the flocks and repairing cities

for their families while the men were away (Num. 32:34–42).

3. Anticipatory matters (Numbers 26–30; 33:50–36:13)

Moses now did several things in anticipation of Israel's entrance into the land. First, he had another census taken (Num. 26). Thirty-nine years of wilderness wandering (with 1,200,000 deaths) had transpired since the census at Mount Sinai. There was need to know Israel's present manpower as she faced the challenge of Canaan. The number counted this time was 601,730 men twenty years and older, in comparison with the earlier 603,550 (Num. 1:46).[101]

A second matter concerned a problem regarding inheritance rights that was raised by the daughters of one Zelophehad, who had died and left no sons (Num. 27:1–11). The directive from God was that daughters should inherit their father's possessions if there was no son so that family claims might be maintained.

A third and very important matter was the appointment of a new leader. Someone had to be selected to take the place of Moses and lead Israel across the Jordan. God's choice was Joshua (Num. 27:15–23), certainly a logical replacement. He and Caleb were the only older men who could enter the land, for all others their age either had died or would die before that time.[102] Joshua had led in battle against the Amalekites (Exod. 17:8–14). He had

---

[101] Seven tribes grew (Judah, Issachar, Zebulon, Manasseh, Benjamin, Dan, and Asher); five lost (Reuben, Simeon, Gad, Ephraim, and Naphtali). The biggest gainer was Manasseh, which grew 20,500 (32,200 to 52,700); the biggest loser was Simeon, which lost 37,100 (59,300 to 22,200).

[102] At the crossing, no other persons could have been more than fifty-eight years old, for all twenty and above thirty-eight and one-half years earlier had now died. Caleb at this time was seventy-nine (Josh. 14:7). Joshua had been entrusted with more leadership than Caleb and also is said to have been "old and well advanced in years" (Josh. 13:1) when Caleb speaks of himself as being yet strong and vigorous. Joshua was probably more than ninety at this time (see p. 154n.68).

accompanied Moses part way up Mount Sinai at the time of receiving the Mosaic Law (Exod. 24:13). He had assisted Moses following Israel's repentance regarding the sin with the golden calf (Exod. 33:11). He had served as one of the twelve spies of Canaan and urged advance into the land along with Caleb (Num. 13:8; 14:6–9).

In all these instances, Joshua had acquitted himself well, demonstrating responsibility and leadership. By these experiences, too, good preparation for the great task now being assigned had been provided. God revealed the selection of Joshua to Moses, who then made proper announcement to the people and gave appropriate charge to the new leader.

Finally, Moses relayed closing instructions, which the people would need when they entered the land. As given in Numbers 28–30, these concerned regular offerings, periodic feasts, and keeping of vows. The instructions in Numbers 33:50–36:13 included destruction of idolatrous inhabitants of Canaan, description of certain borders of the land, identification of those persons who would determine the divisions of the land among the respective tribes, establishment of forty-eight cities for the tribe of Levi (which would include six cities of refuge), and further matters pertaining to inheritance rights.

K. DEUTERONOMY

At the very close of Moses' last days,[103] he delivered the great messages of Deuteronomy orally and then wrote the book. He reviewed for the new generation what God had done for His people since leaving Egypt, including a résumé of the laws revealed at Sinai. Then he set forth new regulations, given by God, relative to Canaan's soon entrance and the more sedentary life to be experienced there.

It had been sometime prior to this that Moses had penned the first four books of the Pentateuch,[104] though how long before is impossible to state. It is clear that Moses had been writing a book of some kind (Exod. 17:14), perhaps a type of daily record (Num. 33:2), from the time of the journey's first stages, and he had probably used this as a historical basis for the more formal production. We know, too, that he had recorded the Book of the Covenant immediately after its revelation (Exod. 24:4–7) and likely had done the same with the more extensive regulations of the two forty-day periods on Sinai, as observed earlier.

But the material in the form now found in Genesis, Exodus, Leviticus, and Numbers was probably not recorded until shortly before the Deuteronomic messages.[105] It certainly had been completed by the time he gave and recorded them, however, and so with Deuteronomy complete, the Pen-

---

[103]According to Deuteronomy 1:3, Moses began these messages on the first day of the eleventh month of the fortieth year, which was only two months and ten days before the Jordan was crossed.

[104]Then as one continuous document, however.

[105]Contrary to the view of higher critics, there is good evidence that Moses did write the Pentateuch: (1) writing was advanced, with even an alphabet in existence which Moses could employ; (2) Moses was capable, both in terms of education and accessibility to necessary information; (3) six times the Pentateuch states that he wrote some respective part of it; (4) the remainder of the Old Testament gives testimony in various ways, implying his authorship of it; and (5) Christ and the New Testament writers give yet clearer testimony to this end, even equating Moses' name with the *torah* (Pentateuch) division of the Old Testament.

tateuch was finished. The Israelites thus had their all-important guidebook ready for the eventful days when they would have crossed the Jordan.

With the work both of leadership and writing complete, and a replacement now appointed, Moses, at age 120, was ready for God's call to heaven. Few men in all history could claim to have had so rich an experience; few so used of God. He was gifted and trained as perhaps none other of his day, and he was entrusted with a task probably greater than any other person of any day. But now his work was done. According to God's instruction, he climbed "to the top of Pisgah, across from Jericho," surveyed the Promised Land, heard God remind him that this was indeed the land that had been promised long before, and then was taken in death by God. He was buried in an unknown grave in a nearby valley (Deut. 34:1–7).

CHAPTER EIGHT

THE CONQUEST

Joshua 1–24

A. THE LAND OF CANAAN

1. Israel's task in conquest

Canaan, across the Jordan from encamped, waiting Israel, was a land of city-states. There was no central government, but there were many cities, each with its own king. To conquer the land meant to defeat each city in turn.

Egypt was nominal overlord. Thutmose III, principal founder of the Egyptian Empire, had added the region to Egypt's domain. His son, Amenhotep II (Pharaoh of the Exodus), had continued strict control. But his son, Thutmose IV, Pharaoh while Israel was in the wilderness—who had married the Asiatic daughter of Artatama, king of Mitanni[1]—was more inclined toward foreign alliances and less interested in military dominance. Then his son, Amenhotep III, who now ruled,

gave little attention to the affairs of empire, concerning himself rather with domestic interests. He did make boasts of conquest, but these were largely empty, for, as Hayes remarks, his "indolent neglect of his Asiatic provinces paved the way for the collapse of Egypt's northern empire."[2] The Tell el-Amarna letters depict him as turning a deaf ear to Canaanite pleas for help against invaders.[3] The individual cities of Canaan were left to themselves as prizes of conquest for Israel.

This does not mean, however, that Israel's task was to be easy. The spies thirty-nine years before had given a true report in speaking of Canaanites as vigorous people and their cities as strongly walled. The people fought frequently among themselves and with outside foes, which kept their warriors

---

[1] Founded late in the sixteenth century, the kingdom of Mitanni came to extend across most of northern Mesopotamia, with its capital at Wasshugani (site uncertain). The population was mainly Hurrian, but the rulers were Indo-Aryan. Their zenith of power came about this time. The kingdom ceased about two hundred years later.

[2] Hayes, *SE*, 2:233; see G. Steindorff and K. C. Seele, *When Egypt Ruled the East*, 2d ed. (Chicago: University of Chicago Press, 1957), pp. 72–75.

[3] For discussion and references, see pp. 82–84.

in fighting trim and well equipped. The cities were built to withstand siege for months at a time.[4] These cities, too, could band together against a common enemy, as they did later against Joshua, in both a southern (Josh. 10) and northern confederacy (Josh. 11). Besides this, the land was mountainous. Once past Jericho, Israel would be in rugged country most of the time, difficult in which to travel and maneuver for war.

2. Canaanite culture advanced

Canaan was advanced in material culture. Cities were well laid out, and houses showed good design and construction. Floors of buildings were often paved or plastered. Drainage systems had been developed. Workers were skilled in the use of copper, lead, and gold. Pottery was among the finest anywhere in the world. Extensive trade was conducted with foreign countries, including Egypt, Northern Mesopotamia, and Cyprus. In technical knowledge, Canaanites were much in advance of Israelites who had spent the past forty years in nomadic conditions of the desert, and the preceding centuries as slaves in Egypt.

In this cultural disparity lay grave danger for Israel—a danger that soon issued in sad reality. History shows that less-developed cultures are often absorbed by those more advanced. Israel was not absorbed by Canaan but was influenced profoundly by the customs of the new land. Had this involved only material culture (such as pottery manufacture, city construction, or methods of farming), there could even have been

benefit; but when it came to include ways of thinking—and especially religious belief and practice—the harm was great. Many of the people accepted the worship of Canaanite Baal rather than Yahweh. The attraction was that Baal was held to be god of rainfall and good crops. No doubt the Canaanites advised their new farming neighbors that technical skill was not enough to insure full larders, but that worship of the right deity was still more important. Such counsel by native inhabitants would have been most influential on incoming Israelites who desired bountiful harvests.

Without question, this was the danger that God sought to avert by commanding that all Canaanites be destroyed or driven from the land (Num. 33:51-56; Deut. 7:1-5). Had Israel complied, all would have been well, but she did not. Many Canaanites were allowed to remain, and Israel suffered the wide-reaching effects of their influence, with consequent loss of God's blessing (Judg. 2:11-15).[5]

3. Plan of attack

Moses' strategy for taking Canaan, no doubt revealed to him by God, clearly had been to attack the land at its approximate midpoint, coming in from the east, and divide it into a south and north section, that each might be conquered separately. We may assume that Moses had shared this thinking with Joshua, so that the new leader had the plan in mind as the people prepared for crossing the Jordan.

---

[4] Samaria withstood the siege of Assyria for more than fourteen months (2 Kings 17:5); and Gaza withstood even the mighty Alexander the Great for five months, in 332 B.C.

[5] Chap. 9, especially pp. 172-75.

B. ENTRANCE TO THE LAND
(Joshua 2:1–5:12)

1. Reconnaissance of Jericho
(Joshua 2:1–24)

Jericho stood as a first and principal objective in the conquest of Canaan. It was a strong city and could not be bypassed safely—an imposing challenge to be met almost immediately.

Joshua sent two spies to make reconnaissance, likely remembering the similar tactic of thirty-nine years before when he had played a vital role himself. The two crossed the Jordan and came to the city where they were protected by a harlot, Rahab, whose house was located on the city wall.[6]

When the men were detected, she hid them beneath drying stalks of flax on the roof and then sent pursuers on a false trail. Convinced that Jericho would fall to Israel, she requested safety for herself and family in return for her favor. The men gave their promise and then, with her further help, succeeded in escaping back to Joshua.

Though the mission of the men likely became known in Jericho too soon for them to observe much detail concerning the city, they did learn from Rahab that the people feared Israel greatly. News of victories over Sihon and Og had reached Canaanite ears. Joshua thus had reason for encouragement.

2. Crossing the Jordan
(Joshua 3–4)

The morning after the spies' return,[7] Joshua ordered the people to move to the bank of Jordan. Shittim,[8] where they had been encamped,[9] apparently was not in immediate proximity to the river, and so the first step in crossing was to move to the river. It was at flood stage here in the spring.[10] At its bank, three days were occupied in final preparations and instructions. We may believe that during these three days the people wondered how all Israel could possibly cross the wide expanse of water flowing by them, but they were soon to learn.

When all was ready, the priests, carrying the ark, moved toward the river, the people, by divine command, following at a distance of three thousand feet (Josh. 3:4). This insured that a maximum number would see the ark as the guiding signal. When the feet of the priests touched the water, it miraculously separated. As if stopped by a dam, the water from upstream that flowed toward them "stood up in a heap." The other water continued its course to the Dead Sea, leaving a wide space for the people to cross. The priests bearing the ark stopped and remained in the middle of the river as the people moved past. During the

---

[6] Here their visit would not be questioned so soon, and also the house, being on the wall, afforded easy escape if necessary.

[7] The spies had been gone longer than expected, being forced to hide in a mountain for an extra three days to avoid pursuers. Joshua may have become somewhat impatient and so moved here immediately after they returned.

[8] The name Shittim (with the article, literally "The Acacias"), probably refers to a small region rather than a town. Its exact location, though frequently conjectured, remains unknown.

[9] Numbers 33:49 mentions their first arrival here. While here, Moses delivered his final instructions, probably including the Deuteronomy messages. Moses began to give these on the first day of the eleventh month, more than two months before crossing.

[10] Joshua 3:15 and 4:18 speak of the Jordan now being "over" (KJV) all its banks (ʿal-kol-gedhothaw). This could mean merely "upon all its banks," indicating that the water only filled the banks without spilling over. The same phrase, however, is used in Isaiah 8:7 where it must mean "over its banks." This and the context argue that Jordan was now at flood stage (see NIV).

time consumed as the people crossed, the water backed up approximately fifteen miles upriver, as far as the city Adam.[11] This gave testimony to each person that God, represented by the ark, was restraining the water. The previous days of wonderment at the river's edge would only have heightened their appreciation now of the power displayed.

Two memorials of this crossing were created—one in the Jordan and one across at Gilgal, where the people encamped (Josh. 4:1–24). Twelve chosen men, one from each tribe, took twelve stones from the Jordan near where the priests stood and brought the stones to the encampment. Then Joshua in turn "set up twelve stones in the midst of the Jordan" (KJV) as a pillar at the place from which the other stones had just been removed.

Both acts were done after all the people had crossed the river and just before the priests with the ark joined the people, who were waiting. As soon as everyone had left the riverbed, the water was released and the river flowed again.

When all the people had arrived at Gilgal, Joshua made the second pillar from the twelve stones brought out of the Jordan. The two pillars were to remind future generations that God had miraculously opened the Jordan so that His people might enter the Land of Promise.

3. Encampment at Gilgal (Joshua 5:1–12)

Gilgal now became a continuing center of Israelite activity. Its exact location is still uncertain,[12] but clearly it was somewhere in the Jordan Valley between Jericho and the Jordan River (Josh. 4:19). From here, Jericho and Ai were soon taken. Later the Gibeonites came to Gilgal seeking a peace treaty (Josh. 9:6). From Gilgal Joshua led his army by forced march to help the Gibeonites against the southern confederacy (Josh. 10:6–7). From here, too, he went north to meet the northern confederacy (Josh. 11:6–14). And here the first allotment of tribal territories was made (Josh. 14:6). While the army was in the field fighting, the people remained at Gilgal as home base.

Three important events transpired soon after encampment. One was the circumcision of all the men (Josh. 5:2–9). This mass observance was necessitated by the fact that the Israelites now living were a new generation, and apparently children had not been circumcised during the long year of the wilderness journey. Now, however, Israel needed to reinstitute the divinely ordained sign of the covenant before the Promised Land could be taken. Accordingly, God ordered its observance and later declared that it here also symbolized the removal of Egypt's reproach.[13]

---

[11] Adam is identified with *ed Damieh* about twenty miles from the Dead Sea. Israel crossed the Jordan opposite Jericho (Josh. 3:16) about five miles from the Dead Sea, so they were fifteen miles from Adam. Since rock slides have occurred near Adam temporarily stopping the Jordan (once in A.D. 1267, in 1906, and July 1927), the suggestion is often made that God used this means here. This is possible, but the record suggests that the waters separated immediately before the priests, which would not have been true if fifteen miles of water had yet to pass.

[12] Muilenburg, *BASOR* 140 (April 1955): 11–27, suggests identification with Khirbet el-Mefjir, which perhaps is the most likely; though Simons, *GTT,* pp. 269–70, rejects it.

[13] This symbolism gave Gilgal its name. *Gilgal* is from the Hebrew root *galal,* meaning "to roll away."

A second event at Gilgal was observance of the Passover (Josh. 5:10). This may have been only the third Passover kept;[14] at least none others are mentioned as having been observed since the occasion at Mount Sinai (Num. 9:1–5). Having now arrived in the land, however, with all males properly circumcised, the people followed God's order to observe this feast, and the Passover was kept on its appointed day, the fourteenth of Nisan.

It should be realized that this was exactly the fortieth year since the Egyptian departure—in accordance with God's word of punishment at Kadesh, declaring that the people would spend one year for each of the spies' days of reconnaissance in Canaan (Num. 14:33–34). God brought them across the Jordan on the tenth day of Nisan (Josh. 4:19), just in time for preparations for this on the fourteenth. Not even the Jordan at flood stage had been reason to miss this appointed occasion in the new land,[15] exactly forty years after leaving Egypt.[16]

The third matter of note at Gilgal was the cessation of manna. God had continued to supply this miraculous food since early in the first year of travel (Exod. 16:14–22). Nearly forty years of this special provision had now elapsed; but, having crossed into the land of promise, the people had no further need for it. The day after the Passover observance, the people no longer found it on the ground. Instead, they ate the produce of the land, which was now available.

C. CONQUEST OF CENTRAL PALESTINE
(Joshua 5:13–9:27)

1. Defeat of Jericho
(Joshua 6:13–27)

With the land entered and preliminary matters accomplished, Joshua turned his attention to the main task of conquest. The first objective, anticipated already in the mission of the spies, was Jericho. The city was near at hand as a constant danger to Gilgal if not taken, and, as noted, was too important as a Canaanite stronghold to be bypassed in any case.

a. The city. Old Testament Jericho is well identified with Tell es-Sultan, five miles west of the Jordan and seven miles north of the Dead Sea. The mound covers about eight acres, though, due to extensive erosion, it is not certain how much was occupied by the city Joshua captured.

If, however, the city of Joshua's conquest was the city Kathleen Kenyon says was taken by Egyptians about 1550 B.C.,[17] then it probably did cover most of the mound. This means that it

---

[14] The first was in Egypt and the second at Sinai. That no others are mentioned could, of course, be due only to a silence in the record. Since circumcision, however, was not observed, which according to Exodus 12:48 was reason alone to prohibit one from the Passover, it seems best to believe that the Passover was not either.

[15] There was reason to cross the Jordan now, too, in the further impression of God's power this would give the Canaanites.

[16] Frequently scholars take these forty years as only approximate, standing for a generation of time. But these years are exact. Aaron died the first day of the fifth month of the fortieth year (Num. 33:38), and the people mourned for one month. Since Moses began the Deuteronomic messages the first day of the eleventh month (Deut. 1:3), which followed the Sihon and Og conquests, Israel had taken five months for the remaining journey and these two campaigns. This left two months and ten days for Joshua to assume leadership and for the Jordan to be crossed by this tenth day of the first month.

[17] See pp. 74–78.

was about average size for the day, though smaller than large sites like Megiddo at fourteen acres, Lachish at eighteen, or especially Hazor at two hundred. Whatever its size, frequent biblical reference to it[18] shows that it was of major importance in the land.

Kenyon's description of the walls of this city is of significance.[19] The walls were of a type which made direct assault practically impossible. An approaching enemy first encountered a stone abutment eleven feet high, back and up from which sloped a thirty-five-degree plastered scarp reaching to the main wall some thirty-five vertical feet above. The steep, smooth slope prohibited battering the wall by any effective device or building fires to break it. An army trying to storm the wall found difficulty in climbing the slope, and ladders to scale it could find no satisfactory footing. The normal tactic used by an enemy to take a city so protected was siege, but Israel did not have time for this if she was to occupy all the land in any reasonable number of months.

b. The conquest. God had other plans for taking Jericho, however, and these were revealed to Joshua in an unusual manner (Josh. 5:13–6:5). One day while Joshua was in the vicinity of the city, perhaps pondering how it might be taken, he was met by one called the "commander of the army of the LORD"[20] and told those plans. The plans were to have "armed men,"[21] led by seven priests carrying the ark, walk around the city once each day for six days and seven times on the seventh. At the close of the thirteenth circuit, the priests should blow trumpets and the people shout with a loud voice. When they did, the walls of the city would collapse and the army could enter.

The plan was executed as given. Those assigned to the daily marching took their places with the ark in their midst.[22] Thirteen times the city was circled and then the walls did fall as the trumpets sounded and the people shouted. The army now took the city with ease, no doubt aided by great fear engendered in the hearts of Jericho's inhabitants. Rahab had testified that they were already fearful at the time of the spies' visit, and now Israel's strange daily encirclement of the city would have added to this emotional state.

All the people of the city were killed, with the exception of Rahab[23] and her family, whose lives were spared in keeping with the spies' promise, and the city was leveled by fire. No Israelite was permitted to enrich himself by spoil, however, God having placed a ban on the city, declaring that it was "devoted"[24] to Himself (Josh.

[18] For example, Numbers 22:1; 26:3, 63; 31:12; 33:48–50; 34:15; 35:1; 36:13; Deuteronomy 32:49; 34:1, 3; Joshua 4:13; et al.

[19] Kenyon, *Digging Up Jericho* (New York: Frederick A. Praeger, 1957), pp. 214–20. She dates these walls only to c. 1550 B.C.; but see contrary conclusion, pp. 74–78.

[20] Another Old Testament appearance of Christ as the Angel of Yahweh. This "commander" called the ground "holy" (Josh. 5:15) as with Moses at the burning bush (Exod. 3:5), and used the personal pronoun "I" as giving Jericho into Joshua's hand.

[21] All two million people did not encircle Jericho. Critics are right in saying this would have been quite impossible. These "armed men" represented the others and likely were not numerous themselves as they accompanied the priests with the ark.

[22] The important object in the marching column was the ark, which represented God. As the ark had earlier held back the Jordan, now it would bring down Jericho's walls.

[23] Here spared, Rahab came to be included in the ancestral line of David and so of Christ (Matt. 1:5).

[24] The Hebrew word is *ḥerem*, used five times in Joshua 6:17–18. The idea "curse," sometimes

6:17–18). The valuable metals, gold, silver, bronze, and iron were placed in God's treasury. Joshua further pronounced a curse on any who should rebuild the city, the reality of which was experienced much later in the reign of King Ahab by Hiel the Bethelite (1 Kings 16:34).

2. Defeat and victory at Ai (Joshua 7:1–8:29)

a. Defeat. This victory at Jericho, however, contributed to a tragic defeat at Ai shortly after (Josh. 7:1–26). The city of Ai was the next objective before Israel. A reconnaissance party sent by Joshua was not impressed by Ai's strength and, apparently overconfident, advised that merely "two or three thousand" would be sufficient to take the city. Joshua sent the larger number, three thousand, but still they were defeated by the men of Ai, who killed thirty-six men as Israel's army fled.

The main reason for the defeat, however, was not the number of Israelite soldiers; it was the existence of sin in Israel's camp. Achan of the tribe of Judah had disregarded God's ban on the "devoted" items from Jericho and took for himself a Babylonian garment, two hundred shekels of silver, and a fifty-shekel bar of gold.[25] Following the defeat, God revealed to Joshua that such a sin had been committed and told him to inquire as to the identity of the guilty party. This was done,[26] and Achan was identified. The man confessed to having taken the items and hidden them in his tent. These were recovered from their hiding place, and then Achan and his family were stoned and then burned with all his possessions. This punishment was necessary, both in view of the serious offense and as a warning to other Israelites.

b. Victory. With the sin punished, Israel was now enabled to conquer Ai (Josh. 8). By night, Joshua sent a large force to hide in ambush in a valley between Ai and nearby Bethel. The next day Joshua led another force in frontal attack on the city as had been done at the time of defeat. This time, however, when the men of Ai came out from the city, Joshua's force retreated as before, the hidden force arose and attacked the army of Ai from behind. Joshua's force then turned, and the enemy was trapped. The result was that all twelve thousand[27] of the male inhabitants of Ai were killed, the king hanged, and the city reduced to rubble.

This time God permitted Israelites to take of the spoil. It should be observed, too, that Joshua employed many more troops in the second attempt on the city, apparently assigning thirty thousand to the ambush alone (Josh. 8:3).[28] He and the people clearly had learned two lessons: the costliness of sin and the error of overconfidence.

---

ascribed to the word is appropriate only in the sense of the thing involved being banned from employment by any other than God.

[25] The common shekel weighed about four-tenths of an ounce, thus making the silver here about eighty ounces and the gold twenty ounces.

[26] Probably by using the official provision for such an inquiry, the Urim and Thummim (Exod. 28:30; Num. 27:21). This revelational device was to be used solely by the high priest.

[27] Either among these, or perhaps in addition to them, may have been men of Bethel. It is stated (8:17) that Bethelites did go with those of Ai in pursuit of Joshua's decoy group.

[28] The relationship between the thirty thousand of verse 3 and the five thousand of verse 12 is not clear. Possibly the thirty thousand refers to the total force and the five thousand to those set in ambush. Even so, thirty thousand is still ten times the number used in the first attack.

c. Location. The location of Ai is still uncertain. The traditional site is et-Tell,[29] about one and one-half miles southeast of Bethel, excavated in 1933–35 by Judith Marquet-Krause and in 1964–72 by Joseph A. Calloway. Their work revealed, however, that this mound was not inhabited between c. 2200 and c. 1000 B.C., and so not in Joshua's day.

Various solutions have been suggested,[30] but the most likely is that et-Tell is not the right location. Some factors favor this explanation. For instance, et-Tell is rather far from Bethel, whereas Joshua 12:9 (see 7:2) states that Ai was "near [*mitsad*] Bethel." Also, et-Tell is a comparatively large mound, whereas Joshua's reconnaissance party described Ai's inhabitants as few.[31]

An alternative to et-Tell as the location for Ai has been suggested as the result of 1981 excavations at Khirbet Nisya, a site mentioned in the 1883 survey of Western Palestine but unknown to the Israel Department of Antiquities until relocated in a 1979 surface survey. Arguing that Beitin, the site currently identified with Bethel, is in the wrong location to satisfy the description of the fourth-century historian Eusebius, David Livingstone theorized that ancient Bethel should be located at modern Bireh, not Beitin. Working from that hypothesis, he located Nisya in the place the biblical description would demand. Nisya is only two to three acres, which correlates well with the biblical description of Ai as a small, but walled city, and is located correctly to be biblical Ai. What's more, its occupation history fits the biblical picture.[32] While only eight squares were excavated in 1981, the initial picture derived from the site offers a tantalizing hope that the correct location of Ai has been found, even though it is still too early to make a definite statement.

d. Bethel. No indication is given of a conquest of Bethel in Joshua's day. Her king is listed as killed by Joshua's forces (Josh. 12:16), but no record is given of a direct attack on the city. The reason may be that her power was broken at the time of Ai's defeat. It was only logical for her to join in assisting Ai against an enemy which she could expect would confront her next, and

[29] The name et-Tell means "the hill" or "heap of ruins" (Josh. 8:28), which is the approximate meaning of Ai (*ha'ay*). This is one reason for the identification, on the assumption that the meaning has carried over to modern time. Simons, *GTT*, p. 270, argues against this, however, pointing out that several sites are today called et-Tell, and also that the name *Ai* need not carry the thought of "ruin" at all, but only of a "heap of stones."

[30] Albright, followed by Wright (*BAR*, p. 80), believes that this account of Ai's fall is really the account of Bethel's conquest, which later became attached to Ai to explain the existence of the continuing ruin near Bethel. But this must be rejected as inconsistent with the veracity of Scripture. More plausible is Vincent's explanation that Ai had become a military outpost of Bethel, which left no permanent remains for the excavator. But Wright counters this idea by observing correctly that Joshua 8 speaks often of the "king of Ai" (ibid).

[31] Simons gives two other arguments: "Et-Tell was not a ruin in the postconquest period, whereas Joshua indicates that Ai was (8:28)"; and "There is no broad valley to the north of et-Tell, whereas Joshua 8:11 indicates the existence of a valley near Ai"; summarized in "Archaeological Digest" of the *American Journal of Archaeology* (July–September 1947), p. 311, as cited by Free, *ABH*, p. 134. Further, as to fewness of inhabitants, the twelve thousand of Joshua 8:25 may have included people of Bethel (see n.27).

[32] Wilbur Fields, "Have We Found Ai?" unpublished paper presented at the annual meeting of the Evangelical Theological Society, 1981.

Joshua 8:17 states directly that she did. Bethel's king may have been killed at this time, though the record mentions only Ai's ruler (Josh. 8:23, 29). Joshua's employment of so many more troops the second time may have been in part due to his expectation that Bethel would join with Ai.

3. Ceremony at Shechem (Joshua 8:30–35; Deuteronomy 27:1–26)

With Jericho, Ai, and Bethel controlled, Joshua took the people, according to God's instruction (Deut. 27:1–26), north to Shechem to renew God's covenant. The intention was to repeat for the benefit of this new generation what had been done forty years before at Sinai when the covenant had been ratified (Exod. 24:4–8).[33] The people were now actually in the land, and it was fitting that there be a reminder of God's requirements and a renewal of the people's promises. Near Shechem, at the foot of Mount Ebal,[34] Joshua built an altar, and the priests made burnt offerings and peace offerings. On prepared stones, Joshua wrote a "copy of the law of Moses" (Josh. 8:32 KJV),[35] apparently as a concrete representation of God's Law among His people. Then half the tribes moved over toward Mount Gerizim, with half remaining near Mount Ebal, and these in turn responded to the blessings and curses of the Law as read by Joshua. Near Joshua as he read was the ark of the covenant representing God's presence. The ceremony must have been impressive, and the people[36] would have remembered it well in succeeding days.

Israel's conquest of this northern, central region where Shechem was a principal city (Gen. 12:6; 33:18–20) is not described in Scripture. The biblical account speaks of the Israelites being able to move north to it, apparently without difficulty, but does not explain how this was possible. Shechem was more than thirty miles north of Ai, and her people would not have considered themselves under Israelite domination simply because the more southern city had fallen.

The most likely explanation is that Israelite forces had moved north to subjugate the area ahead of time, though after Ai's fall. Certain matters suggest this. One is that the account of the Ebal-Gerizim ceremony (Josh. 8:30) begins with the word "then" (*'az,* not merely the simple conjunction *waw*), which could imply lapse of sufficient time for such an intervening conquest. Another is that Joshua 11:19 states that no city other than Gibeon (Josh. 9) capitulated to Israel peacefully, which means that Shechem must

---

[33] See pp. 116–17.

[34] Mount Ebal and Mount Gerizim lie north and south from each other with Shechem between their eastern ends. Before Shechem to the east a plain opens up, in the middle of which Joshua may have stood as he later read the Law to the people on both sides of him.

[35] This can hardly have been all the Mosaic Law, which would have taken very long to inscribe. Various views are held as to how much was included: only the Decalogue, the Decalogue plus the blessings and curses here read by Joshua, the legal portion of Deuteronomy, the 613 commandments of the whole Law (according to Jewish reckoning), or a running gist of the whole Law.

[36] The number of Israelites brought from Gilgal the approximate forty miles to Shechem is hard to determine. Joshua 8:35 speaks of women, little ones, and sojourners besides the men. Certainly the women and children of the two and one-half tribes still across the Jordan were not there, and it is not easy to think of nearly two million others making such a trip, though it is possible. If only a representative group went, at least all ages and both men and women were represented.

have been taken forcibly. And a third is that Joshua 12:17, 18, 24 lists kings of the Shechem area who were killed by Joshua's troops sometime and so probably here at this logical juncture. It should be realized that the biblical account is not explicit on numerous details in the overall conquest.

4. Peaceful homage (Joshua 9)

Returning to Gilgal, the Israelites received unexpected peaceful homage from another important group of people of central Palestine. These were Hivites,[37] representing four major cities generally northwest of Jerusalem a few miles—Gibeon, Chephirah, Beeroth, and Kirjath-jearim—sometimes called the Gibeonite tetrapolis. News of Israel's early successes had spread through the land (Josh. 9:1), and these people saw wisdom in peaceful capitulation.

Doubting that Israel would accept their treaty offer if they were identified with nearby Gibeon, they contrived a trick, wearing wornout clothing and bearing moldy bread, to make themselves appear to have traveled from a distant country. They asked that Israel make a treaty of peace with them, and it was granted. This was contrary to God's instruction (Exod. 23:32; 34:12; Deut. 7:2), however, and the Israelites were held responsible because they had not asked counsel "of the LORD" (Josh. 9:14).[38]

When the ruse was known three days later, Joshua and the elders honored the treaty because it had been made in the name of Yahweh (see 2 Sam. 21:1–14 for a historical sequel), but forced the Gibeonites to serve as "woodcutters and water carriers for the entire community" (Josh. 9:21). While the treaty was a violation of God's command, Israel thus acquired control in the central portion of the land, and this without effort on her part.

D. CONQUEST OF THE SOUTH AND THE NORTH (Joshua 10–12)

At this point Israel had driven a wedge between the northern and southern regions of the land. Jericho, Ai, Bethel, Beeroth, Gibeon, Chephirah, and Kirjath-jearim formed a continuous, slightly curving line across southern central Palestine; and, as we have seen, the fact that Israel had been able to assemble peaceably at Shechem indicates control had been gained in the northern central area as well. The general strategy was working. The South and North were now separated and remained to be taken each by itself.

1. Defeat of the southern confederacy (Joshua 10:1–11)

Contact with the South came soon after the treaty with the Hivite tetrapolis. Among the four cities, Gibeon was the largest and most powerful (Josh. 10:2);[39] and when news of her action

---

[37] One of the seven listed (sometimes only six) national groups of Canaan at the time of the conquest: Amorites, Perizzites, Canaanites, Hittites, Girgashites, Hivites, and Jebusites (Deut. 7:1; Josh. 3:10; 24:11). Little is known of their origin unless they are the same as Horites, for which identification some evidence exists. They are represented as located in a variety of places (Gen. 34:2; 36:2; Josh. 11:3; Judg. 3:3; et al.), thus suggesting little homogeneity.

[38] This was the type of inquiry for which God had given the Urim and Thummim, but it was not employed here.

[39] Excavation at Gibeon (el-Jib, some seven miles northwest of Jerusalem) during 1956, 1957,

reached the king of Jerusalem, he formed a coalition of major southern cities. Four leading cities joined with him: Hebron, Jarmuth, Lachish, and Eglon.[40]

These confederates began their general resistance to Israel by first attacking Gibeon, apparently to force her out of the new alliance with Israel. Gibeon quickly appealed to Joshua in Gilgal, and Joshua brought his troops by forced march the twenty-four-mile distance to Gibeon in one night. He took the attackers by surprise, routed them, and pursued them toward the heights near Beth-horon to the west.[41] Near Beth-horon the fleeing troops turned south in an apparent attempt to reach home cities,[42] but on the way Yahweh sent a fierce hailstorm that killed more of the enemy than did Israel's swords. The five kings, staying close together, succeeded in getting to the vicinity of Azekah[43] and Makkedah, but then sought shelter in a cave.

The pursuing Israelites found the kings in a cave, but, in passing, merely sealed the opening with stones and continued after the fleeing soldiers.

Joshua wanted the troops themselves caught and killed before they could get to the safety of their walled cities. This was accomplished in major part (Josh. 10:18–20), and then attention was again given to the trapped kings. Joshua commanded his military leaders to place their feet on the necks of these rulers while he slew them, thinking, no doubt, that this would bolster their confidence for future battles. Then Joshua had the lifeless bodies of all five hung on trees for his men to see during the remainder of the day (Josh. 10:21–27).

2. A prolonged day (Joshua 10:12–14)

It was earlier that same day, as Joshua stood on a commanding height near Gibeon, likely watching the fleeing enemy outrun his tired troops, that he voiced a poetic call that has caused considerable discussion: "O sun stand still over Gibeon, O moon, over the Valley of Aijalon" (v. 12).[44] These words and the description following have traditionally been taken to mean

1959, 1960, and 1962 has given corroboration; see J. B. Pritchard, *Gibeon Where the Sun Stood Still* (Princeton: Princeton University Press, 1962).

[40] These five cities in their geographical interrelation formed an approximate right triangle. Jerusalem and Hebron formed an eastern north-south leg of about twenty miles. Lachish lay approximately on the southern east-west leg about seven miles from Eglon, which was at the east end of the southern leg, and Jarmuth lay about on the hypotenuse roughly halfway between Eglon and Jerusalem. All are well identified with the possible exception of Eglon.

[41] Beth-horon the upper lay about five miles west and slightly north of Gibeon. Beth-horon the nether was about two miles farther. One should think here merely of the general area.

[42] Since the enemy had not at first fled south toward Jerusalem, the nearest of the five allied cities, it is evident that Joshua had cut off this avenue of escape. Apparently the enemy outstripped Joshua's tired men, however, and so was able to swing south at Beth-horon.

[43] Azekah was located at the head of the valley of Elah where David later fought Goliath (1 Sam. 17:1), about fifteen miles southwest of Beth-horon. Jarmuth, one of the allied cities, was only about three miles west from here. As to Makkedah, see p. 149n.48.

[44] The first words of this poetic call and later words of verse 13, which say that the "sun stayed in the midst [*chatsi,* "half"] of the heavens" (KJV), suggest that the time of day was noon, with the sun directly over Gibeon where Joshua stood. The remainder of the cry, "O moon, over the Valley of Ajalon," suggests that the moon then lay close to the horizon in this valley. Since the valley lies seventeen degrees north of west from Gibeon, the time of year can be figured as July, and the relative positions of the sun and moon indicate that the moon was at third quarter, half full.

that this day was miraculously prolonged.

Numerous scholars take exception to the view, however, including some conservatives. A few have thought that Joshua merely appealed for added strength for himself and his troops. Others have believed that a miracle in refraction of light occurred, so that, though the position of the sun itself did not change in relation to the earth, it appeared to do so and indeed lengthened the day. Still others have suggested that Joshua only requested relief from the burning heat of the noonday sun, which God answered by sending clouds and storm.[45]

The traditional view must be maintained, however, for these alternate explanations do not do justice to the language of the text. Though it is true that the verb *dum* (translated "stand still" in Joshua's call) means basically "be silent," and so could refer to being silent in other ways than retardation of movement,[46] still the verb *'amadh* is also used (twice in v. 13), and it definitely indicates a change in pattern of movement. Further, verse 13 closes with the expression, "and hasted not to go down" (KJV), where the word "hasted" (*'uz*) again speaks of motion, and the phrase "to go down" (*labho'*) is normal in reference to the sun setting. Still further, verse 14 states that this day was unique in history, which suggests a major miracle such as the prolonging of a natural day occurred.

The extent of this prolongation can also be estimated. Since the hour was at noon when Joshua voiced the call, and it is stated that the sun did not go down for "about a full day" (*keyom tamim*), it is likely that the afternoon hours until sunset were prolonged twice their normal length. In other words, the total daylight hours of the day were one and one-half times normal.[47]

There was good reason for Joshua wanting this day prolonged. The five strong kings had brought their armies out from their fortified cities to do battle with Israel in the open. Their thinking likely had been that, since the walls of Jericho and Ai had not helped those cities, it would be better to try a new method. But this left them without their best means of defense, and Joshua knew it. Now he did not want them to get back behind those walls if he could help it.

The violent storm mentioned in connection with this battle must also be taken into account. The destruction brought by the hail would have thrown the Canaanite army into confusion which would have slowed their flight. The accompanying rain would have cooled and refreshed the Israelite soldiers. With the passing of the storm, all that would be needed was enough daylight to make the route complete.

---

[45] For a helpful summary of these and other views, see Bernard Ramm, *The Christian View of Science and Scripture* (Grand Rapids: Eerdmans, 1955), pp. 156–61. Ramm himself favors the "clouding over" view, but see Payne, *BETS* 4 (1960): 95, for refutation.

[46] For instance, as one explanation holds, to be silent in shining with such heat.

[47] As to how this was effected, the closing words of verse 13 "and hasted not to go down about a whole day" (KJV), suggest that the relative positions of the sun and earth did not hold still but merely slowed in their change. This means that the earth simply slowed, in its speed of rotation on its axis, approximately to half that of normal. This did not affect the speed of movement around the sun or the rest of the solar system, which complicating factors have been mentioned in criticism by those advocating other explanations.

Accordingly, Joshua asked God to supply added hours, and God did so, graciously responding to the faith of His servant.

3. Subjugation of southern cities (Joshua 10:28–43)

With this crucial battle won, Joshua pressed on to subjugate cities in all the southern area. He had planned to do this anyhow, following the conquest of central Palestine, and now the situation was most propitious with the armies of the principal cities decimated.

The first assaults were against Makkedah and then Libnah, both close to the cave where the kings had been killed.[48] Each city was taken, apparently without difficulty, with the respective kings and many people killed. However, seemingly little physical harm was done to the cities,[49] a pattern of operation followed for all this southern campaign.

Joshua then moved south to three of the cities of the confederacy: Lachish, Eglon, and Hebron. Another, Jarmuth, had been very near Joshua when he took Makkedah, but no mention is made of fighting there. Perhaps the city, being so near and her king killed with the others, capitulated without sufficient fighting to call for mention. Lachish,[50] about ten miles southwest

of Azekah, was probably the strongest of the three and was attacked first. The city fell on the second day of fighting, and the people were killed as at Makkedah and Libnah, though this time the king had been dispatched already at the cave near Makkedah.

While Israel was so engaged, the king of Gezer,[51] who for some reason felt obligated to Lachish, though his city was some twenty miles north, came with his army to aid Lachish, but he and his men all perished before Joshua in the attempt. Joshua might then have turned to take Gezer, but he did not, probably because it was well out of his way. Instead, he moved on to Eglon,[52] the farthest west of the southern three confederate cities, and then to Hebron,[53] the farthest east. Both fell and were treated as Lachish.

After these earlier and more major conquests, Joshua continued south to subdue all the lower part of the land. His army even reached Kadesh-barnea, where Israel had spent so much time during the wilderness journey. Debir[54] was probably the most important prize in this lower southern area. Finally Joshua returned to Gibeon where the whole effort had started.

Several months must have been occupied in making this extensive campaign. The distances covered were long and

---

[48] Though each is uncertain, Makkedah is best identified with Khirbet el-Kheishum, two miles northeast of Azekah at the head of the Elah Valley, and Libnah with Tell es-Safi four miles west.

[49] At least no mention of general destruction is made. For discussion of significance, see pp. 79–80.

[50] A city of eighteen acres. See p. 78n.71 as to excavation and references.

[51] Identified with Tell Jezer; excavated by R. A. S. Macalister in 1902–05 and 1907–09; see his report, *The Excavations of Gezer,* 1912. Hebrew Union College conducted excavations from 1964 to 1973 (*BA* 30 [February 1967]: 47–62, and *EAEHL,* 2:428-43).

[52] Commonly, though uncertainly, identified with Tell el-Hesi; Albright, *BASOR* 17 (1925): 7.

[53] Hebron still continues as an important city in the midst of the hills of old Judea at its highest point (about three thousand feet). The exact site of the biblical city lies probably east at Gebel er-Rumeidi.

[54] If correctly identified with Tell Beit Mirsim, it lay some thirteen miles southwest of Hebron. Khirbet Rabud, the more recently proposed identification, is about seven and one-half miles southwest of Hebron. See p. 78n.73 as to excavations and references.

the cities taken numerous. Had the cities not fallen with comparative ease, the time would have been much longer, of course. In fact, Joshua then would likely have had to make several campaigns. That he was able to subdue the entire region in this one great effort shows that indeed the cities did capitulate without long periods of siege.

A main reason for this limited resistance was probably a paralyzing fear that had gripped the inhabitants. They had heard of Israel's victories—when she had been beyond the Jordan, after crossing Jordan (at Jericho and Ai), and now over the five southern kings. They had been impressed, too, by the prolonged, miraculous day and also by the unusual storm that had killed so many of the confederate forces. The God who could perform such works must be great indeed! With divine help and with the enemy thoroughly demoralized, Joshua was able to sweep through the land in this single grand campaign.

One main city, however, was not taken. That was Jerusalem, one of the five confederates.[55] It had been out of the way as Joshua had pursued the fleeing enemy on the way south, and perhaps his troops were too weary to attempt the difficult task on the return. It remained a tiny island, not incorporated into Israelite territory, until David seized it much later.[56]

4. Defeat of the northern confederacy (Joshua 11)

News of Joshua's remarkable conquest of the South reached the ears of Jabin, powerful king of Hazor. Hazor[57] was the great metropolis of the North, and her monarch quite automatically found himself leader. Jabin, fearing similar attack on his region, now formed a confederacy. By gathering a greater force, he apparently planned to do better than the southern alliance.

The kings he assembled are listed as representing all parts of northern Palestine: the mountain region still above Hazor, the plain "south of Kinnereth,"[58] the "valley" (KJV, perhaps the Valley of Esdraelon), the western region as far as Dor,[59] and three cities mentioned in particular, Madon, Shimron, and Achshaph.[60] The assembly included Canaanites, Amorites, Hittites, Perizzites, Jebusites, and Hivites. The gathering point was the waters of Merom,[61] and the host numbered like "the sand on the seashore" (Josh. 11:4).

Joshua brought his battle-tried troops north to meet this formidable

---

[55] See Joshua 15:8, 63; 18:28. Jerusalem had led the confederacy.

[56] See 2 Samuel 5:7. Jerusalem was taken once by Judah, but apparently only temporarily (Judg. 1:8).

[57] See pp. 78–79.

[58] Kinnereth probably means the Sea of Galilee. The plain would be the Jordan where many fine cities existed.

[59] Dor lay on the Mediterranean, eight miles north of later Caesarea.

[60] Listed separately, these three cities were likely the strongest. Little is known of them, however; see Joshua 12:20; 19:15 (Shimron of the tribe of Zebulon); 19:25 (Achshaph, farther west, of Asher). Madon is often, though uncertainly, identified with modern Qeren Hattin, west of Tiberias, near Khirbet Madjan, which preserves the ancient name.

[61] Water of Merom may refer to Lake Huleh, recently drained. Some believe, however, the place is better identified with large springs near the modern village of Meiron, ten miles west and slightly south.

enemy. He did not hesitate to attack and thereby probably achieved an element of surprise. God used the move to give his smaller force complete victory. The huge enemy army was routed and chased far to the west. Joshua followed up this triumph by putting "all these royal cities and their kings" "to the sword" (Josh. 11:12). Then he returned to the city of Hazor itself and burned it—something he did not do to the other cities. As noted in chapter 5, most cities were spared, no doubt for the future use of Israelites; but Hazor was apparently seen by Joshua as a prize of psychological value for burning. People would be forced to recognize that any city could have been burned had Israel chosen, if great Hazor could not escape.

These matters make clear that Joshua effected the same thorough conquest of the North as he had of the South. Actually, the fact that Jabin made an alliance to withstand Israel aided Joshua in this full conquest, even as the alliance of the South had helped there. If Joshua had not been able to defeat the strength of the North in one major blow, the individual subjugation of each city would have occupied a much longer time. As it was, the northern campaign appears to have taken even less time than the southern.

5. Summary of conquest

A summary statement of Israel's total conquest is made in Joshua 11:16–23. Joshua was victorious from the extreme south, near "Mount Halak, which rises toward Seir,"[62] to the extreme north "in the Valley of Lebanon below Mount Hermon." The only people who made peace without being attacked were the Hivites of the Gibeonite tetrapolis. It is expressly stated that among those slain were the feared giants, the Anakim, of whom the spies had particularly spoken years before (Num. 13:33). The total number of kings killed was thirty-one, the names of their cities being given in Joshua 12:10–24.

This means that, when Joshua returned to Gilgal from the northern campaign, the military strength of the major part of the land had been broken. Included was the area on the east of the Jordan from the Arnon River in the south to Mount Hermon in the north, and on the west from below the Dead Sea in the south to Mount Hermon again in the north. The cities had been overcome and a large number of the people, including leaders, killed. No record is given that Joshua left controlling garrisons in these cities (probably lacking sufficient men to leave); but the defensive strength of the cities had been broken, and Joshua had reason to believe that actual occupation by the respective tribes should not be difficult.

One principal region had escaped, with enclaves of Canaanites scattered throughout the land. The plain of Philistia, on the Mediterranean coastline, was unconquered[63] (Josh. 13:1–6), although even there Gaza is mentioned as having been affected by Joshua's presence in some respect (Josh. 10:41). Farther north the king of Dor had been defeated and killed as a member of the northern coalition (Josh. 12:23), but, for the most part,

---

[62] "Mount Halak" means smooth, or bald, mountain. This is likely the ridge referred to as the Ascent of Akrabbim (Num. 34:4; Josh. 15:3). It is located southeast of the Dead Sea.

[63] Joshua 13:1 implies that Joshua's age was a factor in God not directing him personally to lead against this coastal area. Joshua had done well to lead as he had and was likely now very tired.

The tribal divisions marked on this map are only approximate since boundary lists are incomplete.

Sidonians

Ijon

Tyre
Beth-anath
Dan

Kedesh
Merom
Bashan
MANASSEH

Achzib

Hazor

Acco
Rehob
Aphek

Chinnereth
Argob

Ashtaroth

Achsaph

Shimron

Edrei

Dor
Jokneam
Remeth
Havoth-Jair
Megiddo
ISSACHAR
Jezreel
Ham
Ramoth-gilead

Taanach
Bethshan
Jabesh-gilead

Hepher
Ibleam

Sucoh
MANASSEH
Tirzah
Shechem
Succoth
Penuel
AMMON

Tappoah

Aphek
Adam

Joppa
Shiloh

EPHRAIM

Bethel
Ai
Abel-keramim?
Rabbath-Ammon
Gezer
Gibeon
Gilgal
Abel-shittim
Ajalon
BENJAMIN
Jericho
Heshbon
Ekron
Beth-jeshimoth
Jebus
Ashdod
Gath
Beth-shemish
Bethlehem
Medeba
Libna
Ashkelon
RUEBEN
JUDAH
Lachish
Debir
Hebron
Gaza
Eglon
Dibon
Aroer
Carmel
Caleb
Eshtemoa
Gerar
Beersheba
Arad
Horma
Aroer
SIMEON Kenites
MOAB

EDOM

Map 6. The Tribal Divisions

the coastal territory had remained untouched, with fighting having occurred only more inland. Judges mentions additional territory that was not conquered, and it says that, even when the tribes had grown strong, they allowed the conquered Canaanites to remain as forced laborers (Judg. 1:27–36). Most of this territory remained in Canaanite hands until the time of David.

E. THE LAND DIVIDED
(Joshua 13–22)

Before the respective tribes could begin occupation, it was necessary to assign territory to the remaining nine and a half tribes. Since there was reason to begin occupation rather soon, while psychological and material advantages from the main campaigns still lingered, there was wisdom in assigning these portions as soon as possible. This was the task to which Joshua set himself on returning to the people still encamped at Gilgal. The procedure had already been indicated when the people were still east of the Jordan; namely, by lot, which placed the decision with God rather than men (Num. 26:55–56; 33:54).

1. Allotments east of the Jordan (Joshua 13)

Reuben, Gad, and half of the tribe of Manasseh had already received their allotted portions. Moses had supervised in this prior to the Jordan crossing (Num. 32:1–42; Deut. 3:13–17; Josh. 13:8–33). The land then assigned stretched from the Arnon River north to Mount Hermon, though how much of this was actually occupied north of the Yarmuk River is uncertain.[64] The line of division between Reuben, assigned the southern section, and Gad, the middle, is quite clear as having run east from the northern tip of the Dead Sea. The division between Gad and half of Manasseh to the North, however, is not clear. The principal boundary certainly was the Jabbok River, since this stream had been Sihon's northern boundary, and it was his kingdom that was divided between Gad and Reuben (Josh. 13:27). Two northern extensions across the Jabbok, however, also seem to have existed, one near the east bank of the Jordan, running as far north as the Sea of Galilee (Josh. 13:27), and one nearer the desert running as far north at least as Ramoth-gilead (Josh. 13:24–28; 20:8).

2. Allotments of Judah, Ephraim, and Manasseh (Joshua 14:1–17:11)

While preparations were being made for allotting portions on the west of the Jordan, Caleb interrupted proceedings with a remarkable request (Josh. 14:6–15). He asked that he might personally be granted the Hebron area, where the giant Anakim had been found, when he, Joshua, and the other spies had surveyed the land before. Joshua had broken the strength of these people in the southern campaign, but apparently some of them still remained; and Caleb wanted to achieve complete extermination. He reminded Joshua that Moses had promised him the region (see Deut. 1:36).

Caleb at this time was eighty-five years old, an age when people normally think of easy tasks; but Caleb asked for

---

[64] North of the Yarmuk, the states of Geshur and Maacah took up much of the territory, and express statement is given that neither came under control of Manasseh (Josh. 13:13).

a hard one, and Joshua, no doubt long an admirer of his close friend, granted the request. Caleb moved at once to the challenging work and did drive the Anakim from the land assigned him (Josh. 15:13–19).

The tribe of Judah, Caleb's tribe, received the first regular allotment of land, which included the area already granted to Caleb. The territory was very large (Josh. 15:1–12). Its eastern border was the Dead Sea, and its western the Mediterranean. Its southern border angled south from the Dead Sea so that Kadesh-barnea was included and its northern border ran irregularly from the northern tip of the Dead Sea west to the Mediterranean, just skirting Jerusalem on the south. Its main cities, as named in Joshua 15:20–63, make a long list.

The next lot was for Ephraim, Joshua's tribe (Josh. 16:1–10). Judah and Ephraim were the two most influential tribes and continued to be until the time of the Exile.[65] Both headed their respective kingdom divisions following the reign of Solomon.[66] Ephraim was given a smaller section than Judah, north of Judah and with room left between for Benjamin. The third lot was for the remaining half tribe of Manasseh (Josh. 17:1–11).[67] This portion bordered Ephraim on the north, stretching again, like Judah and Ephraim, from the Jordan to the Mediterranean. The two Joseph tribes thus were located side by side at the center of the land. The northern boundary of Manasseh was the southern edge of the Esdraelon Valley.

3. Allotting interrupted (Joshua 17:12–18:9)

At this point, before allotting the remaining seven tribes, the people, for some reason, gave themselves to the task of moving camp from Gilgal to Shiloh, where they then erected the tabernacle in the place it was to occupy for many years (Josh. 18:1). They had been at Gilgal between six and seven years during the time of Joshua's campaigns.[68] Now they moved farther into

---

[65] The man Judah had assumed leadership among the brothers (Gen. 43:3; 46:28) and was promised leadership for his tribe by Jacob (Gen. 49:8–12). Ephraim was a son of Joseph and given preference over Manasseh when blessed by grandfather Jacob (Gen. 48:1–22), and also Joshua was from this tribe.

[66] Ephraim assumed a dominant position already in the Judges Period, challenging Gideon for not calling its people to fight the Midianites (Judg. 8:1–3), and similarly challenging Jephthah sometime later (Judg. 12:1–6). Bitterness against Judah became apparent when Ishbosheth, succeeding son of Saul, ruled Ephraim and the northern tribes, and David ruled Judah (2 Sam. 2:1–11), and later again when David returned to Jerusalem following Absalom's rebellion (2 Sam. 19:41–43). After the kingdom's division, Ephraim is identified frequently with all ten tribes (Isa. 7:2, 5, 8, 9, 17; 11:13; Jer. 7:15; 31:9, 18, 20; Ezek. 37:16; Hos. 7:8; et al.).

[67] Comparing Numbers 26:28–34, Joshua 17:1–3, and 1 Chronicles 2:21–23, the rationale for the division of Manasseh appears as follows. The half tribe which settled on the west of Jordan descended from Manasseh's grandson through Machir, namely Gilead, the father of six sons. Zelophehad, the son of one of the sons, had only daughters, and by special decision (Num. 27:1–11; see p. 156) they were permitted to inherit with the sons, with the result that of the ten portions allotted to Manasseh on the west, five were given to these daughters (Josh. 17:3–6). The half tribe on the east of Jordan apparently descended from two grandsons of Manasseh, one through a marriage between a granddaughter of Manasseh through Machir, whose mother is unknown, and Hezron, from whose marriage came Jair, definitely said to have lived within the Transjordan area (1 Chron. 2:21–23).

[68] This length of time is based on Caleb's statement that he had been forty years old at Kadesh-barnea and was now eighty-five (Josh. 14:7, 10), and the fact that over one year of the total forty in the

the land to occupy a city which had just been allotted to Ephraim.

One reason for the interruption certainly was the people's desire to locate the tabernacle in a permanent place as soon as possible, and this desire was realized with the assignment of Ephraim's territory, which included Shiloh.[69] Since, however, there was need to avoid unnecessary delay in allotting, before the advantage of Joshua's campaigns had worn off, there must have been another reason also.

The text suggests one. The remaining tribes suddenly displayed a surprising lack of interest in receiving their portions. This change of attitude seems to have resulted when both Ephraim and Manasseh objected to their allotments.[70] These two tribes complained that their portions were too small, especially since they contained large wooded areas[71] and the Canaanites living there were hard to dislodge (Josh. 17:12–18).

Joshua wisely responded that they should solve their own problems by cutting the trees and driving out the Canaanites, whether strong or not, matters certainly that they should have undertaken without being told. Their objections, however, wrong as they were, evidently were enough to influence the other tribes, which now hesitated to occupy their allotments at all. It is possible that, recognizing the seriousness of the situation, Joshua chose to give the tribes time to reflect, while all moved to the vicinity of Shiloh.

With the people gathered at Shiloh, however, Joshua waited no longer but gave clear orders for reinaugurating and facilitating the allotting procedure (Josh. 18:2–9). He gave instructions that three representatives from each of the remaining seven tribes should form teams to survey the land left to assign. The teams should return with descriptions of the land, which would form a basis for the next allotments. From these descriptions the location of dense woods, the nature of soil, and the density of Canaanite population could be determined, which would help in making proper divisions of the land and also let people know ahead of time what they would find. The decision on which section was to be received by a particular tribe was still to be revealed by lot. Joshua's directions were carried out, and allotting began once more.

4. The seven remaining allotments (Joshua 18:10–19:51)

The first tribe now to receive territory was Benjamin (Josh. 18:10–28). Benjamin's allotment was small, squeezed between large Judah to the south and the important Joseph tribes

wilderness had elapsed by the time the people were at Kadesh. That this much time had been employed in Joshua's campaigns is not surprising in view of all he had done. Joshua himself was probably near one hundred years old when he finished the northern campaign (see p. 176).

[69] What had led to Shiloh's selection is not stated. Probably any site in Judah had been rejected as too far south to serve all the tribes, and Ephraim was next in importance. Some relation may exist to the much-discussed passage Genesis 49:10, but this is not clear.

[70] From this it appears that Joshua had directed each tribe, on receiving allotment, to move immediately to occupy it before allotting another. Likely Joshua had figured a time schedule so that this could be done and still complete the process in reasonable time.

[71] Almost no trees exist in the area today but clearly did then (see 2 Kings 2:24). Heavy woods in this middle region could indicate that few people had lived in these mountains (the Canaanites would have been in the valleys); this situation may have been a factor in Joshua apparently having experienced little fighting in the area prior to this (see pp. 145–46).

to the north. Further, it extended only about half-way to the Mediterranean from the Jordan. It did include the important cities Jericho and Jerusalem.

The next allotment was for Simeon. This time no land area as such was assigned but only cities within the large territory of Judah. Seventeen cities are named (Josh. 19:1–9), which included small population centers near them.[72] One reason for this change in type of allotment was that Judah had been given more land than it needed (Josh. 19:9). Another was that Simeon was now the smallest of the tribes, numbering only 22,200 men at the second census (Num. 26:14)[73] and so could fit into smaller quarters than others. A third, and most important reason, was that its ancestor, Simeon, along with Levi, had received as his "blessing" from Jacob the prediction that he would be scattered in Israel,[74] a consequence clearly of the indiscretion of these two brothers many years before in tricking and brutally slaying the inhabitants of Shechem.[75]

Zebulun received allotment next (Josh. 19:10–16), followed by Issachar (Josh. 19:17–23). Both of these territories were small, about the size of Benjamin, but constituted mainly of fine level land in the fertile Esdraelon Valley. Canaanites, however, were strong in the region, and courage was needed to drive them out. Neither tribe succeeded well in doing this for many years. Zebulun bordered on Issachar's northwest.

Asher received the fifth allotment, a larger section again (Josh. 19:24–31). It lay along the Mediterranean, from Manasseh on the south to Israel's border on the north. The sixth allotment was for Naphtali, the last of the northern tribes (Josh. 19:32–39). Her area was also large, extending from north to south beside Asher, splitting the northern region with her. She bordered both Zebulun and Issachar on the south.

The last tribe to receive allotment was Dan, whose land was in the south (Josh. 19:40–48). This territory was small, pressed between Judah and Ephraim, like Benjamin, which bordered it on the east. Eighteen cities are listed in the division, indicating a heavy Canaanite population, which promised to make occupation difficult.[76] Because Dan was one of the larger tribes numerically,[77] and also because of this difficulty in occupation, many Danites soon migrated.[78] They went far north to Laish, which city they conquered and

---

[72]Apparently Beersheba and Sheba listed in verse 2 are the same city, otherwise the cities listed add to one more than the total figure indicated in verse 6; also a parallel list in 1 Chronicles 4:28–31 does not list a Sheba separately.

[73]See p. 133n.100.

[74]Levi was scattered in that only individual cities were assigned through all the tribes (this, of course, due to being the priestly tribe, Josh. 21:1–41), and Simeon in being given these cities. It is of interest that later a number of Simeonites moved north near to Ephraim and Manasseh (2 Chron. 15:9; 34:6), for which reason the northern kingdom could be called a ten-tribe kingdom when originally only nine tribes were geographically so located.

[75]Genesis 34:1–31; see pp. 56–57.

[76]The Canaanites there would be pressed, too, by the Philistines, later to arrive in large numbers along the immediate coast (see Josh. 19:47; Judg. 1:34; 18:1).

[77]There were 62,700 in the first census (Num. 1:39) and 64,400 in the second (Num. 26:43), making Dan the second largest after Judah.

[78]Not all migrated. This account as given in Judges 18 indicates only six hundred men went at first to seize the land, though probably many others followed. Samson's family, however, were Danites and still lived in the allotted section (Judg. 13:2), and so likely others did, too.

then renamed Dan (Josh. 19:47; Judg. 18).

5. War narrowly averted (Joshua 22:1–34)

A tragic war was narrowly averted at the time when the men of Reuben, Gad, and half of Manasseh returned to their own homes. According to Moses' directive (Num. 32:16–32) seven years earlier, these men had faithfully remained with the main camp on the west of Jordan until the conquest had been completed and the land allotted; but now they returned to their own assigned lands. On the way, they erected a memorial altar at the Jordan River. This action appeared strange to the other tribes. Thinking the altar had been erected as a place of sacrifice, and so was a substitute for the Shiloh altar, they objected strongly, fearing that God would punish all the tribes for what seemed like blatant disobedience.[79]

Wisely, however, before declaring a punitive war against the Transjordan tribes, they sent Phinehas, son of Eleazar the high priest, and ten companions to give the supposed offenders opportunity to explain their action. The Transjordan tribes explained that this altar had not been erected for sacrifice at all but as a fitting object of memorial. These eastern tribes, separated from the others by the Jordan, did not want successive generations to think themselves any less a part of Israel than those on the west of Jordan, and they believed this memorial altar would help. Phinehas and his committee were satisfied with the answer and returned with

it to relieve the troubled minds of the western tribes.

F. INSTITUTIONS

1. Civil government

Upon settlement in the land, Israel's twelve tribes lived with a minimum of government. There was no king and no central ruling body. Each tribe lived quite to itself. The tribes themselves did not have central administrative bodies either. There were few officials at any level to whom people had to render obedience.

The situation was according to God's plan, however. God desired that His people render obedience directly to Him. He would be their Ruler; and if they would live as He directed, they would not need many earthly officers. He had given them His revealed laws so that they would know what He wanted. If they would obey these, they could live together meaningfully and peacefully. Also they would avoid the expense of supporting a human administration. Above all, they would please God, who then would prosper them in their earthly pursuits.

Some government, of course, was necessary to take care of details. This consisted mainly of appointed elders. These persons held jurisdiction over local communities. Elders had carried responsibility since the days of Egypt (Exod. 3:16–18; 19:7; 24:9; Num. 11:16–17), and the office still continued. They are said to have served as judges of persons who had killed someone (Deut. 19:12), conducted inquests (Deut. 21:2), heard family problems (Deut. 21:18–19), settled matrimonial

---

[79]This incident gives clear evidence that altars were not permitted indiscriminately in the land. Altars, other than at the tabernacle, are found used only in unusual religious situations (Judg. 6:24; 2 Sam. 24:25; 1 Kings 18:30) and not generally for offering regular sacrifices.

disputes (Deut. 22:15; 25:7), and settled cases of controversy in the gate of the city (Ruth 4:2).

Courts also existed, many local and one supreme. Each community had "judges and officials" for its local court. These sat in the gate of the city (Deut. 16:18), apparently sharing cases with elders.[80] When cases were "too difficult" for the local court, they could be sent to the supreme court (Deut. 17:8–9). This court sat at the central sanctuary in Shiloh and was composed of priests and lay judges. The latter conducted the investigations (Deut. 19:18), and the former served as legal counsels.

Court decisions required at least two witnesses (Deut. 19:15). If a witness proved false, he received the punishment that the accused would have suffered had he been found guilty (Deut. 19:16–19). Punishment was executed without delay (Num. 15:36; Deut. 22:18) and was sometimes carried out in the presence of the judges (Deut. 25:2–3), even at times by the officials themselves (Deut. 22:18). If the sentence was stoning, many people assisted (Num. 15:36; Deut. 22:21), and the witnesses had to cast the first stones (Deut. 13:9).

2. Central sanctuary

In keeping with the idea of theocracy, with God as chief ruler, the main unifying instrument among the tribes was the central sanctuary at Shiloh, the tabernacle. As in the wilderness, the tabernacle represented God's presence among His people. This religious center was for all the people of every tribe, with no tribe favored over another. Ephraimites, in whose midst it was located, carried no priority for its ministration over Asherites, Reubenites, or any other far away. All could come to the tabernacle and on occasion were commanded to come for their religious expression.

The tabernacle served as the place of sacrifice. Here the priests and Levites ministered in the offerings and ceremonies prescribed in the Law. Offerings were made every day, with more on sabbaths and still more on feast days. All sacrifice was to be made at the tabernacle, private altars not being permitted except in most unusual religious situations.[81] At the tabernacle, too, the prescribed annual feasts were celebrated. To attend at least three of these, every male of each tribe was expected to come to Shiloh (Deut. 16:16).

This situation of the twelve tribes, finding their one bond of unity in a central religious sanctuary, has a parallel in the later leagues of Greece and Italy. Greece called these leagues *amphictyonies*.[82] Two of the better known

---

[80]The Lachish ostraca were discovered in the gate of Lachish. Some of them were part of the evidence in a trial in progress at the time of the city's destruction. See Deuteronomy 21:19; Proverbs 22:22; Amos 5:15. For the ostraca, see H. Torczyner, *The Lachish Letters*, 1935; or *DOTT*, pp. 212–17.

[81]See n.79.

[82]Awareness of the existence of such amphictyonies has influenced numerous liberal scholars to contend that Israel was organized for service at a true central sanctuary. Martin Noth's writings have been particularly important; see *NHI*, pp. 87–88. On the basis of three lists of twelve descendants (Gen. 22:20–24; 25:13–16; 36:10–14) and one list of six (Gen. 25:2), Noth suggests that similar amphictyonic organizations may have existed among the Arameans, Ishmaelites, Edomites, and Keturah's descendants respectively. This position has come under significant criticism from both ends of the theological spectrum. Martin Woudstra, *The Ark of the Covenant from Conquest to Monarchy*

were the Delphic League of central Greece and the Etruscan League of Voltumna, both consisting of twelve member states. Most leagues were composed of either twelve or six members. The member states were not bound by central government but only by a central religious sanctuary, as in Israel. Usually each individual state had more self-government than Israel's separate tribes, however; and their concept of the god (gods) worshiped at the central place differed greatly from Israel's belief in Yahweh.

3. Priests and Levites

Religious personnel were important to the manner of worship that God had instituted in Israel. One entire tribe was devoted by God to provide this personnel, the tribe of Levi.[83] This tribe was considered by God as a substitution for the male firstborn, spared on the night of the initial Passover, and so otherwise claimed by God[84] (Exod. 13:1–15; Num. 3:40–51). Levites numbered twenty-three thousand males one month and older at the time of the conquest.[85] Among them, descendants of Aaron were declared to be priests,[86] and the eldest son of the continuing family was designated high priest.[87] Priests and Levites administered the tabernacle ceremonies. Priests did the sacrificing and Levites assisted. By David's time there were so many priests and Levites that twenty-four divisions were made (1 Chron. 24:1–31), with each division serving in turn for one week. A similar division must have been made at least among Levites already in the period of the Judges, for even then too many existed for all to serve at one time.[88]

(Philadelphia: Presbyterian and Reformed, 1965), pp. 122–25; and Norman K. Gottwald, *The Tribes of Yahweh* (Maryknoll, N.Y.: Orbis, 1979), pp. 345–86.

[83] To maintain the number of tribes at twelve, when one was thus removed, the tribe of Joseph was divided into two, Ephraim and Manasseh. Some liberal scholars believe that the term *Levites* never designated a family but only an office; see Oesterley and Robinson, *Hebrew Religion* (New York: Macmillan, 1930), p. 164. M. J. Meek, *Hebrew Origins* (New York: Harper, 1950), p. 121, himself a liberal says, "The unequivocal testimony of the Old Testament" is that the "Levites were originally a tribe."

[84] At Sinai, Moses numbered Israel's firstborn males older than one month (22,273) and, finding them more than Levites (22,000) by 273 he paid a five-shekel redemption tax for those extra (Num. 3:40–51).

[85] Some scholars question that to be a priest one had to be a descendant of Levi; see G. B. Gray, *Sacrifice in the Old Testament* (Oxford: Clarendon, 1925), p. 240. This questioning is based largely on the following texts: Judges 17:5; 2 Samuel 6:17–18; 1 Kings 3:4; 8:62–64; and especially 2 Samuel 8:18. Each text, however, finds an interpretation fully in keeping with the traditional view that priests had to be Levites; see an unpublished thesis, Leon J. Wood, *The Relationship of the Priests and Prophets in Pre-Exilic Israel as to Their Respective Teaching Functions*, pp. 146–49.

[86] The view of many higher critics that no distinction existed between priests and Levites until the time of Ezekiel must be rejected. The view holds that Ezekiel broached the idea of limiting the term *priests* to descendants of Zadok, and then that later writers broadened the number by assigning Aaron as the progenitor. For discussion, see S. R. Driver, *Introduction to the Literature of the Old Testament* (Edinburgh: T. & T. Clark, 1984), pp. 146–50.

[87] Aaron's two eldest sons—Nadab and Abihu—had died at Sinai (without children, Num. 3:4) for improper ceremonial observance, which left Eleazar and Ithamar, of whom Eleazar was the oldest, and so he became high priest. His eldest son in turn was Phinehas, and his son was Abishua, who—followed by their descendants—were successive high priests. How many other sons Eleazar and Ithamar may have had to help as priests at the time when service at Shiloh began is not known.

[88] If twenty-three thousand were one month and older (Num. 26:62), at least ten thousand must have been twenty-five years and older, the age when service began (Num. 8:24). Even to divide this group into twenty-four divisions would have given over four hundred to serve in any one week.

Map. 7. The Levitical Cities

a. Levitic cities. When at home, priests and Levites lived in specially assigned cities. They were not allotted tribal territory because they had lost tribal significance in being designated for religious service (Josh. 13:14; 21:1-3). These special cities were evenly divided among the tribes, averaging four to a tribe, for a total of forty-eight (Num. 35:1-8; Josh. 21:1-41).[89] Among these forty-eight, also evenly distributed, were six designated as "cities of refuge."[90] To these any person responsible for the death of another could flee and be protected there until determination of his guilt or innocence could be made (Num. 35:9-28; Josh. 20:1-9). If judged innocent, he should remain in safety from any avenger of blood by staying in the city until the death of the current high priest, after which he could return home and apparently be safe.

b. Teaching. Since priests and Levites lived most of the year in their own cities rather than at the tabernacle, and since they were supported by tithes of the people (Num. 18:20-28), which freed them from manual labor, they had time for another important religious function. That was teaching the people the Mosaic Law. Moses had received the Law and recorded it. The two stone tables engraved with the Decalogue were housed in the ark (Exod. 25:16, 21; Deut. 10:1-5), and the copy of the whole Law certainly was kept in or near the tabernacle. It told of Israel's covenantal relation with Yahweh and contained the civil and religious rules by which the people were to live. God had graciously revealed this vital information, but it needed to be communicated throughout the land if people were to respond. Some persons had to act as teachers, and those persons were the priests and Levites. God had commanded them to fill this need (Lev. 10:11; Deut. 33:10), and provided time and opportunity for it.

3. Urim and Thummim

In addition to the revealed, recorded Law, God supplied the priests and Levites with a special device for receiving further information from Himself. This was the Urim and Thummim, apparently consisting of objects (probably two) which could be contained in the pocket-type[91] linen "breastpiece" of the high priest, worn on the front of his ephod (Exod. 28:30; Lev. 8:8; Num. 27:21; Deut. 33:8; 1 Sam. 28:6; Ezra 2:63). The exact method by which God intended these objects to give the revelation is not stated.[92] Whatever it was, when so used, the Urim and Thummim did provide a way whereby God's will might be known, though perhaps limit-

---

[89]There were thirteen cities from Judah, Simeon, and Benjamin designated for priests (Josh. 21:13-19), all of which were not needed until some years had elapsed and priests had become more numerous, and thirty-five cities from the other tribes for Levites (Josh. 21:20-41). The only tribes with other than four cities were Judah and Simeon with nine between them, and Naphtali with three.

[90]On the west of Jordan were Kadesh in Naphtali, Shechem in Ephraim, and Hebron in Judah; on the east, Bezer in Reuben, Ramoth in Gad, and Golan in Manasseh. With this distribution of cities north, central, and south on both sides of the Jordan, no place in the land was more than thirty miles from a city of refuge.

[91]Exodus 28:15-16 describes the "breastpiece" as made of linen "—a span long and a span wide— and folded double [passive participle of *kaphal*]." Since no need existed for this doubling to give added strength, it must be that it was to form a pocketlike pouch.

[92]For discussion of suggested methods, see Leon J. Wood, "Urim and Thummim," *Theolog* (Winter 1964), pp. 25-32.

ed to a yes or no type of communication.[93] The question could be voiced and God would use this means to give answer. Only the high priest could use the objects, a limitation which safeguarded against improper use.

There was good reason for this device. Though the Law gave guidance for many areas of Israelite life, it did not, nor could not, serve all areas. Occasional questions were certain to arise, both of national[94] and local significance, that would not be answered there. A way was needed whereby direct revelation might be received from God. This was all the more true in Israel's theocratic form of government. There was need to be able to hear from God as king in regard to significant decisions. As to questions of local nature, these could be heard by priests and Levites living in the area, who then, if deeming the questions of sufficient importance, could bring them to the high priest for the inquiry.

God might not answer the question. Saul, asking regarding his pending, final battle with the Philistines, was refused (1 Sam. 28:6). This means that God kept full command in respect to Urim and Thummim inquiry. He did not have to give the revelation simply because someone placed a question. But the Urim and Thummim did give God's people a way by which inquiry could at least be inaugurated, and God might then respond and uniquely fill the role of King of His people.

4. Offerings

The law prescribed five types of offerings to be made at the tabernacle. Each symbolized a distinctive religious truth. Some were offered regularly and for the people collectively, others only on occasion and by an individual for himself.

a. Burnt offering (Lev. 1:5–17; 6:8–13). The burnt offering symbolized complete consecration of life to God, being consumed entirely on the altar. It was the principal regular sacrifice offered for the people collectively, and it was also made by individuals for themselves. As a collective sacrifice, a lamb was offered every morning and evening, two lambs on the sabbaths, and still more on feast days (Exod. 29:38–46; Num. 28:3–29:39). For the individual, a lamb, goat, bullock, or ram might be used, and was brought as an act of consecration to God. Certain occasions or situations required it: when priests were consecrated (Exod. 29:15; Lev. 9:12), when women were purified (Lev. 12:6–8), when lepers were cleansed (Lev. 14:19), when ceremonial uncleanness was removed (Lev. 15:14–15, 30), and when the Nazirite vow was broken (Num. 6:11, 14).

b. Meal offering (Lev. 2:1–16; 6:14–23). The meal offering symbolized full dedication of one's material possessions to God. It was unique from others in being bloodless, not involving any animal. Instead, grain was offered, and this might be presented in different

---

[93] Even if so limited, considerable information could be gained by voicing repeated questions. Identifications were actually made in this way, as, for instance, in the case of Achan (Josh. 7:16–18) and later Saul (1 Sam. 10:17–24). Some scholars, however (for instance, J. Barton Payne, *Theology of the Older Testament* [Grand Rapids: Zondervan, 1962], p. 48), believe God communicated directly to the mind of the high priest.

[94] For instance, as to the request of the Gibeonites, who wished for a treaty with Israel (Josh. 9:14). This time an inquiry should have been made and was not.

forms, but always with oil, frankincense, and salt. The meal offering regularly accompanied the burnt offering and was also entirely consumed. It might be brought by an individual, like the burnt offering, and if so, the priest then took only a handful of the presented grain for burning and kept the rest for tabernacle use. Every meal offering was accompanied by a drink offering of wine. The burnt, meal, and drink offerings were those most frequently made.

c. Sin offering (Lev. 4:1–35; 6:24–30). The sin offering was to atone for sins of ignorance.[95] Collective sin offerings were presented regularly on days of prescribed feasts. Individuals were expected to bring sin offerings to cover their own sins at any time. The type of animal prescribed varied partly with the economic status of the offerer (the more affluent the worshiper, the more valuable the animal) and partly with the nature of the offense. The most valuable animal designated was a young bullock, and the least a turtledove or young pigeon, which might be substituted in turn even by a "tenth of an ephah of flour" in case of extreme poverty.

d. Trespass offering (Lev. 5:1–6:7; 7:1–7). The trespass offering was similar to the sin offering except that it atoned for particular sins where restitution for some damage done to another could be made. The Mosaic Law specified that certain sins required the trespass offering (Lev. 5:15, 17; 6:1–2; 14:12; 19:20–22; Num. 6:12), with these usually calling for monetary compensation to the person

offended. The animal prescribed was normally the ram. The offering was always individual in kind; never collective.

e. Peace offering (Lev. 3:1–17; 7:11–34; 19:5–8; 22:21–25). Peace offerings were of three types: the thank offering rendered when unusual blessing had been experienced; the votive offering given in payment of a vow; and the freewill offering presented simply as an expression of love to God. Collective peace offerings were customary on festive occasions (1 Sam. 11:15; 2 Sam. 6:17), and were prescribed for the Feast of Pentecost (Lev. 23:19). Individual peace offerings were given voluntarily and the person might bring any of several types of animals. A primary feature was the sacrificial meal in which portions of the slain animal were eaten to symbolize fellowship between God and the person.

5. Three great feasts

The Israelite calendar called for three main annual feasts. Every male citizen was expected to come to Shiloh for these occasions.

a. Passover and the Feast of Unleavened Bread (Exod. 12:1–13:10; Deut. 16:1–8). This twofold feast was the first feast of the religious year and was the most important. It began on the fourteenth of Nisan (first religious month, March/April) with the observance of Passover. A prescribed meal was eaten in commemoration of the first Passover in Egypt. It then continued seven days with the Feast of Unleavened Bread, named from the

---

[95] Sins of ignorance were sins committed without deliberation. The person who committed deliberate sin, called presumptuous sin, or sin with a high hand, was to be "cut off from his people" (Num. 15:30–31).

163

kind of bread eaten. On the day of Passover a central feature was the slaying of a perfect lamb, selected four days before, as at the first Passover. On the seven following days, numerous sacrifices were offered each day, and the first and seventh days were days of rest and convocation for the people.

b. The Feast of Weeks (Exod. 23:16; Lev. 23:15–22; Num. 28:26–31; Deut. 16:9–12). This feast came at the close of wheat harvest and is thus sometimes called the Feast of Harvest (Exod. 23:16); this was when the first loaves made from the current harvest were offered and is thus sometimes called the Feast of Firstfruits (Lev. 23:17). Since it occurred exactly fifty days after Passover, it is sometimes called the Feast of Pentecost (Lev. 23:15–16; Deut. 16:9). It was observed one day only, with no work allowed and numerous offerings made, including the presentation of two loaves baked from the new harvest.

c. The Feast of Tabernacles (Exod. 23:16; Lev. 23:34–43; Deut. 16:13–15). This feast lasted one week, during which celebrants lived in booths or tents in commemoration of Israel's manner of life during the wilderness journey from Egypt. The feast began on the fifteenth of Tishri, the seventh month (September/October), at the close of the harvest season (thus sometimes called the Feast of Ingathering, Exod. 34:22). Many animals were sacrificed each day of the week, for a total of 71 bullocks, 15 rams, 105 lambs, and 8 goats, more than for any other festival.

6. Other religious occasions

Besides the three main feasts, other religious occasions also were observed by the nation Israel.

a. The Sabbath (Exod. 20:8–11; Num. 28:9–10; Deut. 5:12–15). Foremost and most frequent was the Sabbath, falling on the seventh day of each week, patterned after God's rest on the seventh day of the creation week, and serving as a reminder of God's deliverance of Israel from Egypt. No work was done, and the daily morning and evening sacrifices were doubled.

b. The New Moon (Num. 10:10; 28:11–15). Every new moon was celebrated by the blowing of trumpets and an increase in the daily offerings.

c. The Feast of Trumpets (Lev. 23:23–25; Num. 29:1–6). The new moon of the seventh month (Tishri, September/October) was announced by the blowing of trumpets and celebrated with an increased number of animals sacrificed. This day also marked the beginning of the civil year.

d. The Day of Atonement (Lev. 16:1–34; 23:26–32; Num. 29:7–11). This day, the tenth of the same seventh month, was one of the most important of the year. An elaborate ceremony at the Tabernacle displayed in symbolism the necessity of atonement for sin. On this day, the high priest, for the only time of the year, entered the Holy of Holies as a part of the ceremony in which atonement was made for the priesthood, the Tabernacle itself, and the people collectively. No person was to labor, and all were to fast.[96]

---

[96] "To fast" is the apparent meaning of to "deny yourselves" (Lev. 16:29; see Ps. 35:13; Isa. 58:3). The Day of Atonement was the only day of the year on which fasting was commanded.

e. The Sabbatical Year (Exod. 23:10–11; Lev. 25:1–7; Deut. 15:1–11).

Every seventh year the people were to refrain from working their land or pruning their vines. Spontaneous growth was to be shared by the poor, servants, and strangers. Debts of fellow Israelites were to be canceled.

f. The Year of Jubilee (Lev. 25:8–55; 27:16–25).

After seven consecutive sabbatical years (forty-nine years), a special Year of Jubilee (fiftieth year) was to be observed. Again the land was to rest, meaning that at this time there would be two consecutive rest years (forty-ninth and fiftieth), God promising that the forty-eighth year would be so abundant that all needs would still be supplied for the next two years. In this year all lost family inheritances were to be restored and all slaves who wished to be free were freed.

7. Prophets

Besides priests and Levites, Israel's religious personnel included prophets. Prophets had no prescribed responsibility with the central sanctuary, the offerings, or the festivals,[97] but fulfilled a vital mission of their own. The mission consisted of two basic functions: preaching and receiving revelation.

a. Preachers.

First and foremost, they were preachers of God's message. As noted, the priests and Levites were communicators also, but more in the role of teachers, instructing the people in God's Law, "line upon line, precept upon precept" (Isa. 28:9–13 KJV). Prophets were more preachers, addressing their message to the heart and will. The priests and Levites told the people what God had commanded in the Law; the prophets preached conformity to that standard. They were most frequently called upon to preach repentance and demand reformation after people demonstrated that they would not follow what priests had taught them.

b. Recipients of revelation.

They were also recipients of God's revelations; that is, revelations to supplement and explain the Mosaic Law. The one official recognition of prophets in the Law (Deut. 18:9–22)[98] concerns their place in this capacity. Israelites were not to resort to diviners to determine God's will, as in other countries, but they were to go to the prophet in whose mouth God would place His word. There was a difference between this prophetic revelation and that given through the priestly Urim and Thummim. The latter was a device by which the human instrument might initiate the revelation, as we have seen, but which was limited to mere affirmation or negation. In contrast, the prophet could only wait for God to speak; but then, when the revelation came, he received a full propositional message. Messages so given constituted basic portions of what the prophets preached.

---

[97] The view as held by Haldar, *Associations of Cult Prophets Among the Ancient Semites* (Uppsala: Almquist and Wiksells Boktrycheri, 1945), or Johnson, *The Cultic Prophet in Ancient Israel* (Cardiff: University of Wales Press Board, 1944), that prophets were cultic persons, finds no biblical basis and must be rejected.

[98] The Law recognized the prophets but did not give formal, legal standing or prescription as with priests and Levites.

c. Called to service. Prophets differed from priests and Levites also in that they did not receive their office by inheritance; instead, it was through a special call of God. Undoubtedly, prophets were fewer in number than priests and Levites, but also, being particularly selected, they were men of unusual gift, vision, and dedication. God's assignments led them to many places and situations, often difficult and even dangerous. They needed to be resourceful, courageous, and, especially, men of faith.

d. Number. Though prophets were never as numerous as priests and Levites, clues exist in Scripture that probably Israel was never without prophets and most of the time had a substantial number. This was true even during the Judges Period. Deborah is called a prophetess (*nebhi'ah;* Judg. 4:4), and an unnamed prophet is depicted as coming to warn the people of sin just prior to Gideon's call (Judg. 6:8–10). The casual manner in which each is mentioned suggests that these were in no way the only members of their kind then living. More significant is the indication of 1 Samuel 9:9 that before prophets were called "prophets" they were called "seers." To have reason for such name development, there must have been many representatives then living.[99] It is likely that from the time of Moses, Israel was never without prophets, and that during the early monarchy and especially the divided monarchy they became very numerous. Their influence for good in Israel should never be minimized.

---

[99] It may be added also that Moses' promise of Deuteronomy 18:15–19 suggests that numerous prophets would always be available to fill the task there described.

CHAPTER NINE

THE JUDGES

Judges 1–21; Ruth 1–4; 1 Samuel 1–8

With the Promised Land conquered and allotted to the respective tribes, a day God's chosen people had long anticipated was at hand. Six centuries earlier God had promised that Abraham's seed would become a nation and possess this land. Now the fulfillment of that promise had been realized. While the people had been in Egypt, they no doubt had longed for the day when they would have their own land. In Egypt they had been foreigners and even slaves, and then in the wilderness they had been restless transients. But now they were in a land of their own. They could plan for the future and carve out their own manner of life.

It was also a day of great promise. In that Israel had been raised up by God to be His special people, and in that God would desire such a people to be a fine witness to His glory, there was reason for Israel to anticipate success and prosperity. God indeed had clearly promised unusual blessing, stating that if the people followed Him faithfully, they would be "the head, not the tail" in their world community and so be "at the top" and "never at the bottom" (Deut. 28:1–14; 30:1–10). All that the Israelites needed to do was obey their heavenly Ruler and the most attractive future ever enjoyed by a nation awaited.

This grand future did not come to pass, however, because the people did not meet the condition. They did not remain true to their God or obey His laws. These wonderful blessings, therefore, were forfeited.

A. BACKGROUND MATTERS

1. Book of Judges

The Book of Judges is the main source of information for the period of time now to be considered.

While the Book of Judges is history, it is history of a particular type. Its point of view is that God rewards faithfulness to His covenant with peace and prosperity in the land, but punishes faithlessness with oppression by other nations. This basic theme must be understood if its message is to be appreciated. The key word for Judges is failure, the failure of Israel to live up to her God-given obligation.

A key verse, written twice (Judg. 17:6; 21:25), sounds this note: "Everyone did as he saw fit." The book shows how this was tragically true. The rationale for this type of historical report is found in the need to tell why Israel was not blessed by God as she might have been. She, who had owned such attractive prospects, did not realize them because she did not obey her God. The book depicts the many ways she failed.

Chapter 1 describes Israel's failure to drive the Canaanites from the land. Chapter 2 tells of her consequent acceptance of Canaanite Baal worship. Chapters 3 through 16 depict periods of oppression, brought as punishment, by Mesopotamians, Moabites, Canaanites, Midianites, Ammonites, and Philistines. Each period involved a cycle of Israel sinning, being invaded and severely oppressed, and then delivered by a judge raised up by God. Finally, chapters 17 through 21 narrate two sad episodes which illustrate the depths of religious, moral, and political degeneracy which generally characterized the period.

Even though this motif of failure dominates the book, it is not necessary to assume that the rebellious behavior described here was characteristic of all Israelites. It may not have been normative and certainly was not legally proper. We should be reminded that, while the depressing series of events recorded in Judges was taking place, at the same time the people of Bethlehem were living out apparently quiet lives

governed by law. The idyllic account of Ruth, with the trust in God's providence that underlies it, provides the other side of the coin and reminds us that, at her worst, Israel still contained people for whom the Law and their relationship with God was important.

2. The oppressions

a. Brought by local enemies. Most of the record in the Book of Judges, and most of the time involved in the period concerned, are occupied with the six foreign oppressions. It should be observed that none of these came from large, national powers of the day. Assuming a conquest in the early fourteenth century, the period of the judges was a time in world history when large powers were not engaged in an active domination of the area. Egypt's Eighteenth Dynasty rulers after Amenhotep III were all weaker than he and no longer interested in Canaanite control.[1] Both Seti I and his son, the great Rameses II, of the early Nineteenth Dynasty, did campaign north against the Hittites, but for the most part only passed through the coastal areas of Palestine.[2] Bethshan was occupied by both these rulers, but the valley region in which the city lay was yet under Canaanite control, and Israel still was little affected. Nineteenth Dynasty rulers after these two were again weaker, though Merneptah and later Rameses III of the Twentieth Dynasty did make temporary invasions of the regions.[3]

Great powers to the north did not invade southern Canaan during this period at all. The Hittites, against

---

[1] See p. 137.
[2] See pp. 84–86.
[3] For discussion as to why these inroads are not mentioned in Judges, see pp. 84–86.

whom Egypt particularly battled, were strong but were kept in check by these battles. The country of Mitanni of northern Mesopotamia was still vigorous in Joshua's time but shortly after was seriously curtailed in strength by the rising Hittites under the great Shuppiluliuma.[4] Assyria and Babylonia lay farther to the east and at this time did not play any significant role in the west. Southern Canaan, thus, was left quite to itself. Israel's enemies were the peoples of the area, small like herself. If one adopts a thirteenth-century date for the conquest, the great powers of the Near East had collapsed and were incapable of making inroads into Palestine.

b. Philistines, the most serious. Of all the local enemies, the most serious menace was the Philistines, the one Israel faced last. This people, as we have seen,[5] had been in the land to some extent from the days of Abraham but during the Judges Period came in far greater numbers. As part of the vast movement of the Sea Peoples, some of them had already been repelled by Pharaoh Merneptah (1238–1228), but they came in larger numbers against Egypt in the rule of Rameses III (c. 1195–1164),[6] between his fifth and eleventh years.

They were kept from infiltrating Egypt but not from retreating to and occupying land that Egypt yet claimed along the southern Canaanite shoreline.

Here, in an area previously assigned to Judah and Dan, the Philistines established a pentapolis, in which the five main cities were Ashkelon, Gaza, Ashdod, Ekron, and Gath, each of which had its own ruler (*seren*). After a period of adjustment, assimilating much of the Canaanite culture and religion, the Philistines made their presence known by vigorous military activity, which resulted in Israel's sixth oppression. One of the Philistines' chief sources of strength in their military success was a local monopoly on the manufacture of iron (1 Sam. 13:19–22), the secret of which they had probably learned from the Hittites.[7]

3. The Judges

The Book of Judges is named from the persons God selected to give leadership among His people during this period. Judges 2:16 says that God "raised up judges who saved them." Of most of these persons it is stated that they "judged Israel," and a specified number of years is given. Twelve names are normally included in the honored group. To this list sometimes are added Abimelech, Eli, and Samuel. Abimelech, son of Gideon, however, was more a renegade king than a judge, and both Eli and Samuel, though spoken of as "judging" Israel (1 Sam. 4:18; 7:15–17 KJV), were respectively more high priest and prophet.

For most of the "judges," their commission from God involved far more

---

[4] Shuppiluliuma (c. 1375–1340) was mainly responsible for the rise of the Hittite Empire. He made conquest as far south as the Lebanon mountains; see O. R. Gurney, *The Hittites* (Baltimore: Penguin, 1925).

[5] See p. 45.

[6] Dates uncertain (see p. 85n.102).

[7] Though meteoric iron was known as early as the third millennium B.C., the art of smelting iron appears to have been developed by the Hittites, who accordingly held a monopoly through most of the second millennium. Being much harder than bronze, it gave a monopolizing country enormous advantage over enemies. See Albright, *AP*, p. 110.

Name	Oppression	Reference
1. Othniel	Mesopotamians	3:7–11
2. Ehud	Moabites	3:12–30
3. Shamgar	Philistines	
4. Deborah with Barak	Canaanites	4–5
5. Gideon	Midianites	6–8
6. Tola		10:1–2
7. Jair		10:3–5
8. Jephthah	Ammonites	10:6–12:7
9. Ibzan		12:8–10
10. Elon		12:11–12
11. Abdon		12:13–15
12. Samson	Philistines	13–16

than what we would consider judicial functions. Their work was also military and administrative. Though military activity is only recorded for six of the twelve, this is the aspect for which they are best known, since the most detailed accounts in the biblical record concern tnis aspect. These descriptions of military activity on the part of the six will be noted later in the chapter. There is no record of military activity on the part of four of the judges (Jair, Ibzan, Elon, and Abdon) and only a passing reference for two others (Shamgar and Tola),[8] although it is not certain that these minor judges performed no military function.

All twelve seem to have been occupied for a varying number of years[9] with administrative responsibilities that may have arisen as a consequence of their demonstrated leadership in the military context. It would be natural for people to recognize leadership qualities in the men and women God raised up as deliverers and to continue to look to them for general civic management.[10]

Though the office of judge was not prescribed in the Law, it was approved by God. It is regularly stated that the persons filling it were "raised up" by God (Judg. 3:9, 15, et al.) and also that at least four[11] were especially enabled by the Holy Spirit.

4. A chronological problem

The Book of Judges presents a problem in chronology. The number of years indicated in the book for the numerous periods of oppression or

---

[8] Of Shamgar it is stated merely that he killed six hundred Philistines, and of Tola that he arose "to save Israel."

[9] The number is indicated for seven judges: Tola, twenty-three years; Jair, twenty-two; Jephthah, six; Ibzan, seven; Elon, ten; Abdon, eight; and Samson, twenty. The exact years for the others are not mentioned, though succeeding periods of rest are: Othniel, forty years; Ehud, eighty; Deborah, forty; and Gideon, forty. No figure is given for Shamgar.

[10] This name is the participial form of the verb *shaphat*. Its meaning transcends the concept of the word *judge* in English. The judge in ancient Israel combined judicial, military, and administrative functions. The *NIV* translates the word with "leader" which is much closer to the meaning of the Hebrew word (see Robert D. Culver's article שָׁפַט in *Theological Wordbook of the Old Testament*, 2 vols. [Chicago: Moody, 1980], 2:947).

[11] Othniel (Judg. 3:10), Gideon (6:34), Jephthah (11:29), and Samson (13:25; 14:6, 19; 15:14).

peace, including the time of Samson, add up to 410.[12] But even when the Exodus is placed at the early date, insufficient time exists to allow 410 years for these events.[13]

The reason is that 1 Kings 6:1 states that only 480 years elapsed between the Exodus and Solomon's fourth year, when he began to build the temple. That leaves only 70 years in which to locate the 40-year wilderness period, Joshua's time of leadership (perhaps 16 years), the period between Samson's demise and Saul's inauguration (no fewer than 5 years), Saul's 40-year reign (Acts 13:21), David's 40-year reign, and Solomon's first 4 years— 145 years altogether. Thus, the 410-year total for the events of Judges is at least 75 years too long.

The Book of Judges itself, however, suggests the solution; it implies that certain of these periods overlapped in time. For instance, Judges 3:30—4:1 mplies that Shamgar judged during the eighty years of peace following Ehud's deliverance from the Moabites. Judges 10:7 implies that Jephthah, occupied with the Ammonites east of the Jordan, and Samson, concerned with the Philis-

tines on the west, were contemporary in activity. Certain of the lesser judges, because they were active in particular, separated areas of the land, could well have worked at the same time—as, for instance, Tola, who judged in Issachar (Judg. 10:1–2), and Jair, who judged across the Jordan in Gilead (Judg. 10:3–5).

Careful study reveals that sufficient years may be properly accounted for to solve the problem, without doing injustice to the text. The extent to which this solution may be carried will differ, even within the ranks of conservative scholars.[14] It should be sufficient to note here that the chronologies of Judges may not be consecutive.

5. Canaanite religion

The conquering Israelites were quickly conquered in their turn by the religious practices of the Canaanites who were allowed to remain in the land. It is to this apostasy that the writer of Judges points as the cause for the series of oppressions recorded in the book. Ultimately, it would be the reason for the Exile.

The most significant Canaanite deity

---

[12] Mesopotamian oppression, 8 years (Judg. 3:8); Othniel's deliverance and rest, 40 years (3:11); Moab oppression, 18 years (3:14); Ehud's deliverance and rest, 80 years (3:30); Canaanite oppression, 20 years (4:3); Deborah and Barak's deliverance and rest, 40 years (5:31); Midianite oppression, 7 years (6:1); Gideon's deliverance and rest, 40 years (8:28); Abimelech's rule, 3 years (9:22); Tola as judge, 23 years (10:2); Jair as judge, 22 years (10:3); Ammonite oppression, 18 years (10:8); Jephthah's deliverance and rest, 6 years (12:7); Ibzan as judge, 7 years (12:9); Elon as judge, 10 years (12:11); Abdon as judge, 8 years (12:14); Philistine oppression, 40 years (13:1); and Samson's exploits, 20 years (15:20), totaling 410 years.

[13] See the discussion on pp. 70–71.

[14] For example, Samuel J. Schultz (*The Old Testament Speaks,* 3d ed. [New York: Harper & Row, 1980], p. 104) states that the author of Judges had no intention of producing a complete chronology and that any attempt to provide one is merely a suggestion. Gleason Archer (*SOTI*, pp. 276–77) contends that we "must conclude that many of these careers (of the Judges) overlapped," and that there is reason to assume that several of the judgeships were contemporaneous. It should be stressed that both these men would agree with the general chronological framework presented here, but might disagree on details. For an example of an evangelical scholar who takes a late date for the Exodus and conquest, stretching the position proposed here considerably beyond the limits of our chronological framework, see A. E. Cundall and Leon Morris, *Judges and Ruth* (Downers Grove, Ill.: InterVarsity, 1967), pp. 31ff.

was Baal, the storm god who controlled the rain and hence the fertility of the land. Canaanites believed that prosperity in the form of good crops and large herds depended on the pleasure of Baal. The theoretical head of the Canaanite pantheon was El, the father of the gods, but in practice it was the younger, more vigorous Baal who received the worship of the people.

The religious texts from Ras Shamra (ancient Ugarit) provide a clear picture of the beliefs and practices of the Canaanites.[15] Utilizing the common ancient motif of the dying and rising God,[16] the mythology describes Mot, god of death, killing Baal and holding him captive in the underworld. His death coincided with the annual onset of the dry season.

Then, when the autumn rains began to revive Canaan's parched vegetation, Anath, goddess of war and Baal's sister/wife, won his release to bring renewed fertility to the world. Asherah, though presented as wife of El, at Ras Shamra in lower Canaan appears as consort of Baal; and her carved pole is mentioned in the Old Testament as standing beside his altar (Judg. 6:25–28; 1 Kings 15:13).[17] Ashtaroth, goddess of fertility, love, and war, is also frequently linked with Baal in the Old Testament (Judg. 2:13; 10:16; 1 Sam. 7:3–4; 12:10).

The concepts of all three female deities (Anath, Asherah, and Ashtaroth) were somewhat fluid, tending to change and merge into one another so that clear distinctions were not always maintained. Prescribed worship of these deities involved religious prostitution, and the mythology includes stories of extreme brutality and immorality. Child sacrifice and snake worship were also observed.

The religion was decadent, and Israel sinned greatly and apparently continually by adopting it alongside the worship of Yahweh. The attraction was basically economic. Israelites wanted to be prosperous in their new agricultural pursuits, and they erroneously believed that adherence to the Baal cult was the way to accomplish this (see Hos. 2:5, 8).

B. FAILURE TO OCCUPY THE LAND FULLY
(Judges 1:1–3:7)

The prior chapter has shown that Joshua broke the strength of the Canaanites, but the individual tribes were expected to occupy their respectively assigned portions.[18] Not one tribe succeeded in occupying all the territory allotted, and cities listed as conquered in Joshua needed to be reconquered because of this failure.

Judah, with the help of Simeon (whose assigned cities lay in Judah's territory), pressed the attack first. In

---

[15] See Wright (*BAR,* pp. 106–16), Albright (*ARI,* chaps. 3, 4), and Unger (*AOT,* pp. 168–77).

[16] C. Gordon, however, disputes this commonly accepted viewpoint, denying the death-resurrection cycle. See his *Ugaritic Literature* (Rome: Pontifical Bible Institute, 1949), pp. 4–5; or *ANE,* p. 40.

[17] Some scholars believe that this was an image of the goddess, others that it was merely symbolic of her. See Albright, *ARI,* pp. 77–79; M. Burrows, *What Mean These Stones?* (New Haven: American Schools of Oriental Research, 1941), pp. 212–13.

[18] Liberal scholars have alleged a discrepancy between Joshua's record and that of Judges on this count, saying that Joshua presents the conquest as swift and complete, while Judges shows it as slow and partial. But Wright, *BAR,* p. 69, himself liberal, observes that "It has now become necessary to modify the common scholarly view" in recognizing that Joshua, too, particularly in chapter 13, indicates that much land remained to be occupied after the first successes.

Map 8. Area Actually Settled by Israelites

comparison with other tribes later, they did well, but still they "were unable to drive the people from the plains, because they had iron chariots" (Judg. 1:19). The "plains" here mentioned are likely the flat land toward the Mediterranean known as the plain of Philistia, named for its most famous occupants. Canaanites were still strong there and apparently had adopted the chariot,[19] an effective weapon in this level terrain.

Benjamin, we are told, failed to "dislodge the Jebusites, who were living in Jerusalem" (Judg. 1:21). Jerusalem was a formidable stronghold, and the Benjamites, though the occupation of their relatively small inheritance must not have required inordinate effort, did not succeed in taking it.

Dan, directly to Benjamin's west, was kept out of the fertile lowlands and, like Judah, restricted to the less desirable hill country. As a result, many of them[20] migrated north of Naphtali (Judg. 18).

Ephraim, who had already complained about her portion at the time of allotment, failed to take Gezer on her west (Judg. 1:29). If Gezer is the only place Ephraim failed to take, she did comparatively well, perhaps profiting from Joshua's earlier admonition (Josh. 17:14–18). It is likely, however, that Gezer only stands for rather extensive land in its vicinity, again the better flat land of the allotment.

Manasseh, next north, had problems in level areas, too. She failed to take Bethshan, Taanach, Dor, Ibleam, and Megiddo, with their respective regions (Judg. 1:27), all located either near the

Mediterranean or in the Esdraelon or Jordan valleys.

Issachar and Zebulun both found much of their assigned portions in the Esdraelon Valley, an area held by the Canaanites. The fortunes of Issachar remain unmentioned in Judges, but she probably fell short as well. Cities of the Esdraelon Valley do not evidence Israelite occupation this early, and the same valley saw the Egyptian Pharaohs Seti I and Rameses II make their inroads as far east as Bethshan less than a century later, apparently without greatly disturbing the Israelites.[21] Zebulun failed to take Kitron and Nahalol (Judg. 1:30), neither of which had been well identified but were probably in this valley.

As far as Asher and Naphtali are concerned, Asher failed regarding Acco, Sidon, Achzib, and Aphik, all well identified near the Mediterranean, and also Ahlab, Helbah, and Rehob, less well identified but again probably in the level area (Judg. 1:31–32). Naphtali did not dislodge the Canaanites from Bethshemesh or Bethanath, the latter being rather well identified with modern el-Ba'neh on the western edge of Naphtali.

In summary, the tribes were reasonably successful in the hill country, but not in the more attractive level regions. In those areas Canaanite population would have been larger and opposition greater. The Israelites took the less valuable hills and left the valleys to the former inhabitants. This was directly contrary to God's specific command (Deut. 7:1–4). Canaanites were to be

---

[19] Probably from the Egyptians, who had used the chariot effectively in establishing their empire earlier (see pp. 108–9). Southern Canaan was well within the Egyptian orbit of influence.

[20] See pp. 176–77.

[21] Bethshan, at the border of Manasseh and Issachar, was probably occupied by both Pharaohs; see pp. 84–86.

exterminated lest they turn Israelite hearts away from Yahweh to serve their false gods. This is what did happen in many localities. Accordingly, severe reprimand for unfaithfulness to God came early in the Judges Period, even from the "angel of the LORD" (Judg. 2:1–4), but while briefly prompting a repentant attitude, the rebuke did not significantly change the course on which the people had embarked. Consequently, disciplinary measures in the form of the severe foreign oppressions were necessary.

C. THE PERIOD OF MESOPOTAMIAN OPPRESSION (Judges 3:8–11; 17–21)

The first punishing oppressor came from the far north, Mesopotamia. In addition to considering the suffering and deliverance which resulted from this enemy, it is necessary to look here also at two representative accounts included at the close of the Book of Judges (chaps. 17–21), for they transpired at this same general time.

1. The oppression and deliverance (Judges 3:8–11)

a. Identity of Cushan Rishathaim. The leader of this Mesopotamian invasion bears the name Cushan Rishathaim. His country is called Aram Naharaim, meaning "Aram of the two rivers," a designation for Mesopotamia, which lies between the Tigris and Euphrates. Since this is the only oppressor who came from such a distant land, and since the Mesopotamian region did not otherwise have military

contact as far south as Israel at this time in history, considerable discussion has ensued as to the man's identity.

Some have thought that the spelling of "Aram" (*'rm*), his home country, is a copyist's mistake for "Edom" (*'dm*), so that the attack really came from this nearby southern country; especially since Othniel, the judge who opposed it, was himself a member of the southern tribe of Judah.[22] Garstang suggests differently that Cushan Rishathaim may have been the Hittite king who is known to have conquered Mitanni and later penetrated southward as far as Palestine about this time, leaving traces at Bethshan and elsewhere.[23] But M. Kline's suggestion, noted in chapter 5,[24] is perhaps likely. He believes that Cushan Rishathaim was a Habiru leader, who had entered the land primarily to crush Canaanites and who now, seeing Israel become strong, proceeded to subjugate her as well.

b. Conquest and deliverance. The record does not tell how this conquest was affected, nor how many tribes were involved. None of the other oppressions affected all of the tribes, and so likely this one did not either. The duration is given, however, as eight years. Toward the close of this time the people cried to God for relief, and He gave it through Othniel, younger brother of the renowned Caleb. Othniel had already distinguished himself in seizing Debir (Kiriath-sepher) at a former occasion, when his uncle had promised his own daughter Achsah as wife to the man who would accomplish the feat. Probably his abilities were remembered now, and he was called

[22] See G. Ricciotti, *The History of Israel*, 2d ed. (Milwaukee: Bruce, 1958), 2:244.
[23] John Garstang, *Joshua, Judges* (London: Constable, 1931), p. 62.
[24] See p. 84.

upon to lead against the Mesopotamians. No record is given of how he won the victory. It is significantly stated, however, that "the Spirit of the LORD came upon him" in achieving it. After the victory, the land had rest forty years before the next oppression.

c. Date. Assuming the early date for the conquest, this first oppression may be dated in the early second quarter of the fourteenth century. It cannot have followed Joshua's death immediately, for Judges 2:7 states that the people continued faithful to God during his time and that of the elders who outlived him. Since the oppression was permitted because of unfaithfulness, there had to be time for these elders to die and Israel's apostasy to occur. Given our proposed chronology, Joshua could hardly have died before 1390 B.C.,[25] which means this oppression cannot be placed much before 1375 B.C., fifteen years later.[26]

2. Two representative accounts (Judges 17–21)

Two representative accounts at the close of the Book of Judges fall into this period. One concerns the movement of Danites from their allotted territory to an area north of Naphtali (Judg. 17–18). In the other account, men of Gibeah violated a concubine of a certain Levite, and this resulted in war between Benjamin and the other tribes (Judg. 19–21). The first account must be placed this early in the period of the Judges because the Book of Joshua (19:47) mentions this Danite move, and that book was written while Rahab, rescued from Jericho, was still alive (Josh. 6:25). The other account must be placed this early because Phinehas, son of Eleazar, active during and even before the time of the conquest (Num. 25:7, 11; Josh. 22:13, 31–32), was still high priest (Judg. 20:28). Both accounts are narrated to illustrate the extent of both moral and religious falling away and certainly represent many others that might have been included.

a. Danite movement (Judg. 17–18). The first illustrates the seriousness of religious defection at this time. The Ephraimite Micah was given money by his mother, used it to make a silver idol and establish a private sanctuary, and installed his own son as priest. When a wandering Levite passed by, Micah hired him as his personal priest. About this time five Danites, looking for new and less hazardous land for their tribe, happened by Micah's house, saw this private religious arrangement, and were attracted by it. Later, when leading a contingent of 600 Danites to seize the new northern area they had selected, they again passed Micah's dwelling and urged the Levite to accompany them. The young man, clearly an opportunist, accepted the invitation and then took several of Micah's religious articles with him. Micah's strong protestations did not avail to stop the man or the theft.

The episode involved several factors contrary to the Law. Micah erred in making his own idolatrous sanctuary and consecrating his own son to serve as the idol's priest. The Levite was wrong for engaging in illegal priestly

---

[25] He lived to the age of 110 (Judg. 2:8) and likely was not much over 90 when the Jordan was crossed in 1406 B.C.

[26] Fifteen years may seem like a rather short time, but it would be adequate if we assume that Israel's apostasy began before all the elders died.

activity at the shrine of an idol-worshiping Ephraimite. The Danites were in error for moving from their allotted territory, for establishing their own private sanctuary, and for stealing the property of another to do it.

b. Gibeah outrage (Judg. 19–21).

The second incident reveals the extent of moral degradation in the land. The way in which the author of Judges relates the incident prompts the readers to think of Lot and his angelic visitors. The depravity at Gibeah was on a par with that of the Sodomites!

A Levite stopped with his concubine at Gibeah of Benjamin for the night. During the evening, men of the city came to the house where he stayed, and they demanded to have improper relations with him. The Levite offered them his concubine instead, and she was taken and abused. The Levite found her dead on the doorstep the following morning. In shock and anger he divided her body into twelve parts and sent a part to each tribe, demanding reprisal against Gibeah for the deed. The other tribes then called for the Benjamites to deliver to them the guilty persons, but they refused.

Civil war ensued, and, though Benjamin's force was much smaller,[27] she defeated the other tribes two times. The third time, however, she was defeated, Gibeah was leveled, and all Benjamites were killed, with the exception of six hundred men who fled to the rock of Rimmon. Four months later, the other tribes realized that now one tribe would be exterminated if wives were not provided for these six hundred who had escaped, and unusual measures were taken to do so.[28]

The initial sin involved in this account was the moral outrage committed by the people of Gibeah, first in their desire toward the Levite himself and then toward his concubine. This shows that serious degradation had developed among God's people, similar to that of Sodom in the days of Lot. Beyond that, the serious divisions among the tribes, the destruction of Jabesh-Gilead and the kidnapping of the young women of both Jabesh-Gilead and Shiloh all suggest a wholesale disregard for both the spirit and the letter of the Law. With sins of this magnitude occurring so soon after Joshua's day, the necessity for God's repeated punishments through the oppressions is easily understood.

D. THE PERIOD OF MOABITE OPPRESSION
(Judges 3:12–31)

1. The oppression and deliverance (Judges 3:12–30)

The second oppressing nation, Moab, lived close at hand. Moab lay immediately across the Dead Sea from Judah, south of the Transjordan tribes. It had been their king, Balak, who years before had brought the strange prophet Balaam to curse Israel when she was yet encamped east of the Jordan.

Now the Moabites, assisted in some part by Ammonites and Amalekites,

---

[27] The other tribes had four hundred thousand men (Judg. 20:17), about two-thirds of their potential fighting force (Num. 26:51). Benjamin had only twenty-six thousand (Judg. 20:15), slightly less than two-thirds of its tribal strength (Num. 26:41). See *KD*, 2:449–51, for good discussion.

[28] First, by seizing four hundred unmarried young women from Jabesh-Gilead (the city had not sent soldiers to help in the civil war) and giving these to the six hundred; second, by having some of the six hundred lie in ambush near the dancing area of the "girls of Shiloh" and taking wives from among them. These events clearly show the truth of the repeated statement, "Everyone did as he saw fit."

crossed the Jordan and occupied Jericho. Since Joshua had pronounced a curse on any who should rebuild this city (Josh. 6:26), and since 1 Kings 16:34 states that such rebuilding was done only much later by one Hiel the Bethelite, it is not likely that the Moabites had to dislodge any inhabitants here at this time. Probably the invaders simply moved on to the bare, unoccupied mound, erected a minimum of buildings for their temporary purpose,[29] and brought the Israelites of the area under their control. Eglon, a fat man, was their king. Using Jericho as a center, he kept the Israelites in servitude for eighteen years.

Finally Israel cried once more to God for relief, and God raised up a second deliverer, Ehud of Benjamin. If the date for Ehud is set not long after the civil war of Benjamin and the other tribes, this may have been one of the six hundred Benjamites who escaped to the rock of Rimmon. The deliverance Ehud effected was not through warfare, but through an act of deception in which he succeeded in slaying King Eglon. Ehud presented himself to Eglon to extend a gift from the subjugated Israelites. But having delivered the present, with all servants removed from the room, he drew near the king and plunged a sword into his body, killing him. Leaving the blade enclosed in the fat which engulfed it, he quietly left the room, locked the door after himself, and moved safely away while the deed remained undiscovered. Then Ehud quickly assembled Israelites at the fords of the Jordan where the Moabites, who could now be expected to retreat, would cross. The Moabites did retreat, and Ehud's men killed ten thousand of them. This brought a lengthy peace of eighty years to the land.

2. The eighty years of peace (Judges 3:30)

One reason for this eighty-year extension of peace, the longest such time during the Judges, may be found in the renewed activity of Egypt during this era. Our chronology would place these eighty years in the latter half of the thirteenth century.[30] A correlation of our biblical chronology and Egyptian dates would place these years during the influential rule of the strong Nineteenth Dynasty of Egypt, when power was exerted once again by Egypt in Palestine and southern Syria, particularly by Seti I (1316–1304) and Rameses II (1304–1238). Both rulers campaigned extensively against the Hittites, their forays carrying them through Palestine and bringing new territories in northern Palestine under their control.[31]

Such a display of power would have been well observed by small nations of the region, who, in reaction, would have refrained from undue overt activity that might call attention to themselves. All would have desired to avoid the displeasure of Egypt toward them. Consequently, local wars would not

---

[29] According to Garstang's calculations, the "Middle Building" (so named by him) above the spring could be the main building erected at this time; see pp. 92–95. When using Garstang's conclusions, however, it is only fair to acknowledge that they are repudiated by virtually all current archaeologists.

[30] The forty-year rest period after the Mesopotamian oppression (c. 1375–1367) brings us to c. 1327–1309 for the eighteen years of Moabite oppression, placing this eighty-year peace period c. 1309–1229.

[31] See pp. 84–86.

have been waged so long as Egypt was in the area, thus making for the period of peace.[32]

3. Shamgar
(Judges 3:31)

It was probably during this same eighty-year span that Shamgar lived as third judge. The brief record of his life following directly the record of Ehud's life; and Deborah, the next judge, mentions Shamgar in her victory song (Judg. 5:6) as at least having preceded her. He is called "son of Anath," which suggests that his home town was Bethanath, a southern city of Judah (Josh. 15:59). He later fought Philistines of the south, indicating that he did not come from a similarly named city in Naphtali to the north (Judg. 1:33). Shamgar is not called a judge, nor is he said to have done the work of one. He did, however, win a remarkable victory over Philistines, bringing deliverance to Israelites; and so, since he is listed in the overall account in parallel with other judges, he is best taken as one. His victory is described as a personal one, in which he demonstrated enormous strength and courage, killing no less than six hundred Philistines with nothing but an ox-goad.[33] That this wooden stick was his only weapon likely reflects the lack of iron in Israel, known from other sources as having been true for this time.[34]

E. THE PERIOD OF CANAANITE OPPRESSION
(Judges 4–5)

1. The oppression and deliverance (Judges 4–5)

a. Oppression (Judg. 4:1–3). The third oppression came from Canaanites within the land of Palestine, whom the Israelite tribes should have driven from the land years before. Jabin,[35] king of Hazor, was the leader, and Sisera[36] was his general. The city of Hazor, soundly defeated by Joshua some 170 years before,[37] had again become strong in the land. Sisera employed nine hundred chariots of iron[38] and made Harosheth,[39] about eleven miles northwest of Megiddo on the Kishon River, his center of activity. He was able to assert dominance and maintain control over Israelite tribes of the area for twenty years.

b. Deborah and Barak (Judg. 4:4–9). Israel's principal deliverer this time was a woman, Deborah, unique among the twelve judges, not only

---

[32] Garstang, *Joshua, Judges,* pp. 51–56, believes that there was correspondence between Egyptian activities and all of Israel's peace periods during the time of the judges. He has difficulty making the correspondences, however.

[33] The ox-goad was merely a stout stick, often bronze-tipped, used to guide and impel oxen at work.

[34] Note especially 1 Samuel 13:19–22; see above, p. 169n.7.

[35] Same name as that of the king Joshua defeated; but this does not mean that this account and that found in Joshua 11 are mixed accounts, as held by some liberals; see Myers and Elliott, *Interpreter's Bible,* 2:12–24.

[36] The name *Sisera* has made some scholars think of this general as one of northern origin, who had allied himself with Jabin; see Simpson, *The Composition of the Book of Judges* (New York: Macmillan, 1957), pp. 12–24.

[37] Joshua's defeat was c. 1400 B.C. and the date here c. 1230.

[38] Canaanites had employed chariots for some time (see *ANET,* p. 237), but Israel, confined mainly to the mountains, had little use for them. They are first mentioned as used by Israelites with Absalom, 2 Samuel 15:1.

[39] Probably modern Tell el-Harbaj, a six-acre site on the south bank of the Kishon River, at the foot of Mount Carmel.

because she was a woman, but also because she was acting as judge even before her victorious battle. She is called a prophetess (*nebhi'ah*), and people are said to have come to her for counsel, which no doubt included judicial decisions. She received people under a palm tree located between Ramah and Bethel, some sixty miles south of where the battle with Sisera later took place. Already recognized for leadership, she was the logical one to initiate any deliverance from the Canaanites. She called on Barak, a man of Kedesh, far to the north in Naphtali,[40] to assemble an army. He consented, provided she would participate with him. When she agreed he gathered an army of ten thousand men from Zebulun and Naphtali, apparently the two tribes most affected by the oppression.

c. Deliverance (Judg. 4:10–5:31). Barak brought his army south to Mount Tabor and joined battle with Sisera west of Megiddo (Judg. 5:19) on the banks of the Kishon. From Deborah's later song (Judg. 5:21), it is learned that during the conflict the Kishon overflowed and mired Sisera's chariots. This made victory by Deborah and Barak possible, and they pursued the fleeing enemy back to Harosheth. Meanwhile, Sisera personally fled northward, in an apparent attempt to reach Hazor. On the way, he took refuge in the tent of a Kenite named Jael, who lived near Barak's home town of Kedesh (Judg. 4:11); and she, under

guise of friendship, killed him by driving a tent peg through his skull. Forty years of peace followed.

2. Inroads of Merneptah and Rameses III

Two instances of Egyptian inroads into Palestine in this general time, not mentioned in the Book of Judges, call for notice. The first was by Merneptah (1238–1228) in his fifth year,[41] and the second was by Rameses III (c. 1195–1164).[42]

Merneptah's main activity lay close to the Mediterranean, where he claimed victories at Ashkelon, Gezer, and Yanoam.[43] His contact, therefore, was principally with Canaanites, though he states in general terms that "Israel is laid waste." This last may be something of a boast, however, for he lists no Israelite cities as plundered, and, when he refers to Israel, he does so using the determinative of people and not land.[44] From this it would appear that he defeated Israelite people in battle, but did not gain control of any significant portion of their land.

The fighting of Rameses III seems also to have been limited mainly to the Philistine area, with later battles conducted south of Israelite territory below the Dead Sea.[45] At least he does not list battles fought within Israelite territory proper. He did reach and carry on building activity at Bethshan in the Jordan Valley, but he does not mention any conflicts with Israelites in doing so. The occupation of Bethshan, a bastion

---

[40] Identified with Tell Qades, northwest of drained Lake Huleh.

[41] See p. 80n.82 and p. 85.

[42] See pp. 45, 85, 169.

[43] *ANET*, p. 278. Yanoam was in northern Palestine.

[44] In this inscription otherwise, he uses the "determinative of land" for those conquered. See *ANET*, p. 378n.18, for a different interpretation regarding this change in the determinative.

[45] Regarding Philistines, he boasts of having reduced both the "Tjeker and the Philistines" to ashes; *ANET*, p. 262. See above, p. 85n.105. Regarding the Edom area, see *ANET*, p. 262n.21.

of Seti I and Rameses II,[46] appears to have been relatively peaceful.[47] Apparently, he had marched his army on north after the Philistine action and then turned to move eastward the length of the Esdraelon Valley to Bethshan,[48] accomplishing all this without major conflict.

These two invasions may be correlated with the Judges Period in the following manner. Merneptah's campaign, dating c. 1234 B.C., would have come at the close of the eighty-year period of peace that followed Ehud's deliverance from the Moabites and preceded the Canaanite oppression. As the dominance of Egypt's Nineteenth Dynasty had served to maintain this eighty-year period of peace earlier, this further Egyptian influence could have served to prolong it at the close of the period.[49]

The invasion of Rameses III would have followed the Canaanite oppression, falling in the forty-year peace period that then ensued. It may have played a role in prolonging this season of peace. Why the Book of Judges makes no mention of either invasion has been discussed in chapter 5. In a book designed to describe Israel's deviant behavior and resulting punishments, there simply was no reason to mention foreign campaigns that did not bring punishing oppression on Israel.

F. THE PERIOD OF MIDIANITE OPPRESSION (Judges 6:1–10:5; Ruth 1–4)

A series of annual raids by the Midianites is recorded following the mention of the forty years of peace that ensued after the great victory of Deborah and Barak. This oppression must be considered now as well as the tragic three-year reign of the renegade king, Abimelech, which followed. Two minor judges, Tola and Jair, and the account of Ruth also bear mention.

1. The oppression and deliverance (Judges 6–8)

a. Oppression (Judg. 6:1–6). The fourth oppression was brought by Midianites aided by Amalekites and "other eastern peoples."[50] This combined enemy came from the east to plunder the fine grain-growing areas of Israel, principally the Esdraelon Valley and the Mediterranean coastlands as far south as Gaza (Judg. 6:4). For six years the invaders stripped these areas of both livestock and grain, apparently without opposition. The fearful Israelites' response was to take refuge in caves.

b. Warning (Judg. 6:7–10). When the people cried for relief this time, God first sent an unnamed prophet to warn them concerning their sin. That a prophet was available suggests that prophets were indeed active during the

---

[46] See pp. 84–86.

[47] See Wright, *BAR*, pp. 95–96.

[48] Bethshan, modern Tell el-Hosn, gives indication of almost continuous Egyptian control from the time of Thutmose III to Rameses III. Manasseh had been allotted Bethshan and had found it too difficult to occupy (Josh. 17:16; Judg. 1:27). Opposition to Egyptian occupation, then, would have been from Canaanites, not Israelites. For a brief survey of the Archaeology of Bethshan, see Frances James, "Beth-Shean" in *EAEHL*, 1:207–25.

[49] For dates involved, see above, p. 178n.30.

[50] "Other eastern peoples" seems to have been a general designation for desert tribes, much like the term "Arabs" today.

Judges Period.[51] There is little evidence that his preaching brought repentance; but, even so, God still graciously provided a deliverer, Gideon. God called this one to service through an appearance of the angel of Yahweh.

c. Gideon, the deliverer (Judg. 6:11–7:6).

Gideon lived in Ophrah, a village of Manasseh, likely located in the Esdraelon Valley,[52] the center of the Midianite attacks. The people of Ophrah had accepted Baal worship so completely that they had built their own Baal altar and Asherah symbol.[53] God's first directive to Gideon was to destroy these objects, which he did at great personal risk, showing true courage and faith (Judg. 6:25–32). This act, so unpopular at first that the townspeople wanted to kill Gideon, later served to inspire the people to accept him as leader.[54] Some 32,000 responded from the tribes of Manasseh, Asher, Zebulun, and Naphtali when he called for troops to fight the invading Midianites.[55]

As Gideon saw the enemy host appear, numbering some 135,000 (Judg. 8:10), he believed his 32,000 were too few to do battle. Gideon's request for divine reassurance, using the well-known sign of the fleece, may have been to bolster his flagging faith, or may have been for the benefit of his newly gathered army (Judg. 6:33–40). God granted the request but then said that the 32,000 were really too many, rather than too few. Gideon should reduce the number in order that God might receive credit from the people for the victory when it had been won. Gideon obeyed, first by permitting all who were fearful of heart to return home and then testing to see which men would drink from a brook in a manner showing readiness for battle.

This left him only 300 men, an unbelievably small number to face 135,000. Certainly Gideon's faith was challenged in view of such odds, but God had commanded the reduction, and Gideon prepared for the encounter. No doubt he wondered, however, how the battle could possibly be won.

d. Deliverance (Judg. 7:7–8:32).

The eve of the battle found the enemy encamped in the Esdraelon between Mount Gilboa on the south and Mount Moreh on the north. Gideon's men were gathered near the well of Harod at the foot of Gilboa, armed with trumpets and pitchers containing torches.[56] He divided his tiny force into three sections, deployed it around the edge of the enemy camp, and attacked by night. The simultaneous sounding of the three hundred trumpets and flaring up of the three hundred torches, taken by the Midianites as the signal for a coordinated attack from all sides, ignited panic among the enemy forces. They bolted

---

[51] See pp. 165–66.

[52] The location of Ophrah is uncertain, with modern et-Tayibeh, eight miles northwest of Bethshan, favored. The Esdraelon Valley no doubt had come under Israelite control increasingly after the defeat of the Canaanites by Deborah and Barak.

[53] See p. 172n.17.

[54] When Gideon experienced no harm from Baal (Judg. 6:31), he emerged as victor over Baal and received the name Jerubbaal, meaning "let Baal contend" (Judg. 6:32).

[55] The date was c. 1169 B.C. The Canaanite oppression had lasted twenty years, c. 1229–1209, and the peace period forty years, c. 1209–1169; see above, p. 178n.30.

[56] Chosen likely for two reasons: they were weapons to effect surprise, and probably Gideon had few if any normal weapons in view of enemy dominance for the past seven years.

and ran, heading for the Jordan and home.

Gideon quickly sent word to the Ephraimites to cut off the enemy's escape at the Jordan. They responded, catching the Midianites and killing two of their leaders, Oreb and Zeeb (Judg. 7:23).[57] At this time, too, some of the troops, who had gone home when given the chance, returned to help in the chase (Judg. 7:23). Gideon pursued the enemy to their home country where he completed the rout by killing two main leaders, Zebah and Zalmunna. En route, Gideon had requested food for his troops from the people of Succoth, south of the Jabbok (Gen. 33:17), and also nearby Penuel, but had been refused by both cities, each time in fear of reprisal from the enemy (Judg. 8:6–8). On his return he punished both cities severely.

When he returned home, Gideon was pressed to accept kingship over the people, but he refused, deferring to God as ruler. He did err, however, in accepting gold earrings, taken as spoil, with which to make an ephod, presumably like that worn by the high priest.[58] Gideon sinned in thus presuming to enter upon the prerogative of the priesthood, and the wrong was amplified when later the object came to be worshiped by the people (Judg. 8:24–27). The country had quietness for forty years while Gideon lived.

2. The renegade king, Abimelech (Judges 9)

At Gideon's death, peace was again broken, now not by an outside enemy, but by three years of treachery and bloodshed at the hand of Abimelech, the renegade Israelite who had himself proclaimed king. He was a son of Gideon by a concubine in Shechem (Judg. 8:31), but he did not share his father's love for peace or humility. Instead, he actively sought the kingship. Supported by his mother's family in Shechem, he murdered all but one of his seventy brothers, whom he considered potential rivals. Only Jotham, the youngest, escaped.

Abimelech was crowned by the Shechemites, who were glad to have a king from their own number. He reigned for three years, though the extent of his actual control was probably quite limited. After three years, the Shechemites had experienced enough of his arbitrary ways and revolted, seeking leadership from one Gaal, head of a roving band. In the resulting war, Abimelech was able to crush Gaal's force at Shechem, even burning many of the people alive when they took refuge in the temple of Baal-berith[59] (Judg. 9:23–49). Moving on to Thebez[60] to crush further resistance, however, he was killed when a woman dropped a millstone[61] on his head (Judg. 9:50–57).

---

[57] Timewise this was possible, for the Midianites could have moved only slowly with their flocks and herds. The places mentioned to which they fled near the Jordan, Beth-shittah and Abel-meholah, are best identified south of the original battle area near to the Ephraimite territory. Ephraimites did not have far to go to intercept them.

[58] This was not an image as advocated by some scholars. Gideon, knowing that God had been revealing His will through him, and knowing of probable deficiency in the priesthood in using the true ephod for revelation, somehow improperly believed that he should now assume this "mantle" for himself.

[59] Following Gideon, the people sadly had returned to the old Baal worship (Judg. 8:33–34).

[60] Modern Tubas, about ten miles north of ancient Shechem toward Bethshan.

[61] Likely the upper small millstone, which in grinding grain was moved back and forth on the lower larger one. It was usually about ten inches long and of a size easily gripped.

3. Judgeships of Tola and Jair
(Judges 10:1–5)

Two minor judgeships followed (probably contemporaneous).[62] The two judges served in widely separated parts of the country and so could have been active without mutual interference. Tola, of the tribe of Issachar, judged in Shamir, Ephraim, for twenty-three years. Jair judged in an unidentified city of Gilead across the Jordan for twenty-two years. Little is known of either person. Tola is said to have defended Israel, though without explanation; and Jair is said to have had thirty sons, riding on thirty ass colts, living in thirty cities, which suggests that he was an individual of unusual position and wealth.

4. The account of Ruth
(Ruth 1–4)

The well-known life (especially the marriage) of Ruth transpired in the last half of the twelfth century, possibly during the time of Gideon's judgeship. The general date is ascertained from the fact that Ruth was the great-grandmother of David (Ruth 4:17), who began his rule at Hebron c. 1010 B.C. She was a Moabitess and had married into the Israelite family of Elimelech and Naomi, who had migrated to Moab from Bethlehem-Judah in time of famine. Elimelech died in Moab, leaving his wife, Naomi, and two sons, Mahlon and Chilion. Ruth married Mahlon (Ruth 4:10), and another Moabitess, Orpah, married Chilion. Then both sons died, leaving all three women widows. At this point, Naomi returned to Bethlehem. Both daughters-in-law left with her, but only Ruth continued, vowing never to leave Naomi and to accept Naomi's people as her own. At Bethlehem, Ruth gleaned grain in the field of Boaz (Elimelech's wealthy relative), who then married her. To them was born Obed; to Obed, Jesse; and to Jesse, David.

G. THE PERIOD OF
AMMONITE OPPRESSION
(Judges 10:6–12:15)

The four oppressions considered thus far did not cause the people to change their ways. In fact, their sin seemingly increased as they came to serve not only the false gods of Canaan, but also of Syria, Sidon, Moab, Ammon, and the Philistines (Judg. 10:6). Consequently, God now brought oppression from two quarters simultaneously: from the Ammonites east of the Jordan, and from the Philistines to the far west (Judg. 10:7). The date was c. 1096 B.C.[63] The biblical account narrates the Ammonite oppression first.

1. The oppression and deliverance
(Judges 10:6–11:33)

The Ammonite oppression was experienced mainly on the east of the Jordan, though somewhat also in Judah, Benjamin, and Ephraim on the west (Judg. 10:9). God's deliverer this time was Jephthah, the son of a Gileadite named Gilead and a harlot (Judg. 11:1–3). Gilead's younger sons had driven their older half-brother from home because of his illegitimacy, and

---

[62] See p. 171. The words "after him" of Judges 10:3 (KJV) need refer only to Jair beginning after Tola began and not necessarily after Tola finished.

[63] Since the beginning of the Midianite oppression in 1169 B.C. (see above, n.55), seventy-three years had elapsed in four time periods: Midianites (seven), peace under Gideon (forty), Abimelech (three), and Tola and Jair (twenty-three).

Jephthah had since demonstrated military ability in leading a roving band[64] in the land of Tob,[65] north of Gilead.

When Ammon now invaded the land, elders of Jephthah's home territory found him and asked him to return and lead against this enemy. He agreed, but only upon their promise that he could continue as leader after Ammon had been defeated. Jephthah, rejected earlier, did not want to be insulted again.

Jephthah first tried to reach a settlement with the Ammonite king by negotiation but did not succeed. The foreign ruler would not accept Jephthah's argument that the land now rightfully belonged to Israel since she had held it for three hundred years. Then Jephthah, especially enabled by the Spirit of Yahweh, prepared for open conflict by raising troops from Manasseh and Gilead.[66] Establishing his headquarters at Mizpah in Gilead, he moved against the Ammonite army and won a decisive victory, seizing no less than twenty cities located between Minnith and Aroer[67] in an area formerly allotted to Reuben.

2. Jephthah's vow
(Judges 11:30–31, 34–40)

Eager for divine assistance as he entered battle, Jephthah vowed that if he were victorious he would offer to God whatever first came from his house to meet him on returning home. When he did return, it was his daughter and only child who greeted him. Jephthah lamented deeply, for apparently he had not seriously contemplated this eventuality. He resolved, however, to keep his vow.

This account is one of the more troubling in the Book of Judges. The plain reading of the text would seem to indicate that Jephthah offered his daughter as a human sacrifice. An alternative, and more palatable, interpretation suggests that he devoted her to the service of God at the tabernacle for the rest of her life. A number of arguments can be marshaled in favor of this position.

Three factors weigh against a human sacrifice. First, for Jephthah to have offered his daughter as a human sacrifice would have been contrary both to Mosaic Law (Lev. 18:21; 20:2–5; Deut. 12:31; 18:10) and Israelite practice. Prior to the wicked reigns of Ahaz and Manasseh much later (2 Kings 16:3; 21:6), no record of human sacrifice by Israelites—even by those who followed Baal—is found. Second, Jephthah's respect for God would have kept him from violating the Law and Israelite practice. This respect is demonstrated both in his manner of making the covenant with the Gileadite elders and in his very desire to make the vow at all. Third, if he did sacrifice his daughter, his piety would have led him to do so at the proper place of sacrifice (the tabernacle), but no priest would have been willing to officiate. If he had

---

[64]Perhaps after the pattern of David's later band; see 1 Samuel 22:2; 25:14–16; 27:7–12; 30:1–31.

[65]An area east of the Sea of Galilee. From here soldiers were later hired by Ammon in the Israel–Ammon conflict to fight against David (2 Sam. 10:6–8).

[66]Gilead included land even north of Gad, but since Manasseh (half-tribe on the east of Jordan) is also specified here, it must mean primarily Gad in this instance.

[67]Aroer is well identified on the north bank of the Arnon River about fourteen miles east of the Dead Sea. Minnith is believed to have been located directly north about even with the north end of the Dead Sea.

tried to prepare the sacrifice in his home country, certainly elders there, as well as people generally, would have strongly objected.

Four factors point to perpetual celibacy. First, that Jephthah permitted his daughter to bewail her virginity (Judg. 11:37–38) for two months suits well the idea of her soon being devoted to God in perpetual celibacy. Second, the notice that the daughter "was a virgin" (Judg. 11:39), given as a result of Jephthah having carried out his vow, has particular point if her offering concerned the matter of celibacy. Third, there is evidence for believing that such service for devoted women did exist at the central sanctuary (Exod. 38:8; 1 Sam. 2:22; Luke 2:36–37). Fourth, the pivotal statement of Jephthah in Judges 11:31 ("[It] will be the LORD'S, *and* I will sacrifice it as a burnt offering") may be translated with the conjunction "or." Thus, the first part would refer to what Jephthah would have done if a human first had met him—the second, if an animal.

It should be noted here, however, that if Jephthah did in fact sacrifice his daughter, the text contains no note of approval. Rather, it simply records a reprehensible act that, by this interpretation, reflects the low level of religious understanding found in the land during this dark period.

3. Ephraimite complaint (Judges 12:1–7)

Following Jephthah's victory over the Ammonites, the men of Ephraim complained at not having been asked to assist,[68] showing again that they thought their tribe was of prime importance.[69] Jephthah tried to appease them with words, but to no avail. Their feelings had been hurt, and they intended to make Jephthah realize this by force. They joined in battle against Jephthah on the east of the Jordan. Their army, however, was no match for Jephthah's troops, who won a decisive victory and moved quickly to control the fording places of the Jordan, which retreating Ephraimites would have to use. The victors tested all who wished to cross by making them pronounce the word *shibboleth*. All who said *sibboleth*, using the *s* sound in place of the *sh*, were taken as Ephraimites and killed.[70] A total of forty-two thousand Ephraimites lost their lives either in the battle proper or at the Jordan. This sorry affair serves to illustrate the gulf that had developed between Israel's tribes.

These events completed, Jephthah continued as judge for six years. The promise of the Gileadite elders was kept, for the people did acknowledge him as their leader after the Ammonite victory.

4. Judgeships of Ibzan, Elon, and Abdon (Judges 12:8–15)

Following Jephthah's judgeship there were three minor judges, perhaps somewhat contemporaneous again.[71] Ibzan judged in Bethlehem for seven years and had thirty sons and thirty

---

[68] This was the second such complaint, the first following Gideon's Midianite victory (Judg. 8:1–3).

[69] See p. 154n.66.

[70] Apparently Ephraimites were accustomed to pronouncing the letter *shin* like the *samech*. "Shibboleth" means "flowing stream," a reference here to the Jordan.

[71] Whether they were or were not does not have significance now for the overall chronology, for the Philistine oppression next considered was contemporary with all three either way.

daughters. Elon judged in Ajalon of Zebulun to the north for ten years. Abdon judged in Ephraim, half-way between, for eight years. Abdon's wealth and position are indicated by the fact that he had forty sons and thirty grandsons (sons of sons).

H. THE PERIOD OF PHILISTINE OPPRESSION (Judges 13–16)

1. The oppression (Judges 10:7; 13:1)

The sixth and last great oppression recorded in Judges was brought by the Philistines. According to Judges 10:7, the time was roughly contemporary with the oppression of the Ammonites.[72] The Philistines had come into the land in force during the first quarter of the twelfth century, which by our chronology would have been in the forty-year peace period following the victory of Deborah and Barak over the Canaanites.

It was now approximately one century later, and the Philistines had become firmly entrenched and strong. Their plans for conquered Israelite land differed from those of prior oppressors, who seem to have thought mainly in terms of exploitation by plunder or tribute. The Philistines were interested in more permanent control. The others were members of groups with long standing in the region, but the Philistines were newcomers and ready to challenge old residents for all they could seize. They had a war-like tradi-tion, having been one division of the migrating, rampaging Sea Peoples, and they were prepared in both knowledge and temperament to press their challenge vigorously and long.

It should be realized, too, that Canaanites were as much an object of this aggression as Israel,[73] and there is reason to believe that the Philistines did in time seize land from them as far north as the Esdraelon Valley, and then through the Valley east all the way to the Jordan.[74] The Philistines were able to impose their will on Israel for forty years, the longest of any of the oppressions; and they later continued to do so periodically throughout the reign of Israel's first king, Saul.

2. Samson (Judges 13:2–16:31)

God's man to counter the Philistines was Samson. His father was Manoah, a Danite who had not migrated north with others of his tribe. Importance was lent to Samson's birth by a prior announcement through the Angel of Yahweh (Judg. 13:3–23). The son to be born would be a Nazirite, which means, among other things, that his hair was not to be cut (Num. 6:1–13). Samson's place of birth was Zorah, located at the boundary line between Israelite and Philistine land.

Samson's contact with the enemy was different from that of other judges. He did not lead an army to battle, but he did go alone among the Philistines, working havoc by feats of enormous

---

[72] This contemporaneousness fits other factors, too. With Saul beginning to reign c. 1050 B.C., the battle of Mizpah (1 Sam. 7:7–14) could not have been after c. 1055 B.C., which means the forty-year Philistine oppression (Judg. 13:1) must have begun c. 1095 B.C. The Ammonite oppression came c. 1096 B.C. (p. 184n.63).

[73] This would have tended to make allies of Canaanites and Israelites, something giving further reason for God's original order that Canaanites should be driven completely from the land.

[74] See p. 192n.95.

strength. This strength was not the result of unusually large stature (at least no hint is given in the biblical account to this effect) but of special enablement by the Spirit of God,[75] his dedication to God being symbolized particularly in Samson's uncut hair. Through this strength he was able to kill many of the enemy, but unlike the other judges, Samson only began the deliverance of Israel (Judg. 13:5).

His acts of mayhem apparently disrupted a co-existence between the Philistine lords and their Israelite vassals. It could well be that his contribution to Israel's deliverance was to cause an intensification of Philistine oppression which in turn lead to a new turning to God. Numerous accounts concern Samson's feats, and these may be only representative of others of like kind that could have been included.

3. Samson's feats of strength (Judges 14–15)

a. Wedding incidents. Samson's first demonstrations of strength came in connection with his marriage to a Philistine girl of Timnah.[76] He wished to marry the girl and persuaded his parents to arrange the wedding, in spite of their disapproval.[77] On the way to visit her on one occasion, Samson encountered a lion and killed it with his bare hand. On a later visit he found the lion's carcass holding a swarm of bees and honey, from which fact he propounded a riddle to the Philistine guests at the seven-day feast of his wedding. They were able to solve it only by forcing his bride to deceive Samson into telling her the answer, so that she could tell them. Realizing what they had done, Samson paid the agreed-upon reward, thirty changes of clothing, by slaying thirty Philistines at Ashkelon[78] and taking theirs.

b. Wheat harvest feats. The second demonstrations occurred within a year, during wheat harvest (Judg. 15:1–19). Samson returned to claim his bride, having had time to assuage his first anger, but he was told that she had been given to another. In retaliation, he caught three hundred foxes, tied firebrands to pairs of them joined by their tails, and released them to burn Philistine crops. The Philistines reacted by burning Samson's one-time bride and her father to death. Samson avenged their death by slaughtering many of the enemy. Then he moved back to Israelite territory, taking up a position "in a cave in the rock of Etam,"[79] where three thousand of his own people, afraid of Philistine retaliation, came to capture him. His countrymen promised not to hurt him themselves, so Samson permitted himself to be bound and deliv-

---

[75] This is stressed by mention four times (Judg. 13:25; 14:6, 19; 15:14). Of no other judge is similar mention made more than once.

[76] Rather well identified with Khirbet Tibneh, only four miles southwest of Zorah. Originally allotted to Dan (Josh. 19:43), it was at this time controlled by Philistines and later changed hands more than once (2 Chron. 28:18).

[77] Though Israelite marriage was expressly prohibited only with Canaanites (Deut. 7:3–4), the reasons for this prohibition were as true regarding Philistines. Samson's parents, therefore, were right in believing the marriage improper.

[78] Ashkelon was the port city of the Philistine pentapolis, located about twenty-three miles southwest of Timnah.

[79] The site is unknown but may be the same as an Etam later rebuilt by Rehoboam (2 Chron. 11:6). It must have been in western Judah.

ered to the Philistines in Lehi.[80] But once among them he easily burst his ropes and killed a thousand of the enemy with the use of a "fresh jawbone of a donkey." Extremely thirsty after this effort, he experienced God's gracious provision in water supplied miraculously from the rock where he stood.

c. Twenty-year judgeship. After these experiences Samson remained content to assume a more peaceful mode of life and served as judge in Israel for a period of twenty years (Judg. 15:20). These years may have been spent in Hebron (Judg. 16:3), and on the basis of our proposed chronology would be contemporary with Samuel's judgeship[81] prior to the battle of Mizpah (1 Sam. 7:3–11).[82] Though Samson had experienced the disapproval of his own people, who lived close to Philistine territory, illustrated by the incident just considered, his exploits could have made him quite a champion in an area further removed, like Hebron. Apparently people there were willing to consult with him as judge.

d. Closing events. Toward the close of these years, Samson again visited Philistine territory, stopping at Gaza[83] where he fell victim to lust and sinned with a harlot (Judg. 16:1–3). Rising at midnight, and finding the city surrounded by waiting Philistines, he inflicted marked humiliation on Gaza by breaking away defensive gates and carrying them to a nearby hill on his return to Hebron.

Not long after, Samson once more submitted to lust, becoming infatuated with a scheming woman of the Philistines named Delilah, who lived in the Sorek Valley not far from his place of birth, Zorah. Given promise of massive reward by the Philistine leaders, Delilah sought to entice Samson to reveal the secret of his strength. Each of the five lords of the Phlistines offered her eleven hundred shekels of silver for a total of fifty-five hundred (Judg. 16:5). This sum can be compared with the ten shekels of silver offered to a Levite as a year's wage (Judg. 17:10). The amounts would translate into about 140 pounds for Delilah over against four ounces for the Levite, for the shekel weighed four-tenths of an ounce.

He gave her false answers three times but finally told her the truth regarding his uncut hair. She cut it off while he slept, and the Philistines were able to put out his eyes and make him labor sightless in their prison in Gaza, controlling him at last. When his hair had grown again, however, Samson had his last revenge. Taken to entertain assembled Philistines in the temple of Dagon, he called upon God for a return of his strength, and he was enabled to dislodge two central supporting columns of the temple from their bases, destroying the building and killing more of the

---

[80]The site of Lehi is unknown, but clearly was somewhere between Etam and Philistine land proper.

[81]Samson's twenty-year judgeship fits history between the battle of Aphek (1 Sam. 4:1–11) and that of Mizpah (1 Sam. 7:7–14), twenty years later (1 Sam. 7:2). See discussion regarding Samuel, which follows.

[82]Mizpah is best identified with Tell en-Nasbeh, eight miles north of Jerusalem. Samuel's activity likely centered in this vicinity, well north, then, of Samson's likely area near Hebron.

[83]Identified with Tell el-'Ajjul, some forty miles west of Hebron and twelve miles south of Ashkelon. Perhaps Samson came here to fight some giant-sized descendant of Anak (Josh. 11:22; 2 Sam. 21:15–22).

enemy at the time of his own death than in all his prior years.

4. Evaluation of Samson

a. Characteristics. Samson is one of the perplexing persons of the Old Testament, having both commendable and blameworthy things that can be said about him. Commendable is that fact that his birth, alone among the judges, was fore-announced by no one less than the Angel of Yahweh,[84] implying unusual divine favor in respect to him. Also, more description is devoted in the biblical record to his life than to any other judge except the honored Gideon. Third, he is said to have been especially enabled by the Holy Spirit for his work no less than four times, when this is said of other judges no more than once. Fourth, he called on God for supernatural provision at two different times, and God was pleased to grant it on each occasion (Judg. 15:18–19; 16:28–30). Finally, he is included in the honor roll of faith of Hebrews 11 (v. 32).

Among his blameworthy characteristics, the most notable was his lust for women, from which weakness, in turn, stemmed the violation of his Nazirite standing and his general coldness of heart toward God. It should be realized, however, that the two principal episodes depicting this weakness came at the close of his life, near the end of

his twenty years of service as judge.[85] It may be that the majority of his years serving as judge were lived quite free from similar occasions.

b. Divine assignment. It is quite clear that Samson knew from the first that God had assigned him to combat Philistines. The angel had so instructed his mother (Judg. 13:5), and certainly she would have passed the information along to him. Also it is directly stated that, in spite of the wrong involved in marrying the Philistine girl, Samson did seek thereby an occasion to quarrel with the Philistines[86] (Judg. 14:4). It follows, then, that his consequent contacts with the Philistines were similarly calculated (though perhaps unwisely) and not merely outbursts of temper. The reason that he did not proceed as other judges in raising an army to defeat the enemy is probably twofold: first, God did not direct him to do so, which is clear from the statement of the angel to the mother that Samson would only "begin" to deliver Israel (Judg. 13:5); and second, his fellow Israelites were not of a mind to fight the Philistines, apparently having accepted a coexistence policy which gave the enemy the upper hand (Judg. 15:9–13).

c. Effectiveness. In spite of Samson's decline into sin, his overall work was beneficial for Israel. He did much to confuse and hinder the Philistines in

---

[84] In fact, Samson was here honored along with Isaac (Gen. 18:1–16) and John the Baptist (Luke 1:5–25).

[85] He was likely about forty years old at his death. His birth announcement seems to have been given after the Philistine oppression had started (Judg. 13:5), and the oppression lasted forty years (Judg. 13:1). He was about twenty, then, at his wedding, which just preceded the twenty-year judgeship.

[86] That Judges 14:4 does mean that Samson sought this occasion, rather than Yahweh, as some suggest (though in keeping with Yahweh's pleasure as the verse indicates), follows from the idea of "confront" being implied by the use of *tho'anah* (see 2 Kings 5:7), and also that Samson directly sought a way to prompt this quarrel in propounding the riddle. Apparently Samson had a twofold purpose in mind for the wedding: to marry a girl attractive to him, and to arrange a confrontation.

their designs on the people of Yahweh. Philistine plans were disrupted, and the citizenry was made to respect the God who could so empower a man. They could hardly press on to complete their subjugation of Israel until they had solved the puzzle of this one person. His final slaughter of Philistines in the Dagon temple likely had a direct bearing on the defeat the Philistines experienced shortly after at Mizpah (1 Sam. 7:7–14). Further, the presentation by the Philistines of their own champion, Goliath, about a half century later, may well have been a retaliatory gesture in remembrance of Israel's champion.

Certainly Samson could have accomplished far more had he not fallen prey to the sin of lust, and for this he must be sharply criticized. He affords a strong lesson of warning to others on this count. But this weakness should not cause one to forget his commendable points nor overlook the benefits he achieved for his people.

I. SAMUEL
(1 Samuel 1–8)

During the entire period of Samson's judgeship and feats among the Philistines,[87] one of Israel's great personalities was active in Israel proper. This was Samuel, whose general date is determined by the fact that he had sons old enough to act as judges in Beersheba (1 Sam. 8:1–2) before Saul began to reign in 1050 B.C. This places Samuel's birth hardly later than 1100 B.C.,[88] which was just prior both to the outbreak of the Ammonite and Philistine oppressions and to the birth of Samson.[89]

Samuel is also called a judge (1 Sam. 7:15–17), as these others before him, but he was more than a judge. He was primarily a prophet, so recognized from Dan to Beersheba (1 Sam. 3:20), and he even acted as a priest (1 Sam. 9:12–13; 13:8–13). In these capacities he filled a vital need in a crucial time of Israel's history. His work in correcting religious malpractice, maintaining national morale in the face of major disaster, promoting return to faith in God, and even establishing the new Israelite monarchy was of the greatest importance. He stands as one of the more significant persons in the Old Testament (Jer. 15:1).

1. Early life
(1 Samuel 1–3)

Samuel was the son of a Levite, Elkanah of Ramathaim-zophim (Ramah).[90] Samuel's mother was named Hannah, one of two wives of Elkanah, and she had been barren prior to Samuel's birth. She had prayed for a son and had promised him to God if her prayers were answered. Accordingly, when Samuel was weaned, he was brought to the tabernacle and devoted to service there.

Conditions at the tabernacle were not good at the time, and they were getting worse (1 Sam. 2:12–17). Eli, a descendant from Aaron through Ithamar,[91] was high priest. His two

---

[87] Also while Jephthah was involved with Ammonites across the Jordan and later judged Israelites there for six years.

[88] This agrees with the fact that Ahimelech, high priest in Saul's time, was a grandson of Phinehas, one of the wicked priests in this period (1 Sam. 14:3; 22:9).

[89] Samson was born just the Philistine oppression began (c. 1095 B.C.); see above, nn.72 and 85.

[90] Ramah is best identified with Er-Ram, five miles north of Jerusalem in Benjamin. Elkanah was an Ephraimite (1 Sam. 1:1) because his family had formerly lived in Ephraim, but he was a Levite by tribal descent (1 Chron. 6:33–35).

[91] The family of the high priest had formerly descended from Eleazar (Num. 20:25–29), but now

sons, Hophni and Phinehas, were priests. Eli, himself an earnest follower of Yahweh, was old, and the two sons were in charge of ceremonies. These sons were wicked men, sorely perverting the ritual and profaning the sanctuary by conduct similar to that found in Canaanite temples. As a result, people abhorred to come to worship. Eli was held responsible by God and was rebuked for permitting this continuing abuse by his sons.

Reprimand came first through an unnamed prophet, and later through the lad Samuel (1 Sam. 2:27–3:18). The experience of Samuel when the reprimand came through him must have been both gratifying and fearsome. God honored him by speaking to him audibly during the night, and Samuel had to relay the grim message to Eli, his own teacher, the next morning. Certainly this was a maturing event for so young a boy. The message he conveyed proclaimed grave punishment for Eli's house, and this took on tangible form within approximately fifteen years.[92]

2. The tragic battle of Aphek (1 Samuel 4)

Punishment came through a disastrous battle with the Philistines. Twenty years of Philistine oppression had passed,[93] and Israel attempted to end it by a direct military engagement. The encounter was at Aphek,[94] well north of Philistine territory in the Sharon plain, which signifies that the enemy had already been making sizeable gains against the coastal Canaanites.[95] In the battle that ensued, Israel was badly defeated and lost some four thousand men.

Wrongly thinking that the presence of the ark at the battle front would help in a renewed conflict,[96] the people, finding the degenerate Hophni and Phinehas agreeable, took the ark from Shiloh, contrary to God's will, and brought it the twenty-three miles to camp. But God could not bring favor in the presence of such flagrant disobedience, and again defeat was experienced. This time thirty thousand of Israel fell, including Hophni and Phinehas; and the all-important ark was captured. When news of the major catastrophe reached Shiloh, confusion reigned; and Eli, old and obese, fell from his seat backward and died of a broken neck.

Excavations have revealed that the Philistines now moved directly into Israelite territory, even as far as Shiloh, which they destroyed (Jer. 7:12; 26:6).[97] Probably it was now, too, that they first placed controlling garrisons in

---

with Eli there had been a change to Ithamar's descendants (see 2 Sam. 8:17; 1 Kings 2:27; 1 Chron. 24:3).

[92] If Samuel was about ten years old at the time, which seems reasonable, the date was about 1090 B.C., fifteen years before the battle of Aphek c. 1075 B.C.

[93] The oppression began c. 1095 B.C. (see above, n.72), making the date here c. 1075 B.C. The oppression lasted forty years (Judg. 13:1) until c. 1055 B.C., about five years before Saul became king.

[94] Best identified with later Antipatris, modern Ras el-'Ain, some twenty-three miles west of Shiloh.

[95] Eventual Philistine occupation has been evidenced as far north as the Esdraelon Valley, all through that plain, and even south in the Jordan Valley a short distance.

[96] They were influenced in this by the belief of their neighbors that a physical image insured the presence of the deity. Israel erroneously thought that God's presence could thus be assured.

[97] Shiloh was excavated by Danish expeditions in 1926–29 and 1932, showing that the city was leveled during the eleventh century, no doubt at this time; see Albright, *BASOR* 9 (February 1923): 10–11.

the country (1 Sam. 10:5; 13:3) and, in a move to protect their own iron monopoly, destroyed what metal industry the Israelites may have had, making them completely dependent on the services of the Philistine smiths (1 Sam. 13:19–22).

At such a time, Israelite morale must have been extremely low. It had seriously declined before this because of the deficient religious condition, but this would have reduced it still more, crushing people's spirits to the point of despair. Israel twice had been severely defeated, losing many men and now the ark. The Philistines controlled vast areas of the land. No doubt it seemed to many that the days of Israelite independence were at an end. This foreign power would swallow them completely.

3. The man Samuel
(1 Samuel 7)

This was the situation that Samuel faced as he found himself thrust into the position of Israel's leader. Until this time he had been under Eli's supervision, but now the high priest and his sons were dead. Samuel had already achieved a reputation as a prophet of God among the people (1 Sam. 3:20) and could expect to be looked to for leadership. Prospects for the country were extremely dismal, but the task of bringing order out of near chaos was clearly his.

a. Good preparation. God had prepared Samuel well for the task. There had been the early influence of a godly mother and the careful instruction of the learned Eli. Also, Samuel, having

been raised in the corrupt atmosphere of the tabernacle, knew the dire religious need of the people. He certainly knew, too, the low morale existent everywhere, for Shiloh would have been a center of such information. And Samuel had been divinely granted a courageous heart, a heart that was full of faith in God. Many strong men would have despaired at the task, but Samuel moved into it with ability and strength.

It is evident that his efforts were remarkably productive, for twenty years later, Israel, rather than remaining a weak and miserable vassal of the Philistines, had become a vigorous people, who could and did bring major defeat on the oppressors (1 Sam. 7:3–14). Change of this kind does not happen without due cause, and the only human instrument who could have effected it was the man Samuel.

b. Type of work. The biblical record is silent on how Samuel accomplished so much; Scripture indicates only the results. But conjecture is possible, for certain activities would have been necessary. He would have had to give attention to reestablishment of the tabernacle now that the ark had been taken and Shiloh had been destroyed. It was moved to Nob,[98] where its rightful sacrifice and ceremony would have been renewed after the years of perversion under Hophni and Phinehas. This was a task complicated by the absence of the ark.

Then priests and Levites, in their widely distributed cities, probably needed to be encouraged to review their teaching ministries, which doubt-

---

[98] See 1 Samuel 21:1–9. Samuel is not mentioned as having had contact with the tabernacle at Nob, but it is unthinkable that he would not have been concerned to save the sanctuary at Shiloh and do all possible to move it to another location like this.

less had lagged during the reign of Eli. Careful instruction was important, for the priests and Levites could contact people directly and do much in bringing change of outlook and heightening of morale.[99] We may think of Samuel traveling extensively to make the necessary contacts, always urging people everywhere to a renewal of faith in God.

c. Training schools. Samuel seems to have pioneered a new idea, too, undoubtedly related to the same endeavor: that of training schools for young prophets. We know of these schools only from later passages in which they are mentioned—references to the time of Saul (1 Sam. 10:5–12; 19:19–24),[100] but it seems clear that they had been existent for some time. The best explanation as to why Samuel started these schools is that he realized his need for helpers in this time of crisis. It was impossible for him to be everywhere himself, and so he required assistants. If well-trained,[101] these persons could multiply his efforts, covering much of the ground he could not. Instructing them would have taken valuable time, but Samuel may have

conducted school en route on his travels.[102]

4. The victorious battle of Mizpah (1 Samuel 7:5–14)

After twenty years of this effort (1 Sam. 7:2), Israel was at last enabled to win a decisive victory over the Philistines. Morale had been raised so that the people found courage for another encounter; but, more important, renewal of faith in God had been engendered, so that Yahweh could bless them with a triumph. In fact, the battle occurred as the people were gathered for a time of spiritual revival before God at Mizpah.[103] The Philistines heard of the assembly and, no doubt thinking that it was for the purpose of war, decided to attack directly themselves.

At first the Israelites were afraid when they heard of the enemy's approach; but Samuel called on God for help, and God heard. A violent thunderstorm was sent and struck fear into the hearts of the advancing Philistines, and it was then that the Israelites were enabled to inflict severe defeat, after which they pursued the enemy as far as Beth Car.[104]

---

[99]A prime tendency of the people that would have had to be averted at this time was to align themselves with Canaanites against the common Philistine enemy. It would have taken strong exhortation and careful detailing of dangers involved to offset this natural inclination.

[100]Such a phrase as "training school" is not used in these passages, but only the phrase "company of prophets" (KJV). This group, however, is not mentioned before this and Samuel is said to have been "standing there as their leader" (1 Sam. 19:20). This suggests a training situation, perhaps not formal, but at least informal.

[101]The liberal view that these prophets were ecstatics must be rejected. Saul's strange action of "prophesying" with them and then lying all night minus his outer garment (1 Sam. 19:24) cannot be attributed to sympathetic participation in such ecstasy. To be a participant requires due preparation of mind and desire for it, besides efforts to induce the state. But Saul came in anger because of ineffectiveness on the part of three contingents of policemen, and then began "to prophesy" even before arriving where the prophets were located. His lying all night in this manner is better explained as a fit of emotional despair caused by seeing David in Samuel's approving company.

[102]Naioth in Ramah may have been the headquarters. Naioth means "habitations," and Samuel was there standing head over the young prophets (1 Sam. 19:18–24).

[103]See above, p. 189n.82.

[104]Beth Car must have been a high point, for the reference here is to "below Beth Car," but its location remains unknown.

It should be brought to mind, too, as noted earlier, that Samson's efforts could have played a role in this victory. His slaughter of three thousand Philistines in the temple of Dagon, which likely had just preceded this battle, would have rekindled respect among the Philistines for Israel's God and thereby contributed to the fear experienced in the thunderstorm.

Following this victory, Philistine inroads into Israelite territory increased, until after Saul had been made king (1 Sam. 13). This battle brought the forty-year oppression mentioned in Judges 13:1 to a close.

5. The Ark returned (1 Samuel 5–6). The ark of the tabernacle had been captured in the battle of Aphek twenty years earlier. God had caused a series of events, catastrophic for the Philistines, to bring about its return to Israel just seven months after its capture. First the image of Dagon,[105] beside which the ark had been placed, had twice been made to fall to the floor before it; next, painful tumors had been inflicted on the people, which in some instances brought death; and finally, the land had been overrun with mice.[106] In determining how to send the troublesome ark home, the Philistine priests had tried to save face by employing trickery, whereby the ark would be thrown from the wagon on which it was placed; but God had intervened so the young heifers drawing the wagon, unbroken and with their calves taken from them, had wondrously moved straight along the road to Beth-shemesh[107] in Israelite territory (1 Sam. 6:1–18).

Back in the land, however, the ark still was not returned to the tabernacle at Nob. At Beth-shemesh, it was desecrated when curious people looked into it,[108] and God took the lives of many of them in punishment (1 Sam. 6:19–20). Then, instead of sending it back to the tabernacle, the Beth-shemites sent for men of Kirjath-jearim[109] to come and get it. Apparently these people handled it properly, because they experienced no harm, but still did not return it to the tabernacle. It remained with them for more than seventy years[110] until David brought it to Jerusalem.

There is a question as to why at least Samuel did not insist that the ark be brought to the tabernacle. He must have known of its return to the land, for news of so important an event could not have been kept secret. One would think, too, that he would have desired this as a further means of encouraging the people. Since he did not, all one can say is that there must have been some significant factor, unstated in the bibli-

---

[105]The name *Dagon* may be from *dagh*, meaning "fish," but more likely from *daghan*, meaning "grain," hence an agricultural deity. Temples to Dagon found at Mari, Ugarit, Bethshan, etc,. show that this deity was borrowed from the Canaanites.

[106]This plague of mice is not so described, but the idea is implied in that images of mice were made by the Philistines, as well as of tumors (1 Sam. 6:5).

[107]Beth-shemesh, identified with modern Tell er-Rumeileh and located in an east-west valley leading from Philistine land, was the first city back within Israelite (Judah) territory.

[108]The ark represented God's presence among His people and was to be respected accordingly. These Israelites should have known better than to use it as an object of curiosity.

[109]Commonly identified with Kuriet el-'Enab. (Abu Ghosh), a village nine miles west of Jerusalem on the road to Tell Aviv. It had been one city of the Gibeonite tetrapolis (Josh. 9:17).

[110]The battle of Aphek occurred c. 1075 B.C., and David began to rule in Jerusalem c. 1003 B.C., with the ark being brought there shortly after.

cal record, which caused him to decide against it.

6. The people request a king (1 Samuel 7:15–8:22). Samuel's activities following the Mizpah victory, with priests and Levites now doing their work with reasonable effectiveness once again, became considerably curtailed. It is stated that he covered a relatively small circuit in his work of judging, touching only Bethel, Gilgal, Mizpah, and Ramah, his home town (1 Sam. 7:16–17). To help in the south near Beersheba, he installed his own sons, Joel and Abiah, as judges. In the pattern of Hophni and Phinehas, however, they did not follow the godly example of their father; instead, they took bribes in a perversion of justice.

Their poor conduct stirred the people to make a request of Samuel which disappointed him greatly. They asked that they be given a king (1 Sam. 8:4–6). The failure of these sons was not the main reason for the request, however: the people had seen how nearly they had come to complete disaster under the present governmental system, and now that the situation was improved, wanted a change. The Philistines, or another enemy,[111] might come again. They wanted a king with an organized army "such as all the other nations have."

Samuel took the request as a personal affront, however. He had worked hard for Israel and rightly believed that the country was now in relatively strong condition. The request seemed an indication of a lack of confidence in him. But God told him that this was not so, that really the affront was against Himself—the people no longer wanting the theocracy.

Likely at this point Samuel expected God to tell him to reprimand the people and deny the request. Instead, God told him to comply with the people's request.[112]

God further instructed Samuel to warn them that, along with the king they requested, they would receive heavy burdens in taxation, which they had not experienced under God's theocratic rule. If they had followed God's way, it would have pleased God and been much better for them; but now that they had not, it was best that they have what the other nations had, with all its disadvantages.

---

[111] Nahash, king of Ammon, seems to have been quite in their minds also; see 1 Samuel 12:12.

[112] It should be realized that also earlier indications had been given regarding a coming monarchy (Gen. 49:10; Num. 24:17; Deut. 17:14; 1 Sam. 2:10).

CHAPTER TEN

KING SAUL

1 Samuel 9–31

Palestine was less disturbed by outside powers during the time of Israel's united monarchy than during the period of the Judges. Egypt did not interfere while Saul, David, and Solomon ruled. After Rameses III (c. 1195–1164), no Egyptian king crossed the border of Palestine until the time of Rehoboam, Solomon's son.[1]

Assyria, mired in a dark age that lasted until after the time of Solomon, would not threaten Israel for nearly a century after the division of the kingdom.[2] Prior to the monarchy, there had been only one significant extension of Assyrian power into the west-land, and it was temporary. Tiglath-pileser I (1116–1078) had brought his army as far as the Mediterranean, still far north of Palestine, but other interests kept him from maintaining a hold. No other ruler advanced as far for two centuries following.[3] This means that Israel's first three kings were quite unaffected by large powers,[4] making possible in part the wide expansion of boundaries under King David.

When Saul came to office, his major task was to unify the tribes. Samuel's efforts had contributed significantly, for he had rescued the tribes from complete disaster, restored their morale, and renewed their faith in God. The tribes, however, were still separate entities, with deep-seated differences between them. Jealousies of the past and intertribal warfare were not easily forgotten.

Even more serious was the capture of the ark, the ruin of Shiloh, and the

---

[1] Shishak (Sheshonq I), who founded Egypt's Twenty-Second Dynasty, did so in Rehoboam's fifth year (1 Kings 14:25–26). Earlier he had given refuge to Jeroboam fleeing from Solomon.

[2] Assyria did so for the first time under Shalmaneser III (859–824); see p. 274. King Ahab, a few years earlier, had joined a coalition against this Assyrian at Qarqar (p. 265).

[3] See pp. 261–62.

[4] After 1240 B.C., the Hittites were engulfed in a flow of migration (Sea Peoples) that brought an end to their nation. Boghazkoi, their capital, was completely destroyed. The year 1200 B.C., an arbitrary date for a process that took decades, is frequently given as the end of the age of empire and the beginning of a period in which political power was regional and sporadic.

necessary transfer of the tabernacle to Nob. The central sanctuary had been intended as a principal unifying factor, where people could meet and be reminded of their common heritage as they joined in worship. But Shiloh was no more. The ark had been returned to the land, but not to the tabernacle at Nob. Without it, the tabernacle exerted little of the centralizing influence intended. A strong hand was required if differences were to be forgotten. Saul's task, to weld these twelve long-standing units into one nation, would not be easy.

A. ANOINTING OF SAUL (1 Samuel 9–12)

1. Anointing at Ramah (1 Samuel 9:1–10:16)

a. Anointed by Samuel (1 Sam. 9:1–27). Not long after God revealed to Samuel that the tribes should have a king, He identified who that person should be: Saul, son of Kish, of the tribe of Benjamin. That a member of small Benjamin should receive this honor is significant. Judah and Ephraim were the two leading tribes, with Benjamin lying between. A man chosen from this tribe would prevent the two leading tribes from mutual jealousy, an important consideration when the great need was for unification.

Saul was tall and of striking appearance, being "without equal" in Israel (1 Sam. 9:2). He apparently was humble prior to his anointing, too. At least he was timid, for only after repeated urging by a servant was he persuaded to seek advice from the prophet Samuel at Ramah concerning his lost asses. Samuel first told him that the animals had been found and then the astonishing fact that he was actually to be Israel's first king. What a turn of events for a young man! He had hesitatingly come for the purpose of learning the location of lost animals, and now had been informed that he was to be the chief ruler of all the tribes! Samuel even anointed him with oil the following morning in symbolism of this honor.

b. Confirming signs (1 Sam. 10:1–12). Before Saul left to go home, Samuel also told him of three confirmatory signs that Saul would experience as he traveled. He would meet two men who would tell him that the lost asses had been found and that his father was now seriously concerned about him. Then he would come upon three men, having goats, bread, and wine, who would give him two of the loaves of bread. Third, and most important, he would encounter a company of prophets[5] playing musical instruments as they rendered praise to God.[6] He should join with this last group in giving praise himself, at which time he would experience the "Spirit of the LORD" coming upon him.

These events occurred just as Samuel had predicted, which no doubt served to confirm Samuel's remarkable announcement in Saul's mind. Confirmation would have been needed, for Saul had surely wondered, as he walked along after leaving Samuel, how so great a future could possibly be his. But

---

[5] These were likely young trainees of Samuel's school (see p. 194).

[6] The text says that they "prophesied" (1 Sam. 10:10). But this was not in a spoken message. They prophesied in the sense given the term in 1 Chronicles 25:1–3, where Levites "prophesied, using the harp in thanking and praising the LORD." Samuel's trainees were praising God in song as they came down from the high place.

when these less important matters happened just as foretold, the greater would have become easier to believe. That he did come to believe to a substantial degree follows from his joining in praise with the prophets as instructed. People who knew him were amazed that he did so, for clearly they were not used to seeing the timid Saul engaged in such overt activity. He seemed to be a new person to them, something Samuel also had foretold. It should be noted that Saul had need for this manner of change in personality if he was to become an effective king. He could not then be timid as before, but aggressive for leadership.[7]

2. Identified at Mizpah (1 Samuel 10:17–24)

With Israel's first king now chosen, it remained for Samuel to identify him to the people. Samuel did so at Mizpah, the site of the great victory over the Philistines, an event still reasonably fresh in Israel's memory. He summoned representatives of all the tribes to meet with him there. He did not tell them directly whom God had already chosen but proceeded to make inquiry, probably by the Urim and Thummim,[8] as though no prior information had been given. Apparently Samuel wished the people to witness God's selection firsthand rather than through himself as intermediary.

An identification procedure was followed much like that involving Achan years earlier (Josh. 7:16–18). First Saul's tribe, Benjamin, was identified, then Saul's family, Matri, and finally Saul himself. When the people looked

for Saul, whom Samuel apparently had instructed beforehand to be present, they could not find him. Further inquiry revealed that he had hidden himself among the traveling wagons and baggage. Saul's hesitancy to accept the office might be understood as a natural reluctance to take leadership in a rebellion against the militarily superior Philistines. Saul was now summoned, seen to be kingly in stature, and accepted with shouts of approval by those assembled.

3. Established as king (1 Samuel 11–12)

a. A period of waiting. It is one thing to be approved by representatives, but another to be accepted by people at large. Saul's actual coronation as king was not to follow now as a matter of course. The people had to give their voluntary acceptance, and Saul was still quite unknown to them. There was need that he have public exposure before acceptance could be expected. Also, the tribes were still autonomous units and would naturally hesitate to join such a common venture, no matter the identity of the prospective ruler. Further, there was no capital, palace, staff, or governmental machinery to use. Saul needed an opportunity to prove himself so that he would be accepted and admired by all, before the unification of the tribes and the establishment of the machinery of government could be accomplished.

b. Distinguished at Jabesh-gilead (1 Sam. 11:1–15). Such an opportunity arose soon after the Mizpah iden-

---

[7]This is a better interpretation of his being "changed into a different person" (1 Sam. 10:6) than that he became an ecstatic as believed by some.

[8]Though the Urim and Thummim device is not mentioned in the text, it was the normal method of inquiry in such circumstances; see Num. 27:21; and above, pp. 161–62.

tification. The Ammonites, under King Nahash, now attacked the city of Jabesh-gilead[9] across the Jordan. The inhabitants of this city sent for help from all the tribes, apparently not knowing that Saul had been chosen king.

Their appeal came to Saul's attention, nonetheless, and he immediately saw it as both a responsibility for him and the opportunity he needed. In a dramatic gesture, he butchered a yoke of oxen and sent pieces to all the tribes. Messengers taking them declared that all who did not respond to Jabesh-gilead's call by joining Saul would have their own oxen treated in similar fashion. The response was excellent. A total of thirty thousand presented themselves from Judah, and three hundred thousand from the other tribes, here collectively called Israel.[10] From this group[11] Saul selected three army contingents, which he led against the Ammonites, winning a decisive victory.

The result was as Saul desired. The fancy of the Israelites was caught, and they now did accept him as king. The formal ceremony was conducted at Gilgal, with Samuel again leading the proceedings. Saul was crowned as first king, amidst an offering of sacrifices and general rejoicing.[12]

c. Samuel's word of exhortation (1 Sam. 12:1–25). Following the coronation, Samuel delivered a parting exhortation to the people.[13] It was an emotional moment for the great prophet and retiring leader. He had acceded to the people's request for a king, at God's own direction, and now he voluntarily served in crowning him. Samuel, who had worked so well and to whom the people owed so much, was now stepping down. But further, Samuel knew that the sin which had caused the former system of rule to fail could also affect the new one. Exhortation was needed because the people must be made to realize that change of heart was more important than change of rule.

Samuel began by soliciting the people's acknowledgment of his own righteous activity before them. Then he reminded them of their past failures and strongly urged them to obey God's Law. This they must do if they were to experience God's blessing. Further, as a way of stressing the importance of his words, he called for God to send a thunderstorm in this time of wheat harvest, normally the dry season.[14] God did so, and the people cried out in fear as the thunder rolled and the rain fell. He closed with brief words of further exhortation, promising in addi-

---

[9] Identification is uncertain, but Glueck argues rather convincingly, *BASOR* 89 (February 1943) and 91 (October 1943), for Tell Abu-Kharaz on Wadi Yabis, two miles from the Jordan and nine miles from Bethshan.

[10] In this twofold division, there is an early hint of the basic conflict between Judah and the other tribes, which was to break out fully after Solomon. Probably representatives of Simeon were with Judah, but the rest would have been with Israel.

[11] We need not think of all 330,000 as an army, but as those who expressed approval of Saul's action and who responded. From these Saul could choose the actual fighting force.

[12] The date was c. 1050 B.C. Saul ruled forty years (Acts 13:21), and David's period following is generally accepted as c. 1010–970.

[13] Though Samuel would live many more years, and continue to be influential in the government (even anointing David in time, 1 Sam. 16), this was his last act as chief. From now on a king would be the main leader.

[14] The dry season lasts from about mid-April to the first of November. Wheat harvest comes in June.

tion that he would himself pray unceasingly for them.

B. THE RULE OF SAUL
1. Simple and inexpensive

The government Saul established was simple—no doubt purposely so. There had been time for Saul to plan, and he had evidently recognized that the people were in no mood for elaborate government. It would not be easy to impose rigid controls when the people had never had them; and, though Samuel had warned that taxes would come, it was apparent that time and education would be necessary before the people would accept them. Accordingly, the government was kept simple and inexpensive.

The capital Saul established was at Gibeah,[15] his own home town. The palace itself was of simple design. Excavation has revealed that it was more of a fortress than a lavish residence.[16] There is no suggestion that he gave the capital city any special privilege in the land, something which, if done, could have stirred criticism among people unaccustomed to the ways of royalty. Still further, no elaborate court was created. Indeed, in the biblical record there is only one officer named; he is Abner, captain of the army and cousin of Saul[17] (1 Sam. 14:50). Monthly meetings at the time of the new moon may have been the set occasions for discussing problems and planning strategy (1 Sam. 20:24–27).

2. Little basic change

It is clear, too, that Saul instituted few policies which caused appreciable change in the life patterns of people. For instance, old tribal borders continued to be observed. Saul did not do away with them or seek to change them as a means of achieving unity, though the tribes were no longer to think of themselves as separate entities. No doubt Saul realized that any new central form of government could only succeed if it won voluntary allegiance on its own merits. Tradition-defying orders might stir rebellion.

Likely the people were pleased that Saul instituted this manner of rule. They had the satisfaction of a king like other nations, and yet they did not suffer irritating interference in their private lives. Radical new laws, systems, or institutions had not been imposed, and taxes had not been greatly increased.[18] It was good to know that a chief ruler was in charge to lead in battle, which seemed important after years of repeated oppressions. There was a sense of security, too, in having a standing army that was ready to fight in their behalf. They were quite willing to fill army quotas if they could avoid the fearful invasions of past years. All this Saul apparently realized and he acted accordingly. His manner of beginning the rule showed both wisdom and foresight.

---

[15] Well identified as Tell el-Ful, located at the northern outskirts of present-day Jerusalem. The serious crime of the Judges Period, when civil war followed, had occurred here.

[16] Excavated by W. F. Albright (1922–23). See L. A. Sinclair's more recent study, "An Archaeological Study of Gibeah (Tell el-Ful)," *AASOR* 34 (1960), and Wright, *BAR*, pp. 122–24.

[17] Since the biblical record speaks only of Abner, Saul himself, Jonathan his son, or David his son-in-law as leading the army, it may be that Saul intentionally kept military leadership confined to his own family.

[18] The biblical record gives no hint that any of these were instituted, but rather implies that they were not.

Map 9. The Kingdom of Saul

C. THE REJECTION OF SAUL
(1 Samuel 13—15)

Saul's manner of continuing the rule, however, did not show the same good judgment; for even though reasons existed for not starting with strong government, before many years had passed he should have begun to institute policies and measures toward unification. If the tribes were to be welded into a nation, these were needed. But no evidence exists that Saul ever tried to effect them.

Saul's lack of discernment in such matters likely stemmed in part from two causes: first, his personal deficiency in self-control, of which more will be seen presently; and second, his serious wrong of harboring a rebellious heart toward God. Because of these matters, Saul did not rule long before God told him, through Samuel, that he had been rejected as king. This rejection was voiced in connection with two military episodes, separated by an undetermined period of time.

1. The first rejection
(1 Samuel 13—14)

The first was a renewed conflict with the Philistines, which occurred at Michmash. The Philistines had been quiet since their sound defeat at Mizpah; but now, only two years after Saul's inauguration (1 Sam. 13:1),[19] they again entered the land and encamped at Michmash,[20] just four miles northeast of Gibeah, the capital of Israel.[21] They had come to avenge a victory wrought by Jonathan over a garrison of Philistines stationed at Geba (1 Sam. 13:2—3). Their forces included three thousand chariots,[22] six thousand horsemen, and a host of foot soldiers.

The presence of such an army caused terror among Israelites of the vicinity, many fleeing to caves and thickets to hide, and others crossing the Jordan. Saul quickly assembled a force at Gilgal to withstand them and waited for Samuel to come and offer sacrifice prior to the impending battle.

It was at this point that he committed the sin that prompted the first rejection. Having waited seven days, the impatient Saul assumed the priestly office, which in turn demonstrated that he had a proud, self-sufficient, rebellious heart. In this respect, considerable change in character had taken place since the day he had been first anointed.

God still gave Saul victory in this battle, however, mainly through the effort of his able son, Jonathan. Prospects were dark until Jonathan achieved a minor but brilliant victory. The Israelite forces were much smaller than the Philistines, and the only swords were those held by Saul and Jonathan them-

---

[19] This verse is somewhat unclear in Hebrew. Rather than depending on textual criticism to resolve the difficulty, the two-year period mentioned is regarded here as a statement of the time elapsed between the beginning of Saul's reign and the battle of Michmash, rather than a garbled statement of the total length of Saul's reign.

[20] Present-day Mukhmas, on the northern ridge of Wadi Suweinit, east of Bethel on the way to Jericho.

[21] Usually the Philistines liked to fight in level areas where they could use their chariots best. They had come, however, to retaliate for Jonathan's victory and also, no doubt, seize Saul's capital if possible.

[22] While the Hebrew text reads thirty thousand, other ancient texts read three thousand, a number that still represents a formidable chariot force and is more compatible with known chariot contingents from the ancient world. It is assumed that the text had been damaged in transmission.

selves.[23] Also, Saul's own army was apparently suffering from daily desertions (1 Sam. 13:15; see 13:2), while the Philistines remained capable of sending foraging troops in three directions at the same time (1 Sam. 13:16–18).

But then came Jonathan's daring triumph. Accompanied only by his armorbearer, he crossed from Geba[24] on the south of Wadi Suweinit to Michmash on the north, descending and climbing steep ridges en route, and attacked and defeated an entire Philistine garrison (1 Sam. 14:1–14). News of so courageous an exploit spread rapidly, bringing new hope to the Israelites and resulting in the return of many deserters to Saul's army. At this time, too, God intervened to bring an earthquake, which resulted in more confusion among the enemy. Saul took advantage of the quick change of events to attack and was enabled to defeat the frightened Philistines and drive them as far west as Ajalon.

Saul almost defeated his own cause in the course of the victory, however. He foolishly imposed a restriction on the men of his army, forbidding any to eat food for all of one day (1 Sam. 14:24–46). He apparently hoped to give more incentive and time to pursue the enemy, but what he accomplished was to deprive his men of badly needed nourishment for the chase. Further, Saul nearly took the life of his son because of the order. Jonathan, who had not heard the command, did eat; and Saul, believing his word must be maintained even at the cost of his son, would have killed him but for the pleas of the people.

2. The second rejection (1 Samuel 15)

The second instance of disobedience came with Saul's battle with the Amalekites, approximately twenty years later.[25] During the intervening years, Saul had been militarily active, and had not experienced censure. Among his opponents had been the countries of Moab, Ammon, Edom, and Zobah,[26] besides the Philistines in an ever-continuing struggle. He appears to have been relatively successful.

Then came the Amalekite battle. Samuel gave Saul specific instruction regarding it. Saul was to initiate this encounter as a retaliatory measure for the hit and run raids on Israel by Amalek years before, during the wilderness journey (Exod. 17:8–14),[27] and to completely destroy the people and all their livestock. Saul carried out the

---

[23] Due to the Philistine iron monopoly; see p. 169n.7.

[24] Identified with Modern Jeba, located opposite old Michmash. Geba must be distinguished from Gibeah, Saul's capital, three miles southwest.

[25] This twenty-year span is determined as follows. David was anointed soon after the Amalekite battle (1 Sam. 16:1–13). Since he was thirty years old at his inauguration to kingship (2 Sam. 5:4) in 1010 B.C., he was born in 1040 B.C. He could hardly have been less than fifteen years old when anointed (he had been left to attend sheep alone) which means about 1025 B.C., and the earlier battle of Michmash had occurred about 1047 B.C., two years after Saul's inauguration.

[26] A rather large state located just north of Damascus, hence much farther from Saul's home base than his other opponents.

[27] God speaks more strongly against the Amalekites than any other foe Israel encountered. In Exodus 17:14 He promises complete annihilation, and in Deuteronomy 25:17–19 Moses reminds the people of this promise. Here Saul is told to carry it out. Apparently it was the manner of their attack on Israel (hitting and running, taking advantage of Israel's weak position) which prompted the severe censure.

mission, defeated the foe, and in large part obeyed in slaying all the people and their animals. He disobeyed, however, in sparing King Agag and some of the finest sheep and oxen. When Samuel asked the reason, he explained that the animals were for sacrifice. Samuel, however, sternly replied that God desired obedience more than sacrifice. Samuel rebuked the king and told him once more that God had rejected him as the head of Israel's ruling family. Samuel then killed King Agag with his own hands.

Israel's first king failed in the sight of God. He would not obey divine commands. God had not given His people a king to act according to his own will, but to be God's intermediary. Saul, having started well, was affected by his role as chief, and forgot that God was the supreme Head. It may be assumed, too, that these two crucial occasions were not the only instances of disobedience on his part, but rather were representative of many others and of a general rebellious attitude. Because these were particularly pointed, the official rejection was voiced only regarding them.

The rationale for the permitted lapse of twenty years between these two times seems to be as follows. The first rejection was more of a warning than a final pronouncement.[28] That is, Saul might have made amends had he taken heed. For this reason he continued to experience success in other military endeavors. He did not, however, profit from the warning, but continued in disobedience, which was climaxed in the Amalekite encounter. This brought the final rejection, with God's enabling Spirit then being taken from him (1 Sam. 16:14).[29]

D. SAUL AND DAVID
(1 Samuel 16–20)

1. David's divine selection
(1 Samuel 16:1–13)

With Saul now rejected by God, there was need for one to take his place. Accordingly, God soon instructed Samuel regarding procedure in locating such a one. He was to go to Bethlehem[30] and anoint there a son of Jesse. Samuel went to Bethlehem and had Jesse bring his sons before him. Seven were brought, but each was refused by God. David, the eighth and youngest, had been left to care for the family's sheep. Samuel insisted that he be brought, and God indicated him to be the one. As the father and brothers watched, Samuel then anointed the young man, who was probably about fifteen years of age, as Israel's second king. He was not destined actually to rule for a few years, but already at this time the Spirit of God came upon him for special enablement, in anticipation of that day (1 Sam. 16:13). Though not stated, Samuel very likely also warned the family not to let information regarding this anointing be made public to protect David from possible reprisals by Saul.[31]

---

[28] It is true that Samuel's words to Saul the first time sound final, but this does not mean that there was no provision for repentance. Jonah's words to Nineveh sound final also, but God was ready to change the order when repentance was shown (Jonah 3:4, 10).

[29] With no mention of the Spirit since the time of His coming on Saul prior to the Jabesh-gilead battle (1 Sam. 11:6), the assumption is valid that the Spirit had remained on him after that time to enable him for ruling and had remained until this instance about twenty-two years later.

[30] Not a long distance, for only about ten miles separate Ramah, Samuel's home town, from Bethlehem south; see p. 191n.90.

[31] Secrecy must have been maintained, for no intimation is made that anyone else ever knew of this

2. Saul's emotional instability

Saul had imposing stature and did not lack in courage, but he was emotionally unstable. This weakness came to the fore soon after his second rejection as king. As long as the Spirit of God remained upon him for special empowerment, he was able to maintain self-control. But with the Spirit departed, periods of severe depression came upon him, prompted in large part, no doubt, by the divine rejection.[32] Consequently, a person was sought as court musician, whose music might sooth the king during these attacks. In God's providence, the one chosen was David, who was skilled with the harp. His music did help, but it was not a cure.

Saul became jealous very easily. David, who at first was a favorite of the king, soon experienced this jealousy as the people came to give him higher plaudits than the king. Saul also at times became extremely angry, even to the point of insanity. In this state he twice attempted to strike David with his spear.

Further, Saul was subject to paranoid tendencies, thinking himself to be persecuted by all around him. At one time this tendency led to the slaughter of eighty-five innocent priests (1 Sam. 22:7–19). Such a man could not command the respect of his people indefinitely. Actions so abnormal and frequent would have become widely known, with people losing confidence accordingly. What gains he may have made in achieving goodwill early in his reign were no doubt lost in his later years.

3. David's rise to prominence (1 Samuel 16:14–18:7)

Under God's blessing, though David did not become king after his anointing, he did quickly rise to prominence in the land. The first step was being made court musician to Saul, as just observed. David was a man of many talents, of which musicianship was one.[33] He must have displayed military ability before the king as well, for he was soon made a royal armorbearer (1 Sam. 16:21).

The next step, and a big one, was David's victory over the Philistine giant, Goliath (1 Sam. 17:1–58).[34] The Philistines had attempted to enter Israel through the Elah Valley, a natural approach into the mountains of Judah. They assembled for battle between Shochoh and Azekah.[35] Saul led his army to meet them, while David for some reason was at home. For forty

---

original anointing. Though the brothers were jealous of David, they would not have wanted to talk to others about him having been so honored over themselves.

[32] These periods were the result of "an evil spirit from the LORD" troubling Saul. Apparently this was God's way of showing His rejection rather than immediate dismissal from office.

[33] Few could match him: a trusted shepherd; a skilled harpist; an outstanding poet, writing many of the Psalms; an expert with the sling; a man of strength, dexterity, and courage to kill both a lion and bear with only his hands; a military genius who did not lose battles; an outstanding statesman when he became king; and above all a man of great faith in God.

[34] Second Samuel 21:19 attributes Goliath's death to one of David's men, Elhanan. First Chronicles 20:5, however, says that Elhanan killed Lahmi, brother of Goliath. The apparent conflict is best resolved in terms of a textual error in the Samuel passage. The Hebrew text of Samuel is one of the most poorly preserved in the Old Testament. The view of some that the Chronicler sought deliberately to maintain David's right to the honor by changing the truth must be rejected, for this assumes a fallible text.

[35] This places the battle about four miles south of Beth-shemesh or seventeen miles southwest of Jerusalem in modern Wadi es-Sant.

days Goliath, a Philistine over nine feet tall, dared any Israelite to meet him in personal combat and so decide the whole contest;[36] but no one accepted the challenge.

David came to the camp at the end of the forty days on a mission for his father, to inquire about the welfare of three of his brothers who were there as soldiers. When he realized the shameful situation, he quickly volunteered to meet the giant. Saul at first doubted the wisdom of this but, seeing David's earnestness and faith, let him go. David refused normal armor but took only weapons to which he was accustomed, a sling and five suitable stones. Goliath met him, covered with armor from head to foot and with a shield-bearer before him. When Goliath first saw David approaching, he disdained him, thinking himself humiliated by such an unlikely opponent. David, however, came not in his own strength, but in the name of Yahweh, God of Israel.

One stone was all that David needed. It struck Goliath in the one vulnerable place, his forehead, and he fell to the ground dead. David quickly ran to him and, using Goliath's own sword, for David had none, cut off his head. A brilliant victory was won for Saul and Israel by this display of great courage and faith.[37]

News of such an achievement spread rapidly among the people. Soon David found himself known and honored on all sides (1 Sam. 18:1–7). The people sang his praises, and Saul himself now rewarded him by making him commander of the army, though David was still a young man.[38] About this time, too, Jonathan, Saul's able and eldest son, developed a deep friendship with David. The mutual respect and love between the two lasted for the remainder of their lives. As army commander, David continued to achieve outstanding success, adding to his growing reputation throughout the land.

4. Saul's jealousy (1 Samuel 18:8–20:42)

Soon David came to be ascribed higher honor than Saul, and Saul's emotional weakness showed itself by intense jealousy. He could not accept the people singing that David had slain his "ten thousands" and Saul only his "thousands." He attempted to take David's life numerous times and ways.

a. Attempts to kill David (1 Sam. 18:8–19:24). The first attempts were direct, for Saul tried twice to kill David with his spear (1 Sam. 18:8–11). These attempts came as David continued to play the harp in the king's presence.

David was able to avoid both attacks, and then Saul sought to work more indirectly. As a seeming reward for David's service,[39] Saul promised him

---

[36] This type of two-warrior contest was not unknown in the ancient world. Several examples are related from the Greco-Roman time. One is found regarding the Near East in the "story of Sinuhe" (see *ANET,* p. 20, for the text).

[37] Because Saul asked regarding David's identity after this exploit (1 Sam. 17:55–58), some scholars believe that David could not have been court musician prior to this. It is doubtful, however, if Saul would have let him fight Goliath at all if he had not known him beforehand. Probably the inquiry concerned David's family and background which had not seemed too significant before; see 1 Samuel 17:25. The biblical order of events must be maintained.

[38] Probably in his early twenties, since he started to rule in Hebron at age thirty (2 Sam. 5:4).

[39] In that Saul had promised his daughter (besides riches and tax-free status, 1 Sam. 17:25) to whoever would kill Goliath, David should have been given Saul's eldest daughter, Merab (of whom

Michal, his daughter, as wife. But he asked David to supply a hundred Philistine foreskins as dowry, hoping that David would be killed in acquiring them. David delivered two hundred safely, however (1 Sam. 18:20–27). Saul next attempted to work through his servants, commanding that they take David's life, but Jonathan intervened to have the order changed (1 Sam. 19:1–7).

Shortly after, another signal victory wrought by David over Philistines prompted a further direct attack by Saul to strike David with the spear, but once more David avoided the king's effort. Saul quickly ordered servants to follow David to his home and kill him the next morning, but Michal worked against her father by letting David down from an outside window (1 Sam. 19:8–17).

David fled from the palace area, realizing the intensity of Saul's hatred, and came to Samuel at Ramah about two miles north. Saul sent three different companies of men there to seize David so that Saul could have him executed. When all three failed, Saul himself went. When he found David, however, in the approving company of Samuel and his young prophets (besides the three companies Saul had earlier sent, all engaged in rendering praise to God),[40] Saul did not apprehend him but fell into a fit of despair and lay all night in a deep stupor (1 Sam. 19:18–24).[41]

b. David's flight from the palace (1 Sam. 20:1–42). These repeated attempts to take David's life made the young man realize that living any longer at the palace was too hazardous. Though Saul had been shamed at Ramah, there was good reason to believe that he would soon forget and try again. David accordingly sought the counsel of Jonathan, and the two planned a final test to determine the continuing intention of the king. The test was planned in connection with a regular feast of the new moon where David's presence would be expected.[42] He would intentionally not appear, however; and the test would concern the attitude displayed by the king in view of his absence, which Jonathan would then report to his friend. The next day at the feast Saul demonstrated his attitude to be no different than before, and so Jonathan, regretfully but faithfully, brought the word to David. Both agreed that David would have to leave the palace area, and they parted with great emotion. David began the life of a fugitive.

E. SAUL'S LAST YEARS (1 Samuel 22:6–19; 28:1–25; 31:1–13)

1. Further degeneration of conduct (1 Samuel 22:6–19)

How many years of life remained for Saul after the flight of David is not clear. No definite clues exist. It is not likely, however, that David's fugitive

---

Saul did speak to David, though then gave her to another, 1 Sam. 18:17–19), and this without dowry.

[40] See p. 198n.6.

[41] See p. 194n.101.

[42] Since this feast lasted two days (1 Sam. 20:5, 27), it was considered important. The new moon was a religious feast time; but this feast at the palace was something additional, for it took place in civil surroundings with apparently only civil personnel present (1 Sam. 20:25). It was probably a regular monthly meeting, which was scheduled at new moon time, to determine affairs of state.

experiences lasted more than a few years, perhaps four or five at the most. Certainly the greater part of Saul's reign had elapsed by this time.[43]

What years did remain were spent in continued frustration and wasted effort. Most of the time seems to have been occupied in trying further to apprehend David. Saul's principal motivation in this was his recognition that David was the divinely chosen successor to the throne. He did not have to be told about the official anointing ceremony at Bethlehem to realize this. God's evident blessing on the young man, as well as the general approval of the people, were all too significant. Saul was intent on forcing a change in the divine plan if possible and lent strong effort to that end. Further rebellion of heart toward God was manifested in this, of course.

At one time Saul cruelly took the lives of eighty-five defenseless priests in retaliation for an imagined act of disloyalty (1 Sam. 22:6–19). As David had fled from Gibeah, he had stopped at Nob,[44] then site of the Tabernacle, to ask for food, a weapon, and apparently advice.[45] Ahimelech,[46] then high priest, had cooperated,[47] while Doeg, chief herdsman of Saul, who happened to be present, observed.

Not long after, Doeg, an opportunist interested in royal favors, told Saul what he had seen. Saul immediately summoned Ahimelech and the priests attendant in Nob, numbering eighty-five, to answer for assisting David. Ahimelech gave his answer, and Saul then ordered his men to kill Ahimelech and all eighty-five priests. When they refused to harm the priests, Saul turned to Doeg, who willingly carried out the king's command. After this, Saul also had the city of Nob itself destroyed, including women, children, and all animals. Certainly this was one of Saul's most despicable actions.

2. Final Philistine conflict (1 Samuel 28:1–25; 31:1–13)

When David fled from Saul, Israel lost her ablest military leader. The Philistines had been kept in check as long as David led Israel's forces against them, but Saul had no one of equal ability to replace him.[48]

After David's departure, nothing is heard from the Philistines for a time,

---

[43] Over twenty-two years had elapsed by the time of David's anointing (p. 204n.25), which means that about thirteen years had been consumed in David's coming to the palace as musician, experiencing life as army commander when high plaudits were rendered by the people, and suffering Saul's numerous attacks on his life.

[44] Site uncertain, but apparently within viewing distance of Jerusalem (Isa. 10:32; Neh. 11:32). The best suggestion is Ras Umm et-Tala on the eastern slope of Mount Scopus, northeast of Jerusalem. If correct, David had only about two miles to get there, heading southeast.

[45] That advice was given is not indicated in the account itself (1 Sam. 21:1–9), but is in the reports later of both Doeg (v. 10) and Ahimelech (v. 15).

[46] Ahimelech was a son of Ahitub, grandson of the wicked Phinehas, and great grandson of Eli, descendant of Ithamar. Earlier, Ahimelech had aided Saul in making inquiry for him at the battle of Michmash (1 Sam. 14:3, 36–42, where he is called Ahijah).

[47] Though David did not tell Ahimelech that he was fleeing from Saul, it is clear that Ahimelech suspected the fact; first by his question in 1 Samuel 21:1 and then by his defense of David here before Saul (1 Sam. 22:14–15). He had taken a chance in helping David and is to be commended for his courage.

[48] Though Abner was still captain of the army, he is never seen leading in victory. Jonathan is (Michmash battle), but not Abner, who may have been a better administrator than military strategist (see 1 Sam. 17:55–57; 20:25; 26:5, 7, 14, 15; 2 Sam. 2:8, 12–31; 3:6–37).

but their thrusts into the land gradually became more pronounced, as revealed by two particular incidents. One occurred when fugitive David went to the town of Keilah, located well within the hill country of Judah southwest of Bethlehem,[49] to assist in withstanding a Philistine attack there. On this occasion, Saul did not attempt to defend territory belonging to him (1 Sam. 23:1–5). The other was an instance, not long after, when Saul did quickly pull back from pursuit of David on being informed of a Philistine inroad into the country, and apparently he did make a defense (1 Sam. 23:27–28). The particular place of Philistine penetration this time is not indicated.

The decisive and final battle for Saul with the Philistines came at Mount Gilboa (1 Sam. 28:1–25; 31:1–13). The Philistines first gathered at Aphek, the site of their important victory over Israel some sixty-five years earlier.[50] Then they marched in force through the Esdraelon Valley and encamped at Shunem[51] near Mount Gilboa. Saul moved to meet them and took up quarters in that mountain.

Fearing the coming encounter, he sought information on its outcome from God, but was not answered "by dreams, or Urim or prophets" (1 Sam. 28:6). He longed to consult Samuel, who was now dead (1 Sam. 25:1), and in desperation he broke God's law (Lev. 20:27) and his own regulation (1 Sam. 28:9) by visiting a witch who lived at Endor[52] (1 Sam. 28:7–25). Through what was apparently a resulting supernatural appearance of Samuel, at which the witch herself was terrified, Saul was warned of tragic defeat on the morrow.

The battle was joined, and the prediction came true (1 Sam. 31:1–13). Israel was severely defeated, and Saul's three sons (Jonathan, Abinadab, and Melchi-shua) were killed. Saul was sorely wounded and, not wanting to be captured alive, fell on his own sword.[53] The Philistines found the four bodies of the royal family and hung them for public viewing on the wall in the nearby city of Bethshan.

The men of Jabesh-gilead, upon hearing of the tragedy and remembering their debt to Saul (1 Sam. 11:1–13), came by forced march at night and rescued the bodies and gave them a decent burial. Several years later, David likewise showed grace toward his predecessor by transferring his bones, as well as Jonathan's, from Jabesh-gilead to Saul's homeland, Benjamin, for permanent interment (2 Sam. 21:12–14).

3. Estimate of Saul

Sad indeed was the end of Israel's first king. He had started well but ended shamefully. His tragic death on

---

[49] Identified as Khirbet Qila, six miles east of modern Beit Guvrin, eighteen miles southwest of Jerusalem, three miles south of Adullam.

[50] See p. 192n.93.

[51] Identified with modern Solem in the territory of Issachar at the eastern foot of "Little Hermon" (hill of Moreh, Judg. 7:1), about eight miles from where Saul would have camped in Mount Gilboa. This is doubtless the town where the Shunammite later provided a special room for Elisha (2 Kings 4:8–10).

[52] Endor, modern 'En-dur, was located about nine miles straight north of where Saul encamped. The Philistines were far enough east at Shunem to permit him access to the city.

[53] The later account told by the Amalekite to David (2 Sam. 1:2–10), that he had killed Saul, was very likely a fabrication. At the most, he only finished what Saul had already done in falling on his own sword.

Mount Gilboa suited the perverted manner in which he had ruled during his last years. Saul is an example of what can happen to a man of promise who does not obey God. He had good potential and even was selected by God for his task. He had an attractive appearance. He had the certainty of God's blessing, if he would only follow God's will. But his reign proved to be one of almost continual frustration and lack of accomplishment. In their initial request, the Israelites had wanted one like him to rule so that their country might be strong against enemy attack; but when Saul died, after forty years of rule, the country had actually become weaker than when he began.

Saul was plagued with an emotional problem from the beginning. He probably fought continually to overcome his timidity. This inborn lack of confidence may have influenced him, for instance, in not imposing strong unifying regulations on the people, a policy which was wise at first, as observed, but should not have been continued. Saul's main problem, however, was his pride and rebellious spirit toward God. Fame apparently affected him, and he did not control his actions. He forgot that God was still Head of His people. For this reason he was rejected by God.

The country was probably as disunited at Saul's death as at his inauguration. Any gains during early years were likely lost during the later years. Waning confidence in Saul as a man would have soon led to loss of confidence in the united nation for which he stood. This distrust on the part of the people no doubt played a significant role in Saul's final defeat on Mount Gilboa. Few men responded to his call to serve in the army, and this left him quite incapable of meeting the Philistine challenge. He had ample reason to fear, which is why he resorted to the witch of Endor.

For this reason the Philistines won an easy victory. Israel's army was destroyed and the king killed, leaving the country helpless before the enemy. There is little doubt that the Philistines now moved into the land in strength. This is reflected in the fact that when Ishbosheth, Saul's son and successor, set up his capital, he did so, not at Gibeah, but at Mahanaim across the Jordan (2 Sam. 2:8–9). It is reflected also by the panic in Gibeah when news of the Gilboa disaster was received— panic that, for instance, caused the nurse of Mephibosheth, Jonathan's son, to flee with him in her arms, and drop him in her anxiety (2 Sam. 4:4). As Saul fell on his sword he must have realized that such a situation would now result. What a picture with which to die! He had been promised much when young, but ended with little. Favored above all of his day, he had failed in his great opportunity.

F. DAVID AS FUGITIVE
(1 Samuel 21–27, 29–30; 2 Samuel 1)

1. David's situation

When David fled from Saul, the change in his relation to the king presented difficulties. For one thing, he had to face a new kind of life, requiring a psychological adjustment not easy to make. He had been the favorite in the land, the leader of Israel's victorious army, and applauded on every hand. Now he was a fugitive, legally an outlaw, hunted by the king. Such an adjustment is hard, but David had to make it if he was to keep a clear mind in his new role.

Another matter concerned his relation to the people as their future king, for which he had been anointed by Samuel. How would this new life affect the people's opinion of him? Until now he had enjoyed excellent prospects, with good public exposure and even marriage to the king's daughter. Would his new role change this thinking regarding him?

Still a third matter concerned his own protection from Saul. Certainly the king would pursue him, and David would be forced to seek safety somewhere. How should he proceed and where should he go? Two possible avenues confronted him. One was to move outside the land, where Saul could not follow; but this would involve risk, for he had been leader of Israel's army and might be recognized. The other was to remain in the country, gather a substantial protective band of men, and remain mostly in sparsely populated areas where pursuit would be difficult. This, however, had the drawback of requirements for food and shelter, and he could not really hope to gather a force sufficiently large to withstand Saul's army. The events now to be traced show him trying both avenues.

2. David's course of action (1 Samuel 21–26)

When David left the capital, Gibeah, after bidding farewell to Jonathan, he went, as we have seen, first to Nob, where Ahimelech served as high priest at the tabernacle.[54] Here David received some of the sacred bread for food, Goliath's sword for a weapon, and, most important, an indication through Ahimelech of God's will (1 Sam. 21:3–9; 22:10–15).[55] With a few personal servants,[56] David then directed his steps to the Philistine city, Gath,[57] apparently determined to try the foreign alternative first. However, he was soon recognized there by the servants of King Achish, and he quickly feigned madness that he might escape harm.

David then tried the second alternative. He returned to his homeland and took up residence in a cave near Adullam,[58] where be began gathering a protective force of men. Since he was within ten miles of his home in Bethlehem, he was near enough for his father and brothers to visit him. Somehow David was able to make known, perhaps in part through the help of his family, his need and desire for volunteers. Four hundred responded—men described as in distress, in debt, and discontented (1 Sam. 22:1–2; 1 Chron. 12:8–15). Many may have been political refugees in common with David, having fled from the capricious Saul. It is not likely that David would have harbored persons guilty of gross crimes.

---

[54] The tabernacle was probably intact here yet, minus only the ark. It seems to have been in good condition still later when at Gibeon (2 Chron. 1:3).

[55] No indication is given as to the nature of the communication, but only that it was given, probably by the Urim and Thummim. A likely guess is that it was an approval for the flight.

[56] Ahimelech's indication that David was alone (1 Sam. 21:1) is in terms of David having no army with him, which apparently was unusual. It is clear, however, that a few attendants were there (1 Sam. 21:4–6).

[57] Often identified with Tell el-'Areini, but better with Tell es-Safi, about twenty-three miles southwest of Gibeah; see A. F. Rainey, "Gath of the Philistines," *Christian News From Israel* 17 (September 1966): 31–38.

[58] Identified with modern Tell esh-Sheikh Madhkur, Adullam was about nine miles east of Gath, halfway between Gath and Bethlehem.

With the band assembled, David again tried the foreign expedient, this time moving east to Moab.[59] He took his parents with him now, no doubt fearing reprisals against them by Saul. For some reason, however, Gad, a prophet who had joined David's band, soon counseled him to leave this country; and David moved once more back to Judah, this time to an area called "the forest of Hereth," unknown today.

Here Abiathar, son of Ahimelech, fleeing from Saul, came to David (1 Sam. 22:20–23). The time was soon after Saul's slaughter of the eighty-five priests of Nob, from which Abiathar had escaped. He was high priest now, since his father had just been killed. He brought the priestly ephod with him, apparently including the Urim and Thummim for divine inquiry.[60] We can imagine David's grief at news of the atrocity, but also joy that Abiathar had been able to reach him, especially bringing the Urim and Thummim.

It was not long before David had opportunity to put this divine means of inquiry to use. He learned that the Philistines were preying on the inhabitants of Keilah,[61] and desiring to make friends wherever possible and wanting to help these people, he sought God's will as to giving them assistance (1 Sam. 23:1–13). The answer to the inquiry was affirmative, and David came to the relief of Keilah and helped defeat the Philistines. In spite of the benefit given, however, further inquiry revealed that the people of Keilah would now turn him over to Saul if he remained, and he soon left.

At this point David moved southward, to the region of Ziph and Maon below Hebron.[62] Here Saul made his first attempt to seize David, for the Ziphites had informed him of David's position. He was unsuccessful, however, for from here he had to return to fight Philistines (1 Sam. 23:14–28). David then moved east to En-gedi[63] on the shore of the Dead Sea where Saul again pursued him after the Philistine encounter (1 Sam. 24:1–22). It was here that David spared Saul's life for the first time. Saul had entered a cave where David was hiding, and David could have killed him, but instead he merely cut off part of Saul's clothing for evidence of his proximity. When Saul learned of David's gracious sparing of his life, as David later showed him the severed cloth from a distance, Saul outwardly repented and asked for David's continued mercy.

David next moved back again to the region of Maon. Now he sought food for his men from a wealthy landholder named Nabal, who lived near his camp (1 Sam. 25:2–42). David believed that he had a right to ask for assistance, since his men had been giving protection to Nabal's flocks (1 Sam. 25:7, 14–17). But Nabal, a surly person, was of no mind to accede, and David prepared to punish him. Nabal's wife,

---

[59] Moab had been defeated by Saul a few years earlier (1 Sam. 14:47) and perhaps David reasoned that they would be friendly with one who was now fugitive from Saul. Too, David's ancestress, Ruth, had come from Moab, and it held natural ties for him.

[60] See p. 199n.8.

[61] See p. 210n.49.

[62] Ziph, identified with modern Tell Zif, is three and one-half miles southeast of Keilah. Maon, identified with Khirbet Ma'in, is five miles south of Ziph.

[63] En-gedi is still called by the same name, after a fresh flowing spring. It is sixteen miles straight east from Ziph.

Abigail, however, of a different temperament, intervened to supply the food needed. Nabal died ten days later, perhaps in part from shock in learning from his wife what David had planned to do. David then took Abigail as his own wife.

Not long after, the Ziphites once more tried to curry Saul's favor by telling him of David's hiding place (1 Sam. 26:1–25). Saul came, and for a second time David spared his life when he could have killed him. David, accompanied by Abishai,[64] went to where Saul slept under the guard of Abner and the army, and took away Saul's own spear and jug of water. Once again, the following day, Saul, shown the articles by David, repented and promised not to pursue David any longer.

3. David at Ziklag
(1 Samuel 27, 29–30;
2 Samuel 1)

a. To Ziklag (1 Sam. 27:1–4). Following this second instance of sparing Saul's life, David went once more to the foreign area of the Philistines, for he feared that he could not always escape these attempts by Saul. There was, no doubt, an additional reason for this move—one suggested by the fact that he had recently requested food from Nabal. David's troops now numbered six hundred (1 Sam. 27:2; see 1 Chron. 12:1–7, 19–22), and it would not have been easy to keep them in provisions. The Philistines, like many people of the day,[65] employed mercenary troops; and, if they would now accept his band as such, this problem would be solved. Also, Saul would not follow him here.

With these advantages in mind, David made the move, chancing another unfavorable reception, and offered his services to Achish, king of Gath. Achish accepted David this time, no doubt persuaded that David was a proven refugee from his enemy, Saul, and also by the six hundred David now led, a military unit that Achish could use. He gave David the city of Ziklag,[66] well south in Philistine territory, as a base of operations.

b. Precarious activity at Ziklag (1 Sam. 27:5–12). David played a dual role at Ziklag. Pretending to serve Achish as a good mercenary, he attacked southern tribes that had been perennial enemies of Israel, particularly the Geshurites, Gezrites, and Amalekites.[67] He let Achish believe that he was distressing southern Judah, thus maintaining standing with him while he distributed booty among cities of southern Judah (1 Sam. 30:26–31) to

---

[64] Abishai was a brother of Joab, and became David's general. They were sons of David's sister, Zeruiah (possibly half-sister, see 1 Chron. 2:16; 2 Sam. 17:25). This is the first mention of either, and both may have first associated themselves with David at this time.

[65] Mercenary troops were not uncommon. Ittai, the Gittite (of Gath), had a band of six hundred men (2 Sam. 15:18–22) and later joined himself to David at the time of Absalom's rebellion. Hanun, king of Ammon, hired twenty thousand Syrians and a thousand Macathites to help fight Israel (2 Sam. 10:6).

[66] Tentative identification has been made with Tell al-Khuwailfa, twenty-three miles nearly straight south of Gath and twelve miles north northeast of Beersheba. Ziklag had been one of the cities allotted to Simeon (Josh. 19:5), but apparently had been taken by the Philistines, though far from the center of Philistine activity.

[67] The Geshurites were of Geshuri, south of Philistine land (Josh. 13:2), not of Geshur in Syria (2 Sam. 15:8). Gezrites are unknown, but were not of Gezer to the north. Amalekites are well known as inhabitants of the northern Negeb.

keep their favor toward the day when he would need support in becoming their king.

This was a precarious path to tread, but David apparently did it with success. This is not to say, however, that God was pleased. It seems clear that David's time of sojourn among the Philistines was not one of high spiritual standing.

c. Spared from fighting Israel (1 Sam. 28:2; 29:11). After sixteen months of this activity (1 Sam. 27:7), the final Philistine battle with Saul drew near, and David found himself in difficulty. He apparently had committed himself to Achish to a degree where he could not remain uninvolved without endangering his own position. Consequently, he purported to go along with the Philistine plans. It is unthinkable that he really wished to participate,[68] however, even though he did accompany Achish on the way to battle as far as Aphek, the place of general assembly. Accordingly, he must have been greatly relieved when other Philistines objected to his presence and he was sent home to Ziklag.[69]

d. Amalekite encounter (1 Sam. 30:1–25). Catastrophe met David on his return to Ziklag. The Amalekites, perhaps in retaliation for David's earlier raids, had ravaged the town and taken his wives and the wives of all his men, besides much booty. David's men, ordinarily faithful to him, now came near mutiny. It may be that they had earlier disagreed with David regarding the

whole Philistine policy, and so blamed him here for this.

But David was quick to act. He set out in pursuit of the captors. Learning the location of the Amalekites from a captured Egyptian, who had been left behind because of illness, David stormed the camp and recovered both wives and booty. This alleviated the wounded feelings of the men, and peace was restored. The booty he took exceeded what had been lost, and there was even enough to distribute elsewhere. He did so in thirteen listed Judean towns, where he had received friendly assistance in recent months, and whose friendship he wished to maintain in view of his coming kingship (1 Sam. 30:26–31).

e. News of Saul's death (2 Sam. 1:1–27). It was on the third day after returning from this pursuit that he received word of Israel's tragic defeat at Mount Gilboa and the death of Saul and his sons. The news was brought by one who had escaped the slaughter and who now thought he might obtain favor from Israel's next king by claiming to have killed the prior one. He said that Saul, realizing that the battle was lost and that the enemy was pressing hard upon him, had called to the young man and asked that he kill him, which the young man (who was an Amalekite) said he had done. He carried Saul's crown and bracelet as evidence to support his story.

This was convincing to David, who had no reason to doubt his testimony,[70] and he responded by weeping

---

[68] David's words to Achish never directly indicate that he wanted to go, but are carefully phrased to have made Achish think so. Had David really found it necessary to go he may have defected to aid Saul, even as the Philistine captains suspected. Certainly he would not have fought against Saul, whom he recognized as God's anointed.

[69] It is about forty-eight miles straight south from Aphek to Ziklag, a distance which took David sometime into the third day to cover (1 Sam. 30:1).

[70] The crown and bracelet were evidence that the man had been on hand at least shortly after Saul's

and fasting until the evening of that day. Then he returned to see the young man once again, not to honor him (as the man had hoped) but to order his death for having put his hand on the anointed of Yahweh. This gesture was in keeping with David's own earlier refusal to touch the king's life. David's sincere and touching words of lamentation for both Saul and Jonathan are recorded in 2 Samuel 1:17–27.

David's mourning came from his heart, but, on the other hand, he was obviously aware that this news sounded the note for the time for him to return to Israel. David would have no part in bringing about Saul's death, but at the same time it was what he had been waiting for since the long-past day of his own anointing. The way was now clear for him to return home and receive the kingship.

---

death. However, they were not evidence that he had actually killed Saul, and he probably had not, in view of the account in 1 Samuel 31:4–5. See p. 210n.53.

CHAPTER ELEVEN

DAVID

2 Samuel 1–24; 1 Kings 1:1–2:11; 1 Chronicles 12–29

In contrast to the rule of Saul, David's reign was one of unification and development of the kingdom. He brought the tribes together, established an efficient government, organized the priesthood, and maintained an army that scarcely lost a battle. He inherited a divided, war-torn land and, when he died, left an empire. David was not only a strong king in contrast to his predecessor, he was the strongest king Israel ever had. He was the measure of others. To be a king like David came to be the highest accolade a successor could have.

A. DAVID AT HEBRON
(2 Samuel 1:1–5:5)

Though Saul was dead, David was still not to rule all twelve tribes for seven years. He was readily accepted as king by Judah, but not by the tribes of the north. They crowned Ishbosheth, a remaining son of Saul. In this division of loyalties, a basic separation among the people was evidenced, which has been noted earlier[1] and which came to fruition after Solomon. David ruled over Judah for seven and one-half years and later over all Israel for thirty-three, making a total reign of forty and one-half years (1010–970; 2 Sam. 5:5).

1. David made king of Judah
(2 Samuel 2:1–4)

At the time of Saul's death, David was better known by the people of Judah than by those of the other tribes. His hometown was Bethlehem of Judah, and most of his activity had been south of Saul's capital, Gibeah. This had been true during the time when he had led Saul's army against the Philistines, who lived southwest, and also during his life as a fugitive.

It was logical for him, therefore, as he returned to his own people,[2] to go first to Hebron, a central, principal city

---

[1] Regarding the time Saul called for volunteers to go against Ammonites in behalf of Jabesh-gilead; p. 200n.10.

[2] Returning from Ziklag (see p. 214n.66) he would have had only seventeen miles to travel northeast to get there.

of Judah, and for the people located there to proclaim him king. He had been their champion for many years, and his gifts and favors had been distributed among their cities. Moreover, he had proved his ability in leadership, especially warfare, much in contrast to the performance of the prior regime. No doubt a large majority were glad for the opportunity to make him king at last, giving them one in whom they could place confidence. Accordingly, when David arrived at Hebron with his own household—in addition to the households of all his six hundred followers (2 Sam. 2:3)—the men of Judah promptly assembled and anointed him "king over the house of Judah."

2. Ishbosheth made king of Israel (2 Samuel 2:8–10)

The situation was different for the other tribes,[3] because they did not know David so well. Stories would have circulated among them regarding his prowess against the Philistines, when he was still Saul's army commander; but, after he fled from the king, he probably dropped from their attention.

Consequently, on learning of Saul's death, logic led them to think first of Saul's surviving son, Ishbosheth.[4] Three sons had died with Saul, but this one remained, along with two daughters, Merab and Michal. Abner, who somehow had survived the slaughter on Mount Gilboa, was instrumental in establishing Ishbosheth as king, choosing Mahanaim[5] across the Jordan as the new capital.

This change in location of capital was caused by the Philistine domination of Israel since the Gilboa rout. At Mahanaim the young man was proclaimed king of both sides of the Jordan, though the extent to which people west of the river either benefited or felt responsible is questionable. Their main concern was with the threatening presence of the Philistines.

How did the Philistines react to the crowning of David and Ishbosheth over their respective countries? Did they consider them dangerous enemies, did they view them as helpful vassals, or were they unconcerned? Regarding the Israelite king, they probably were quite unconcerned. His influence at most would be minimal west of the Jordan where they were interested.

Regarding David, it is conceivable that they still thought of him as only a vassal. He had been among them, served well under Achish, and should not be difficult to control as ruler over small Judah. Certainly they were pleased that the nation of Israel was now divided, and they no doubt thought in terms of soon taking over the entire country anyway.

---

[3] From here on in Scripture, the term *Israel* is used with some regularity to mean the tribes north of Judah; for instance 1 Samuel 2:9, 10, 17. When David eventually comes to reign over all twelve tribes, he is said to reign over "all Israel and Judah" (2 Sam. 5:5).

[4] Ishbosheth was formerly called Ishbaal (1 Chron. 8:33; 9:39). Similarly, Gideon's later name, Jerubbaal (Judg. 6:32), was afterward changed to Jerubosheth (2 Sam. 11:21). The element "baal," meant "master" or "possessor" but came into disrepute because of the foreign god, Baal. The element, "bosheth," chosen as substitute (see also Mephibosheth, 2 Sam. 9:6) meant "shame," referring to shameful Baal.

[5] The site of Mahanaim is not certain. It is commonly identified with Khirbet Mahneh, twelve and one-half miles north of the Jabbok, but is better placed nearer the Jabbok, for it was at Gad's northern border (Josh. 13:26–30). It was some distance east of the Jordan in view of 2 Samuel 2:29.

3. Struggle between David and Ishbosheth (2 Samuel 2:12–4:12)

a. Early conflict. Conflict between Judah and Israel was almost inevitable from the beginning. It broke out first in a minor skirmish at Gibeon[6] of Benjamin, six miles northeast of Jerusalem (2 Sam. 2:12–32). There Abner met David's chief, Joab,[7] by the pool of Gibeon.[8] At first only twelve men of each side fought, but the conflict widened and a small war ensued. Finally David's force emerged victorious. Following the main struggle, Asahel, younger brother of Joab, was killed by Abner as he fled from the battle scene, a deed Joab was not to forget.

b. David's increase in strength. As months passed, David continually grew stronger in his rule, while Ishbosheth became weaker. Abner, who had been the true ruling voice in Mahanaim from the first, finally quarreled with his king and decided to offer his services to David (2 Sam. 3:7–16). In this, Abner was showing his recognition of inevitable developments. He had gained respect for David's ability long before, when both had been active in Saul's inner circle. Now that David was definitely becoming stronger in his position, Abner could see that any future for him lay with David.

Sending a message to David, he agreed to deliver all Israel into David's hands in return for his own safety and, no doubt, an honored position. David first made him agree, however, to return Michal, David's former wife. She had married one Phaltiel after David became a fugitive, and David now wanted her back. Apparently his love for her had not waned; and, further, the marriage tied him with the house of Saul, which should help gain the allegiance of the northern tribes.

Abner gave assent and brought about Michal's return, much to the sorrow of her present husband, who followed her weeping as far as Abner would permit. Abner also communicated with elders from the various tribes, urging that they now turn their allegiance to David, apparently with some success.

Before he could really effect this change of allegiance, however, he was killed by Joab (2 Sam. 3:17–27). This wanton act by David's leader was committed in retaliation for the death of Asahel, though one wonders how much Joab's fear of a rival for his position may also have contributed. David, desiring to court favor with the northern tribes, now did all he could to disassociate himself from the deed, making a public display of his sorrow that it had happened (2 Sam. 3:28–39).

c. Ishbosheth assassinated. With Abner's control gone, two of the lesser officers of Ishbosheth assassinated their king in his palace and carried his head to David, thinking they would be rewarded (2 Sam. 4:1–12). But, as with the messenger of Saul's death, David again reacted in an unexpected way, having both immediately killed. Probably two reasons accounted for

---

[6] See p. 146n.39.

[7] Abishai, brother of Joab, was mentioned earlier (p. 214n.64), but this is the first mention of Joab, himself. Asahel was the youngest of the three.

[8] A pit identified with this pool has been excavated. It was dug to a depth of thirty-five feet in the rock with a descending stairway. Further steps were found to lead another forty feet down a tunnel to a water chamber.

this reaction: first, David's respect for one who had been duly appointed king of Israel (particularly since he was a son of Saul) and, second, David's desire once more to disassociate himself from a deed that could bring disfavor of the northern tribes toward him. The image of one who schemed and killed to attain his goals was undesirable. He wanted to be known as he truly felt, and he did have personal revulsion against such actions. Similar thinking had earlier caused him to extend his appreciation to the inhabitants of Jabesh-Gilead for their act in giving Saul and his sons an honorable burial (2 Sam. 2:4–7).[9]

4. David made king of all Israel (2 Samuel 5:1–5; 1 Chronicles 12:23–40)

Seven years and six months of ruling at Hebron (2 Sam. 5:5) had passed when David was formally anointed king over all Israel.[10] By this time, people spontaneously desired him. Leaders from all the tribes, accompanied by sizable armies,[11] came to Hebron to make the formal request and reach an agreement.

Since the biblical record specifically states that a "covenant" (KJV) was made at the time, it is likely that some

negotiation transpired. The people wanted David as king, but he would have wanted some commitments in return, guarantees that would insure a true central government. He had seen enough laxity during Saul's rule to realize that regulation, organization, and taxation were necessary if unity was to be achieved. Apparently he also recognized that the time to procure promises was before the rule started. Moreover, negotiation would have been necessary between Judah, which was present as well (Simeon, too, 1 Chron. 12:24–25), and the northern tribes. The people of Judah would have had to agree to share their king, perhaps demanding some concession in return, and also to accept the same regulations that David now demanded of the other tribes.

The thinking of all the tribes in weighing such demands is not difficult to conjecture. They needed a king, and they needed a strong one—indeed, one with the kind of ability David had earlier shown as head of Saul's army. If David could lead them out of their present subjection to the Philistines, any terms, at all reasonable, would not be too high to meet. Agreement was reached, the terms were accepted,[12] and David was anointed for the third time in his life.[13]

---

[9]David had been told of this kindness of Jabesh-gilead immediately after arrival in Hebron. Years later he went further and brought the bones of Saul and Jonathan back to Gibeah for burial (2 Sam. 21:12). He could not do this now, for Benjamin was not yet in his jurisdiction.

[10]In 2 Samuel 2:10, Ishbosheth is said to have ruled over Israel only two years, some five and one-half years less than David over Judah. This difference may be accounted for as follows. With confusion reigning and Philistines dominant, Abner may have waited many months before proclaiming Ishbosheth king; a brief time elapsed between Ishbosheth's death and the northern leaders getting together (with Abner also dead and so not able to give leadership) to ask David to rule them; and several months again elapsed after their request and the actual move of David to Jerusalem, during which time he had to make plans and fight Philistines in two battles.

[11]These armies totaled 339,600 men (1 Chron. 12:23–40). If all these came, as seems indicated, this was a great showing of enthusiasm for David to accept the Israelite throne.

[12]Evidence that they were is seen in the manner of strong rule that David did establish, much in contrast to that of Saul.

[13]The first had been by Samuel in anticipation, the second by the people of Judah seven and one-half years before, and now over all the land.

B. DAVID ESTABLISHES THE KINGDOM OF ISRAEL (2 Samuel 5:6–8:18; 10:1–19)

David's genius for rule was apparent from the start. His initial problem concerned the Philistines. Though the northern tribes had accepted him as their king, the Philistines still were dominant there. Before David could fully rule, this dominance had to be removed. David succeeded brilliantly in the task.

1. Struggle with Philistines (2 Samuel 5:17–25)

David did not have to ponder the problem long before it was thrust upon him, for the Philistines themselves initiated military action. They had remained quiet while David was king of Judah only; but, with the kingdom now united, their policy changed. It was clear that David was no longer a vassal. He was once again a chief enemy and should be dealt with accordingly.

a. First battle. The Philistines made their attack in the Valley of Rephaim, just south of Jerusalem. The strategy is apparent. They already had a garrison in Bethlehem (2 Sam. 23:14), probably established after the Mount Gilboa victory, and they wanted to supplement it and divide the country, making it impossible for David to effect the agreed-upon union of the nation. David established his headquarters northeast of Hebron at the cave of Adullam[14] (2 Sam. 23:13–14), where he had first assembled his band when a fugitive. His army still consisted mainly of the faithful group gathered during fugitive days. It was a closely knit band of men, willing to risk their lives if their leader wished for as much as a drink from a spring behind enemy lines (2 Sam. 23:15–17). God assured David of victory, and David attacked at Baal-perazim (location unknown), defeating the Philistines. The victory was so complete that the enemy left images of their gods behind as they fled, apparently in panic. These images were burned by David.[15]

b. Second battle. The Philistines were not through, however. They regrouped and came into the same valley again, attempting a similar divisive tactic. This time God's instruction was for David to change the direction of his attack and come at them from the rear at an opportune moment, which God Himself would signify by a sound in nearby balsam trees. This strategy made use of the mobility of David's small, disciplined band to surprise the enemy. The ensuing attack brought decisive victory once again, and David this time drove the Philistines as far as Gezer.[16] This major triumph ended the domination of the Philistines over Israel.[17] What further contacts there were in later years occurred on Philistine soil and were relatively minor in significance

---

[14] See p. 212n.58.

[15] The KJV renders the verse in this way. Modern versions (NIV, NEB) generally read, "David and his men carried them off." The parallel passage (1 Chron. 14:12) records the burning of the Philistines. It is most reasonable to read the two texts as complementary, Samuel recording the capture of the idols and Chronicles their destruction.

[16] See p. 149n.51. Gezer, at the northeast boundary of Philistine territory, was at least fifteen miles from the point of this battle.

[17] That David had lived and fought with the Philistines helped him to know their ways and plan his own strategy. This certainly helped also to break their monopoly on iron.

(2 Sam. 21:15–22; 1 Chron. 18:1; 20:4–8).

Thus, David's beginning as king was most auspicious. In two brief encounters, he had solved the problem of the Philistines. The impression on the northern tribes, which had long been oppressed by this formidable enemy, must have been very great. These tribes had sought David as their king, especially that he might rid them of this oppression, and here he had done so already, with apparent ease. Without question, his task of asserting himself as king, with the imposition of organization and regulation that involved, was made much easier by this signal achievement.

2. A new capital (2 Samuel 5:6–12; 6:1–7:29; 1 Chronicles 13, 15–17)

With the Philistine menace eliminated, David could think in terms of an appropriate capital.[18] Hebron was central for Judah (but too far south to serve the whole country), like Shechem was central for Israel (but too far north for Judah). Gibeah, Saul's former capital, had been destroyed by the Philis-tines and had not been a particularly good location anyhow. Apparently its only water supply had been a cistern, excavation having found no trace of a spring.[19]

a. Jerusalem made capital. David's choice fell on Jerusalem, a city still held by Jebusites.[20] It lay exactly on the border between Judah and Israel, had a good water supply in the Spring of Gihon,[21] its position was readily defensible, and it had no existing tribal affiliations. To occupy it would also eliminate a Canaanite stronghold within the country, so David captured it, apparently without difficulty,[22] and fortified it. There is no indication that he destroyed the former inhabitants, which means that a majority of the city's population may have been foreign for some time.[23]

b. Religious capital. David desired to make Jerusalem the religious capital as well. It was not long, therefore, before he sought to bring the ark, which had been at Kirjath-jearim for seventy years,[24] to the city (2 Sam. 6:1–11; 1 Chron. 13). However, David did not transport it correctly, using an open

---

[18]Though 2 Samuel 5:6–9 records David's taking Jerusalem before telling of the Philistine battle, the intention cannot be to indicate that this transpired first. Second Samuel 5:17 says that the Philistine encounter came as soon as the Philistines heard of the agreed union. Also, if David had then already taken Jerusalem, the Philistine attack at Rephaim to divide the country would not have made sense. Further, 1 Samuel 23:13–14 indicates that David made his headquarters at the cave of Adullam, which would have made no sense at all if he already had the stronghold of Jerusalem.

[19]See p. 201n.16.

[20]Jebusites were Canaanites who had continued to live in Jerusalem. Jerusalem even carried the alternate name, Jebus (Josh. 18:16, 28; Judg. 19:10). The name *Zion* is introduced in 2 Samuel 5:7 and probably referred to the hill on which the city stood, which later was only one of other hills occupied as the city grew. See also p. 150n.56.

[21]A fine flowing spring in the Kidron Valley east of Jerusalem, from which Hezekiah later had a tunnel cut; see p. 305.

[22]Second Samuel 5:8 suggests that some strategy involving a waterway was used to take the city. Since the Jebusites already had a slanting tunnel to the Spring of Gihon, it may have been this tunnel that David's men employed.

[23]That Jebusites did continue to live in the area is indicated also by the fact that Araunah, at whose land a plague in David's latter days was stopped, was a Jebusite (2 Sam. 24:16–17).

[24]See p. 195n.110.

cart rather than poles as prescribed by God. As a result, one of the attendants, Uzzah, son of Abinadab in whose house the ark had resided, was struck dead when he attempted to keep it from falling from the cart. David then left the ark at the nearby home of one Obed-Edom, whose household was greatly blessed by God as a result. Three months later David returned to finish the task, this time proceeding according to divine direction (2 Sam. 6:12–23; 1 Chron. 15:1–29). He placed the ark in a tent which he had prepared in Jerusalem amidst great rejoicing and offering of sacrifices.

David desired to build a fine temple for the ark, but God did not allow it (2 Sam. 7:1–17; 1 Chron. 17:1–15). The prohibition came through the prophet Nathan, who is first mentioned here and was active throughout David's reign. He announced that God would greatly bless David, that his family would never be replaced on the throne by another, but that, since he was a man of war, he should not be the one to build a temple. His son, who would be a man of peace, would be the man to do so. David's admirable reaction to these disappointing words was to voice a prayer of submission and thanksgiving before God (2 Sam. 7:18–29; 1 Chron. 17:16–27). He then proceeded to gather substantial quantities of material toward the day when his son would build it (1 Chron. 22:1–5, 14–16).

The contrasting attitudes between David and Saul toward the ark and the priesthood would not have escaped the people. Saul not only neglected the ark, but killed many of the priests. David, on the other hand, brought the long-displaced ark to the new capital early in his reign; and also installed the priests, Abiathar and Zadok,[25] along with Levites, to assist in ministering before it (2 Sam. 8:17; 15:24–36; 1 Chron. 15:11). David's genuine concern for the religious elements of Israel must have pleased all devout Israelites, further strengthening their allegiance.

3. David's conquests
(2 Samuel 8; 10; 12:26–31;
1 Chronicles 18–20)

a. Consolidation of the tribes. The biblical record includes little information regarding David's consolidation of the Israelite tribes into a centralized government. Much more is stated regarding his foreign wars. Since these, however, could not have been waged without a strong nation at home, it is certain that he did achieve true unity, something that Saul never did.

Several factors would have contributed to this unification. For one thing, David had assumed the throne of the northern tribes by the acclamation of the people (2 Sam. 5:1–3), whose elders entered into a covenant relation with him. For another, he had earned the goodwill of the people by his scrupulous dealings with Saul and his survivors and by his early success against the Philistines. Also, he was able to work with people and bring them to agree with his thinking. Still

---

[25] Zadok is first mentioned at this time. He probably is the one who is listed with others as having come to David in Hebron, as head of twenty-two captains of his father's house (1 Chron. 12:28). He was a descendant of Eleazar, third son of Aaron, while Abiathar was descendant of Ithamar, the fourth son (1 Kings 2:27; 1 Chron. 24:3). Since he came with others from the northern tribes, he must have been recognized there as high priest, which suggests that Saul had so appointed him following the flight of Abiathar after the Nob slaughter.

further, he was a man of conviction and confidence who would have inspired others to follow. These matters would have prompted the people to accept his leadership; and his own good judgment, coupled with experience gained while a member of Saul's government, would have contributed to the successful unification of all twelve tribes.

This tribal consolidation would also have involved the acquisition of land originally allotted but never occupied. Until now, Israelites had been confined mostly to the hills, with the Philistines and Canaanites holding the better lowlands. But this situation changed under David. The implication of Scripture[26] is that Canaanite holdings along the Mediterranean to the north, across the Esdraelon Valley, and through the Jordan Valley were now brought under Israelite control. The Philistines were not driven from the plain of Philistia in Israel's southwest, but they were confined to a much restricted territory.

Aside from this small Philistine enclave, all the formerly unconquered territories now fell under Israelite control, and David ruled from north of the Sea of Galilee to Beersheba in the south and on both sides of the Jordan River. As a result, Israelites could know for the first time that they did exist as a true nation. The tribes had become genuinely united, controlled almost all their allotted land, and had a fine king of whom they could be proud.

b. David's army. To make extensive foreign conquests, David needed a strong army. Again, little detailed information is available about its constituent parts; but certain facts may be pieced together from scattered references. In general, the army consisted of three sections: (1) the original faithful six hundred from David's fugitive days, a group to which probably some replacements and additions were made, (2) troops levied from the people, constituting a sort of revolving standing army, and (3) foreign mercenaries.

The core at all times seems to have been the six hundred, the group referred to as *gibborim,* "mighty men"[27] in several places. This term appears to be used for them, for instance, when a group is mentioned as being with David in his flight from Absalom (2 Sam. 16:6); also when his supporters are listed at the revolt of Sheba (2 Sam. 20:7); later when supporters of Solomon are named at the attempted rebellion of Adonijah (1 Kings 1:8, 10); and still later when attendants are listed on the occasion of David's closing admonitions (1 Chron. 28:1).

It was probably from this six hundred that the special "mighty men" were selected (2 Sam. 23:8–39; 1 Chron. 11:10–47), all perhaps commanders. A recorded list of "thirty" may be of captains over divisions of twenty each; and another five named may have served over them.[28] The high

---

[26] Evidenced by the continuous route taken by David's census people somewhat later (2 Sam. 24:5–8), and also by the description of the land which later was passed along to Solomon (1 Kings 4:7–19).

[27] The term *gibborim* is used for armies other than David's, but almost always with an added term, such as *hayil,* "of valor." This is never true for David's group. Also, when used of David's army, the term, especially in 1 Kings 1:8, 10 and 1 Chronicles 28:1, seems to carry a particular reference rather than general as at other times.

[28] The elite five are listed in two classes: first, Jashobeam, Eleazar, and Shammah; second, Abishai (brother of Joab, with Joab himself not named) and Benaiah, each listed with corresponding exploits.

caliber of these troops is indicated both by the exploits described (2 Sam. 23:8–39) and by the exemplary conduct of one of them, Uriah the Hittite, who, when called back from battle by David, would not even go to his own home, since this comfort would be out of keeping with his duty as a soldier (2 Sam. 11:11; 23:39).

David also kept 24,000 in service as a regular standing army, changing the personnel once every month (1 Chron. 27:1–15). This means that he had 288,000 trained men, prepared at all times for immediate call to service as needed. At the time of Absalom's revolt, this group turned against David when Absalom called on them, and their number is then described as "the sand on the seashore" (2 Sam. 17:11).

Then David kept foreign mercenaries, who appear to have served as his private bodyguard, made up of Cherethites and Pelethites[29] (2 Sam. 8:18; 15:18; 20:7; 1 Kings 1:38, 44). They may not have gone to war frequently with the regular army but stayed with the king for his personal protection.

c. Foreign conquests. With the home country firmly consolidated and controlled, and with an effective army available, David was in a position to wage war on foreign soil as need arose.

There is no suggestion that he intentionally sought conquest, however, or that he gave himself to creating an empire. For the most part, he simply entered battle situations as they arose and sought to win them. His victories did result in the country's borders continually enlarging.

(i) Moab and Edom. The first war listed[30] was with Moab, on the east of the Dead Sea (2 Sam. 8:2; 1 Chron. 18:2). David had found refuge there for a time when pursued by Saul, but now he inflicted a complete defeat upon the country. The cause of the war is not indicated, but David's harsh measures point to serious provocation. The result was that Moab became a vassal state, apparently keeping her own king but having to pay tribute.

Sometime later, David fought and defeated Edom, located south of the Dead Sea (2 Sam. 8:13–14; 1 Chron. 18:12–13). Again little description is given. The battle occurred in the "Valley of Salt";[31] severe reprisals once more were effected;[32] and Israelite garrisons were installed, signifying that Edom also was made a vassal state. These two victories gave David sovereignty on the east and south of the Dead Sea to the Gulf of Aqaba, an important waterway for trade.

The "thirty" (actually thirty-two are named, probably indicating later additions) are listed without exploits. First Chronicles 11:41–47 adds sixteen additional names, suggesting further additions.

[29] Believed to be Cretans and Philistines on the basis of name comparisons. They remained loyal to David in the rebellion of Absalom (2 Sam. 15:18; see 2 Sam. 20:7). They were present and last heard from at Solomon's anointing to kingship (1 Kings 1:38, 44). There is no intimation of how David obtained the service of such a group.

[30] Both 2 Samuel 8:1 and 1 Chronicles 18:1 list a preceding engagement with the Philistines. This was a minor battle, however, for only a few towns were taken.

[31] A part of the Arabah (see 2 Kings 14:7) and not the Wadi el-Milh (Valley of Salt) near Beersheba. An offensive war with Edom is not likely to have been waged that far into Israelite territory.

[32] This severity is brought out especially in 1 Kings 11:15–18, where Joab is said to have killed "all the men of Edom," likely meaning the men of the Edomite army, remaining in the land six months to do so. First Chronicles 18:12 indicates that eighteen thousand were killed. Likely the royal household was also killed, with only Hadad and some servants escaping to Egypt.

(ii) Damascus, Zobah, Hamath. In the north, David achieved victory over strong Zobah,[33] from whose king, Hadadezer, he seized one thousand chariots, seven thousand horsemen, and twenty thousand foot soldiers (2 Sam. 8:3–12; 1 Chron. 18:3–11). David killed the horses except enough for one hundred chariots. Evidently he did not believe that he had use for more in his own army, probably because much of his fighting was done in mountain areas, where chariots were of little value.

When Arameans of Damascus came to assist Zobah, apparently arriving after the main battle, David defeated them, demanded tribute, and received it. Also, voluntary tribute was now extended by Hamath, located further north on the Orontes River. No details are given regarding these interchanges. David placed garrisons in Damascus as he had in Moab and Edom, indicating that this region, too, became a vassal state, though how far north of Damascus this degree of control extended is not clear. Certainly it did not reach Hamath, which only acknowledged David's sovereignty; and the status of Zobah, between Damascus and Hamath, is uncertain. As for the coastal region along the Mediterranean, David had already made a treaty with Hiram, king of Tyre, which provided material and labor for building David's palace (2 Sam. 5:11) and established a cooperative relationship in that direction.

(iii) Ammon and Zobah. An important war with Ammon, again to the east, is described in greater detail (2 Sam. 10; 1 Chron. 19). Chronologically, this engagement probably preceded the northern struggle just noted,[34] though its record follows in the biblical account. David's kindness toward Hanun, a new king of Ammon, had been misunderstood; and messengers sent by David had been insulted. Ammon, fearing reprisal from David, immediately prepared for war. King Hanun hired mercenaries from the Aramean states, Bethrehob (in Coele-Syria, north of Dan; see Judg. 18:28), Zobah, and Maacah (south of Mount Hermon).[35] David sent Joab with Israel's army to meet this combined force, and Joab won a decisive victory through his skill as a military strategist.

Joab returned to Jerusalem, but Hadadezer, defeated king of Zobah, came again with fresh troops for a return battle. David's army moved across the Jordan to meet him at Helam[36] and once more won a complete victory. The opposing army, now sorely depleted in numbers, retired from the scene acknowledging Israelite supremacy.

Joab then laid siege to Rabbah,[37] capital of Ammon, evidently in a continuation of the struggle begun earlier

---

[33] An Aramean state north of Damascus and east of the Anti-Lebanon mountains, which controlled nomadic tribes as far north as the Euphrates. It was the most powerful of the Aramean states at this time.

[34] Because Zobah is involved at this time, too, and actively engaged against Israel, whereas in the northern struggle she was fully subdued and so no longer in a position to assist should Ammon or any other have called.

[35] For discussion of the location of each, see Merrill F. Unger, *Israel and the Arameans of Damascus* (London: James Clark, 1957), pp. 42–45.

[36] Helam is best identified with modern ʿAlma, thirty miles east of the Sea of Galilee, considerably north of Ammon where the previous battle was fought.

[37] Rabbah is well identified with modern Amman, present capital of Jordan, twenty-two miles east of the River Jordan.

by Ammon (2 Sam. 12:26–31; 1 Chron. 20:1–3). It was during this siege that David sinned with Bathsheba and killed her husband, Uriah, by placing him at the point of heaviest fighting (2 Sam. 11:1–27). Rabbah was finally taken and David assumed the crown of Ammon, thus annexing this country to his own kingdom.

d. David's empire. This was the extent of David's recorded conquests. The breadth of his authority was now most impressive. As for the kingdom proper, this included all land originally allotted to the twelve tribes (less reduced Philistia), plus the kingdom of Ammon. As for vassal states, keeping their own kings but controlled by David's troops, these included Moab and Edom (east and south of the Dead Sea) and the area around Damascus northeast, which may have involved even all Zobah.

As for territory that acknowledged Israelite sovereignty through the payment of tribute, this included the northern region (of which Hamath was capital). Since its boundary reached northeast to the Euphrates, and since this country acknowledged Israelite sovereignty, David's authority extended from the Gulf of Aqaba and the River of Egypt[38] in the south all the way to the Euphrates in the north. This was the area that God had promised to Abraham for his posterity centuries before (Gen. 15:18). It did not rival the vast territories of Egypt, Assyria, Babylonia, etc., in their empire days; but in David's time it was one of the larger land areas held, and David was

probably one of the strongest rulers of his age.

C. DAVID'S GOVERNMENT

1. The state

The successes of David's reign must have had a profound impact on Israel's perception of its place in history. Before his rule, they had been the object of attack, for they had been weak and other nations, especially the Philistines, had been strong. But now matters were reversed. They had become the dominant nation, and those nearby feared them. Never before in history had it been this way. God's promise to their father Abraham had at last come true.

King David was the central figure in this new status. The Israelite people had followed and marveled as he led the way. To him belonged the honor. Israel was David's kingdom more than David was Israel's king.

Little information is given concerning the administrative measures David enacted. There is indication that he placed general supervisors over every tribe except Gad and Asher, though their duties are not described (1 Chron. 27:16–22). He also appointed heads over treasuries, storehouses, and various agricultural departments (1 Chron. 27:25–31). Certainly high taxes were imposed to support the program, though considerable foreign tribute was received, which would have helped.

2. The court

Two similar lists of leading members of David's court are recorded (2 Sam. 8:15–18; 20:23–26). Serving in a

---

[38] River of Egypt (*nahal misrayim;* Num. 34:5) is best taken to mean Wadi el-ʿArish, reaching the Mediterranean forty-five miles southwest of Gaza and eighty miles east of the Pelusiac mouth of the Nile. For discussion, see K. Kitchen, "Egypt, River of," *NBD,* pp. 353–54.

HAMATH

Lebo-hamath

Byblos

ARAM-ZOBAH

Beeroth

Berothai

SIDONIANS

Damascus

Sidon

BETH-REHOB

Beth-zaith

Zarephath

ARAMEANS

Ahlab

Ijon

Tyre

Dan

Hosah?

Kedesh

MAACAH

Acco

Chinnereth

Ashtaroth

Kenath

Dor

Tob

Megiddo

Bethshan

Ramoth-gilead

Salchah

I S R A E L

Shechem

Mahanaim

Joppa

AMMON

Rabbath-Ammon

Bethel

Ashdod

Ekron

Jerusalem

Ashkelon

Gath

Madeba

PHILISTINES

Hebron

Aroer

Gaza

Gerar

JUDAH

Sharuhen

MOAB

Beersheba

Kir-hareseth

Zoar

Brook of Egypt

Kadesh-barnea

Tamar

Bozrah

EDOM

Teman

Kingdom Proper

Vassal States

Acknowledged Israelite
sovereignty

Elath

Map 10. The Kingdom of David

military capacity were Joab, commander of the army, and Benaiah, commander of the two foreign divisions, the Cherethites and Pelethites. Superintending civic duties were Jehoshaphat, the *mazkir* ("one who reminds"), whose task likely was to keep records and remind the king of appointments and responsibilities; Seraiah, the *sopher* ("scribe"), who carried on official correspondence; and Adoram, minister over the *mas* ("tribute labor"),[39] probably composed of foreign laborers serving on public works. Leading in religious matters were Zadok and Abiathar, the two high priests. Besides these, the chronicler (1 Chron. 27:32–34) lists four others high in rank: Jonathan, an uncle of David, as counselor; Jehiel as governor of David's children; and Ahithophel and Hushai as two other counselors.

David's own family was large. When various lists are combined (2 Sam. 3:2–5; 5:13–16; 1 Chron. 3:1–8; 14:4–7; 2 Chron. 11:18), the names of eight wives and twenty-one children are revealed. Besides the wives named, other unnamed "wives and concubines" were added when David assumed his rule in Jerusalem. The number of these is not given; but, at the time of his flight from Jerusalem before Absalom, at least ten concubines were left to keep the palace (2 Sam. 15:16). It was customary in that day for powerful kings to keep large harems, and David apparently followed the practice.

Besides these persons mentioned, others also sat at the king's table. One was Mephibosheth, to whom David showed kindness because he was a son of Jonathan (2 Sam. 9:1–13). Barzillai, a wealthy Gileadite who befriended David in his flight from Absalom, was invited; and, though he refused, he was represented by Chimham, likely a son. David's select "mighty men" (KJV), noted above, being highly honored by him, also probably ate at the palace with some regularity.

3. Religious personnel

a. Gad and Nathan, prophets. Among David's religious personnel, the prophets Gad and Nathan were outstanding. Gad had been with David when he was a fugitive (1 Sam. 22:5), and later in David's reign he was the one who offered David the choice of three punishments from God for his sin in census-taking (2 Sam. 24:10–15). Nathan told David that God would not permit him to build the temple (2 Sam. 8:2–17). Later he rebuked David for his sin with Bathsheba (2 Sam. 12:1–15), and finally he played a prominent role in Solomon's acclamation as king (1 Kings 1:11–45).

b. Zadok and Abiathar, high priests. As noted, David, contrary to Mosaic Law (which allowed for only one), recognized two high priests, Zadok and Abiathar. The circumstance, however, was unusual. Abiathar had escaped Saul's slaughter of the eighty-five priests of Nob (1 Sam. 22:20–23) and come to David. He had been with David ever since, certainly high in David's honor and affection. On assuming the rule of all Israel, however, David had found Zadok also recog-

---

[39] Probably the same man as called Adoniram in Solomon's day (1 Kings 4:6; 5:14), whose task was essentially the same. Since his name appears in only the second of the two lists (2 Sam. 20:24) from David's rule, it is likely that he was not needed until late in David's reign when this type of conscript labor had come to be used.

nized as high priest, probably appointed by Saul following the slaughter.[40]

Both were descendants of Aaron, Abiathar through Ithamar and Zadok through Eleazar, and so both had inheritance rights to the title. Zadok appears to have been favored by David over Abiathar by being placed in charge of the ark (2 Sam. 15:24–29). Later, when Abiathar supported Adonijah, Zadok helped in the anointing of Solomon as king (1 Kings 1:7–8). As a result, Zadok and his family continued in the office of high priest after David's rule, whereas Abiathar was expelled (1 Kings 2:26–27).

c. *Organization.* These two high priests were over the priests and the Levites. All these descendants of Levi were reorganized.[41] The priests were divided into twenty-four specific courses, each course given a turn to serve for a week at the central sanctuary; thus, each averaged a total of two weeks service during any one year (1 Chron. 24:1–19).[42]

Similarly, David divided the Levites, who had been previously sectionalized into musicians, gatekeepers, officials and judges, and general priestly assistants.[43] Of these, at least the musicians, and probably the other sections as well, were divided into twenty-four courses (1 Chron. 25:1–31), as were the priests.[44] David was rightly concerned with the religious life of the people and believed that efficient service by the priests and Levites, as enhanced by this manner of organization, would be crucial in making it the highest possible. David himself contributed to this religious emphasis and growth by the numerous psalms he wrote, some of which came to be used in the official religious services.[45]

D. SIGNIFICANT DEEDS

Several significant deeds of David while king are narrated in the biblical

---

[40] See p. 223n.25.

[41] The main reason being that priests and Levites numbered too many to serve at one time. Since this condition would have existed also in the Judges Period, David may have had precedent for what he did. When the ark was away from the tabernacle, this system could have fallen into disuse, with David now reviving and strengthening it.

[42] Until the temple was built by Solomon, this service presumably was conducted at the tabernacle, located in David's time at Gibeon (2 Chron. 1:3) and at the special tent David erected for the ark in Jerusalem. An altar requiring priestly service was located at this tent as witnessed by Joab running there for safety (1 Kings 2:28). Certain Levites were assigned to the tent (1 Chron. 16:4–6). Zadok and others were assigned to Gibeon (1 Chron. 16:39).

[43] When these distinctive Levitic groups came into existence is not indicated. At least the gatekeepers were a distinct group from the time of Moses (1 Chron. 9:17–26). The "singers" (KJV) were the religious musicians, the "gatekeepers" (KJV) were the guardians of the sanctuary (with gates assigned, 1 Chron. 26:13–19), and the "officials and judges" (*shoterim, shophetim*) were seemingly special recorders and court judges assigned to various tribes (1 Chron. 26:29–32). Most Levites conducted the more normal Levitic duties, as described in 1 Chronicles 23:28–32.

[44] David's census revealed thirty-eight thousand Levites of service age, of which four thousand were musicians, four thousand gatekeepers, six thousand officials and judges, and the remaining twenty thousand for general service (1 Chron. 23:3–5).

[45] Superscriptions attribute seventy-three psalms to David. His musical ability is witnessed by his early appointment as court musician to Saul. Some of his poems are recorded outside the Psalms (2 Sam. 1:18–27; 3:33–34; 23:2–7). Psalm 18 is given also in 2 Samuel 22:2–51 and attributed to him. He is called "Israel's singer of songs" (2 Sam. 23:1). Even Amos, three hundred years later, refers back to him as a musician (6:5). First Chronicles 16:7 tells of David giving parts of Psalms 96, 105, and 106 to Asaph for use in rendering thanksgiving to God.

record. Some are commended by God; others are condemned.

1. Commended deeds
(2 Samuel 9; 21:1–14)

a. Kindness to Mephibosheth. One of David's finest actions was his gracious gesture toward Jonathan's lone surviving son, Mephibosheth. As noted above, David granted him a place of honor in the kingdom (2 Sam. 9:1–13). Early in his reign, David took the initiative in looking for a descendant of Saul, whom he might honor in memory of Jonathan. When informed of Mephibosheth, he immediately instructed that he be brought to the palace.

Mephibosheth, made lame by a fall in the midst of panic in Gibeah following the Mount Gilboa disaster, came with much fear, for a summons to a member of a deposed royal family could mean death. But David quieted his fears and then rejoiced his heart by giving him all the land which Saul, his grandfather, had owned, besides granting him a place at the royal table. David further assigned Ziba, a previous servant of Saul, who had informed David concerning Mephibosheth, to become overseer for Mephibosheth.

In this action, David showed a great heart. Monarchs of the day normally disposed of all members of rival families; seldom did they honor them. There was benefit for David in being gracious, however, for he would have further endeared himself to those northern subjects who still felt loyalty to Saul's departed house.

b. Justice to Gibeonites. A later commendable deed was his rectification of a wrong committed by Saul against the Gibeonites (2 Sam. 21:1–11), who years before had tricked Joshua into making a league with them (Josh. 9:1–27). Though the pact never should have been made, God still held His people responsible to respect it. But Saul had not done so; he killed many Gibeonites, appropriating their possessions for himself and his family.

A famine of three years prompted David to inquire of God concerning some possible wrong, and the misdeed of Saul was cited. David immediately sought to make amends. He asked the Gibeonites what they would like him to do, and they requested that seven sons of Saul be delivered to them for hanging. David carried out the request,[46] sparing Mephibosheth; and the Gibeonites then hanged the seven in Gibeah, Saul's old home town. It may be that all seven had earlier benefited from spoils Saul had taken from these people and so were justly punished.

2. Condemned deeds
(2 Samuel 11:1–12:25; 24:1–25; 1 Chronicles 21)

a. Sin with Bathsheba. Two of the recorded acts of David are condemned by God. The first occurred early in his reign, while his army under Joab was laying siege to the Ammonite capital,

---

[46] Second Samuel 21:8 states that five of these were sons of Michal. If so, they must have been born when she was married to Phaltiel, for she was barren with David as a result of her criticism of him for dancing before God (2 Sam. 6:20–23). However, there is textual evidence of a copyist error involved in which "Michal" was substituted for "Merab." Also, the husband cited in 2 Samuel 21:8 is Adriel, whom Merab, Saul's older daughter, married (1 Sam. 18:19), not Michal. It is, of course, possible that Michal raised these children for Adriel (Merab perhaps having died). If so, David's action in taking them from her would have been difficult for David as well as for her, for, though they had quarreled, she likely still lived in the palace.

Rabbah (2 Sam. 11:1–27). David, upon seeing Bathsheba washing herself as he looked from a palace window, sent for her and committed adultery with her. When she informed him later that she was pregnant, he had Uriah brought home from the battlefront so that he might be with his wife in an attempt to deceive him into thinking the child his wife was carrying was his. But Uriah would not go to his home while his men slept in tents in the field, and David, in desperation, had him assigned a deadly position in the battle. There he was killed as David planned, and David took Bathsheba as his wife.

For this sin, God reprimanded David severely through Nathan the prophet. David repented immediately (2 Sam. 12:1–23), but, in keeping with Nathan's prediction, Bathsheba's baby died at birth. David's mourning at this time is evidence of both his grief at the loss of his newborn son and his remorse for his sin.[47] The death of this little one was only the beginning of continuing family difficulties for David, also in keeping with Nathan's forewarning.

b. Sin in census taking. The other disapproved deed of David, the taking of a census of the people (2 Sam. 24:1–25; 1 Chron. 21), came many years later in his reign.[48] The nature of the sin, which certainly was more than merely counting people, is not clear, but must have been very serious. Even cold-hearted Joab urged the king to refrain from the action, and the degree of God's displeasure is indicated by the severity of the punishment inflicted as a result. The real sin may have been a plan to impose high taxes and possibly even conscription of labor.

Other countries used the *corvee*, or system of conscripted labor, for construction of public works, and David may have thought to do the same. We know at least that a second list of David's officers (2 Sam. 20:24), as observed above, did include the name of one Adoram, who was supervisor of "forced labor." The phrase used here normally refers only to foreign labor, but David may have decided to add levies from his own people—as Solomon did later on (1 Kings 5:13–14), much to the dislike to the people then (1 Kings 12:4).

Whatever David's purpose, he insisted that the census be taken, clearly in an act of pride (see Ps. 30:6),[49] and Joab obeyed in directing the work. The census, which revealed eight hundred thousand men of military age in Israel and five hundred thousand in Judah,[50]

---

[47] Psalm 51 and likely 32 were written at this time, as expressions of David's grief and repentance.

[48] However, not at the very close of David's rule, as one might think from the fact that the account is placed at the end of 2 Samuel. Parts of Scripture are arranged in terms of content instead of chronological order. A census like this would have had a goal in view—such as a king would set in his years of strength. Perhaps the place of reporting it in 1 Chronicles (chap. 21) is significant, between the Ammonite battle and David's organization of the priests and Levites.

[49] Psalm 30, for "the dedication of the temple," may have been composed at this time; see 1 Chronicles 22:1.

[50] Counting women and children, the total population was about four million, approximately double what it had been at the time of Joshua's conquest (Num. 26:1–65). That Judah's number is so large in comparison with that of all the other tribes combined shows that Simeon's number was probably included, and also much of Dan's, since not all of Dan had migrated to the north. Danites who remained in the south likely amalgamated with Judah. The chronicler adds that this number did not include the people of Levi or Benjamin, for Joab did not complete the count since the whole matter was so offensive to him (1 Chron. 21:6).

took more than nine months to complete. When the work was done, Gad the prophet was sent by God with three choices of punishment, from which David was to choose one. David chose "three days of plague," which resulted in seventy thousand of David's newly counted people dying. The plague which killed them was stopped just outside of Jerusalem at the threshing floor of Araunah the Jebusite, where Solomon later built the temple. In repentance, David purchased the floor and also oxen from Araunah, and offered sacrifices to God.

E. LAST YEARS OF DAVID (2 Samuel 13–20; 1 Kings 1:1–2:11; 1 Chronicles 22; 28–29)

David's final years were marked by continual problems within his own family. These came as further punishments for David's sin and carried overtones of repeated struggle for succession to the throne.

1. The succession problem

As David's reign drew to a close, the problem of who should succeed him became increasingly acute. There was no question that the people wanted the monarchial form of government to continue, for David's benefit to them had been great; but it was not clear who should take his place. Since the

dynasty of the first king, Saul, had ended at his death, no pattern of succession had been established. Because David was an excellent king, and God had promised to establish his house on the throne of Israel, it was to be expected that one of his sons would be the successor. But which son and how he should be designated was unclear.

With David so strong, certainly most expected him to make the selection, but no public announcement was made. Actually, David did make his choice, designating Solomon at his birth,[51] but for some reason he did not make this generally known, perhaps since the time was yet early in his reign. But with no announcement made, people were left to wonder who the selection might be. If David's other sons knew, they sought to circumvent it, perhaps taking it merely as a passing whim of the king.[52] In any event, a serious struggle for the throne ensued, involving two sons, Absalom and later Adonijah.

2. Absalom's revolt (2 Samuel 12–19)

Absalom made the more concerted effort of the two. He was David's third son, born of an Aramean princess of Geshur[53] named Maacah (2 Sam. 3:3). But Amnon, the eldest, had been killed at Absalom's own hand to avenge the humiliation of Absalom's sister, Tamar

---

[51] This designation by David is not recorded in the account of Solomon's birth, which does, however state that God loved Solomon (2 Sam. 12:24). Yet, when Adonijah attempted much later to seize the throne, Nathan, who was aware of the designation, reminded Bathsheba, who also knew of it (1 Kings 1:13); she in turn reminded the king (1 Kings 1:17); and David himself then referred to it (1 Kings 1:30).

[52] For all David's strong points, being a stern disciplinarian was not one of them. The sons' actions toward him indicated this, and also the direct statement made concerning Adonijah: "His father had never interfered with him by asking, 'Why do you behave as you do?' " (1 Kings 1:6). David's hesitancy to hurt any of his sons could have influenced him not to make the selection public knowledge until after Solomon was grown, and to keep postponing it even then.

[53] Geshur was an Aramean city east of the Sea of Galilee. It was allotted to Manasseh, but according to Joshua 13:13, the Geshurites had never been expelled. See Deuteronomy 3:13–14; Joshua 12:5.

(2 Sam. 13:1–29). The deed was done at a feast Absalom held for the royal princes. The second son, Chileab,[54] son of Abigail (former wife of Nabal the Carmelite), is not mentioned again after the notice of his birth, which suggests that he likely had died while still young. This left Absalom as the logical heir to the throne.

a. The plot (2 Sam. 13:30–15:12). It is difficult to tell at what point Absalom decided to plot for the throne. The idea probably arose gradually and likely was present at least by the time he killed Amnon. Absalom's first act, following this murder, was to flee in fear of David to Geshur, where Talmai, his grandfather (mother's father) ruled. He could do little there in furthering the plan, but he did not dare return to Israel until he was summoned by David. After three years, Joab, probably urged by Absalom,[55] persuaded David to permit the return, but the king would still not see his son (2 Sam. 14:1–24). After another two years, David did consent to see him, and then forgave him (2 Sam. 14:25–33). Now Absalom was in a position to effect his plan in earnest.

First he curried favor with the people (2 Sam. 15:1–6). He was a handsome person and, if we may judge from Joab's advocacy, a young man who exhibited real potential for leadership.

He assembled the nucleus of what was probably intended to be a personal army like his father's. He played on the still present tribal jealousies by intercepting those with problems before they would get to the king's appointed officers, and, if they proved to be from "Israel" (i.e., the north), he told them the king would not give them a fair hearing but that he would if he were king. He was clever and convincing, so that these efforts did bring many people to favor him.

After four years,[56] when Absalom believed sufficient goodwill had been generated, he took the second step. He went to Hebron[57] with the king's unsuspecting permission,[58] assembled his followers, and had himself anointed king (2 Sam. 15:7–12).[59] With a considerable force of men, he then marched north against his father in Jerusalem, and David, taken unawares, found his only recourse was to flee (2 Sam. 15:13–17).

An undercurrent of discontent must have existed in the country to make possible the degree of success thus implied for Absalom. It is clear that some people did have grievances, for these were the persons Absalom specially had worked with in his plotting. Perhaps, too, taxes had become very high, causing unrest. Further, with the development of the empire, the king's interests had become wider than his

---

[54] Called Daniel in 1 Chronicles 3:1. Apparently he had two names.

[55] Joab likely believed that Absalom would be the next king and here desired to maintain favor with him.

[56] The number forty, given in 2 Samuel 15:7, seems impossible to reconcile with the fact that David ruled only a total of thirty-three years in Jerusalem. It is generally thought to be a copyist's error, the actual time being four years (as in the Arabic, Syriac, Vulgate, et al.).

[57] Perhaps Absalom chose Hebron for this anointing since David had been anointed there twice.

[58] Absalom's low state of spiritual maturity is indicated both by his desire to revolt at all and by his willingness to use the excuse of an unpaid vow (2 Sam. 15:7) for obtaining the king's permission to go to Hebron at this time.

[59] It is not directly stated that he was anointed at Hebron, but this follows from the account when taken as a whole.

own land, and many may have thought themselves neglected. Still further, any regime loses sympathizers and gains enemies with time; and David was now toward the close of his rule.

Absalom was attractive and likely caught the fancy especially of younger people who had not witnessed the marked contrast of what David had achieved for the country with what had existed under Saul. Even some persons close to David were swept along. Ahithophel, long-time adviser to David (1 Chron. 27:33), whose very son was one of David's "mighty men" (2 Sam. 23:34 KJV), came at Absalom's call (2 Sam. 15:12). Amasa, close relative of both David and Joab (2 Sam. 17:25; 1 Chron. 2:15–17), became his military commander.

b. David's flight (2 Sam. 15:13–17:29). Those who left Jerusalem in flight with David were his personal bodyguard, the Cherethites and Pelethites; his faithful six hundred; and numerous servants. Also Zadok and Abiathar, the two high priests, desired to follow and bring the ark; but David sent them back, instructing them to inform him, through their two respective sons, Ahimaaz and Jonathan, regarding the plans of Absalom (2 Sam. 15:24–29).

David also told his own remaining official counselor, Hushai, to return and seek to counteract whatever advice Ahithophel might give Absalom about pursuing David, and then tell Zadok and Abiathar what Absalom decided to do (2 Sam. 15:30–37). Hushai did this, was successful in his effort, and

then informed the two high priests as directed (2 Sam. 17:1–23). Vital information thus came to David regarding Absalom's plans, so that the king was able to group his forces at Mahanaim, former capital of Ishbosheth, and make preparation for the attack of his son (2 Sam. 17:24–29).

Along the way from Jerusalem to Mahanaim, a distance of more than fifty miles,[60] David experienced varied reactions from people. As one would expect, most were sympathetic, weeping at the sad scene they witnessed; however, not all were so inclined. As a matter of fact, Shimei, a descendant of Saul and still loyal to the former ruler, seeing this as an opportunity to bring long-awaited reprisal, met the king at Bahurim[61] to inveigh curses and throw stones. David refused to bring action against him (2 Sam. 16:5–13). Ziba, appointed servant to Mephibosheth, appeared sympathetic by offering saddled asses and prepared food for the king's family; but he was only seeking to further his own cause against his master, Mephibosheth (2 Sam. 16:1–4; 19:24–30). On arrival at Mahanaim, David received a most gratifying reaction. An Ammonite named Shobi and a Gileadite named Barzillai brought furniture, dishes, and food in large quantity for his weary followers.

c. The battle (2 Sam. 18:1–19:29). The battle occurred near Mahanaim, in an area called the "forest of Ephraim" (2 Sam. 18:1–18). Absalom had gathered the general troops of Israel, having taken time to do so as counseled by Hushai. David divided his compara-

---

[60] The exact distance depends on the correct location of Mahanaim; see p. 218n.5.

[61] Identified with modern Ras et-Tmim to the east of Mount Scopus. It was at Bahurim also that Ahimaaz and Jonathan, messengers to David, had to hide from Absalom's pursuers (2 Sam. 17:17–21).

tively small force into three groups, headed respectively by Joab, Abishai, and a Gittite named Ittai. Though fewer in number, David's men were hard-core troops for whom Absalom's hastily gathered soldiers were no match in morale or ability. With the blessing of God, David's men won a decisive victory.

Contrary to David's explicit order, however, and with the real battle won, Joab killed Absalom, who, because of his long hair, had become ensnared in a tree. When David learned of the deed, as well as the victory, his reaction was to express grief for his son rather than joy at the victory. David's love for his undeserving son is touching, but grief at this time hardly encouraged the loyal men who had fought so hard and well (2 Sam. 18:19–19:8). The death of Absalom broke the revolt, and what remained was for David to return to Jerusalem.

d. Sheba's revolt (2 Sam. 19:9–20:22). Developments at this point led to another revolt, however, but this time it was less serious. This was initiated by Sheba, a Benjamite, who called for secession on the part of northern tribes at the time of David's return across the Jordan.

A general movement had arisen among the northern tribes to bring David back, and David had taken special steps to encourage Judah also to take part, not wishing his own tribe to think that because they had aided Absalom they were now in his disfavor. He even promised to make Amasa, Absalom's general, his own chief commander in place of Joab, who had killed

Absalom. The men of Judah quickly responded that they did wish to take part, and David left for the trip home.

Previous to the outbreak of the revolt, David had significant encounters with three different persons as he came to the Jordan River. Shimei, now fearful because of his vindictive actions when David fled, was among the first to meet David there, and humbly he pled for mercy, quite in contrast to his former insolence. David granted the mercy, though he really did not forgive him, as shown by his later command to Solomon to take his life (2 Sam. 19:17–23; 1 Kings 2:8–9).

Another who met him was Mephibosheth, also seeking mercy in view of the deceitful actions of his servant Ziba (2 Sam. 19:24–30). David then divided Mephibosheth's property equally between Mephibosheth and Ziba, an action certainly unfair in view of Mephibosheth's sincere and truthful words in contrast to those of Ziba.[62]

The third person involved was eighty-year-old Barzillai, who had benefited the king so greatly with provisions earlier (2 Sam. 19:31–39). Now he crossed the Jordan with David, who urged him to continue to Jerusalem and receive a permanent residence in the palace. But the aged Barzillai refused, desiring instead to return to his own city where he felt more at home.

Then the trouble started. The men of Judah had been the first on hand to escort the king across the Jordan and on to Gilgal.[63] Only a part of Israel's representatives had yet arrived, and when others came later to Gilgal, jeal-

---

[62] Mephibosheth gave evidence of true sorrow, expressed appreciation for past generosity, showed no bitterness at David's decision, and was willing to let Ziba have all if David so desired.

[63] For location, see p. 140n.12.

ousies broke out anew as the northern tribes thought they saw favoritism on David's part. Heated words were exchanged, and finally Sheba, particularly vocal, induced the northern tribes to secede from David's kingdom and follow him.[64]

It must have been most disquieting to David, who had just gone through one revolution, to have another break out. He remained undaunted, however, for upon arrival back in Jerusalem, he immediately dispatched Amasa, his new general, to gather an army from Judah to put down the outbreak (2 Sam. 20:3–22). When Amasa took longer than the three days allotted him, David, believing haste was important, commissioned Abishai,[65] Joab's brother, to take the hard-core troops instead and quell the rebels.

Though Joab was not in charge, he accompanied the force; and when Amasa was encountered along the way, Joab proceeded treacherously to kill him (much as he had Abner years before). This was a shocking action, but the troops did not delay because of it, no doubt in part due to their knowledge of Joab and his violent ways. They pressed on in pursuit of Sheba and finally caught up with him far north at Abel of Bethmaacah.[66]

A serious battle did not develop, however, as David had feared, for the townspeople, led by a "wise woman," were quite willing to deliver Sheba's severed head to David's army in exchange for their own safety. Apparently the initial revolt had been hasty rather than deep-seated, and Sheba had soon been left without extensive support. He clearly had not been able to assemble an army of any real strength, and he had fled northward mainly to escape David's forces. Now that he was dead, the revolt was finished.

3. Solomon's accession (1 Kings 1:1–2:9; 1 Chronicles 22:6–23:1; 28–29)

Solomon was crowned king while David still lived, meaning that a brief coregency existed. Adonijah, fourth son of David, had made an abortive attempt to seize the throne after Absalom had failed, and Solomon was hastily made king in his place.

The attempt of Adonijah to rule likely came soon after David returned to Jerusalem following the brief exile caused by Absalom. This follows from several facts taken together. First, it is known that David ruled a total of no more than forty years, and that Absalom was born after those years began (2 Sam. 3:2–3). Then it is clear that Absalom had grown to adulthood by the time of Amnon's crime against Tamar, which places that sad event at least something more than twenty years after David's first anointing at Hebron. Further, ten more years had now elapsed since that crime (2 Sam. 13:38; 14:28; 15:7), which means a minimum at this point of more than thirty years. Lastly, we know that David lived a short while after Solomon's accession. These matters together suggest that Absalom's try for the

---

[64] Another outbreak of the same deep-seated division that was to flower fully in the day of Rehoboam.

[65] Purposely bypassing Joab here in favor of the brother who had also performed well in leadership before this, and was one of David's five among the "mighty men" (2 Sam. 23:18–19 KJV).

[66] Probably modern Tell Abil near recently drained Lake Huleh. Called Abelmaim when later taken by Arameans (2 Chron. 16:4).

throne may have been made about David's thirty-fifth year, and Adonijah's within two or three years following.

Adonijah's attempt to take the kingship was no doubt influenced by Absalom's. As David's fourth son, he was next in line should Absalom fail. With Absalom dead, and with no public announcement yet given by the king as to his choice of successor, Adonijah made his try (1 Kings 1:5–9).[67] He assembled for himself "chariots and horses . . . with fifty men to run ahead of him" even as Absalom had done, and also persuaded two key persons of David's official family, Joab and the high priest Abiathar, to support him.[68] When he believed that the time was right, he assembled these and other less influential persons at the spring En-rogel, that he might be formally anointed.

But news of this clandestine gathering soon came to the attention of opposition forces, comprised principally of Nathan the prophet, Zadok the other high priest, Benaiah the leader of David's bodyguard in company with that guard, and the elite "mighty men" (1 Kings 1:10, 38 KJV). These constituted a formidable group, which accounts for Adonijah's secrecy. Nathan, working through Solomon's mother, Bathsheba, took the lead in calling David's attention to the situation (1 Kings 1: 11–53). When so informed, the long-overdue announcement regarding Solomon was finally made by David—at least to the small number gathered before him—and he gave direction for the young man to be anointed immediately at the Spring of Gihon. When the people shouted at the moment of anointing, the sound carried as far as Adonijah's assembled group at En-rogel.[69] These in fright quickly dispersed. Adonijah then submitted to Solomon, and civil strife was averted.

David spent the remaining short span of his reign in preparing both the new king and the people for the period of rule before them. He had Solomon's new position publicly proclaimed (1 Chron. 28:1–8) and charged Solomon with the weighty responsibilities that faced him (1 Kings 2:1–9; 1 Chron. 28:9–10), involving especially the building of God's temple (1 Chron. 22:6–19; 28:11–21). Also, he spoke parting encouragement and instruction to the people (1 Chron. 29:1–22). Then he died "at a good old age, having enjoyed long life, wealth and honor," and was buried in Jerusalem (1 Kings 2:10–11; 1 Chron. 29:26–28).

F. ISRAEL'S GREATEST KING

David was Israel's greatest king. People looked back to his reign as the high point in their history. Jerusalem came

---

[67] Though both Absalom and Adonijah clearly thought in terms of the eldest living son having right to the throne, neither believed that the king was thinking in these terms or else they would not have tried to seize the crown as they did.

[68] Joab, opportunist that he was, had at first favored Absalom. Now with David's favor being turned from him, he found it easy to follow Adonijah. The reason for Abiathar's action is not apparent, unless it was jealousy of Zadok who seemingly had taken the lead over him under David; this in view of Zadok's being mentioned first and also having charge of the ark (2 Sam. 8:17; 20:25; 15:24, 27, 29, 35, 36). He may have thought he could do better with Adonijah.

[69] En-rogel is about two thousand feet south of Gihon and hidden from it by an intervening hill, thus near enough for this sound to have been heard without Adonijah's party having been able to see the anointing ceremony itself.

to be thought of as the "City of David" (1 Kings 2:10; 3:1; 8:1; Neh. 3:15), for it had been established by David and was the "city where David settled" (Isa. 29:1). He became the measure for evaluating succeeding kings. It was for David's sake that God did not destroy Judah in times of serious sin (2 Kings 8:19). Most important, the coming Messiah was to be the descendant of David. For this reason, Christ is called the "Son of David" (Matt. 1:1), and the people praised Christ in His triumphal entry to Jerusalem with the words, "Hosanna to the son of David!" (Matt. 21:9, 15).

CHAPTER TWELVE

SOLOMON

1 Kings 2:12–11:43; 2 Chronicles 1–9

A marked contrast existed between the kingships of Solomon and David, a contrast caused by the diverse backgrounds of the two rulers. David had been raised in the open, watching sheep, and later had experienced the rigors of a fugitive life. Solomon, however, had known only the ease of the palace, with its attendant luxuries. Accordingly, David, aggressive and efficient, became a king of action, who could personally lead armies to victory. Solomon became a king of peace, happy to stay at home and content merely to retain the land his father had gained. David's court never grew larger than the requirements of his government, but Solomon's became lavish in the manner of other Near Eastern courts. As a result, Solomon needed greater revenue than David, and he raised taxes accordingly. He also engaged more in foreign trade, showing adeptness, indeed, and enjoying marked success. David was more a man of the people; Solomon was a man of the court. More significant, David maintained a vibrant faith in God as a "man after God's own heart," while Solomon, though beginning well in spiritual devotion, failed to hold this basic relationship before God, fell into sinful ways, and finally came under God's censure.

A. ESTABLISHED AS KING (I Kings 2:12–46; 3:4–28; 2 Chronicles 1:1–17)

1. Consolidation of power (1 Kings 2:12–46)

As long as the coregency between Solomon and David continued, matters went smoothly between Solomon and those who had opposed him; but when David died, the situation changed. Adonijah, whose claim to the throne was strong enough to win the support of Abiathar and Joab, would have remained a threat to Solomon's throne as long as he remained alive. He provided Solomon with a reason to have him eliminated when he approached Bathsheba, Solomon's mother, with a request to marry Abishag, a beautiful Shunammite girl who had ministered to David in his old age (1 Kings 1:1–4). Solomon promptly refused and had this older brother killed for what was probably a threat to his rule. Custom of the day required that a man's concubines should become a part of the inheritance of his heir (1 Kings 2:22; see 2 Sam. 16:21). It is probable that Solomon's suspicions concerning his brother's true intentions were correct, for Adonijah believed that he had the favor of the people (1 Kings 2:15), a condition essential if one is to usurp the throne.

With Adonijah removed as an opponent, Solomon turned to Adonijah's main supporters, Abiathar and Joab. He deposed Abiathar from his office as high priest, banishing him to his land in Anathoth (1 Kings 2:26–27). This left Zadok as sole high priest, solving the thorny problem David had avoided. This development carried ominous overtones for Joab, who now sought refuge for himself "at the horns of the altar,"[1] located at the tent David had erected for the ark. Solomon, in turn, following his father's instruction (1 Kings 2:5–6),[2] directed Benaiah, former chief of the guard under David, to kill Joab at the altar, since Joab refused to leave (1 Kings 2:28–34). Thus this man received his due at last. He had killed both Abner and Amasa in

his jealousy, while military commander himself; and now he was killed in turn by Benaiah, Solomon's selection to fill that position.

David also had instructed Solomon to take the life of Shimei, who had cursed David when he fled from Jerusalem at the time of Absalom's rebellion (1 Kings 2:8–9). At first Solomon merely confined the man to his home in Jerusalem;[3] but later, when Shimei left the city to recover two escaped servants, Solomon did take his life (1 Kings 2:36–46). If Shimei had been so opposed to David when David was weak, Solomon could know that likely he had not become a friend since; so he killed him in a further move to consolidate power. Solomon's opponents now had been removed, and he ceased from taking more lives. The kingdom was firmly established in his hand.

2. Promise from God (1 Kings 3:4–28; 2 Chronicles 1:1–17)

Shortly after this, Solomon received an unusual token of God's favor (1 Kings 3:5–15). Commendably recognizing the need for God's blessing, Solomon sacrificed "a thousand burnt offerings" at Gibeon where the tabernacle now stood.[4] Gibeon apparently

---

[1] Joab here was acting on the basis of Exodus 21:13–14 but apparently only thinking in terms of his involvement in the recent plot. David's charge to Solomon to take his life, however, had been on the basis of his having killed Abner (2 Sam. 3:27–28) and Amasa (2 Sam. 20:8–9), which murders were beyond any safety the altar might afford.

[2] David's attitude toward Joab is difficult to assess. When provoked so many times, why David had not punished the man long before causes one to wonder. One factor certainly was that Joab unquestionably was capable. Also, after the Uriah incident, David was under an embarrassing obligation to him for having cooperated in putting this fine soldier in a deadly position. In this instruction to Solomon, he seems to have been taking an easy way out to bring the deserved punishment.

[3] Shimei is described as a man of the family of Saul (2 Sam. 16:5), who apparently agitated in favor of a return to the former dynasty. By confining him to Jerusalem, Solomon thought to curtail any insurrection he might attempt.

[4] The tabernacle had been moved from Nob (see p. 212n.54) probably after Saul's tragic slaughter of the priests of Nob (1 Sam. 22:18–19).

was selected for this occasion of sacrifice, rather than David's tent in Jerusalem, because the altar there was no doubt larger and more suitable for the extensive sacrificing Solomon proposed.[5]

While the king was there, God showed His pleasure by appearing to him in a dream by night,[6] inviting him to make a request. Solomon was pleased at this and humbly requested wisdom in his rule. In further approval, God indicated not only that this request would be granted, but promised Solomon "riches and honor" to the extent that no person of his day would be like him. Solomon's later life portrayed the fulfillment of this gracious word from God. Thrilled at these promises, knowing besides that his opponents had been disposed of and having inherited an extensive and prosperous country from his father, Solomon truly had bright prospects for a happy, successful rule.

B. SOLOMON'S KINGDOM

1. Defense measures

A prominent feature of Solomon's rule was the development of extensive defenses. This was in keeping with his general interest of maintaining the present boundaries of his country rather than expanding them. His major defense measure was the fortification of key cities that ringed Israel's heartland (1 Kings 9:15–19). These were Hazor to the extreme north, Megiddo (at the strategic north-south pass into the Esdraelon Valley), and Gezer, Beth-horon, and Baalath (which guarded the western approaches from Philistine territory). Tadmor[7] is also listed, but if identified with Palmyra, the famous trading center 175 miles northeast of Damascus, it cannot have been an inner defense center. It may have been an outer command point, however, to give early warning of enemy movement from the northeast.

Troops quartered in the inner defense cities would have provided a wall of protection from foreign attack and could have moved quickly to put down attempts at revolution from within. In Jerusalem itself, Solomon built both a "wall"[8] and the "Millo"[9] (KJV; NIV "supporting walls") to give added strength.

Another significant defense feature was Solomon's employment of the chariot, in which he differed from David (2 Sam. 8:4).[10] Canaanites had

---

[5] This is probably the significance of the phrase in 1 Kings 3:4, "for that was the most important high place." The altar there was likely the great brazen altar still, prescribed by God, seven and one-half feet square and four and one-half feet high (Exod. 27:1–8). David's altar likely was smaller.

[6] A type of dream-vision in which Solomon was awake and conscious to the extent of being able to formulate a rational response to the question posed.

[7] The Kethib reading in 1 Kings 9:18 is "Tamar." This, however, is not the best reading, in view of 2 Chronicles 8:4 having Tadmor. If the same locality is not intended in both passages, a "Tamar" did exist south of the Dead Sea which would have been a logical defense post toward the south.

[8] From 1 Kings 11:27 we learn that David's wall still had a gap (perets) somewhere. Solomon probably closed it and added more wall to enclose the new temple area within the city confines. It probably enclosed his palace too (1 Kings 3:1).

[9] The Millo was existent in David's time (2 Sam. 5:9), and apparently Solomon added to it. Hezekiah added still more under threat of an Assyrian invasion (2 Chron. 32:5). Its exact identity is uncertain, but clearly was related to defense, perhaps a tower or fortress. See J. Simons, *Jerusalem in the Old Testament* (Leiden: Brill, 1952), pp. 116–17; 131–44. Richard M. Mackowski (*Jerusalem: City of Jesus* [Grand Rapids: Eerdmans, 1980]) suggests that it was a terrace or platform on which Solomon's palace was built.

[10] See pp. 226; evidently, David even destroyed enemy chariots rather than keeping them for

used this weapon for years, and Solomon now followed their lead, assembling as many as fourteen hundred chariots and twelve thousand horsemen, and four thousand stalls to house the horses (1 Kings 10:26; 2 Chron. 9:25).[11] Besides Hazor, Gezer, and Megiddo[12] mentioned above, both Tanaach and Eglon[13] have also revealed, through excavation, strong defenses and chariot stables from this same time. To staff these cities with adequate military personnel and maintain such chariot forces, Solomon had to keep a large standing army, calling for enormous amounts of food and other provisions.

2. Solomon's court

Solomon's court was larger than David's. Two principal officials are listed besides those in David's government: one named Azariah, who was "in charge of the district officers" (*'al hannissabim*), likely meaning over the district officers; and one named Zabud who was a type of prime minister (*'al habbayith*). There were also additional minor officials: twelve who superintended districts (likely under the Azariah just named; 1 Kings 4:7–28) and

as many as 550 supervisors of labor (1 Kings 9:23).

Solomon's own family was large. If David had adopted the common custom of maintaining a large harem, Solomon did so with a vengeance. His wives ultimately numbered seven hundred and his concubines three hundred (1 Kings 11:3). The number of his children is not given but must have been sizable. All these ate at court expense. The enormity of Solomon's court and his dependents may be guessed from his ration list. One day required no less than thirty *kor* [14] of fine flour, sixty *kor* of meal, ten fat cattle, twenty pasture-fed cattle, one hundred sheep, and other animals (1 Kings 4:22–23).

3. Financial support

Fortification of cities, support of a standing army, and provisions for a lavish court called for a very large income. Solomon's sources appear to have been of four types.

a. Taxation. Solomon divided the country into twelve districts[15] to facilitate the collection of taxes. He assigned an officer over each as chief tax collector. Each district was to furnish provi-

---

himself. His fighting was much in the mountains, however, whereas these defense cities of Solomon were largely in flat areas, where the chariot could be used.

[11] The forty thousand figure in 1 Kings 4:26 must be a scribal error in view of the four thousand figure in 2 Chronicles 9:25 and the fact that fourteen hundred chariots suggests four thousand horses, not forty thousand.

[12] While archaeologists once interpreted finds at Megiddo as "Solomon's Stables" these 450 "stalls" were redated by Yadin to the time of Ahab (see "New Light on Solomon's Megiddo," *BA* 23 [1960]: 62–68). More recently the function of these structures as stables has been called into question (J. B. Pritchard, "The Megiddo Stables: A Reassessment," *Near Eastern Archaeology* [1970], pp. 268–76). Yadin still maintains their identification as stables ("The Megiddo Stables," in *Magnalia Dei*, ed. F. M. Cross, W. E. Lemke, and P. D. Miller, Jr., [Garden City, N.Y.: Doubleday, 1976], pp. 249–50).

[13] See Albright, *AP,* pp. 124–25. On Hazor, see pp. 78–80.

[14] The *kor,* or *homer* (same measure), was the largest capacity measure and was probably equal to 58.1 gallons liquid measure or 6¼ bushels dry; see R. B. Y. Scott, "Weights and Measures of the Bible," *BA* 22 (1959): 22–40.

[15] These did not always conform to old tribal boundaries, which may not mean that Solomon deliberately tried to break up old loyalties, but people must have felt emotional alarm that old established lines were not observed.

sions for the court for one month per year (1 Kings 4:7–28). There was need for barley and straw to feed horses, as well as food for his dependents. Such a burden must have been oppressive and makes understandable the cry for relief when Rehoboam later came to the throne (1 Kings 12:3–4).

b. Labor conscriptions. Solomon maintained a program of labor conscription, or corvee, which was common in the ancient world, but it was always intensely disliked. David had used foreign labor, even having a minister of cabinet rank in charge of it toward the close of his reign (2 Sam. 20:24), indicating that he came to depend greatly on this labor source. This, too, Solomon did, using large numbers of Canaanites still living in the country (1 Kings 9:21–22). But he also resorted to conscription of Israelites themselves (1 Kings 5:13). While building the temple, he sent thirty thousand (ten thousand per month) to Lebanon to help bring the cedar trees he needed. Men so conscripted simply worked for the government without pay, for the length of time designated.

c. Foreign tribute and gifts. A third source of revenue imposed no burden on the Israelites themselves. It con-

sisted of tribute and gifts received from foreign countries. Details on the amounts are not supplied, but the indication is that many countries sent representatives with silver, gold, fine garments, valuable spices, and animals (1 Kings 10:24–25). The Queen of Sheba, whose visit is described at some length (1 Kings 10:1–13), brought one such gift of 120 talents[16] of gold besides large quantities of spices and precious stones.

d. Trade. Solomon developed far-flung trade relationships, which also produced considerable revenue. One avenue of trade was through the Red Sea to the south. David's southern conquest had reached to the Gulf of Aqaba, making this sea route accessible. With the aid of Phoenician experts, Solomon constructed and provided crews for a fleet of ships leaving Ezion-geber at the tip of the Gulf (1 Kings 9:26–28). The ships went as far as Ophir,[17] no doubt stopping at many ports en route, for the trip took three years[18] (1 Kings 10:22). When the ships left Ezion-geber, the cargo may have been limited to copper;[19] but it is recorded that on their return voyage they carried gold, silver, hardwood, precious stones, ivory, and animals (1 Kings 10:11, 12, 22).

---

[16] Stone talent weights from ancient Palestine vary in weight from 75 to 80 pounds. The Israelite talent is figured at 75.6 pounds. Setting an arbitrary price for gold of $400 per ounce, each talent would be worth $483,840 and the total value of the gift $58,060,800!

[17] The identity of Ophir is unknown. Four sites are suggested: southwest Arabia, southeast Arabia, Somaliland, and Supara in India. In favor of the last is the long time of the journey, that all items imported are from India, and that trade is known to have existed that far away at the time. Albright, however, favors the third suggestion: see *ARI*, pp. 133–35.

[18] "Three years" means no more than three and a half years and no less than all of one year and some part of the prior and following years. Three years is not an unreasonable length of time.

[19] Solomon's ships are called ships "of Tarshish" (1 Kings 10:22 KJV). While some have argued that these were refinery ships, from a proposed etymology of the name (see Unger, *AOT*, pp. 225–26; Albright, *BASOR* 83 [Oct. 1941]: 21), this may also describe a large, ocean-going cargo ship of a type that might make the trip to Tarshish (Spain?). R. F. Youngblood, "תַּרְשִׁישׁ," *Theological Wordbook of the Old Testament*, ed. R. Laird Harris, Gleason L. Archer, Jr., and Bruce K. Waltke, 2 vols. (Chicago: Moody, 1980), 2:981.

A site (Tell el-kaleifeh) near the Gulf of Aqaba was once interpreted by Nelson Glueck as the ancient Ezion-geber. Its location, a structure Glueck took to be a smelter, and "slag heaps" nearby all seemed to suggest this as a center for Solomon's mining activities. Glueck himself later retracted this interpretation, however, and further work has uncovered harbor installations and walls of a type identified with Solomon elsewhere in the region.[20] Located farther to the southwest, this installation is a more likely site for Solomon's harbor.

Solomon also carried on trade involving horses and chariots. He not only purchased many for his own use, but he took advantage of his strategic position along north-south trade routes to buy and sell for others. He bought them mainly from Egypt and Kue (Cilicia),[21] and sold them to Hittites and Arameans (1 Kings 10:28-29).

C. FOREIGN RELATIONS

Because he inherited a land area of empire size and conducted such trading operations, Solomon's involvement in foreign affairs became extensive. A clear indication of this is his many marriages to foreign women. Marriages are common seals of foreign alliances. That he had among his wives Moabites, Ammonites, Edomites, Sidonians, and Hittites (1 Kings 11:1) suggests that he had entered into alliances with all these people.

1. Alliance with Egypt

It is directly stated that Solomon made an alliance with Egypt, sealing it with his marriage to the Pharaoh's daughter (1 Kings 3:1). While Egypt under the weak Twenty-First Dynasty was far removed from its former glory, Pharaoh's daughter must have been the most significant of Solomon's wives. In an age when Assyria had not yet begun its expansion into Palestine, Solomon's marriage to Pharaoh's daughter must have signified that he held high standing in the world of his day.[22] The alliance was one of his earlier ones, and the honor accorded by the Pharaoh really must be attributed more to David than Solomon.

In keeping with the importance of the alliance, Solomon built a special house for the Egyptian bride (1 Kings 7:8). Solomon also gained the city, Gezer,[23] through this marriage. The Pharaoh had previously seized Gezer, slaying its occupants, and now gave it to his daughter, Solomon's wife, as a present (1 Kings 9:16). Solomon fortified it as a defense city.

---

[20] Nelson Glueck, *BA* 28 (1965): 70–87, and Beno Rothenberg, "Ancient Copper Industries in the Western Arabah," *PEQ* 94 (1962): 5–71.

[21] The Hebrew word *miqweh* in 1 Kings 10:28 (translated "linen yarn" in KJV) is best taken in reference to the Asia Minor country, Kue, and so translated "from Kue." Horses were a comparatively late introduction to Egypt, though by Solomon's time they could have had sufficient stock for some export. Asia Minor is known to have had fine horses. Egypt had fine chariots, introduced apparently by the Hyksos. For discussion, see Albright, *ARI*, pp. 135–36.

[22] At one time Egyptian Pharaohs did not give their daughters even to kings of Babylon or of Mitanni. However, Egypt had slipped in world position by this time. The Pharaoh involved would have been one of the last of the Twenty-First Dynasty.

[23] First Kings 9:16 states that Pharaoh burned Gezer at this time, and it is archaeologically questionable if Gezer here suffered this form of destruction. Some believe that a textual error had crept into the text and that it should read "Gerar." It is also possible that Gezer was already in Israel's hand at this time in view of David's victories in the Philistine area. See Albright, *ARI*, pp. 213–14.

2. Alliance with Tyre

Solomon made another important alliance with the Phoenician king, Hiram I (c. 978–944). Solomon's wife of the "Sidonians"[24] (1 Kings 11:1) was likely a daughter of this ruler. Tyre, rebuilt by the Phoenicians in the twelfth century, was now capital of this maritime country, which controlled about 150 miles of the Mediterranean coastline north of the Bay of Acre. Phoenicia held colonies at many points around the Mediterranean, and her trade with them and other countries was widely known.

Solomon was particularly interested in her cedar, for which he was willing to trade wheat and fine oil (1 Kings 5:2–11). Hiram had already supplied cedar to David in anticipation of the temple, and now he was pleased to continue this with Solomon. He also loaned Solomon 120 talents of gold (1 Kings 9:10–14), which indicates that Solomon did not have enough revenue to do all he wished, even though his resources were extensive.

At the end of twenty years, when the temple and other buildings had been completed, Solomon sought to repay Hiram for both the cedar and gold by giving him twenty cities, presumably located near Phoenicia. However, Hiram was not happy with the cities, for apparently they were poor; and he voiced displeasure to Solomon and returned them (1 Kings 9:12, 13; 2 Chron. 8:2). The form Solomon's repayment then took is not stated. At least the incident did not disrupt the treaty between the two countries, for Hiram joined Solomon in the maritime venture from Ezion-geber, already noted, sometime later. It may be, indeed, that this joint enterprise involved Solomon's repayment; Hiram perhaps receiving a major part of the proceeds for some time.

3. Visit of the Queen of Sheba (1 Kings 10:1–13; 2 Chronicles 9:1–12)

Among Solomon's distinguished visitors from foreign lands was a Sabean queen from the southern tip of Arabia, the land of Sheba. This country is roughly identified with the modern state of Yemen.[25] Solomon's ships had likely been stopping at ports in this land.

In fact, the Queen's long, arduous journey (some twelve hundred miles) may have been motivated in part by mercantile advantages that she saw in personal confrontation with the one who had sent the ships. Southwestern Arabia was well known for trade in spices and incense, and this queen may have felt that her business by caravan route was jeopardized by Solomon's merchant fleet.[26] She came also, as she says, to see Solomon himself, having heard, probably from sailors of the ships, concerning his great wealth and wisdom.

She brought a large gift to Solomon of 120 talents of gold, was duly impressed with what she saw at his

---

[24] The Sidonians were principally inhabitants of Sidon, but the term came to be used for Phoenicians generally. Tyre and Sidon were the two principal cities of Phoenicia, with Sidon the older. Tyre, however, had by this time become the more important and the residence of the king. See 1 Kings 16:31.

[25] Regarding Sabean settlement, see Albright, *ARI*, pp. 132–35. Modern explorations in Yemen are described by W. Philips, *Qataban and Sheba* (New York: Harcourt, Brace, 1955).

[26] On Sabean trade, see Albright, *ARI*, pp. 132–35.

luxurious court, received in turn all that she desired (perhaps including trade agreements) along with a large gift, and returned satisfied to her country. Significantly, 1 Kings 10:15 states that part of Solomon's revenue from trading came from spice merchants of the kings of Arabia, indicating that, whatever agreements may have been made with the queen, Solomon continued with his trade in the area.[27]

D. BUILDING ACTIVITY
(1 Kings 5:1–9:9; 2 Chronicles 2–7)

Besides fortifying defense cities, Solomon erected several splendid buildings in Jerusalem, the most important of which was the temple.

1. Building the temple
(1 Kings 5–6; 7:15–51; 2 Chronicles 2–4)

As noted in the previous chapter, David had wanted to build the temple, but he was forbidden by God. He did gather extensive material for it, however (1 Chron. 22:1–5; 14–16),[28] and he also passed along to Solomon written plans that had been revealed to him by the Spirit of God for the structure of the temple (1 Chron. 28:11, 12, 19).

It has been noted that Solomon contracted with Hiram of Tyre for cedar wood and supplied a levy of ten thousand workers per month to assist in cutting and transporting it. Cedar was considered a fine wood for such building.[29] Hiram took responsibility for conveying the logs by sea to a Palestinian port of Solomon's choosing. He also supplied stonecutters to help prepare the great quantity of stone needed (1 Kings 5:18).

Actual building began in the spring of Solomon's fourth year (c. 966 B.C.; 1 Kings 6:1), and it was completed seven years later in the fall (1 Kings 6:38). The building was located on Mount Moriah (2 Chron. 3:1), the site of Araunah's threshing floor, where the plague had stopped in David's day (2 Sam. 24:16–25). In fact, it was most likely the place where Abraham long before had been commanded to sacrifice Isaac (Gen. 22:2). Mount Moriah was immediately adjacent to David's city on the north.

The plan of the temple proper called for a building similar to the tabernacle but twice the size.[30] It was ninety feet long and thirty feet wide, and it contained the same two divisions: the Holy Place and the Holy of Holies, occupying two-thirds and one-third of the total, respectively. Though built of stone, it was paneled with cedar overlaid with gold.

The Holy of Holies housed the ark

---

[27] A clay stamp from South Arabia was found at Bethel by James Kelso. It dates about the time of Solomon and shows that trade was existent at the time. The stamp was originally about three by four inches and probably was used to seal bags of cargo. See G. W. VanBeek and A. Jamme, "An Inscribed South Arabian Clay Stamp from Bethel," *BASOR* 151 (October 1958): 9–16.

[28] The amount David gathered in gold and silver is described as one hundred thousand talents of gold and one million talents of silver. At about $400 an ounce (see above, n.16), the gold alone would have been worth about $48,384,000,000. The weight of the gold would have totaled 3,780 tons.

[29] Gudea (c. 2100 B.C.), ruler of Lagash, had acquired cedar from this region already in his day. The Egyptian Wenamon came to Lebanon for cedar for Egypt (c. 1100 B.C.); see Barton, *AB*, pp. 449–50, 455.

[30] This plan finds close parallel with a temple at Tell Tainat of northern Syria unearthed in 1936. More recently, one discovered at Hazor also bears marked resemblance; see Yadin, *BA* 22 (1959): 3–4.

of the covenant (along with its mercy seat and two cherubim). Two additional[31] cherubim were of carved olive wood overlaid with gold and stood fifteen feet high (1 Kings 6:23–28; 2 Chron. 3:10–13). In the Holy Place were the altar of incense or "golden altar" (1 Kings 7:48; 2 Chron. 4:19), ten golden lampstands standing five on each side (1 Kings 7:49; 2 Chron. 4:7), and ten tables of showbread (1 Kings 7:48; 2 Chron. 4:8). In front of the Holy Place was a porch thirty feet wide and ten feet deep, and on the porch stood two bronze pillars called Jachin and Boaz (1 Kings 7:15–21),[32] elements missing from the tabernacle.

Along the sides and rear of this structure were chambers three stories high, providing storage area (1 Kings 6:5–10). Around the whole building lay a court similar to that which surrounded the tabernacle. Found in it were the great brazen altar, thirty feet square and fifteen feet high (2 Chron. 4:1); a large laver, or "Sea of cast metal," fifteen feet across the brim (1 Kings 7:23–26); and ten small lavers, five on opposite sides of the building. This court, as well as the temple proper, was restricted to the priests, but around it was a "large court" (2 Chron. 4:9) intended for the people.

2. Dedicating the temple (1 Kings 8:1–9:9; 2 Chronicles 5–7)

A building of this grandeur and significance called for appropriate dedication ceremonies. Solomon first ordered that the all-important ark of the covenant be brought from the tent David had made and be placed in the Holy of Holies. Other articles of furniture might be newly made but not this one. Since it was the same ark constructed earlier at Mount Sinai in the time of Moses, it had represented God's presence in the tabernacle and would continue to do so in the temple.

Significantly, when it was placed in its assigned location, the "cloud" of God's glory filled the building (1 Kings 8:1–11; 2 Chron. 5:1–14), even as it had the tabernacle. Then Solomon preached a brief sermon to those gathered (1 Kings 8:12–21; 2 Chron. 6:1–11) and offered a longer prayer of dedication (1 Kings 8:22–53; 2 Chron. 6:12–42). When he finished, miraculous fire fell from heaven to ignite the burnt offering placed on the brazen altar (2 Chron. 7:1–3).[33] Then Solomon continued with other sacrifices until the enormous total of 22,000 oxen and 120,000 sheep had been offered, during seven days of celebration (1 Kings 8:62–66; 2 Chron. 7:4–11).[34] Following this,

---

[31] Since the two cherubim of the mercy seat were made of one piece with it (Exod. 25:18–19), these two large cherubim were additional.

[32] These pillars seem to have been freestanding, being described only as "in the front of the temple" (2 Chron. 3:17). They were each twenty-four feet high, counting their capitals which were topped with "bowls" (KJV; *gulloth*). Their names, Joachin and Boaz, may have been the first words in sayings ascribed to them. *Jachin* would fit such a saying as "Yahweh will establish (*yakin*) thy throne forever"; *Boaz*, "In the strength (*beoz*) of Yahweh shall the king rejoice." For discussion of parallels, see Albright, *ARI*, pp. 144–48.

[33] See p. 124 as to miraculous fire in connection with the tabernacle. Other instances of special fire from God are recorded in Judges 6:21; 1 Kings 18:38; 1 Chronicles 21:26.

[34] Solomon of course did not offer these sacrifices himself. But with the numerous priests and

God showed His favor by appearing to Solomon a second time, once more promising blessing if Solomon would obey God's commandments as David his father had done (1 Kings 9:1–9; 2 Chron. 7:12–22).

3. Other fine buildings
(1 Kings 7:1–12)

Solomon erected several other buildings as well, probably locating them near the temple in the new part of the city—a part then under construction. One of them was his personal residence, the palace. It must have been an elegant structure, for it took thirteen years to build, even six years longer than the temple. Another was the "Palace of the Forest of Lebanon," perhaps so named because it was supported by rows of cedar pillars. It was used at least in part to store arms (1 Kings 10:16–17; Isa. 22:8).

A third building was the "Hall of the Pillars" (KJV), perhaps a sort of splendid passage building, lined with pillars, between the "Palace of the Forest of Lebanon" and a fourth building, the "Hall of Justice." In this last structure, which was used for judgment, Solomon sat on a six-step throne of ivory overlaid with gold (1 Kings 10:18–20). Next came Solomon's own palace, probably joined to the "Hall of Justice" for ease of access. Last was the special house made for Solomon's honored wife, the daughter of Pharaoh.

The temple was built first and then these other buildings later, during the thirteen years ascribed for the palace construction, for a total of twenty years (1 Kings 9:10). Apparently Hiram continued to help with material, workmen, and gold during all this time, with Solomon then granting in partial payment the twenty cities that, as noticed, were refused.

E. LITERARY AGE

The time of David and Solomon is commonly called Israel's "golden literary age." David had marked ability in fine arts, and Solomon followed him in skill as a writer. Their common interest, in turn, encouraged others to develop like talents. It was a day which lent itself to artistic expression: a day of optimism and prosperity, a day of importance for Israel as a world member, a day of sufficient wealth to give time for leisure and reflection, and especially a day when stress lay on true worship of God.[35]

1. Historical writing

The age saw works of history produced. Both David and Solomon had official court scribes, and from their formal records histories of the reigns of both kings were written. Nathan the prophet wrote one that covered the rule of both David (1 Chron. 29:29) and Solomon (2 Chron. 9:29). Gad, his counterpart, wrote one which covered the reign of David alone (1 Chron. 29:29). The history of Solomon given in 1 Kings seems to have been taken mainly from "the book of the annals of Solomon," whose author is not identified (1 Kings 11:41). The prophets Ahijah and Iddo, both of whom continued to live after Solomon, wrote histories which included accounts of his reign (2 Chron. 9:29).

Levites on hand, and likely additional altars temporarily placed conveniently near for this special time, the number of animals indicated could have been offered in the seven days reported.

[35] True worship continued for all David's reign and half or more of Solomon's.

2. Music and psalmody

Another area of literary activity included music and psalmody. David, in anticipation of the day when the temple would be built, gave specific instructions regarding music in worship. Some four thousand Levites were designated as "singers" (KJV), and they were divided into twenty-four courses to serve for a week at a time.[36] Instruments were to be played, including lyres, harps, and cymbals (1 Chron. 25:1–6), and David designated 288 of those "trained and skilled in music" to join in a choir (1 Chron. 25:7). Seventy-three psalms, some of which were to used in temple service, are attributed to David, although he may have written more.

He appointed Asaph as chief of choral worship (1 Chron. 16:4–5), and this man in turn penned twelve psalms that have been included in the Bible. The sons of Korah seem to have been a particular singing group from the Levites, and ten psalms are ascribed to them, either as authors or performers (see 1 Chron. 6:31–32). Ethan and Heman, two men compared for wisdom with Solomon (1 Kings 4:31), are credited with one psalm each, and two are ascribed to Solomon. It is clear that Solomon, upon completing the temple, in no way lessened the place of music in service, and may have stressed it even more (2 Chron. 5:12–13; 9:11).

3. Wisdom and dramatic literature

Third, wisdom and dramatic literature was produced. Some of the psalms are to be classed as wisdom literature, but the finest Old Testament examples are the Books of Proverbs and Ecclesiastes. While there is a wide range of opinion about the extent of Solomonic participation in the actual writing of these books, even among Evangelicals, tradition says that Solomon wrote all of the latter and most of the former.[37] The Book of Job also falls under this classification but may have been written earlier.[38] Solomon also wrote the Song of Solomon, classed by some as semi-drama. In summary, most of the third division of the Hebrew Bible, called the "writings" (*Kethubim*), came from this golden age of literature.

F. SPIRITUAL DECLINE AND PUNISHMENT
(1 Kings 11; 2 Chronicles 9:29–31)

1. The decline
(1 Kings 11:1–8)

Solomon was capable as an administrator. The country continued strong and outwardly prosperous during his rule. For the most part the empire remained intact. The people had never had such a good life as during the reigns of both David and Solomon, though taxes continued to rise, which produced dissatisfaction by the close of Solomon's rule.

Religiously, however, Solomon

---

[36] See p. 230.

[37] Solomon himself excelled in wisdom, of course, and would have encouraged this quality in others. He spoke 3,000 proverbs and composed 1,005 songs, including as subject matter items pertaining to trees, hyssop, beasts, birds, creeping things, and fish (1 Kings 4:32–33). Most of Proverbs (chaps. 1–24) is directly ascribed to him (1:1; 10:1); chapters 25–29 are also, though said to have been compiled by Hezekiah's people. Only 30–31 are given to others, namely Agur and Lemuel.

[38] A problem regarding its historical accuracy (in view of its detailed conversational content) arises if written in Solomon's time. It may have come from the hand of Job himself.

brought the disfavor of God upon himself. He had started well. Divine approval had been uniquely signified by Yahweh's promise of wisdom, riches, and honor, but Solomon did not remain faithful to his early religious commitments. He compromised the convictions he had expressed in his prayer at the temple dedication. When he experienced this spiritual decline himself, his country was influenced as well.

A principal reason for this sad development is found in Solomon's international affairs and the resulting effect upon him. He permitted the thinking and customs of other nations to influence his decisions and manner of living. This situation developed especially as a result of his marriages to foreign women. These marriages, initially symbolic of the establishment of foreign alliances, became far more than that for Solomon; for the wives "turned away his heart after other gods" (KJV). The extent of his defection is indicated by the notice that he built a "high place" (*bamah*) to "Chemosh the detestable god of Moab," and to "Molech the detestable god of the Ammonites," and apparently also to the false gods of "all his foreign wives" (1 Kings 11:7–8).

It is not clear at what point in Solomon's reign this defection began seriously to show itself. No signs of it are evident at the completion of the temple, eleven years after his inauguration, when he offered his grand sermon and prayer. It may be presumed to have come gradually and perhaps after the midpoint of his reign, when the bad influence of the foreign wives and contacts could have had time to work. Commendably, however, prior to his death Solomon did realize what had

happened and turned back to God, as evidenced in his final book, Ecclesiastes, where he concludes that the "whole duty of man" is to "fear God and keep his commandments" (12:13).

2. The punishment (1 Kings 11:9–43)

Early in Solomon's reign, God had warned him against such defection (1 Kings 3:14; 9:4–9). His failure in this area brought inevitable judgment, for God told him that most of his kingdom would be ruled by someone other than his son. During the latter years of Solomon's reign, God's punishment came through three men who arose to trouble Solomon.

a. Jeroboam (1 Kings 11:26–40). The first was Jeroboam, who later became the first king of the northern kingdom of Israel. Evidently a capable man, Jeroboam had been placed in charge of the work force from the northern tribes building the Millo for Solomon. One day, when on leave, he was met by Ahijah the prophet, who tore his new garment symbolically into twelve parts and gave Jeroboam ten. He explained that these ten pieces represented ten tribes over which Jeroboam would rule when Solomon was dead. He told him the reason for this punishment being meted out to Solomon and promised Jeroboam rich blessing on his own reign if he would avoid similar defection.

Solomon somehow learned of Ahijah's words to Jeroboam and immediately sought to take Jeroboam's life, much in the pattern of Saul with David years earlier. But Jeroboam fled, as had David (though in this instance he fled all the way to Egypt), and was given protection by Pharaoh Shishak (Sheshonq I, 940–920). From Egypt Jeroboam eventually returned to Israel after Solomon's death to assume the rule over the northern ten tribes.

b. Hadad of Edom (1 Kings 11:14–22). The second man to trouble Solomon was Hadad of Edom, whose activity served to diminish Solomon's control over the empire in the south. Hadad had been the sole survivor of the royal family in Edom at the time of Joab's great slaughter there during David's reign.[39] He had sought asylum in Egypt, as Jeroboam did later. On learning that David and Joab were dead, he returned to Edom and probably became head of his country, which was under Solomon's jurisdiction as a province.

But Hadad, remembering Joab's atrocities, was a bitter enemy of Israel and made continual trouble for Solomon. He probably did not succeed in actually removing Edom from Israelite jurisdiction, for Solomon's copper and maritime operations from Ezion-geber apparently continued for all his reign; but certainly he put forth a strong effort to this end and did cause serious difficulty for Solomon's interests. No doubt Hadad's opposition grew great in Solomon's latter days as God's favor came to be increasingly withdrawn.

c. Rezon of Damascus (1 Kings 11:23–25). The third person who caused major problems for Solomon was Rezon, whose power in Damascus weakened Solomon's control over the empire in the north. Rezon had been a supporter of Hadadezer, the king of Zobah, whom David had defeated early in his reign (2 Sam. 8:3–9). Rezon apparently had escaped unharmed from

that battle and then formed a small army of his own to further his personal desire for power. His main prize was Damascus, and he succeeded in becoming ruler there. Damascus had not been particularly strong before this, but he made it so.

He clearly was capable as a military figure and gathered an efficient force behind him. He gradually increased the position and influence of his new center and thus was able to cause serious trouble for Solomon. No indication is given, however, that he was able actually to remove Damascus from provincial status while Solomon reigned. Indeed, the fact that Solomon saw fit to invest in construction at Tadmor (Palmyra; 1 Kings 9:18), far north of Damascus, is quite out of keeping with the idea—though this building activity may have been carried out quite early in Solomon's reign, when Rezon's threat had not yet developed.

Toward the close of Solomon's rule, however, this man did create severe opposition to Israel, again in keeping with the withdrawal of God's favor from Solomon. It may be that effective control by Solomon in both Edom and the Damascus region was all but lost by the time of his death.

G. SOLOMON THE KING

Solomon's reign was long, lasting forty years (970–931) as had his father's before him. It was a rule of prosperity and peace, and it was a time of genuine accomplishment. As a result of extensive building, trading, and international relations, Israel became known through all the Near East. Beside this, the arts, particularly music and literature, were advanced. Further,

---

[39] See p. 225n.32

true worship of God at the temple assumed a form of dignity in keeping with the regulations of Moses' Law. All this can be said to Solomon's credit. He stands as one of Israel's most significant rulers.

However, he could have stood much higher had he remained faithful to God. Few rulers have had greater opportunity or prospects. He had an empire by inheritance, and he had God's particular promise of wisdom, riches, and honor. All the hard work of consolidation and enlargement of Israel to empire size had been done by David. With excellent groundwork laid and attractive possibilities ahead, Solomon had only to continue his father's efforts to witness the finest of achievements.

The greater world powers were not at this time in a position to give him great opposition either. The place Israel might have achieved in world affairs was most significant.

But Solomon failed to meet God's standard. He did not remain faithful to God's will and way. Consequently, this great potential for Israel was not realized; but instead there came a gradual diminishing of world position in Solomon's last years. In fact, he had to be informed before his death that only a small part of his realm would be passed on to his son. As he died, he must have felt deep regret that he had not remained faithful, as God had instructed him early in his reign.

CHAPTER THIRTEEN

THE NORTHERN KINGDOM

1 Kings 12–22; 2 Kings 1–17

The division of kingdom—a division that God predicted to Jeroboam through Ahijah—had a background reaching far back into Israel's history. The tribes of Judah and Ephraim had been jealous of one another since the days of Egypt. Judah was the largest and had been honored with the leading position as the tribes moved through the wilderness. Ephraim, in contrast, was one of the smaller tribes,[1] but had descended from Joseph and had been given precedence over Manasseh by Jacob. Also, the great leader, Joshua, had been of her number. Ephraim had displayed her sense of importance twice during the Judges Period: once to Gideon (Judg. 8:1–3) and later to Jephthah (Judg. 12:1–6), complaining each time that she had not been properly recognized in doing battle with the enemy.

At the founding of the monarchy the existence of this intertribal hostility was recognized in God's choice of Israel's first king from small Benjamin, located between these two rival tribes. The split was accented after Saul's death, when only Judah crowned David and the northern tribes turned to Ishbosheth. It also showed itself following Absalom's rebellion and David's return to rule, when the northern tribes once more went their own way, led by Sheba of Benjamin, though this time only for a few days (2 Sam. 19:41–20:22). What Ahijah predicted and what Solomon feared in causing Jeroboam to flee to Egypt, then, was only a new outbreak of an old condition. In view of this, any king coming to Israel's throne should have been careful not to give cause for a new instance of division, especially when discontent already existed, as was true at Solomon's death. Rehoboam, Solomon's son, however, did not exercise this manner of care and so brought on the final cleavage.

---

[1] In the wilderness, the number of Ephraim fell from 40,500 to 32,500 (Num. 1:33; 26:37), making her then larger only than Simeon. In contrast, Judah grew from 74,600 to 76,500 (Num. 1:27; 26:22).

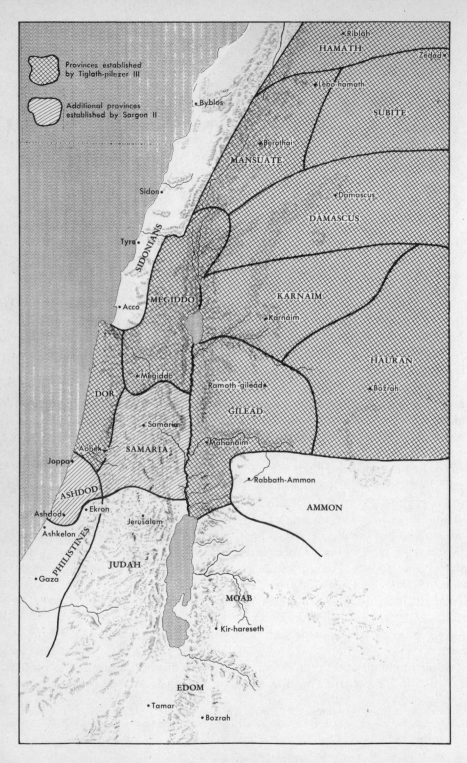

Map 11. The Campaigns of Tiglath-pileser III

A. THE REVOLT
(1 Kings 12:1–24;
2 Chronicles 10)

That Rehoboam was, in a measure, aware of the difficult situation facing him is indicated by his willingness to go to Shechem to meet with the leaders of the northern tribes. Had things been normal, they would have come to him at Jerusalem, the capital, for the inaugural ceremonies. Undoubtedly Shechem was selected now because of two reasons: it was central ground for the discontented tribes, and it had historical significance.[2] Jeroboam, too, returning from his place of refuge in Egypt, came to the meeting. Apparently he had been summoned by the northern tribes, who somehow had learned of Ahijah's anointing and Solomon's revenge. He was now received by them as their champion to lead in negotiations.

The assembled tribes knew what they wanted from Rehoboam, if they were to accept him as king. Solomon's heavy load of taxation and labor conscription should be reduced. They had suffered long enough and were committed to forcing a change. The demand was voiced, apparently by Jeroboam, and then Rehoboam sought counsel regarding how he should respond.

He turned first to older men, who had lived through Solomon's harsh years, and later to those his own age. The younger men, no doubt wanting to enjoy a continuing lavish court, counseled refusal, and Rehoboam listened. The ten tribes immediately seceded from Rehoboam's kingdom and set about establishing their own kingdom, making Jeroboam the first king, as Ahijah had predicted.

While still at Shechem, Rehoboam made an effort to continue his authority over the North by sending his chief tax collector, Adoram, to demand tax money from the people; but the man was stoned to death for his effort. Rehoboam wisely and hastily then retreated to the safety of Jerusalem. There he assembled an army of 180,000 from his two tribes, Judah and Benjamin,[3] determined still to force his will on the rebels. God, however, through the prophet Shemaiah forbade the action and Rehoboam properly desisted. The schism would continue, as God had predicted through Ahijah, and Rehoboam would have to be content with ruling only two tribes.

B. THE EARLY YEARS
(931–885; 1 Kings 12:25–16:20)

1. Jeroboam as king
(931–910; 1 Kings 12:25–14:20)

a. The new kingdom. As Jeroboam took over as first ruler of the new ten-tribe nation of Israel, he had the challenging task of establishing a new kingdom. It would be interesting to know what steps he took to do so and what the nature of his administration was; unfortunately, no information is given. A working government was put into operation, however; and it surely took careful thinking and diligent labor on his part, demonstrating that he was a capable person. It is to be presumed that he followed the familiar patterns

---

[2] See p. 36n.19 and p. 145n.36.
[3] Few of these would have been from Benjamin at this time. Likely Benjamin, which historically had aligned itself with the northern block of tribes, only gradually came under Rehoboam's control; see pp. 285–86.

that had been developed by David and Solomon. In view of the demands made to Rehoboam by the people, it is safe to assume that he tried to keep taxes at a minimum and that he undoubtedly avoided labor conscription entirely.

The capital was established initially at Shechem, the place of the meeting with Rehoboam (1 Kings 12:25). Since Jeroboam soon directed building activity also at Penuel, across the Jordan on the Jabbok River, he may have had this as an alternate residence. However, he eventually established his permanent capital at Tirzah (1 Kings 14:17; 15:21, 33; 16:6, 8, 9; et al.), thought to be modern Tell el-Farah,[4] about six miles northeast of Shechem.

b. Substitute worship. Religiously, Jeroboam sinned in the sight of God by establishing a substitute worship for his northern people (1 Kings 12:26–33). He reasoned that if he did not do this, the people, in returning to Jerusalem to worship, would be tempted to reunite the two countries. He established new worship centers at Dan in the far north and Bethel in the south.[5]

As symbols for the new program, he erected gold images of calves at each center. The intent was still to worship Yahweh—but in a new way.[6] He built a temple ("house of high places"), presumably to house the image and an altar (1 Kings 12:31, 33) at each cen-ter, and appointed priests of the common people (non-Levites) to serve them. One reason for not using Levites, as required in the Mosaic Law, was that many of them, perhaps most, had left for Judah, evidently in rebellion against these innovations (2 Chron. 11:13–14). Jeroboam further made provision for an annual feast, substituting it for the legal Feast of Tabernacles, setting its time of observance just one month later.

2. Jeroboam rebuked and punished (1 Kings 13:1–14:18)

These acts of Jeroboam constituted a serious offense in the sight of God. They were in direct violation of the Mosaic covenant, and they introduced a potential syncretism of true worship with the fertility cult of Baal. Without question, Jeroboam's innovation made the later introduction of Baal worship into the land under Ahab and Jezebel (1 Kings 16:30–33) much easier. The Canaanites, too, made calves in connection with their religious exercises, thinking of Baal or Hadad as standing on their backs.[7]

Accordingly, God soon sent a messenger to rebuke Jeroboam. Called merely "a man of God," the messenger came north from Judah, spoke against the Bethel altar, and predicted that a prince of the rival house of David,

---

[4] For discussion of excavation, see DeVaux, *RB*, 1947–52.

[5] Bethel was located just north of the Benjamite boundary (Josh. 18:13) and so near Judah's territory that Abijam, successor to Rehoboam as king in Judah, was able to take control of it at one time during Jeroboam's reign (2 Chron. 13:19). Jeroboam then may have wished he had not placed this center so far south.

[6] Jeroboam apparently wished to parallel the Jerusalem worship of Yahweh in an effort not to offend Jerusalem sympathizers more than necessary. Accordingly, Albright believes these calves were not intended as representatives of Yahweh but only animals on which the people were to think of Yahweh standing in invisible form, a manner of thinking common to Canaanites in reference to Baal or Hadad; see Albright, *FSAC*, pp. 203, 229.

[7] For pictures of gods so represented standing on the backs of animals, see *ANEP*, figs. 500, 501, 522, 534, 537.

Josiah by name,[8] would one day burn the bones of Jeroboam's priests upon that very altar (1 Kings 13:1–3; 2 Kings 23:15–16). Jeroboam, angry at the warning, pointed his hand at the messenger and ordered nearby attendants to seize him, but miraculously his hand "shriveled up." Jeroboam then besought the messenger to ask God to restore it, which the messenger did; and God made the hand well again. The incident must have caused Jeroboam to rethink his program, but no indication is given that he made any changes.

Later, in remarks spoken to Jeroboam's wife, Ahijah the prophet spoke against this false worship (1 Kings 14:1–18). The queen had disguised herself and come to Ahijah to inquire if her son would recover from a serious illness. Ahijah, informed by God beforehand that she would do so, took the occasion not only to inform her that the boy would die but also to denounce the royal family for its sin and predict the destruction of the entire household. Jeroboam, in sending his wife to inquire of the prophet, had concluded that because Ahijah had favored him once in predicting his rule, he would do so again.

He discovered, however, that God's prophets are not in the business of courting royal favor; instead, they are busy proclaiming God's truth whatever the effect might be. The child did die, as Ahijah foretold, and the entire family was destroyed later by a successor, Baasha.

3. Loss of territory

In addition to this, Jeroboam did not fare well in maintaining all the land that he had received on becoming king. It may be assumed that the entire area that had been controlled by Solomon, apart from that which was retained by Judah, came under his jurisdiction at the inauguration. If it did, significant sections were lost during the early reigns of Israelite kings, and then more territory was lost during Jeroboam's reign.

One such section was in the north, around Damascus. Substantial loss in degree of control had occurred there even while Solomon reigned; this came about because of the vigorous opposition of Rezon. But during Jeroboam's rule, the region itself was lost; this is known from the fact that, when Rezon died, he left Damascus as capital of an independent Aramean state.[9]

Another section was in the southwest, where the Philistines now became active again, reclaiming some of their lost territory. Nadab, Jeroboam's son and successor, found it necessary to try to regain Gibbethon from them in his reign, though without success (1 Kings 15:27). In the east, at least Moab was lost, for the Moabite Stone[10] records her reconquest by Omri, Israel's sixth king.

Besides loss of such territories, Jeroboam's country suffered at least one serious invasion into its heartland by a foreign enemy. This came at the hands of Shishak (Sheshonq I), king of Egypt, who had earlier given asylum to Jeroboam when he fled from Solomon.

---

[8] One of the remarkable "name" prophecies of the Old Testament, made here nearly three centuries before the man named began to rule.

[9] For evidence and general discussion of Aramean history at this time, see Merrill F. Unger, *Israel and the Aramaeans of Damascus* (London: James Clarke, 1957), pp. 38–57. Unger believes that this Rezon was likely the Hezion of 1 Kings 15:18, who is listed also on the votive stele of Benhadad I.

[10] See pp. 262–63.

Now, however, after first devastating Judah to the south, Shishak marched into and through Jeroboam's territory, inflicting widespread destruction of life and property.[11]

4. Jeroboam's death
(1 Kings 14:19–20;
2 Chronicles 13:20)

Jeroboam himself did not die at the hand of an assassin, an aspect of God's punishment that was reserved for his son, Nadab. Jeroboam died a natural death after twenty-two years of rule. He had shown some ability, but, because of sin, he forfeited God's blessing. He founded the new country, but he failed to move it to strength and vigor as an independent state. Indeed, he left the country sowed with seeds of discontent that were to sprout in numerous royal assassinations, a rapid succession of dynasties, and frequent periods of weakness.

5. Nadab
(910–909; 1 Kings 15:25–31)

Nadab[12] succeeded his father, reigning at Tirzah two years. His only recorded endeavor was his siege of Gibbethon[13] in Philistine territory, noted above. While maintaining this siege, he was assassinated by Baasha (1 Kings 15:27–28), probably one of his generals, who then ruled in his stead. Baasha proceeded to destroy all the house of Jeroboam according to Ahijah's prediction.

Religiously, Nadab followed in the footsteps of his father. Specifically, he is said to have continued "walking in the ways of his father and in his sin, which he had caused Israel to commit" (1 Kings 15:26). This descriptive phrase is repeated with some variations in connection with most of Jeroboam's eighteen successors (see 1 Kings 15:34; 16:19, 26, 31; 22:52; et al.); it refers to the sin of worshipping at Dan and Bethel. All eighteen rulers continued this substitute form of worship, and God held it against each as serious sin.

6. Baasha (909–886; 1 Kings
15:32–16:7;
2 Chronicles 16:1–6)

Baasha ruled for a long period (twenty-four years). Little, however, is recorded of his reign except for the general fact that he continued in conflict with Judah. One particular episode is described. Baasha sought to fortify Ramah, just four miles north of Jerusalem and well within Benjamite territory. His intention was to control north-south traffic above Judah's capital, clearly a tactic more economic than military.

Asa, king of Judah, retaliated by persuading Benhadad I (c. 896–874), king of the rising Aramean power at Damascus, to attack Baasha's northern cities. Benhadad did so, likely not needing much excuse, and Baasha had to cease his efforts at Ramah to protect his own land. What is not indicated is the degree to which Benhadad was

---

[11] For discussion of this invasion, see pp. 288–89.

[12] Nadab may have been Jeroboam's second son, depending on whether Abijah, who died of illness, was the eldest or not. This is not made clear, but is likely.

[13] Gibbethon is best identified with modern Tell el-Melat, three miles east of 'Aqir (likely Ekron) and three miles west of Gezer. Though small in area, it must have been considered important; for twenty-six years later Omri, then general under King Elah, besieged it again (1 Kings 16:15–17). See Simons, *GTT*, pp. 201, 337, 359, 510.

successful against him at this time. At least Baasha was not able to accomplish all that he had intended against Judah.

Religiously, Baasha continued in the way of his two predecessors and accordingly was warned through Jehu the prophet that his house would suffer a fate similar to that of the house of Jeroboam (1 Kings 16:1–7).

7. Elah and Zimri
(886–885; 1 Kings 16:8–22)

Elah succeeded his father Baasha and ruled two years. The Philistine city of Gibbethon was attractive to him, as it had been to Nadab, and he sent his general, Omri, to lay siege to it once more. While Omri was there, Zimri, another military figure, conspired against and killed Elah. Zimri proceeded to destroy all the house of Baasha, according to Jehu's words, and proclaimed himself king. Meanwhile Omri, at Gibbethon, learning of the assassination, had himself declared king by his army and returned to Tirzah to put down Zimri's rebellion. This was accomplished, and Zimri committed suicide, burning the palace over him, after a rule of only seven days.

With Zimri dead, Omri's claim to the throne was still not unchallenged, however. A certain Tibni, otherwise unknown, was now set up as ruler by a part of Israel. A divided rule existed for four years,[14] before Omri, with the backing of his army, was able to emerge victor and establish Israel's fourth ruling family.

C. THE DYNASTY OF OMRI
(885–841; 1 Kings 16:23–22:53;
2 Kings 1–8)

1. Political situation

With Omri, the political situation in Israel became stabilized once more. It may be presumed that this pleased the people. Omri represented the third ruling family within the short span of three years. Elah had ruled only two years, and Zimri's reign had lasted a mere seven days; and the struggle between Omri and Tibni had been disturbing to all. But with this division settled, Omri began a dynasty that was to last three generations.

Stabilization came none too soon. The Aramean state to the north, with its capital at Damascus, was rapidly rising in power. Asa of Judah had already asked assistance from her king, Benhadad I, against Baasha. Benhadad was aggressive. A stele left by him near Aleppo shows that he was able to make his power effective as far as northern Syria by c. 850 B.C.[15] Had Israel remained weak much longer, she would have had little chance of competing with a ruler so strong. Ahab, Omri's son, was to find matters difficult as it was.

In addition to the potential threat of Damascus, a greater source of danger was rising further east. Assyria—which had been bidding to become a world power for a few decades but had been contained by the Mittanians and Hurrians and later by Aramean groups of the upper Euphrates region—was now

---

[14] Omri ruled twelve years (1 Kings 16:23), from Asa's twenty-seventh (1 Kings 16:15) to Asa's thirty-eighth year (1 Kings 16:29). The notice of his beginning to reign in Asa's thirty-first year (1 Kings 16:23), then, must be in reference to his sole rule.

[15] For discussion of this stele, see Albright, *BASOR* 87 (October 1942): 23–29; Albright and Della Vida, *BASOR* 90 (April 1943): 30–34. For text, notes, and picture, see *DOTT*, pp. 239–41, and text and notes, *ANET*, p. 501.

breaking out from its confinement.[16] This took place particularly under Ashur-nasir-pal II (883–859), who was known for his extreme cruelty and ruthless methods.[17] With him the period of Assyrian empire is said to have begun, as he marched his army across the Euphrates and occupied land as far west as Byblos, Sidon, and Tyre on the Mediterranean.[18] Omri ruled in Israel at the time; and, although his country was not yet touched by this conqueror, it was by Ashur-nasir-pal's successor, Shalmaneser III.

2. Omri's reign
(885–874; 1 Kings 16:23–28)

Omri was a strong ruler, easily the most capable and aggressive Northern Israel had yet known. Marked testimony of this is provided by an unexpected source. Assyrian rulers, living a century later, still referred to Israel as the "land of Omri."[19] Though the biblical record says little about him, his exploits must have been remarkable to so impress rulers of this strong state. Three accomplishments are especially noteworthy.

a. New capital, Samaria (1 Kings 16:24). The biblical account does tell of one achievement of this king. Omri built a new capital for Israel, the city of Samaria. Tirzah had been capital from the time of Jeroboam. Omri continued residence there while still in conflict with his rival, Tibni, but two years later he purchased a new site, the hill of Samaria, where he built an entirely new city.[20] A decisive move of this kind bespeaks a man of vision and courage. His motivation clearly lay in the desire to have a capital that was more easily defended against military attack. Further, like Jerusalem, the capital belonged to the king by right of purchase.

History witnesses to his wisdom in choice of site, for Samaria proved to be an almost impregnable stronghold. Excavation has also revealed that excellent workmanship characterized the building activity.[21] The city Samaria, named after the former owner of the hill on which it was built, continued as capital until Israel's fall to the Assyrians in 722 B.C.

b. Conquest of Moab. A second accomplishment is known from the inscribed Moabite Stone.[22] This valuable monument was found by a German missionary in 1898; it was lying on the ground near the Arnon River. Written by the authority of Mesha, king of Moab (2 Kings 3:4), it states that "Omri, king of Israel" had conquered Moab in the days of Mesha's father. Mesha's point is to say that,

[16] For brief discussion, see p. 197.

[17] He boasts of his cruelty even in his annals; see Finegan, *LAP,* pp. 202–3 for sample quotations, taken from Luckenbill, *Ancient Records of Assyria and Babylonia* (Chicago: University of Chicago Press, 1926), vol. 1, secs. 443, 447; also *ANET,* pp. 275–76, or Barton, *AB,* p. 457.

[18] See his inscription, *ANET,* pp. 275–76.

[19] For instance, Adad-nirari III (810–782; *ANET,* pp. 281–82), Tiglath-pileser III (745–727; *ANET,* pp. 283–84), and Sargon II (721–705; *ANET,* pp. 284–85).

[20] The hill of Samaria, named after its owner, Shemer, is located seven miles northwest of Shechem and stands three hundred feet high, quite by itself, though ringed by other mountains, so that attackers had to charge uphill from any side. It was strategically located also in that it commanded north-south trade routes.

[21] See A. Parrot, *Samaria, the Capital of the Kingdom of Israel* (London: SCM, 1958).

[22] For text and discussion, see *ANET,* p. 320; for the same and a picture, see *DOTT,* pp. 195–99.

under the pleasure of his god Chemosh, he was able to throw off the tribute that Omri had imposed.[23]

. Omri, then, was capable of raising a sufficient army from his country, so recently weakened by insurrection, to defeat a land of the standing of Moab. This means that he was an able person—not only in maintaining but also in enlarging the land he had. From this it follows, too, that he must have experienced some measure of success over the Arameans of Damascus, for it is not likely that he would have chanced this attack on Moab, to the southeast, if he could have been threatened from Damascus to the north.

c. Phoenician alliance. Still a third accomplishment is implied in the marriage of his son, Ahab, to the Phoenician princess, Jezebel. It is likely that he made a treaty with her father, King Ethbaal;[24] for, as observed earlier, such marriages were normal seals of formal alliances. A pact between Israel and Phoenicia would have been mutually advantageous, too: Israel gaining cedar from Lebanon and fine imported merchandise from maritime Phoenicia; and Phoenicia gaining grain and olive oil from Israel, besides valuable trade routes to customers further south. In addition, each would have experienced additional strength against the rising Aramean power in Damascus.[25] This alliance and resulting marriage, though diplomatically wise and politically expedient, proved to be a religious disaster; for it opened the way for the introduction of state-sanctioned Baal worship into Israel.

3. Ahab and Jezebel (874–853; 1 Kings 16:28–34; 20:1–22:40)

a. Introduction of Baal worship. Probably the two most familiar names in the history of Northern Israel are King Ahab and Queen Jezebel. But they are known because the biblical record says they did evil in the sight of God more than all before them (1 Kings 16:30). The main reason for this indictment is that they introduced Jezebel's native religion, the cult of Baal-Melqart,[26] to Israel.[27] Worship of Baal, the Canaanite deity, had been

---

[23] See 2 Kings 3:4–27 for the account of Mesha's rebellion and of Israel's attempt to force continued payment (pp. 268–69).

[24] In 1 Kings 16:31, Ethbaal is called "king of the Sidonians," when actually his capital was Tyre. See p. 247n.24.

[25] It is possible, however, that Benhadad of Damascus had already himself made alliance with Tyre. His stele found near Aleppo (see above, n.15) is dedicated to the Tyrian god, Baal-Melqart, suggesting that at least a friendly relation existed between the two countries, if not a treaty. If so, the political advantage of Omri's treaty with Tyre lay mainly with Israel, while it would have been economically advantageous to Tyre to assure peaceful relations with its nearest trading partners.

[26] This Tyrian god is called Melqart. Melqart is the Tyrian expression of the almost universal Palestinian fertility god, Baal.

[27] Actually this introduction was due primarily to Jezebel rather than Ahab. Ahab permitted it, and so was responsible; but Jezebel was its sponsor. The Baal prophets were those who ate "at Jezebel's table" (1 Kings 18:19); she was the one who ordered the "LORD's prophets" killed (1 Kings 18:4); and she sent the threatening note to Elijah (1 Kings 19:2). As for Ahab, he called for prophets of Yahweh when he wanted advice (1 Kings 22:6–12) and named his children with Yahweh-type names: Athaliah, Ahaziah, Jehoram. Baal names were also common, however, as suggested by names listed on ostraca found at Samaria: see J. W. Jack, *Samaria in Ahab's Time: Harvard Excavations and Their Results* (Edinburgh: T. & T. Clark, 1929), p. 37. Though these ostraca have been dated in the reign of Jeroboam II, about one century after Ahab, the names they show likely had been used for many years. For commentary and text, see *ANET,* p. 321, and *DOTT,* pp. 204–8.

observed among Israelite tribes in pre-monarchical days, and Samuel had found it necessary to fight vigorously against it. It is likely that, under vigorous and orthodox kings like David, such worship was at least suppressed. While it probably continued to be practiced as an underground religion when suppressed, under Ahab and Jezebel it acquired the status of a sanctioned religion.

Jezebel, persistent and dominant as she was, was not content with having her religion merely coexist with that of Yahweh worship. She wanted it to supplant what had been before and lent every effort that it would. She came near to accomplishing her purpose, too, as is indicated especially by her vicious slaughter of the native prophets of Yahweh (1 Kings 18:4), something she, being the foreigner, would not have dared undertake unless she had already been well in command of religious matters.[28] The earlier sin of Jeroboam, establishing the shrines at Dan and Bethel, with their golden calves, had been serious enough; but this introduction of the Baal cult was much worse. It involved an outright substitution of deity—even polytheism for monotheism—and degrading, licentious observances, including religious prostitution.

b. Capable rule. Apart from these serious religious faults, however, Ahab was a capable ruler, seeking to follow the pattern of his father. For one thing, Ahab continued a building program. Excavation at Samaria has revealed that he built an impressive casemate wall around the acropolis, or royal quarter of the city. This was a double wall divided into rooms by partitions. To the north, the outer wall was about six feet thick, the inner about four feet, and the space between about twenty-three feet.

The ivory plaques and fragments found at various points throughout the city suggest the "ivory" palace criticized by Amos (3:15; 6:4). These were used as inlays in paneling and furniture and are of great beauty. They reflect the cosmopolitan interests of Israel's king, as the artistic influences that shaped them come from both Egypt and Mesopotamia.[29] It is stated further that Ahab built cities for the people (1 Kings 22:39).

c. Experiences in warfare. In spite of his religious failings, Ahab appears to have been an effective military leader. On two occasions he defeated Aramean forces in accordance with predictions of "a prophet" of Yahweh (1 Kings 20:1–34). In the second instance, the advisors of Benhadad[30] instructed him to attack Israel in a valley, rather than on a mountain as the first time; for Yahweh, Israel's God, was, they explained, a God only of the hills and not of the valleys. Benhadad did so but found that the place made no differ-

---

[28] People normally react more quickly at native clergy being harmed by an outsider than almost anything else. Jezebel must have felt very confident even to attempt it. With them killed, too, it meant more than ever that she had things her own way. It is also possible that the people of Israel were sufficiently apostate at this period that their support for Yahwism was nonexistent.

[29] See Nahman Avigad, "Samaria" in Michael Avi-Yonah and Ephraim Stern, *EAEHL*, 4:1032–50.

[30] This must be Benhadad II, son of the Benhadad whom Asa had employed to attack Baasha long before; because in 1 Kings 20:34 he speaks to Ahab of his father having privileges in Samaria, and the father of Benhadad I was Hezion, who died long before Samaria was built. Unger, *Israel and the Aramaeans*, pp. 59–61, takes the opposite view.

ence. This time Ahab inflicted an even greater defeat than in the first instance, and the Arameans were forced to sue for mercy. Benhadad was surprised at the leniency of Ahab's terms of surrender,[31] however, as was Yahweh's prophet (1 Kings 20:35–43).

Ahab's motive for this leniency may be found in a threat then posed by the great Shalmaneser III (859–824), king of Assyria. If Benhadad were to be helpful to Ahab and other rulers of the west in resisting this greater common foe, he should not be deprived of his army. It is significant, indeed, that not many months later, in 853 B.C., both Ahab and Benhadad did join in a northern coalition to stop Shalmaneser's mighty army at Qarqar on the Orontes River. To this coalition, Ahab was able to contribute two thousand chariots and ten thousand soldiers, and Benhadad twelve hundred chariots, twelve hundred horsemen, and twenty thousand soldiers.[32]

Still the same year,[33] Ahab again fought with Benhadad, this time at Ramoth-gilead,[34] and was killed, thus fulfilling a prediction and warning by the fearless prophet Micaiah (1 Kings 22:13–39). Jehoshaphat, king of Judah, had allied himself with Ahab for the battle and was nearly killed himself when mistaken for Ahab by the enemy forces. Ahab had distinguished himself in view of Micaiah's prediction but was killed in spite of the precaution.

d. Alliance with Judah. That Jehoshaphat was with Ahab in this battle was almost certainly due to an alliance between Israel and Judah. Ahab's daughter Athaliah had been married to Jehoshaphat's son Jehoram, the normal seal of such a pact (2 Kings 8:26). Peaceful conditions, conducive to a mutual agreement, had now existed between the two countries since the beginning of Omri's rule. Also, other times of assistance by Jehoshaphat to Ahab's sons were to follow, which further indicate this formal relationship.[35] Though likely producing benefit economically, the alliance was harmful religiously for Judah. The influence of Baal worship from Israel— the result especially of the marriage involved—brought serious corruption to the religious life of Judah.

4. The prophet Elijah (1 Kings 17–19; 21; 2 Kings 1:1–2:11)

During the reign of Ahab, one of Israel's outstanding prophets ministered. This was Elijah. Without the extensive record of this man's activities, far less would be known about Ahab and Jezebel.

a. Famine and fire (1 Kings 17–19). Elijah came from backward Gilead across the Jordan and dressed simply in camel's hair clothing (2 Kings 1:8). He demonstrated outstanding courage and faith in opposing

---

[31] Cities formerly taken from Israel were to be restored and Ahab was to have certain "market areas" assigned him in Damascus, as Damascus had enjoyed formerly in Samaria. But no surrender or reduction of army or arms was required, which is certainly most unusual.

[32] For the text from Shalmaneser, see Barton, *AB*, p. 458, *ANET*, pp. 278–79, and *DOTT*, pp. 46–49.

[33] See Thiele, *MNHK*, p. 66n.7, for an explanation of both battles occurring the same year.

[34] Best identified, according to N. Glueck's suggestion (*BASOR* 92 [December 1943]), with Tell-Ramith, some twenty-eight miles east of the Jordan and fifteen miles south of the Sea of Galilee.

[35] Very likely the significance, too, of 1 Kings 22:44 and 2 Chronicles 18:1.

Jezebel's introduction of the Baal-Melqart cult. His first recorded prophetic act was to announce to Ahab that God was about to send a dreadful drought and famine upon the country because of this religious defection (1 Kings 17:1).[36] Then Elijah hid from Ahab during the forty-two months of the famine (Luke 4:25; James 5:17)—first at the brook Cherith and then in foreign Zarephath between Tyre and Sidon (1 Kings 17:2–24), much to the displeasure of Ahab, who looked for him even in foreign countries (1 Kings 18:10).[37]

Following this, he reappeared to Ahab at God's direction and persuaded the king to cooperate[38] in arranging a contest on Mount Carmel for the purpose of demonstrating which god was true, Yahweh or Baal-Melqart (1 Kings 18:17–20). When the contest was held, Elijah challenged the prophets of Baal to prove their god by calling down fire from heaven to consume their sacrifice. Baal failed, but Yahweh's fire consumed the drenched sacrifice, the water, and the very stones of the altar (1 Kings 18:38). Then Elijah succeeded in persuading the influential spectators[39] not only to acclaim Yahweh as true God orally but to do so actively by helping to slay the opposing prophets of Baal (1 Kings 18:39–40).[40]

b. Failure and renewal. At this point, prospects for national revival of true Yahweh worship were excellent; but Elijah himself, in a moment of weakness, spoiled them. He ran from the country when threatened by Jezebel (1 Kings 19:1–3), an act that could only have shocked and disillusioned those who so recently had committed themselves to religious change on Mount Carmel.[41] Accordingly, when Elijah reached Mount Horeb sometime later, he was reprimanded by God; but then he was given instructions for a new and different type of ministry and sent back to Israel (1 Kings 19:8–18).[42]

An aspect in the new instructions was to acquire a helper (Elisha), which he did. The two worked together for about ten years[43] in continued resis-

---

[36] Baal-Melqart, god of storm and good crops, was directly challenged in this prediction of drought. Could Baal bring rain when Yahweh said none would fall? For forty-two months the people were to learn the answer as a way of preparation for the climaxing contest on Mount Carmel.

[37] It was necessary for Elijah to remain secluded until the full impact of the supremacy of Yahweh over Baal might be impressed upon the people, in anticipation of the contest on Mount Carmel.

[38] Royal cooperation was necessary to insure that the Baal prophets, who had nothing to gain by such a contest, would be on hand; also to reassure potential spectators, who otherwise had reason to fear reprisal by the vindictive Jezebel, that no harm would result for them.

[39] These spectators must have approximated 1,500 in number to be able to keep 450 Baal prophets from escaping (1 Kings 18:40). They would also have been important, influential persons. Elijah's purpose was to influence all Israel, and so he would have wanted Ahab to invite those whose word to others would carry weight.

[40] This action, repulsive in itself, was necessary as the first act in ridding the land of the foreign cult. It was an act of obedience to God's own order (Deut. 13:6–9; 17:2–7) and a device by which these spectators might commit themselves, by act, to the religious change desired.

[41] Jezebel would have taken full advantage of this fact and spread her version of Elijah's flight rapidly all through the country. It would be in keeping with her other actions if she even went further and killed those who had helped in slaying her Baal favorites. Many of the fifteen hundred may have died in the next few days.

[42] This time of reprimand and instruction came in the form both of an object lesson (wind, earthquake, and fire, followed by a still, small voice) and a spoken word. The new type of ministry indicated was to be of the "still, small voice" variety, in contrast to the preceding dramatic measures.

[43] The figure, ten years, is not given, but can be estimated. A few years had to elapse for Israel,

tance to the religious and moral decadence of the regime of Ahab and Jezebel.

c. Three later episodes. From these later years of service, three incidents are recorded. In one, Elijah rebuked King Ahab for his unjust seizure of a vineyard near his alternate palace in Jezreel (1 Kings 21:1–29). Jezebel led in arranging for the death of the owner, Naboth, by means of a staged court trial, and Ahab took possession. But Elijah met him at the vineyard, rebuked him, and warned him of coming destruction on his household.

In a second episode, Elijah rebuked Ahab's son and successor, Ahaziah, for asking the priests of Baal-zebub, god of the Philistine city Ekron[44] to predict Ahaziah's chance of recovery from wounds suffered in a fall (2 Kings 1:2–16). Elijah intercepted the messengers and sent them back to the king with the information that Ahaziah would die, and included a rebuke for sending outside Israel for such information, as though there were no God in Israel. Elijah eventually appeared before Ahaziah to rebuke him further. But before he, at God's command, made this appearance, God had, by fire, destroyed two fifty-man contingents sent by Ahaziah to bring Elijah to him.

In the third incident, Elijah was taken to heaven by God, as his fellow prophet and assistant, Elisha, watched (2 Kings 2:1–11). This was a great honor bestowed on Elijah and implies unusual approval by God on his ministry. Elisha took up Elijah's mantle, which had fallen from the great man's shoulders as he was being taken, and wore it himself as a symbol of God's anointing now upon him.

Elijah's main impact on Israel lay, as intended, in his vigorous opposition to the cult of Baal-Melqart promoted by Jezebel. His total effect is hard to assess, but certainly was considerable. As noted, it may have been much greater had he not run when Jezebel threatened him; but still the overall influence of the famine, the contest on Mount Carmel, and the later faithful ministry conducted with Elisha must have left lasting results. The entrenchment of Baal worship in Israelite life would have become far deeper had not Elijah lived and worked as he did.

5. Ahaziah
(853–852; 2 Kings 1:2–18)

Two sons of Ahab succeeded him: first Ahaziah, then Jehoram. Ahaziah ruled only two years and died without sons to succeed him, thus giving opportunity for the second son, Jehoram. Ahaziah died from wounds received in a fall, apparently through an upper, latticed window. As noted, messengers were sent to Ekron's Baal-zebub to inquire about his chance for recovery but were intercepted by Elijah and then returned with rebuke by the prophet.

Two other matters from his reign are recorded. One is that Mesha, king of Moab, revolted against the heavy trib-

---

ravaged by famine, to regain sufficient strength to do battle again with the Arameans; then at least two years for the two battles described in 1 Kings 20; then the Qarqar battle of 853 B.C. allied with Benhadad, followed by the Ramoth-gilead battle in which Ahab was killed; then the two years (not necessarily twenty-four months, however) of rule by Ahaziah; and finally the year or so involved of Jehoram's reign until Elijah's translation to heaven (2 Kings 2:1–13).

[44] Most commonly identified with ʿAqir, ten miles northeast of Ashdod. It was near the boundary between Philistine and Israelite lands and often changed hands (Judg. 1:18; 1 Sam. 5:10; 7:14; 17:52). Whether it was in Israelite or Philistine control at this time is unknown.

ute imposed by Jehoram's grandfather, Omri.[45] Results of this uprising were experienced later in Jehoram's rule as well. The other is that Ahaziah entered into a joint maritime venture with Jehoshaphat, doubtless in keeping with the alliance his father had made with Judah (2 Chron. 20:35–37). The venture proved disastrous, however, when the ships built were all destroyed, apparently even before their maiden voyage. The destruction was in accordance with the prophet Eliezer's prediction, which pronounced God's displeasure at this second instance[46] of Jehoshaphat aligning himself with the wicked kings of Israel.

6. Jehoram
(852–841; 2 Kings 3)

Jehoram ruled longer than his brother, a total of twelve years (2 Kings 3:1). The many incidents told from his reign make it seem more significant than twelve years would suggest. Two matters account for this detailed record: first, during his time the Arameans of Damascus were especially active in respect to Israel; and second, the great prophet Elisha was then at the height of his ministry.

a. Religious viewpoint. Concerning Jehoram's attitude toward the Baal cult, it is stated that he removed an image of Baal made by his father (2 Kings 3:2); and so one might think that he banned Baal worship, or at least was unsympathetic to it. Other matters, however, show that this was not so. At a later

time, for instance, he was ironically bidden by Elisha to seek help from the prophets of his father and mother in a time of need, implying that this was his normal practice (2 Kings 3:13). Also, Jehu, his successor, later found it necessary to slay Baal prophets of the land when he came to the throne (2 Kings 10:19–28). That Jehoram could be expected to have continued the Baal cult follows from the fact that his domineering mother Jezebel still lived throughout his reign (2 Kings 9:30–33). The image in Samaria which Jehoram removed may have been particularly objectionable to a population segment that he wished to appease.

b. Revolt of Moab (2 Kings 3:4–27). Another item to notice from Jehoram's reign is the direct result of the recent revolt of Moab during Ahaziah's reign. Mesha, Moab's king, refused to send the tribute imposed years earlier by Omri, no doubt encouraged by Ahab's death at the hand of the Arameans. But Jehoram missed the economic advantage the tribute had afforded his father and, with the aid of Jehoshaphat, took steps to force its continuance.

By agreeing, Jehoshaphat began a third joint venture with Ahab's house, in keeping with the alliance made with Ahab but adding to his sin before God. The combined armies,[47] on their way to attack Moab, found themselves facing death in an arid land for lack of water. Only by Elisha's timely intervention were they spared.[48] The armies

---

[45] See pp. 262–63.

[46] The first instance was when Jehoshaphat went to aid Ahab in his battle at Ramoth-gilead and was nearly killed; p. 265.

[47] By this time, three armies, for Jehoram and Jehoshaphat had been joined by the king of Edom as they rounded the southern end of the Dead Sea (2 Kings 3:9).

[48] This was a significant occasion: three kings able to do nothing to help themselves had to go to one of Yahweh's prophets! Yahweh's instruction through Elisha was for ditches to be dug in the valley

then moved into the land of Moab and inflicted severe damage before Mesha could retaliate—this because they had traveled by an unexpected southern route and taken Mesha by surprise.[49]

But Mesha recovered in time to save his country from complete destruction and was finally able, through a dramatic sacrifice of his eldest son, to effect full withdrawal of the enemy forces. The exact connection between this sacrifice and the withdrawal is not made clear, but it is possible that the army of an apostate Israel feared the intervention of Chemosh in response to this supreme sacrifice. The biblical account, however, does support Mesha's boast on the Moabite Stone[50] that deliverance from Israel's dominance was achieved in his day.

7. Aramean episodes in Jehoram's reign (2 Kings 5–7; 8:28–29)

Though contacts between Israel and the Arameans continued from the reign of Baasha through most of Israel's history, more is related about them during the rule of Jehoram then during the reigns of all the other kings combined.[51] These particular contacts were significant from the biblical point of view because they involved the great prophet Elisha.

a. Naaman, Aramean general (2 Kings 5). The first episode recorded concerns the general of the Aramean armies, Naaman, who served under Benhadad II. It is likely that Naaman had held this position for some time and had led in the battles with Ahab noted earlier. But now he sought help from Israel, for he had become afflicted with leprosy and had been told by a captive Israelite girl that a prophet in Israel could heal him. Benhadad, willing to find such assistance for his valuable officer anywhere, sent appropriate official letters with Naaman to Jehoram in Samaria; but the immediate reaction of the Israelite king was to believe that war was somehow being instigated.

Elisha, however, hearing of the situation, asked that the foreign commander be sent to him, thus easing Jehoram's mind. Naaman, who expected due recognition of his high position, then felt insulted when told by Elisha merely to wash seven times in the Jordan River for his recovery and so nearly missed the physical healing available. Counsel by a wise servant, however, persuaded him to comply, and he then did experience a remarkable restoration. By this he became convinced of the supremacy of Israel's Yahweh and promised henceforth to worship Him alone.[52]

---

where they were encamped. Rain was then sent which flowed down the valley, filled the ditches, and so supplied the armies with ample, clear water.

[49] With Israel located northwest from Moab, Mesha would have expected an attack from the north. By circuiting the southern end of the Dead Sea, Jehoram and Jehoshaphat were able to move into the southern section of Moab before Mesha was aware of their presence.

[50] See p. 262n.22.

[51] This assumes that the stories in 2 Kings 5–8 all relate to his reign, which is likely. With no time indications given, some scholars have suggested that these may have come from the reign of Jehu or even Jehoahaz. The placing and order of the stories, however, argue that all occurred in the reign of Jehoram.

[52] Naaman even asked to take "as much earth as a pair of mules can carry" (2 Kings 5:17) back to Damascus, to the end of worshiping Yahweh. Heathen ideas related deity and land; and Naaman here thought that he had to have some of Yahweh's land if, even in this unusual manner, he was to worship

b. *Blinded Arameans (2 Kings 6:8–23).* Sometime later an entire military contingent was sent by the Arameans to capture Elisha, but they were struck blind for their trouble. This unusual episode was occasioned by Elisha's informing Jehoram more than twice (2 Kings 6:10) of when and where Aramean attacks on Israel were to be directed.[53] When Benhadad's advisors informed him of the secret of Jehoram's success, the Aramean king sent troops to capture the prophet at Dothan where he was residing. Elisha's servant was terrified on seeing the besieging host, but Elisha reassured him and asked God to open his eyes that he might see the greater protective hosts of God. Elisha then requested God to smite this army with blindness and, when God did, led them like sheep the ten miles south to the capital, Samaria. Here their eyes were reopened to see their dangerous situation, but Elisha instructed Jehoram to treat them kindly by supplying food and permitting their return to Damascus.

c. *Siege of Samaria (2 Kings 6:24–7:20).* Several months later the Arameans returned to Israel in greater force and laid siege to Samaria. The prolonged siege brought starvation to the city, with some people even driven to eat their own children (2 Kings 6:28–29). Elisha was blamed by Jehoram, likely due to some earlier warning that such a siege might happen as a punishment for sin, but the prophet then revealed that everyone would have all the food he desired on the following day. This came true when

the Arameans fled in the night at the imagined sound of chariot wheels, which they took to indicate a relief force of Egyptians. Panic prompted them to leave food and all else behind. Starving lepers, resorting, in desperation, to the Aramean camp, learned of the flight. They brought the city the good news of available food in the abandoned camp, and all the people did in truth have the nourishment they needed the following day.

d. *Wounded by Arameans (2 Kings 8:28–29).* A final conflict with the Arameans led to Jehoram's death. Like Ahab his father, he met the Arameans in battle at Ramoth-gilead, and, like him, he had help in the encounter from a king of Judah, now Ahaziah, suggesting that the formal alliance between the two countries still existed. Jehoram was seriously wounded and returned to Jezreel, alternate capital of Omride rulers, to recover. Later, Ahaziah, who had returned to Judah after the battle, came to Jezreel to visit him; and, while there, he was caught in a wave of destruction launched by Jehu, which resulted in the death of both kings.

8. The prophet Elisha

a. Background information. Elisha's work as a prophet was basically the same as Elijah's: resistance to the cult of Baal-Melqart. He requested, at Elijah's translation to heaven, that he might have a double portion of Elijah's spirit (2 Kings 2:9), probably a request to be named principal heir to the prophetic ministry of his mentor. Elisha may have come from a wealthy family, for when

---

Him. This showed his heathen ignorance, but it also showed his sincerity; and Elisha apparently agreed to the request.

[53] It would be interesting to know whether Naaman, recently converted to the worship of Yahweh, led in these battles. No indication, however, is given.

he was first called by Elijah (1 Kings 19:19), he was plowing with a team of oxen in a field where twelve other teams also worked, presumably all owned by his father. If so, he contrasted sharply on this count with his master, Elijah, who had been raised in the poor area of Gilead near the desert. But Elisha's decision to follow Elijah had been final and decisive. He killed his own oxen to prepare a farewell feast for relatives and friends, and he used the wood from his tools as fuel for the fire (1 Kings 19:21).

Elisha's period of ministry lasted much longer than Elijah's. He began in Jehoram's early years, continued through the reigns of Jehu and Jehoahaz, and died sometime while Jehoash ruled (2 Kings 13:20), a period of about fifty years (c. 850–800). Though having the same objectives in his ministry as Elijah, his manner in reaching them was somewhat different. In keeping with his contrasting background, Elisha was more at home in cities and even at the palace and was often in the company of kings. Also, Elijah had been more a man of moods, either strongly courageous or despairing to the point of death; but Elisha was self-controlled and even-tempered, found neither in dramatic staged contests nor sulking in the desert. It may be, too, that Elisha was more interested in the needs of people; for many of his miracles, again in contrast to Elijah, were to aid, heal, and give relief to persons he encountered.

b. Elisha's experiences. The Bible records a series of eighteen separate episodes that involve Elijah. This is in contrast to the record of Elijah's ministry, which is found mainly in three consecutive chapters (1 Kings 17–19). The narratives regarding Elisha fall mostly in Jehoram's reign, and so are not separated greatly in time, but still they do not constitute one continuous account.

Several of these episodes have already been noticed. The others need only be listed: the making of foul water sweet for drinking (2 Kings 2:19–22); slaying those who mocked him (2:23–25); supplying oil that a widow's debts might be paid (4:1–7); praying that a woman of Shunem, who had been kind to him, might give birth to the child she so much wanted, and later restoring that child to life (4:8–37); making edible some food in which a poisonous herb had been mistakenly mixed (4:38–41); multiplying food in time of famine to feed a hundred young prophets (4:42–44); pronouncing leprosy on his servant Gehazi for telling a falsehood (5:20–27); recovering an axhead lost in the Jordan (6:1–7); arranging for restoration by the king, of property belonging to the woman of Shunem, after she had left the land due to famine at Elisha's advice (8:1–6); anointing Hazael as king in Damascus, and Jehu, captain under Jehoram, as king to succeed Jehoram in Samaria (8:7–15; 9:1–10); and much later, in the reign of Jehoash, predicting three victories by him over the Arameans (13:14–19).

One of Elisha's main interests was training young prophets for service (2 Kings 2:3–7, 15–18; 4:38–41; 6:1; 9:1).[54] Elijah likely had started the program, establishing schools at Gilgal, Bethel, and Jericho; but Elisha contin-

---

[54]An interest similar to that of Samuel years before. Whether schools had continued during intervening years is not indicated, but probably they had not.

ued and expanded it. He is seen frequently in the company of students, called "sons of the prophets" (KJV). His purpose was to provide dedicated, trained men to do the work of true prophets in the manner of Elijah and now himself. Sinful, Baal-worshiping Israel needed them desperately.

D. THE DYNASTY OF JEHU (841–753; 2 Kings 9:11–10:36; 13; 14:16–29)

The two strongest ruling families of Israel reigned consecutively: first, the family of Omri, just considered; and second, that of Jehu. Jehu's dynasty ruled longer than Omri's—eighty-nine years as against forty-four—and it included five generations (Jehu, Jehoahaz, Jehoash, Jeroboam II, and Zechariah), in comparison with Omri's three. Jehu's dynasty, however, was not as strong as Omri's, for during its time Israel experienced heavy loss to both the Arameans and the Assyrians. Religiously, each dynasty was seriously deficient, but at least that of Jehu did not foster Baal worship as had that of Omri.

1. Jehu's destruction of the house of Omri (2 Kings 9:11–10:28)

Jehu, first king in this Fifth Dynasty, is best known for his slaughter of the Omrides, who preceded him. Before this time, God had foretold through Elijah twenty years (1 Kings 19:15–17; 21:21–24) that such a

time of punishment would come to this house. With the urging of Elijah and Elisha, Omri's family had been given opportunity enough to repent of its sin in Baal worship and wanton destruction of life. Now came the hour of retribution.

Elisha himself ignited the conflagration, which Jehu then fueled. Elisha sent one of the "company of the prophets" to anoint Jehu as king in Jehoram's place and to instruct him regarding the purging (2 Kings 9:1–10). Jehu, Jehoram's military captain, was still at Ramoth-gilead, the site of the last battle, and readily accepted the honor. His men were pleased as well, and all moved quickly across the Jordan to Jezreel to carry out instructions.

King Jehoram himself, still recovering from wounds, was slain first.[55] Ahaziah, Judah's king who was visiting, fled for his life from Jezreel, but was later caught and killed by pursuers sent by Jehu.[56] Jehu rode into Jezreel and ordered the attendants of Jezebel to throw her from an upper window from which she was looking. They readily complied, and hungry dogs ate her flesh as Elijah had predicted long before (1 Kings 21:23). At Jehu's insistence, Ahab's seventy sons were then killed by Samaria's leaders. Their heads were delivered to Jehu at Jezreel.

After this he left for Samaria, and on the way met and killed forty-two relatives[57] of Ahaziah coming to visit the two kings, not knowing they were

---

[55] Jehoram's body was cast into the field of Naboth, taken by Ahab years before, in fulfillment of Elijah's prediction (1 Kings 21:19). The judgment had been stayed in respect to Ahab himself because of his repentance (1 Kings 21:27–29), but now fell upon Jehoram, his son.

[56] Apparently Ahaziah fled toward Megiddo, with Jehu's men smiting him at Gur (unknown), but he reached Megiddo before dying. At some point Ahaziah hid in Samaria (2 Chron. 22:9), perhaps going there first and later moving northwest to Megiddo; the details are not clear.

[57] These could not have been immediate brothers of Ahaziah, for they had been killed before this by an attack of Philistines and Arabians (2 Chron. 21:16–17).

already dead. Soon after he met Jehonadab, son of Rechab,[58] who, on profession of sympathy and support of Jehu's cause, was taken along in Jehu's own chariot to assist in the revolution. Jehu arrived at the capital and killed all the officials there as well, presumably including the men who had earlier sought favor by killing Ahab's sons. Lastly, Jehu called all the prophets and priests of Baal to their temple in Samaria, as if to extend favor to them, but then sent eighty of his men into the temple to kill them to the last man. Seldom has history witnessed a more thorough blood purging of a previous royal family and favored religious order than this.

2. Jehu as king (841–814; 2 Kings 10:29–36)

Jehu's zeal to rid the land of Omri's house was not matched by his capacity to rule. His twenty-eight years as king were marked by unrest and turmoil, with serious social and economic abuses rife among the people.[59] Neither was he able to prevent inroads and humiliation at the hands of both the Arameans and Assyrians.

Religiously, Jehu received God's commendation at the beginning of his rule because of obedience in destroying the house of Omri (2 Kings 10:30), but then he failed to follow the path he had started. God gave His approval of the blood purge—even though Jehu certainly killed more than divinely intended—for this constituted the punishment decreed against the wicked family years before, and it dealt a shattering blow to the cult of Baal-Melqart. Accordingly, God promised that four generations of Jehu's family would succeed him on the throne. Jehu, however, then chose to perpetuate Jeroboam's worship centers at Dan and Bethel (2 Kings 10:29) and so forfeited the divine approval after all, and consequently experienced difficult times.

a. Hazael's havoc in Israel (2 Kings 10:32–33). Humiliation of Israel at the hands of foreign powers was especially pronounced during Jehu's reign. This came mainly from the Arameans, led by Hazael, in further fulfillment of God's prediction through Elijah (1 Kings 19:15–17).

The fulfillment was first begun when Elisha went north to Damascus to anoint Hazael as the Aramean king (2 Kings 8:7–15). Elisha wept when he did so, for he knew the havoc this man would bring on Israel. The anointing took place shortly before that of Jehu.[60] Though there is no record of how Hazael brought about this havoc, the extent of it is evidenced. He succeeded in seizing all Transjordan from Israel, including the tribal territories of Manasseh, Gad, and Reuben (see Amos

---

[58] Jehu's attitude toward this man indicates respect for him. Jehonadab was loyal to Yahweh and strict in his manner of life. He became tribe-father of the Rechabites, an ascetic group whose faithfulness to regulations prompted admiration by Jeremiah years later (Jer. 35:1–19; see 1 Chron. 2:55 for identity of Rechab).

[59] This fact is evidenced especially by the writings of Amos and Hosea, both prophets to Israel who wrote about one-half century after Jehu's rule. The abuses of which they speak had existed during his time.

[60] The time here is evidenced by inscriptions from Shalmaneser III. In one from his fourteenth year (845 B.C.), he mentions Hadadezer (Benhadad II) as still king in Damascus, and in another from his eighteenth year (841 B.C.) he mentions Hazael. This means that Hazael came to the throne between 845 and 841, and probably just before 841 in view of the manner of notice made regarding him.

1:3). Then, though it is not directly stated, he also must have made serious inroads into Israel west of the Jordan; for a notation from the time of Jehoahaz, son of Jehu, states that Hazael by then was able even to dictate how many horses, chariots, and footmen Israel's king could have in his army (2 Kings 13:7).[61]

Still a further indication from Jehoahaz's time can be seen in a comment regarding King Joash of Judah. It says that Hazael was able to advance as far south as the Philistine city of Gath,[62] seize the city, and force Joash to pay tribute, so that the same would not be done to Jerusalem (2 Kings 12:17–18). If Hazael could impose his will to this extent as far south as Gath and Jerusalem, he must have brought Israel first to a position of extreme subservience, a process no doubt begun as early as the reign of Jehu.

b. Humiliation before Assyria. Israel also suffered at the hands of Assyria during Jehu's rule. In fact, the Assyrian invasion came prior to that of Hazael, and brought even greater harm to Hazael's land than to Israel. The occasion is known only from Assyrian records.[63]

Shalmaneser III, the great Assyrian ruler of the time, was the same man against whom Ahab and Benhadad had combined in a twelve-member coalition at Qarqar a dozen years before. Now, for the sixteenth time, he crossed the Euphrates in military campaign. He succeeded in leading his large army all the way to Damascus, effecting extensive damage on the city, though without actually capturing it, and then went on to force Jehu in Israel to pay heavy tribute.[64]

On his famous Black Obelisk,[65] found at Nimrud in 1846, Shalmaneser lists the tribute and depicts the Israelite king in bas-relief bowing low in submission while presenting his payment. Though Shalmaneser does not claim to have wrought destruction in Israel, the heavy tribute he demanded was humiliating and economically oppressive. Shalmaneser made one more attack in the general area three years later,[66] claiming success once more, but nothing is known of the details. No Assyrian army came again for a generation, which permitted Hazael to regain the strength to inflict the aforementioned harm on Israel.

c. Reasons for Jehu's weakness. Some factors that entered into Jehu's inability to defend his country are suggested by the overall account. One of the more important certainly was his slaughter of able leaders in the blood purge of Omri's house. Jehu went beyond what

---

[61] He was permitted only fifty horsemen, ten chariots, and ten thousand footmen, a marked contrast to the two thousand chariots Ahab had brought to Qarqar!

[62] Gath formerly belonged to the Philistines, but Rehoboam included it in a list of cities which he fortified, indicating that it then, and probably still at this time, belonged to Judah (2 Chron. 11:8). Hazael may have acted as an ally of the Philistines in now seizing Gath from Judah, for the city appears to have been in Philistine hands again by the time of Uzziah (2 Chron. 26:6).

[63] Left by Shalmaneser III. For all his inscriptions, see *ANET,* pp. 276–81.

[64] Shalmaneser also lists Tyre and Sidon as paying tribute.

[65] This four-sided black limestone pillar stands six and one-half feet high, with five rows of bas-reliefs and explanatory cuneiform inscriptions on all sides. In the second row on one side appears Jehu, the only extant representation of an Israelite king. The obelisk resides in the British Museum. For text, see *ANET,* p. 280; for pictures, see *ANEP,* figs. 351–55.

[66] Text in *ANET,* p. 280. This was Shalmaneser's twenty-first year.

God had intended in this purge and unnecessarily killed many who might have helped him, particularly court officials from Jezreel and Samaria. One does not quickly replace men of experience.

Another reason was that some of his people no doubt refused to cooperate with him, in view of his ruthlessness during the purge. He may have had to work with quite a segment of dissident people. Still another was that the earlier alliances with Judah and Phoenicia would now have ceased, as a further result of the purge. Judah would have broken relations because of the death of King Ahaziah and his kinsmen,[67] and Phoenicia because of the slaughter of Jezebel and the priests of Baal-Melqart.

But perhaps most significant, Jehu himself clearly lacked necessary ability. He must have been qualified in military science, for he had been captain under Jehoram; but he lacked in diplomacy and in judgment, as made evident by his reckless slaughter of the former regime. All these factors, of course, were under God's control as He permitted the country to experience punishment in accordance with His announcement to Elijah long before (1 Kings 19:15–17).

3. Jehoahaz
(814–798; 2 Kings 13:1–9)

Jehoahaz succeeded Jehu his father and reigned seventeen years. Little is related regarding his rule, apart from a further degree of subjection to Hazael. The only item stated in addition is that he sought help from God against Haza-el and was given a "deliverer" (2 Kings 13:5). This "deliverer," strange to say, must have been the Assyrian emperor, Adad-nirari III (810–783), who came to the throne during Jehoahaz's reign. He did serve as "deliverer" to Israel in that he attacked and crushed Damascus in 803 B.C.,[68] thus bringing relief to Israel from the Aramean oppression. It is true that Israel, along with Tyre, Sidon, Edom, and Philistia, was forced to pay tribute, but it did not experience the devastation wrought on Damascus. The Aramean state was hurt sufficiently so that Israel was now able to start on a long road toward a new position of strength.

4. Jehoash
(798–782; 2 Kings 13:10–25;
14:15–16)

At Jehoahaz's death, his son Jehoash assumed the throne. During his rule, Israel made rapid strides on this road to recovery. Soon after assuming office, Jehoash was promised a resurgence in military position by Elisha. Elisha, an old man now, called the new king to him and predicted victory over Damascus. He instructed Jehoash to smite the ground with arrows. This king did so, but only three times; and Elisha rebuked him for not smiting it more, explaining that he would have defeated Damascus a corresponding number of times. He would, however, still be victorious on three occasions. Succeeding years saw Jehoash experiencing the fulfillment of this prediction, enabling him to recover all the cities Damascus

---

[67] Athaliah, daughter of Ahab, who had married Jehoram, now ruled in Judah, having seized the throne by treachery. Actually it was good for Judah to be free from this alliance, but Israel no doubt was hurt both economically and militarily.

[68] For the text of Adad-nirari III, see *ANET*, pp. 281–82; also *DOTT*, pp. 50–52. By the time of this attack, Benhadad III, son and successor of Hazael, had ascended the throne in Damascus.

had earlier taken from Israel (2 Kings 13:25).

Jehoash also became strong enough to withstand an attack by Amaziah, king of Judah (2 Kings 14:8–14). In fact, he was able to inflict a major defeat upon him, a matter to be treated more in the following chapter.

An item of further significance is that Jehoash appointed his son as coruler. Jeroboam II became coregent when Jehoash had ruled only five of his sixteen years.[69] The likely reason is found in the war of Jehoash with Judah. Before engaging in the conflict, he placed his son on the throne to rule while he was away, apparently anticipating a prolonged effort.[70]

5. Jeroboam II
(793–753; 2 Kings 14:23–29)

Jeroboam II was the third successive descendant of Jehu to occupy the throne, and he proved to be one of Israel's most capable rulers. Under him, Israel rose to a position of remarkable influence. No description of Jeroboam's battles in accomplishing so much is given, but the end achievement is made clear: Jeroboam was able to establish roughly the same boundaries on the east and north that had existed in the empire days of David and Solomon. It is stated that he placed Israel's northern limit at the "entering of Hamath" (2 Kings 14:25 KJV), the same phrase that describes Solomon's northern boundary (1 Kings 8:65).

It is also stated that "he recovered for Israel both Damascus and Hamath" that had belonged "to Judah" (2 Kings 14:28), the last no doubt a reference to David and Solomon's time, since these cities had not belonged to either Judah or Israel since. It may be observed, too, that this comparative form of reference implies the restoration of the same general relationship between the cities and Israel as had then existed. Still further, by gaining this control over Damascus, he must also have recovered all Transjordan which Hazael had seized. With these boundaries restored, Israel was the largest and most influential country along the eastern Mediterranean. The name of Jeroboam II must have come to be widely known and respected.

At least three factors would have contributed to this marked change of status for Israel. The first, already noticed, is that rival Damascus, formerly the leading country, had been weakened by the attack of Adad-nirari III. The second is that Jehoash, and especially Jeroboam II, were capable rulers (demonstrated in Jehoash's successful encounter with Judah [2 Kings 14:8–14; 2 Chron. 25:17–24] and in Jeroboam's case by the accomplishments just noted). The third is that Assyria, who might have interfered if

---

[69] Evidenced by comparison of certain passages. According to 2 Kings 14:23, Jeroboam II came to the throne in the fifteenth year of Amaziah of Judah, 782 B.C. But 2 Kings 15:1 indicates that Azariah, successor of Amaziah in Judah, began to reign in Jeroboam's twenty-seventh year, which year is known to have been 767 B.C. If this was Jeroboam's twenty-seventh year, then he must have begun to reign in 793 B.C., the fifth year of Jehoash's reign. This means that 2 Kings 14:23 dates from his first year of sole rulership. See Thiele, *MNHK,* pp. 77–81.

[70] Not only does the time of Jehoash's war with Judah fit this beginning of coregency, but so does an unusual second reference to the close of Jehoash's rule in 2 Kings 14:15–16 (first one given in 2 Kings 13:12–13). This second statement falls immediately after the account of this war (2 Kings 14:8–14), as though the war occurred during the coregency and was a cause for it. For discussion, see Thiele, *MNHK,* pp. 84–85.

able, was now experiencing a period of decline caused by the rising menace of northern Urartu people, internal dissension within Assyria itself, and a succession of weak rulers.[71] During their reigns, Assyria lost nearly all her foothold west of the Euphrates and could not hinder the expansionist designs of faraway Israel.

6. Eighth-century prophets

Prophets had existed in Israel from the time of Moses.[72] Of these, the more significant were Samuel, Nathan, Gad, Ahijah, Elijah, and Elisha. Others, frequently unnamed, ministered throughout the early years of Israel's nationhood. It may be that these various biblical accounts represent only a fraction of all the prophetic activity during these years.

In the eighth century, however, a change came in their methods.[73] While continuing the same basic message of obedience to Yahweh's Law, the prophets came to address it to the people collectively, on a national level. Also, the sins rebuked were the sins of the nation, rather than those of individuals. Still further, many prophets now began to write their messages as well as speak them. As a result, prophetic literature which forms an important part of the Old Testament came into existence.

Three of these writing prophets ministered during some part of the reign of Jeroboam II. One was Jonah (2 Kings 14:25), sent on a mission to Nineveh, the great city of Assyria. His time of arrival there, with the consequent repentance of the inhabitants, is best located at the period of Assyrian weakness just noted. Such a period is more conducive to repentance than one of prosperity and strength. Not only was Assyria weak politically and militarily; it had also been ravaged by a series of epidemics that had swept through the land, bringing death to large numbers. Besides, a total eclipse of the sun, June 15, 763 B.C., added to a widespread atmosphere of dread.[74] In this atmosphere, Jonah's message of impending doom for Nineveh would have carried great weight, thus making the remarkable repentance recorded understandable.

The two other prophets are Amos and Hosea, mentioned earlier. Amos, a herdsman of Tekoa, was a citizen of Judah, but was sent north to Israel to bring God's warning in the days of Jeroboam (Amos 1:1). Hosea, a citizen of Israel, also prophesied in the "reign of Jeroboam" (Hos. 1:1). Hosea may have begun his ministry slightly after Amos, for he says that he continued during the reigns of Uzziah, Jotham, Ahaz, and Hezekiah, kings of Judah,[75] while Amos mentions only Uzziah. The almost unprecedented prosperity of Jeroboam's rule led to luxury, idleness, and other sin, all of which were con-

---

[71] They were Shalmaneser IV (783–773), Asshur-dan III (773–754), and Asshur-nirari V (754–746).

[72] Moses called himself a prophet and predicted that others like himself would arise (Deut. 18:15–22).

[73] Likely both Obadiah and Joel ministered already in the last half of the ninth century, though as prophets of Judah.

[74] See A. T. Olmstead, *History of Assyria* (Chicago: University of Chicago Press, 1923), pp. 169–74.

[75] This means a minimum duration of twenty-five years to an impossible maximum of just over a century, depending on how soon in Uzziah's reign he began and how long in Hezekiah's he continued.

demned by these prophets.[76] Much of Hosea's message was based on his own sad experience in marriage, having been left by his profligate wife. He likened her unfaithfulness to that of Israel with God.[77]

7. Zechariah
(753 B.C.; 2 Kings 15:8–12)

Jeroboam's son, Zechariah, succeeded him, making Zechariah the fourth successive descendant of Jehu to sit on the throne. He did not rule long, however, for within six months of assuming the throne, he was assassinated by his successor, Shallum.[78] Nothing else is indicated regarding Zechariah except that he continued the first Jeroboam's false worship at Dan and Bethel. He probably was not as capable as his father, one reason that explains why an assassination plot could be successfully planned and perpetrated.

E. THE DECLINE OF ISRAEL
(752–722; 2 Kings 15:13–17:41)

The reign of Jeroboam II was the northern kingdom's one period of brilliance. With the death of his son, however, the nation rapidly declined in both strength and position. This period of decline closed with the fall of Israel's capital, Samaria, to the great Assyrian war machine in 722 B.C.

1. Shallum
(752 B.C.; 2 Kings 15:13–15)

Shallum killed Zechariah and set himself up as ruler, thus instituting Israel's sixth ruling family. He reigned only one month, however, when Menahem, possibly as military leader under Zechariah, retaliated by killing him. Nothing further is recorded regarding Shallum.

2. Menahem
(752–742; 2 Kings 15:16–22)

Menahem now set himself up as Israel's ruler, thus instituting Israel's seventh ruling family. He ruled for a total of ten years. He is said to have come "from Tirzah" (2 Kings 15:14) at the time that he killed Shallum in Samaria. The implication appears to be that he had held authority in Tirzah,[79] probably his own interest in assuming the throne. It is possible that he experienced opposition in this, however, from the city of Tiphsah,[80] for on becoming king he proceeded to have many of the people there executed.

During Menahem's rule, the power of Assyria was once more experienced by the countries on the Mediterranean. Tiglath-pileser III (745–727), perhaps Assyria's strongest ruler (in marked contrast to his immediate predecessors), had now come to the throne and restored Assyria's empire. He had achieved success first to the south (in Babylonia) and also the north (against the Urartu) before crossing the

---

[76] Amos 2:6–8; 5:10–12; 6:1–8; 8:4–6; Hosea 2:14–23; 4:1–6, 13–19; 7:4.

[77] Hosea 2:2–13; 3:1–5. Israel's unfaithfulness to God receives testimony also in the Samaritan Ostraca, dated from this time (see p. 263n.27). A high percentage of names on these ostraca are compounded with "Baal," showing that significant allegiance was still directed toward this pagan deity which Jehu had supposedly driven from the country.

[78] In keeping with a prediction of Amos (7:9).

[79] See pp. 258, 260, 261, 262.

[80] Location uncertain. Possible identification with Thapsacus (on the west bank of the Euphrates) has been made, but this location would hardly fit the account, for Tirzah was not far from Samaria.

Map 12. Palestine Under Assyrian Control

Euphrates and coming again into the west. He was successful in this direction, too; and, in conjunction with his conquests, he instituted policies that differed from those of previous rulers. Former kings had been satisfied merely with nominal control and a reception of tribute, but this approach had resulted in constant revolt. Tiglath-pileser incorporated conquered land as Assyrian provinces and deported native leaders who might instigate revolution. The policy proved effective and was copied by successors.

His campaign of 743 B.C.[81] reached all the way to Israel and involved Menahem.[82] Tiglath-pileser was not yet able to incorporate the area as a province, but he did exact tribute from Menahem.[83] The imposed sum of one thousand talents of silver was raised by Menahem through a head tax that was assessed against all "wealthy men" in the country at the rate of fifty shekels each.[84] By means of this payment, Menahem was able "to strengthen his own hold on the kingdom." In doing so, however, he became another vassal to the Assyrian ruler (2 Kings 15:19–20).

3. Pekahiah
(742–740; 2 Kings 15:23–26)
and Pekah
(752–732; 2 Kings 15:27–31)

At Menahem's death, his son, Pekahiah, succeeded him. He ruled only two years, though, when Pekah, one of his military leaders, assassinated him at the palace in Samaria and set himself up as king, thus instituting Israel's eighth ruling family.

According to the Old Testament, Pekah ruled for a total of twenty years. Chronological correlations, however, seem to require that these twenty years include years when Menahem and Pekahiah ruled. Pekah's last year clearly was 732 B.C.,[85] so his twenty-year period began in 752 B.C., the year of Menahem's accession, leaving only eight years for Pekah's sole reign.

Thiele suggests the explanation that Pekah had ruled before this across the Jordan in Gilead as a rival to Menahem and Pekahiah. This was before he had gained sufficient courage and support to cross the Jordan with fifty Gileadites, do away with Pekahiah, and seize the throne.[86] If this is correct, the first

[81] The date of this campaign is often given as 738 B.C., but Thiele makes a strong case for 743 B.C. on the basis of a careful study of records of Tiglath-pileser III. See Thiele, *MNHK*, pp. 94–115; Unger, *Israel and the Aramaeans*, p. 97.

[82] In this same year Tiglath-pileser met a northwest coalition, of which Uzziah (Azariah), king of Judah, was leader. See discussion in the next chapter.

[83] Tiglath-pileser lists several other kings who also paid tribute, including Kistashpi of Hummuh, Rezin of Damascus, Hiram of Tyre, Urikki of Kue, Pisiris of Carchemish, Tarhulara of Gurgum, and Sulumal of Melid. For text, see *ANET*, p. 283; *DOTT*, pp. 54–55.

[84] With one talent equal to 3,000 shekels, 60,000 persons would have been assessed. The total would have been 66,000 pounds of silver which, at an arbitrary $10 an ounce, would be worth $10,560,000.

[85] Indicated by the fact that 2 Kings 15:30 and 2 Kings 17:1 establish that the last year of Pekah, the first year of Hoshea, the twelfth year of Ahaz of Judah, and the twentieth year of Jotham of Judah were all the same year, thus giving a correlation with Judean kings, which makes that year 732 B.C. It is determined also by Tiglath-pileser's notice (see *DOTT*, p. 55) that he deposed Pekah, establishing Hoshea in his place, which came during his western campaign of 734–732. See the dating indications for Ahaz and Jotham of Judah in the following chapter.

[86] Thiele, *MNHK*, p. 124–25; see also H. G. Stigers, "The Interphased Chronology of Jotham, Ahaz, Hezekiah, and Hoshea," *BETS*, 9 (Spring 1966): 84–86. Reasons favoring this suggestion are: (1) that Pekah had a band of Gileadites with him when he killed Pekahiah (2 Kings 15:25);

twelve years of his rule were over Gilead only, with sovereignty acknowledged successively to Menahem and Pekahiah. This would explain how he could have been called "chief officer" under Pekahiah (2 Kings 15:25). It has been pointed out by Merrill Unger that an anti-Assyrian party may have developed in Israel as a result of Menahem's head-tax program, and it is this that may have paved the way for Pekah's revolution.[87] This suggestion would go along with the fact that Pekah did take a strong anti-Assyrian position when he became king in Samaria; at that time he aligned himself with Rezin of Damascus against the great eastern power.

In Pekah's sixth year of sole rule, 734 B.C., Tiglath-pileser III returned to the west to put down this rebellious alliance. He had come at the request of Ahaz, king of Judah, who had been besieged in Jerusalem by Pekah and Rezin (2 Chron. 28:5–8; Isa. 7:1–2). The two allies had hoped to force Ahaz to join their rebellion, but Ahaz would not; instead, he asked for aid from the Assyrian ruler.[88]

Tiglath-pileser readily complied by conducting his well-known campaigns of 734–732.[89] He first (734) moved down the Mediterranean coast as far as Philistia and subdued cities there, especially Gaza, apparently to cut off possible Egyptian assistance to the coalition. Later (probably 733) he marched into Israel, destroying cities all across Galilee[90] and taking many people captive (2 Kings 15:29).

Finally, in 732, he moved against Damascus, likely his prime target from the beginning, devastating the country, capturing the capital city, and executing Rezin the king. Tiglath-pileser himself did not kill Pekah, Israel's king, because Hoshea, who succeeded Pekah, did it for him—without doubt in concert with the Assyrian conqueror, however, as Tiglath-pileser claims to have placed Hoshea on Israel's throne (2 Kings 15:30).[91]

4. Hoshea
(732–722; 2 Kings 17:1–6)

Having slain Pekah, Hoshea assumed rule, thus instituting Israel's ninth and last royal family. Israel, at the time of Hoshea's accession, was no longer large. The Assyrians had taken both the north (Galilee) and Transjordan, incorporating these areas as Assyrian prov-

---

(2) Shallum, killed by Menahem, was a "son of Jabesh" (2 Kings 15:13), which suggests a background in Jabesh Gilead, which area, when Shallum was killed by Menahem, would have given support to such a rival as Pekah instead of Menahem; (3) that Menahem, in giving tribute to Tiglath-pileser, is said to have done so "to strengthen his own hold on the kingdom," which suggests that he had such a rival as Pekah, who desired to take it out of his hand; (4) that Pekah had not dared to seize the throne in Samaria earlier would follow in view of the support of Tiglath-pileser which Menahem had gained by the tribute given; and (5) that Pekah appears in friendly relation with Rezin, king of Damascus, shortly after his seizure of Samaria (Isa. 7:1–2), finds ready explanation in an earlier Gileadite-Damascus league, when Pekah ruled only in Gilead near Damascus.

[87] Unger, *Israel and the Arameans,* p. 99.

[88] See pp. 301–2.

[89] For inscription, see *ANET,* pp. 283–84. More complete inscriptions can be found in Luckenbill, *Ancient Records,* vol. 1, secs. 777–79.

[90] Excavation has revealed this devastation, particularly at Megiddo, level III (see Wright, *BAR,* p. 164) and at Hazor, level V, where one sherd was found bearing the name *Pekah, pqh* (see Yadin, *BA* 19 [February 1956]: 2–11; 20 [May 1957]: 34–47; 21 [May 1958]: 30–47; 22 [February 1959]: 2–20).

[91] See *ANET,* p. 284, for text.

inces,[92] leaving Hoshea only hill country west of the Jordan. Hoshea himself was merely a vassal. Little of the glory that had been Israel's under Jeroboam II remained. Even so, Hoshea soon turned in revolt once more against the hated Assyrians, to whom apparently he had submitted only for the sake of expediency. The insurrection came soon after Tiglath-pileser was succeeded by his son Shalmaneser V (727–722). Hoshea foolishly made a pact with Egypt, now weak, divided, and therefore unable to give the assistance Hoshea needed. So allied, he refused to pay the annual tribute to Assyria.

In 724 B.C., Shalmaneser V marched on Israel (2 Kings 17:3–6). Hoshea went to meet him, now bringing his overdue tribute, but this no longer satisfied the Assyrian monarch. Hoshea was immediately taken captive and Shalmaneser moved on to Samaria, placing the capital under siege. He expected it to fall quite readily, no doubt, since the king had already been imprisoned; but it stubbornly resisted. The siege lasted from 724 to 722.[93] Finally, however, the inevitable happened and Samaria fell, bringing the days of Israel as a sovereign nation to a close.[94]

F. ISRAEL UNDER ASSYRIAN CONTROL

After Samaria's fall, an Assyrian governor was placed over the land, thus incorporating all of Israel into Assyria's provincial system. Many Israelites were taken captive by Assyria,[95] either prior to the final collapse or at that time, and in place of these a foreign upper class of people was imported.[96] This manner of mixing populations had also been instituted by Tiglath-pileser III, as a means of diminishing chances of rebellion among subjugated peoples.

No doubt it served that purpose here in Israel, but it also worked religious havoc. The foreigners brought with them their own native ideas of deity and of manner of worship. This influx resulted in a syncretized religion, in which both the false deities and Yahweh were revered (2 Kings 17:29–41). This mixing of population resulted also in intermarriage between the Israelites who were left in the land (of which there were many) and the

---

[92] The Damascus territory had also been similarly incorporated; see Bright, *BHI,* pp. 257–58, for discussion and references.

[93] Indicated as from Hoshea's seventh year to his ninth (2 Kings 17:6; 18:9–10). Put more precisely, taking Hoshea's year of accession as 732/731, this places the siege at 725/724–723/722. See Thiele, *MNHK,* pp. 141–42. The "three years" indicated (17:5; 18:10) means all of one year and some part of both the preceding and following. This means that the siege lasted a minimum of fourteen months.

[94] Though Sargon II, successor of Shalmaneser V, claims to have been the ruler when Samaria fell (see *ANET,* pp. 284–85; or *DOTT,* pp. 58–63, for texts), several reasons argue that this was an empty boast and that Shalmaneser still reigned: (1) 2 Kings 17:1–6 implies that Shalmaneser took Samaria; (2) Sargon's early notices say nothing of taking Samaria, but only the Khorsabad texts from his fifteenth and sixteenth years, which were intended to display his feats; (3) Sargon did not begin to reign until December 722 B.C., too late to qualify as Hoshea's ninth year, which would have closed nine months before. For discussion, see A. T. Olmstead, "The Fall of Samaria," *AJSL* 21 (1904–1905): 179–82; Thiele, *MNHK,* pp. 141–47; Unger, *Israel and the Aramaeans,* pp. 106–8; H. Tadmor, "The Campaigns of Sargon II of Assur: A Chronological-Historical Study," *JCS* 12 (1958): 39.

[95] Sargon lists 27,290, which, if correct, must have been taken following the fall of Samaria proper. Many more had been taken by Tiglath-pileser and probably Shalmaneser.

[96] According to 2 Kings 17:24, these were brought from "Babylon, Cuthah, Avva, Hamath, and Sepharvaim," areas widely scattered in the Assyrian domain.

734 B.C.

732 B.C.

733 B.C.

Damascus

A R A M

Ijon

Abel-beth-maachah

Tyre • Dan

Kedesh

SIDONIANS

Yiron

Merom

Hazor

Karnaim

Acca

Jotbah

Kanah • Chinnereth

Ashtaroth

Hannathon

Dor

Megiddo

Ramoth-gilead

Bethshan

I S R A E L

Samaria

Mahanaim

G I L E A D

Aphek

Joppa

Rabbath-Ammon

Bethel

Gezer

Ajalon

Heshbon

AMMON

Ashdod

Ekron

Jerusalem

PHILISTINES

Sochoh

Medeba

Lachish

Hebron

Dibon

Gaza

JUDAH

Beersheba • Arad

M O A B

to the
Brook of Egypt

Kir-hareseth

Map. 13. The Kingdoms of Israel and Judah Shortly After the Division new foreign people (who were fewer in number). The descendants of these marriages came to be called Samaritans.

G. SUMMARY

Israel continued as a nation for just over two centuries, 931 to 722 B.C. Nineteen kings reigned, representing nine ruling families. Eight kings were either assassinated or committed suicide. Not one of the nineteen was considered good by God, because each followed either the substitute worship at the golden-calf centers or the more evil cult of Baal. For this reason, God's blessing was withheld.

Through Elijah and Elisha, warning was given to the house of Omri concerning the excessive sin of turning to Baal-Melqart. When no heed was given, punishment was meted out, first in the destruction of the Omride family by Jehu and then in the abject humiliation of all Israel before the Arameans of Damascus.

Once again warning came through Amos and Hosea to the house of Jehu during the prosperous days of Jeroboam II, for gross wickedness related to the material affluence then existent. Nevertheless, again the people would not hear. Thus, a second time God permitted major national humiliation—in this instance at the hands of mighty Assyria. This occasion did not end until Samaria had fallen and Israel ceased to exist as a sovereign power. Israel had been given opportunity to repent, but would not. God's wrath fell upon her.

CHAPTER FOURTEEN

THE KINGDOM
OF JUDAH

1 Kings 14:21–15:24; 22:41–50; 2 Kings 8:16–29; 11–25;
2 Chronicles 10–36

Judah's history paralleled that of Israel, but ran nearly a century and a half longer.

A. A PERIOD OF CONFLICT WITH ISRAEL
(931–870; 1 Kings 14:21–15:24; 2 Chronicles 10–16)

The nation left to Rehoboam, following the secession of the northern tribes, consisted primarily of the tribe of Judah. Rehoboam held basically the same area that David did when he was initially made king at Hebron. When Ahijah first spoke to Jeroboam concerning the division, he mentioned only one tribe as remaining loyal to Solomon's descendant (1 Kings 11:31). At the time, however, he gave Jeroboam only ten of the twelve pieces of the rent garment in symbol of the tribes he would rule, implying that another tribe would be added to Judah. Benjamin was that added tribe, though at first her loyalty was likely with the seceding tribes (1 Kings 12:20).

Historically, Benjamin had always aligned herself with the northern group.[1] But now she came to follow Rehoboam[2] and was soon referred to regularly as part of the southern nation.[3] How this change came about is not indicated, but likely Rehoboam simply brought pressure to bear on her leaders to switch loyalty, employing ominous threats and/or attractive inducements. Jerusalem, after all, lay directly on the Benjamite border, and a buffer zone was sorely needed between it and the new northern kingdom.

---

[1] Listed with the tribes over which Ishbosheth ruled (2 Sam. 2:9). Also the revolt at the time of David's return to Jerusalem, following Absalom's death, was led by a Benjamite, Sheba (2 Sam. 20:1–22).

[2] Perhaps Rehoboam's control never extended over all of Benjamite territory, however. Bethel, made religious center by Jeroboam, was on the border between Benjamin and Ephraim (Josh. 18:13) though in Ephraimite territory (1 Chron. 7:28); and later Baasha was able to fortify Raamah, only four miles north of Jerusalem, well within Benjamite land (2 Chron. 16:1). Probably the actual border shifted from time to time.

[3] For instance, 1 Kings 12:21–23; 2 Chronicles 11:1, 3, 10, 12, 23; 14:8; 15:2, 8, 9; et al.

A question arises regarding the tribe of Simeon, to whom Joshua had allotted eighteen cities within the territory given to Judah (Josh. 19:1–9; 1 Chron. 4:28–33). Why were her people not included in the southern nation? The answer is best found in an apparent movement of many (perhaps most) Simeonites, sometime prior to the division of the kingdom, north to the region of Ephraim and Manasseh, perhaps more specifically northern Manasseh. In both 2 Chronicles 15:9 and 34:6 Simeon is mentioned along with Ephraim and Manasseh in a way suggesting that all three tribes were then (time of Asa and following) geographically linked together.[4]

1. Rehoboam
(931–913; 1 Kings 14:21–31; 2 Chronicles 10–12)

Rehoboam became king at the age of forty-one and ruled for seventeen years. He did evil in the sight of God, not following the pattern of his grandfather, David. He was influenced too much by the religious failures of Solomon's latter days. Rehoboam built high places (*bamoth*), images (*masseboth*), and Asherim poles (*'asherim*), and also permitted male prostitutes (*qadesh*) in the land (1 Kings 14:23–24).

These infractions represent a return to the Canaanite religion, which David had largely put out of the country. That Rehoboam was now restoring it came probably as a result of pressure from continuing adherents, who had remained silent until the reign of this more sympathetic king. Because of the existence of Canaanite worship during the Judges Period, God had withheld His blessing then, and Rehoboam should have recognized that He would do so again.

a. Success against Jeroboam (1 Kings 14:30; 2 Chron. 11:5–13).
Rehoboam had military encounters with two main enemies, Jeroboam of Israel and Shishak of Egypt. With the first he was generally successful, but with the second he suffered tragic loss as God's punishment for the religious defection.

The Bible states that Rehoboam had continual conflict with Jeroboam (1 Kings 14:30). There is no indication that this was in violent, open warfare, however; in fact, violent conflict had been directly forbidden by God (2 Chron. 11:1–4). The strife likely centered in repeated border disputes, especially involving the Benjamite area. Rehoboam felt that he needed Benjamin as a buffer zone, and Jeroboam naturally would have wanted it, too. In that Benjamin does come to be listed with Judah, it follows that Rehoboam won in these disputes more often than Jeroboam. The victories would have involved military clashes at the border and persuasion in winning the allegiance of the Benjamites. Rehoboam needed both the land and good will of the people.

In keeping with Rehoboam's success in Benjamin are his endeavors in building the defenses of his nation. He demonstrated an aggressive spirit in

---

[4] Second Chronicles 34:6 suggests the location as being more specifically northern Manasseh, in that Naphtali, still farther north, is associated with Simeon. Rationale for Simeon's move lies in Simeon's humbled situation in being assigned only cities when all other tribes had been assigned territories. This humbled status was no doubt related to Jacob's prediction that Simeon would be scattered in Israel (Gen. 49:5–7) and Simeon's small number upon entering Canaan (only 22,000, the smallest tribe). See Leon J. Wood, "Simeon, the Tenth Tribe of Israel," *Theolog* 4 (Fall 1966): 6–10.

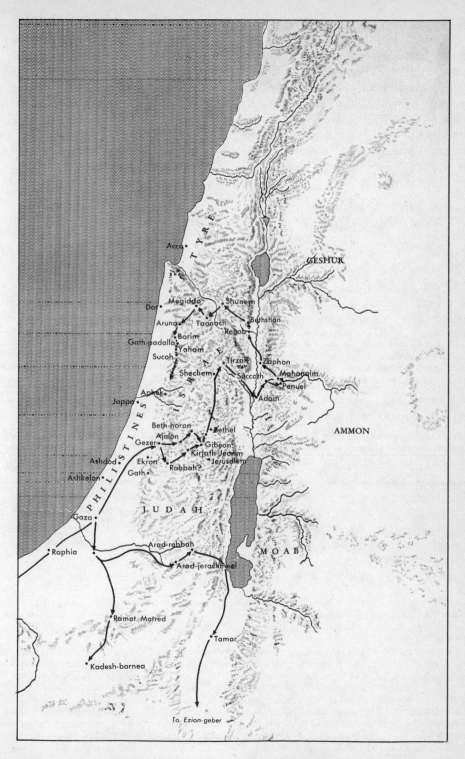

Map 14. The Campaign of Shishak

fortifying no less than fifteen cities (2 Chron. 11:5–10), located in both Judah and Benjamin.[5] Since they are all either to the south or west from Jerusalem, it appears that they were mainly in defense against Egypt and Philistia, rather than Israel to the north. If so, this fortification likely was undertaken following the invasion of Shishak from Egypt in Rehoboam's fifth year.

b. Defeat by Shishak of Egypt (1 Kings 14:25–27; II Chron. 12:2–12).

The Egyptian king, Shishak (Sheshonq I, c. 945–924), was a native of Libya and founder of Egypt's Twenty-Second Dynasty. He had earlier given asylum to Jeroboam in his flight from Solomon (1 Kings 11:40). Now in Rehoboam's fifth year he made a strong attempt to reassert Egyptian supremacy in Palestine. Shishak lists no less than 150 cities that he overran in this campaign.[6] Many are located in southern Judah and still farther south in Edom. Though unlisted by Shishak, Debir, and possibly Beth-shemesh, which give evidence of having been destroyed about this time, may have felt his might.

No cities of central Judah, however, are mentioned by the conqueror, which is strange, in that the biblical record speaks of Shishak taking vast treasures from Jerusalem itself (1 Kings 14:26;

2 Chron. 12:9). It may be that Rehoboam simply gave this treasure as tribute to Shishak to keep him from destroying Judah proper. This would be in keeping with a promise given by God through the prophet Shemaiah to the Judean king. The prophet had come to the king, warning him that, due to Rehoboam's sin, God would use Shishak as His instrument of discipline. Rehoboam repented, so God promised to give "them deliverance" (2 Chron. 12:6–7). For all central Judah to have been spared serious damage would have constituted a meaningful form of this "deliverance."

In the north, Israel too felt Shishak's power, as noted in the previous chapter. Numerous cities listed by Shishak are from Israel. A fragment of a victory monument bearing Shishak's name has been found in the ruins of Solomon's Megiddo, giving testimony of the extent of his conquests. The Egyptian army even crossed the Jordan into Gilead, and numerous cities from there are listed. All this means that Shishak covered a wide area in the campaign and was remarkably successful. His country at home, however, apparently was too weak for him to maintain a permanent hold. His design of establishing Egyptian authority in Palestine was not realized.[7]

As mentioned above, it was probably

---

[5] The two most northern were Zorah and Ajalon, originally allotted to Dan (Josh. 19:41–42). Since 2 Chronicles 11:10 indicates that the fifteen cities were from Benjamin as well as Judah, it must be that these two cities (the nearest to Benjamite territory) had been absorbed by Benjamin after the Danite migration (Judg. 18).

[6] Carved on the exterior of the south wall of the Amon temple at Karnak. Shishak is pictured smiting the Asiatics as the god Amon presents to him ten lines of captives which symbolize the cities listed. See ANEP, fig. 349 for a picture; for translation, discussion, and bibliography of publications, see J. Simons, Handbook for the Study of Egyptian Topographical Lists Relating to Western Asia (Leiden: Brill, 1937), pp. 99–101, 178–86.

[7] Shishak may have maintained a fortification at Sharuhen (modern Tell el-Farah), southeast of Gaza for a time, however. A formidable brick wall, twenty-three feet wide, found there has been ascribed to him, which, if correct, would show an intention to remain at least in this one city, affording a foothold in the land. See Wright, BAR, pp. 149–50.

after this campaign that Rehoboam fortified his fifteen cities, for Shishak does not seem to have been hindered by them at the time. The effort could well have been made later to forestall a repetition of what had been experienced.

2. Abijam
(913–911; 1 Kings 15:1–8; 2 Chronicles 13:1–22)

The son and successor of Rehoboam was Abijam,[8] who ruled for three years. He continued in the sin of his father. He also continued his father's struggle with Jeroboam, and with still greater success. At one time a major battle broke out between the two sides (2 Chron. 13:3–19) in the area of Ephraim near Mount Zemaraim (likely east of Bethel). Abijam, though having a smaller force, was victorious and gained control even over Bethel, the important southern religious center of Israel. In addition, he took less important Jeshanah and Ephron nearby. This advance did not last long, however, for Asa, his son[9] and successor, was hard pressed again by Baasha, who even moved for a time as far south as Ramah, just four miles from Jerusalem, with an occupying force.

3. Asa
(911–870; 1 Kings 15:9–24; 2 Chronicles 14–16).

Asa ruled forty-one years and was the first of the religiously good kings of the southern kingdom. Eight of Judah's total nineteen kings are said to have been good in God's sight, which is in marked contrast to none out of Israel's nineteen, all of whom are described as evil. This does not mean that all eight in Judah's history pleased God to the same degree, but only that each intended to conduct himself and the kingdom according to the Mosaic Law and carried out this desire to a meaningful extent.

a. Religious activities (1 Kings 15:11–15; 2 Chron. 14:2–5; 15:8–18). Several good acts of Asa are mentioned. For example, he put male prostitutes (*qedeshim*) and idols (*gillulim*) out of the land. Also, he removed his (grand)mother from being queen mother because she had made an idol to the goddess Asherah. In his fifteenth year, following a victory over an Egyptian army (noted below) and encouragement by the prophet Azariah (2 Chron. 15:1–7), he called for an assembly of people from Judah and Benjamin, also including Israelites from the tribes of Ephraim, Manasseh, and Simeon, to renew their covenantal promises with God. Sacrifices were offered of the seven hundred oxen and seven thousand sheep taken as spoil in the recent conflict. He also added some newly dedicated furnishings to the temple and in some way renewed the altar of God. One thing that he did not

---

[8] Called Abijah in 2 Chronicles 13:1–2. *Abijam* means "father of the sea," and Abijah, "father is Yahweh." Apparently he was called by both names.

[9] Because Abijam and Asa are said to have had mothers and grandmothers of the same name (1 Kings 15:2, 10; 2 Chron. 15:16), some scholars believe they were brothers and not father and son, as indicated in 1 Kings 15:8 and 2 Chron. 14:1; see Abijam's short reign of only three years. But Abijam was old enough to have sons (indeed, according to 2 Chron. 13:21 he had twenty-two sons and sixteen daughters from fourteen wives). It is likely that the mother, Maacah, and grandmother, Abishalom, were really grandmother and great-grandmother to Asa. Because of Abijam's short reign, Maacah had carried over as queen mother and was the one deposed by Asa for worshiping a false idol (1 Kings 15:13; 2 Chron. 15:16). See Albright, *ARI,* p. 158.

do, however, was to remove the old Canaanite high places.

In the latter days of his life, sad to say, Asa did not do as well in God's sight. He seems to have become proud and self-reliant. This is evidenced by his imprisonment of Hanani, a prophet, for a rebuke Asa deserved. It may also be indicated by his trust in physicians rather than God when he became diseased in his feet (2 Chron. 16:12). The physicians he consulted almost certainly practiced a combination of very primitive medicine and magic, in which case the criticism implied in the text (v. 14) would have been directed at the magical elements of their craft.

b. Victory over Egypt (2 Chron. 14:9-15).

Asa experienced two instances of major foreign conflict. The first was with Egypt and it ended in a splendid victory. The Egyptian force was led by one Zerah from Ethiopia, likely a military leader under Osarkon I (c. 914-874),[10] king of Egypt. He may already have been serving as commander at an Egyptian outpost, possibly left at Sharuhen by Shishak. Approximately thirty years had elapsed since Shishak's attack, assuming that Zerah's campaign came in Asa's fifteenth year, which is likely.[11] Zerah's

attack was launched in the general region of Sharuhen, involving specifically Mareshah[12] and Gerar. Asa looked to God for assistance and received it, enabling him to defeat the larger force and take much spoil for Israel.

c. Self-reliance in respect to Israel (1 Kings 15:16-22; 2 Chron. 16:10).

Perhaps this success in Egypt was in part what caused Asa to become sinfully self-reliant and to turn from the commendable trust in God that he had been displaying. At least it was the very next year, Asa's sixteenth,[13] when the second foreign conflict ensued, that he showed this change of spirit.[14]

The new struggle was with Baasha, king of Israel; and its nature was more economic than military. Baasha had penetrated the northern border of Judah for the purpose of fortifying Ramah, only four miles north of Jerusalem, that he might establish control over north-south Jerusalem traffic.

In retaliation, Asa, rather than seeking guidance from God, relied on his own judgment and sent for help from Benhadad I of Damascus. Benhadad, just rising to a position of power, was happy to comply and test his strength against Israel. He attacked certain

---

[10] Some have identified Zerah with O(serak)hon, but the identification is not likely: due to a basic change in spelling for the two; Zerah not being called a Pharaoh; and Osarkon being of Libyan descent and not Ethiopian, as indicated for Zerah. See G. Ricciotti, *The History of Israel*, 2 vols., 2d ed. (Milwaukee: Bruce, 1958), 1:359.

[11] So argues Thiele, *MNHK*, pp. 57-62. His argument hinges on his belief that the chronological notation of "the thirty-sixth year," in 2 Chronicles 16:1, is in reference to the duration at that time of Judah's history rather than to Asa's sole reign. He has convincing arguments as against Albright, "The Chronology of the Divided Monarchy," *BASOR* 100 (December 1945): 16-22.

[12] Mareshah has been identified with Tell Sandahannah, near Keilah and Achzib (Josh. 15:44; Mic. 1:14-15). Less than two miles north is modern Beit Guvrin.

[13] On the basis of Thiele's chronology (*MNHK*, pp. 59-60).

[14] It should be realized that between the two conflicts, however, Asa's fine assembly for the renewal of the covenant with God was called in Jerusalem. In fact, the seven hundred oxen and seven thousand sheep then offered were largely from the spoil taken, and no doubt the whole occasion was prompted by a spirit of thanksgiving for God's favor then shown. For all this good result, however, Asa could still have subconsciously been affected with a proud spirit, as a consequence of the success.

northern cities of Baasha, and the Israelite king was forced to withdraw from Ramah and protect his own interests. Asa in turn appropriated supplies which Baasha had collected at Ramah and used them to strengthen defenses at Geba and Mizpah.[15]

Thinking himself wise in this maneuver, Asa was quite taken aback and then angered when Hanani, the prophet, did not praise him but brought stern rebuke for trusting in himself rather than God. The prophet told him that what he had really accomplished was to bring Judah under obligation to a foreign power and to set the stage for further conflict, rather than to achieve true benefit as Asa had thought. Hanani implied that had Asa trusted in God, he would have gained a genuine victory over Baasha, even as he had over Zerah of Egypt the prior year (2 Chron. 16:8–9), and he would not have involved his country in these detrimental relationships.

B. A PERIOD OF ALLIANCE WITH ISRAEL
(873–835; 1 Kings 22:41–50; 2 Kings 8:16–29; 11:1–16; 2 Chronicles 17:1–23:15)

The next period is marked by good relations with Israel to the north. The fighting which had characterized the prior period ceased. This was the day of the house of Omri in Israel, and peace reigned between the two countries. As noted in the previous chapter, even a treaty—though working religious ill for Judah—was likely signed between them. Athaliah, the last to rule over Judah in this time, was actually the daughter of Ahab, son of Omri.

1. Jehoshaphat
(873–848; 1 Kings 22:41–50; 2 Chronicles 17–20)

Asa's son and successor was Jehoshaphat, who ruled for thirty-five years beginning at the age of twenty-five. Three of these years were as coregent with his father.[16] Asa developed a serious disease in his feet and may have become sufficiently incapacitated to require his son to act for him. He proclaimed him actual king along with himself. This was the first instance of coregency in either Judah or Israel, following the brief co-rule of Solomon with David. Israel's employment of the idea came more than a century later.[17]

a. Commendable religious activity (1 Kings 22:43, 46; 2 Chron. 17:3–9; 20:3–33). Religiously, Jehoshaphat was the second good king of Judah. He followed in his father's footsteps by further ridding the land of Baal's cultic features, even removing the high places (*bamoth*) now to some degree.[18] Further, he gave special orders to Levites and others to teach the "Book of the Law" throughout all Judah. A prime task of the priests and Levites from the beginning had been this teaching,[19] but apparently they had been lax in

---

[15] Asa likely reestablished the boundary near Benjamin's northern limits. Geba, which he fortified, is mentioned in Josiah's reign later as then having been near the northern border (2 Kings 23:8). For location, see p. 204n.24; for Mizpah, p. 188n.82.

[16] See Thiele, *MNHK*, pp. 64–66 for evidence.

[17] At the close of Jehoash's reign; see p. 276.

[18] Both 1 Kings 22:43 and 2 Chronicles 20:33 state that the high places were not removed, while 2 Chronicles 17:6 says that they were. The situation likely was that the better-known high places were, while those in which many of the common people worshiped (1 Kings 22:43) were not.

[19] See p. 161.

recent years. Jehoshaphat correctly recognized that if the people were to obey God's Law, they needed first to be instructed in it.

An illustration of Jehoshaphat's commendable faith in God is seen in connection with an attack made against him by a coalition of Moab, Ammon, and Edom (2 Chron. 20:1–30). Learning of the invasion, Jehoshaphat did not despair but called for a time of fasting and prayer in Jerusalem. God responded to the prayer, voiced by the king himself through an attendant prophet, and promised victory. When Jehoshaphat's troops, led by singing Levites, came to where the enemy was located, they found that interarmy rivalry had led to armed conflict between them. The only task of the Judean force was to collect the booty of the dead opponents.

b. Strong rule (2 Chron. 17:10–19).

It should not be thought, in view of this instance, that Jehoshaphat was a weak ruler with a weak army. He had, in fact, a strong army consisting of five divisions, three from Judah and two from Benjamin. Perhaps he was caught off guard somewhat by the suddenness of the above attack. Jehoshaphat also gave attention to strengthening the defenses of his country, building both fortresses and store cities. His might became known abroad, and other countries feared to make war against him, perhaps accounting for the tripartite nature of the invading enemy referred to above. Both the Philistines and Arabians sought to maintain his good will by bringing valuable presents.

c. Judicial provisions (2 Chron. 19:4–11).

Jehoshaphat took steps to improve juridical procedures in the land. In view of the nature of the changes he made, it appears that the Mosaic Law was not being followed in civil matters. Jehoshaphat now called for the divinely ordained regulations to be reinstated. He appointed judges in important cities, thus making more local courts (legally prescribed: Deut. 16:18; 19:12; 21:18–19; 22:13–14), and he urged that those appointed be fair in all decisions. He also appointed certain priests, Levites, and recognized leaders to serve in a central court in Jerusalem (prescribed Deut. 17:8–13). When the matter to be considered at this court involved religion, Amariah, the high priest, was to act as chairman; when it involved a civic question, Zebadiah, a civic leader, was to officiate. In these provisions, Jehoshaphat displayed a true heart towards God and towards the people, as well as commendable ability in statesmanship.

d. Alliance with Israel (1 Kings 22:44, 48, 49; 2 Kings 3:4–27; 2 Chron. 18:1–19:3; 20:35–37).

Jehoshaphat's alliance with the house of Omri has already been noted.[20] That he made it demonstrated further the statesmanlike qualities he possessed; and, in terms of economic and military values, it may have made some contribution to his country. In terms of God's all-important approval, however, great loss was suffered. For one thing, it involved the tragic marriage of his son Jehoram to Ahab's daughter Athaliah, who followed in the ways of her mother, Jezebel.[21] Jehoshaphat had

---

[20] See p. 265.

[21] She is not specifically stated to have been Jezebel's daughter (2 Kings 8:16–24), but this is extremely likely.

abundant reason to regret this marriage many times in years to come.

Other problems arose from this alliance. These resulted from the three specific times that Jehoshaphat aided Israelite kings, in keeping with the pact, as noted briefly in the previous chapter. He helped Ahab in his battle with Benhadad at Ramoth-Gilead and was nearly killed for his trouble (1 Kings 22:29–33; 2 Chron. 18:29–34). He joined Ahab's eldest son, Ahaziah, in shipbuilding at Ezion-geber on the Gulf of Aqaba, and every vessel was destroyed before its maiden voyage (1 Kings 22:48–49; 2 Chron. 20:35–37). Finally, when he allied himself with Ahab's second son, Jehoram, in a military offensive against Moab to coerce tribute-paying to Israel, he nearly perished, along with the attendant armies, for lack of water (2 Kings 3:4–27).

Prophets of God were involved each time: (1) Micaiah in warning that the Ramoth-Gilead battle would be lost, a fact that should have stirred Jehoshaphat to withdraw immediately,[22] (2) Eliezer, less known, in warning that Jehoshaphat's ships would be broken due to God's displeasure at the alliance, and (3) Elisha, in revealing God's way of deliverance for the allied kings in their dire need for water. Jehoshaphat should have learned a lesson the first time, but he did not.

2. Jehoram
(853–841; 2 Kings 8:16–24; 2 Chronicles 21)

Jehoshaphat, following the pattern of his father, appointed his son Jehoram as coregent for the last four years of his reign.[23] Since the time of the appointment coincides with the year of Jehoshaphat's assistance to Ahab at Ramoth-Gilead, Jehoshaphat's incentive in this may have been to have a son ruling at home while he was away for what might turn out to be a prolonged war. During these years of coregency, Jehoram should have learned from his godly father; and perhaps he did in secular matters, but it is certainly not evident in religious matters. Jehoshaphat had been one of Judah's best kings in God's sight, but now Jehoram is characterized as one who did evil. A contributing reason was doubtless his marriage to the wicked Athaliah (2 Kings 8:18). He ruled alone for eight years after his father's death (2 Chron. 21:5), and five unhappy events marked the time.

The first was his slaughter of his own six brothers, all of whom their father Jehoshaphat had previously given gifts of gold, valuable articles, and fortified cities (2 Chron. 21:2–4). Jehoram's purpose must have been to insure his own rule against rivals, a procedure that was common throughout the ancient world but was almost without precedent in Judah. Jehoram and his wife, Athaliah—who, after the deaths of her husband and then her son, seized the throne and massacred her own grandchildren (2 Chron. 22:10–12)— are the primary examples of dynastic murder in the history of the southern kingdom.

The second and third unhappy events concerned two successful instances of revolt against his rule. One was by the country of Edom (2 Kings

---

[22] Also, following this near miss with death, Jehoshaphat was directly rebuked for the alliance by another prophet, Jehu, son of Hanani (2 Chron. 19:1–3).

[23] See 2 Kings 1:17 and 3:1. For argumentation, see Thiele, *MNHK,* pp. 64–68.

8:20–22; 2 Chron. 21:8–9), who earlier had helped Jehoram and Jehoshaphat against Moab (2 Kings 3:4–27). The submission of Edom to Judah likely dated from Jehoshaphat's still earlier triumph over a coalition that had included Edom (2 Chron. 20:1–29).[24] It may also have been at that time that an Edomite deputy was installed as ruler in place of a king (1 Kings 22:47). Jehoram fought to put down the revolt at this time but was not successful. The other revolt was by a city, Libnah (2 Kings 8:22).[25] Apparently this one, too, was successful, for no indication is given that Jehoram even made an attempt to retaliate.

The fourth was an invasion of his country by Philistines and Arabians,[26] in which Judah suffered substantial loss. Material goods were seized, and all of Jehoram's own wives and sons (with the exception of Ahaziah, the youngest) were captured (2 Chron. 21:16–17).[27] Little could be more tragic and humiliating for a king than this.

The fifth was the gruesome death of Jehoram himself. He died of a fearful disease of the intestines, in accordance with a warning given by Elijah[28]

(2 Chron. 21:12–15, 18–20). In all, one must say that Jehoram's reign was disastrous politically, militarily, and religiously.

3. Ahaziah
(841 B.C.; 2 Kings 8:25–29; 9:27–29; 2 Chronicles 22:1–9)

Ahaziah succeeded his father Jehoram and ruled less than one year. He was the youngest son of the family,[29] and he alone had survived the raid by the Philistines and Arabians. Unfortunately, Ahaziah was strongly influenced by his mother, Athaliah, who "encouraged him in doing wrong" (2 Chron. 22:3).

Though Ahaziah had escaped the hands of the Philistines and Arabians, he was not able to escape Jehu. As observed in the previous chapter, he traveled north to visit his wounded uncle, Jehoram; and Jehu killed both in his destruction of the house of Omri. Ahaziah had earlier helped his uncle in a battle against the Arameans, when Jehoram had received his wound. Ahaziah did escape the initial blow of Jehu at Jezreel but was later caught and killed by Jehu's men, dying finally at Megiddo.[30] His servants brought his body back to Jerusalem for burial.

---

[24] The control in Edom gained by David had been lost by the time of Rehoboam's reign. The new conquest by Jehoshaphat was of prime importance because it reopened the vital trade route to the South.

[25] Libnah is sometimes identified with Tell es-Safi, four miles west of Azekah at the head of the Elah Valley, but probably better with Tell Bornat, six miles south; see Albright, *BASOR* 15 (December 1924): 19.

[26] Philistines and Arabians were the ones who had earlier feared and even paid tribute to Jehoshaphat (2 Chron. 17:11).

[27] This son is called Jehoahaz in 2 Chronicles 21:17 (see 22:1). Jehoahaz and Ahaziah are basically the same names, with the compound elements "Ahaz" and "Jah" simply transposed.

[28] Elijah probably died about 850 B.C., shortly after the accession of Jehoram in Israel in 852 B.C. Jehoram of Judah began his reign as coregent in 853, which means this letter came early in his reign, likely while Jehoshaphat still lived.

[29] His age of twenty-two, given in 2 Kings 8:26, is correct and not forty-two as given in 2 Chronicles 22:2. His father, Jehoram, was only forty when he died (2 Kings 8:17). A copyist's error, confusing the letter *kaph* (twenty) with the *mem* (forty), may be responsible.

[30] See p. 272n.56.

4. Athaliah (841–835;
2 Kings 11:1–16;
2 Chronicles 22:10–23:15)

a. Cruel, wicked rule (2 Kings 11:1–3; 2 Chron. 22:10–12). Athaliah, mother of Ahaziah, was a true daughter of her mother, Jezebel. She pursued the same goals and displayed the same hard, vindictive character.[31] The two women stand quite alone in biblical history for their forwardness and cruelty. Athaliah had already demonstrated the kind of person she was prior to Ahaziah's death. She may have influenced her husband to kill rival brothers. She sought to install the cult of Baal in Judah as her mother had in Israel (2 Kings 8:18, 27; 11:18), though fortunately with less success.

With her son dead, however, she perpetrated a still worse crime. She had Ahaziah's children (her own grandchildren) slaughtered so that she might herself seize the throne. Human decency, apart from a normal grandmother's love, called for her to go into mourning and seek to comfort and care for her son's offspring, but this was not Athaliah's way. All the children died with the exception of a baby, Joash, who was rescued by an aunt, a sister of Ahaziah, named Jehoshabeath. Because Ahaziah's brothers had already been killed in the Philistine–Arabian attack, the power-hungry woman did not have to take their lives. It may be, indeed, that their earlier deaths were what prompted Athaliah first to think of trying for the throne. With all sons now dead and the grandchildren really too young[32] to give any challenge, the way apparently seemed open to the place of power she wanted.

After this initial, ignominious deed, Athaliah ruled for six years. Seemingly none wished to withstand her, either in the first seizure of power or during the following years, for no report is given of any challenge. We are not told either of any of her activities during these six years, but we may be sure that she did all she could to foster Baalism. The fact that Jehu had dealt a serious blow to the cult in Israel by his well-known blood purge probably motivated her to do even more in Judah to perpetuate it, but it may also have contributed to greater opposition against her.

b. Crowning of Joash (2 Kings 11:4–16; 2 Chron. 23:1–15). The baby Joash, rescued by Ahaziah's sister, reached the age of seven during Athaliah's sixth year of rule. This was old enough for Jehoiada, high priest and husband of Jehoshabeath, who had waited and planned for Athaliah's overthrow, to take action in placing the young boy on the throne in her place. Military and religious leaders were brought into the plan, which was made easier by widespread discontent with her rule. All went well as the seven-year-old was brought forth from his hiding place and crowned. A large number of assembled people clapped their hands and shouted, "Long live the king." Athaliah heard the shout, came to see the cause, and cried in despair, "Treason, treason." Jehoiada ordered

---

[31] This was true of Athaliah in spite of almost unparalleled catastrophe that she had experienced: the body of her mother had just been eaten by dogs; her brother, Jehoram of Israel, had been killed at the same time by Jehu in the blood purge of Omri's house; her husband, Jehoram, had recently died of a fearful disease of the bowels; her son Ahaziah had just been killed by Jehu's pursuing men; and her other sons had shortly before been captured by raiding Philistines and Arabians.

[32] Ahaziah himself was only twenty-three at his death (2 Kings 8:26).

her execution, and this was promptly carried out.

C. FOUR GOD-APPROVED KINGS
(835–731; 2 Kings 12–15; 2 Chronicles 23:16–27:9)

Four successive kings, called good in the sight of God, now ruled. These four, plus Asa, Jehoshaphat, Hezekiah, and Josiah, make a total of eight good kings of Judah. None of the present four receive so high a commendation as either Hezekiah, Josiah, or Jehoshaphat; but still, together, they gave Judah her longest span of God-approved rule, a period of over one hundred years.

1. Joash
(835–796; 2 Kings 12; 2 Chronicles 23:16–24:27)

Joash, who ruled forty years, led the way. The young king needed an advisor; and the aged, pious high priest, Jehoiada, who had already protected and anointed him, served in this capacity. To Jehoiada must go most of the credit for the fine record of Joash's early years.

a. Religious reformation (2 Kings 12:2–16; 2 Chron. 23:16–24:14). After Athaliah's advocacy of the Baal cult, religious reform was needed in Judah. Joash, through Jehoiada, set about the task. Religious articles imported by Athaliah were destroyed, including the Baal-Melqart temple, its altars, and its images. The Baal priest, Mattan, was killed, and the personnel and offerings prescribed in the Mosaic Law were

reinstituted. True worship of Yahweh was again observed, though some of the high places still continued to be used.

Many years later, when Joash had come to an age to act for himself, he gave orders for the temple to be repaired of damage done to it by Athaliah's sons (2 Chron. 24:7). The priests and Levites were slow, however, in collecting funds for the purpose, which prompted Joash, in this twenty-third year, to suggest a new method of raising the necessary money. A box was placed at the side of the altar for people to give when they came with their sacrifices. They did so enthusiastically. Workers were hired and the required repairs made, with money enough left over to provide new furnishings. A high spirit of true worship prevailed in the land.

b. Declension and punishment (2 Kings 12:17–21; 2 Chron. 24:15–27). So long as Jehoiada continued as high priest, Joash ruled as a God-fearing king; but when Jehoida died, the king changed. This development came sometime after Joash's twenty-third year, for it was then that he gave the order relative to offerings for temple repair just noted, but how long after is not indicated. Jehoiada died at the age of 130 (2 Chron. 24:15),[33] which was sometime in the latter part of Joash's reign. Following the great man's demise, the king began to listen to new advisors who were more sympathetic to the deposed cult of Baal-Melqart (2 Chron. 24:17–18). In fact, he was so influenced that he

---

[33]This was much above the average for the day. Jehoiada had been born while Solomon yet reigned, and so likely served as high priest for some of Asa's rule and all of Jehoshaphat's. He probably had been responsible in part for their good records. He would have been about one hundred years old when he anointed Joash. His wife, Jehoshabeath, granddaughter of Jehoshaphat, was obviously much younger.

had Jehoiada's own son, Zechariah, stoned to death for rebuking him for sinful actions (2 Chron. 24:20–22).

The close of the year in which Zechariah was stoned saw great loss for Joash at the hands of Hazael, king of Damascus.[34] Having brought a crushing defeat on Israel, Hazael marched south as far as Gath in Philistia and seized it. Then he turned toward Jerusalem. He brought destruction through Judah generally and took many lives, including those of a number of princes (2 Chron. 24:23–24). Only by giving Hazael large tribute[35] did Joash succeed in persuading him to not completely destroy Jerusalem (2 Kings 12:17–18).

As a further punishment, Joash was assassinated by conspirators (2 Kings 12:19–21; 2 Chron. 24:25–27). Even his own servants took part, prompted by their disapproval of his reversal in policy after Jehoiada's death. To die in this manner was a bitter close to Joash's life, especially when for years his reign had been a cause for rejoicing in Judah.

2. Amaziah
(796–767; 2 Kings 14:1–20; 2 Chronicles 25)

Amaziah succeeded his father—the assassination not bringing an end to the dynastic line—and he ruled twenty-nine years, though the last twenty-four were in coregency with his son, Uzziah. Amaziah stood approved of God in life and reign as his father, but also like him, he did not remove all the high places. One of Amaziah's first actions was to punish his father's assassins by having them all killed (2 Kings 14:1–6).

a. Victory over Edom (2 Kings 14:7; 2 Chron. 25:5–16). Two major battles were fought by Amaziah, the first of which was with Edom and ended in complete victory. Edom, lost as a result of revolt against Jehoram, continued to be attractive to Judah because of the southern trade routes to which it gave access.

Amaziah made ambitious plans to regain control there, even hiring soldiers from Israel for one hundred talents of silver to support his own troops. He was rebuked by a "man of God" for securing them, however, and so sent them back home, much to their displeasure.[36] He later found he did not need them anyway, for he was able to achieve victory alone. He killed ten thousand of the enemy and took another ten thousand captive, only to slay them by casting them from the top of a high rock. Following the victory, however, he greatly displeased God by bringing images of Edom's false gods back to Judah and worshiping them. A prophet bringing rebuke pointedly asked, "Why do you consult this people's gods, which could not save their own people from your hand?"

b. Defeat by Israel (2 Kings 14:8–14; 2 Chron. 25:17–24). The second battle was with Israel. Amaziah, made proud and self-confident by his Edomite victory, challenged Jehoash of

---

[34] See pp. 273–74.
[35] Described as all the "sacred objects" of his fathers and of himself, plus all the gold deposited in the temple treasury and that of the palace.
[36] This displeasure was demonstrated in their attack, whether in taking an indirect route home or sometime later, on cities of northwest Judah in the area of Bethhoron. They killed three thousand people and took much spoil at the time (2 Chron. 25:13).

Israel. Israel recently had suffered extensive harm at the hands of Hazael of Damascus, but by now she was experiencing a resurgence, which Amaziah apparently did not realize.

Jehoash, commendably, tried to dissuade the Judean ruler;[37] but Amaziah insisted and war did ensue near Beth-shemesh, west of Jerusalem. Judah was defeated, and Jehoash then proceeded to Jerusalem, destroying some six hundred feet of city wall, a sign of total subjugation, and seizing substantial booty and many captives. It is likely that among these captives was even Amaziah himself (2 Kings 14:13), which, if so, was a humiliation of the gravest kind. The chronicler states that all this came in punishment for Amaziah having "sought the gods of Edom" (2 Chron. 25:20). If Amaziah was taken captive (which, significantly, fits with the beginning of his son's coregency), he likely was kept in Israel as long as Jehoash of Israel lived (2 Kings 14:17) and was then allowed to return to resume the rule of Judah.[38]

c. Death (2 Kings 14:18–20; 2 Chron. 25:26–28). No information is given regarding Amaziah's rule after he returned except the unhappy note that he, too, as his father, saw a conspiracy formed against him. He tried to escape death by flight to Lachish, but was followed and killed there. His body was returned to Jerusalem for burial.

3. Uzziah
(Azariah; 791–739; 2 Kings 14:21–22; 15:1–7; 2 Chronicles 26)

Amaziah's son and successor is called by two names, Uzziah and Azariah, names closely associated in meaning and perhaps used interchangeably.[39] Uzziah was one of Judah's most capable rulers. For the most part he followed the positive life-patterns of his two predecessors; and God, in approval, used his native ability to restore a high status for Judah in the world. This improvement in Judah's position came at approximately the same time as Israel's enlargement under the able Jeroboam II. Between the two men, the total land-area finally controlled came to rival even that of the days of David and Solomon.[40]

a. Coregencies. Uzziah ruled longer than any prior king of either Judah or Israel—fifty-two years (2 Kings 15:2; 2 Chron. 26:3). The first twenty-four were in coregency with his father, and the last twelve were similarly served with his son Jotham, leaving only sixteen years of solitary rule.[41] Uzziah would have been sixteen years of age

---

[37] Jehoash showed better sense than Amaziah, though in attempting dissuasion he used an allegory which belittled the Judean king and may have served to incense him rather than to change his mind.

[38] Thiele, *MNHK,* pp. 83–87, argues to this conclusion: (1) in that 2 Kings 14:13 seems to mean that Amaziah was taken captive; (2) that 2 Kings 14:17 unexpectedly says that Amaziah lived for fifteen years after Jehoash died, a rationale for which could well be that Amaziah was released after Jehoash's death and then returned to reign in Judah for these fifteen years; and (3) that Uzziah's becoming coregent at this time thus finds good explanation.

[39] The name *Uzziah,* is found quite often (2 Kings 15:13, 30, 32, 34; 2 Chron. 26:1, 3, 11, et al.; Isa. 1:1; 6:1; Hos. 1:1; Amos 1:1; Zech. 14:5). Azariah is used less frequently (2 Kings 14:21; 15:1, 6, 8, 17, 23, 27; 1 Chron. 3:12). Azariah (*'azaryah*) means "Yahweh has helped"; Uzziah (*'uzziyah*), "Yahweh is my strength."

[40] See p. 276.

[41] See Thiele, *MNHK,* pp. 81–83, for arguments as to a coregency with Amaziah, and see pp. 120–23 for argument as to the same with Jotham.

(2 Kings 15:2) at the time of his father's likely captivity by Jehoash of Israel. He would have ruled as supreme head the nine years[42] his father was captive, then in a secondary capacity in the period when his father resumed his reign.

The occasion for his son Jotham's coregency, spanning Uzziah's last twelve years is almost certainly Uzziah's becoming a leper at the beginning of that period. The disease was inflicted as punishment from God for intruding into the priest's office (2 Chron. 26:16–21). Uzziah attempted personally to offer incense in the temple, though warned against doing so by eighty-one priests. The chronicler states that from the time of this affliction the king had to live in a separate house and that Jotham was then "over the king's house, judging the people" (2 Chron. 26:21; 2 Kings 15:5 KJV).

b. Expansion of territory (2 Chron. 26:6–16).

Uzziah assumed sole rule of Judah some fifteen years after Jeroboam II became supreme head of Israel. Equally talented, he was able to follow the example set by Jeroboam in land acquisition and even, after the demise of Jeroboam, to attain a role yet more influential in the world.

Toward the south, Uzziah maintained the control his father, Amaziah, had gained over Edom and in addition built port facilities at Elath on the Gulf of Aqaba for the purpose of trade (2 Kings 14:22; 2 Chron. 26:2). Toward the east, he accepted gifts from the Ammonites, indicating a domination imposed on them. Toward the west, he warred successfully with the Philistines, seizing several cities, including Gath, taken earlier by Hazael from Amaziah at the time of his captivity. Uzziah also made his own country stronger through additional fortification, particularly at Jerusalem. He installed ingenious engines for shooting arrows and catapulting stones from the walls. He seems also to have reorganized the army, thus likely increasing its effectiveness.

In summary, besides strengthening home base, Uzziah established or maintained effective control east of the Dead Sea, south to the important Gulf of Aqaba, and southwest to the river of Egypt. This, with the extensive holdings of Jeroboam II to the east and north, made the total territory now by far the largest of any time following the kingdom's division and, in truth, approximately that of the united monarchy period.

c. Zenith of influence.

It was following the death of Jeroboam II, however, that Uzziah reached his zenith. By 743 B.C., the year of the first western campaign of Tiglath-pileser III of Assyria, Uzziah had become the strongest ruler along the Mediterranean coast. Since the defeat of Damascus by Adad-nirari III a half century earlier, Jeroboam II had been the strongest; but following his death, Israel had become seriously weakened by inner turmoil and a rapid succession of kings.[43] Syrian states north of Damascus had long been kept weak by continued Assyrian aggression and could not lead in resisting Tiglath-pileser. Consequently, Uzziah, who had become known because of his success in the south, was now recog-

---

[42] The number nine is determined from chronological correlations showing that Jehoash of Israel ruled until 782 B.C., which is nine years after Uzziah's first accession in 791 B.C.

[43] See pp. 278–82.

nized by these others and given leadership of a coalition to withstand the coming Assyrian conqueror.

Tiglath-pileser himself gives record of this coalition and encounter, indicating definitely that it was led by one "Azriau of Yaudi," which can only mean Azariah (Uzziah) of Judah.[44] Uzziah was no longer young at the time, for this was the forty-eighth year of his rule, when he was sixty-four.[45] It would have been a memorable occasion to find himself thus honored by fellow rulers.

4. Jotham
(750–731; 2 Kings 15:32–38; 2 Chronicles 27)

Jotham succeeded his father, Uzziah, and reigned twenty years,[46] though the first twelve, as noted, were as coregent with his father. If his father was able to lead in the northern coalition just mentioned, it follows that he was not seriously incapacitated by his leprosy during these years; so Jotham may have been installed co-ruler mainly as a "front" man, to meet people and convey orders worked out and given by the capable Uzziah.

Jotham in turn installed his son Ahaz as his coregent. Correlations show that this was done about twelve years before Jotham died,[47] which means surprisingly that coregencies here overlapped. That is, Jotham made his son Ahaz his coregent while he was still coregent with his father, Uzziah. During four years,[48] Judah had Uzziah as chief ruler, Jotham as his coregent, and Ahaz as Jotham's coregent.

The year of Ahaz's accession as Jotham's co-ruler was 743 B.C., the same year that Uzziah went north to lead in the coalition. The most likely explanation for this unusual situation is that Jotham, now left alone in Jerusalem, fearful of the consequences for his father in this battle, and probably thinking that Tiglath-pileser would bring vengeance on Uzziah's own country if he won victory over the coalition, sought strength by making Ahaz co-ruler with him.[49] He may have doubted seriously that his father would return.

Jotham was the fourth successive God-approved king of Judah. Accordingly, he continued to experience blessing in his reign and was able to

---

[44] Some scholars, because of alleged chronological difficulties and the fact that this encounter transpired far north of Judah, have suggested that this Azariah was a king of some northern Syrian state. However, it is extremely coincidental that there could have been two kings of the same name, from states of the same name and at the same time. For discussion, see Thiele, *MNHK*, pp. 93–94; Unger, *Israel and the Aramaeans of Damascus* (London: James Clarke, 1957), pp. 96–98. For text, see *ANET*, p. 282, or *DOTT*, pp. 53–56.

[45] Uzziah would already have been a leper eight years, but evidently not greatly impaired in military skill or leadership ability. Tiglath-pileser claims a victory over the coalition.

[46] Second Kings 15:30 gives him twenty years, and correlations with other kings require it. The sixteen years mentioned in 2 Kings 15:33 and 2 Chronicles 27:1 must concern his rule until terminated at the insistence of Ahaz; with Jotham, however, yet living four more years to make the full twenty. See H. G. Stigers, "The Interphased Chronology of Jotham, Ahaz, Hezekiah, and Hoshea," *BETS* 8 (Spring 1966): 86–88.

[47] For discussion, see Stigers, "Interphased Chronology," pp. 86–88.

[48] Of Jotham's total twenty years, he co-ruled with his father the first twelve and with his son the last twelve, making the middle four the years of overlap.

[49] Since Ahaz presented a pro-Assyrian policy when he became head ruler, it may be that a pro-Assyrian party in Judah was influential in forcing this early coregency. If so, this would have been a second reason for the unusual situation.

maintain his country's strong position. Only one military engagement is mentioned, that with the Ammonites, which battle he won. As a result, Israel received payment of tribute[50] from Ammon for three years. Jotham also carried on extensive construction activity. In Jerusalem he built an important temple gate and added to the "wall of Ophel." Elsewhere he enlarged cities and erected "forts and towers" as means of fortification.

But prosperity often leads to religious neglect, and it did here in Judah. This is evidenced by the words of the prophet Isaiah, who rose to ministry at this time.[51] He speaks much of the sin of a people made proud and selfish through comfort. He warns that punishment would come if changes were not made. Indeed, punishment was already at hand at the time of Jotham's death. Pekah, king of Israel, and Rezin, king of Damascus, were at the gate of Jerusalem, laying siege to force Judah to cooperate in a revolt against Assyria (2 Kings 15:37). Ahaz had this distressing situation to face as he took over as chief ruler.

D. YEARS OF ASSYRIAN DOMINANCE
(743–640; 2 Kings 16–21; 2 Chronicles 28–33)

The might of Assyria now made itself felt in Judah much more directly and seriously than at any previous time. Until this period, Damascus and Israel had served as terminating points for Assyrian campaigns, but now their resistance was waning and soon was to cease entirely. Ominously, Judah was next in line.

1. Ahaz
(743–715; 2 Kings 16; 2 Chronicles 28)

Ahaz ruled for a total of twenty-eight years, though only sixteen[52] were as supreme head (2 Kings 16:2; 2 Chron. 28:1). Twelve years were spent while his father yet lived, and thirteen after his son, Hezekiah, was made coregent with him, leaving only three years of sole rule.

From the beginning of his reign, Ahaz was pro-Assyrian in his policies. There is reason to believe that he was able to assume power over his father while Jotham yet lived.[53] If so, the reason must be that the Jerusalem nobles believed they were better off in submitting to Tiglath-pileser of Assyria than in resisting him, and accordingly supported the sympathetic Ahaz in grasping the throne.

a. The Siege by Pekah and Rezin (2 Kings 16:5–9; 2 Chron. 28:5–21).
Because of the pro-Assyrian feeling in Jerusalem, Pekah, king of Israel, and Rezin, king of Damascus, had joined as allies to besiege Jerusalem and force

---

[50] It consisted of one hundred talents of silver, ten thousand measures of wheat and ten thousand of barley.

[51] Isaiah received his call (or recommissioning) in the year King Uzziah died (Isa. 6:1–8), and may have started ministering a short time before. He continued into the reigns of Jotham, Ahaz, and Hezekiah (Isa. 1:1).

[52] From 735 B.C., when he took over as head ruler (Jotham yet living four years), until 719 B.C., when his son, Hezekiah, in turn took over from him (while Ahaz yet lived four years). See Stigers, "Interphased Chronology," pp. 88–89, for discussion. Admittedly, the dating of Ahaz and Hezekiah is difficult. See Payne, *BS* 126 (1969): 40–52, for a treatment of the main problems. The dates here set forth seem to fit the scriptural evidence best.

[53] For reasons, see Stigers, "Interphased Chronology," pp. 87–88.

Judah to support a revolt against Assyria. The siege came in Jotham's closing years, as noted, but since Ahaz had already assumed leadership, the task of resistance was mainly his. Recognizing his inability to meet the combined foe in combat, and wishing to keep in the good favor of Assyria, he sought help from Tiglath-pileser III, the same conqueror against whom his grandfather, Uzziah, had led the northern coalition only nine years before.

Ahaz now, by letter, asked Assyria to enter the region and attack both Damascus and Israel, thus forcing the two to lift the siege and return home. He gave the Assyrian monarch considerable gold and silver as an inducement. Ahaz's plan worked, for Tiglath-pileser did come,[54] and Pekah and Rezin were forced to return to their respective countries. Before they did so, however, they wrought extensive damage in Judah, killing 120,000 people and taking 200,000 captives.[55] These captives, however, were permitted to return home to Judah almost immediately, as a result of admonition by God's prophet, Oded.[56]

Ahaz received a rebuke from God for his manner of finding relief from the siege. Isaiah brought it at the time that Ahaz was considering sending his letter and gift to Tiglath-pileser (Isa. 7–8). The prophet told him that his real enemy was not these smaller, neighboring kings, but the mighty Assyrian host whose assistance he was about to seek. The truth of Isaiah's statement is borne out by the havoc Tiglath-pileser then

inflicted in the general region during the next three years, apparently even forcing Ahaz himself to pay tribute, in addition to the initial gift (2 Chron. 28:20–21). It is borne out, too, by the further devastation in Judah of succeeding Assyrian rulers, in years immediately following.

b. Religious defection (2 Kings 16:2–4, 10–18; 2 Chron. 28:1–4, 22–25). Religiously, Ahaz ended the tradition of godly rule established by the four kings who had preceded him. He made images of Baal, observed infant sacrifice in the Valley of Hinnom, and worshiped in the high places. While meeting with Tiglath-pileser in Damascus, at the close of the conqueror's devastating campaign, Ahaz saw and admired a certain pagan altar there and sent a plan of it home to Uriah the priest to copy for Jerusalem. When he later returned, he established this altar as the official place of sacrifice at the temple, in place of the brazen altar prescribed in the Mosaic Law. Besides this, he intentionally damaged several of the sacred vessels of the temple and even closed the doors of the temple, thus forcing people to worship where and as he wanted.

c. Military reverses (2 Chron. 28:16–19). In view of this conduct, it is not surprising to read of numerous military reverses. The first reverse came at the hands of Edom, who once again revolted, even carrying captives from Judah, reversing Amaziah's earlier treatment of Edom. The important

[54] In his famous campaign of 734–732; see p. 281.
[55] To account for this loss of life, certainly large battles were fought sometime during this general time of siege. From Isaiah 7:6 it is clear that the alliance had intended actually to replace Ahaz with one ben Tabeel; see Bright, *BHI*, p. 256n.11.
[56] Oded met the host at Samaria and the captives were then taken to Jericho where they were released, some embarrassment evidently being spared in not returning them directly to Jerusalem.

port of Elath on the Gulf of Aqaba was once again lost to Judah, when it was seized by Rezin of Damascus for his country (2 Kings 16:6). Another defeat occurred when the Philistines once again invaded Judah and inflicted severe destruction, even seizing several cities. The chronicler implies that Ahaz, in his letter to Tiglath-pileser, had requested that the great Assyrian press an attack on both Edom and Philistia, besides Israel and Damascus. For this reason, an indication by Tiglath-pileser that he did smite the Philistines and receive tribute from Edom, as well as from other countries, is significant.

2. Hezekiah
(728–686; 2 Kings 18–20; 2 Chronicles 29–32)

Hezekiah succeeded his father, ruling for forty-two years, though the first thirteen were as coregent. There is reason to believe that he assumed chief rule, however, some four years before his father died,[57] likely at the insistence of a growing anti-Assyrian party that objected to further pro-Assyrian actions by Ahaz. It is probable, indeed, that this first accession as co-ruler had been

at the insistence of this group, though then Ahaz was still permitted to keep the top position.[58]

a. Approved of God (2 Kings 18:4–7; 2 Chron. 29:2–31:21). Hezekiah was one of Judah's finest kings in the sight of God. He is given the high accolade of having acted as David, his father,[59] and also of being the peer of all Judah's kings in trusting God (2 Kings 18:5).

After the deliberate idolatry of Ahaz, drastic reform was necessary, and Hezekiah effected it. The doors of the temple were again opened, and the priests and Levites were instructed to remove all foreign cult objects. Then they were to clean and restore all the proper items so that true worship might be reinstated. A grand time of sacrificing and celebrations marked the return of the true Mosaic ceremonies (2 Chron. 29:20–36).

Further, Hezekiah ordered the Passover to be observed once more. Apparently this had been neglected for many years, even before the rule of Ahaz. Hezekiah invited Israelites from Beersheba to Dan to take part in the festal occasion (2 Chron. 30:1–27).[60] Many

---

[57] Evidenced as follows: (1) 2 Kings 18:13 says that it was in his fourteenth year that Sennacherib attacked, which attack, according to Assyrian records, came in 701 B.C., which sets the beginning of his reign at 715 B.C. But (2) 2 Kings 16:1–2 states that Ahaz reigned only sixteen years after Pekah's seventeenth year (735 B.C.), which would be to 719 B.C., some four years prior to 715 B.C. The answer must be that Hezekiah took over as head in 719, with Ahaz still living to 715, from which date Hezekiah's sole rule is figured in 2 Kings 18:13. See Stigers, "Interphased Chronology," pp. 86–90. Thiele does not recognize this coregency for Hezekiah and so does not account for chronological notations in 2 Kings 18:1, 9, 10.

[58] Hezekiah would have only been about twelve years old at the time; see Stigers, "Interphased Chronology," p. 83. Note that the chronological indications of 2 Kings 18:1, 9–10 are in terms of Hezekiah and not Ahaz who yet lived.

[59] This was said also of Asa (1 Kings 15:11) and Jehoshaphat (2 Chron. 17:3), and is again of Josiah (2 Kings 22:2), but not of Joash, Amaziah, Uzziah, or Jotham, the four good kings who immediately preceded Ahaz. In fact, of Amaziah it is stated that he did not measure up to David's standard (2 Kings 14:3). David's reign continued to be a measure for later rulers.

[60] The celebration probably occurred in Hezekiah's first year (2 Chron. 29:3), but likely the first year of his sole reign, which means 715 B.C. Samaria had been taken captive six years before, which made proper the general invitation as far north as Dan. This makes it appear that Hezekiah made some

responded, and a time of feasting and worshiping followed such as had not occurred since the reign of Solomon (2 Chron. 30:26). This in turn led to a cleansing of the land generally; thus it was that high places (*bamoth*), images (*masseboth*), Asherah poles (*'asherim*), false altars (*mizbehoth*), and even the brazen serpent that Moses had made in the wilderness centuries before (Num. 21:5–9) were destroyed. Still further, Hezekiah revitalized the organization of priests and Levites and their support by the tithes of the people (2 Chron. 31:1–21). Never before had the land undergone so thorough a reformation.

b. Hezekiah and the Assyrians.

Hezekiah was anti-Assyrian, in contrast to his father. He did not, however, openly rebel against the eastern power as long as Sargon II was ruling (722–705).[61]

Sargon, who resettled Israelite territory with persons taken captive from other subjugated countries, was a capable ruler and military leader. Within one year of Samaria's fall, he brought the Assyrian army into the west again to put down a revolt headed by Hamath.[62] He next fought successfully in Asia Minor, and then gave attention

to a revolution in Carchemish, whose population he deported. He followed this by finally breaking the power of the hated kingdom of Urartu[63] to the north, which his predecessors had been unable to do. More significantly for Hezekiah, he came in 711 B.C. to the Philistine territory and crushed a revolt led by Ashdod, then the leading Philistine city.[64] Hezekiah had been asked to join the Ashdod alliance but wisely had refused.[65]

c. Hezekiah and Sennacherib (2 Chron. 32:1–8).

When Sargon's son, Sennacherib (705–681), came to the throne, however, Hezekiah did join such a pact. A change in kings was always seen as a propitious time for rebellion, as subject people tested the strength of the new ruler. This new alliance was composed of more members than before, with Tyre the leading city[66] and a new Egyptian king, Shabaka (c. 710–696), who gave promise of providing more support, having come to the throne. Hezekiah made thorough preparations for an expected retaliation by Sennacherib, however (2 Chron. 32:1–8). He constructed further fortifications, made new weapons, and reinforced his military

---

effort at reform in Israel as well as Judah. See Keil, *KD,* 7:454–62, however, who argues for a later year in Hezekiah's reign.

[61] After Tiglath-pileser III (745–727) came Shalmaneser V (727–722) and then Sargon II; see pp. 281–82.

[62] Sargon's inscription states that both Damascus and Samaria had a part in this Hamath-led uprising; see G. Ricciotti, *The History of Israel,* 2 vols., 2d ed. (Milwaukee: Bruce, 1958), 1:356–57.

[63] Strong, troublesome foe of Assyria for many years; see E. A. Speiser, "Introduction to Hurrian," *AASOR* 20 (1940–41).

[64] Ashdod apparently had taken the lead following Gaza's devastation by Tiglath-pileser in 734 B.C. The new Twenty-Fifth Dynasty in Egypt had promised aid in this rebellion, and (as Sargon indicates) Judah, Edom, and Moab had been invited to enter. When Sargon put down the revolt, the assistance of Egypt did not materialize, and the rebel leader, when he fled to Egypt for protection, was even handed back to the Assyrians! See *ANET,* p. 286, for text.

[65] That he did not was likely due in large part to the advice of Isaiah; see Isaiah 20:1–6.

[66] Leadership now swung to Tyre because Gaza and Ashdod had been terribly hurt in 711 B.C., and were slow to join any new coalition. Ashkelon and Ekron did join, however. Ekron's king, Padi, who refused to join, was removed from his position. See *ANET,* p. 287, for text.

strength. He gave special attention to stopping the water supplies that the enemy might use. At the same time he provided a more convenient access to water for his own people by digging the now-famous Siloam Tunnel from the Spring of Gihon, through the hill of Ophel to a place within the city lower than the starting point; a truly remarkable piece of engineering.[67]

d. Sennacherib's invasion (2 Kings 18:13–19:37; 2 Chron. 32:9–21; Isa. 36–37).

During Sennacherib's first four years of rule, he was occupied with maintaining Assyrian control over Babylon; but in 701 B.C., he came to put down this revolt in the west.[68] He dealt first with Tyre, the leading city, by crushing resistance there, and Tyre's King Luli fled to Cyprus. At this point, many of the coalition's less enthusiastic members capitulated, including the kings of Byblos, Arvad, Moab, Edom, and Ammon. Then Sennacherib moved south along the Mediterranean and punished another leading city, Ash-kelon, deporting her king, Sidqia, to Assyria. It was probably at this point, with the coastline in his control, that Sennacherib moved inland toward the third leading city, Jerusalem.

On the way he stopped to lay siege to Lachish.[69] While here he received tribute from Judah, indicating Hezekiah's recognition that the cause of the revolt was lost (2 Kings 18:14–16).[70] About this time, too, Hezekiah released Padi, the former king of Ekron, who had been deposed by the coalition and imprisoned in Jerusalem when he refused to cooperate in the rebellion.[71] But Sennacherib was not satisfied with this show of submission by Hezekiah, so he sent three lieutenants[72] and a large force of men to pursue psychological warfare against Hezekiah and his people (2 Kings 18:17–37; 2 Chron. 32:9–16; Isa. 36:1–21). Their threats were effective in causing the people to fear and in prompting Hezekiah to consult with Isaiah, from whom the king received a comforting word from God.

---

[67] An inscription found near the mouth of the tunnel (see *ANET*, p. 321, for text) states that diggers worked from both ends. Their place of meeting shows a slight jog but the degree of skill in maintaining the right slope and direction is incredible. The inscription says that the tunnel was 1,200 cubits long. Measurement today reveals the distance in feet to be 1,777 (others give 1,749), which indicates the length of the cubit to have been just under eighteen inches. See 2 Kings 20:20; 2 Chronicles 32:30.

[68] Sennacherib left a record of this campaign on a prism, called the Taylor Prism, now in the British Museum. See *ANET*, pp. 287–88; *DOTT*, pp. 64–68.

[69] Sennacherib does not speak of this move toward Jerusalem nor of the Lachish siege on the prism, though he pictures the Lachish siege in his palace at Nineveh (see *ANEP*, figs. 371–74). For a description of this picture and of evidence from excavation at Lachish, including a pit where as many as fifteen hundred people were buried in mass, see Wright, *BAR*, pp. 167–72.

[70] Sennacherib lists this tribute as thirty talents of gold and eight hundred of silver, while the Bible mentions thirty of gold and three hundred of silver (2 Kings 18:14). For discussion relative to the difference in silver talents, see Robinson, *The Bearing of Archaeology on the Old Testament* (New York: The American Tract Society, 1941), p. 100. Sennacherib claims that the tribute included also precious stones, inlaid couches and chairs, elephant hides, Hezekiah's own daughters, concubines, and musicians.

[71] The biblical record does not mention this king of Ekron, but Sennacherib does.

[72] Names given for them (2 Kings 18:18) were titles of high Assyrian officials: Tartan (*turtannu*), meaning "second in rank"; Rabsaris (*rabushareshi*), meaning "chief eunuch"; and Rabshakeh (*rab shaqu*), meaning "chief officer"; see M. Burrows, *What Mean These Stones?* (New Haven: American Schools of Oriental Research, 1941), pp. 43–44.

At this juncture, Sennacherib heard that Egypt's army under Tirhakah,[73] was coming to the aid of the coalition, and turned to meet it rather than continuing on immediately to Jerusalem. He sent a letter to Hezekiah at the time, however, in which he stated the threats already made by the lieutenants. With this letter in hand, Hezekiah sought further reassurance from God, which was given through Isaiah. This time the prophet told the king that Sennacherib would not capture Jerusalem, nor even come near it (2 Kings 19:8–34; Isa. 37:8–35).

From Sennacherib's report, we learn that he did encounter an Egyptian force and defeat it in the plain of Eltekeh, near Ekron.[74] He also speaks of capturing the nearby cities of Eltekeh, Timnah, and Ekron, and reinstalling her former king, Padi, in the latter, establishing him now as ruler over the whole general region. Sennacherib further states that he conquered a total of forty-six strong cities of Hezekiah, besides numerous villages, and seized over 200,000 prisoners.

The biblical record gives the final note, however, in stating that all this activity was suddenly brought to an end by the slaying of no less than 185,000 troops of Sennacherib by the "angel of the LORD."[75] Of this Sennacherib says nothing, as one might expect. His account, however, indirectly corroborates the fact, because he does not claim to have captured Jerusalem, which would be most unusual otherwise, since Jerusalem was certainly one of his prime objectives from the first. His own words speak only of shutting Hezekiah in Jerusalem "like a bird in a cage."[76]

e. Hezekiah's illness and fame (2 Kings 20; 2 Chron. 32:22–33; Isa. 38–39). Two other episodes in Hezekiah's life, both related to this Assyrian campaign, are recorded. One concerns a time of severe illness from which the king recovered only because of God's gracious hand of healing. The time was

---

[73] Because Tirhakah was not yet king of Egypt in 701 B.C. (became king in 689 B.C.), and because some believe he was not even born until 709 B.C., numerous scholars hold that two campaigns by Sennacherib are represented in the biblical story: one in 701 B.C. and one after 689 B.C. Sennacherib's own inscriptions are lacking for his last eight years and do not help. The biblical record, however, gives no hint of a second campaign, and implies in 2 Kings 19:8–9 (Isa. 37:8–9) that Sennacherib's encounter with Tirhakah followed the siege of Lachish immediately. Therefore, it is better to accept only one campaign. As to the problem regarding Tirhakah, perhaps this army commander was someone other than the later king of Egypt. He is called in the text "king of Ethiopia," rather than king of Egypt, which might be a clue, though Egyptian kings at this time were Ethiopian in lineage. The view that Tirhakah, king of Egypt, was born only in 709 B.C., put forth by M. Macadam, has also been challenged, making it possible that proleptic speech is used in 2 Kings 19:9, when it calls Tirhakah, "king of Ethiopia"; see Kitchen, *AOOT,* p. 83. B. Oded, in *JAIH,* asserts that Tirhakah was old enough to have participated in this war (p. 448). Albright, for instance, advocates the two-campaign view: see *BASOR* 130 (1953): 8–11; 141 (1956): 23–27; Bright, *AHOI,* 3d ed., pp. 298–309, argues for the plausibility of this two-campaign view.

[74] This encounter with the Egyptians may have preceded the Tirhakah battle, however. If so, Sennacherib fought the Egyptians twice.

[75] An account by Herodotus had led some scholars to suggest a way in which God destroyed these soldiers. Herodotus says that Sennacherib's host was attacked by field mice swarming over the camp and devouring quivers, bows, and shield handles. The suggestion is that the plague, which is carried by rats and mice, was the method God used. This explanation may be doubtful, but at least Herodotus's story provides an indirect confirmation of the biblical miracle, for his account is what might be expected in view of such a miracle. See Herodotus 2.141; Finegan, *LAP,* pp. 213–14.

[76] *DOTT,* p. 67.

during, or just prior to, Sennacherib's invasion of the land.[77] Hezekiah prayed to God that he might recover; and God answered through Isaiah, promising the king fifteen more years of life, as well as deliverance from the Assyrian power. It is likely that Hezekiah's concern over his sickness was accented by his anxiety for the country (if it was now left without a leader). In consideration of his emotional distress, God gave Hezekiah a remarkable sign as evidence that the promise would be fulfilled: the return of the sundial shadow ten degrees.

The other episode concerns the visit to Jerusalem by messengers from Merodach-baladan, king of Babylon. This occurred shortly after Hezekiah's recovery from illness (Isa. 39:1).[78] While the group came ostensibly to congratulate the Judean king on his recovery, the true reason no doubt lay in the anti-Assyrian cause common to both Babylon and Judah. Babylon had long been in a power struggle with Assyria, and Merodach-baladan had been personally involved for at least twenty years. Help was desired from whatever source it might be found. The messengers brought lavish gifts to Hezekiah, and Hezekiah in turn showed them his wealth. For this, however, he was severely rebuked by Isaiah, who told him that the homeland of these men would one day come and seize all this treasure for itself. This did occur one century later, when the great Nebuchadnezzar II came to power.

3. The prophets Isaiah and Micah

a. Isaiah. It has already appeared that the prophet Isaiah was important to his country. He had remonstrated with Ahaz over his alliance with Assyria, and he had advised and comforted Hezekiah. It is likely, too, that these episodes only represent many more of similar nature. For instance, Isaiah must have had contact with the pious Jotham earlier and have had much to do with the God-pleasing reforms effected by Hezekiah. Even with Ahaz, who outwardly scorned him, Isaiah's influence could not have gone unnoticed.

Probably the prophet Isaiah had much to do with the establishment of Hezekiah's coregency with Ahaz, when Hezekiah was only a lad of twelve. When Hezekiah ruled alone, Isaiah was heard to speak strongly against alliance with Egypt (Isa. 30:1-7; 31:1-3), which certainly influenced Hezekiah's refusal to join the pact of 711 B.C. In this, however, Isaiah was opposed by false prophets (Isa. 30:8-11); and their influence, in turn, may have had a part in Hezekiah's change of mind regarding the coalition of 701 B.C. When Hezekiah, however, turned again to Isaiah for help in the trouble that resulted, the prophet did not react against him but cooperated freely. He understood the king's difficult position and saw genuine sincerity, which was enough to prompt his support.

b. Micah. Another writing prophet of the time was Micah. He ministered

---

[77]This is indicated not only by the promise to Hezekiah (Isa. 38:6), but also chronological considerations. Hezekiah ruled a total of twenty-nine years as supreme king (2 Kings 18:2), and so, subtracting fifteen (the years of life now added to him) from this, the year of his illness results as the fourteenth, the same as the year of Sennacherib's attack (2 Kings 18:13).

[78]Merodach-baladan ruled Babylon 721–710 and again 703–702. After 702 he continued his opposition to Assyrian control as a refugee in Elam. It was likely during this time that he sought the support of Judah by means of this embassy.

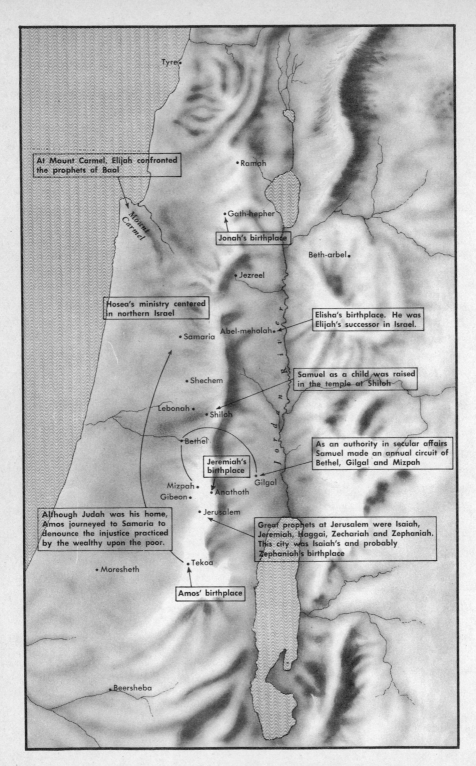

Map 15. Cities of the Prophets

THE KINGDOM OF JUDAH

during the reigns of Jotham, Ahaz, and Hezekiah (Mic. 1:1), evidently beginning shortly after Isaiah and continuing contemporaneously with him. Micah came from the village of Moreshath in southwest Judah. He is never depicted at the court as is Isaiah, but Jeremiah (26:17–19; see Mic. 3:11–12) does speak of him as having influence, especially with Hezekiah. Micah's main message addressed the themes of social abuse and unfaithfulness to Yahweh. These emphases and his pointed warning of coming punishment, reinforced similar words of Isaiah.

4. Manasseh
(697–642; 2 Kings 21:1–18; 2 Chronicles 33:1–20)

Manasseh succeeded his father, Hezekiah, and ruled fifty-five years, the longest of any king in either Judah or Israel. The first eleven, however, were as coregent with his father,[79] making him the fifth consecutive Judean prince to begin reigning in this manner.

a. Religious defection (2 Kings 21:2–16; 2 Chron. 33:2–10). Manasseh did not learn from his godly father in religious matters; instead, he followed the pattern of his Law-defying grandfather, Ahaz, in doing evil in the sight of God. He restored the offensive cultic objects that Hezekiah had de-stroyed, placed altars of Baal throughout the land and even in the temple, and recognized the Ammonite deity, Molech, by sacrificing children in the Valley of Hinnom. He approved various forms of pagan divination and even erected an image of the Canaanite goddess, Asherah, in the temple. He killed those who protested, thus shedding much innocent blood. It may be that Isaiah was among these, as tradition testifies.

In all this, the combined influence of current Assyrian practices in religion and of the older Phoenician worship of Baal-melqart may be discerned. Manasseh is said to have caused the people to do more evil than nations whom God had dispossessed from the land centuries before (2 Kings 21:9). Prophets of God duly warned the king concerning his ways, but he did not take heed.

b. Punishment and repentance (2 Chron. 33:11–20). Punishment from God was not long in coming,[80] taking the form of Manasseh's personal captivity[81] by an Assyrian king.[82] Little is known about this captivity. It was brought about by either Sennacherib's son, Esarhaddon (681–669), or grandson, Ashurbanipal (669–633), in the successive reigns of whom Assyria reached the zenith of her power. Both rulers campaigned with success as far

---

[79]Thiele argues for this coregency on the basis that it is the most logical way to account for an extra eleven years, which result when the reigns of the remaining kings of Judah are fitted into the total number of years left until the captivity; *MNHK*, pp. 156–59.

[80]Later and still greater punishment came in the form of Judah's captivity by Babylon. Second Kings 23:26 explicitly states that even all of Josiah's reform could not offset the provocations of Manasseh in God's sight.

[81]Described (2 Chron. 33:11) as being taken in hooks and fetters. The practice was to bind the prisoner with fetters and place a hook in his lips by which to lead him in abject submission; see Ricciotti, *History of Israel*, pp. 389–90, for discussion and evidence.

[82]Second Chronicles 33:11 states that he was taken to Babylon. Some scholars believe that an error in location exists here, Babylon being substituted for Nineveh. Esarhaddon, however, rebuilt Babylon after its devastation by his father, Sennacherib, and made it an integral part of the Assyrian domain once again. Manasseh may well have been held captive there. For texts, see D. D. Luckenbill, *Ancient Records of Assyria and Babylonia* (Chicago: University of Chicago Press, 1927), vol. 1, secs. 646, 647.

south as Egypt for the first time in Assyrian history; and Ashurbanipal made significant conquest, even in the treacherous mountains of Elam to the east.

In favor of Esarhaddon being the one who took Manasseh is the fact that—on an inscription that has been dated as being from 678 B.C.—this ruler specifically mentions Manasseh, along with twenty-one other kings, as his vassal, stating that all these were required personally to bring valuable building materials to Nineveh.[83] The language used, however, hardly characterized the occasion as one of captivity, though it may have been.

In favor of Ashurbanipal is the fact that he put down a revolt of southern Mediterranean states in which Manasseh probably was involved,[84] an occasion when such a captivity could easily have resulted. The revolt was widespread, even including Babylon to the east, and it lasted over a period of five years (652–648). Since the biblical record speaks only of "captains" (KJV; Hebrew, *sare*) of the host effecting the captivity, it may be that the Assyrian king himself was not present, which may explain why no official notice was entered in the Assyrian record. Furthermore, the latter view better correlates with the biblical story, which implies that Manasseh's captivity came toward the close of his reign, following his many years of idolatrous practice. With the earlier occasion, he would have reigned only seventeen of his fifty-five

years when taken; while with the latter, about forty-six.

Manasseh was eventually permitted to return to Judah as a result of God's favor gained by Manasseh's repentance while a captive. In being restored to the throne, he commendably sought to make amends for his earlier wickedness. He removed the foreign cultic items and reestablished true worship at the temple. How many years of this manner of rule remained for him after the return is not revealed, but perhaps four or five.[85]

5. Amon
(642–640; 2 Kings 21:19–26;
2 Chronicles 33:21–25)

Amon succeeded his father but ruled only two years. He reverted to the idolatrous practices his father had pursued for the major part of his rule, apparently not being impressed by the reform of the closing years. Perhaps his own servants came to be repulsed by his actions, for some of them banded together in conspiracy and killed him in his own house. The people at large, not approving assassinations in any case, took the lives of the conspirators. Amon's eight-year-old son, Josiah, became king.

E. BABYLON BECOMES DOMINANT
(640–586; 2 Kings 22–25;
2 Chronicles 34–36)

With the accession of Josiah, Judah entered her closing period of history.

---

[83] Inscribed on Prism B of Esarhaddon; see *ANET,* p. 291, for text.

[84] Ashurbanipal lists Manasseh along with twenty-one other kings as submitting before him as he marched against Egypt (see *ANET,* p. 294, for text). There is no direct indication, however, that he was then taken back to Assyria as captive.

[85] There is no way to know how long Manasseh was held captive. It is stated only that during this time he did repent and God did give him deliverance. If he was taken in his forty-sixth year, he could have been there four or five years and still have had four or five after returning to Jerusalem.

No longer was there reason to fear Assyria, for Ashurbanipal's last years witnessed little military activity, and only weak rulers followed him until Nineveh's fall in 612 B.C. Babylon, however, soon took over as world leader, bringing in the period known as Neo-Babylonian. This shift of power came at the close of Josiah's thirty-one-year reign. His time of rule, then, was relatively free from foreign interference and dangers, but those of his three successors were much involved with the new great power, by whom Judah was finally taken captive.

1. Josiah
(640–609; 2 Kings 22:1–23:30; 2 Chronicles 34–35)

The three decades of Josiah's reign were among the happiest in Judah's experience. They were characterized by peace, prosperity, and reform. No outside enemies made war on the nation, the people could concentrate on constructive activity; and Josiah himself sought to please God by reinstituting adherence to regulations commanded in the Mosaic Law.

Josiah was made king when he was merely a boy of eight. Religious idolatry was rampant as a result of Amon having reverted to Manasseh's earlier practices. But apparently the lad had God-fearing advisors who offset any influence of his father, for Josiah returned to following the way of Yahweh. At the age of sixteen, he began of himself "to seek the God of his father David" (2 Chron. 34:3). At the age of twenty he began to cleanse Jerusalem and Judah of the idolatrous objects his father and grandfather had brought into the land (2 Chron. 34:3–7). Successful in his own land, he even pursued similar activity to the north in Israel, where Assyria now held nominal control, removing altars and images of false deities.[86]

a. Josiah's reformation (2 Kings 22:3–23:25; 2 Chron. 34:8–35:19).

At the age of twenty-six (622 B.C.), Josiah, pleased at what had been accomplished but seeing much more that needed to be done, put forth still greater effort to bring about what is called the most thorough reform in Judah's history. This special endeavor was prompted in particular by the discovery[87] of "the Book of the Law of the LORD that had been given through Moses" (2 Chron. 34:14).[88] The discovery was made by Hilkiah the high priest while workmen repaired the temple.[89] Shaphan, a scribe, brought the book to Josiah's attention and read to him from it.

Josiah was disturbed at the deviation he recognized between the require-

---

[86] That he could do this in spite of Assyrian control is no doubt tied in with the growing Assyrian weakness of the day.

[87] Manasseh may have destroyed all copies of the Law that he could find, which prompted someone to hide this one so well that it became lost to knowledge. It is possible, too, that this copy had been placed in the temple cornerstone by Solomon, a practice not uncommon for the day.

[88] Probably a copy of the five books of Moses. Josiah's detailed keeping of the Passover at this time requires it to have been more than merely Deuteronomy, as many hold (see G. Wright, *Interpreter's Bible*, 2:311–30). It should be observed also that nothing in the record suggests that this book had recently been written, as negative criticism has long believed. Indeed, Josiah had already been effecting reforms, as well as Hezekiah earlier, showing that they knew what God desired in His Law without having to find this particular copy. The discovery here added detail to Josiah's knowledge.

[89] As in the former time of Athaliah, the wicked reigns of Manasseh and Amon had led to temple neglect and even purposeful changes through pagan innovations.

ments it set forth and the actual practices in the land. The counsel of Huldah, a prophetess, was sought; and she warned that punishment was inevitable for the country because of this deviation. However, her message from God also included the fact that it would not come in Josiah's day, since he sought to do what God desired. Josiah proceeded to have this law read to the people, and along with that he issued orders for the reform.

All foreign cult objects were removed from the temple, from the city of Jerusalem, and from all corners of the Promised Land. In addition, the idolatrous priests were removed from their positions, and houses of religious prostitution were destroyed, and child-sacrifice to Molech in the Valley of Hinnom was abolished. Moreover, horses dedicated to the sun were removed from the entrance to the temple, and their chariots were burned with fire. Finally, high places to false deities, erected by Solomon just outside Jerusalem, apparently still in use, were razed (2 Kings 23:4–14).

Josiah, not content to effect this reform merely in Judah, gave orders respecting the north as well, taking advantage of Assyria's period of general weakness. A particular place of interest was Bethel, long the center of golden-calf worship. According to a prophecy given over three hundred years before,[90] Josiah burned the bones of the false priests; he did this on the altar that Jeroboam I had erected, and then he destroyed both the altar and its high place.

Perhaps the most significant feature of Josiah's reform was the observance of the Passover in the eighteenth year of his reign (2 Kings 23:21–23; 2 Chron. 35:1–19). The record states that a Passover had not been kept as carefully since the days of Samuel the prophet (2 Chron 35:18).[91] The original command of God in the Mosaic Law had been that the feast was to be observed with care annually, but the people had not obeyed. Josiah made sure that this year the feast was kept in strict accordance with God's law.

b. Josiah's death (2 Kings 23:28–30; 2 Chron. 35:20–27). Josiah was an able king. The sweeping reforms he instituted, in spite of the opposition that no doubt arose, could not have been brought about by a mediocre leader. He made his authority felt even in the erstwhile provinces of Israel, as mentioned above, thus enlarging Judah's sphere of influence. However, when he attempted to intervene in the affairs of the world powers, he exceeded himself and brought about his own death.

The occasion involved his endeavor to stop a northward march of Pharaoh Necho II of Egypt in 609 B.C. Necho was moving to the aid of the Assyrians, who were attempting to stop Babylonia from becoming the new world leader. Assyria's two main cities, Assur and Nineveh, had fallen in 614 and 612 B.C., respectively, to attacks by the

---

[90] Brought by the "man of God" to Jeroboam just after the establishment of the false worship of the calves; pp. 258–59.

[91] This means that it was observed now with yet greater care and detail than in Hezekiah's reforms (see pp. 303–4).

Carchemish
Haran
Euphrates River
Aleppo
Orontes River
Hamath
HAMATH
Arvad
Riblah
Byblos
Lebanon Mountains
Anti-Lebanon Mountains
Damascus
Tyre
Mediterranean Sea
Megiddo
Josiah's Battle
Rabbath-Ammon
Ashdod
Ashkelon
Jerusalem
Gaza

Map 16. Necho's Route and Josiah's Battle

Medes and Babylonians;[92] and the remnants of Assyria's army, under Ashur-uballit II, had fled westward to Haran.[93] In 610 B.C., Haran fell to Nabopolassar, king of Babylon, which all but finished the Assyrians.

Now, in 609 B.C., Necho, who had just succeeded Psammetichus I as king of Egypt[94] and who wanted Egypt to regain world prominence instead of Babylonia, was marching northward to help Assyria's few remaining forces. Josiah, in a probable indication of favor toward Babylonia, attempted to stop the Egyptians at strategic Megiddo, and he was killed in the effort. His body was returned to Jerusalem and was buried there.

2. Seventh-century prophets

Josiah's day was one of outstanding prophets—perhaps three or four writing prophets. Jeremiah began to minister in Josiah's thirteenth year (Jer. 1:2), 627 B.C., and continued after Jerusalem's fall to Babylonia in 586 B.C. Zephaniah also dates his book to Josiah's reign (1:1) and likely began his ministry about the time that Jeremiah did, at least prior to Josiah's reforms, for he speaks of foreign cults yet existing in the land (1:4). Nahum does not date his book to the reign of a king but is best placed in Josiah's time, too, for the main theme he pursues concerns the fall of Nineveh, which came in 612

B.C., three years before Josiah's death. Habakkuk's prophecy as well must be located either at the close of Josiah's rule or during the succeeding reign of Jehoiakim, for he speaks of the Babylonian invasion being near at hand (1:5–6).

At no other time in the history of either Israel or Judah was there such a concentration of writing prophets. The significance must be that God was giving Judah one last intensive warning of impending punishment. No doubt, too, much of the credit for the reform Josiah effected must go to these stalwart men. The king had to lead the way, but these prophets probably aided greatly, both encouraging his movement and prompting the people to accept it.

Jeremiah, for instance, speaks harshly of the inexcusable idolatry filling the land (2:5–13), warning of punishment if repentance were not forthcoming (3:1–5, 19–25). Zephaniah predicts severe punishment for Judah's sin (2:4–3:7). Nahum's warning was more indirect, telling of Nineveh's coming destruction; but the message that God brings punishment on all who do wickedly could not have been missed. Habakkuk again speaks directly of the Babylonians coming against Judah as an instrument of God's justice (1:1–11).

---

[92] The barbaric Scythians from northern Mesopotamia also had some part. These people had been making their presence felt in recent years. They had passed through Philistia about 627 B.C., in Josiah's early years (see Jer. 6:22–26), creating fear in Judah; had been stopped by Psammetichus I of Egypt by prayers and presents (Herodotus 1.105); had defeated Cyaxares of Media in 624 B.C.; and now had switched sides to aid Media and Babylonia against Assyria.

[93] A fragment of the "Babylonian Chronicle," dealing with events of the years 616–609, discovered in the British Museum by C. J. Gadd, has thrown considerable light on this period; see *ANET*, pp. 303–5, for text; *DOTT*, pp. 75–83, for text and discussion; and D. J. Wiseman, *Chronicles of Chaldean Kings* (London: British Museum, 1956) carries a full treatment.

[94] Psammetichus had already shown favor toward Assyria, even having taken an army in 616 B.C. to assist in checking Nabopolassar in Mesopotamia. Necho was following his lead.

3. Jehoahaz
(609 B.C.; 2 Kings 23:31–33;
2 Chronicles 36:1–3)

Josiah had three sons, and each in time ruled over Judah. No other king in either Israel or Judah had this distinction.[95] Yet all three failed to follow their father in obeying God.

The first to rule was the middle son, Jehoahaz. The people bypassed the eldest in selecting him as Josiah's successor at the age of twenty-three. He had ruled only three months, however, when Pharaoh Necho, now in authority over Judah since the defeat of Josiah, ordered his replacement by the older brother, Eliakim, whose name was now changed to Jehoiakim.[96] Apparently Necho had reason to believe that Jehoahaz would not cooperate with him but that the older son would.[97] At this time, too, Necho demanded tribute from Judah, requiring one hundred talents of silver and a talent of gold. Jehoahaz was taken prisoner to Egypt, where he died as predicted by Jeremiah (22:11–12).

4. Jehoiakim
(609–597; 2 Kings 23:34–24:7;
2 Chronicles 36:4–8)

Jehoiakim was twenty-five, two years older than his deposed brother, when he was placed on the throne. Jehoiakim did evil before God and was an inefficient ruler. Perhaps his failings were already evident when the people earlier chose his younger brother as his father's successor. Jeremiah shows disdain for him by declaring that Jehoiakim would be buried with "the burial of a donkey" (22:13–19).

The particular act of Jehoiakim that prompted this remark was his construction of a new palace. Apparently dissatisfied with the one his father had, he used state funds and forced labor to build it. Jehoiakim also foolishly cut and burned Jeremiah's book, written at the direction of God, apparently thinking that this would in some way offset its dire warnings (Jer. 36:23). Measures of this kind—along with a hated head tax, imposed to pay Necho's tribute (2 Kings 23:35)—would have irritated the people and stirred deep unrest. Contributing further to the unsettled conditions were great political upheavals of the day, with Babylonia now emerging as the new world power.

5. Babylon's rise to power

Babylon's dominance in the Mediterranean countries had not come by 609 B.C., when Necho marched to meet the Babylonians. The Egyptian Pharaoh was unsuccessful at the time in retaking Haran from Nabopolassar, but he did keep the Babylonians from pressing their claim further. Egypt remained dominant in the west for another three years.[98] Nabopolassar and his talented son Nebuchadnezzar had to remain content to strengthen their present holdings in anticipation of another day.

Early in 605 B.C., that day came,

---

[95] Ahab in Israel came the nearest, having two sons to rule: Ahaziah and Jehoram.

[96] Since the meaning of Eliakim ("God has established") is basically the same as Jehoiakim ("Yahweh has established"), Necho, who seems to have ordered also the name change, must have wanted only to demonstrate his authority to do so.

[97] At the time, Necho was at Riblah on the Orontes River, where he had established his camp for the encounter with Babylonia. Jehoahaz was summoned there to receive the news of his dismissal.

[98] Necho's authority in Judah to replace one king by another was only representative of control in all these Mediterranean countries.

315

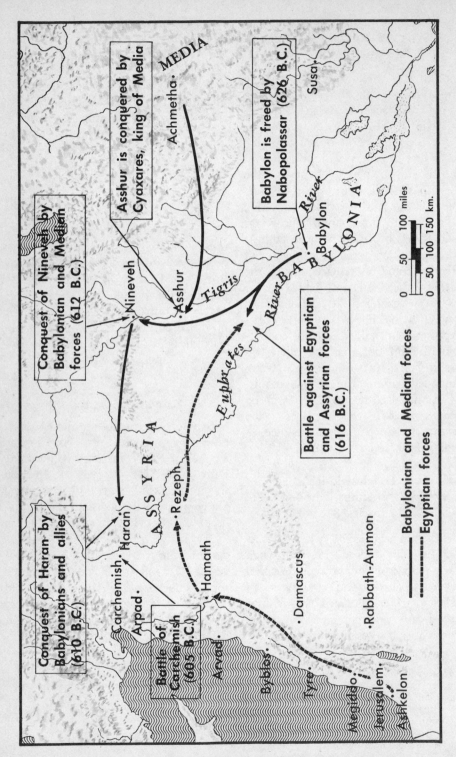

Map 17. Fall of Assyria and Rise of Babylonia

Asshur is conquered by Cyaxares, king of Media

Babylon is freed by Nabopolassar (626 B.C.)

Conquest of Nineveh by Babylonian and Median forces (612 B.C.)

Battle against Egyptian and Assyrian forces (616 B.C.)

Conquest of Haran by Babylonians and allies (610 B.C.)

Battle of Carchemish (605 B.C.)

MEDIA

Achmetha.

Susa

BABYLONIA

Babylon

River

Nineveh

Asshur.

Tigris

Euphrates River

A S S Y R I A

Rezeph.

Haran.

Carchemish.

Arpad.

Hamath.

Damascus.

Rabbath-Ammon.

Arvad.

Byblos.

Tyre.

Megiddo.

Jerusalem.

Ashkelon.

Babylonian and Median forces
Egyptian forces

100 miles
150 km.

0   50   100
0   50   100

when the two sides clashed in the Battle of Carchemish on the Euphrates. Nebuchadnezzar now led Babylon, for his aged father was confined with illness at home. The young Babylonian displayed his genius by sending the Egyptians reeling in headlong defeat. Necho fell back to Hamath on the Orontes River, hoping to regroup; but Nebuchadnezzar gave him no opportunity as he followed hard after him and all but annihilated what remained of the Egyptian force.[99] Thus, Nebuchadnezzar won the control his father had desired, and Babylonia became the new world leader.

The "whole of the land of Hatti,"[100] meaning all Syria and Palestine to the border of Egypt, now lay exposed to the new conqueror. All he had to do was assert control, which he began doing immediately, moving as far south as Jerusalem, where he forced the submission of Jehoiakim and of other kings of the area.

As Nebuchadnezzar moved through the newly won country, he desired not only the submission of leading cities but also the procurement of able young men, whom he planned to relocate in Babylon as prospective government personnel. It is likely that each city was forced to give him their finest. Among those from Jerusalem[101] were Daniel and his three friends—Hananiah, Mishael, and Azariah.[102] While involved in this activity, Nebuchadnezzar was suddenly interrupted by the death of his ailing father, Nabopolassar, in August of 605 B.C., and quickly returned to Babylon to receive the crown as Nebuchadnezzar II.

The following fall saw him back in the west again, however, continuing the work. Mentioned by him as a major prize during the summer of 604 B.C. was the Philistine city of Ashkelon, which was taken by him after a fierce struggle (see Jer. 47:5–7).[103] Subsequently, in 601 B.C., Nebuchadnezzar moved against Egypt and was met by Necho near the border. Both sides lost heavily in the engagement, and neither could claim victory. As a result, Nebuchadnezzar was repulsed and had to return to Babylon.

6. Jehoiachin and the capture of Jerusalem in 597 B.C. (2 Kings 24:8–16; 2 Chronicles 36:9–10)

Nebuchadnezzar's withdrawal gave only brief respite to the region, however; for in 597 B.C. he returned to bring severe devastation. The cause was rebellion on the part of Jehoiakim, who

---

[99] Besides references in n. 93, see for details, Thiele, *MNHK,* pp. 22–27; D. N. Freedman, *BA* 19 (1956): 50–60; Albright, *BASOR* 143 (1956): 28–33; H. Tadmor, *JNES* 15 (1956): 226–30; J. P. Hyatt, *JBL* 75 (1956): 277–84.

[100] Nebuchadnezzar's own designation; see *DOTT,* p. 79.

[101] This was the third year of Jehoiakim (Dan. 1:1) on the basis of Tishri reckoning, but the fourth year (Jer. 46:2) on Nisan reckoning; see Thiele, *MNHK,* 165–66.

[102] The seventy-year captivity of Judah (Jer. 25:11–12; 29:10) is figured from this time of Daniel's deportation rather than that of either 597 or 586 B.C., when many more people were taken. The return occurred in 538–537 B.C. Many young men were taken at this time (Dan. 1:1–6). This instance of captivity is commonly called the first aspect of the total captivity, with those of 597 and 586 B.C. called the second and third aspects.

[103] See *DOTT,* pp. 79–80; and H. L. Ginsberg, *BASOR* 111 (1948): 24–27, who discuss the probability of an Aramaic letter discovered in Egypt, pleading for help from the Pharaoh, having been written by the king of Ashkelon at this time. But see A. Malamat, "The Last Kings of Judah and the Fall of Jerusalem," in 1ed *Israel Exploration Journal* 18 (1968): 142–43, for a contrary opinion.

now looked once again to Egypt for support (2 Kings 24:1).[104] For a time the Babylonian monarch sent only contingents of his army, reinforced by Aramean, Moabite, and Ammonite troops (2 Kings 24:2; Jer. 35:11), to keep the revolt in check; but he finally saw the need of a major campaign and came himself.

In December of 598 B.C., Nebuchadnezzar left Babylon, and the same month Jehoiakim died in Jerusalem.[105] Jehoiakim's eighteen-year-old son,[106] Jehoiachin, replaced him on the throne and received the blow of the Babylonian attack the following March, 597 B.C. Egyptian support hoped for by Jehoiakim did not materialize. Jehoiachin was taken captive to Babylon, along with the queen mother, princes, servants, and booty. The prophet Ezekiel was taken at this time, too (Ezek. 1:1–3), and with him ten thousand leading citizens, including a thousand craftsmen and smiths (2 Kings 24:11–16).

7. Zedekiah and the captivity of 586 B.C.
(2 Kings 24:17–25:21; 2 Chronicles 36:11–21; Jeremiah 39:1–10)

Nebuchadnezzar proceeded to install Jehoiachin's uncle, Mattaniah, Josiah's third son, on the throne. He was twenty-one at the time, fifteen years younger than Jehoiakim, the oldest of the three sons. Nebuchadnezzar changed his name to Zedekiah, as Pharaoh Necho had done in giving Eliakim the name Jehoiakim. The people of Judah seem never to have accepted Zedekiah as their true king, however. Instead they still ascribed this honor to Jehoiachin, though in captivity.[107] As a result, and because of Zedekiah's own poor judgment and general inability, his reign was beset by continual agitation and unrest. Ultimately Zedekiah gave ear to the anti-Babylonian voices among his advisors. In view of Nebuchadnezzar's earlier harsh treatment of Jerusalem, one would think that the Judean people would have remained docile, but they did not.

a. Revolt against Babylon (2 Kings 24:20; 2 Chron. 36:13). A strong anti-Babylonian group in Jerusalem brought pressure for the revolt and urged Zedekiah to look again to Egypt for help. A new coalition was being formed by Edom, Moab, Ammon, and Phoenicia (Jer. 27:1–3); and this Jerusalem group wished Judah to join. False prophets aided their cause in declaring that God had already broken the yoke

---

[104]See Wiseman, *Chronicles,* pp. 26–28.

[105]The exact time is established by comparing the Babylonian Chronicle with 2 Kings 24:6, 8. Jeremiah's scathing predictions as to the nature of Jehoiakim's death and burial (Jer. 22:18–19; 36:27–32), may suggest that he was killed in a battle with one of the marauding bands and in a situation which prevented a normal, honorable burial. It is also possible, indeed likely, that he was assassinated by his own people in an attempt to appease Nebuchadnezzar.

[106]Second Kings 24:8. Second Chronicles 36:9 gives only eight years, but this must be due to a copyist's error, simply omitting a *yodh,* which is a number designated "ten."

[107]Evidence exists from the discovery of jar handles, both at Tell Beit Mirsim (possibly Debir) and Tell er-Rumeileh (probably Beth-shemesh), stamped with the words, "Eliakim, steward of Jehoiachin," which indicates that royal property was still thought to belong to Jehoiachin in Zedekiah's time. Then, in Babylon, documents bearing the title for Jehoiachin, "king of Judah," have been found in the palace, showing that he was resident there, in keeping with 2 Kings 25:27–30, and suggesting that he was still considered Judah's king. For text, see *ANET,* p. 308. For discussion, see H. G. May, *AJSL* 56 (1939): 146–48; Albright, "King Jehoiachin in Exile," *BA* 5 (1942): 49–55.

of Babylon and that within two years Judah's captives would return home to Jerusalem (Jer. 28:2–4). In opposition, Jeremiah denounced this message declaring it false and urging continued acceptance of Babylonian lordship (Jer. 27:1–22).

Two other developments outside Judah helped fan revolutionary flames in Zedekiah's fourth year: in Egypt, Necho was succeeded by Psammetichus II, and a minor rebellion was staged in Babylon itself. Still, however, Zedekiah was not persuaded to listen to the anti-Babylonians. Instead he sent a representative to Nebuchadnezzar in Babylon (Jer. 29:3; 51:59)—perhaps even going himself—to express Judah's loyalty.

But five years later Zedekiah chose to revolt, and he looked to Egypt for support. The details of this alliance are lacking, but it is certain that some formal pact had been made with Egypt at the time.[108] Hophra succeeded his father, Psammetichus II, as Pharaoh of Egypt in 588 B.C., and he was even more aggressive in furthering a policy of Asian intervention. As a result, early in 588 B.C., Nebuchadnezzar once more marched to the west,[109] and his army laid siege to Jerusalem. The siege was lifted temporarily when the Egyptians sought to honor their alliance by sending troops, but apparently the Babylonians had little trouble in meeting and inflicting defeat on the force before it was able to reach those besieged.

Nebuchadnezzar's army was soon back outside Jerusalem's walls.

b. Jeremiah's suffering at the hands of his countrymen. During these months, Jeremiah suffered great hardship at the hands of his fellow Judeans. At the time of the temporary lifting of the siege, he gave due warning that the Babylonians would soon be back and was promptly imprisoned by the Jerusalem princes (Jer. 37:11–16). The worried Zedekiah visited him there, received further prediction that Jerusalem would fall to the enemy, and released the prophet to the freedom of the court of the guard (Jer. 37:17–21).

The princes, however, not happy with this, once more forced his confinement, only this time in a miry cistern (Jer. 38:1–6). How long he was held in this wretched place is not stated, but finally the king permitted one of his servants, Ebed-melech, to draw him out (Jer. 38:7–13). Despite the persecution, however, Jeremiah faithfully continued to give God's warnings and advice.

c. Fall of Jerusalem (2 Kings 25:1–21; 2 Chron. 36:17–20; Jer. 39:1–10). In accordance with Jeremiah's warning, the city fell to the Babylonians in July of 586 B.C.[110] Zedekiah tried to flee but was captured near Jericho and brought to Nebuchadnezzar's headquarters at Riblah. Zedekiah's sons were slain before his eyes, and then his own eyes were put out.

---

[108] One of the Lachish Letters indicates an official visit to Egypt by "the commander of the host, Coniah son of Elnathan"; see *ANET*, p. 322.

[109] He established headquarters at Riblah on the Orontes River, north of Palestine. He may have sent army contingents in various directions from there. He besieged Tyre from 587 to 574 B.C. The Lachish Letters indicate devastation all through Judean cities; see *DOTT*, pp. 212–17. Ammon may have been a target, too; see Ezekiel 21:18–32.

[110] Siege began in the tenth month of Zedekiah's ninth year (January 588 B.C.) and continued until the fourth month of his eleventh year (July 586 B.C.), a total of eighteen months.

He, with many of the people, was taken captive to Babylon, while Jerusalem suffered severe damage at the hands of Nebuzaradan, an officer of Nebuchadnezzar. The complete destruction of the great temple built by Solomon, which had stood for four centuries, made such an impact that it is still commemorated in synagogues today.

According to the Lachish Letters,[111] devastation was experienced through all Judah at this time. In one letter, an officer stationed at an observation post writes to the Lachish commander that the signal of Azekah can no longer be seen, which suggests that this city had just fallen to the Babylonian forces. Jeremiah indicates that Azekah and Lachish were two of the last cities to remain before the fearful onslaught (Jer. 34:6–7). The Babylonian monarch intended that Judah should never again revolt.

---

[111] These are twenty-one ostraca, dating from this time, which were found in the gate of Lachish. At least some of these are military correspondence to the governor of Lachish. Besides the reference included in n. 108, see Albright, *BASOR* 82 (1941): 18–24, for discussion.

CHAPTER FIFTEEN

EXILE AND RETURN

2 Kings 25: 22–30; 2 Chronicles 36:22–23; Ezra; Nehemiah; Esther;
Jeremiah 40–44; Daniel 1–6

The fall of Jerusalem and the exile of her leading citizens brought an abrupt change in the national life of Judah. The temple, which had been the center of religious activity, was now destroyed. Jerusalem had served as the center of civic life, but now it lay in ruins. The more able and influential of its citizens had been deported to Babylon, which left less capable people to make decisions and form policies. But though life did change, Judah's history continued both in exile and in the Promised Land. The deportation was partial, and a populace, made up of the common people, carried on.

A. DEVELOPMENTS IN JUDAH (2 Kings 25:22–26; Jeremiah 40–44)

1. General situation

Like the Assyrians before them, the Babylonians took the influential people of conquered nations as hostages. With the leadership, and especially the sons of the leadership, in captivity, the conquered nation was much less likely to rebel. Of further advantage to the conqueror was the opportunity to train the captive sons in the thought and statecraft of Babylon, rendering them valuable both as hostages and eventually as members of the bureaucracy of empire.

The difference between Assyria's policy and Babylon's is significant. The Assyrians mixed populations, deporting Israel in 722 B.C. and repopulating their land with conquered people from other parts of the empire. Those Israelites left in the land after the fall of Samaria intermarried with the non-Israelite deportees.[1] Judah was at least spared this temptation during its exile.

Judah was now a province of Babylon. She no longer had her own king, but was ruled by a governor appointed by the foreign authority. The first

---

[1] The Samaritans descended from mixed marriages in Israel. As for Judah, some intermarriage had come into existence by the time of Ezra's return to Jerusalem (458 B.C.); but this was with neighboring peoples, not imported foreigners (Ezra 9:1–2).

governor was Gedaliah, son of Ahi-kam,[2] grandson of Shaphan[3] (2 Kings 25:22). With Jerusalem destroyed, Gedaliah established a new capital at Mizpah.[4] Perhaps he was active earlier in the court of Judah during the reign of Zedekiah. A seal found at Lachish and bearing the inscription, "Belonging to Gedaliah who is over the house,"[5] is archaeologically dated to the time of the general destruction of 586 B.C. If reference is to the same Gedaliah, the man had filled a supervisory position in Zedekiah's palace.

The people governed by Gedaliah are called "the poorest people of the land" and were left to cultivate the soil (2 Kings 25:12). Their number had been greatly reduced,[6] both by the captivity and death from the wars. Many had died in the war of 597 B.C., and Jehoiachin and ten thousand captives (2 Kings 24:14) had then been deported. Many more had perished in the long siege of 588 to 586 B.C., and again a large number had been taken to Babylon. Excavation has revealed that the Babylonian destruction reached all across Judah, for numerous cities show evidence of being burned at this time. Lachish, for instance, gives evidence of devastation at both 597 and 586 B.C. The land, both in size of population and general appearance, little resembled what it had been only a few years before.

2. Assassination of Gedaliah (2 Kings 25:23–26; Jeremiah 40:7–41:18)

Gedaliah had been governor for only two months[7] when he was murdered by Ishmael, a member of the royal family. Ishmael was among a number who had fled from Judah at the first approach of the Babylonian army and taken residence in Ammon. When Gedaliah was made governor in Mizpah, Ishmael with others returned to Judah and professed loyalty to the new regime. Gedaliah was warned by his military aide, Johanan, that this profession was false, but Gedaliah refused to believe him.

Then Ishmael, with the backing of Baalis, king of Ammon (Jer. 40:14), both of whom were apparently jealous of Gedaliah, successfully plotted Gedaliah's death and also killed a small garrison of Babylonians at Mizpah and some Judean assistants. So secretly was the treachery carried out that it remained unknown outside the governor's house for two days. On the second day, Ishmael and his men found it necessary to kill a visiting group of pilgrims—after which they fled in haste for Ammon, apparently fearing now that news of the bloody action might become known. Ishmael took a number of hostages, including daughters of Zedekiah, who had been entrusted to

---

[2] He had once saved Jeremiah from death (Jer. 26:24).

[3] Probably the same as Josiah's scribe, who was active in the reformation movement of Josiah's time (2 Kings 22:3).

[4] For location, see p. 189n.82.

[5] For discussion, see H. G. May, *AJSL* 56 (1939): 146–48.

[6] Albright's figure of less than twenty thousand must be too low, however; see Albright, *BP,* pp. 49, 59–60, 62–63. Others suggest a less extensive devastation. P. R. Ackroyd, *Exile and Restoration* (Philadelphia: Westminster, 1968), pp. 20–31.

[7] Killed in the seventh month (2 Kings 25:25). Though the year is not given, the implication is strong that this was the same year in which the destruction had taken place, 586 B.C. Jerusalem had fallen in the fifth month (2 Kings 25:8).

Gedaliah's care and whom Ishmael for some reason had not killed.

At this point, Johanan, the military leader, who had earlier warned Gedaliah, became aware of the atrocity and gave pursuit. He caught Ishmael's force at Gibeon, where he succeeded in liberating the hostages; but Ishmael and eight of his men made good their escape to Ammon.

3. Jeremiah gives counsel (Jeremiah 40:1–6; 42:1–43:3)

The Babylonian general had, at Jeremiah's own request, left him in the land. Given his choice of going to Babylon or remaining in the land, he had decided to stay. He took up residence in Mizpah, where he could be near the new governor, Gedaliah. Upon the assassination of the governor, Jeremiah was consulted by Johanan and his companions, who needed advice now that the Babylonians had been given cause for retaliation. The people feared further reprisal, which they believed would come as a result of this slaying of the Babylonian governor and soldiers left to keep order. They asked Jeremiah to seek word from God and promised to follow whatever the word might be.

Ten days later Jeremiah received God's revelation, which instructed the people to remain in the land and not to fear, for the Babylonians would not retaliate. Jeremiah communicated this good information to the people, warning particularly against seeking shelter in Egypt. The people, however, now broke their promise and refused to accept the word he brought. Instead they accused him of speaking falsely, followed the dictates of their own hearts, and did exactly what he told them not to do. They made plans to go to Egypt.[8]

4. Descent to Egypt (Jeremiah 43:4–44:30)

The number of Judeans who made the trip was relatively large. Jeremiah 43:5–6 speaks of the group as those who had returned from surrounding countries, as had Ishmael, and those who had been placed under Gedaliah's charge. Jeremiah went as well, certainly against his will, but likely in an effort to keep God's Word before the people as best he could. The land of Judah may have been quite depopulated after the group had left. The migrants came to Tahpanhes,[9] in the eastern Delta of Egypt, where apparently all took up residence for a time. There Jeremiah, at God's direction, hid stones in the pavement at the entry of a royal palace, and he delivered God's prediction that Nebuchadnezzar would one day conquer and establish his pavilion on that very place (Jer. 43:8–13).[10]

From Jeremiah 44:1, 15, it appears

---

[8] Trust had been placed in Egypt before, always with disappointment, but never had there been a mass flight there. Perhaps the scarcity of numbers contributed to the unwise decision.

[9] Identified as Tell Defenneh, located twenty-seven miles south southwest of Port Said. The same consonantal spelling, *thpnhs,* has been found in a Phoenician letter in Egypt of the sixth century (see A. Dupont-Sommer, *PEQ* 81 [1949]: 52–57). Petrie excavated the site in 1883–1884 and discovered the foundation of a castle, perhaps the one before which Jeremiah buried the stones; see Barton, *AB,* p. 28.

[10] The prediction was fulfilled. A British Museum tablet tells of a successful campaign by Nebuchadnezzar in his thirty-seventh year (568–567) against Pharaoh Amasis. Amasis had replaced Pharaoh Hophra who had been defeated by Nebuchadnezzar in 572 B.C. Now when Amasis rebelled, Nebuchadnezzar marched into Egypt and inflicted a further defeat. See Wiseman, *Chronicles,* p. 94; also Finegan, *LAP,* p. 131.

that Judeans had taken up residence throughout Egypt. Jeremiah warned them that, because of continuing unfaithfulness to God, none would be permitted to return to Judah (vv. 12–14). An extrabiblical source indicates that a colony of Jewish mercenaries lived in a military settlement on the island of Elephantine, at the first cataract of the Nile in southern Egypt. This evidence comes from the well-known papyri found on the island of Elephantine. The papyri date from near the close of the fifth century.[11]

B. THE BABYLONIAN PERIOD (605–539)

The time when the Judeans were taken captive was that of the great Neo-Babylonian Empire, when Babylonia reached its zenith of world influence. Nebuchadnezzar fashioned this empire early in his rule; and it continued until 539 B.C., when Persian forces under Cyrus the Great took control from his heirs. Judean captives lived in the vicinity of Babylon from near the beginning of this time and remained well into the Middle Ages.

1. Nebuchadnezzar (605–562)

Nebuchadnezzar ruled forty-three years and maintained his country's supreme position as long as he lived. For good reason the image dream interpreted by Daniel depicted him as the "head of gold" (Dan. 2:38), for he stands as one of the great rulers of ancient time. Those who succeeded him were not equal to the task of holding what he had conquered. Under their rule the country decayed from within, outlasting Nebuchadnezzar by a scant twenty-three years.

a. Military activity. Nebuchadnezzar was proficient in warfare. His conquests through the time of Jerusalem's destruction have been noted, but he did more. The siege of Tyre, apparently begun during the same campaign in which Jerusalem fell, was continued for thirteen years. At the end of this period, he received the city's acknowledgment of Babylonian suzerainty, though he does not appear to have actually taken the strong island fortress.[12] Jeremiah states (52:30) that Nebuchadnezzar forced another deportation from Judah (582 B.C.),[13] and the same year he campaigned successfully in Coele-Syria, Moab, and Ammon.[14]

Then in 568 B.C. he invaded Egypt shortly after Pharaoh Amasis had replaced Pharaoh Hophra.[15] The time was one of weakness and confusion in Egypt, and the Babylonian ruler took advantage of it. Nebuchadnezzar's goal does not seem to have been permanent conquest, however, but only punitive action for Egypt's past interference in Syria-Palestine. He was successful, for peaceful relations existed between the two great powers in ensuing years.

---

[11] For discussion and references, see p. 370.

[12] A prediction by Ezekiel (26:1–14) finds partial fulfillment in this Babylonian campaign. The complete fulfillment came later, however, when Alexander the Great of Greece drew the remains of old Tyre into the Mediterranean to make a causeway out to the fortress on the island offshore.

[13] Jeremiah states that 745 persons were taken this time, probably along with others from Syria, Moab, and Ammon, whom Nebuchadnezzar also defeated the same year.

[14] See Josephus (*Antiquities* 10.9.7). An undated text of Nebuchadnezzar, speaking of a campaign into the Lebanon mountains, may refer to the same time; see *ANET*, p. 307.

[15] See above, n.10.

b. Building activity. Nebuchadnezzar was an active and successful builder. The words of Daniel 4:30 are apt, as the Babylonian ruler is quoted as saying, "Is not this the great Babylon I have built as the royal residence, by my mighty power and for the glory of my majesty?" He constructed an intricate system of fortifications, including Babylon's own defenses and a chain of fortresses both north and south of the capital city. He built temples, palaces, canals, and streets. A processional avenue leading to the city's sacred area was lined with brightly colored, enameled brick, adorned with rows of bulls and dragons in bas relief. The street led through the famous gate of Ishtar, similarly decorated.[16] In the sacred area proper was the grand ziggurat that Nebuchadnezzar rebuilt from a former day,[17] and the great temple of Marduk, likewise restored.

Most famous of all were the hanging gardens, built in terraces by Nebuchadnezzar to please his Median queen, who missed her native mountains. The Greeks were so impressed by the gardens that they classed them as one of the seven wonders of the world.

2. Nebuchadnezzar's successors (562–539)[18]

None of the successors of Nebuchadnezzar could match his achievements, and Babylonia's glory began to fade soon after his death. He was succeeded by his son, Amel-marduk, who ruled only two years (562–560). The Bible mentions him (Evil-merodach) as the one who released Jehoiachin from prison and gave the deposed Judean king a place of privilege at the Babylonian court (2 Kings 25:27–30; Jer. 52:31–34).

Amel-marduk was murdered by his brother-in-law, Neriglissar (Nergal-shar-usur), who was then enthroned in August 560 B.C. The identity of this man with the Nergal-sharezer of Jeremiah 39:3, 13—who, as the official (*rab mag*) under Nebuchadnezzar, had played a part in releasing Jeremiah from prison in 586 B.C.—is generally accepted. If correct, he was at least middle-aged at the time of his accession. As king, he is known mainly for building activity and a major military venture across the Taurus Mountains. In the latter, he was successful at first, but then suffered defeat and withdrew to Babylon in 556 B.C., shortly before his death. He was succeeded by his young son, Labashi-Marduk, who was assassinated only a few months later by a group of courtiers, including Nabonidus, who now seized the throne.

3. Nabonidus (556–539)

Nabonidus (Nabu-na'id), son of an Aramean nobleman from Haran,[19] was probably the most capable ruler following Nebuchadnezzar.[20] Of priestly line-

---

[16] See *ANEP*, figs. 760–62, for pictures.

[17] A. Parrot reconstructs this ziggurat as 298 feet square and 300 feet high, rising in seven stages. A. Parrot, *The Tower of Babel* (London: SCM, 1955), pp. 46–51.

[18] For details of this chronology, see R. A. Parker and W. H. Dubberstein, *Babylonian Chronology, 626 B.C.–A.D. 45* (Chicago: University of Chicago Press, 1942).

[19] His mother may have been Nitocris, widowed wife of Nebuchadnezzar; see Sidney Smith, *Babylonian Historical Texts* (London: 1924), pp. 37, 43, for discussion. Another view is that he may have married this Nitocris, who was either the widowed wife of Nebuchadnezzar or his daughter, see Dougherty, *Nabonidus and Belshazzar* (New Haven: 1929), pp. 59–60. Either view would explain how Nebuchadnezzar could be called the father of Belshazzar (Dan. 5:2).

[20] Herodotus states that he had been the Babylonian representative in 585 B.C. when a peace treaty

age and a devotee of the moon god, Sin, he gave himself to antiquarian religious interests. He rebuilt the temple of Sin in Haran, excavated temple sites in Babylonia, and restored long abandoned rites. He did not hesitate to innovate religious practices, many of which were not pleasing, however, to the establishment of the Marduk priesthood. His devotion to Sin, rather than Marduk, indeed, caused marked irritation and finally outright opposition.

Though not given to military activity, Nabonidus did make two campaigns early in his reign: one against Cilicia (554 B.C.) and another against Syria (553 B.C.). An unusual act was his transfer of residence to Tema, southeast of Edom in the Arabian desert. The reason is obscure, though it likely had to do with his religious interests again. He remained in Tema for a period of ten years, leaving the kingdom in the hands of his able son, Belshazzar (Bel-shar-uzur). Actual kingship was entrusted to the young man, which coincides with Belshazzar's portrayal in the Book of Daniel.[21]

In Babylon, with Nabonidus absent, the annual New Year celebrations were suspended for several years. Always of great importance to the people, their omission stirred serious discontent among more than just the Marduk priests. In 539 B.C., Nabonidus returned to Babylon and ordered the festivities reinstated but apparently too late to offset the harm already done. By this time, Nabonidus was considered by many people as unfit to rule. This prompted a spirit of revolt and made the time ripe for the conquest of Cyrus.

C. CAPTIVE JUDAH

1. Daniel
(Daniel 1–6)

One of the most significant of the Judean captives was Daniel, who wrote the biblical book bearing his name.

a. Daniel's honor. Daniel, along with his three friends[22] and others of his age,[23] was taken to Babylon in the summer of 605 B.C. Nebuchadnezzar's reason was not to inflict hardship but to educate these young men, that he might pick from them the most capable to staff various offices of his kingdom (Dan. 1:4). Before three years[24] had passed, Daniel, as a result of interpreting a dream for Nebuchadnezzar (Dan. 2:1–45), was elevated to the important position[25] of chief of the "wise men," upon whom the king depended for

---

between the Medes and Lydians had been drawn (Herodotus 1.74; see R. P. Dougherty, *Nabonidus and Belshazzar* [New Haven: 1929], p. 36).

[21] Daniel 5:1–31 tells the story of Daniel's reading the miraculous writing on the palace wall for Belshazzar. For this he was made "third ruler in the kingdom" (5:29 KJV), suiting the fact that Belshazzar was himself the second ruler. For pertinent texts of Nabonidus, see *ANET*, pp. 312–15; *DOTT*, pp. 89–91.

[22] All four were given Babylonian names: Daniel, Belteshazzar; Hananiah, Shadrach; Mishael, Meshach; and Azariah, Abednego.

[23] Probably in their middle teens, in view of the purpose for which they were brought and the advanced age to which Daniel lived (at least until 536 B.C.).

[24] During Nebuchadnezzar's second year (Dan. 2:1). Since Nebuchadnezzar was crowned in September 605 B.C., immediately after his return to Babylon, his first year would have begun in the spring (Nisan) of 604 and his second in the spring of 603. Daniel's elevation came, then, sometime between the spring of 603 and the spring of 602 B.C.

[25] The plan had been for the young men to be educated for a minimum of three years (Dan. 1:5), but apparently David was awarded his position prior to that time. However, training may have continued.

counsel.[26] Daniel apparently retained this position for a long time, because years later Nebuchadnezzar still referred to him as "chief of the magicians" (Dan. 4:9).[27]

Change came for Daniel, however, by the time of Belshazzar's rule, for this king needed to be reminded that Daniel was indeed available to interpret the miraculous writing on the palace wall (Dan. 5:10–12). But by this time sixty-three years had elapsed since Daniel's first appointment, and he may have held numerous positions since.

At the time of the Persian conquest of Babylon, when Daniel could not have been less than eighty years,[28] he was still retained by the new regime in a position of high responsibility. In fact, he was made one of the three presidents who superintended the respective governors of Persia's 120 provinces (Dan. 6:1–2).[29]

b. Daniel's influence. With Daniel holding these high positions at the Babylonian court, it is reasonable to assume that he was able to play a significant role in securing pleasant conditions for his captive countrymen.

Daniel may also have exerted influence to bring about the elevation of Jehoiachin to a place of honor by King Amelmarduk (2 Kings 25:27–30). This type of act toward a captive king suggests the interests of a special friend working in his behalf. Further, Daniel may have had much to do with the decree which permitted Jews to return to Palestine.[30] He held his highest position at the time of this return and could have exerted his greatest influence. It is certain that he desired this permission to be granted, for he specifically included it as a request in prayer (Dan. 9:1–19). One can imagine him broaching the idea to the Persian king and doing all that he could to encourage its realization.

2. Among the captives

a. Number. The number of persons taken captive from Judah to Babylon is difficult to determine. Only regarding the second deportation (597 B.C.) is a definite figure given: ten thousand, which included seven thousand men of might and one thousand craftsmen (2 Kings 24:14–16). Concerning the first deportation (605 B.C.), all that can

---

[26] Divination was a highly practiced art, and many methods were employed; see A. Guillaume, *Prophecy and Divination Among the Hebrews and Other Semites* (London: Hodder & Stoughton, 1938); A. Leo Oppenheim, *The Interpretation of Dreams in the Ancient Near East* (Philadelphia: Transactions of the American Philosophical Society, 1956). That Daniel, in becoming head of these wise men, did not himself practice their arts is clear from the story overall and particularly from Nebuchadnezzar's consultation with him separately when the king dreamed again in chapter 4 (vv. 7–9 especially).

[27] Since it was shortly after the dream of chapter 4 that Nebuchadnezzar, in fulfillment of the dream, became apparently demented (Dan. 4:28–37), the date must have been toward the conclusion of his forty-three-year reign.

[28] It is not likely that the age of those taken captive with Daniel was less than an average of fifteen years, which would have made him no less than eighty-one in 539 B.C.

[29] That Daniel was so retained is most remarkable in the light of a change in government and also his own advanced age. It speaks highly of Daniel's ability, but even more of God's particular blessing on him and God's desire that he continue in this place of influence.

[30] The decree was issued in Cyrus' first year (2 Chron. 36:22; Ezra 1:1) when Daniel was yet active. The fact that Cyrus permitted other captive peoples to return to their homelands also (see *ANET*, p. 316, for inscription) need not militate against this possibility. The Jews may have been the first to receive this permission, which privilege was then accorded to others as well.

Reviser's note: While it would be foolhardy to argue that Daniel's involvement in the edict of Cyrus is impossible, it should be noted that the suggestion is speculative and without corroborating evidence.

be said is that at least some other young men besides Daniel and his three friends were involved. Respecting the third deportation (586 B.C.), when Jerusalem as a city was devastated, those seized are designated as all but "the poorest people of the land" (2 Kings 25:11, 12, 21), and no doubt included the largest number.[31] That a total of many thousands were taken is indicated also by the sizable number of persons who returned from the captivity in 538 B.C., namely 42,360 (Ezra 2:64; Neh. 7:66).[32]

b. Ezekiel. Ranking with Daniel and King Jehoiachin, the prophet Ezekiel was one of the most illustrious captives. Nothing is revealed regarding him prior to captivity, but he played a significant role among the exiles. He was God's messenger among them, rebuking them for sin and comforting them with promises of deliverance. He made it clear that their captivity was in no way the result of limitation in God's power to protect them but solely a punishment permitted by Him for their sin. Positively, he declared that God would yet vindicate His sovereignty in working their deliverance and bringing retribution on their captors. Ezekiel was given a better hearing than some of his predecessors, for official elders came to him to seek counsel and hear the word of God (Ezek. 8:1; 14:1; 20:1). During the years of captivity, the people did change favorably in spiritual outlook and personal relationship to

God. In this, Ezekiel was certainly a main influence.

3. Life in Babylon

There is evidence that life for the Judean captives was comparatively pleasant; much different, surely, than the condition of bondage experienced by their ancestors in Egypt.

a. Institutions maintained. One aspect of this evidence is that some of Judah's own institutions were maintained. For instance, elders, long employed in the local government of Judah, were still active. As just noted, elders came to Ezekiel, acting as representatives of the people, to seek counsel. Also, the prophets and priests (in their respective teaching ministries) were retained; for when Jeremiah addressed a letter to the captives, he mentioned first the elders, then both prophets and priests, and finally the people generally (Jer. 29:1).

b. Freedom of movement. The captives enjoyed freedom of movement in the land. Ezekiel did, even having his own house (Ezek. 8:1). Also, the elders were at liberty to visit him there. The freedom accorded Jehoiachin, after liberation from prison by Amel-marduk, testifies similarly. He was given food and other provisions at the court for the remainder of his life and may even have been granted some authority to rule, for it is stated that he was given a "seat of honor" (throne?) above that of other kings with him in Babylon

---

[31] Jeremiah 52:30 mentions a fourth deportation as occurring in Nebuchadnezzar's twenty-third year (582 B.C.); see p. 324n.13. The smallness of the total number of captives Jeremiah lists (52:28–30) may be explained in terms of possible copyist's errors, or in terms of Jeremiah desiring to list only particular classes or groups of captives; see Keil's discussion, *KDC,* Jeremiah, 2:327–31.

[32] Not all returned either, as indicated by the large number still living in the east in Esther's day (see pp. 346).

(2 Kings 25:28). Cuneiform tablets found by Weidner[33] in Babylon agree with these biblical notations. They identify Jehoiachin as "King of the land of Judah," and indicate that he and his five sons received liberal allowances of oil and food. They state further that the sons were in the care of an attendant, suggesting that servants were actually provided for the family.[34]

c. Correspondence privileges.

Further, the Judeans had correspondence privileges, for they could write letters to friends back in Judah. Jeremiah speaks of such letters (29:25) and also wrote to the captives in Babylon himself (29:1). That communication of this kind must have been carried on is evidenced also by people in Judah knowing of Jehoiachin's status, so that they were able to hope for his return as king (Jer. 28:3–4).

d. Employment opportunities.

Perhaps the most significant evidence comes from indications of favorable employment opportunities being open to the captives. One is found in the type of person Nebuchadnezzar chose to deport. He took craftsmen and artisans, particularly in the captivity of 597 B.C. (2 Kings 24:14–16). Apparently Nebuchadnezzar planned to put them to work in skilled trades. The other is found in the many business tablets discovered at Nippur on the canal Kabari, which contain Jewish names in a context showing that they were active in business: renting, buying, and selling.[35] The tablets date from the fifth century[36] and so represent the Jewish situation after the exiles had been in Babylonia for more than a hundred years, but they imply that similar conditions had existed for some time.

e. Fertile land on which to live.

Still further, Jews were permitted to live on fine, fertile land. Many resided along or near the river Chebar (Ezek. 1:1, 3; 3:15, 23; et al.), which is likely the same as the canal Kabari (*nari kabari*, meaning "great river"), known from one of the texts just mentioned. It flowed out of the Euphrates above Babylon, passed Nippur, and then entered the Euphrates again. The city Tel-abib, where Ezekiel at one time remained with resident captives for seven days (Ezek. 3:15), was on the canal. Modern Tilabub, near which Israelite pottery had been discovered, probably marks the site. The canal supplied irrigation for a rich farming area,[37] which means that Jews were favored by an advantageous land for farming, whether for themselves or in working for others.

f. Still a punishment.

That the captivity was intended as a punishment from God need not militate against the pleasantness of this picture. The experi-

---

[33] E. F. Weidner, *Jojachin, Konig von Juda, in babylonischen Keilschrifttexten* (Melanges syriens offerts a Monsieur Rene Dussand, II, Paris, 1939). The texts date from the tenth to the thirty-fifth year of Nebuchadnezzar. Three texts are reproduced in *ANET,* p. 308.

[34] For discussion, see William F. Albright, "King Joiachin in Exile," *BA* 5 (1942): 49–55.

[35] Found in the ruins of a business house, Murashu Sons. Many are in the form of contracts, showing names of participants in business transactions. See H. V. Hilprecht and A. T. Clay, *Babylonian Expedition of the University of Pennsylvania,* ser. A, vols. 9–10, 1893, 1904; *ANET,* pp. 221–22; *DOTT,* pp. 95–96.

[36] During the reigns of the Persian kings Artaxerxes I (464–423) and Darius II (423–404).

[37] See G. Contenau, *Everyday Life in Babylon and Assyria,* English trans. (New York: St. Martin's Press, 1954), pp. 41–43.

ence did serve as a punishment, if only because the people had been uprooted from their homes and were forced to endure the humiliation that comes with even the best of captivities. This sense of humiliation would have been felt most keenly at the beginning of the period, probably the time when Psalm 137 was written, speaking as it does of weeping by the rivers of Babylon. The false prophets, who urged rebellion against Babylon (Jer. 29:4–10), very likely were more vocal in the earlier years as well. Jeremiah urged them, and the captives in general, to accept their status and make their lives as pleasant as possible—in keeping with the apparent ease that did result.

D. THE PERSIAN PERIOD

Old Testament prophets had predicted not only the captivity of Judah but also its restoration to the Promised Land. The duration of the Exile was set by Jeremiah at seventy years (25:11–12; 29:10). The end of that period was marked by a change in world leadership that saw the short-lived Babylonian Empire collapse before the armies of Persia. The next two hundred years of Judean history would pass under the domination of this new power.

1. Conquest of Babylon

a. Preliminary victories of Cyrus. Persia's rapid rise to power, under the brilliant leadership of Cyrus the Great (559–530),[38] was climaxed by the conquest of Babylonia. His father was Cambyses I, the vassal king of Anshan under Astyages (the Mede). When Cyrus took the throne on his father's death, he consolidated the various Persian tribes under his rule and began to plot the overthrow of the Median king, who was also his grandfather. Nabonidus, last king of Babylon, had ambitions to rebuild the temple of the moon god Sin at Haran, and he entered into an alliance with Cyrus to take the city out of the control of the Medes. With the assistance of Babylon, Cyrus rebelled against Astyages and by 550 B.C. had added Media to his burgeoning empire.

Nabonidus now began to fear Cyrus and made alliances with both Amasis of Egypt (569–525) and Croesus of Lydia (560–546). To counter this threat Cyrus marched, virtually unopposed, through northern Mesopotamia and into Cappadocia (eastern Asia Minor), where he fought an indecisive battle against Croesus. Croesus withdrew to his capital, Sardis, where he intended to wait out the winter, assuming Cyrus would not attack until spring. Cyrus, by making a forced march through the harsh mountain winter, caught Croesus off guard and without the assistance of his absent allies (547–546). In their decisive engagement, Cyrus neutralized the Lydian cavalry by stationing his camels in a forward position so that the unfamiliar scent of them would make the enemy horses unmanageable. With his victory over Croesus, Cyrus extended his boundaries as far west as the Aegean Sea.

b. Fall of Babylon. With Nabonidus's one ally defeated, and the other inactive,[39] Babylon was soon to fall before

---

[38] Predicted by name a century and a half earlier by Isaiah (44:28; 45:1) as one who would conquer rapidly and would be God's "servant" (KJV) in effecting deliverance for the Jews.

[39] It is likely that the agreement with Egypt now failed, Pharaoh Amasis wanting no part of it any longer.

the mighty conqueror. At first, after returning from the western sweep, Cyrus spent time enlarging his eastern boundary as far as India.[40] But in 539 B.C. he marched on the main prize, Babylon, which now stood alone against him. The people of Babylon, as well as the priests of Marduk, wasted none of their loyalty on Nabonidus, who had alienated them with his religious innovations and cavalier disregard for their sensibilities. They were eager for a change. Cyrus was quite ready to oblige them, though how much of the discontent was known to him is uncertain. In any case, his task was remarkably easy.[41]

The decisive engagement was not fought at Babylon but at Opis on the Tigris to the north, where Cyrus was victorious. His officer, Ugbaru,[42] was then able to take Babylon itself without a fight. This was in October 539 B.C. Nabonidus himself, who had earlier fled before the oncoming Persian force, was taken prisoner shortly after. Cyrus personally entered Babylon a few weeks later, and was actually welcomed as liberator by both the Marduk priests and the general populace.[43]

The Persian monarch treated Babylon with consideration. The city was not looted, nor were the religious or civil institutions greatly changed. The result was that a transfer of allegiance to him was brought about with a minimum of resentment or disturbance. With this conquest of Babylonia completed, Cyrus held sway over more land than any ruler before him: from the Aegean Sea to India.

2. Persian rulers[44]

Cyrus ruled as supreme monarch for nine years following this Babylonian victory.[45] He appears to have been as skillful in rule as in conquest, knowing when to be firm and when to be charitable, so that friend and foe alike admired him. Finally, in 530 B.C., while leading his army into the far north, he was fatally wounded. His body was returned to Pasargadae, the Persian capital, for burial.

---

[40] See A. T. Olmstead, *History of the Persian Empire* (Chicago: University of Chicago Press, 1948), pp. 45–49; R. Ghirshman, *Iran from the Earliest Times to the Islamic Conquest,* trans. from French (Baltimore: Penguin, 1954), p. 131.

[41] Important inscriptions describing the occasion exist from both Cyrus (Cyrus cylinder) and from Nabonidus (Nabonidus Chronicle), and they agree in basic facts. For Cyrus' record, see *ANET,* pp. 315–16; and Thomas, *DOTT,* pp. 92–94. For Nabonidus' record, see *ANET,* p. 306; and *DOTT,* pp. 81–83.

[42] John C. Whitcomb finds reason for distinguishing between the Ugbaru, who, in Nabonidus' inscription, took Babylon for Cyrus, and the Gubaru, whom Cyrus appointed governor of Babylon sometime later. Many scholars equate the two under the general name, Gobryas. But in this same inscription of Nabonidus, Ugbaru is said to have died on the eleventh day of the month, Arahshammu, which was only a matter of days after the fall of Babylon, whereas Gubaru is mentioned in numerous other texts as ruling as governor in Babylon for several years. Whitcomb identifies this Gubaru (Gobryas) with Darius the Mede, mentioned several times in the Book of Daniel (5:31; 6:1, 2, 3, 6, 7; et al.). See Whitcomb, *Darius the Mede* (Grand Rapids: Eerdmans, 1959). Another view, suggested by D. J. Wiseman, states that Darius may have been Cyrus himself; see Wiseman, "The Last Days of Babylon," *Christianity Today* 2 (November 1957): 7–10.

[43] Neither Cyrus nor Nabonidus mention Belshazzar in their reports to help us know how to fit the story of Daniel 5 into this conquest. Belshazzar's death may have come when Gobryas first entered Babylon in October 539 B.C., or it may have come somewhat later when the sacred citadel fell.

[44] For details, see A. T. Olmstead, *Persian Empire,* pp. 45–49; or R. Ghirshman, *Iran,* p. 131.

[45] Whitcomb argues that Gubaru (Gobryas) ruled the province of Babylon all during Cyrus' nine years and even during the first five years of Cambyses; Whitcomb, *Darius,* pp. 15–16, 23–24.

a. Cambyses (530–522). Cyrus was succeeded by his son, Cambyses II, who had acted as deputy to his father in Babylon. Cambyses, in establishing himself on the throne, did away with his brother Smerdis (Bardiya), whom he considered a rival. Cambyses's greatest accomplishment was his conquest of Egypt, which he added to his already huge territory in 525 B.C. He first met the Egyptian army at Pelusium[46] and won a clear victory. He was significantly aided by the defection of the commander of Greek mercenaries, whom Pharaoh Amasis had hired.

At this time Amasis died and was succeeded by his son, Psammetichus III. But the new ruler had little more success against the Persians, and they now moved on into the rich Delta region. Soon Cambyses held control of the entire country,[47] organizing it as a satrapy[48] of the empire. He was not successful, however, in his attempt to extend his control farther, either westward toward Carthage or southward to Nubia and Ethiopia.

When en route home in 522 B.C., encamped near Mount Carmel in Palestine, Cambyses received news that one Gaumata had seized the Persian throne, masquerading as Smerdis, the brother whom Cambyses had secretly assassinated.[49] Cambyses's sudden death at this point has given rise to numerous conflicting stories. It is frequently assumed that he committed suicide, although this is far from certain.

b. Darius Hystaspes (522–486). One of Cambyses's officers, Darius I, son of the satrap, Hystaspes, and a descendant of a secondary branch of the royal line of Persia, now assumed command of the army and marched home to put down the insurrection and seize the throne. He was successful in both, putting the pretender to death. He found the empire generally in foment, however, with some areas in open rebellion. He showed himself equal to this challenge also and, within two years, had matters well in hand. He considered the overall triumph sufficiently important to have a record made of it for future generations high on a mountain cliff beside the road to Ecbatana. This inscription, which has come to be called the Behistun Inscription, was written in three languages and has proven invaluable in modern time for providing the key to reading Old Akkadian.[50]

Darius went on to become one of

---

[46] Located near the Mediterranean, twenty miles east of modern Port Said, at the mouth of the most easterly (Pelusiac) branch of the Nile, long since filled with silt.

[47] Cambyses followed the same policy as his father in respecting native religious customs and institutions. He lacked his father's consideration for people and buildings, however, working cruelty and senseless destruction. The Elephantine papyri indicate that the Jewish temple on the island of Elephantine was left intact but that the temples of the Egyptian gods were pulled down; see *ANET*, p. 492; and *DOTT*, pp. 262–63, for Elephantine texts.

[48] Persia divided her many provinces into twenty larger divisions called satrapies, the viceroys of which were called satraps.

[49] Olmstead, however, argues that Smerdis had not been killed prior to this time and that this person really was Smerdis, Cambyses's brother; see Olmstead, *Persian Empire*, pp. 107–16.

[50] Written in Persian, Elamite, and Akkadian, this inscription can be seen on a mountainside some 350 feet above the main road between old Babylon and Ecbatana. Primarily through efforts of H. C. Rawlinson, who in 1835 scaled the cliff and made copies and squeezes, this inscription was made to yield the secret for reading the cuneiform characters. More recently, detailed study of the inscription has been made by George C. Cameron. See Cameron, *JNES* 2 (1943): 115–16; also Cameron, *National Geographic Magazine* 98 (1950): 825–44.

Persia's most capable rulers. He demonstrated skill in reorganizing the empire. Cyrus had added conquered kingdoms without changing established boundaries; but Darius, having just suffered the effects of serious revolt, now changed boundaries by dividing all into newly designed satrapies. Judges with fixed circuits were appointed, and an intricate postal system for effective communication was established. Darius proved himself to be an able military leader by directing his armies to repeated successes. Basing his strategy on the false assumption that the divided Athenians would not offer significant resistance, Darius's commander suffered a humiliating defeat at the hands of the Greeks in the famous battle of Marathon, 490 B.C. He planned revenge, but a revolt in Egypt demanded his attention for a time, and his own death came in 486 B.C. before he was able to retaliate.

c. Xerxes I (486–465). Xerxes I succeeded his father. His first two years were occupied in quelling revolutions, especially in Babylon which he finally incorporated with Assyria.[51] Then in his third year he planned his greatest military campaign, which he hoped would avenge his father's defeat by the Greeks. His plans were thorough, and the number of troops assembled was enormous. At first he was victorious, even capturing Athens and burning the Acropolis. But then his fine fleet of ships was routed at Salamis, and his army, under the command of his general, Mardonius, was cut to pieces at Plataea the following year (479 B.C.). Xerxes, who had returned to his capital following the defeat at Salamis, now gave up on his attempt to annex Greece by military means and entered into a vigorous building program.

d. Artaxerxes Longimanus (465–425). The last Persian ruler of note is Artaxerxes Longimanus. He succeeded to the throne when the commander of the palace guard, one Artabanus, assassinated his father. Artaxerxes's first task was to dispose of all rivals for the throne. Then, in 460 B.C., he faced a serious revolution in Egypt, which was put down only after several years of fighting by his satrap of Abarnahara[52] (Syria and Palestine), Megabyzus. Difficulty with the Greeks led to further humiliation for the Persian monarch, as he signed a treaty (449 B.C.) permitting Greek cities in Asia Minor to be free to join in league with Athens. Neither Artaxerxes nor Xerxes attained the stature of their predecessor, Darius. The rulers succeeding them were still less talented, and, at the coming of Alexander, the empire was taken by the Greeks.

E. THE FIRST RETURN TO JUDAH
(Ezra 1–6)

During these years of Persian history, significant events transpired for the Jews.[53] Principal among these were

---

[51] See Olmstead, *Persian Empire,* pp. 236–37. For Xerxes's own list of countries ruled and those where a condition of revolution existed at his accession, see *ANET,* pp. 316–17.

[52] This is the Aramaic form of the Persian *'Ebirnari'.* It means "beyond the river." It was the district created by Darius in his reorganization which, according to Herodotus (*Historiae* 3.89–97), included "All Phoenicia, Palestine, Syria and Cyprus." See Michael Avi-Yonah, *The Holy Land* (Grand Rapids: Baker, 1966), pp. 11–12.

[53] From this point in time it is common to speak of "Jewish" history. Most of those who returned from captivity were of the tribe of Judah, which gave rise to the name.

three separate returns from captivity. The first came shortly after the Persian conquest of Babylon (538 B.C.; Ezra 1:1), led by Sheshbazzar. The second came eighty years later, in the seventh year of Artaxerxes Longimanus (458 B.C.; Ezra 7:7), led by Ezra. And the third came thirteen years after the second, in the twentieth year of Artaxerxes Longimanus (444 B.C.; Neh. 2:1), led by Nehemiah.

1. Edict of Cyrus
(2 Chronicles 36:22–23; Ezra 1:1–4; 6:3–5)

The tolerant attitude of Cyrus toward his subjects included permission for people, who had been deported by Babylon, to return to their homelands.[54] Cyrus extended this permission to the people of Judah in his first year;[55] but as suggested earlier, this may have been due to the influence of Daniel.[56]

Cyrus' edict is recorded twice in Scripture: Ezra 1:2–4 and 6:3–5.[57] The accounts are not identical, which suggests that the original edict was longer than either and contained the items which both together possess. In summary, they give orders that the Jerusalem temple be rebuilt, with the cost defrayed from Cyrus' own treasury; that certain specifications be met in this rebuilding; that all Jews who wished could return to their homeland, with those Jews who remained in Babylon being urged to assist with financial contribution; and that the gold and silver vessels taken by Nebuchadnezzar be returned to Jerusalem. The degree of favor for the Jews shown in this edict is remarkable,[58] and causes one to wonder if it may not have been originally penned by Daniel himself.

2. The return
(Ezra 1:5–2:70)

Presumably the return occurred soon after the issuance of the decree, likely in 538 or 537 B.C. It was led by Sheshbazzar, called a "prince of Judah" (Ezra 1:8).[59] Those who made the journey are listed in Ezra 2, with their number indicated as 42,360, besides 7,337 servants (Ezra 2:64–65). This is a substantial number, but it did not include all the Jews who lived in the East. In fact, it probably did not include a majority; for, just over a half century later, in the

---

[54] Cyrus himself states this policy on his famous cylinder; see *ANET*, p. 316; *DOTT*, p. 93.

[55] See Noth, *NHI*, pp. 307–8; Bright, *BHI*, pp. 343–44.

[56] See p. 327.

[57] The first is written in Hebrew and has the form of a royal proclamation. The second is in Aramaic and has the form of a *dikrona*, which is a memorandum of an oral royal decision. See Bright, *BHI*, pp. 342–43; E. J. Bickerman, "The Edict of Cyrus in Ezra I," *JBL* 65 (1946): 244–75; and R. A. Bowman, *Interpreter's Bible*, vol. 3 (1954), pp. 570–73, 613–16.

[58] That Cyrus speaks highly of "The LORD, the God of heaven" (Ezra 1:2) is not so surprising in itself, however, for he speaks similarly of Marduk; see *ANET*, pp. 315–16. To speak this way of foreign deities was in keeping with his conciliatory policy.

[59] Sheshbazzar may be the same as Zerubbabel. Both are called "governor" of Judah (Ezra 5:14; Hag. 1:1), and both led in building the temple (Ezra 5:16; 5:2). However, since both names are Babylonian (Zer-Babel and Shin-ab-usur), there is little reason for them differing unless they refer to different men. See William F. Albright, "Recent Discoveries in Bible Lands," in Robert Young, *Analytical Concordance to the Bible*, rev. ed. (Grand Rapids: Eerdmans, n.d.), p. 36. Apparently Sheshbazzar was succeeded by Zerubbabel, who likely was in the group who came under Sheshbazzar and may already have then been active. If Sheshbazzar is the same as Shenazar (1 Chron. 3:18), which is likely, since both make good abbreviated forms of the Babylonian Sinabusur ("May Sin protect the father"), then Zerubbabel was his nephew; see Wright, *BAR*, pp. 203–5; Albright, *JBL* 40 (1921): 108–10. Both were descendants of Jehoiachin (1 Chron. 3:16–19; Matt. 1:11–13).

time of Esther,[60] enough Jews yet lived there to kill as many as 75,000 of their enemy neighbors in two days of fighting (Esth. 9:16). As has been noted, Jews had been living in the East under surprisingly pleasant conditions, with many having established themselves in lucrative businesses. They did not find it easy now to leave; and a large number did not. Those who did choose to return to the Promised Land made the trip apparently without serious incident.

3. Building the temple (Ezra 3–6)

A prime order of business on arriving in the homeland was the rebuilding of the temple. Its immediate construction was imperative for the restoration of temple worship for the spiritual well-being of the returned exiles and as a witness of Jewish devotion to Yahweh before the neighboring people.

a. A good beginning. Construction on the temple did begin soon after arrival in the land. Ezra 3:8 states that the people were led in this by Zerubbabel and Joshua (Jeshua), the high priest,[61] though apparently Sheshbazzar was in general charge (Ezra 5:16). They first erected the altar and reinstated the prescribed sacrifices in the seventh month of the first year of their return. Shortly after, in the middle of the same month, the people observed

the Feast of Tabernacles, since its prescribed time was then at hand. Later, in the second month of the second year, they commenced work on the temple proper.

The first step was laying the foundation, which seems to have been accomplished rather quickly. When it was completed, the people celebrated. Many rejoiced, but others, who could remember the glory of the former Solomonic temple, wept openly (Ezra 3:8–12). They could see that the new temple would be more modest than the former. At this point, opposition from Samaritans to the north began (Ezra 4:1–5).[62] The Samaritans seem to have thought that the territory of Judah was theirs to control, though this was not a legitimate assumption on their part.[63] Besides this outside interference, the Jewish workers on the temple began to use more of their time for rebuilding their own houses and farming their own lands (Hag. 1:3–11).[64] It was not long before all work ceased, with the result that the temple remained little more than a foundation until the second year of Darius (520 B.C.; Hag. 1:1), some sixteen years later.

b. Construction resumed. In Darius's second year, the prophets Haggai and Zechariah urged that building operations be resumed. They addressed both the people in general and Zerubbabel and Joshua (who were still in com-

---

[60] Esther married the Persian ruler Xerxes I (Greek name for the Persian *Khshayarsha,* an equivalent to the Hebrew *Ahasuerus,* Esth. 1:1), who reigned 486–465.

[61] Joshua was son of Jehozadak (Josadak), who was among those taken into captivity, a descendant of Eleazar through Zadok (1 Chron. 6:15).

[62] These Samaritans first asked to assist and were properly refused (their worship of God being mixed with foreign deity worship, 2 Kings 7:29–41) by Zerubbabel, and then they openly opposed.

[63] See the discussion in Avi-Yonah, *Holy Land,* p. 13.

[64] Likely these workers were composed almost entirely of those who had returned from captivity. Jews who had continued to live in Judah during the Captivity may not have been very cooperative, for now they would have to share their housing and lands, which may have led to some friction. Strife of this kind could have contributed also to the failure in building the temple.

mand) in particular. Sheshbazzar, who would have been an old man at the time of the return, apparently died soon after his arrival at Jerusalem, to be succeeded by Zerubbabel, who had now held his position for some time. Their prophetic efforts were fruitful and work did begin in the sixth month of the year (Hag. 1:15; Ezra 5:1–2).

Again opposition arose, this time from the satrap of Abarnahara himself, Tattenai by name. It does not seem to have been serious. He first asked the Jews regarding their authority to do this building, and then he wrote directly to Darius for his confirmation. After he had received word that the Jews did have official Persian approval, he ceased opposition and even lent assistance, according to Darius's order (Ezra 5:3–6:14). Four years later, in the sixth year of Darius (March 515 B.C.; Ezra 6:15), the temple was completed.

F. THE SECOND RETURN
(Ezra 7–10)

Fifty-eight years elapsed between the completion of the temple and the second return to Judah. Only a few clues exist concerning the history of those years.

1. Intervening years

Darius ruled Persia until 486 B.C., followed by Xerxes I, who ruled until 465 B.C. It was during the rule of Xerxes that Esther was queen. Then came Artaxerxes Longimanus, during whose seventh year the second return occurred. It was led by Ezra, a descendant of Aaron, skilled in teaching the Law (Ezra 7:6, 10).[65] Ezra was known to Artaxerxes, for this Judean had attained a position of some standing at the court. He may have held an office like Minister of Jewish Affairs. In some undisclosed manner he persuaded the king to permit him to travel to Judah for the purpose of effecting needed reforms.

Three matters give indication concerning life in Judah during these intervening years. From Haggai's indictment of the people for failing to complete the temple earlier (Hag. 1:3–11), we know that they were rebuilding comfortable houses and farming their land. Indeed, they had become so occupied that they had failed to complete God's temple. From the fact that Nehemiah found it necessary much later (444 B.C.) to come and build Jerusalem's walls, it is clear that little was done in reconstructing the capital city apart from erecting private homes. From Ezra's confession of the people's sin in intermarriage with surrounding pagans (Ezra 9:1–15), we know of interaction with neighboring peoples, which raised the possibility of a return to the old idolatrous worship which always seemed to accompany intermarriage.

Politically, Judah was a part of the large Persian satrapy of Abarnahara, which included land southwest of the Euphrates to the border of Egypt, principally Syria and Palestine. In this larger unit, Judah constituted one province over which a governor normally (*tirshatha*, meaning "He who is to be

---

[65] Some scholars hold to a date for Ezra as the seventh year of Artaxerxes II (398 B.C.), and others to the thirty-seventh year of Artaxerxes I (428 B.C.). Both must be rejected; but for discussion, see Rowley, "The Chronological Order of Ezra and Nehemiah," in *The Servant of the Lord and Other Essays on the Old Testament* (London: Lutterworth Press, 1952), pp. 131–59; Bright, *BHI*, pp. 375–86; or J. S. Wright, *The Date of Ezra's Coming to Jerusalem*, 2d ed. (London: Tyndale, 1958).

feared"; Ezra 2:63; Neh. 8:9; 10:1) ruled.[66] It may be that at times Judah did not have its own governor and was ruled directly by the district satrap. In any event, the satrap had authority to intervene at any time, as Tattenai did in connection with the renewal of temple construction in 520 B.C.

2. The royal letter (Ezra 7:11–26)

Like Sheshbazzar eighty years before, Ezra, too, received notable privileges from the Persian monarch in connection with his return. These privileges included authority to take as many of his countrymen with him as desired the opportunity; to receive from Jews in Persia, as well as from Artaxerxes himself and his court counselors, gold and silver for the Jerusalem temple; to draw upon the royal treasury of the satrapy of Abarnahara for needs that might arise; to purchase animals for sacrifice at the temple; to exempt temple personnel from Persian taxation; and to appoint civil magistrates in the land of Judah to enforce the laws of Yahweh, with power of life and death over the guilty. Ezra's interest and assigned task was thus not to build the country materially, as it had been with the first return and would be again with the third, but to build the people socially and spiritually. Reform was needed that the people might live more pleasingly in the sight of God.

3. Return and work (Ezra 7:27–10:44)

a. The journey (Ezra 8). Ezra assembled those who wished to return at the river Ahava (unknown, but probably near Babylon). The size of the group is indicated by the number of men, approximately 1,500, a number much smaller than that of the first return. When no Levites were found in the group, Ezra delayed while 38 Levites were persuaded to join, and they were accompanied by 220 Nethinim[67] as helpers. Final departure occurred the twelfth day of the first month (458 B.C.) and arrival in Jerusalem the first day of the fifth month (Ezra 7:9; 8:31), a journey of just over three and one-half months.

b. Problem of intermarriage (Ezra 9). The main area of reform which confronted Ezra was the intermarriage of a number of Jews with surrounding peoples. Jewish people had permitted their sons to marry heathen daughters of neighboring nations, and even the priests, Levites, and civil leaders were involved. Ezra was told of this defection from the Law soon after his arrival and reacted with remorse. He rent his clothing, pulled hair from his head, and sat confounded until the evening. Then he offered a prayer of confession. When he finished, those standing by were deeply moved and expressed their conviction that the marriages should be dissolved. Ezra agreed and solicited approval from certain of the more

---

[66] See Avi-Yonah, *Holy Land,* p. 12.

[67] The term *Nethinim* ("given ones") is used outside of Ezra and Nehemiah only in 1 Chronicles 9:2. With Sheshbazzar, 392 persons so named returned to Jerusalem (Ezra 2:58), and with Ezra, 220 (Ezra 8:20). They probably were descendants of foreign prisoners, such as the Gibeonites (Josh. 9:27), who had such duties as drawing water and carrying wood for the Levites in temple service. David had assigned Nethinim to serve in this way (Ezra 8:20); the names ascribed to Nethinim in Ezra 2:43–58 are foreign in type; and both 1 Esdras 5:29 and Josephus (*Antiquities* 11.5.1) call them "temple slaves."

sympathetic religious and civil authorities as well. Details were worked out to accomplish this difficult and grievous task.

c. Dissolving the marriages (Ezra 10).

Decision was made that each case be judged separately. To insure justice, it was determined that judgments should be passed by the elders and the appointed judges from the villages of the respective parties. They would know the situations better than someone who was unacquainted with the facts. Judging began as soon as arrangements could be made and was completed within three months (Ezra 10:16–17).

Without question, such large scale separation of marriage partners worked hardship and heartbreak in many cases, but the issues were serious. From the time of Moses, God's Law had demanded that separation from foreign peoples be maintained lest Israelites be influenced to worship pagan deities. If intermarriage had occurred already, and to this extent, so soon after the return from captivity, the situation could soon lead to serious consequences. Ezra recognized the hard fact and took the unpleasant but appropriate action. It may be, indeed, that news of the condition had reached him even in Babylon and had particularly prompted him to make the journey to Jerusalem in the first place.

G. THE THIRD RETURN
(Nehemiah 1–13)

The third return, that of Nehemiah, came in the twentieth year of Artaxerxes (444 B.C.; Neh. 1:1). No indication is given regarding the number of Jews who went along in this return, but there were enough to warrant the Persian king providing "army officers and cavalry" (Neh. 2:9) to act as guards. Nehemiah himself, of course, was the principal person. Nehemiah's purpose lay in the rebuilding of Jerusalem's walls. Strange to say, the walls of the city had not been restored though the people had been back in the land nearly a century.

1. A thwarted attempt at wall building
(Ezra 4:6–23)

One abortive attempt at wall building likely had been made, however; though only a few years before Nehemiah's return. Knowledge of this comes from a letter written to Artaxerxes by the Samaritans,[68] recorded in Ezra 4:6–23. The letter urges the Persian king to require that the Jews, who were already building "walls" and "foundations" in Jerusalem, be stopped. Artaxerxes responded by an order to this effect, and the work did cease.

The date during Artaxerxes's reign,[69] to which this instance is best assigned, falls during the thirteen-year interval between the returns of Ezra and Nehemiah (458–445)[70] It is not likely that

---

[68] Quite likely Judah did not have her own governor at this time (see below, n.72), and so the Samaritans felt free to interfere in this manner.

[69] Ezra 4:6–23 was placed where it is, probably to group similar subject matter together. Chronologically, the passage is out of place because: (1) the two kings named in it, Ahasuerus (Xerxes, 486–465) and Artaxerxes (465–425), ruled much later than the time of temple building described elsewhere in the chapter; (2) the type of building activity set forth in the letter concerns "walls" and "foundations" of the city, not the temple; and (3) the Persian king was unable to find Cyrus's original edict when this letter was received, but he did when a letter sent in 520 B.C. (Ezra 5:7–6:5) came, which makes better historical sense if this letter of Ezra 4 came after that of 520 B.C., rather than before.

[70] For discussion, see H. H. Rowley, "Nehemiah's Mission and Its Background," *BJRL* 73 (March

it came in the short seven-year span preceding Ezra's return, for then one would expect him to have mentioned it in its proper historical context in his book.[71] If it came, however, following Ezra's return and shortly before that of Nehemiah, it could have had a part in motivating Hanani to journey to Persia to seek the help of his brother, Nehemiah, for this rebuilding, as set forth in Nehemiah 1:1–4. In turn, it may have augmented Nehemiah's own desire to heed Hanani's request. Someone directly from the capital, armed with authority,[72] apparently was needed to counteract Samaritan opposition, if Judah's capital was to have her walls rebuilt.[73]

2. Nehemiah (Nehemiah 1:1–2:10)

Nehemiah held a responsible position at the Persian court, as cupbearer to King Artaxerxes. In this he was more than merely a domestic servant, as is shown by his access to the king to speak intimately regarding a return to Jerusalem, by the king's considering him able enough to act as Judah's governor when he went there, and by the king's requesting Nehemiah to return to his present position when the new task had been completed (Neh. 2:4–6). Furthermore, Nehemiah was granted unusual privilege, like Sheshbazzar and Ezra before him, in connection with the return.

Sometime in the month Kislev (December),445 B.C., Hanani came to his brother, Nehemiah, at Susa, the Persian capital, with his sad report concerning matters in Jerusalem. Nehemiah was grief-stricken and spent days in intercession for his people. Not until four months had passed, however, did he ask the king if he might go and render assistance. He seems to have waited for an opportune time, desiring every advantage when the request would be given. Perhaps he was remembering Artaxerxes's earlier refusal, voiced through the Samaritans, as to rebuilding Jerusalem's walls.

But in the spring of 444 B.C., the opportunity came. The king noticed sadness on Nehemiah's part one day and asked the reason. Nehemiah told him of Jerusalem's plight, asked if he might journey there to help, and even requested letters to officials in Abarnahara to grant him safe passage and material aid for rebuilding. The Persian monarch responded with an affirmative answer and granted him all for which he asked, thus cheering and encouraging his faithful servant's heart. He

1955): 528–61. Rowley dates this opposition just prior to Nehemiah's return of 445 B.C. He places Ezra's return, however, after that of Nehemiah.

[71] Ezra returned in Artaxerxes's eighth year. That Ezra did not mention it in a historical context coming after his return is understandable, for he did not treat history after 458 B.C. He completed his book with the account of marriage dissolutions, which were concluded within eight months (see Ezra 7:9; 10:17) of his first arrival. This means that, if Ezra was to include this letter at all, it had to be placed out of historical context. Ezra's mention of "wall" in Ezra 9:9 can hardly be taken as a reference to the abortive instance of wall-building.

[72] In that no prior governor was displaced by Nehemiah on arrival in Judah, it is probable that none immediately preceded him. Ezra, though still living and active, did not serve as governor.

[73] This means, of course, that Artaxerxes must have changed his mind between replying to the Samaritan letter and giving Nehemiah permission to go. Conditions of unrest in the west, known both from secular history (see n. 74) and from Ezra 4:6–23, could have prompted this change. A governor in Judah of Nehemiah's stature, loyal to the throne, could be a significant stabilizing force; and to have him rebuild the walls of his city could add to the prestige he would need.

further assigned army officers and cavalry to convey Nehemiah safely over the many miles of travel.[74]

3. Nehemiah builds the wall (Nehemiah 2:11–6:19)

On arrival, Nehemiah set himself quickly to the task of rebuilding Jerusalem's walls.

a. Preparation. Within three days he made a secret[75] nocturnal inspection of the walls[76] to determine their exact condition. Apparently he wanted firsthand knowledge, that he might make the most effective plan of action. With facts assembled, he gathered the Jerusalem leaders and presented his ideas. Whatever opposition may have existed among the group, due to the previously thwarted attempt or to possible disinterest, was overcome by the force of Nehemiah's enthusiasm and care in planning. Good response was forthcoming and a positive decision made. Workers were quickly recruited, both from Jerusalem and outlying cities; and all were assigned particular sections of the wall on which to labor.

b. Opposition. The work moved forward with surprising rapidity—but only under severe opposition from the outside. The king had given Nehemiah full authority for the task, in contrast to the aborted earlier attempt; but enemies still did their best to hinder the work. Apparently neighboring provinces, especially Samaria, had benefited from Judah's weakness and did not wish to lose this advantage. Heading the opposition was the governor of Samaria, Sanballat the Horonite (of Bethhoron; Neh. 2:10).[77] His daughter later married into the family of Eliashib, high priest in Jerusalem (Neh. 13:28). He was helped by Tobiah, called "the Ammonite official" (Neh. 2:10), who may have been governor of Ammon.[78] A third opponent was Geshem (Gashmu) the Arabian (Neh. 2:19; 6:6), often identified with a powerful chieftain of Kedar in northeastern Arabia.[79] With so much opposition, many men would have lost heart, but not Nehemiah.

At first these adversaries were content merely to mock (Neh. 2:19–20;

---

[74] Although matters were now better in Abarnahara than they had been (see p. 333), still unrest continued. From the first of his rule, Artaxerxes had been bothered by Grecian attacks on Cyprus and in 460 B.C. had encountered a serious rebellion in Egypt supported by Greece. This rebellion had continued until 454 B.C., when Megabyzus, satrap of Abarnahara, had finally brought it to an end. But five years later, Megabyzus himself had rebelled, and Artaxerxes had only recently achieved control once again. These matters no doubt influenced the king to provide this military guard for Nehemiah and his group.

[75] No doubt in order to keep any word of his intentions from leaking to the opposition. Apparently Nehemiah anticipated that trouble would come, probably in view of that experienced earlier.

[76] For description of topography encountered, see J. Simons, *Jerusalem in the Old Testament* (Leiden: Brill, 1952), pp. 432–33.

[77] He is called governor of Samaria in the Aramaic papyri from Elephantine; *ANET,* p. 492; *DOTT,* p. 264. Sanballat (Sinuballit) is a Babylonian name, but his two sons were given Jewish names, Delaiah and Shelemiah.

[78] It is likely that he was an ancestor of the Tobiads, who governed Ammon for generations following this time, as indicated by the Zeno papyri (third century) and by palace and tomb remains at 'Araq el-Emir near present Amman, Jordan. An inscription at the family burial site, bearing the name *Tobiah,* may come from the very time of this Tobiah. For discussion of the Tobiads, see C. C. McCown, *BA* 20 (1957): 63–76; R. A. Bowman, *Interpreter's Bible,* vol. 3 (1954), pp. 676–77.

[79] Mentioned in a memorial inscription from ancient Dedan (modern el-'Ula) and an Aramaic dedication on a bowl in the Egyptian delta; see F. M. Cross, *BA* 18 (1955): 46–47; I. Rabinowitz, *JNES* 15 (1956): 2, 5–9.

4:1–3). Then plans were laid to attack Jerusalem, with Arabians and Ashdodites, in addition to Ammonites, to take part (Neh. 4:7–8). News of this terrorized the Jews, but Nehemiah responded by dividing the builders into two groups, one to continue building and the other to bear arms. In this way the work progressed, though more slowly. A schedule was kept from dawn until dark to achieve as much speed as possible. During the night, a heavy guard was posted to protect what had been accomplished. All this was effective and resulted in the main attack being called off, though smaller raids were conducted on outlying districts. Josephus tells of these, stating that in them many Jews lost their lives (*Antiquities* 11.5.8).

The opponents tried four times to lure Nehemiah away from Jerusalem and the work, but he saw through their schemes and did not go (Neh. 6:1–4). Then they threatened to bring to the Persian king an accusation of disloyalty on Nehemiah's part (Neh. 6:5–9). Still further they attempted to bring reproach on Nehemiah in the sight of his own people through a false prophet Shemaiah (Neh. 6:10–14). But Nehemiah was equal to all the strategy they devised. The work of rebuilding was completed in only fifty-two days,[80] amazing in view of the opposition, and much to the consternation and displeasure of the enemies.

4. Nehemiah as governor (Nehemiah 7–12)

After completion of the wall, Nehemiah continued as governor of the province, according to Artaxerxes's appointment.

a. Size of Judah. The size of Judah in this postexilic time was substantially smaller than it had been prior to the captivity. This was the result mainly of a change in the southern boundary, which now seems to have run only at an approximate east and west line just north of Hebron,[81] well north of Beersheba, the former southern limit. The northern boundary apparently was about the same, including such cities as Gibeon (Neh. 3:7) and Mizpah (Neh. 3:15, 19); also the eastern, including at least Jericho (Neh. 3:2); and the western, though of this more question exists.[82] The whole was roughly rectangular in shape, extending north and south about twenty-five miles. This area seems to have already been divided into districts when Nehemiah arrived, for he used them in assigning people to work on the walls (Neh. 3:2–27).[83]

b. Remission of debts (Neh. 5:1–19). One of Nehemiah's first actions was to remit the debts of poor people. This he

---

[80] Because fifty-two days is a short time, some scholars (for instance, Albright, *BP,* p. 52; or Bright, *BHI,* p. 365) favor the indication of Josephus (*Antiquities* 11.5.8) that the period was really two years and four months. There was, however, great urgency, many workers, and only a portion of the total wall to be rebuilt.

[81] South of Judah the province of Idumaea (Diodorus 19.95.2; 98.1) had been established. It was inhabited by Edomites and included Hebron to the north and Beersheba to the south, minus the coastal plain. See Avi-Yonah, *Holy Land,* pp. 25–26.

[82] The question concerns whether a strip reaching into the coastal plain, containing the three cities, Lod, Hadid, and Ono, was included. Since, however, it was near Ono that Sanballat proposed to meet Nehemiah (Neh. 6:2), desiring likely a neutral area, it is not probable that this strip was a part of Judah.

[83] For discussion, see Noth, *NHI,* pp. 325–26; Avi-Yonah, *Holy Land,* pp. 14–22.

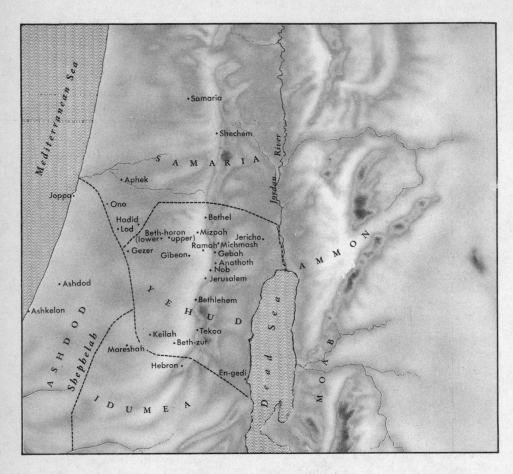

Map 18. Post-exilic Judah

did likely during the early time of building the wall, for record of it is included along with the story of that great effort. The province of Judah was in dire economic straits as a result of high Persian taxes and successive poor crops. In this situation, some of the more wealthy had taken advantage of the poor by bringing them into debt and dispossessing them of property. Nehemiah appealed to the consciences of these people, urging them to stop the practice and restore what they had taken, even exacting an oath before God. Nehemiah himself set a fine example by refusing the customary gubernatorial remuneration for his services.

c. Security measures (Neh. 7:1–4; 11:1–36). With the wall completed, it was necessary to take security measures. Placed in general charge were Hanani, the brother of Nehemiah, who had made the trip to Susa to request aid, and one Hananiah. Musicians and other Levites were recruited to help the gatekeepers in watching the gates and walls. Apparently the population in Jerusalem proper remained small, for Nehemiah now required that one-tenth of the population from other cities, chosen by lot, move to the capital.[84] This action involved an inspection of registrations, and by it Nehemiah came across an old list of those who had returned to Judah under Sheshbazzar. This list is repeated in Nehemiah

7:6–73 almost without variation from that in Ezra 2:1–70.

d. Reading God's Law (Neh. 8–10). Nehemiah, interested in the religious life of the people, encouraged all to assemble for the reading of God's Law. This was in the fall of 444 B.C., shortly after the wall's completion. Ezra, still active thirteen years after his arrival, did the reading.[85] He was joined by other Levites in explaining the meaning, perhaps by translating from Hebrew to the Aramaic adopted during the Exile.

When that part of the Law prescribing the Feast of Tabernacles (Lev. 23:39–43) was read, the people expressed desire to keep it immediately, since it was then the time of year for it. This was done, and in careful detail. All this in turn was followed by a public confession of sin by the people and a further separation from pagan influence.[86] Finally a covenant to keep faithfully all that God required in the Law was signed by both Nehemiah and numerous representatives of the people (Neh. 10:1–39). A fine spirit of renewed commitment to God was demonstrated, which augured well for days to come.

e. Dedication of the walls (Neh. 12:27–47). Formal dedication of the walls was now made. The time was likely still 444 B.C., though at the close of the year. Civil and religious leaders were assembled from all parts of the province. They formed two proces-

---

[84] The register of names given in Nehemiah 11:3–36 represents the population as existent in the time of Nehemiah. The register of priests and Levites in Nehemiah 12:1–26 represents those from the time of Zerubbabel on to this time of Nehemiah.

[85] Since Nehemiah was not a priest, he properly gave room to Ezra, who was. Surprisingly, Ezra is not mentioned often by Nehemiah. Apparently he was not greatly involved in the civil matters that occupied Nehemiah's attention.

[86] Perhaps more in other areas than mixed marriages, now that Ezra had dealt with that problem just thirteen years before, though Nehemiah did have to face it again by 430 B.C. (see the following paragraphs on p. 344).

sions, marching in opposite directions around the walls, meeting together at the temple. The people raised their voices in enthusiastic singing heard at great distance. The dedication proper was followed by a further organization of priests and Levites, this especially regarding the collection and care of the tithes and contributions of the people (Neh. 12:44–47).

5. Nehemiah's second term (Nehemiah 13)

Nehemiah served in Jerusalem during two periods of time. He remained as governor the first time twelve years, from the twentieth to the thirty-second years of Artaxerxes (444–433; Neh. 1:1; 13:6). Then he went back to his former position in the Persian court, no doubt according to the original agreement (Neh. 2:6), but was permitted to return to Jerusalem after an interval probably of only a year or two. The exact time of the interval is not indicated, nor the circumstances of his being permitted to go again to Jerusalem. Probably he simply was unhappy about being away from his people in Judah, and the king allowed him to return to where his interest lay.

a. Reforms. Upon arriving the second time, Nehemiah was grieved at a return to laxity toward God's Law, which had arisen during his brief absence. Most shocking was the fact that Eliashib, the high priest, had allowed Nehemiah's old enemy, Tobiah the Ammonite, to live in a room of the temple intended for the storage of the tithes of the people. Nehemiah, without hesitation, ordered the room cleared of all Tobiah's effects and restored to its original purpose (Neh. 13:4–9). Then he commanded that the

collection of tithes be carried out with greater care, which would have as a side benefit the insurance that all such rooms would be necessarily used (Neh. 13:10–14). It would seem that the directives of but twelve years before (Neh. 12:44–47) were already being neglected.

Nehemiah next addressed a pervasive disregard for the Sabbath (Neh. 13:15–22). Not only did Jews themselves desecrate the holy day by working and doing business, but they permitted resident Tyrians to bring in merchandise and conduct trade. Nehemiah closed the city gates and posted guards to enforce his prohibition of all such merchandising.

Nehemiah also had to deal with return to the practice of mixed marriages (Neh. 13:23–28). In spite of Ezra's earlier efforts in 458 B.C., and his own in 444 B.C., here in c. 430 B.C. the problem existed once more. Nehemiah found children who could not even speak Hebrew, because Jews had married foreign partners, especially from Ashdod, Ammon, and Moab. Apparently the marriages were not dissolved this time, as in Ezra's reform, but the people were made to swear that no more would be contracted. When Nehemiah found that one of the grandsons of Eliashib the high priest had married none other than a daughter of his former enemy, Sanballat, he expelled him from Judah.

b. Duration unknown. How long Nehemiah remained in Judah this time, or whether he ever went back to the Persian capital, is not indicated. He may have remained in Jerusalem until his death, the time of which also is unknown. There is evidence that he was no longer governor of Judah at least in 407 B.C., for an Elephantine papyrus gives the governor's name then as Bagoas.[87]

6. Malachi, the last Old Testament prophet

The last of the writing prophets, Malachi, probably ministered during Nehemiah's time. Nehemiah does not refer to him, but certain references made by Malachi show the probability. He implies that the temple had been in existence for some time (Mal. 1:7–10; 3:8), so the date was well after that of Haggai and Zechariah, who only urged rebuilding to continue. He speaks of a governor (Mal. 1:8) as being familiar to the people, which locates his day generally in the Persian period. But, more particularly, he writes of sins of his time that are identical to those Nehemiah encountered: absence of personal piety, especially among the priests (Mal. 1:6–8); existence of foreign marriages (Mal. 2:10–12); and laxity in paying tithes for temple support (Mal. 3:7–10).

H. ESTHER (Esther 1–10)

Many Jews lived outside of Judah during the postexilic time. The Old Testament supplies information regarding those who continued to live in the east at one important juncture. This was the time when Esther was appointed queen in the Persian court and was providentially instrumental in delivering the Jews from terrible slaughter. The account, recorded in the Book of Esther, covers the third to the twelfth years of Xerxes's rule (483–471; Esth. 1:3; 3:7).

1. The account

The narrative begins in the third year of Ahasuerus (Xerxes).[88] While an extended feast was in progress,[89] Ahasuerus demanded that his queen, Vashti, display her crown and beauty before his festive, drunken guests; and, when she refused, he deposed her in a burst of anger. This, he said, was to provide a proper example, so that all wives would henceforth honor their husbands (Esth. 1:1–22).

The situation called for the selection of a new queen, and a contest was arranged for doing so. Maidens were brought from all parts of the empire to provide a choice for the king. Among these was a Jewish orphan, Esther,[90] descendant of Kish, who had been among the captives brought years before from Jerusalem. She had been brought up in the home of her cousin, Mordecai,[91] who held an office in the palace at Susa.[92] Beautifying prepara-

---

[87] For text and discussion, see *DOTT,* pp. 260–65.

[88] Not only is "Ahasuerus" a good Hebrew equivalent for Xerxes's Persian name "Khshayarsha" (see above, n.60), but the history reflected in the Book of Esther fits well the history involving Xerxes, and the temperament of Ahasuerus as reflected in Esther suits that of Xerxes in secular history.

[89] Likely the feast when Xerxes planned his famous campaign against the Greeks.

[90] Her Hebrew name was Hadassah (Esth. 2:7), meaning "myrtle." Esther probably refers to the Babylonian "Ishtar," the name of an important goddess.

[91] Babylonian name based on the name of the deity Marduk.

[92] Susa was located on the Karkheh River in southwest Persia, about 150 miles north of the Persian Gulf. It was the capital of Elam in earlier years. Under the Achaemenids, it served as one of three capitals. Darius I built a fine palace here, covering more than two acres. Apparently Esther lived in this palace. French excavators, under the leadership of M. Dieulafoy, worked here between 1880 and 1890. The excellent objects found are housed in the Louvre in Paris. See R. Ghirshman, *Iran from the Earliest Times to the Islamic Conquest* (Baltimore: Penguin, 1954).

tions lasted a full year. When the contest was finally held, Esther won his favor, so he made her queen in the seventh year of his reign.[93]

Shortly after this selection, Haman, the leading member of Ahasuerus' court, conspired to kill all Jews. Mordecai, whose identity he knew, had been refusing to do him the homage he thought was due. Haman persuaded Ahasuerus to sign a decree that on the thirteenth of Adar (the twelfth month) all Jews should be executed. He argued that these people were dangerous to the empire and that the king would receive a significant gain in the confiscation of their property. At the time, Ahasuerus did not know that Esther was one of their number.

Mordecai informed Esther of the decree, and she courageously went to the king without benefit of normal summons to request an additional decree that the Jews be permitted to fight back against their executioners. The request was presented at a special banquet at which Haman was present. When the king demanded to know who had plotted against Esther's people, she identified Haman. Ahasuerus was angry at his subordinate and ordered his immediate execution on the very gallows that Haman had intended to use to hang Mordecai. Also he granted Esther's request regarding the further decree. In the fighting that followed between Jews and their would-be exe-

cutioners, seventy-five thousand of the latter were killed (Esth. 9:16).[94]

2. The significance

a. Number of Jews. This account implies that a surprisingly large number of Jews yet lived in the east, for the slayers must have outnumbered the seventy-five thousand who were slain. These Jews were probably centered in a few particular areas of the empire.[95] The main concentration no doubt was near Babylon, where they had early established themselves in businesses, as noted. It could be expected, too, that after Persia took control, a significant group had moved to important Persian centers, such as Susa, where Esther was queen. Pockets of them would still have been found also in cities of old Assyria, where captives had been taken from Israel in 722 B.C.

These would have been the chief localities where fighting transpired and the seventy-five thousand died. As for the province of Judah itself, the decrees would have been valid there, too; but no indication is given of fighting. Very likely Jews were simply too strong in their home country for any opponents to dare to attempt an execution.

b. Freedom. Another fact demonstrated is that Jews continued to enjoy freedom to live and work as they pleased.[96] Mordecai was prominent in a court position and later was raised to Haman's former place of honor. Esther

---

[93] The Grecian campaign had occupied the intervening time since the third year (see p. 333). Esther was chosen queen late in 478 B.C.

[94] When the Jews were highly successful on the one day in slaying opponents, Esther requested that a second day be given for the same activity, and the king agreed. The seventy-five thousand were killed over the two days.

[95] The king did send the decree to all 127 provinces (Esth. 3:13; 8:9), but this does not necessarily mean that Jews were found in all 127. All decrees likely were sent to every part of the empire.

[96] Tablets found at Nippur mentioned earlier (p. 329) actually come from this time. They show clearly that Jews were active in business.

was elevated to the place of queen. That she could have entered the "beauty contest" in the first place, and have been chosen by the king without his knowing her nationality, gives signal witness that Jews were not a marked people. They were permitted to live and move about as other people, apparently without discrimination.

c. Jewish enemies. A third matter of note is that Jews did have enemies, however, as they have had continually since that day. Haman was a leader in this. He knew of the Jews as a distinct people in the empire and identified them collectively as an object of hatred. So strong was his feeling that, when irritated by one of them, he wanted to destroy all. Probably he was not alone in this, so one must believe that Jews of the day were considered by a number of people to be an undesirable social element. Anti-Semitism, wrong as it is, is not modern.

d. Providential care. A fourth significance is that God's special care was being extended toward these Jews of the east, even though they had chosen not to return to the homeland when they had the opportunity. This care, evidenced particularly in the precise timing of events for the Jews' benefit, is in fact the outstanding feature of the account.[97]

Esther became queen just in time to become instrumental in thwarting Haman's plot. Mordecai's attention was called to a previous plot against the king just in time to give the king reason to honor him at a most opportune moment. The king, experiencing insomnia, had court records read to him, one of which concerned this good and unrewarded deed of Mordecai, the very night before Haman arrived to ask that Mordecai be hanged. This resulted in the king honoring Mordecai in a manner most humiliating to Haman, just before Haman could make his own request to hang Mordecai.

These crucial time sequences led to some remarkable reversals in expected happenings. The honor which the Jew-hating Haman believed was designed for himself came to be given to the Jew Mordecai. The gallows that Haman had made for Mordecai came to be used for himself. The edict that was designed by the Jew-hating Haman for doing away with all Jews became instead the instrument for slaying Jew-haters generally. Only God's special providence could account for such astonishing developments.

e. Feast of Purim. A fifth significance is that this occasion gave rise to the Jewish feast of Purim. The name *Purim* comes from the word *pur,* meaning "lot."[98] Haman cast lots for determining the particular day on which the Jewish slaughter should take place (Esth. 3:7).[99] Since this event turned to the good of the Jews, the feast was instituted and named accordingly. It

---

[97] This fact makes the presence and interest of God real in the book, which otherwise does not mention Him by name.

[98] M. Dieulafoy, who excavated at Susa, discovered a quadrangular prism which has the numbers one, two, five, and six engraved on its sides. This no doubt was the type of die used in this determination. The word *pur* is derived from the Assyrian *puru,* meaning a "pebble" or "small stone."

[99] Further providential influence is seen in the result of the lot casting. It was cast in the first month of Ahasuerus's twelfth year, and the lot selected the twelfth month, giving ample time for the new order permitting the Jews to retaliate.

has long been one of the more popular Jewish observances.

I. THE ELEPHANTINE COLONY

Another area of Jewish occupation outside Judah was located on the island of Elephantine in the Nile River of Egypt. This island is situated at the lower end of the first cataract, about five hundred miles south of the Mediterranean. Numerous papyri written in Aramaic were found there, most of them in 1903.[100] They date from the fifth century B.C. As suggested earlier, this group of Jews may have descended from those who took Jeremiah with them when they fled from Judah, years earlier, in fear of Babylon. The colony served as a southern military garrison for the Persians who were stationed in Egypt. It appears to have ceased existence shortly after the beginning of the fourth century.

The contents of the papyri vary considerably in character. One papyrus gives a copy of the famous Behistun Inscription, placed by Darius II high on a mountainside near Ecbatana, Persia.[101] Another is a marriage document. Still another, dated c. 419 B.C., surprisingly instructs the Elephantine Jews, by the authority of the Persian government, to keep their own Passover Feast, according to the practice of the temple in Jerusalem.

A matter of major significance is that these Jews had a temple to Yahweh (*Yahu*). This means that, though far from Jerusalem, they had not forgotten the one true God. The worship of Yahweh was not pure, however; for the names of at least three other deities, who were worshiped by some of the residents, have been found.[102]

In 410 B.C., a revolt broke out, led by Egyptian priests of Khnum in cooperation with the Persian commander, and the temple to Yahweh was destroyed. This prompted a letter to be sent by the Elephantine Jews to Johanan, high priest in Jerusalem, asking that help be given to rebuild it; but no answer was forthcoming. Then, in 407 B.C., a further letter was sent to Bogoas, governor of Judah, and one also to Delaiah and Shelemaiah, sons of Sanballat, governor of Samaria. This led to the matter being brought to the attention of the satrap, Arsames, who apparently gave assistance; for recently published papyri indicate that the temple was rebuilt at least by 402 B.C.[103]

Certain matters of historical significance also call for notice. One is that regular communication existed between this Egyptian group and the Jews in Judah. Another is that this group expected, and at times received, financial help from the motherland. A third is that correlating information is given regarding certain persons mentioned also in the biblical record. One such person is Sanballat, governor of Samaria, spoken of as father of Delaiah and Shelemaiah,[104] and no doubt the

---

[100]The early finds were published by A. Cowley, *Aramaic Papyri of the Fifth Century, B.C.* (Oxford: Clarendon, 1923); see *ANET*, pp. 491–92; and *DOTT*, pp. 256–69, for selections. A later group was published in America; see E. G. Kraeling, *The Brooklyn Museum Aramaic Papyri* (New Haven: Yale University Press, 1953). Still another group was published by Godfrey R. Driver, *Aramaic Documents of the Fifth Century B.C.* (Oxford: Clarendon, 1954; abridged and revised, 1957).

[101]See p. 332.

[102]For text, see *ANET*, p. 491; for discussion, *DOTT*, p. 257.

[103]See E. G. Kraeling, *Brooklyn Aramaic Papyri*, p. 63.

[104]Mentioned in line 29 of the letter addressed to Bogoas, governor of Judah, asking help to rebuild the temple; see *ANET*, p. 492; *DOTT*, p. 264.

same as the opponent of Nehemiah. Another is Johanan, mentioned as high priest in Jerusalem,[105] said in Nehemiah 12:10–11, 22–23 to be grandson of Eliashib, who was high priest in Nehemiah's time (Neh. 3:1). A third is Hananiah, writer of the so-called Passover Papyrus of 419 B.C.[106] who may be the same as the man Nehemiah made superintendent over Jerusalem along with Nehemiah's brother Hanani (Neh. 7:2).[107]

---

[105] Line 18 of the letter addressed to Bogoas.

[106] Line 2 of this papyrus, see *ANET,* p. 491; *DOTT,* p. 259.

[107] For enlargement of Elephantine significances, see I. M. Price, O. R. Sellers, and E. L. Carlson, *The Monuments and the Old Testament* (Philadelphia: Judson, 1958), pp. 320–32.

CHAPTER SIXTEEN

BETWEEN THE TESTAMENTS

For most Christians, Israel's history stops abruptly with the prophet Malachi, to be resumed briefly four hundred years later in the New Testament period. But these four hundred "missing years," known as the intertestamental period, were alive with activity that shaped the world into which Jesus was born, a world that is confusing indeed if the events and changes that took place between the Testaments are ignored.

The Old Testament period ended under the imperial auspices of Persia. In the New Testament, Rome is in command. In the interim, a series of Hellenistic rulers vied for ascendancy. Alexander the Great wrested control from the declining Persian Empire. But he died a little more than a decade later, and one of his generals, Ptolemy Lagus, assumed the throne of Egypt and Palestine. After a century of rivalry, the Ptolemies gave way to the Seleucids, descendants of another of Alexander's generals. The policy of radical Hellenization imposed on Israel by Antiochus Epiphanes eventually led to the Macca-

bean revolt, in which a family of native Israelites took the throne. Their dynasty, the Hasmonean, was brought to an end by the Roman general Pompey, who took the Near East, and Israel with it, for the Roman Senate.

Internal politics during these years were often violent and acrimonious. A variety of parties developed in response to an increasingly complex set of forces within Judaism. The three most notable parties, which continued into the New Testament era, were the Sadducees, the Pharisees, and the Essenes. The Pharisees and the Sadducees appear often in the Gospels and represent the official opposition to Jesus. The Essenes, who do not figure in the New Testament narrative, were nevertheless important. Their monastic retreat at Qumran, on the shores of the Dead Sea, produced some of the most important documents to survive to the present—the Dead Sea Scrolls.

The thought world of the intertestamental period was fertile. The clash between Greek and Hebrew ideas, the experience of persecution for the sake of righteousness, the continual frustration of the hopes of Jews who had come to anticipate a miraculous military victory over the forces of the gentile world—all these produced a rich literary tradition. Of greatest interest for the Christian reader are the Apocrypha, the apocalyptic writings, and the Dead Sea Scrolls. During this period, a movement that has been erroneously called "normative Judaism" was taking shape. The development of the oral law, which would later become the Talmud, began with this movement, which ultimately became the religion of the Rabbis.

It should be obvious that, while Old Testament canonical history concludes with Malachi, the history of Israel continues its vigorous course well beyond that prophet's time.

A. ISRAEL AS A VASSAL STATE

In one sense, the entire intertestamental period can be called "silent." Malachi's promise of the return of Elijah apparently marked the end of Old Testament prophetic activity, and the people awaited its fulfillment. It is evident that by the time of the Maccabees there is no expectation of divinely inspired prophetic utterance until some time in the future.[1] Jesus' identification of John the Baptist as the promised Elijah[2] marks the end of the divine silence; God began to speak once more, this time not merely through the mouths of prophets but through His Son. Josephus also gives testimony to the belief that the voice of prophecy had ceased.[3]

Historically, however, only the first two hundred years of the intertestamental period are silent. When the Book of Malachi was written, the minor province of Judah was a part of the Persian Empire and mired in a historically mute period. The Old Testament writers take us just past the work of Nehemiah—and there the story ends. Both biblical and secular history are all but silent about the affairs of the people of God during the two centuries that follow; the primary sources for the intertestamental period pass over these years with scant mention.[4] The second half of these four hundred years, on the other hand, comes to life in a rich historical record. Some of Judaism's most stirring events of faith and heroism as well as of persecution and infamy took place in this time.

A few bits of information are available about the time from Malachi to Alexander, but they are of limited importance.[5]

The appearance of Alexander initi-

---

[1] A verse in 1 Maccabees (9:27) speaks of a tribulation greater than anything experienced since the voice of prophecy was stilled. Another passage in the same book (4:46) puts off any decision on the reconsecration of the altar until a prophet came to instruct them, and yet another passage (14:41) puts the intended duration of Simon's hereditary high priesthood "until a prophet should arise."

[2] Matthew 11:14.

[3] In *Contra Apion* 1.8 he acknowledges that there has been some writing of Jewish history since Artaxerxes, but it is a history without divine authority because "there hath not been an exact succession of prophets since that time." Here he uses the usual Jewish understanding of what Christians call the historical books. For the Jew, the history of the Old Testament is also the work of prophets, and this group of books is referred to as the "Former Prophets."

[4] Josephus, *AJ* 11.7–8.

[5] Donald E. Gowan, *Bridge Between the Testaments* (Pittsburgh: Pickwick, 1976), pp. 61ff. Solomon Grayzel, *A History of the Jews,* 2d ed. (New York: Mentor, 1968), pp. 46–47, points out that the events of these years are primarily accessible through deduction based on a comparison of earlier and later events. For a summation of these years, see Martin Hengel: *Jews, Greeks and Barbarians: Aspects of the Hellenization of Judaism in the Pre-Christian Period* (Philadelphia: Fortress, 1980), pp. 1–12.

ated one of the most turbulent epochs in Israel's history. Alexander may be considered an ideological conqueror.[6] Raised under the tutelage of Aristotle, he dedicated himself to the establishment of a world unified by the influence of Greek culture.[7] Had it not been for his policy of establishing Greek cities as centers for Greek culture, the military conquests of Alexander would have had little more impact on Israel than those of the Assyrians, the Babylonians, or the Persians. As it was, the challenge of Hellenism to the religion of Israel was as dangerous as the cult of Baal had been; indeed, it was even more insidious because much of the Greek way of life was attractive, sophisticated, and economically appealing.

The military acquisition of Palestine came quickly, easily, and without much historical notice. Alexander's defeat of the Persian army at Issus (333 B.C.) left the way open for the acquisition of Persia's holdings in Syria and Palestine. Resistance came only from the Phoenician city of Tyre and the southern city of Gaza. Alexander marched through Palestine on his way to Egypt, where the Egyptians, who were hostile to Persia, greeted Alexander as a liberator and acclaimed him as Pharaoh. While the final defeat of Darius' forces still lay ahead, the acquisition of Egypt completed the conquest of the western portion of the empire. Alexander went on to claim the rest of Persia's holdings, pushing as far east as India before he died of fever in the ancient city of Babylon at age thirty-three.[8]

As impressive as Alexander's military conquests were, they were merely a prelude to events that would shake the world of Judaism. Following Alexander's death, his generals began a series of wars and intrigues and eventually apportioned his conquests among themselves. After approximately forty years of struggle, the families of two of the generals had acquired control of most of the Near East.[9] Ptolemy I (Lagus) took and held Egypt, founding the Ptolemaic dynasty, which would be the last dynasty to rule over Egypt. Farther to the north, Seleucus I (Nicator) acquired Mesopotamia, Syria, and Asia Minor. Palestine, however, would remain a bone of contention between the Ptolemies and the Seleucids. An agreed-upon division of conquered territory had given Palestine to Seleucus, but when he made his claim he found Ptolemy already in possession.[10] Be-

---

[6] Some—such as Michael Grant, *From Alexander to Cleopatra* (New York: Scribner, 1982), pp. 49–52—would argue that Hellenization was merely a side effect of military and economic expansion. It is true that the location of Hellenistic cities throughout the Seleucid empire served military and economic purposes, but this does not account for all the phenomena of Hellenism. According to Grayzel, *History of the Jews*, pp. 52–53, the cities also provided a focal point for an attempted homogenization of an unwieldy, diversified empire. Solomon Zeitlin, *The Rise and Fall of the Judaean State*, 2 vols. (Philadelphia: Jewish Publication Society, 1962), 1:43–44, takes the opposite position to an idealistic extreme. Purely economic and military explanations fail to do justice to a rapid, vigorous, and aggressive spread of the Greek language and culture.

[7] John Bright, *AHOI*, p. 414; D. S. Russell, *The Jews from Alexander to Herod* (London: Oxford University Press, 1967), pp. 7–9.

[8] The career of Alexander is amply covered in numerous, essentially repetitive, histories. Their primary differences lie in their assessment of the intangibles of his character and motivations. A good summary of the sources for Alexander and the problem of writing about more than the outline of his career see Tom B. Jones, *Ancient Civilization* (Chicago: Rand McNally, 1960), pp. 283–84.

[9] Gowan, *Bridge Between the Testaments*, p. 78.

[10] Victor Tcherikover, *Hellenistic Civilization and the Jews* (Philadelphia: Jewish Publication Society, 1966), pp. 50–58.

tween 320 B.C. and 301 B.C., Ptolemy invaded and controlled Palestine and Phoenicia three times.

The conflict between these two dynasties continued for a hundred years (301–198 B.C.). The Seleucids and the Ptolemies waged war intermittently throughout that period (276, 260, and 246 B.C.), but the Ptolemies remained in control of Palestine.[11] A short-lived peace was reached in 241 B.C.

Antiochus III (the Great) came to the Seleucid throne in 223 B.C. It took him twenty-five years, but Antiochus ultimately wrested control of Palestine from the Ptolemies.[12]

The century of Jewish life under the Ptolemies is poorly documented in the ancient texts, but some general observations are possible. Taxes were high[13] and the administration of the region was probably conducted from Acco (renamed Ptolemais). While there is some limited evidence of the kind of syncretism that would eventually bring Judaism into a life-and-death conflict with Hellenism,[14] the general impression this period leaves is one of comparative religious freedom in a setting of economic oppression.[15]

This economic oppression lay primarily in the planned economy imple-

mented by the Ptolemies. A cornerstone of this was a practice called "tax farming." The Ptolemies sold a franchise for the collection of taxes in a given area to the highest bidder. The "tax farmer" who won the franchise was then free to collect as much in taxes as he was able. The end result was an economic system that enriched a few and impoverished the many.[16]

The transfer of control from the Ptolemies to the Seleucids in 198 B.C. was made easier by the dissatisfaction of the Jewish populace. The Ptolemaic garrison was expelled from Jerusalem with the help of Jewish forces,[17] which had gone over to the Seleucid side; they welcomed Antiochus the Great into Jerusalem and supplied provisions for his armies and war elephants. While the motives behind this change of allegiance were no doubt complex,[18] the result was predictable. In the aftermath of his victory, Antiochus the Great granted concessions to the people of Judea, thus marking the beginning of more than two decades of Jewish freedom.

This royal favor was not without its negative aspects. The concessions, which were fairly common for the pacification of subject peoples,[19] pro-

---

[11] W. Stewart McCullough, *The History and Literature of the Palestinian Jews from Cyrus to Herod, 550 B.C.–4 B.C.* (Toronto: University of Toronto Press, 1975), pp. 85–86.

[12] Russell, *The Jews*, p. 17.

[13] Gowan (*Bridge Between the Testaments*, p. 80) cites the example of taxes set on grain at 33% and on fruit at 50%.

[14] S. K. Eddy, *The King Is Dead: Studies in the Near Eastern Resistance to Hellenism* (Lincoln, Neb.: University of Nebraska Press, 1961), pp. 196–204.

[15] McCullough, *History and Literature*, pp. 89–90; Martin Hengel, *Judaism and Hellenism*, (Philadelphia: Fortress, 1974), pp. 35–57. Hengel's detailed analysis of the social, political, and economic conditions in Palestine points to the economic difficulties of the orthodox in a context of passive, rather than overt, Hellenization.

[16] The most notorious tax farmer was Joseph ben Tobias (Grayzel, *History of the Jews*, p. 59; *AJ* 12.4.2–5). Grant (*From Alexander to Cleopatra*, p. 44) calls the Ptolemaic system of taxation "of a size and diversity unknown in the ancient world."

[17] *AJ* 12.3.3.

[18] Eddy, *The King Is Dead*, pp. 200–201; Hengel, *Jews, Greeks and Barbarians*, pp. 37ff.; Tcherikover, *Hellenistic Civilization and the Jews*, pp. 79–89.

[19] Hengel, *Jews, Greeks and Barbarians*, p. 43. In fact, Hengel points out that the exemptions granted Jerusalem were comparatively small.

vided the context for the continued growth of a Hellenized elite within Judea. The Ptolemies had encouraged the cooperation of the upper classes by offering them a share in the fruits of Hellenistic rule.[20] The Seleucids continued these policies, and by the time the full light of intertestamental history illuminates Judea, the aristocracy had become thoroughly Hellenized and active participants in the foreign governance of Palestine. These Hellenized Jews held the primary political, economic, and religious positions under the Seleucids and had a vested interest in maintaining a cooperative relationship with the ruling dynasty.

The Hellenization of the upper classes was even more pronounced under the Seleucids than it had been under the Ptolemies.[21] Under the leadership of the pro-Seleucid high priest Jason (Joshua), Jerusalem was allowed to incorporate as a Greek city (*polis*). Jason, who had purchased the priesthood from Antiochus IV in 175 B.C., used his position to establish the Greek *gymnasium* in Jerusalem. This thoroughly Greek educational institution with its classical education and nude athletics horrified the orthodox members of the community.[22]

A speech in the pseudepigraphal *Book of Jubilees*, supposedly delivered by Abraham, reflects this reaction; the patriarch warns against Israelites who refuse circumcision for their children (15:33–34). Earlier, *Jubilees* says the Law of God, as recorded in "the

heavenly tablets," commands Jews not to "be uncovered as the Gentiles are uncovered" (33:31), i.e., in the Greek games. The apocryphal Ecclesiasticus speaks pointedly about the wise, who will not hate the Law (33:2), and the lawless, whose sacrifices are blemished and unacceptable (34:18–19). What military conquest had not accomplished, cultural and religious syncretism was threatening to do.

It is in this setting of Greek political and cultural dominance that the writer of 1 Maccabees resumes the systematic recording of Jewish history.

Antiochus IV (later to be called Epiphanes), the great villain of this historical work, came to the throne of the Seleucid dynasty during a time of great international ferment. To the west, Rome had emerged as a threatening world power. Parthia menaced the eastern frontier, and to the south, Antiochus' ambitions to control Egypt would lead to war and to his ultimate humiliation at the hands of Rome. Jerusalem itself was in the throes of internal disorder created by the scheming of opposing Hellenizing factions, aggravating the already strong hostility of the more conservative, largely disenfranchised populace.

During the Ptolemaic period Jerusalem had been treated as if it were a Hellenistic temple state with the high priest as the chief political figure.[23] It is not surprising to see the struggle for power that swirled about the politicized high-priestly office. The extent to

---

[20] Ibid., p. 112.

[21] McCullough, *History and Literature*, pp. 89–90, calls the Ptolemies the "least culturally aggressive of all Hellenistic dynasties," and the Hellenism experienced by Palestinian Jews as "mild."

[22] Grant, *From Alexander to Cleopatra*, pp. 72–73.

[23] Gowan, *Bridge Between the Testaments*, pp. 61–62, postulates a gradual increase in the power of the high priest, ultimately giving him tax collecting power and placing him as the primary intermediate between Judea and the ruling Greek dynasty.

which the high priesthood was subject to the control of the Greek kings and the economic benefits that might accrue to the family holding the office are demonstrated again and again. Onias II withheld tribute from Ptolemy III and lost his franchise to collect taxes to his nephew Joseph ben Tobias, who was probably a descendant of the Tobiah who had vied for power with Nehemiah.[24]

In 174 B.C., rivals for the high priesthood questioned the Seleucid loyalties of Onias III. Antiochus IV then deposed him and made Jason, his brother, the new high priest. This intervention marked the beginning of a period when the traditionally hereditary nature of the high priesthood was set aside, and the Seleucid and later Roman rulers saw it as their right to appoint high priests.[25]

Jason was an aggressively Hellenistic Jew whose appointment outraged the people of Judea; but when he was replaced by Menelaus, a non-Aaronide whose only qualification for the office was that he had offered Antiochus IV a larger bribe, the outrage eventually erupted into rioting.[26] However, it was events outside Judea that would pave the way for the climactic conflict with Greek authority.

Antiochus IV took the throne of a badly divided, financially stricken empire, threatened by enemies on all its borders.[27] In 169 B.C., Ptolemy VI declared war on Antiochus but was routed by the Seleucid forces. While Antiochus was in Egypt, rumors spread in Palestine that he had been killed, and the deposed Jason moved against his successor, Menelaus, to reclaim the priesthood. The fighting that followed produced no advantage for Jason, even though Menelaus had to seek refuge in the newly established Greek citadel (Acra). Jason was eventually forced into exile because of his brutality to the residents of Jerusalem.[28] Antiochus interpreted these events as a rebellion against his rule; and when he returned from Egypt, he unleashed his armies on the city. He reconfirmed Menelaus as high priest and, in cooperation with Menelaus, proceeded to plunder the temple.[29]

The unrest in Judea took on new significance for Antiochus the following year (168 B.C.), when he attempted to assume control of Egypt. Rome, which was beginning to show an interest in the east, sent a senatorial embassy to Egypt ordering Antiochus out of Egypt. Having been a hostage in Rome, Antiochus was well aware of the power that confronted him, so he withdrew. The threat of Roman power on his southern border, coupled with his recent experience in Jerusalem, convinced him that to continue the policy of tolerance for the Jews—a policy that had prevailed since Alexander's time— would be a mistake.[30] The intent of his militant policy of Hellenization seems to have been to incorporate Judea into his kingdom at a new level.[31]

It has been argued convincingly that

---

[24] See pp. 340, 344.
[25] Jones, *Ancient Civilization*, p. 299.
[26] 2 Maccabees 4:25–26.
[27] Russell, *The Jews*, p. 32; Grant, *From Alexander to Cleopatra*, pp. 49–56.
[28] 2 Maccabees 5:5–10.
[29] 1 Maccabees 1:20–28; 2 Maccabees 5:11–21.
[30] Jones, *Ancient Civilization*, p. 341; Zeitlin, *Rise and Fall*, pp. 87–88.
[31] 1 Maccabees 1:41–42.

the original impetus for forceful Hellenization came not from Antiochus himself but from the Tobiad high priest, Menelaus.[32] It is highly unlikely that Antiochus could have been adequately informed of conditions and sentiments in Judea unless he was informed by someone close to the situation.[33] Thus, what began in many respects as a civil war between the Hellenistic innovators and the orthodox majority was escalated by Jewish complicity into the persecution that precipitated the Maccabean rebellion. However, it is still true that the power of the Seleucid king made the persecutions possible; Antiochus must still bear the stigma of being the first pagan monarch to persecute Jews for their faith.

In 167 B.C., Antiochus sent Apollonius to Jerusalem to punish the rebels. Entering the city on the Sabbath, he slaughtered its unresisting citizens, plundered and burned the city, tore down its defensive walls, and fortified the Acra, the Hellenistic city established by Jason.[34] Later he would enforce an imposed, syncretized worship and prohibit circumcision, Sabbath observance, and the Jewish dietary laws.[35] Pagan altars were established throughout Judea, and Jews who refused to offer sacrifice on those altars and eat the flesh of pigs were sentenced to death. On 15 Kislev (December 6),

167 B.C., Antiochus committed the ultimate blasphemy; he erected a statue of Olympian Zeus in the temple and ten days later offered a sacrifice of swine's flesh on the altar of burnt offering.

Initially, the response of the Jews to this program was passive resistance. Rather than defile themselves with unclean food, pagan worship, and a profanation of God's command, they fled to the wilderness or chose death. This commitment is recorded in 1 Maccabees in almost journalistic style; 2 Maccabees expands the motif in a clearly legendary and embellished style that nevertheless conveys a powerful impression of the dedication of the orthodox to withstand the temptation to violate Torah, even in the face of death.[36]

B. THE MACCABEES
(1 Maccabees 2; *AJ* 12.6)

Mattathias, a priest of the family of the *Hashmonaim* (Hasmoneans) from the village of Modin, enters the story at this point. He was already an old man when, as both priest and leader of his village, he was ordered by a Syrian emissary to offer sacrifice on a pagan altar. He refused, only to see a Jewish apostate step forward to take his place. Enraged, Mattathias killed the apostate and the Syrian officer, striking the blow that would change Jewish response

---

[32]Elias Bickerman, *From Ezra to the Last of the Maccabees* (New York: Schocken, 1962), pp. 104–17; Gowan, *Bridge Between the Testaments*, pp. 97–100; Hengel, *Judaism and Hellenism*, pp. 283–92.

[33]McCullough, *History and Literature*, p. 115. Because most of the available sources are written from the Palestinian perspective, it is all too easy to assume that the focus of Antiochus' attentions was there. In fact, through much of intertestamental times, Judea enjoyed extensive periods of Seleucid absence as the regime's attention was diverted by more important problems elsewhere.

[34]1 Maccabees 1:29–40; 2 Maccabees 5:24–26.

[35]It is unlikely that, according to 1 Maccabees, the laws and religions of all the people of the Seleucid empire were to be abrogated. Such a decree would have been pointless in the religiously tolerant Near East.

[36]1 Maccabees 1:60–64; 2 Maccabees 6:4–7:42.

from passive to militant. After they had dismantled the pagan altar, Mattathias and his five sons—John, Simon, Judas, Eleazar, and Jonathan—fled to the hills.[37]

In the early stage of the revolt, Jewish fugitives had been attacked on the Sabbath and had refused to defend themselves. Mattathias and his followers, however, reasoned that if all the Jews followed that example, there would soon be no Jews left. So they determined to fight back, even on the Sabbath.[38] During this same period they were joined by the Hasidim (the Pious),[39] a sect that appears to have been less concerned with political or nationalistic matters than with the defense of the Law.[40]

The goals of this coalition seem to have been rather limited at first. Operating as a guerrilla army, they wreaked havoc on apostate Jews, destroying pagan altars and forcing circumcision on any uncircumcised males they encountered.[41] Within a year the elderly Mattathias succumbed to age and the rigors of the fugitive existence, and Judas, whom they came to call *Maccabeus* (the Hammer),[42] assumed command (166 B.C.).

1. Judas Maccabeus and the Armed Rebellion (166–160 B.C.; 1 Maccabees 3:1–9:22; 2 Maccabees 8:1–15:37; AJ 12.7–11)

The early phase of the rebellion under Judas seems to have been primarily religious. His allies the *Hasidim* had no interest in political power or objectives[43] other than the reestablishment of orthodox worship and the expulsion of the radical Hellenizers who controlled Jerusalem. Judas's coalition, therefore, was strong only so long as the threat to orthodoxy existed. After centuries of foreign domination, the majority of Jews had reoriented their allegiance from the nation to the temple and were willing to die for their faith but not for their state.

But the forces of Judas were not the only threat to the Syrians during these years. His early triumphs came while the armies of Antiochus IV were on the empire's eastern frontier, leaving the control of such peripheral areas as Judea in the hands of auxiliary troops under the command of local governors.[44] Consequently, Judas's first encounters with Syrian forces were amazingly successful.

---

[37] 1 Maccabees 2:15–30.

[38] 1 Maccabees 2:32–41.

[39] The *Hasidim* were apparently, from the role they play in the early years of the Maccabean revolt, already a party of considerable power.

[40] This pietistic sect would ultimately give rise to both the Pharisees and the Essenes. Jonathan A. Goldstein, *Anchor Bible Commentary,* vol. 41, *1 Maccabees* (Garden City, N.Y.: Doubleday, 1976), pp. 5–6.

[41] 1 Maccabees 2:44–48.

[42] There is not universal acceptance of the derivation of the name from the Hebrew word for "hammer." Grayzel, *History of the Jews,* pp. 67–68, offers the suggestion that it derives from the first letters of the Hebrew sentence, "Who is like unto Thee among the mighty, O Lord," supposedly the motto of the Maccabees. A less flattering derivation is offered by Zeitlin, who rejects Grayzel's suggestion out of hand (*Rise and Fall,* p. 96). He explains that it means "hammer-head" a name that described the shape of Judah's skull!

[43] As evidenced by their withdrawal from the rebellion when religious freedom was returned and the Aaronide Alcimus was named high priest (1 Macc. 7:12–17).

[44] Bickerman, *Ezra to the Maccabees,* p. 115.

Even before his first encounter with regular Syrian forces, Judas routed three auxiliary units under the command of some local Syrian commanders. The first of these was a contingent of mercenaries, possibly under the same Apollonius who had led the massacre in 167.[45] Then Seron, a local commander who tried to advance his career, was defeated near Beth-Horon.[46] Finally, an army commissioned by Antiochus' regent, Lysias, was routed near Emmaus. Apparently this last force was so considerable that local slave traders, certain of Syrian victory, accompanied the army to collect the Israelite survivors for sale.[47] While these victories did not have a major impact on the Seleucid empire, they emboldened the resistance and provided an abundant source for weapons and money.[48] Finally, Lysias himself marched against Judas and was defeated.[49]

After Lysias withdrew to Antioch, Judas and his followers moved on to Jerusalem, where, with the exception of the Acra, they took control of the city and the temple area. Judas assigned a contingent to guard the citadel where the Hellenizers and a small Syrian garrison had barricaded themselves, while select priests purified the temple, dismantled the desecrated altar, and built a new one with unhewn stones. On the 25th of Kislev, 164 B.C., sacrifice was renewed; this date henceforth marked the beginning of the eight-day celebration of *Hanukkah,* the feast of dedication.[50]

We must assume that during the months that followed, the Syrian forces were occupied farther to the north, for Judas and his armies spread out through the areas that had once been Israelite territory to rescue Jews being persecuted by their Gentile neighbors.

The political situation in Judea at this point was complex. The purpose of the rebellion had been accomplished—the temple was once again in Jewish hands, the syncretistic cult had been banished, and the Syrians had been expelled, at least temporarily. At the same time, the Romans were offering to intervene on behalf of Judea. The accepted ruler,

---

[45] See 1 Maccabees 1:29–35; 3:10–12; 2 Maccabees 5:24–26; and Grayzel, *History of the Jews.* Josephus identifies him as the governor of Samaria mentioned in a letter he records (*AJ* 12.5.5). Goldstein sees this as a likely identification (*1 Maccabees,* p. 245).

[46] 1 Maccabees 3:13–14. After Goldstein (*1 Maccabees,* p. 246), who argues that he was the commander of "an independent, tactical unit in the Seleucid army."

[47] 1 Maccabees 3:41; 2 Maccabees 8:10–11.

[48] 1 Maccabees 6:6.

[49] With an army that Josephus records at 40,000 infantry and 7,000 cavalry, it is unlikely that Lysias would have withdrawn merely because he had lost 5,000 men. It has been suggested (Goldstein, *1 Maccabees,* pp. 270–71) that, at the urging of Menelaus, Lysias made a tactical withdrawal aimed at removing the Syrian army from view, thus robbing Judas of the unifying effect of such a potent visible threat. Zeitlin (*Rise and Fall,* p. 101) suggests that the withdrawal was prompted when Lysias received word of Antiochus Epiphanes' death.

[50] The two accounts in the Apocrypha (1 Macc. 4:52–59; 2 Macc. 10:1–8) of the founding of this festival do not contain the legend of the Hanukkah lights. Josephus (*AJ* 12.7.6–7) mentions the festival but omits the legend as well. It is not until the *Gemara,* a collection of discussions and elaborations on the *Mishnah,* that the story of the miracle of the Hanukkah lights is found. According to this story, the Seleucids had defiled all the oil for the temple *Menorah*; and, when the Maccabees attempted to rekindle the *Menorah,* they were able to find only one small flask with enough oil for one day. Nevertheless, this small supply burned for eight days, hence the eight-day duration of the festival. The origins of Hanukkah may be more complex than any of these stories suggest (Hayyim Schauss, *The Jewish Festivals: History and Observance* [New York: Schocken, 1962], pp. 208–18).

however, was not Judas but the despised Menelaus.[51]

Judas, recognizing that the present conditions were only temporary, fortified Beth Zur (Zechariah)—a major fortress protecting the southern approach to Jerusalem—and Mount Zion itself. It is conceivable that Judas' military forays into surrounding territories were, at least in part, motivated by a desire to hamper an anticipated Syrian invasion.

The Acra remained a thorn in the flesh of the Maccabees and their followers, and it now became the object of Judas' military operations. He launched a siege of the Acra sometime in the spring of 163 B.C. But within a matter of months, escapees from the Acra had warned Lysias and the young Antiochus V of Judas' hostile activity. As a result, the Jewish forces were for the first time confronted with a major contingent of the Syrian army, cavalry, and war elephants. During this engagement, Eleazar became the first of the sons of Mattathias to be killed. The Jewish forces were routed, and some took refuge in the recently fortified temple area.

After a lengthy siege, Lysias had to withdraw to respond to a threat from Philip, another of Antiochus IV's commanders, who had returned from Persia with the king's army and was attempting to take control at Antioch. In his withdrawal, Lysias agreed to rescind all prohibitions against the free exercise of Jewish religion, promised not to intervene in the internal conflict between the Hellenizers and the orthodox, and deposed and executed Menelaus.[52] An Oniad named Alcimus was appointed high priest in his place, at which the Hasidim, convinced that their religious objectives had been realized, withdrew their support from Judas and gave their allegiance to the new high priest. Alcimus proved as perfidious as Antiochus, however, later seizing and killing sixty of their number.

At about this same time (162 B.C.), Demetrius, the son of Seleucus IV who had been held hostage in Rome, escaped and returned to claim the throne. Supported by the army, he deposed Antiochus V, who was executed along with Lysias, his guardian. His first act as king was to send Bacchides (his general) and Alcimus (who had asked for royal help) against the Maccabees.[53] The attempt to take Judas and his followers was unsuccessful; so Bacchides withdrew, but he left a military contingent to back Alcimus.

Judas and a faithful core of followers, refusing to recognize Alcimus, returned to active guerrilla warfare throughout Judea. In response, Demetrius sent his general Nicanor. Judas' first encounter with Nicanor resulted in a victory for the Maccabees, but it was to be his last.

With the Syrian force rebuffed and Nicanor killed, Judas reasserted his control over Judea and sent ambassadors to Rome to request an alliance against Demetrius. Rome was more than happy to accommodate the request, and, late in 161 B.C., a treaty was formalized.[54] Demetrius responded, mobilizing his regular army as soon as the spring campaigning season began and sending Bacchides back to Judea. The impact of the arrival of this formi-

---

[51] 2 Maccabees 11:16–33.
[52] Bickerman, *Ezra to the Maccabees,* pp. 117–18; Goldstein, *1 Maccabees,* pp. 66–67.
[53] 1 Maccabees 7:8–11.
[54] The negotiations and agreement are recorded in 1 Maccabees 8.

dable force was so great that all but eight hundred of Judas' men deserted him. Terribly outmanned, Judas chose, against the advice of his followers, to die on the field of battle. With Judas dead, the rebellion lost its first great military leader, thus ending the first phase of the war.

Judas' efforts can be evaluated from two perspectives. If, as the traditions depict him, he was a simple fighter for religious freedom, then he was a success. Stepping onto the stage of history in a time of religious oppression, with the Jewish faith ready to succumb to the enticements of the cosmopolitan Greek world and the promises of political and economic reward they offered, he stemmed the tide of religious syncretism and foreign domination, if only imperfectly.

If, on the other hand, one is inclined to see him as a man in quest of larger political goals,[55] then he must be seen as a leader who overreached himself. His military accomplishments were remarkable, given the conditions under which he operated, but he was a local leader whose successes were to a large extent dictated by external forces. His alliance with Rome may be seen as a diplomatic coup, but (as Bickerman suggests) it was of no immediate value and may be considered the act that brought about his final and fatal encounter with Bacchides and laid the groundwork for the appeal to Rome that, in 63 B.C., would make Judea a Roman province.

As was so often the case with the Judean and Israelite kings who preceded him, his religious fervor was a thing to be honored and emulated, but his entanglements with external politics were largely fruitless.

2. Jonathan and the Diplomatic War (160–143 B.C.; 1 Maccabees 9:23–12:53; AJ 13.1.1–13.6.6; WJ 1.2.1)

Judas' death brought an end to the initial military phase of Maccabean resistance. Jonathan, who assumed the mantle of leadership, was reduced to hiding in the wilderness of Tekoa with the remnant of followers that had survived. During this time, while hard pressed by Bacchides, the third brother (John) was killed by Nabateans. In response, Jonathan attacked and destroyed a Nabatean caravan. This brought Bacchides down on his small army—which escaped, under heavy pressure from its enemies, only by swimming the Jordan. This event illustrates the weakness of what was left of the Maccabean movement in 160 B.C. following Judas' death. In 159 B.C., the high priest (Alcimus) died, and, for whatever reason, Demetrius failed to replace him.

---

[55] As is sometimes the case. Judas' treaty with Rome was certainly without religious motivation and, in fact, violated a well-established Old Testament principle against reliance on foreign powers. His refusal to accept a biologically, if not spiritually, acceptable high priest is not as clear an indication, but it does hint at a more political agenda (see Russell, *The Jews,* pp. 50ff.). The question of whether Judas was motivated by pure religious goals is, however, a modern one. From its inception, the nation of Israel had been a religious state. To see Judas as a champion of purely religious emancipation for Judea would be to interpret him from the secularist perspective of the twentieth century. A devout Jew of the second century B.C. would have seen political freedom as an integral part of religious freedom. Given the rising messianic expectations of intertestamental Judaism, a purely religious answer to the challenge of Hellenism under the Seleucids seems totally inadequate. It might, however, be valid to suggest that the emphasis of the Maccabean rulers shifted as events shaped the Maccabees and the taste of power became its own motivation.

After fortifying sites around Jerusalem and garrisoning them with Syrian troops, Bacchides took the sons of Judea's leaders as hostages, imprisoned them in the Acra, and then returned to Antioch. Within two years the Hellenizers became alarmed at Jonathan's growing strength and again appealed to Antioch for help. Bacchides returned to deal with the threat, but he suffered a defeat at Jonathan's hand and made preparations to withdraw. It is at this point that Jonathan distinguished himself as a negotiator and politician. He took advantage of his temporary position of strength and sued for peace. Bacchides, apparently angered at the Hellenizers for involving him in an unsuccessful campaign and glad to have the conflict with Jonathan behind him, agreed. He left Jonathan in control of the hill town of Michmash, where, we are told, "he began to judge the people, and he destroyed the ungodly out of Israel."[56]

Jonathan remains in relative obscurity until Alexander Balas, claiming to be the son of Antiochus IV,[57] sought to take the throne away from Demetrius. Rome, Ptolemy VI, and other lesser powers backed Alexander, so Demetrius turned to Jonathan for mercenary soldiers. To win his favor, Demetrius granted Jonathan the right to raise and arm troops and then released the hostages he had held in the Acra. Jonathan immediately moved to Jerusalem, which he refortified.

But Alexander offered Jonathan a far more tempting inducement—the high priesthood. In October of 152 B.C., Jonathan assumed that office as a patron of the Seleucid king. In 150 B.C., Demetrius was killed in battle by Alexander, and Jonathan was appointed governor of Judea. In the ten short years since the death of Judas, the Maccabean family had reversed what seemed ultimate defeat and had consolidated both religious and political power.

Jonathan's reign as governor and high priest takes an intricate course through the conflicts of his Greek overlords, a course that, until the very end, he charted with a skill that testifies to his acumen as a politician. His patron, Alexander Balas, ruled for only five years before he was dethroned and killed by Demetrius II, son of Demetrius I. During the transition from Alexander to Demetrius II, Jonathan laid siege to the Acra once again. Demetrius called him to account for this, but Jonathan brought a large delegation of Jewish leaders and— probably more impressive—extravagant gifts for the new king. Demetrius II was won over; he confirmed all the honors already bestowed on Jonathan, increased the territory of Judea, and reduced taxes.

When one of the generals of Alexander Balas revolted against Demetrius, Jonathan used the situation to win an agreement from Demetrius that the Greek garrison be withdrawn from the Acra. Demetrius agreed, and Jonathan and his men fought heroically to save the king's life. Their heroism proved misplaced, however. The crisis past, Demetrius went back on his agreement with Jonathan. In retaliation, Jonathan transferred his allegiance to Antiochus

---

[56] Jonathan was allowed to "retire" and establish himself as a village sheik ruling over a limited sheikdom in the Judean hill country.

[57] A claim that is not challenged by Josephus or the author of 1 Maccabees but was generally questioned by other ancient sources (Goldstein, *1 Maccabees,* pp. 398–99).

VI (Alexander's son) and Tryphon. Once again, his prior honors were confirmed, and Simon, his brother, was appointed governor "from the ladder of Tyre to Egypt."[58]

With the territory of Judea greatly expanded, Jonathan made contact with Rome to reaffirm the earlier alliance. Rome's response was favorable, and, after further military success for both Jonathan and Simon, the refortification of Judea was undertaken.

Tryphon, who was scheming to displace Antiochus VI, made plans to eliminate Jonathan as a threat to his own ambitions. Luring him into the city of Ptolemais, Tryphon had Jonathan taken captive and his bodyguard massacred.

Simon quickly stepped in to rally the Jews and to complete preparations for war. Tryphon, with Jonathan in custody, offered to release him for the payment of a hundred talents of silver and the presentation of two of Jonathan's sons as hostages. Simon paid the ransom, but Tryphon refused to release Jonathan. After attempting unsuccessfully to break the continuing siege of the Acra, Tryphon killed Jonathan and returned to Syria.

Jonathan was an able general, but his contribution to the revolt lies in the diplomatic realm. By deftly choosing the right side in a series of power shifts, Jonathan and Judea were able to more than double their territory. In nine years, between his enlistment by Demetrius I against Alexander Balas (152 B.C.) and his death at the hands of Tryphon (143 B.C.), Jonathan rose from village chief to high priest and governor.

His brother also received a governorship under the Seleucids and was in a strong position to step in when Jonathan died. Jonathan must be judged a success in achieving almost unthinkable political advancement for himself and his brother and in laying the foundation for the imminent political liberation of Judea.[59]

3. Simon the Hasmonean (142–134 B.C.; 1 Maccabees 13–15:41; 16:11–17; *AJ* 13.6.3–7.4)

Simon is a transitional figure in Jewish history. Under his direction the Maccabees moved from the struggle for independence to its realization. The high priesthood, a political appointment for decades, became the hereditary possession of the family of the Maccabees. But, as the final figure in the heroic battle for freedom, he was also the first in a line of kings—the Hasmonean dynasty—that distinguished itself for its impiety and treachery. Simon's four brothers had died bravely in the face of their enemies, but Simon himself was murdered at a banquet where he and two of his sons had drunk too much.

It would probably be wrong to condemn him too harshly, however. The Maccabees were a family of unusual gifts and abilities. While their revolution took a wrong turn, the events of history shape people as surely as people shape history. As the last of the Maccabees, Simon must be regarded as the culmination of a heroic

---

[58] 1 Maccabees 11:52–59. This would include the coastal area from Phoenicia (modern Lebanon) to the southern limit of Seleucid control.

[59] For an evaluation of Jonathan's accomplishments, see Zeitlin, *Rise and Fall,* p. 142.

struggle for freedom. Simon was, by all accounts, a good man who took his priestly office seriously and was well regarded by his subjects.[60] He was also a typical Hellenistic king. We may generalize and say that the better qualities he exhibited during his reign were the residue of his past; his worse qualities, the somber promise of the future.

Simon began his reign by transferring allegiance from the perfidious Tryphon back to the equally untrustworthy Demetrius II. In exchange for his support, Simon was released from what the writer of I Maccabees refers to as "the yoke of the heathen"—the payment of tribute to the Seleucids. This release was a tacit admission of Judea's independence,[61] which is also reflected in the dating of documents; 142 B.C. becomes "the first year of Simon the great high priest, the governor and leader of the Jews," rather than the 170th year of the Seleucid reign.[62]

Simon convened a meeting of the priests, elders, and leaders of the people in 141 B.C. to legitimize his high priesthood. Mattathias had come from a priestly family, but he was not of the Zadokite line, the only lineage accepted for the hereditary office of high priest. Furthermore, the offices of king and high priest had always been carefully kept separate during the monarchy, and it required a specific act to overturn this. The Great Synagogue noted the contributions of Simon and his family on behalf of the people and the temple and agreed to accept him and his descendants as high priest and governor until the appearance of a true prophet. This qualification allowed for the overturning of (1) the provision recorded in the Torah that the high priest should be of the line of Phinehas[63] and (2) the tradition that can be traced back to the time of David that only the line of Zadok out of all the line of Phinehas was the rightful high priestly line.

Simon made use of his newly won independence and completed the siege of the Acra; he expelled the surviving Hellenizers from the citadel and turned it into his own palace. For the first time in four decades, Jerusalem was free of the stigma of Hellenistic dominance. To safeguard the route between Jerusalem and the seaport of Jaffa, he took the fortress of Gazara (Gezer).

The predictable ongoing struggle for the Seleucid throne allowed Simon the freedom to pursue his own goals. In 139 B.C., Demetrius II marched into Babylon in an effort to drive out the Parthians. There he was captured, and Tryphon returned to claim the throne once again. He was challenged by Antiochus VII, the brother of Demetrius II. Antiochus confirmed Simon's position and granted him the right to mint his own coinage. However, he also demanded the return of the Hellenistic cities taken by Simon—including the Acra. This conflict continued during Simon's lifetime, but it was not until after his death that the Syrians made good on their demands.

Simon died ignominiously at the hand of his own son-in-law. With his death the Maccabean era ends and the Hasmonean era begins. It seems appropriate that a dynasty noted for its

---

[60] 1 Maccabees 14:4–15.
[61] Goldstein, *1 Maccabees,* pp. 477ff.
[62] 1 Maccabees 13:41-42.
[63] Numbers 25:12–15.

bloodshed and internal conflict should be inaugurated with the intrafamilial murder of its founder.

C. THE HASMONEAN ERA

The Hasmoneans would rule over an independent Israel that, for a time, would equal the boundaries of David and Solomon. This, however, is not an indication that all was well. They ruled in a manner that gave evidence of the increasing secularization of the power of the state and the king. The high priesthood degenerated during these years to a level not far above its nadir under Menelaus. The polarization of Judean society was nearly complete; rival parties, using the power of the throne to their own advantage in the name of theology, grew, while others simply withdrew in anticipation of some final, apocalyptic righting of matters. The Maccabees had successfully thrown off the foreign yoke, only to have it replaced by the not noticeably less objectionable dominance of their descendants.

1. John Hyrcanus
(135–104 B.C.; *AJ* 13.8–10; *WJ* 1.2.3–8).

Antiochus VII invaded Judea during the first year of the reign of Hyrcanus. He besieged Jerusalem and won the return of the cities outside Judea that had been captured by Jonathan and Simon; he also required tribute of five hundred talents of silver and withdrew only after taking hostages and dismantling Jerusalem's walls.

This humiliating state of affairs was to continue for only a short time. In 128 B.C., Antiochus VII was killed in a war with the Parthians, and Demetrius

II returned to reclaim his throne. John Hyrcanus took advantage of the weakness of Syria, reaffirmed Judea's relationship with Rome, and began a series of campaigns aimed at expanding Judea's borders and recapturing what had been lost. His campaigns are the first systematic and planned conquests of the Hasmonean era.[64]

In the south, he conquered Idumea, subjecting its residents to forced conversion and circumcision. (The ancestors of Herod, the Idumean, probably became "Jewish" in this way; thus, he could claim to be Jewish while the Jews could hate him as an outsider.) To the north, he razed the city of Shechem and the Samaritan temple on Gerizim and added southern Galilee to his holdings, gaining control of the rich valley of Esdraelon all the way to Mount Carmel on the coast. Late in his reign, he took the Greek city at Samaria.

His conquests were impressive, but the rumor spread that he paid his foreign mercenary soldiers by plundering King David's tomb. Whether true or not, the story, coupled with his use of foreigners in the army and his increasingly Hellenistic style of rule, created a rift between Hyrcanus and the Pharisees, a party that came into prominence during his reign. According to Josephus, Hyrcanus began as a supporter of the Pharisees; but when a Pharisee named Eleazar challenged his right to hold the high priesthood, his support swung to the Sadducees.

The Essenes were another party derived from the earlier Hasidim. They apparently became so disenchanted with the Hasmonean regime at this time that they withdrew to the desert and established the Qumran commu-

---

[64]Tcherikover, *Hellenistic Civilization and the Jews,* pp. 245–46.

nity, which produced the manuscripts that today are known as the Dead Sea Scrolls.[65]

2. Aristobulus
(104–103 B.C.; *AJ* 13.11, *WJ* 1.3)

The brief reign of Aristobulus is noteworthy for several reasons. Hyrcanus had minted coins in his own name, but Aristobulus was the first Hasmonean to formally take the title "King."[66]

He also was the first of the Hasmoneans to imprison his brothers to keep them from making a claim on his throne. It had been his father's intention that his widow would succeed him and that Aristobulus would serve as high priest. But Aristobulus imprisoned his mother and three of his brothers, taking both offices for himself. He allowed his mother to starve to death in prison and had Antigonus, the one brother he did not imprison, put to death.

Aristobulus also conquered the territory of the Itureans in the north of Galilee, forcing them to undergo circumcision and to adhere to the Mosaic Law.[67]

3. Alexander Jannaeus
(103–76 B.C.; *AJ* 13.12–15, *WJ* 1.4)

Released from prison by Aristobulus' widow, Salome Alexandra (whom he later married), Alexander took the throne and, for the first fifteen years of his reign, continued the expansionist policies begun by John Hyrcanus. He officially claimed the title of king and used Greek motifs and inscriptions on his coinage, in some of which he is identified as king.

During these years, he was so successful militarily that he extended the boundaries of Israel to match those of Solomon's kingdom, but off the battlefield this Hasmonean was a dismal parody of the founders of the dynasty. Noted for his immorality and drunkenness, more the soldier chieftain than the pious high priest, he earned the enmity of the Pharisees and the common people. While officiating at the Feast of Tabernacles in the temple, the crowd of worshipers expressed their displeasure with him by hurling insults and citrons at him. Jannaeus responded by loosing his mercenaries on the crowd and, according to Josephus, killing six thousand.

Following an unsuccessful foray into the Nabatean realms, he returned to a civil war that lasted six years, during which fifty thousand Jews were killed by Greek mercenaries. In desperation, the Pharisees called on Demetrius III (Eukairos), a Seleucid ruler. Thus, we find successors of the Hasidim, who are in league with the descendants of Antiochus Epiphanes, fighting against

---

[65] Russell, *The Jews*, p. 67.

[66] Ibid., p. 68, points out that Strabo calls Alexander Jannaeus the first to assume that title. He suggests, plausibly, that Aristobulus may have refrained from calling himself king among his own people, though he did so in his dealing with outsiders.

[67] Later Jewish attitudes to "Galilee of the Gentiles" were probably compounded out of its openness to Gentile influences and the Gentile population that had been forcibly converted to Judaism. The view of Galilee as a religiously simple, less than orthodox, source of trouble for Jewish authorities runs through Grayzel's (*History of the Jews*, pp. 131–36) condescending summary of the life of Christ. As a Jewish scholar once expressed it to this writer, "If a new religion was going to emerge out of Judaism, I would have predicted it would come from Galilee."

the descendants of the Maccabees.[68] Jannaeus was routed and went into hiding. Ironically, some of his former enemies threw their support to him, and Demetrius' victory was short-lived.

As soon as Jannaeus had reasserted his authority, he began the persecution of the Pharisees who had instigated the revolt. While he drank and caroused with his concubines, he had eight hundred Pharisees crucified before him and had their wives and children killed before them as they died. Because of the brutality of his reign and his persecution of the Pharisees, many scholars see Jannaeus in the Wicked Priest of the Habakkuk commentary from Qumran,[69] although there is no consensus on this.

Josephus records that Jannaeus's hard drinking brought on some ailment that plagued him for three years but could not keep him from going to war. The combination of fever and exertion finally took him to the grave.

4. Salome Alexandra
(76–67 B.C.; *AJ* 12.16, *WJ* 1.5)

Salome, whose brother was Simeon ben Shetah, the leader of the Pharisees, succeeded her husband. She reversed his pro-Sadducean policy and reinstated the Pharisees and their laws. While Pharisaic theology taught humility and forgiveness, in practice they used their new position of power to avenge themselves on the Sadducees. Salome Alexandra appointed her son Hyrcanus II as high priest.

Her other son, Aristobulus, was pro-Sadducee. He was prominent in a deputation that asked permission to establish Sadducean fortresses outside Jerusalem. They argued that their safety was in jeopardy and that, without such refuges, they would be forced to take up residence among the Gentiles. Salome acceded to this request, thus giving Aristobulus and the Sadducees a significant advantage in the power struggle that followed her death.

5. Aristobulus II
(67–63 B.C.; *AJ* 13.16–14.4, *WJ* 1.6–7)

Upon his mother's death, Hyrcanus II (the favorite of the Pharisees) was named high priest and king; but within three short months Aristobulus II (the favorite of the Sadducees and the aristocracy) had forced his resignation and withdrawal from Jerusalem. At this point Antipater II, father of Herod the Great, entered the picture. Appointed governor of Idumea by Jannaeus, he now moved to increase his own power by convincing Hyrcanus II to escape his brother's reach. Hyrcanus fled to Petra, where the Nabatean king Aretas agreed to help him regain the throne. The defeat of Aristobulus at the hands of Aretas led to a complete rift between the priestly establishment and the common people, who followed the Pharisees. In the struggle between these two brothers and their followers the hard-won Hasmonean realm evaporated.

The Roman army had marched into Syria under the leadership of Pompey, one of Rome's most gifted generals. Both Hyrcanus and Aristobulus appealed to Pompey for support for their respective causes. Pompey, eager to claim the Eastern Mediterranean for Rome, took control of Judea, thus ending the Hasmonean dynasty.

[68] Russell, *The Jews,* p. 71.
[69] Menahem Mansoor, *The Dead Sea Scrolls,* (Grand Rapids: Eerdmans, 1964), p. 93.

The conquest was not accomplished without bloodshed. After a siege of three months, Pompey took Jerusalem; he and his army entered the temple and killed the priests at their sacrifices. Pompey himself entered the Holy of Holies, a desecration that shocked all Judeans, regardless of their political affiliation.

In the chaotic world of the pre-Roman Near East, the establishment of the kingdom of Judea had been a remarkable achievement, but its internal strength had been sapped by the religious conflicts that arose out of the Hasmonean attempt to combine temple and throne. Therefore, the independent kingdom of Judea ended much as it had begun, with factional struggles for supremacy.

But as sordid and depressing as this story is, it is holy history in the truest sense; God continued to work through it all to prepare His people for the coming of Messiah. Those preparations are more clearly seen in the social and religious developments of this period than in its history.

D. SOCIAL DEVELOPMENTS

1. Hellenism

Hellenism looms large in the history of Israel, as it does in the subsequent history of the Western world. It was an important formative element in the development of the Judaism of the New Testament era. One of its facets is the rise of a dispersed Judaism, enriched by crossfertilization with the ideas of the Greek world but ultimately strengthened in its faith by the pressures exerted by that world.

A simple definition of Hellenism is found in Aristotle's description of a Jewish sage: he "not only spoke Greek, but had the soul of a Greek."[70] Hellenism was, in Bickerman's words, "a supranational culture based on reason and faith in reason,"[71] not simply the spread of Greek ideas and language to the East. It was as much a world view as a definable body of information, and it developed into a syncretistic system that incorporated Greek structures and language into a matrix of Near Eastern customs.[72]

The Jews of the intertestamental period encountered two forms of Hellenism. The militant, aggressive Hellenism imposed by Antiochus IV and the Jewish Hellenizers was met and defeated on the fields of battle and of diplomacy. The more subtle form of Hellenism, which came into Judea as a world view shaping perceptions and determining methodologies for thought, was far more influential. While it can be said that the Maccabees expelled militant Hellenism, it can also be said that the thought world of Hellenism shaped later Judaism.

The most notable example of the blending of Greek and Hebrew ideas is probably the work of the Alexandrian Jewish philosopher Philo. In his attempt to blend the philosophical systems of Greece with the Law of Moses,

---

[70] Salo Baron, *A Social and Religious History of the Jews*, 18 vols. (New York: Columbia University Press, 1952), 1:184.

[71] Bickerman, *Ezra to the Maccabees*, p. 178.

[72] Gowan (*Bridge Between the Testaments*, pp. 71–72), Russell (*The Jews*, pp. 23–29; *The Method and Message of Jewish Apocalyptic* [Philadelphia: Westminster, 1964], pp. 18–19), and Samuel Sandmel (*Judaism and Christian Beginnings* [New York: Oxford University Press, 1978], pp. 3–4) are only a few of the numerous authors who might be consulted on the nature of Hellenism and its impact on Judaism.

he raised the art of allegorization to a previously unheard-of level.[73] Using his allegorical hermeneutic, he was able to show (at least to his own satisfaction) that Moses had anticipated the philosophy of the Greeks.

While Philo and the Hellenized aristocracy of the pre-Maccabean period represent an extreme of Jewish Hellenism, it can hardly be denied that even the most orthodox of Palestine's citizens were touched by its pervasive intellectual climate. For example, one of the main vehicles for Hellenization was the adoption of the Greek language, and history shows that Greek was in widespread use in Palestine.[74] The author of *The Letter of Aristeas,* which contains the legend of the translation of the Septuagint, reports the Greek names of many of the translators and takes for granted that seventy-two orthodox scholars, able to work effectively in both the Hebrew of the original and the *Koine* of the translation, could be found.

Jesus ben Sirach, that eloquent spokesman for orthodoxy, was also subtly influenced by Hellenism. He stressed the value of travel and a broad base of experience, referred to merchants and their activity frequently, and

identified himself in his book—all practices that were foreign to earlier Near Eastern authors, yet characteristic of Hellenistic writers and concerns.[75] He praises the beauty of women[76] in a way unheard of in earlier wisdom literature, which denigrated beauty in favor of character.[77] Other examples might be cited,[78] but we can conclude that, though ben Sirach chose to write his wisdom in the Hebrew language, his thoughts were unconsciously influenced by Hellenism.

Similarly, the Book of Jubilees, while it is a spirited apology for the Law and orthodoxy, "succumbs to the seduction of the Greek penchant for rationalization."[79]

Even the Pharisees, the custodians of mainline Jewish orthodoxy, were to some extent influenced by Hellenism. Commercial law, as regulated by the Talmud, derived much of its technical vocabulary from Greek commerce.[80] In their drive to make the descendants of Abraham holy through education, the Pharisees attempted to set "the crown of Torah . . . before every man." Yet, this idea that a person is improved through education and that individual betterment betters the nation is essentially Platonic.[81] Their attempt to sys-

[73] For a good summary and evaluation of Philo, see Gordon H. Clark, "Philo Judeus," in *The Zondervan Pictorial Encyclopedia of the Bible,* ed. Merrill C. Tenney, 5 vols. (Grand Rapids: Zondervan, 1976), 4:773–76.

[74] See Martin Hengel, *Judaism and Hellenism,* pp. 58–65. Hengel also points to the popularity of Greek names as evidence of Hellenization in Palestine.

[75] Tcherikover, *Hellenistic Civilization and the Jews,* pp. 143, 149; Bickerman, *Ezra to the Maccabees,* pp. 64–65. Harrison (*HIOT,* pp. 1231–32) would disagree.

[76] Ecclesiasticus 26:16–18; 36:22.

[77] As in Proverbs 11:22. The epitome of womanhood, as described in Proverbs 31:10–31, ends with a characteristic evaluation: charm is a delusion, beauty is fleeting, but the fear of the Lord, toil, and labor are enduring.

[78] Hengel, *Jews, Greeks, and Barbarians,* pp. 122ff.

[79] Bickerman, *Ezra to the Maccabees,* pp. 62–63.

[80] Daniel Jeremy Silver, *A History of Judaism,* vol. 1, *From Abraham to Maimonides* (New York: Basic Books, 1974), p. 174.

[81] Bickerman, *Ezra to the Maccabees,* pp. 161–65, cites other significant Hellenistic strains in Pharisaism.

tematize the Law and its observance is, in itself, more in keeping with the spirit of Hellenism than with the Old Testament.

This is not to suggest that there was a single, monolithic, "normative" Judaism. On the contrary, even Pharisaism preserves a bewildering diversity of opinions concerning the Mosaic Law and its proper observance. Judaism in the years between the Testaments was not a monolithic structure but was home to a multiplicity of theologies, ideas, and approaches. But early Judaism, for all its factions and diversity, was held together by a central and unshakable commitment to Torah.[82]

The Essenes emphasized the sinfulness of the body; they frequently prohibited marriage and practiced an ascetic lifestyle—all witness to the incorporation of Hellenistic ideas.

2. Diaspora Judaism

The Letter of Aristeas makes reference to Jewish mercenaries in the army of the Egyptian King Psammetichus II (594-589 B.C.). The Elephantine Papyri contain correspondence from a Jewish garrison and show that Jewish mercenaries continued in Egypt long afterward, at least as late as 400 B.C.[83] Contingents of Jewish soldiers could be found throughout the Greek-speaking world.[84] From this it is reasonable to assume that Jewish fighting men had begun taking employment with foreign powers even before the Exile and thus were part of the first wave of emigration from Palestine.

This emigration was accelerated by the Exile. A significant proportion of the population of Judah was carried off to Babylon, and most of the remaining people of importance sought refuge in Egypt after the murder of Gedaliah.[85] These Jewish enclaves on foreign soil continued to exist after the Exile, flourishing as extraterritorial pockets of Judaism. Josephus states that Jews beyond the Euphrates were "countless myriads whose numbers cannot be ascertained,"[86] while by the first century the Jewish colony at Alexandria was estimated at between a half a million and one million, nearly two-fifths of the population of the city.[87] It is likely that by the time of Christ there were more Jews outside Palestine than in it; estimates of their numbers run as high as ten percent of the total population of the Roman Empire.[88]

The effects of this wide dispersion were mixed. While it was all but impossible to find a city in the Empire without some Jewish population, Jews of the diaspora frequently became the object of anti-Semitism. A significant body of anti-Semitic literature flourished toward the end of the Hellenistic era. Jews, who rejected all pagan gods, were attacked as atheists or slandered

---

[82] See Sandmel's discussion, *Judaism and Christian Beginnings*, pp. 12–15. The only problem with Sandmel is that he seems to want to limit the diversity by excluding apocalyptic. While it would be difficult to prove in this limited space, the pseudepigraphic and apocalyptic writings must have constituted an important element in the religious consciousness of Judaism. Sandmel himself seems to acknowledge this in his definition of synagogue Judaism (p. 16).

[83] See p. 324.

[84] Hengel, *Judaism and Hellenism*, pp. 15ff.

[85] Jeremiah 43:1–7.

[86] *AJ* 11.5.2.

[87] Population figures from this period are seldom reliable, but, even if exaggerated, this witnesses to a perception of a huge Jewish population in Egypt.

[88] Baron, *Social and Religious History*, pp. 170–71.

with stories designed to make them appear either sinister or ridiculous.[89] On the other hand, religiously sensitive pagans frequently found themselves drawn to Judaism, which, with its high ethical standards and monotheistic faith, stood in sharp contrast to other religions. This popularity caused, of course, further hostility. A byproduct of this period are numerous Jewish *apologias*.[90]

The adoption of a Hellenistic veneer on the part of these dispersed Jews might indicate that the Judaism of the *diaspora* was of an inferior sort,[91] but current scholarship has been uncovering evidence of the general homogeneity of early Judaism.[92]

3. The Synagogue

The origin of the synagogue is undocumented and hence hotly debated. The name, a Greek word referring first to the act of assembly and then also to the place of assembly, is an indication of the impact of Greek on Judaism. Sandmel offers the most reasonable explanation of its origin. Jews who lived faraway from the temple and were separated from its ritual felt the need

for a religious center. Over a period of time, therefore, the synagogue became the local Jewish religious center, quite independent of temple ritual and hierarchy.[93] Simple as this may seem today, the shift from a priestly to a popular religious center was radical. It was a first step toward the democratization of Judaism.[94]

While its origin is of interest as a topic for scholarly debate, it is the institution as it appears fully developed in intertestamental history that occupies us here. Of major importance is the fact that, wherever Jews went, ten men could gather and form a synagogue. Thus, Judaism was freed from the geographical restrictions of temple and land. The focus on the Torah and on study and prayer and, after A.D. 70, the complete replacement of sacrifice with prayer, made Judaism a portable religion. It is unlikely that Judaism outside of Palestine would have survived without the synagogue.

E. PARTIES WITHIN JUDAISM

Josephus identifies three major parties within the Judaism of his day.[95] The Pharisees and the Sadducees are

---

[89] Tcherikover, *Hellenistic Civilization and the Jews,* pp. 360–77.

[90] Baron, *Social and Religious History,* pp. 173–79.

[91] As implied by Werner Foerster, *From the Exile to Christ: Historical Introduction to Palestinian Judaism,* ed. Gordon E. Harris (Philadelphia: Fortress, 1964), pp. 32–33. For a summary of the welter of opinions that have arisen out of this false dichotomy between "Palestinian" and "Hellenistic" Judaism, see George Eldon Ladd, *A Theology of the New Testament* (Grand Rapids: Eerdmans, 1974), pp. 361–62.

[92] Bickerman, *Ezra to the Maccabees,* pp. 179ff.; Sandmel, *Judaism and Christian Beginnings,* pp. 12–15.

[93] Zeitlin, "The Origin of the Synagogue: A Study in the Development of Jewish Institutions," in *The Synagogue: Studies in Origins, Archaeology, and Architecture,* ed. Joseph Gutman (New York: KTAV, 1975), pp. 20ff. proposes a typically idiosyncratic theory that the synagogue, which was begun as a kind of town meeting, acquired its religious significance when the Pharisees legislated a new, communal meaning for the daily sacrifice. For a more mainstream formulation, see W. White, Jr., "Synagogue," in *Zondervan Pictorial Encyclopedia of the Bible,* ed. Merrill C. Tenney, 5 vols. (Grand Rapids: Zondervan, 1976), 5:555–56. Joseph Gutman, "The Origin of the Synagogue: The Current State of Research," in Gutman, *The Synagogue,* pp. 72–76, summarizes the dominant views.

[94] Silver, *History of Judaism,* pp. 189–90.

[95] *AJ* 13.5.9.

familiar to all readers of the Gospels as the religious authorities who opposed Jesus. But the Essenes, Josephus' third party, were an obscure sect known only from extrabiblical writings—and generally only by specialists—until the discovery of the Dead Sea Scrolls in 1947. Other sects and subdivisions in Judaism also developed during the intertestamental period, but these three are of greatest importance for subsequent biblical history.

1. Pharisees

The origins of the Pharisees cannot be traced with certainty, but it is often contended, with some merit, that the work of Ezra led to the development of a class of biblical interpreters.[96] The Pharisees as a party derive from the Hasidim of the Maccabean period. They are first mentioned in Josephus' account of their fall from favor under Hyrcanus.[97]

The continued vitality of the Pharisaic movement is explained by the ability of the Pharisees to accommodate themselves to the changing situations of later eras.[98] This accommodation was made possible by the Pharisaic doctrine of *oral law*—what the New Testament refers to as "your own tradition."[99] Since the written law was fixed and nothing could be done to alter it, some of the more specific laws that applied to the agrarian world of Moses

and early Israel seemed irrelevant in the cosmopolitan world of the intertestamental period. More importantly, many situations had arisen for which there was no specific biblical teaching.

To deal with this, the Rabbis taught that God had given both a written law and an oral law to Moses on Mount Sinai. The oral law formed the core of the Talmud, which, because nothing could be added to the written Law (and thus by implication to the oral law once it was written down), remained oral until a century after Christ.[100] In the oft-quoted statement from the tractate *Pirke Aboth,* rabbinic tradition states that a "hedge" should be made for the Torah. Since many situations were not covered specifically in the written law and one could therefore break the law without realizing it, the oral law applied the precepts of the written law to situations not specifically covered in the latter. By keeping the ordinances of the oral law the Jews could be sure to avoid breaking the written law.[101] This desire to make the law relevant to a new age and to avoid the past disasters sent by God in punishment for previous transgression lies at the root of the Pharisaic enterprise.

Whatever their motives, the Pharisees became a party with considerable popular influence. Josephus describes them as having the ability to sway the masses, even against kings or the high

---

[96] As in Hermann L. Strack, *Introduction to the Talmud and Midrash* (New York: Atheneum, 1931), pp. 8–9; C. K. Barrett, *The New Testament Backgrounds* (New York: Harper Torchbooks, 1961), p. 139.

[97] *AJ* 13.10.5.

[98] Max Dimont, in his interpretive history of Judaism (*Jews, God, and History* [New York: Signet, 1962], p. 98), refers to the Pharisees' tradition of oral law as a "do-it-yourself jurisprudence kit to keep up with changing times."

[99] Mark 7:9; Matthew 15:3.

[100] Strack, *Talmud and Midrash,* pp. 10–11.

[101] R. Travers Herford, *The Ethics of the Talmud: Sayings of the Fathers* (New York: Schocken, 1962), p. 21.

priest.[102] This power no doubt derived from the fact that the temple was becoming more and more removed from the private lives of Jewish worshipers as it became increasingly political and aristocratic. The Pharisees were the party of the synagogue, deriving authority from the interpretation of Scripture and the rigor of their adherence to that interpretation.

We cannot overestimate the importance of the Pharisees, of their association with the synagogue, and of their emphasis on the study of Torah. The Pharisees themselves became the spiritual progenitors of modern Judaism; the synagogue became the prototype of the early church; and the Christian emphasis on Scripture as the Word of God, although in a somewhat different form, has antecedents in the writings of the Rabbis.

2. Sadducees

The Sadducees are of less enduring interest than the Pharisees, primarily because they were linked inextricably to the temple. Their party came to an end in A.D. 70—when the temple was destroyed. They were aristocratic, drawing their base of support from the upper class and the priesthood. The Sadducees were the dominant political force in Palestine prior to A.D. 70.

In many ways, the Sadducees were more conservative than the Pharisees. Rejecting the additions of the oral law, they accepted only the Pentateuch as canonical and interpreted it literally.[103] The religious sensibilities of the Sadducees, tied as they were to the uninterrupted operation of the temple, were not offended by accommodation with

Hasmoneans or Romans, which makes them seem more liberal than the Pharisees to the modern reader.

Even though the name of the Sadducees is familiar to us, we have little information about their beliefs or their organization. Each of the Synoptics does, however, point out that they denied any resurrection (Matt. 22:23; Mark 12:18; Luke 20:27).

3. Essenes

While the Sadducees tied themselves to the political status quo and the Pharisees withdrew from the political arena to mark out a unique religious approach to accommodate to life in this world, the Essenes withdrew from society to prepare for an apocalyptic conclusion to history. Although much more is known about the Essenes now than before the discovery of the Dead Sea Scrolls and the excavation of the Qumran monastery, there are still large gaps in our understanding. It is still debated whether or not the Qumran sectaries were, in fact, Essenes; it is generally accepted that the residents of Qumran were of the same spirit as the Essenes known from Josephus and the Damascus Document, but scholars generally hedge on an exact identification, since what is known about the Qumran group differs from what was previously known about the Essenes.

William S. LaSor offers a plausible resolution to the problem of these differences. He argues that it is not necessary to insist on absolute uniformity between one Essene community and another, since variations could have developed easily among the isolated groups.[104] It is also conceivable

---

[102]*AJ* 13.10.5.
[103]Gowan, *Bridge Between the Testaments*, p. 181.
[104]William Sanford LaSor, *The Dead Sea Scrolls and the Christian Faith*, rev. ed. (Chicago: Moody, 1972), pp. 85–86.

that the differences represent different stages in the development of Essenism.[105]

The Essenes, like the Pharisees, stressed personal piety and a separation from life's impurities. The Essenes, however, took the notion of separation to far greater lengths than did the Pharisees. Because of what they considered to be the religious corruption of mainline Judaism, they withdrew, refusing to participate in the sacrificial system.[106] What distinguished the Essenes from other Jewish sects was their conviction that they alone represented the true remnant of Israel and that therefore only their understanding of Scripture was valid.[107]

The apocalyptic elements in Essene theology are evident in the sectarian documents of Qumran.[108] The War Scroll in particular describes an apocalyptic Armageddon in which the Sons of Light (the Qumran sectaries) would fight for God against the Sons of Darkness. The attitude of the sectaries toward the rest of Judaism was extremely negative; they would have considered all those outside their sect (and especially the Jerusalem priesthood) the Sons of Darkness.[109] They looked forward to the coming of two (and possibly even three) Messiahs—one kingly, another priestly.[110]

Their strictness seems excessive, even when compared with the Pharisees. The Manual of Discipline prescribes severe punishments for seemingly trivial offenses.[111] Like the Sadducees, they appear to have tied their existence to a particular situation, namely, the impending apocalyptic conclusion of history, and, like the Sadducees, they did not survive the disruption of Israel that took place in A.D. 70.

The Essenes, particularly the Qumran Essenes, are important for the firsthand evidence they provide of the importance of apocalyptic thought for early Judaism. They are also the only sect of Judaism to leave extensive contemporaneous writings about themselves, thus providing important background for both the study of intertestamental Judaism and the New Testament. Finally, their library, preserved in the caves around the Dead Sea, provides Old Testament scholarship with the most ancient manuscripts of biblical texts known to be in existence.

F. LITERATURE OF THE INTERTESTAMENTAL PERIOD[112]

1. Apocalyptic literature

Known to most Protestants from the biblical books of Daniel and Revela-

---

[105]Gowan (*Bridge Between the Testaments,* pp. 212–13) expresses typical reticence, while coming out in favor of identifying Qumran with the Essenes.

[106]Although they did bring flour and oil offerings (Mansoor, *Dead Sea Scrolls,* pp. 127ff.).

[107]Geza Vermes, *The Dead Sea Scrolls in English,* 2d ed. (Baltimore: Penguin, 1975), pp. 35ff.

[108]Especially, the Manual of Discipline, the War Scroll, and certain of the Hymns of Thanksgiving.

[109]Silver, *History of Judaism,* p. 188; LaSor, *Dead Sea Scrolls,* pp. 199ff.

[110]Mansoor, *Dead Sea Scrolls,* p. 157.

[111]For example, to "guffaw foolishly" was punished with thirty days of penance, gesticulating with the left hand warranted ten days of penance, and to murmur against leadership resulted in expulsion from the community.

[112]The study of intertestamental literature is both technical and specialized. No detailed analysis will be attempted here. For apocalyptic literature, see D. S. Russell, *The Method and Message of Jewish Apocalyptic* (Philadelphia: Westminster, 1964); Leon Morris, *Apocalyptic* (Grand Rapids: Eerdmans, 1972); H. H. Rowley, *The Relevance of Apocalyptic,* rev. ed. (New York: Association, 1963); S. B.

tion, apocalyptic is a uniquely Judaeo-Christian literary genre that apparently enjoyed immense popularity during the late intertestamental period. Apocalyptic is easier to identify than it is to define: nearly everyone knows when he or she is reading apocalyptic, but there is no consensus as to its definition. Simply stated, apocalyptic is a literary genre characterized by a unique style and a particular theological content. By this definition, the prophecies of Zechariah would not be apocalyptic because, while their language fits the definition, the particular theological emphases are absent. The writings of Paul, on the other hand, are informed by apocalyptic theology but are almost totally free of apocalyptic imagery.[113]

Following the lead of Daniel,[114] Jewish apocalyptic literature developed in response to an ongoing history of frustration and oppression. In many ways, apocalyptic is a literature of theodicy. In the dark centuries following the Babylonian captivity, it must have seemed that the glorious prophecies of restoration given to Israel by God had failed. Taking their cue from the earlier prophets, the writings of the apocalyptists were an attempt to explain why a people chosen by God and, according to their understanding, living righteously before Him, should experience the kinds of suffering that had characterized Jewish life since the Exile. Their answer was that hope did not lie in the orderly progression of history but in its cataclysmic resolution. In this final act of judgment, God's ways could be vindicated and His people would be restored.

Although modern authors do not agree on a definition of apocalyptic,[115]

Frost, *Old Testament Apocalyptic: Its Origins and Growth* (London: Epworth, 1952); Paul D. Hanson, *The Dawn of Apocalyptic: The Historical and Sociological Roots of Jewish Apocalyptic Eschatology,* 2d ed. (Philadelphia: Fortress, 1979); Klaus Koch, *The Rediscovery of Apocalyptic* (London: SCM, 1972). These provide a range of position, with Morris the only evangelical author.

For the Apocrypha, the commentaries in the Anchor Bible series contain good background studies and verse-by-verse commentary: Goldstein, *1 Maccabees*; Jonathan A. Goldstein, *The Anchor Bible,* vol. 41A, *II Maccabees* (Garden City: Doubleday, 1983); Jacob M. Myers, *The Anchor Bible,* vol. 42, *I & II Esdras* (Garden City: Doubleday, 1974); David Winston, *The Anchor Bible,* vol. 43, *The Wisdom of Solomon* (Garden City: Doubleday, 1979); Carey A. Moore, *The Anchor Bible,* vol. 44, *Daniel, Esther, and Jeremiah: The Additions* (Garden City: Doubleday, 1978). The classic work of R. H. Charles, *The Apocrypha and Pseudepigrapha of the Old Testament,* 2 vols. (Oxford: Clarendon, 1913), is still worthy of attention. James Charlesworth, *The Old Testament Pseudepigrapha,* 2 vols. (Garden City: Doubleday, 1984, 1985), may replace Charles as the basic text. For valuable introductions, see Bruce M. Metzger, ed., *The Oxford Annotated Apocrypha* (New York: Oxford University Press, 1965); Bruce M. Metzger, *An Introduction to the Apocrypha* (New York: Oxford University Press, 1957); Leonhard Rost, *Judaism Outside the Hebrew Canon* (Nashville: Abingdon, 1976); George W. Nickelsburg, *Jewish Literature Between the Bible and the Mishnah: A Historical and Literary Introduction* (Philadelphia: Fortress, 1981).

The early years of Qumran studies produced a near embarrassment of riches in terms of publications. In recent years, publication has slowed considerably, with most of the current material too specialized for a general bibliography. We will suggest a few basic introductions to the Scrolls: Vermes, *Dead Sea Scrolls*; Mansoor, *Dead Sea Scrolls*; Yigael Yadin, *The Message of the Scrolls* (New York: Simon and Schuster, 1957); Millar J. Burrows, *The Dead Sea Scrolls* (New York: Viking, 1955); and *More Light on the Dead Sea Scrolls* (New York: Viking, 1958); LaSor, *Dead Sea Scrolls.* For bibliographical data, see J. A. Fitzmyer, *The Dead Sea Scrolls: Major Publications and Tools for Study* (Missoula, Mont.: Scholars, 1975).

[113] Paul D. Hanson—in his article "Apocalypticism" in *Interpreter's Dictionary of the Bible, Supplement* (Nashville: Abingdon, 1976) and more extensively in his *The Dawn of Apocalyptic,* 2d ed. (Philadelphia: Fortress, 1979)—would add a third, "religio-social" element to the definition.

[114] Daniel 7–12.

[115] While a scholarly pessimism has emerged about our ability to define "apocalyptic," (see especially

there are some traits that would appear representative. Apocalyptic uses bizarre and sometimes mythological imagery and numerological symbols; with a pessimistic portrayal of history's downward course, it divides time into identifiable periods; it presents a dualistic picture of observable reality on earth as opposed to the divine realities visible through divine revelation only to the eye of faith.[116]

The literary characteristics of the genre, however, are secondary to the theological emphases that typify it. The messianic idea takes on new dimensions in apocalyptic literature.[117] The increasing emphasis on the Messiah as a supranatural figure breaking into the flow of human history from the outside is coupled with the apocalyptic doctrine of the two ages. This present age is evil and the domain of Satan. The coming messianic age stands in opposition to this age and its prince.[118] It is in the conflict between the ages that the world view of apocalyptic works itself out. The suffering of Israel is attributable to the satanic opposition that characterizes this present evil age. God's hand is not readily visible in this age because it is functioning above the stage of human history and is accessible only by means of direct revelation. It was through this suprahistorical understanding that Israel's expectations were lifted from the territorial and nationalistic realm and made to conform to the highest expressions of God's promises in the Old Testament.

2. The Septuagint

According to the legendary Letter of Aristeas, the Old Testament was translated into Greek in the reign of Ptolemy Philadelphus (283–245 B.C.). The story describes Ptolemy's desire to acquire a copy of the Jewish law, in Greek, for the library at Alexandria. The author styles himself a courtier of Ptolemy and one who witnessed and assisted in the translation. Seventy-two scholars, six from each of the twelve tribes, were called to Alexandria, where, sequestered on the Island Pharos, they produced the translation in seventy-two days.[119] Philo asserts that all of the translators were inspired and that they miraculously produced identical translations.[120] The name "Septuagint," which means "seventy," derives from this legend (the Roman numeral for seventy, LXX, is used as its abbreviation).

While no modern scholar takes this account as anything but legendary,[121] it does contain a germ of truth. The

---

Hanson, *Dawn of Apocalyptic,* pp. 428ff.) it must be insisted that literary genres do have literary characteristics. While Hanson disallows lists of such characteristics, it seems impossible to speak of genre, as he does, without also admitting that lists of characteristics generally present in that genre are not only possible but essential.

[116] Russell provides a much more extensive listing of characteristics in *Method and Message of Jewish Apocalyptic,* p. 105. Also see Klaus Koch, "What is Apocalyptic? An Attempt at a Preliminary Definition," in Paul D. Hanson, *Visionaries and Their Apocalypses* (Philadelphia: Fortress, 1983), pp. 21–24.

[117] The Messiah is certainly present in the Old Testament, though in a form that was not readily comprehensible to the average reader.

[118] See Ladd, *Theology of the New Testament,* pp. 61-69, 364–65, 550, for references to the impact of this doctrine of the two ages on the eschatology of the New Testament.

[119] Aristeas, on the other hand, reports that they compared their work and preserved the consensus translation.

[120] *The Life of Moses,* 2.56–77.

[121] Barrett, *New Testament Backgrounds,* pp. 209–10; Nickelsburg, *Jewish Literature,* pp. 168–69.

Torah, or Pentateuch, was probably translated sometime in the third century B.C. in Alexandria, possibly during the reign of Ptolemy Philadelphus, while the balance of the Old Testament was completed in the course of the next two centuries.[122]

The Septuagint became the Bible of the Diaspora. It differs somewhat from the Hebrew Bible; the LXX version of some books (most notably Jeremiah) is significantly different from the Masoretic text. It also contains books and portions of books that are not part of the Hebrew canon. Moreover, the books are in a different order.[123] These differences may be explained by the Dead Sea Scrolls, which bear witness to the fact that the LXX was based on a Hebrew original that diverged from the text on which modern translations are based.[124] Rejected by the Jewish community shortly after the time of Christ, the Septuagint had already become the Bible of the church, and it was this adoption by the Christian community that preserved the translation.[125]

The language of the LXX exercised a profound influence on the language of the New Testament. Based as it was on the Hebrew, the Septuagint provided Greek words for their Hebrew equivalents, frequently changing the meaning of a Greek word to accommodate the Hebrew idea—and sometimes the opposite.[126]

The impact of the LXX was immense. The use of a Greek-language Bible made Judaism accessible to a non-Jewish audience, which opened the way for the proselytism mentioned in the New Testament.[127] Most importantly, the spread of Christianity was facilitated by the ready availability of the Scriptures in the *lingua franca* of the day.[128]

3. The Apocrypha

The word *apocrypha* is derived from a Greek verb meaning "to hide." The designation "hidden [books]" probably derives from 2 Esdras 14:46, where Esdras (Ezra) is instructed to publish the twenty-four books that constituted the Hebrew canon but to keep hidden the remaining seventy books given to him by inspiration. It is assumed that these "hidden" books included the collection known to Protestants today as the Apocrypha—in addition to numerous other books then in circulation.[129]

When Jerome translated the Bible

---

[122]Gowan, *Bridge Between the Testaments,* pp. 307–8.

[123]It is sometimes argued that there were two canons—one Palestinian and one Alexandrian. It is more likely that, among the Writings, the canon remained fluid until after the time of Christ. The Pentateuch and the Prophets were evidently set in the second century B.C.; see Ecclesiasticus, where the translator refers to "the Law, the Prophets, and the writers who followed in their steps" (NEB).

[124]Shemaryahu Talmon, "The Old Testament Text," pp. 1–41, and William F. Albright, "Early Recensions of the Hebrew Bible," pp. 140–46, in F. L. Cross and Shemaryahu Talmon, *Qumran and The History of the Biblical Text* (Cambridge, Mass.: Harvard University Press, 1975).

[125]Schurer, in his classic work, *The Literature of the Jewish People in the Time of Jesus* (New York: Schocken, 1972), pp. 163–64, attributes the rejection of the Septuagint by Jews as a reaction to its adoption by the church.

[126]Bickerman, *Ezra to the Maccabees,* pp. 77ff.

[127]Matthew 23:15.

[128]Barrett, *New Testament Backgrounds,* pp. 208–9.

[129]Many of which are lost today, but it is reasonable to assume that at least some of the works that are known as Pseudepigrapha were among the hidden books intended by the writer of 2 Esdras. For a summary of the Pseudepigrapha, see W. Ward Gasque, "Pseudepigrapha," in *Zondervan Pictorial Encyclopedia of the Bible,* 5 vols. (Grand Rapids: Zondervan, 1976), 4:969–70.

into Latin (the translation known as the Vulgate), the outside books (books that appeared in the Septuagint but not in the Hebrew canon)[130] had been in common use among Christians for three hundred years. While Jerome did not consider them authoritative, he nevertheless translated them—but with a disclaimer. In the centuries that followed, his translation became the basis for other translations, but the disclaimer was forgotten.[131]

During the Reformation, the Reformers desired a return to the original Greek and Hebrew texts of the Bible. Their translations bypassed Jerome's Vulgate in favor of the more selective Hebrew canon.[132] The Council of Trent (1546), reacting to this rejection, gave the full weight of Roman authority to the Apocrypha, excluding only the books of 1 and 2 Esdras and the Prayer of Manasseh.[133] This decision has perpetuated the canonical tradition begun in the intertestamental period, while the canon of the Reformers reaches back in an unbroken line to the Scriptures in their original form.[134]

The works that constitute the Apocrypha, as defined by Protestants, can be grouped in several categories. Some are additions to canonical books. For example, Esther is expanded by the addition of 107 verses, which "correct" the original by adding the overtly religious elements that many have felt were needed.[135] Daniel is expanded by the addition of two stories ("Bel and the Dragon" and "Susannah"). "The Song of the Three Young Men" and "The Prayer of Azariah" were also added to Daniel.

One book (1 Esdras) is a paraphrastic rendition of Ezra and portions of 2 Chronicles and Nehemiah. Another (2 Esdras) is an apocalyptic work probably written after the fall of Jerusalem in A.D. 70.[136] Historical writing in the Apocrypha is represented by the rather sober, straightforward account of the Maccabean revolt in 1 Maccabees and the somewhat bizarre, moralistic accounts of 2 Maccabees.

Judith and Tobit purport to be true accounts of the goodness and heroism of their main characters, but they are

---

[130] Gowan, *Bridge Between the Testaments,* pp. 337–38.

[131] *HIOT,* p. 1188.

[132] Luther considered the Apocrypha "good and useful for reading" but not canonical (Floyd V. Filson, *Which Books Belong in the Bible* [Philadelphia: Westminster, 1957], p. 74).

[133] Ibid., p. 89.

[134] The books in the Apocrypha have not been and should not be accepted as Scripture by the Protestant churches. They fall short of the mark of authority that belongs to the inspired Scriptures. Floyd V. Filson presents a convincing case against the Apocrypha as Scripture. To summarize, he begins by arguing that, had the early church been familiar with the Hebrew canon, it is unlikely that the Apocrypha would have been accepted in the first place. There is no evidence that there ever was a canon for the Septuagint, and, in fact, there is no evidence that Jesus and the writers of the New Testament considered the books of the Apocrypha authoritative. The sermons in Acts completely ignore the Apocrypha as a part of the continuous record of divine revelation. Historically, the church has exhibited ambivalence and confusion about the value of the Apocrypha; and a body of literature over which so much disagreement has been expressed can hardly provide a solid base for authoritative teaching. From a purely pragmatic perspective, Filson goes on to contend that the Apocrypha adds nothing essential to the faith (Filson, *Which Books Belong,* pp. 90–100).

We may champion the scholarly study of the Apocrypha, yet only in the same way that we might champion the study of Josephus, Philo, or the Gnostic texts from Nag Hammadi. For all their value and influence, they are less than Scripture.

[135] Metzger, *Oxford Annotated Apocrypha,* p. 96.

[136] Russell, *The Jews,* pp. 62ff.

transparently fictional works. Both reflect the Jewish piety of the Hellenistic period,[137] which encouraged Jews to endure hardship in expectation of God's vindication.

Baruch, the Letter of Jeremiah, and the Prayer of Manasseh form a group by themselves, since each is presented as the writing of one of those biblical characters. The Prayer of Manasseh, considered a "little classic of devotion,"[138] is a prayer reminiscent of the penitential Psalms, supposedly offered by the contrite Manasseh as he was held in exile in Babylon.[139] The Letter of Jeremiah is a polemic against the worship of idols, while Baruch—the book of which it forms a part—is a composite work on the sin, punishment, and forgiveness of Israel.[140]

The remaining books are late representatives of the wisdom genre. The Wisdom of Solomon is a hybrid; it praises wisdom and exhorts its readers to follow wisdom in the traditional Hebrew fashion, but the wisdom it champions is more Greek than Hebrew.[141] Ecclesiasticus (or the Wisdom of Ben Sirach) is the culmination of the Hebrew wisdom tradition, although it also reflects the influence of Hellenism.[142]

The influence of the Apocrypha in Western literature and thought has been great,[143] and, even though they cannot be accepted as canonical, this group of books has great value for the Christian's understanding of the New Testament world.[144] They can also be read with as much benefit as much of the modern popular devotional literature. While not inspired, the religious sensibilities of the pious authors of these ancient writings often ring true for the modern reader.

4. The Dead Sea Scrolls

The initial discovery of scrolls in 1947 and the subsequent excavations in the caves in the Judean desert constitute one of the major document finds in archaeological history. Albright even called it "the greatest manuscript discovery of modern times."[145] It captured the imagination of the general public in a way that few discoveries have. The result of this interest was the publication of an avalanche of books—technical, semitechnical, and popular. The early writing about the scrolls, often based on misinformation and sometimes on particular biases, tended to be sensational and, in many cases, misleading.[146] With the publication of the scrolls and the scholarly examination that followed, all but a few extrem-

---

[137]Metzger, *Oxford Annotated Apocrypha*, p. 76.

[138]Ibid., p. 219.

[139]2 Chronicles 33:11–13.

[140]*HIOT*, p. 1240.

[141]Winston, *Wisdom of Solomon*, pp. 18ff.; *HIOT*, pp. 1229–30.

[142]*Supra*, p. 381.

[143]Bruce Metzger, "The Apocrypha and Pseudepigrapha," in *The Expositor's Bible Commentary*, ed. Frank E. Gaebelein, 12 vols. (Grand Rapids: Zondervan, 1976–   ), 1:173–74; *Oxford Annotated Apocrypha*, pp. xvi–xx.

[144]See Julius Scott's excellent summary in "On the Value of Intertestamental Jewish Literature for New Testament Theology," in *JETS* 23 (December, 1980), pp. 315–24.

[145]William F. Albright, editorial, *BASOR* 110 (April, 1948) pp. 2–3; reprinted in *BA* 40:3 (Sept. 1977), p. 130.

[146]One is reminded of the recent furor and controversy over the Ebla discoveries. LaSor, *Dead Sea Scrolls*, pp. 207–22, addressed some of these controversies in his excellent, if dated, study.

ists have adopted a much more sober stance toward the scrolls.

What we know about them today is that they represent the library of a Jewish sect dating from the Maccabean period through the fall of Jerusalem in A.D. 70. The scrolls[147] were apparently stored in jars in caves to protect them from the anticipated destruction of the monastery at Khirbet Qumran during the first Jewish revolt. Excavations, conducted under extremely difficult and sometimes dangerous conditions, uncovered scrolls and scroll fragments in eleven caves.[148]

Some of the most spectacular of the finds came from cave 1, where the two Isaiah scrolls (1QIs[a], 1QIs[b]), the Manual of Discipline (1QS), the Habakkuk Pesher (1QpHab), the Genesis Apocrypha (1QapGen), the War Scroll (1QM), and the Thanksgiving Hymns (1QH) were found.[149] Two copper scrolls found in cave 3 record the hiding places of sixty treasure hoards. If they are true and the ancient landmarks could be found, these scrolls would lead searchers to over two hundred tons of gold and silver![150] The most recent of the scrolls to be published is the Temple Scroll,[151] which Yigael Yadin acquired from an anonymous Jerusalem antiquities dealer.

The scrolls and fragments of biblical books are probably of greatest interest to students of the Bible for their impact on the study of the biblical text. Every Old Testament book with the exception of Esther is represented among them. The St. Mark's Monastery Isaiah scroll is a complete text of the book of Isaiah—measuring twenty-four feet in length—and is the oldest extant biblical book in the world. Such ancient copies of the books of the Old Testament demonstrate the consistency of their transmission over the approximately one thousand years between their transcription in the Scriptorium of Khirbet Qumran (beginning in the second century B.C.) and the standardization of the Masoretic text (in the eighth and ninth centuries A.D.). They have been valuable also in clarifying obscure readings in the more recent copies of the biblical books.[152]

The Old Testament Apocrypha and Pseudepigrapha are amply represented in the scrolls, providing added information for a burgeoning field of study. Because the sectarian documents illuminate the life and beliefs of the Qumran sectaries in greater detail than is available for any of their contemporaries, they are of importance for the study of intertestamental Judaism. Commentaries on biblical books help to clarify some obscure biblical readings and

---

[147] A misnomer to a certain extent, because relatively few complete scrolls were found. Fragments of scrolls, however, account for over six hundred different manuscripts.

[148] The most compelling recitation of the recovery of the major scrolls from cave 1 can be found in Yadin, *Message of the Scrolls*, pp. 15–51. A general summary of the scroll discoveries can be found in most of the works cited in n. 112.

[149] These titles may vary from work to work. For precision, a system of cataloguing has been developed that identifies each work individually. For example, 1QIs[a] refers to the first ([a]) scroll of Isaiah (Is) found in cave 1 (1Q). The lower case "p" in the Habakkuk commentary and the "ap" in the Genesis Apocryphon designations refer to the type of literary work.

[150] LaSor, *Dead Sea Scrolls*, pp. 33–34. Vermes, *Dead Sea Scrolls*, pp. 271ff., while not providing a translation of the scroll, does evaluate the arguments for the authenticity of the treasure described.

[151] Yigael Yadin, *The Temple Scroll*, 3 vols. (Jerusalem: Israel Exploration Society, 1983).

[152] See Mansoor, *Dead Sea Scrolls*, pp. 82–87, for a valuable summary of the scrolls' contributions to biblical study.

provide enlightening examples of the hermeneutical methods of at least one segment of early Judaism.

G. CONCLUSION

The foregoing summary should demonstrate the vitality and diversity of the world of Judaism in the centuries before Christ. More importantly, it should demonstrate the work of divine providence in continuing to shape and prepare God's people for the coming of Messiah.

We should never assume that because the intertestamental period has not been recorded in inspired Scripture, God stopped working in human history when He stopped speaking to Israel through His prophets. Quite to the contrary, the preparation of a people to receive and understand God's gracious gift of redemption in His Son continued until time could hold no more and eternity broke through in its overflow. Beneath every event in this survey of Israel's history, from Abraham through the last of the Hasmoneans, the Spirit of God whispers, "Soon, but not yet," and in the escalating expectations that reach their focus only in the New Testament's revelation of the Incarnation, we hear the early echoes of John's fervent prayer, "Amen. Come, Lord Jesus."

BASIC FURTHER READING

HISTORY

Albright, William F. "The Biblical Period." In *The Jews: Their History, Culture, and Religion*, ed. L. Finkelstein, 3–65. New York: Harper & Row, 1949. Reprint. Pittsburg: The Biblical Colloqium, 1950.

————— "The Old Testament World." In *The Interpreter's Bible*, ed. George A. Buttrick, 12 vols. (Nashville: Abingdon, 1951–57), 1:233–71.

————— "The Role of the Canaanites in the History of Civilization." In *The Bible and the Ancient Near East*, ed. George E. Wright, 328–62. Garden City: Doubleday, 1961.

Breasted, James H. *A History of Egypt*. New York: Scribner, 1954.

Erman, Adolf. *The Literature of the Ancient Egyptians*. Trans. A. M. Blackman. New York: E. P. Dutton, 1927.

Fairservis, Walter A., Jr. *The Ancient Kingdoms of the Nile*. New York: Mentor, 1962.

Frankfort, Henri. *Ancient Egyptian Religion*. New York: Columbia University Press, 1948.

————— *The Birth of Civilization in the Near East*. Garden City: Doubleday/Anchor, 1956.

Gardiner, Alan. *Egypt of the Pharaohs*. Oxford: Clarendon, 1961.

Gordon, Cyrus H. *The Ancient Near East*. 3d. ed. New York: W. W. Norton, 1965. Formerly issued as *The World of the Old Testament*. Garden City: Doubleday, 1958.

Grant, Michael. *From Alexander to Cleopatra: The Hellenistic World*. New York: Scribner, 1982.

Guillaume, A. *Prophecy and Divination Among the Hebrews and Other Semites*. London: Hodder & Stoughton, 1938.

Gurney, O. R. *The Hittites*. 2d ed. Hammondsworth: Penguin, 1954.

Hallo, W. W. and Simpson, W. K. *The Ancient Near East: A History*. New York: Harcourt, Brace, Jovanovich, 1970.

Hayes, William C. *The Scepter of Egypt*. Cambridge: Harvard University Press; Part I, 1953; Part II, 1959.

Hitti, Philip K. *History of Syria, Including Lebanon and Palestine*. New York: Macmillan, 1951.

Hooke, Samuel H. *Babylonian and Assyrian Religion*. London: Hutchinson's University Library, 1953.

Jakobsen, Thorkild. *The Treasures of Darkness: A History of Mesopotamian Religion*. New Haven: Yale University Press, 1976.

Jones, Tom B. *Ancient Civilization*. Chicago: Rand McNally, 1960.

Macqueen, James G. *The Hittities: and Their Contemporaries in Asia Minor*. Boulder, Colo.: Westview, 1975.

Mendenhall, George. *Law and Covenant in Israel and the Ancient Near East*. Pittsburgh: The Biblical Colloqium, 1955.

Moscati, Sabatino. *Ancient Semitic Civilizations*. Eng. trans., London: Elek Books, 1957.

O'Callaghan, R. T. *Aram Naharaim*. Rome: Pontifical Biblical Institute, 1948.

Olmstead, A. T. *History of Assyria*. New York: Scribner, 1923.

————— *History of the Persian Empire*. Chicago: University of Chicago Press, 1948.

————— *History of Palestine and Syria to the Macedonian Conquest*. New York: Scribner, 1931.

Oppenheim, A. Leo, *Ancient Mesopotamia*. Chicago: University of Chicago Press, 1964.
─────── *The Interpretation of Dreams in the Ancient Near East*. Philadelphia: Transactions of the American Philosophical Society, 1956.
Roux, Georges. *Ancient Iraq*. Baltimore: Pelican, 1964.
Saggs, H. W. F. *The Greatness That Was Babylon*. New York: Mentor, 1962.
Schwantes, Siegried. *A Short History of the Ancient Near East*. Grand Rapids: Baker, 1965.
Steindorff, George, and Seele, Keith C. *When Egypt Ruled the East*. Rev. ed. Keith C. Seele. Chicago: University of Chicago Press, 1957.
Unger, Merrill F. *Israel and the Aramaeans of Damascus*. London: James Clarke & Co., 1957.
Van Seters, John. *The Hyksos*. New Haven: Yale University Press, 1966.
Wilson, John. *The Burden of Egypt*. Chicago: University of Chicago Press, 1951.
Wiseman, Donald J., ed. *Peoples of Old Testament Times*. Oxford: Oxford University Press, 1973.

ARCHAEOLOGY, CULTURE, GEOGRAPHY, TEXTS

Aharoni, Yohanan. *The Land of the Bible: A Historical Geography*. Trans. A. F. Rainey. Philadelphia: Westminster, 1962, 1967.
Aharoni, Yohanan, and Avi-Yonah, Michael. *The Macmillan Bible Atlas*. Rev. ed. New York: Macmillan, 1977.
Albright, William F. *Archaeology and the Religion of Israel*. 5th ed. Baltimore: Johns Hopkins Press, 1956.
─────── *The Archaeology of Palestine*. Rev. ed. Hammondsworth: Penguin, 1956.
Avi-Yonah, Michael. *The Holy Land*. Grand Rapids: Baker, 1966.
Avi-Yonah, Michael and Stern, Ephraim. *Encyclopedia of Archaeological Excavations in the Holy Land*, 4 vols. Englewood Cliffs, N.J.: Prentice-Hall, 1975, 1976, 1977, 1978.
Baines, John and Malek, Jaromir. *Atlas of Ancient Egypt*. New York: Facts on File, 1980.
Baly, Denis. *The Geography of the Bible*. 2d ed. London: Lutterworth, 1974.
Barton, George A. *Archaeology and the Bible*. 7th ed. Philadelphia: American Sunday School Union, 1937.
Beyerlin, Walter, ed. *Near Eastern Texts Relating to the Old Testament*. Trans. John Bowden. Philadelphia: Westminster, 1978.
Blaiklock, Edward M. and Harrison, Roland K., eds. *The New International Dictionary of Biblical Archaeology*. Grand Rapids: Zondervan, 1983.
Burrows, Millar. *What Mean These Stones?* New Haven: American Schools of Oriental Research, 1941.
Childe, Gordon. *New Light on the Most Ancient East*. London: Routledge, Kegan, and Paul, 1952.
De Vaux, Roland, *Ancient Israel: Its Life and Institutions*. Trans. J. McHugh. 2 vols. New York: McGraw-Hill, 1961.
Erman, Adolf. *The Ancient Egyptians: A Sourcebook of Their Writings*. New York: Harper, 1966.
Finegan, Jack. *Archaeological History of the Ancient Middle East*. Boulder, Colo.: Westview, 1979.
─────── *Light From the Ancient Past*. 2d ed. Princeton: Princeton University Press, 1959.
Free, Joseph P. *Archaeolgy and Bible History*. 8th ed. Wheaton: Scripture Press, 1964.
Garstang, John, and Garstang, J. B. E. *The Story of Jericho*. Rev. ed. London: Marshall, Morgan & Scott, 1948.
Glueck, Nelson. *The Other Side of the Jordan*. New Haven: American Schools of Oriental Research, 1940.
Kenyon, Kathleen. *Archaeology in the Holy Land*. 4th ed. New York: W. W. Norton, 1979.
─────── *Digging up Jericho*. New York: Frederick A. Praeger, 1957.
Kitchen, Kenneth A. *The Bible in Its World: The Bible and Archaeology Today*. Chicago: InterVarsity, 1978.
Lichtheim, Miriam. *Ancient Egyptian Literature*. 3 vols. Berkeley: University of California Press, 1975, 1976.
Livingston, G. Herbert. *The Pentateuch in Its Cultural Environment*. Grand Rapids: Baker, 1974.
McCown, C. C. *The Ladder of Progress in Palestine*. New York: Harper & Row, 1943.

May, Herbert G., ed. *Oxford Bible Atlas*. Revised by John Day. New York: Oxford University Press, 1984.

Millard, Alan. *Treasures from Bible Times*. Belleville, Mich.: Lion, 1985.

Monson, J., ed. *Student Map Manual*. Jerusalem: Pictorial Archive, 1979.

Owen, G. F. *Archaeology and the Bible*. Westwood, N.J.: Revell, 1961.

Pfeiffer, Charles F. *Baker's Bible Atlas*. Grand Rapids: Baker, 1961.

————— *The Biblical World*. Grand Rapids: Baker, 1966.

Pritchard, J. B., ed. *Ancient Near Eastern Texts Relating to the Old Testament*. 3d ed. with suppl. Princeton: Princeton University Press, 1969.

—————, ed. *The Ancient Near East in Pictures Relating to the Old Testament*. 2d ed. rev. with suppl. Princeton: Princeton University Press, 1969.

Schoville, Keith. *Biblical Archaeology in Focus*. Grand Rapids: Baker, 1978.

Simons, J. *The Geographical and Topographical Texts of the Old Testament*. Leiden: E. J. Brill, 1959.

Simpson, W. K., ed. *The Literature of Ancient Egypt: An Anthology of Stories, Instructions and Poetry*. New ed. New Haven: Yale University Press, 1973.

Thomas, D. Winton, ed. *Archaeology and Old Testament Study*. Oxford: Clarendon, 1967.

—————, ed. *Documents From Old Testament Times*. New York: Harper & Row, 1958.

Thompson, John A. *The Bible and Archaeology*. Grand Rapids: Eerdmans, 1962.

Unger, Merrill F. *Archaeology and the Old Testament*. 4th ed. Grand Rapids: Zondervan, 1960.

Wiseman, Donald J. *Illustrations from Biblical Archaeology*. Grand Rapids: Eerdmans, 1958.

Wright, George Ernest. *Biblical Archaelogy*. Philadelphia: Westminster, 1957.

————— *Shechem*. New York: McGraw-Hill, 1965.

Wright, George Ernest, and Filson, Floyd Vivian, eds. *The Westminster Historical Atlas to the Bible*. Rev. ed. Philadelphia: Westminster, 1956.

HISTORY OF ISRAEL

Albright, William F. *The Biblical Period From Abraham to Ezra*. New York: Harper & Row, 1963. Liberal.

————— *From the Stone Age to Christianity*. 2d ed. Garden City: Doubleday/Anchor, 1957. Liberal.

Anderson, Bernard W. *Understanding the Old Testament*. Englewood Cliffs, N.J.: Prentice-Hall, 1957.

Anderson, George W. *The History and Religion of Israel*. London: Oxford University Press, 1966. Liberal.

Archer, Gleason L., Jr. *A Survey of Old Testament Introduction*. Chicago: Moody, 1964. Conservative.

Baron, Salo W. *A Social and Religious History of the Jews,* vol. 1. New York: Columbia University Press, 1952.

Bickerman, Elias. *From Ezra to the Last of the Maccabees*. New York: Shocken, 1962.

Bright, John. *A History of Israel*. 3d ed. Philadelphia: Westminster, 1981. Liberal.

Bruce, F. F. *Israel and the Nations*. London: Paternoster, 1963. Conservative.

De Vaux, Roland. *The Early History of Israel*. Philadelphia: Westminster, 1978. Liberal.

Eichrodt, Walther. *Theology of the Old Testament*. Trans. J. A. Baker. Philadelphia: Westminster, 1961. Liberal.

Eissfeldt, Otto. *The Old Testament, An Introduction*. Trans. P. R. Ackroyd. New York: Harper & Row, 1965. Liberal.

Garstang, John. *Joshua, Judges*. London: Constable, 1931. Liberal.

Donald E. Gowan, *Bridge Between the Testaments*. Pittsburgh: Pickwick, 1976.

Grayzel, Solomon. *A History of the Jews*. 2d ed. New York: Mentor, 1968.

Harrison, Roland Kenneth. *A History of Old Testament Times*. London: Marshall, Morgan & Scott, 1957. Conservative.

————— *Introduction to the Old Testament*. Grand Rapids: Eerdmans, 1969. Conservative.

Hayes, John H. *An Introduction to Old Testament Study*. Nashville: Abingdon, 1979. Liberal.

Hayes, John H., and Miller, J. Maxwell. *Israelite and Judaean History*. Philadelphia: Westminster, 1977. Liberal.

Hengel, Martin. *Judaism and Hellenism*. Philadelphia: Fortress, 1974.

Herrmann, Siegfried. *A History of Israel in Old Testament Times*. Trans. John Bowden. Philadelphia: Fortress, 1975. Liberal.

Hunt, Ignatius. *The World of the Patriarchs*. Englewood Cliffs, N.J.: Prentice-Hall, 1967. Liberal.

Kaufmann, Yehezkel. *The Biblical Account of the Conquest of Palestine*. Trans. M. Dagut. Jerusalem: Hebrew University Press, 1953. Liberal.

Kitchen, Kenneth A. *Ancient Orient and Old Testament*. Chicago: InterVarsity, 1966. Conservative.

LaSor, William Sanford, Hubbard, David Allan, and Bush, Frederic William. *Old Testament Survey: The Message, Form, and Background of the Old Testament*. Grand Rapids: Eerdmans, 1982. Moderate.

McCullough, W. Stewart. *The History and Literature of the Palestinian Jews from Cyrus to Herod, 550 B.C.–4 B.C.* Toronto: University of Toronto Press, 1975.

McKenzie, John L. *The World of the Judges*. Englewood Cliffs, N.J.: Prentice-Hall, 1966. Liberal.

Maly, Eugene. *The World of David and Solomon*. Englewood Cliffs, N.J.: Prentice-Hall, 1966. Liberal.

Merrill, Eugene H. *An Historical Survey of the Old Testament*. Nutley, N.J.: Craig, 1966. Conservative.

Noth, Martin. *The History of Israel*. 2d ed. London: A. & C. Black, 1958. Liberal.

Oesterley, William O. E., and Robinson, Theodore H. *A History of Israel*. 2 vols. London: Oxford University Press, 1932. Liberal.

Payne, J. Barton. *An Outline of Hebrew History*. Grand Rapids: Baker, 1954. Conservative.

_____ *The Theology of the Older Testament*. Grand Rapids: Zondervan, 1962. Conservative.

Ramsey, George W. *The Quest for the Historical Israel*. Atlanta: John Knox, 1981. Liberal.

Ricciotti, G. *The History of Israel*. 2 vols. 2d ed. Milwaukee: Bruce, 1958. Liberal.

Robinson, Henry W. *The History of Israel*. Ed. L. H. Brockington. Geneva, Ala.: Allenson, 1964.

Rowley, H. H. *The Faith of Israel*. London: SCM, 1956. Liberal.

_____ *From Joseph to Joshua*. London: Oxford University Press, 1950. Liberal.

_____ *The Servant of the Lord and Other Essays on the Old Testament*. London: Lutterworth, 1952. Liberal.

Russell, D. S. *The Jews from Alexander to Herod*. London: Oxford University Press, 1967. Liberal.

Sandmel, Samuel. *Judaism and Christian Beginnings*. New York: Oxford University Press, 1978.

Schultz, Samuel J. *The Old Testament Speaks*. 3d ed. San Francisco: Harper & Row, 1980.

Silver, Daniel Jeremy. *A History of Judaism*, vol. 1, *From Abraham to Maimonides*. New York: Basic Books, 1974.

Tcherikover, Victor. *Hellenistic Civilization and the Jews*. Philadelphia: Jewish Publication Society, 1966.

Thiele, Edwin R. *The Mysterious Numbers of the Hebrew Kings*. Rev. ed. Grand Rapids: Eerdmans, 1965. Conservative.

Whitley, Charles. *The Exilic Age*. Philadelphia: Westminster, 1957. Liberal.

Young, Edward J. *An Introduction to the Old Testament*. Grand Rapids: Eerdmans, 1949. Conservative.

Zeitlin, Solomon. *The Rise and Fall of the Judaean State*, 2 vols. Philadelphia: Jewish Publication Society, 1962.

CHRONOLOGICAL CHART

2150 B.C.	2100 B.C.	2050 B.C.	2000 B.C.

ABRAHAM — 175 years

2166

2091 2080 — Ishmael Born

2030 — Sarah Died

2020? — Married Keturah

1991

ISAAC — 180 years

2066 2056? — Mt. Moriah Sacrifice

2026 — Marries Rebekah

JACOB — 147 years

2006

UR III (Middle date)

2130 2022

ISIN-LARSA

MIDDLE KINGDOM
1991

Amenemhet I

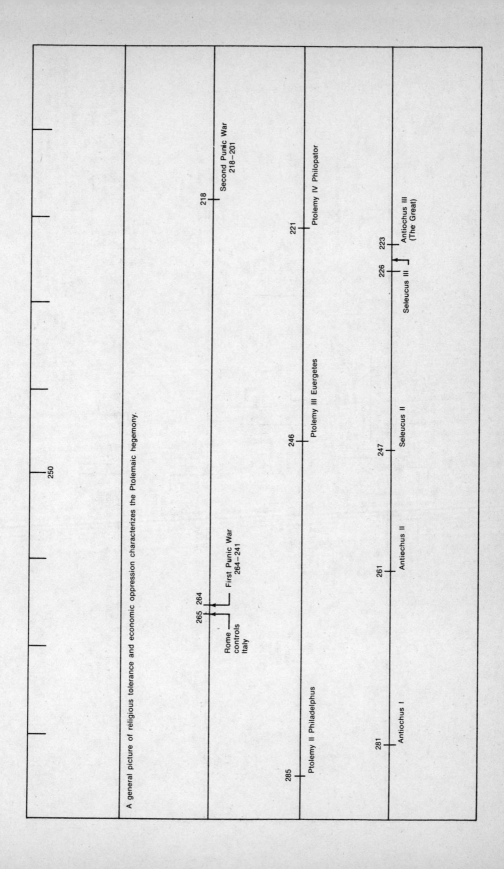

A general picture of religious tolerance and economic oppression characterizes the Ptolemaic hegemony.

250

285 — Ptolemy II Philadelphus

281 — Antiochus I

265 264 — Rome controls Italy

First Punic War 264–241

261 — Antiochus II

247 — Seleucus II

246 — Ptolemy III Euergetes

218 — Second Punic War 218–201

221 — Ptolemy IV Philopator

226 — Seleucus III

223 — Antiochus III (The Great)

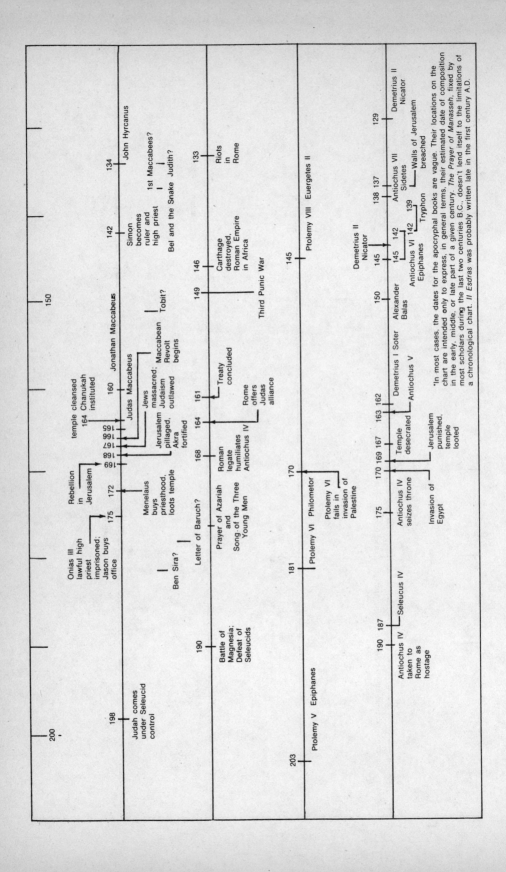

200

198 Judah comes under Seleucid control

Onias III lawful high priest imprisoned; Jason buys office

175 Menelaus buys priesthood, loots temple

172 Rebellion in Jerusalem

169

168 Jerusalem pillaged, Akra fortified

167
166
165

164 temple cleansed Chanukah instituted

Judas Maccabeus

Jews massacred; Judaism outlawed

160 Jonathan Maccabeus

Maccabean Revolt begins

150

142 Simon becomes ruler and high priest

134 John Hyrcanus

1st Maccabees?

Bel and the Snake Judith?

133

Ben Sira?

181 Letter of Baruch?

Prayer of Azariah and Song of the Three Young Men

168 Roman legate humiliates Antiochus IV

Tobit?

161 Treaty concluded

Rome offers Judas alliance

149 Carthage destroyed. Roman Empire in Africa

146 Third Punic War

190 Battle of Magnesia; Defeat of Seleucids

203 Ptolemy V Epiphanes

181 Ptolemy VI Philometor

170 Ptolemy VI fails in invasion of Palestine

145 Ptolemy VIII Euergetes II

190 Antiochus IV taken to Rome as hostage

187 Seleucus IV

175 Antiochus IV seizes throne

Invasion of Egypt

170 Temple desecrated

169
167 Jerusalem punished, temple looted

163 Demetrius I Soter
162 Antiochus V

150 Alexander Balas

145 Demetrius II Nicator
Antiochus VI Epiphanes
142 Tryphon
139

138 137 Antiochus VII Sidetes

Walls of Jerusalem breached

129 Demetrius II Nicator

*In most cases, the dates for the apocryphal books are vague. Their locations on the chart are intended only to express, in general terms, their estimated date of composition in the early, middle, or late part of a given century. *The Prayer of Manasseh*, fixed by most scholars during the last two centuries B.C., doesn't lend itself to the limitations of a chronological chart. *II Esdras* was probably written late in the first century A.D.

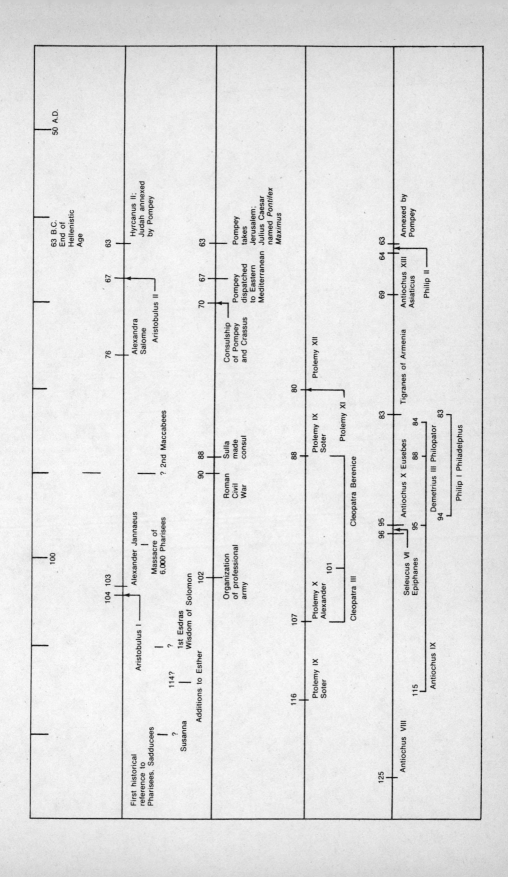

SUBJECT INDEX

SCRIPTURE INDEX

THE NEAR EAST IN THE TIME
OF THE PATRIARCHS

Caspian Sea

Persian Gulf

Black Sea

Mediterranean Sea

Red Sea

ELAM

Susa

Tigris River

Erech

UR

Nippur

Babylon

BABYLON

Eshnunna

Arrapkha

Tutul

ASSYRIA

Asshur

Nineveh

Euphrates River

Mari

MITANNI

Tadmor

HURRIANS

Haran

Carchemish

Aleppo

Ebla

Hamath

Qatna

Kadesh

Damascus

Laish (Dan)

Hazor

Megiddo

Ugarit

Byblos

Sidon

Tyre

AMORITES

Shechem

Salem
(Jerusalem)

Bethel

Beersheba

Gaza

Zoar

CANAAN

CYPRUS

HITTITES

Hattusa

Kanish

Gordium

ARZAWA

Troy

MYCENAEANS

Mycenae

Cnossus

MINOANS

On

Memphis

Thebes

Nile River

SCHEMATIC PLAN
OF UR

N

Ziggurat

Western
Harbor

Northern
Harbor

Temple

Palace

Canal

Fortress

Dwelling
Quarter

Dwelling
Quarter

Later
Babylonian
Quarter

Temple
of Enki

Euphrates

Canal

200 yards
200 meters

0   100
0   100

Empire of Hammurabi,
early 18th cent. B.C.
Empire of Thutmose III c.1468 B.C.
Egyptian sphere of influence
Hittite sphere
Abraham's wanderings
(late 3rd or early 2nd
millennium B.C.)
Major route

300 miles
400 km

100   200   300
100   200   300   400

© Carta, Jerusalem

1

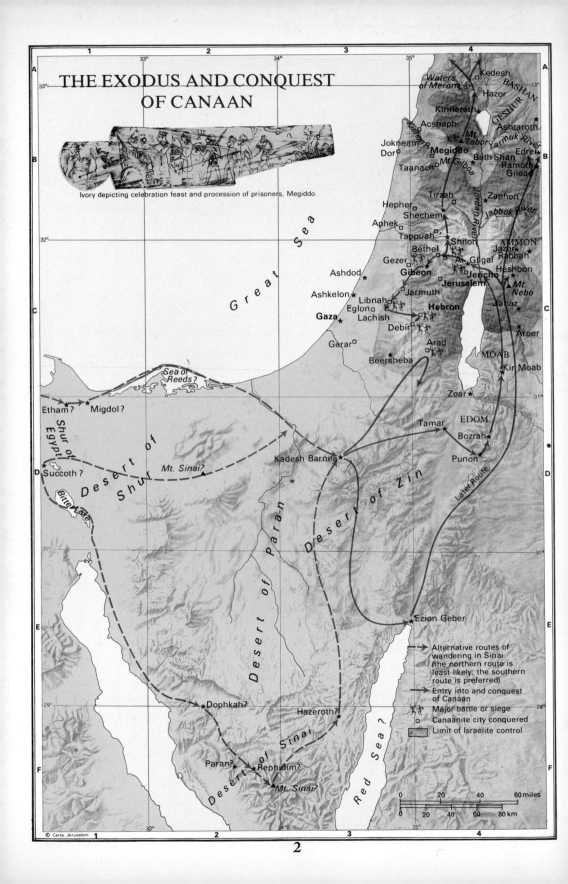

THE EXODUS AND CONQUEST
OF CANAAN

Ivory depicting celebration feast and procession of prisoners, Megiddo.

Great Sea

A
Waters of Merom
Kedesh
BASHAN
Hazor
Kinnereth
Acshaph
Ashtaroth
GESHUR
Jokneam
Kishon R.
Mt. Tabor
Edrei
Dor
Megiddo
Yarmuk River
Taanach
Mt. Gilboa
Beth Shan
Ramoth Gilead
Tirzah
Zaphon
Jordan River
Jabbok River
Hepher
Shechem
Aphek
Tappuah
Shiloh
AMMON
Bethel
Jazer
Rabbah
Gezer
Ai
Gilgal
Heshbon
Gibeon
Jericho
Ashdod
Jerusalem
Mt. Nebo
Ashkelon
Libnah
Jarmuth
Eglon
Jahaz
Gaza
Lachish
Hebron
Debir
Aroer
Gerar
Arad
MOAB
Beersheba
Kir Moab
Zoar

Sea of Reeds?
Etham?
Migdol?
Shur of Egypt?
Succoth?
Desert of Shur
Mt. Sinai?
Kadesh Barnea
Tamar
EDOM
Bozrah
Punon
Bitter Lake
Desert of Paran
Desert of Zin
Later Route
Ezion Geber

→ Alternative routes of
wandering in Sinai
(the northern route is
least likely; the southern
route is preferred)
→ Entry into and conquest
of Canaan
✕ Major battle or siege
□ Canaanite city conquered
▨ Limit of Israelite control

Dophkah?
Hazeroth?
Desert of Paran
Red Sea?
Paran?
Rephidim?
Mt. Sinai?
Desert of Sinai

| 0 | | 20 | | 40 | | 60 miles |
| 0 | 20 | 40 | 60 | 80 km |

© Carta, Jerusalem

2

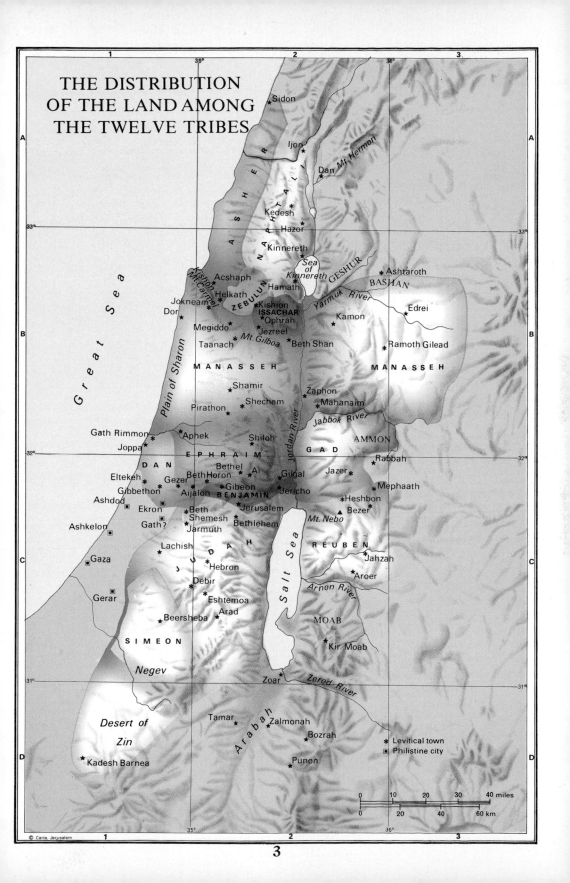

THE DISTRIBUTION OF THE LAND AMONG THE TWELVE TRIBES

Sidon

Ijon

Dan *Mt. Hermon*

A S H E R

N A P H T A L I

Kedesh

Hazor

Kinnereth

Sea of Kinnereth GESHUR Ashtaroth

Acshaph Hamath BASHAN

Helkath Edrei

Jokneam *Mt. Carmel* ZEBULUN Kishion

Dor ISSACHAR Ophrah Kamon

Megiddo Jezreel

Taanach *Mt. Gilboa* Beth Shan Ramoth Gilead

M A N A S S E H *M A N A S S E H*

Shamir Zaphon

Shechem Mahanaim

Pirathon *Jabbok River*

Gath Rimmon Aphek Shiloh AMMON

Joppa *G A D*

E P H R A I M Rabbah

D A N Bethel Ai Jazer

Eltekeh BethHoron Gilgal Mephaath

Gibbethon Gezer Gibeon Jericho

Ashdod Aijalon BENJAMIN Heshbon

Ekron Beth Jerusalem Bezer

Ashkelon Gath? Shemesh Bethlehem *Mt. Nebo*

Jarmuth *R E U B E N*

Lachish *J U D A H* Jahzah

Gaza Hebron Aroer

Debir *Arnon River*

Gerar Eshtemoa

Arad *M O A B*

Beersheba

S I M E O N Kir Moab

Negev

Zoar *Zered River*

Desert of Tamar Zalmonah

Zin Bozrah

✱ Levitical town

◘ Philistine city

Kadesh Barnea Punon

| 0 | 10 | 20 | 30 | 40 miles |

| 0 | 20 | 40 | 60 km |

Great Sea

Plain of Sharon

Jordan River

Salt Sea

Arabah

Kishon

© Carta, Jerusalem

3

THE EMPIRE OF DAVID AND SOLOMON

CYPRUS

Great Sea

Orontes River

Aleppo ★

Euphrates River

Tiphsah ★

Hamath ★

Arvad ★

Tadmor ★

Lebo Hamath ★

Gebal ★

PHOENICIANS

Litani River

Mt. Hermon

ARAMEANS OF DAMASCUS

Sidon ★

Damascus ★

Tyre ★

Dan ★

Kedesh ★

Hazor ◉

GESHUR

Acco ★

Kinnereth ★

Ashtaroth ★

Kenath ★

Dor ★ Jezreel Megiddo ◉

Yarmuk River

Beth Shan ★

Ramoth Gilead ★

Sharon

Shechem ★

Gilead

Jordan River

Jabbok River

Aphek ★

Mahanaim ★

Joppa ★

Bethel ★

AMMON

Gezer ◉

Rabbah ★

Ashdod ★

Jerusalem ◉

Ashkelon ★

Beth Shemesh ◉

Medeba ★

Gaza ★

Gath ★

Hebron ★

Ashan ★

PHILISTINES

Sharuhen ★

Arad ★

Salt Sea

MOAB

Beersheba ◉

Kir Moab ★

Baalath Beer ★

Zoar ★

Brook of Egypt

Tamar ★

Kadesh Barnea ★

Bozrah ★

Arabah

Hazar Addar ★

EDOM

Desert

Ezion Geber ★ Elath ★

	Saul's kingdom c. 1050-1010 B.C.
	Israelite kingdom of David and Solomon, c. 1010-930 B.C.
◉	Solomon's major building projects
★	Fortified under Solomon

0   20   40   60   80 miles
0   40   80   120 km

© Carta, Jerusalem

TRADE UNDER SOLOMON

Gozan ★

Carchemish ★

Nineveh ★

Horses

Arvad ★ Hamath ★

Tiphsah ★

Asshur ★

Mediterranean Sea

Gebal ★

Tribute

Tadmor ★

Sidon ★

Tribute

Damascus ★

Timber

Tyre ★

Grain, oil, wine

Joppa ★ Jerusalem ★

Gaza ★

Dumah ★

On ★

Chariots

Memphis ★

EGYPT

Ezion Geber ▲

From Arabia: tribute, gold, silver

From Ophir: gold, ivory, gems monkeys, sandalwood

Tema ★

Red Sea

From Sheba: spices, perfumes, gold, gems

Solomon's kingdom

▲ Copper mining

0   100   200 miles
0   100 200 300 km

4

THE DIVIDED KINGDOM

Byblos
Lebo Hamath

Sidon

PHOENICIANS

Litani River

Mt. Hermon
Dan
Damascus
ARAMEANS OF DAMASCUS

Tyre

Kedesh
Hazor

Bashan

Karnaim

Dor
Valley of Jezreel
Jezreel
Megiddo
Mt. Carmel
Kishon
Sharon

Yarmuk River

Ramoth Gilead

Samaria
Tirzah
Shechem

Jordan River

Succoth
Jabbok River

Great Sea

Joppa
Aphek

AMMON

Gezer
Mizpah
Jericho
Jerusalem

Rabbah

Heshbon

Ashdod
Ashkelon

PHILISTINES

Lachish

Hebron
En Gedi
Arad

Salt Sea

Dibon
Arnon River

MOAB
Kir Hareseth

Gaza

Beersheba

JUDAH

Wadi of Egypt

Tamar

Negev

Bozrah

Zered River

Kadesh Barnea

EDOM
Arabah

Teman

Elath

Sphinx, ivory carving, Samaria.

Israel	} Divided Kingdom	
Judah	10th cent. B.C.	
Israel (Jeroboam II)	} Maximum extent	
Judah (Uzziah)	mid 8th cent. B.C.	

0   20   40 miles
0   20   40   60 km

© Carta, Jerusalem

5

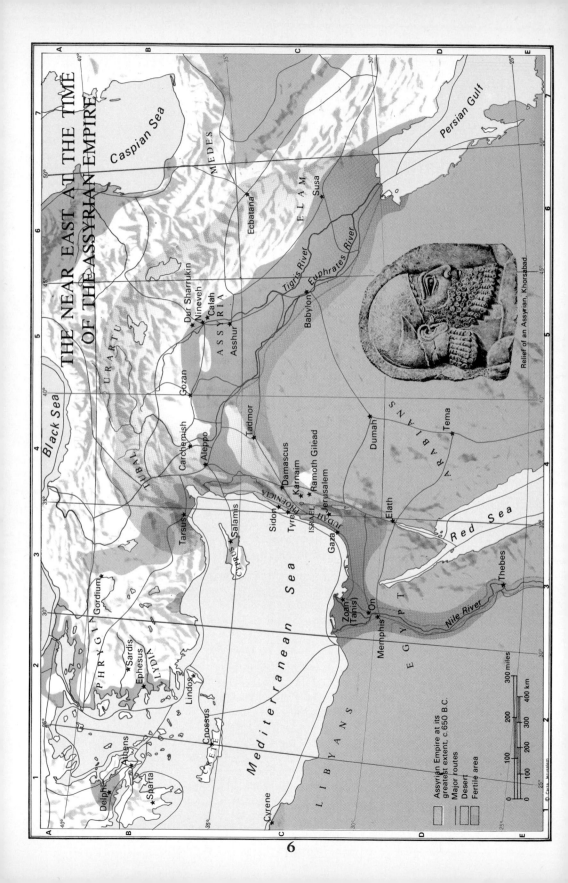

THE NEAR EAST AT THE TIME OF THE ASSYRIAN EMPIRE

Relief of an Assyrian, Khorsabad

Black Sea
Caspian Sea
Mediterranean Sea
Red Sea
Persian Gulf

MEDES
URARTU
ELAM
ASSYRIA
PHRYGIA
LYDIA
TUBAL
CYPRUS
CRETE
PHOENICIA
ISRAEL
JUDAH
EGYPT
LIBYANS
ARABIANS

Ecbatana
Susa
Babylon
Dur Sharrukin
Nineveh
Calah
Asshur
Gozan
Tadmor
Carchemish
Aleppo
Damascus
Karnaim
Ramoth Gilead
Dumah
Tema
Tarsus
Salamis
Sidon
Tyre
Jerusalem
Gaza
Elath
Gordium
Sardis
Ephesus
Lindos
Cnossus
Athens
Delphi
Sparta
Cyrene
Zoan (Tanis)
On
Memphis
Thebes

Tigris River
Euphrates River
Nile River

Assyrian Empire at its
greatest extent, c. 650 B.C.
Major routes
Desert
Fertile area

300 miles
400 km
0   100   200   300
0   100   200   300   400

© Carta, Jerusalem

6

THE BABYLONIAN AND PERSIAN EMPIRES

THE RETURN TO ZION 538–445 B.C.

Median Empire c. 556 B.C.
Babylonian Empire c. 539 B.C.
Persian Empire c. 500 B.C.
Persian royal road
Persian royal city
ARIA   Satrapy (Province) under Darius I.
Exile of Jews from Judah 605 to 582 B.C.
Flight of Jews to Egypt c. 586 B.C.

© Carta, Jerusalem

7

SOLOMON'S TEMPLE

CROSS-SECTIONS

1 Holy of Holies
2 Main hall
3 Inner courtyard

GROUND PLAN

JERUSALEM AT THE TIME OF DAVID AND SOLOMON

Gate of Benjamin (?)

Palace of the Forest of Lebanon

Gate of Ephraim (?)

Temple

Solomon's Palace

Hall of Justice

OPHEL

Gihon Spring

Kidron Valley

Stairs

Valley Gate

The Valley

David's city

Solomon's additions

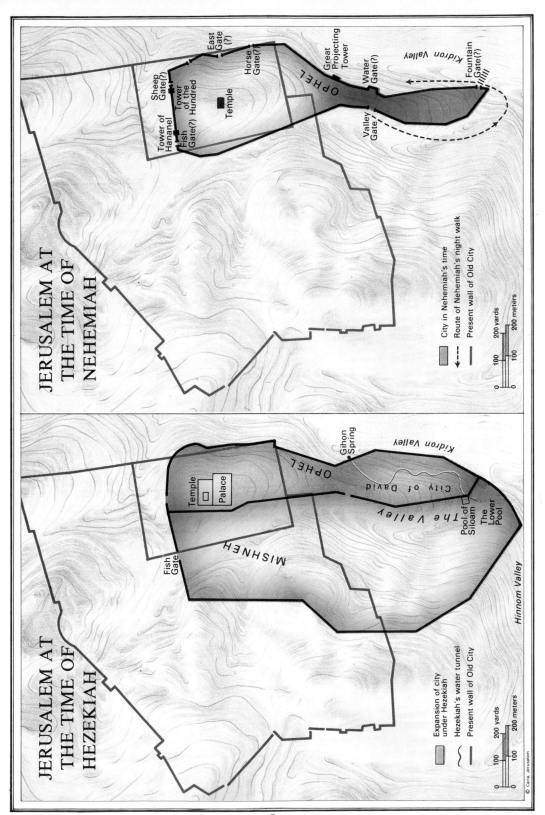

JERUSALEM AT THE TIME OF NEHEMIAH

Kidron Valley

East Gate (?)

Horse Gate (?)

Great Projecting Tower

Water Gate (?)

OPHEL

Fountain Gate (?)

Sheep Gate (?)

Tower of the Hundred

Temple

Valley Gate

Tower of Hananel

Fish Gate (?)

City in Nehemiah's time

Route of Nehemiah's night walk

Present wall of Old City

0   100   200 yards

0   100   200 meters

JERUSALEM AT THE TIME OF HEZEKIAH

Temple

Palace

MISHNEH

Fish Gate

OPHEL

Gihon Spring

Kidron Valley

City of David

The Valley

Pool of Siloam

The Lower Pool

Hinnom Valley

Expansion of city under Hezekiah

Hezekiah's water tunnel

Present wall of Old City

0   100   200 yards

0   100   200 meters

© Carta, Jerusalem

9

JESUS' LIFE AND MINISTRY

Sidon
Damascus
Zarephath
S Y R I A
Tyre
Caesarea
Philippi
P H O E N I C I A
G A U L A N I T I S
Seleucia
T R A C H O N I T I S
Ptolemais
(Acco)
Korazin
Mt. of Beatitudes
Bethsaida
Heptapegon
Cana
Capernaum
Naveh
Sepphoris
Tiberias
Sea
of
Galilee
Hippus
Dium
Nazareth
G A L I L E E
Mt.
Tabor
Gadara
Abilene
Nain
Scythopolis
(Beth Shan)
Caesarea
Pella
D E C A P O L I S
S A M A R I A
Samaria
Gerasa
Shechem
Sychar
Joppa
Gedora
Antipatris
J o r d a n   R i v e r
Diospolis
(Lod)
Mt. of
Temptation
Philadelphia
(Rabbah)
Jamnia
J U D E A
Emmaus
Jericho
Jerusalem
Bethany
Site of
Baptism
P E R E A
Azotus
(Ashdod)
Bethlehem
Ashkelon
Dead   Sea
Gaza
Hebron
Machaerus
I D U M E A
En Gedi
Masada
Raphia
Beersheba
Elusa
N A B A T E A
Zoar
Mampsis
Flight to Egypt and return to Nazareth
Baptism and temptation in the desert
Journeys in Galilee
and to Caesarea Philippi
Journey to Tyre and Sidon
Journey to and from Jerusalem
Site of major event in Jesus' life
Road
Eboda

M e d i t e r r a n e a n   S e a

0   10   20   30   40 miles
0   20   40   60 km

© Carta, Jerusalem

10

THE TEMPLE AT THE TIME OF JESUS

THE TEMPLE MOUNT

Tower

Royal Porch

Balustrade

INNER TEMPLE
Inner Court
Temple
Altar
Court of Men
Court of Women

Antonia Fortress

Court of Gentiles

Sheep Gate

Tower

Colonnades

Tower

0   50   100 yards
0   50   100 meters

After Prof. Avi-Yonah

Viewed from the east

JERUSALEM AT THE TIME OF JESUS

Hinnom Valley

THE UPPER CITY

Place of the Last Supper

House of Caiaphas

Herod's Palace

Tower of Mariamne

Tower of Phasael

Tower of Hippicus

Tomb of Jesus

Golgotha

Judgment Gate

Way of the Cross (?)

THE LOWER CITY

Palace of Herod Antipas

Tyropoeon Valley
Street

'Robinson's Arch'

Stairs

"Wilson's Arch"

Praetorium (Antonia Fortress)

Kidron Valley

Main Entrance

TEMPLE MOUNT

The Temple

Pool of Bethesda

Garden of Gethsemane

Mt. of Olives

Site of Stoning of Stephen (?)

0   100   200 yards
0   100   200 meters

© Carta, Jerusalem

11

PAUL'S FIRST AND SECOND MISSIONARY JOURNEYS

A R M E N I A

M E S O P O T A M I A

C A P P A D O C I A

BITHYNIA AND PONTUS

Black Sea

THRACIA

MYSIA
Troas

Pergamum
Thyatira
Sardis
Philadelphia
Ephesus
Smyrna
Laodicea

S I A

Rhodes

GALATIA

PHRYGIA

Antioch
Iconium
Lystra
Derbe

PISIDIA

ANTIPAMPHYLIA
Attalia Perga
LYCIA

L Y C A O N I A

C I L I C I A
Tarsus

Seleucia
Antioch

S Y R I A

P H O E N I C I A

J U D A E A

A R A B I A

Caesarea

Jerusalem

CYPRUS
Salamis
Paphos

Mediterranean Sea

CRETE

E G Y P T

C Y R E N E

SAMOTHRACE

MACEDONIA
Philippi Neapolis
Thessalonica Amphipolis
Berea
Apollonia

EPIRUS

Aegean Sea

A C H A I A
Athens
Corinth
Cenchrea

Lamp with bull's head and cross-shaped handle, Beth Shan

First missionary journey A.D. 46-48
Second missionary journey A.D. 49-52
Seven churches of Western Asia Minor

200 miles
300 km
100
100
200
0

© Carta, Jerusalem

12

PAUL'S THIRD MISSIONARY JOURNEY AND TRIP TO ROME

ARMENIA

MESOPOTAMIA

CAPPADOCIA

BITHYNIA AND PONTUS

Black Sea

SYRIA

Antioch

Tarsus

CILICIA

Seleucia

PHOENICIA

Sidon

Tyre
Ptolemais
Caesarea
Antipatris
JUDAEA
Jerusalem

ARABIA

LYCAONIA

GALATIA

Iconium

CYPRUS

ASIA

PHRYGIA

Pergamum
Thyatira
Sardis Philadelphia
Smyrna Laodicea
Ephesus
Miletus

LYCIA

AND PAMPHYLIA

Myra

Patara

Troas
Assos
Mitylene
CHIOS
SAMOS
Cos
Cnidus
Rhodes

MOESIA

THRACIA

Philippi

Thessalonica

Berea

MACEDONIA

EPIRUS

ACHAIA

Corinth

CRETE

Lasea Salmone

Fair Havens

Mediterranean Sea

EGYPT

CYRENE

DACIA

ILLYRICUM

Adriatic Sea

ITALIA

Rome
Three Taverns
Forum of Appius

Puteoli

Rhegium

Syracuse

SICILIA

SARDINIA

CORSICA

MALTA

PROCONSULAR AFRICA

Third missionary journey A.D. 53-57
Journey to Rome and Imprisonment
Seven churches of Western Asia Minor

300miles

100   200   300
0
400 km

© Carta, Jerusalem

13

THE ROMAN EMPIRE
IN NEW TESTAMENT TIMES

Senatorial province under Augustus
Imperial province under Augustus
Conquered or annexed after Augustus
Provincial boundary
Major road

ROME (A.D. 1ST-3RD CENTURIES)
Earliest Christian sites

14

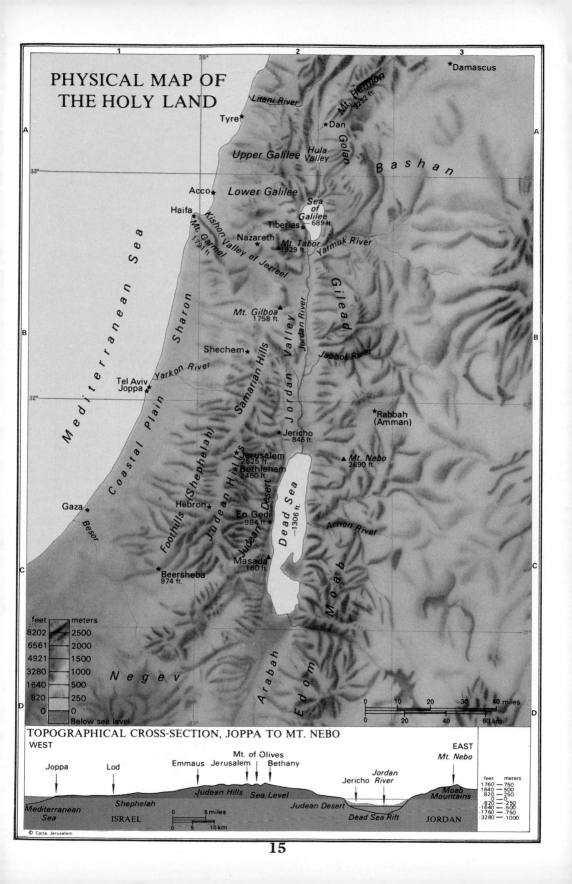

PHYSICAL MAP OF THE HOLY LAND

★ Damascus

Litani River

Mt. Hermon
9232 ft.

Tyre ★

★ Dan

Upper Galilee

Hula Valley

Golan

B a s h a n

Acco ★ · Lower Galilee

Haifa

Sea of Galilee
-689 ft.

Kishon · Tiberias ★

Mt. Carmel
1791 ft.

Nazareth ★ · Mt. Tabor
1929 ft.

Valley of Jezreel

Yarmuk River

M e d i t e r r a n e a n   S e a

Gilead

Sharon

Mt. Gilboa
1758 ft.

Shechem ★

Samarian Hills

Jordan River

Jordan Valley

Jabbok River

Yarkon River

Tel Aviv
Joppa ★

★ Rabbah
(Amman)

Coastal Plain

Jericho
-846 ft.

Foothills (Shephelah)

Jerusalem
2625 ft. ★
★ Bethlehem
2460 ft.

▲ Mt. Nebo
2690 ft.

Gaza ★

Hebron ★

Judean Hills

Judean Desert

Dead Sea
-1306 ft.

En Gedi
-984 ft. ★

Besor

Arnon River

Masada
160 ft. ▲

Moab

Beersheba ★
974 ft.

feet	meters
8202	2500
6561	2000
4921	1500
3280	1000
1640	500
820	250
0	0
	Below sea level

N e g e v

Arabah

Edom

0 10 20 30 40 miles
0 20 40 60 km

TOPOGRAPHICAL CROSS-SECTION, JOPPA TO MT. NEBO

WEST

EAST
Mt. Nebo

Joppa   Lod   Emmaus Jerusalem Bethlehem
Mt. of Olives

Jordan River

Jericho

Moab Mountains

Judean Hills

Sea Level

Mediterranean Sea

Shephelah

Judean Desert

Dead Sea Rift

ISRAEL

0   5 miles
0 5 10km

JORDAN

feet	meters
1760	750
820	250
0	0
-820	-250
-1640	-500
-1760	-750
-3280	-1000

JERUSALEM TODAY (CENTER)

ARCHAEOLOGICAL DIGS AND REMAINS FROM OLD AND NEW
TESTAMENT TIMES.

1 Second Temple tombs
2 "Tomb of the Kings"
3 Remains of (Third) Wall
4 First Temple tombs
5 Garden Tomb
6 First Temple tombs
7 "Sanhedrin tombs"
8 Mamilla Pool
9 "Tomb of Herod's family"
10 Remains of (Third) Wall
11 Wall and gate, Second Temple
12 "Solomon's quarries"
13 "Zedekiah's Cave"
14 Sitti Maryam (Mary's) Pool
15 Sheep pools
16 Struthion Pools
17 First Temple tombs
18 "Ecce Homo Arch"

19 Second Temple tombs
20 Second Temple period wall
21 Second Temple period wall
22 Remains from First Temple period
23 Second Temple enclosure remains
24 Sacred Rock
25 "Hezekiah's Pool"
26 Warren's Gate
27 Wilson's Arch
28 Temple enclosure remains
29 Hulda Gates and Single Gate
30 "Solomon's Stables"
31 Hellenistic tower
32 Wall and gate, Second Temple period
33 Building, first Temple period
34 Building, Second Temple period
35 Israelite tower and building
36 Hezekiah's wall

37 Lower aqueduct
38 Building and pool
39 Robinson's Arch
40 Temple enclosure remains
41 Tower of Hippicus
42 Towers and building
43 Second Temple period walls
44 First Temple period tombs
45 Building ("House of Caiaphas")
46 Jason's Tomb
47 Tombs/monuments, "Absalom", Zachariah, Bene Hezir
48 "Tombs of the Prophets"
49 Gihon spring, Jebusite wall
50 First wall remains
51 Tomb of "Pharaoh's Daughter"
52 Siloam Pool
53 Second Temple period cisterns
54 Second temple period tombs

Map legend:
- Archaeological Digs
- Inter-urban (Shetut/Tsel)
- Police Station
- First Aid Station
- Synagogue
- Church
- Mosque
- Museum, Art Gallery
- Theater, Concert Hall
- International Club
- Sports and Recreation Center
- Hotel
- Christian Hospice
- Important Structure

0   200   400 yards
0   200   400 meters

© Carta, Jerusalem

16